Journal of Comparative Poetics
No. 30, 2010

alif

# Trauma and Memory

*The following people have participated in the preparation of this issue*:
Omneya Mohallal Ali, Mona Amuyni, Sanaa Anaselwugud, Bushra Azzouz, Asef Bayat, Nagla El Baz, Anna Bernard, Carol Clark, Elliot Colla, Sharif Elmusa, Abdel Aziz EzzelArab, Alaa Abdel Hadi, Madiha Doss, Ira Dworkin, Hoda Elsadda, El Sayyid Fadl, Ahmed Shams el Din el Haggagi, Hussein Hammouda, Abdel Nasser Hassan, Ashraf Atiyya Hashem, Nicholas Hopkins, Zeinab Ibrahim, Ananya Kabir, Pauline Kaldas, Susan Kollin, David Konstan, Huda Lutfi, Joseph Massad, Mona Misbah, Amy Motlagh, Nadya Mujahid, Steve Nimis, Everett Rowson, Salah El Sarwi, Mounira Soliman, Suzanne Stetkevych, Sherine El Taraboulsi, Mona Tolba, Mohammed Younis.

Cover illustration: "Breaking the Habits 8" by Sara Dolatabadi.

Distributed by AUC Press.
Dar el Kutub No. 3464/10
ISBN 978 977 416 407 1
ISSN 1110-8673

*Earlier issues of the journal include* (back issues available at prices listed):

*Alif* 1: Philosophy and Stylistics
*Alif* 2: Criticism and the Avant-Garde
*Alif* 3: The Self and the Other
*Alif* 4: Intertextuality
*Alif* 5: The Mystical Dimension in Literature
*Alif* 6: Poetics of Place
*Alif* 7: The Third World: Literature and Consciousness
*Alif* 8: Interpretation and Hermeneutics
*Alif* 9: The Question of Time
*Alif* 10: Marxism and the Critical Discourse
*Alif* 11: Poetic Experimentation in Egypt since the Seventies
*Alif* 12: Metaphor and Allegory in the Middle Ages
*Alif* 13: Human Rights and Peoples' Rights in the Humanities
*Alif* 14: Madness and Civilization
*Alif* 15: Arab Cinematics: Toward the New and the Alternative
*Alif* 16: Averroës and the Rational Legacy in the East and the West
*Alif* 17: Literature and Anthropology in Africa
*Alif* 18: Post-Colonial Discourse in South Asia
*Alif* 19: Gender and Knowledge
*Alif* 20: The Hybrid Literary Text
*Alif* 21: The Lyrical Phenomenon
*Alif* 22: The Language of the Self: Autobiographies and Testimonies
*Alif* 23: Literature and the Sacred
*Alif* 24: Archeology of Literature: Tracing the Old in the New
*Alif* 25: Edward Said and Critical Decolonization
*Alif* 26: Wanderlust: Travel Literature of Egypt and the Middle East
*Alif* 27: Childhood: Creativity and Representation
*Alif* 28: Artistic Adaptations: Approaches and Positions
*Alif* 29: The University and Its Discontents: Egyptian and Global Perspectives

*Printed at*: Elias Modern Publishing House, Cairo.

*Price per issue*: Egypt: LE 20; Other Countries: Individuals: $20, Institutions: $40.

*Electronic version*: issues 1-26 are available at http://www.jstor.org

*Correspondence, subscriptions, and manuscripts should be addressed to*:
*Alif*, Department of English and Comparative Literature,
The American University in Cairo
PO Box: 2511, Cairo 11511, Egypt
Telephone: 2-02-27975107; Fax: 2-02-27957565
E-mail: alifecl@aucegypt.edu
Website: www.aucegypt.edu/academics/dept/eclt/alif

Contents

## English Section

## Arabic Section

Memory has the fragrance of a weeping night flower arousing in the exile's blood a need for singing.

— Mahmoud Darwish

Le lieu que l'on ne voit plus, cesse d'être notre lieu. L'exilé est un aveugle sans territoire . . . . Il suit deux chemins parallèles: celui de sa mémoire et celui de ses pas. Il arrive que ses pas le trahissent; jamais sa mémoire.

— Edmond Jabès

## Trauma and Memory

This issue of *Alif* focuses on trauma and loss and their presence in collective and individual memory. The question of traumatic events has been recognized in psychology, psychoanalysis, and literature, but scholarly studies have mostly concentrated on traumas enacted in the West—World Wars and the Holocaust. This issue attempts to extend the field of trauma and memory studies to include other parts of the world: Algeria, Egypt, Iraq, Iran, India, Ireland, Lebanon, Palestine, Pakistan, multi-ethnic America, and ancient Greece. Whether the Lebanese civil war or the Peloponnesian war, the *Nakba* of 1948 or the *Naksa* of 1967, the articles and personal testimonies in this issue explore the impact of such tragic events on literary genre, films, fiction, folk culture, poetry, drama and visual arts.

*Alif*, a refereed multilingual journal appearing annually in the spring, presents articles in Arabic, English, and, occasionally, French. The different traditions and languages confront and complement each other in its pages. Each issue includes and welcomes original articles. The next issues will center on the following themes:

*Alif* 31: The Other Americas.
*Alif* 32: The Imaginary and the Documentary: Cultural Studies in Literature, History, and the Arts.
*Alif* 33: The Desert: Human Geography and Symbolic Economy.

# Forms of Memory: Partition as a Literary Paradigm

**Anna Bernard**

"Partition lives on in post-colonial times to such an extent that we should truly prefer the phrase 'partitioned times' to the more common 'post-colonial times'" (Jassal and Ben-Ari, 19, citing Samaddar 21). With this spirited epigraph, the editors of a recent collection on the 'partition motif' assert the centrality of partition to any discussion of the formerly colonized world. Their claim is symptomatic of a growing insistence on the importance of the comparative study of partition in the humanities as well as the social sciences, signaled not only by books like Jassal and Ben-Ari's (both are anthropologists), but also within the far more developed field of Indian partition studies, where humanities scholars regularly note the relationship between the partition of the subcontinent and other twentieth-century partitions (Pandey, *Remembering Partition* 1; Francisco 372; Kaul xiii).[1] There are evidently pressing historical reasons for a turn to partition studies in the last twenty-five years: several scholars cite the reunification of Germany and the break-up of the former Yugoslavia as motivation (Cleary 1-2; Radha Kumar 3; Bose, "The Partition Evasion" n. pag.), and in Indian partition scholarship the 'intercommunal' violence in Indian cities in the 1980s and 1990s is often described as having triggered collective memories of Partition violence, which in turn compelled historians to break the long official and academic silence surrounding the atrocities (Didur, *Unsettling Partition* 4; Pandey, *Routine Violence* 5). At the current time, given the serious consideration of proposals to partition Iraq—including a non-binding resolution passed in the United States Senate in 2007, sponsored by then-Senator Joe Biden (see Johnson 142, n. 9; Bose, "The Partition Evasion" n. pag.)—the need for a more comprehensive and interdisciplinary approach to the comparative study of the legacies of twentieth-century partitions, one which is motivated by a commitment to social justice and not only the 'security' concerns that tend to dominate policy studies, seems especially urgent.

However, despite this clear political and intellectual impetus, what remains less certain is what kinds of methodologies partition studies should entail, particularly in the humanities, and what kinds of insights might be gained from the act of comparison itself. This article will speculatively address one aspect of this problem by proposing a basic method for comparing works of 'partition literature,' which I define as texts that represent either the event of territorial partition or its consequences (see also Cleary 94 and 238, n. 64; Harlow). I contend that it is possible to identify distinct genres, plotlines, and esthetic modes within the category of partition literature, with specific reference to the romance, the *Bildungsroman*, and the fragmented narrative. My examples come from the postcolonial partitions of India, Palestine,[2] and Ireland only, in which conflicting claims to self-determination based on 'ethnic' or 'communal' conflict have been the primary rationale for partition in the moment of decolonization. Ethnic conflict has also been the motivation for partition in the former Yugoslavia and Cyprus, though not at the point of imperial withdrawal, while the Cold War partitions of Germany, Korea, and Vietnam were engineered as part of the US-Soviet struggle for global dominance. Nevertheless, in each case, partition was imposed or overseen by a stronger polity at the expense of a weaker one, instigating a "moment of nationalisation" (Pandey, *Remembering Partition* 17) which produced reconfigured or completely new national identities (see also Cleary 1-3 and 20; Fraser 2). Since this experience of dramatic, and often violent, territorial reorganization is common to all twentieth-century partitions, it is my hope that the narrative forms I identify will also be recognizable across a much broader range of partition contexts.

My approach builds on previous efforts to describe common characteristics among partition literatures, most notably Joe Cleary's book *Literature, Partition and the Nation-State*, as well as the existing scholarship on comparative approaches to twentieth-century partitions and the cultural effects and legacies of partition in particular locations. However, it also departs from this scholarship by accounting not only for the functions of partition literature, but also for what I identify as the unexpected and suggestive convergence of its techniques. I first briefly discuss the main conclusions of the scholarship on partition and partition literature, which I situate in relation to my own method for reading these texts. The second part of the article examines the narrative strategies I focus on in more detail, with attention to the *Bildungsroman* and the fragmented narrative. I argue that both of these forms seek to critically replicate the processes through which the event of partition is memorialized. They do this not only by testifying to the physical and psychic violence inflicted by partition and in its aftermath, as many commentators have noted, but also by creating "counterfactual" representations of pre-partition history or the post-partition present (see Gopal 82-86). Here I follow Crystal Bartolovich's definition of "critical counterfactualism" as the "reclaiming of still incomplete revolutionary projects" (64; see also Gopal 84). While the texts I discuss are not all revolutionary in the sense she means, and they often do not actually depict alternative pasts or presents, they all contest the current order by evoking a yearning for what "might have been" (Bartolovich 66). This "critical counterfactualism" challenges the retrospective assertion of either the inevitability or the necessity of partition, and it encourages the reader to consider other forms of social and political organization that could have (or could still) come into being.

This approach requires a form of distant reading not unlike the general method proposed by Franco Moretti; thus, I pay more attention to the similarities between the texts I consider than to their many differences, and I do not attempt to account for partition narratives that cannot be classified as belonging to one of the genres I describe. My comparisons of particular texts are necessarily limited: The four main texts under consideration deal with the effects of partition within the Israeli state and the Punjab only, and their languages are Urdu (which I read in translation), Hebrew, and English, omitting Arabic and the many other languages of Indian partition literature. I also leave out major narrative forms of partition literature such as the short story (important in Urdu and Bengali in particular), memoir, and testimonial, as well as poetry and drama. A final limitation is that by emphasizing the counterfactual tendencies of the specific forms I consider, I do not fully account for partition literature that consolidates partition rather than challenges it, to use Cleary's vocabulary (59; see also Harlow 87).

However, by suggesting a provisional template for reading partition fiction that can be used in reference to different geopolitical contexts, I aim to contribute to the development of a methodology that can avoid some of the pitfalls of the "case-by-case approach" to partition studies (Radha Kumar 4), which in the realm of policy can lead to a failure to learn lessons from other partitions, and in literary criticism, to tautology (i.e. the claim that 'these narratives of partition are all about partition'). If we are to make meaningful comparisons between partition texts, it is necessary to refine our mode of enquiry, which I think is best done through a focus on shared narrative techniques. More polemically, though I agree with Cleary that partition literature is not necessarily contestatory, I would like to suggest that the propensity towards counterfactualism can be seen as *inherent* in the particular genres I identify. This is a different claim from the commonplace assertion that fictional accounts of partition "interrupt" (Pandey, *Routine Violence* 15), "destabilize" (Didur. *Unsettling Partition* 11-13), or "expose" (Hasan 39) the new national narratives formed in the aftermath of partition. On the contrary, I argue that literature can do more than counter official narratives, and that it is not necessarily or even typically anti-nationalist. Instead, partition fiction has a special capacity to gesture towards and, in some cases, formally construct, visions of collectivity and nationhood based on solidarity, not separation.

**Comparing Partitions**

The existing approaches to the comparative study of partition can be broadly characterized by discipline, by their attitude to partition, and by what it is that they seek to compare. In policy-oriented fields like political science, international relations, or peace and conflict studies, it is often taken for granted that a comparative approach to partition studies can determine the utility of partition—or lack thereof—as a means of resolving 'ethnic conflict' (a term which assumes that such conflicts are fuelled by atavistic, 'tribal' allegiances rather than, for example, the divide-and-rule policies practiced under colonial governance). Although some contemporary political theorists hold that partition is a viable option "when all else fails" (Kaufmann; Johnson; Waterman), many others contend that twentieth-century partitions have consistently produced more problems than they have solved. As one vehement rebuttal to the pro-partitionists puts it, partition is "an effectively useless policy tool" since "effective partition is unlikely to occur except through ethnic cleansing during war" (Horowitz and Weisiger 203). It follows that the study of the failures of past partitions can potentially reveal "broad, comparative lessons for making peace" (Bose, *Contested Lands* 5) in regions that are still suffering partition's after-effects, or where partition is still considered to be a possible solution (e.g. Iraq or Israel/Palestine). The basis for comparative study then is not only the common structural features that twentieth-century partitions have shared—such as the use of partition as an imperial exit strategy—but also, and more importantly, the desire to construct a prescriptive framework for resolving ethnic conflict (or otherwise set the terms of national independence, as in the Cold War partitions) that can be adapted to different contexts, whether or not partition is seen as an acceptable means of resolution.

Partition scholarship in the humanities tends to take a less overtly instrumentalist—or interventionist—approach. Rather than viewing partition through the lens of conflict resolution theory, humanities scholars have typically been more skeptical of claims for the obduracy of ethnic divisions, and have identified partition itself as a form of social violence. Recent scholarship in history, literature, and cultural studies has focused on the artistic and testimonial evidence of the lasting suffering partition has engendered, in both material terms (murder, rape, dispossession, and displacement) and psychic terms (trauma, nostalgia, and the formation or suppression of collective memory). This approach might seem to enable comparison between different partition contexts on the basis of a shared experience of partition-induced trauma, an approach already suggested by the number of studies of the Indian partition of 1947[3] that draw on Holocaust and trauma studies (e.g. Didur, *Unsettling Partition*; Kabir; Priya Kumar; Jassal and Ben-Ari 48; 46). Yet very little comparative study of partition has so far taken place in the humanities, whether from a trauma studies perspective or otherwise. Instead, the vast majority of work on the cultural effects of partition has addressed the Indian partition, where, as Ritu Menon has argued, there is little comparison of the experience of Partition "from a cross-border, three country perspective" (159), let alone between the Indian partition and other partitions.

The focus on India helps to explain the pronounced emphasis on human suffering in existing scholarship. Not only were the immediate effects of Partition particularly catastrophic, especially in the Punjab, but they were also suppressed from most histories of the period in favor of celebratory nationalist accounts of the birth of the two new nations of India and Pakistan (Hasan 12-18; Pandey, *Remembering Partition* 1-20). Fictional accounts of the Indian partition have been a key part of the effort to counter the "collective amnesia" (Pandey, *Routine Violence* 23) enabled by such triumphalism, since fiction, in both literature and film, was the arena in which the most sustained engagement with the human cost of the partition took place. However, the idea that Partition literature is best read as a counter-nationalist document of suffering now threatens to achieve hegemonic status. Partition fiction is regularly described, often with reference to the work of Gyanendra Pandey and Menon and Bhasin, as a means of filling in the gaps in the official historical record (e.g. Rastegar 26); like subaltern testimony, it is seen to serve as one of the "small voices" of history (Pandey, *Remembering Partition* 203). Literature, in other words, is understood as an "eloquent witness, and perhaps the only witness, to an unspeakable and inarticulable history" (Kumar 202; Hasan 17). Deepika Bahri goes so far as to suggest that Bapsi Sidhwa's *Cracking India* (first published as *Ice Candy Man*), which I discuss in more detail below, positions the *reader* as a "belated witness who must now share the pain, the blame, the guilt" (228) with those who lived through Partition.

The problem with this approach is not that it sees all literary accounts of the Indian partition as necessarily oppositional; Pandey, for one, explicitly distinguishes between critical and consolidatory texts when he suggests that the northern Indian partition literature published in the 1950s and 1960s "conforms pretty much to the secular nationalist problematic" that mourns partition violence but sees it as an inexplicable aberration (*Routine Violence* 23). Instead, the trouble is that when the value of literature is located in its capacity to bear witness to personal trauma (or indeed, to position the reader as a proxy witness to such trauma), the line between literature and survivors' testimony is blurred, and the specific work that literature is able to perform in partition contexts—as opposed to other contexts of mass dispossession, violence, or war—becomes much harder to describe. Jill Didur makes a similar point when she warns against reading Partition narratives as either "record" or "gossip": If we are to be able to attend to the "literariness of [partition] literature," we have to approach literary texts as discursive *interventions* into existing representations of the history of partition ("Lifting the Veil?" 10ff; Didur, *Unsettling Partition*; Marx 599). This is not to suggest that the affective or traumatic dimension of the experience of partition is unimportant, but rather that it is inseparable from the particular kinds of reconceptualizations of social and political space that twentieth-century partitions have entailed. While fiction and testimony are both able to represent individual suffering, fiction is better placed to contextualize it, and to reexamine the political certainties that have produced it.

One of the reasons that the comparative study of partition literatures is useful is that it can help shift the focus from reading this literature as testimony to reading it as an imaginative response to the common guiding logic of partition, which has held that political space must be reorganized in order to "accommodate" (Cleary 29) ethnic or other forms of political conflict. If the rationale for comparing (for instance) Khushwant Singh's *Train to Pakistan* with Mukul Kesavan's *Looking Through Glass*—two texts which were written forty years apart, and which make use of documentary realism and magical realism respectively—is that both of them represent the partition of India, it is very tempting to conclude that the reason to read these two texts together is to glean different kinds of information about the event of Partition itself: one more immediate, and the other as evidence of the continued "haunt[ing] of the collective memory of the subcontinent" (Priya Kumar 215). But if one compares *Train to Pakistan* with the Palestinian writer Ghassan Kanafani's *Men in the Sun* (*Rijal fi al-shams*), with the rationale that each of them represents a response to partition, it is clearly impossible to rely on coincident or divergent representations of the same events as a basis for comparison. If we are to understand the relationship between these texts as sharing something more than the recourse to a universalized notion of trauma—which would not solve the problem of what distinguishes partition literature from other kinds of conflict literature—it is necessary to find links between their respective political imaginaries.

Cleary has come closest to proposing a methodology for this kind of comparison by suggesting that partition narratives can be compared in terms of their effort to either advance the goal of complete separation or promote convergence and reintegration (59). However, he does not suggest particular literary strategies which might be adopted across different contexts, focusing instead on the local and text-specific articulations of the functions he identifies. Thus, though he does note at one point that dreams of reconciliation are registered at the level of form, he limits this insight to Irish partition literature only (110). My aim is to demonstrate what Cleary leaves implicit by accounting for some of the formal and generic similarities that I have found to be common among literary narratives of partition. If, as Jason Francisco puts it, the literature of partition "rightly forces us to reckon sides and to choose" between partition and coexistence (373), it does so by formally re-enacting the conditions of that choice, and by refusing to concede—sometimes in spite of itself—that partition could ever have produced a just or equitable outcome.

## Genres of Partition

### 1. Romance

One of the major forms common to partition narratives from India/Pakistan/Bangladesh, Israel/Palestine, and Ireland/Northern Ireland is the "romance-across-the-divide" (Gopal 72-73; Cleary 110 and 112-14). The basic model for this plot is a heterosexual romance between lovers on opposite sides of the partition, which typically is either tragically thwarted or can only be realized in exile. In Singh's *Train to Pakistan*, for example, the romance between a Sikh man and a Muslim woman (admittedly a rather violent and misogynistic affair; see Kaul 16) ends in disaster: Juggat Singh manages to stop the train carrying Nooran to Pakistan from being blown up, but he is killed in the process. In *Arabesques*, a novel witten in Hebrew by the Palestinian Israeli writer Anton Shammas, the romance is similarly, though less violently, truncated. The novel initially takes the form of letters from the Palestinian Israeli protagonist to his Jewish Israeli lover, but in a self-consciously allegorical reversal, the woman's husband, an officer in the Israeli army, finds the letters and cuts off their correspondence. Conversely, in Joan Lingard's Kevin and Sadie series (1970-1976), Catholic Kevin and Protestant Sadie are able to stay together, but only by leaving Belfast for England. Over the course of the remaining books, they get married, have a child, and finally settle in Wales, but they never return permanently to Northern Ireland. Another variation appears in Sidhwa's *Cracking India*. In the early part of the novel, the Hindu Ayah's multi-confessional group of lovers represents a pre-partition pluralist idyll which is already retrospectively tinged with nostalgia; when this circle of lovers is forcibly narrowed to her Muslim abductor Ice-candy-man, Ayah's abduction is made even more horrific by the loss of the pre-partition innocence of the possibility of the cross-communal romance, which, after partition, can only be falsely staged through violence and coercion.[4]

Clearly, the "romance-across-the-divide" is not a genre that is limited to partition contexts; as Doris Sommer has famously shown, the genre was commonly used in nineteenth-century Latin America as a means of imaginatively unifying newly independent states made up of economically and ethnically diverse populations. Yet while Sommer's national reconciliations tend to be figured by happy-ever-after narrative resolutions, the tragic endings common to partition romances tend to represent unification as unrealizable in the present. Whether because of the seeming irreversibility of the loss of pre-partition innocence, or the inability to imagine a state structure in which the lovers' romance would not be taboo (Cleary 115), narrative resolution is typically only achieved in these novels through the confirmation, not the refutation, of the divide between the 'national' groups. Indeed, the desired union of the two lovers often has the effect of intensifying the divide rather than undermining it (Gopal 73). Thus, though A. B. Yehoshua's *The Lover* is a 'successful' partition romance, insofar as it ends with Dafi and Na'im's physical consummation of their mutual attraction, this union is made possible by Na'im's increasing desire to identify as a Jew rather than an Arab (242; Ramras-Rauch 143). Reconciliation can only be achieved through Na'im's willing capitulation to Jewish Israeli hegemony, which makes the lives of what the novel designates as 'real' Palestinian Arabs (represented by Na'im's brother, a militant killed in action) seem even more remote from Jewish Israeli experience.

What distinguishes the failed partition romance from other kinds of failed cross-border romances—including Romeo and Juliet's—is its particular form of counterfactualism, in which the social order where the lovers might be united is *not* unimaginable (*pace* Cleary), because historical alternatives can be found in the pre-partition period, when other forms of political organization—including federation, regional autonomies, and economic unions (see Fraser)—were not only imagined but seriously considered. In each of the examples I've mentioned, the yearning of the lovers enables us to envision the possibility of an undivided India, Ireland, or Palestine: Their romance challenges the collective naturalization of partition by attempting to defamiliarize the communal boundaries used to rationalize it. The eventual frustration of that yearning—or the colossal compromises that one or both lovers must make to satisfy it—does not negate its affective power or its imaginative affiliation with past alternatives to partition. Even Yehoshua's novel, which is hardly anti-partitionist in content, has to work very hard to combat the logic of its genre; it does so in part by turning the adolescent romance into a rather comic, lighthearted affair that signifies the Jewish state's capacity to accommodate its Palestinian Israeli minority, rather than presenting a tragic passion doomed by the history of Palestinian expulsion and dispossession. By equating romantic love with a desired social harmony as a genre, the partition romance directly challenges the political logic of partition, even if individual texts attempt to mitigate or neutralize that challenge.

Partition romance is a form in which the relationship between narrative structure and the critique of partition is readily apparent. The next two genres I consider are less easily identifiable, either as discrete narrative forms or as forms that are intrinsically linked to, let alone critical of, partition. These caveats notwithstanding, I want to argue that both the *Bildungsroman* and the fragmented narrative offer provocative ways of thinking about how the naturalization of partition might be confronted, since, as I suggested above, both forms seek to undermine the seeming fixity of social and territorial boundaries in the post-partition period by critically reproducing the history of the creation of those boundaries, and by trying to make alternatives to partition thinkable once again.

### 2. *Bildungsroman*

In the case of the *Bildungsroman*, this project is sometimes attempted by aligning the narrator's coming of age with the event of partition itself, as in *Cracking India* and in the non-fictional childhood memoirs by Amos Oz and Ghada Karmi; or, alternatively, by figuring coming of age as an awareness of the legacy of partition, as is the case in Salman Rushdie's *Midnight's Children*, Seamus Deane's *Reading in the Dark*, Edward Said's memoir *Out of Place*, and Shammas's *Arabesques*. In each of these texts, young adulthood is metonymically associated with the traumas (or for Oz, the temporary triumph) of partition: The pre-partition period, or the period before the awareness of partition, is identified with childish innocence, while the post-partition or post-awareness period equals adult disillusionment. Like the partition romance then the partition *Bildungsroman* is a pessimistic genre, in which the pre-lapsarian age before partition is—like childhood—irrevocably lost, and the dystopia of the present seems extremely difficult to overcome. At the same time, however, the nostalgia for that time of innocence is constitutively anti-partitionist, and so it holds onto the possibility of a different kind of future. Even in Oz's memoir, as one reviewer notes, the young Oz's entry into adulthood is marked not just by his mother's death, but also by "the death of the socialist-Zionist dream of a just society" (Leonard n. pag.); the event of partition simultaneously signifies the realization and the negation of the fantasy of total separation, as it becomes almost immediately clear that partition has not ended Palestinian and Arab resistance to Zionism.

*Cracking India* and *Arabesques* share more than a dual reliance on the genres of the partition romance and *Bildungsroman*, since both have had the dubious honor of having received a great deal of critical attention in English.[5] A more compelling link, however, can be seen in the novels' common use of the *Bildungsroman* form, both featuring a semi-autobiographical protagonist (who in *Arabesques* is also named Shammas), as a means of simultaneously rehearsing and challenging the seeming inevitability of partition. The specific political projects of the two novels are by no means equally radical: *Cracking India* restages partition from the vantage point of an upper-class family in

Lahore whose Parsee origins place them 'outside' of the conflict and in a position to offer charity to its victims (see Hai), while *Arabesques* takes the riskier route of "deterritorializing Hebrew" (Hever; Hochberg) by using it to tell a story of Palestinian dispossession. Yet both demonstrate the *Bildungsroman*'s particular capacity to highlight the contingency of partition, in part by drawing attention to the responsibility, and not just the victimization, of those who were present and those who live with its consequences.

*Cracking India* is in many ways a fairly conventional example of the *Bildungsroman*, following its protagonist-narrator's journey from an almost total innocence of all forms of injustice, including discrimination on the basis of gender and disability, to a level of familiarity with social, sexual, and physical violence that leaves her, if not traumatized, certainly far less capable of wonder or trust. While critics have normally located the novel's effort to defamiliarize the event of partition in its use of Lenny's naïve narrative perspective, signified most obviously through her "collapse of the figurative and literal uses of language" (Didur, *Unsettling Partition* 72; Bhatia 203-04; Hai 388-89), this progression from innocence to experience is in fact a more important intervention. Partition is made uncanny (Gopal 81) not just because the reader is meant to imagine what it might be like to share Lenny's innocence, but because, like her, we are encouraged to contrast the time of pre-partition innocence with that of post-partition disillusionment.

The novel is almost comically packed with moments of confusion and epiphany that make up what might be understood as Lenny's sentimental—or perhaps political—education. In one of the novel's most frequently cited passages, Lenny takes the news that India is to be "broken" literally: "Can one break a country? And what happens if they break it where our house is? Or crack it further up on Warris Road? How will I ever get to Godmother's then?" (101). This retrospective staging of childish credulity is not always believable or consistent—as Hai points out (394), few five-year-olds would casually refer to pubic hair or white slave trafficking (Sidhwa 68-69)—but it is nevertheless used to establish Lenny's innocence, which is allegorically paralleled, like Ayah's meetings in the park with her admirers, with the pre-partition innocence of the population. However, Lenny's climactic loss of innocence comes not from her position as a witness to violence, as some critics have claimed, but from her own actions: When she betrays Ayah's hiding place to Ice-candy-man (Sidhwa 194), she becomes implicated (again, like the population as a whole) in the violence against Ayah that follows (Kabir 184). At this point, her role as naïve informant, to paraphrase Gayatri Spivak (6), is dramatically decreased: She plays no role in narrating the novel's most harrowing episode, the massacre in Ranna's village (207-20), and she is unable to offer much information about Ayah's abduction, rape, or recovery, despite the centrality of this event to the narrative (Hai 402). According to the logic of the *Bildungsroman* form then Lenny is socially incorporated by becoming complicit with partition violence: She comes of age by passing from the role of witness to the role not of victim (that is taken by Ayah) but of participant.

The critical emphasis on the novel's preoccupation with witnessing (Bahri) seems to overlook this essential structural element of the text, which is foreshadowed earlier in the novel by the delight Lenny takes in the bullying of the family's Hindu servant, Hari (126). Lenny's culpability works on an allegorical level—she is a representative of her class (the Parsees benefited from colonial rule as a group, as the novel itself makes clear)[6] as well as the general population—but it also signals Lenny's sense of her own individual agency as a perpetrator of division and violence. Aijaz Ahmad has written that "what we witnessed [after Partition] was not just the British policy of divide and rule, which surely was there, but our own willingness to break up our civilizational unity, to kill our neighbours, to forgo that civic ethos, that moral bond with each other, without which human community is impossible" (119; see also Gopal 82). This is a damning but also, from a counterfactual perspective, a productive insight, for if the Indian partition and the violence that followed it were not only the result of colonial policy and the competing self-interests of Congress and the Muslim League, but also a product of the agency of non-elites, then Partition violence can be less easily conceived of as an agentless disaster. In this light, Lenny's incorporation into post-partition society is also an assumption of political responsibility.

While *Arabesques* draws on the *Bildungsroman* form much more subtly and selectively than *Cracking India,* and is far more difficult to summarize as a result, the novel's use of the genre also stages the progression from innocence to knowledge as a process of coming to understand one's own complicity with partition. The novel's most distinctive feature is its structural opposition between two alternating narratives. "The Tale" ("*Ha-sipur*," also "the narrative") is a folkloric account of the fictional Shammas's natal village of Fassuta, a Christian village in the Galilee, set mainly before 1948 but also during Shammas's childhood in the 1950s; "The Teller" ("*Ha-mesaper*," also "the narrator") is a linear, realist narrative set in the protagonist's adult life as an author and journalist writing in Hebrew in the 1980s. It is easy to map this formal division onto the national division set up by partition, and one of the ways in which this novel works to defamiliarize partition is by gradually destabilizing the split between "oral Arabic" and "scribal Hebrew" (Brenner 440), for instance by allowing characters from one part of the narrative to migrate to the other.

What is less immediately apparent, however, is that the complex process of *Bildung* that is staged in "The Tale" is also part of this effort. The magical realism of the early part of the narrative—signaled most obviously by the mythical rooster Ar-Rasad, who guards the village's gold-filled cave (Ginsburg 190)—aligns Shammas's childhood innocence with the image of pre-partition Palestine as a bucolic, pre-modern idyll, in contrast with the Israeli dystopia of the present. As the novel progresses, however, "The Tale" begins to lose its fantastic quality and coalesce into "hard political history" (Feldman 382), as the adult narrator moves back in time and recounts events that took place before he was born: before and during partition. Some of this account details Israeli atrocities against Palestinians, including the expulsion of the residents of the nearby Muslim village of Deir el-Kasi in 1948. Yet the narrative is more centrally concerned with the role that "corruption and weakness," infighting, greed, and revenge killings played in the "drown[ing of] the rebellion" of 1936 (Shammas 190) and the Palestinian defeat in 1948, as represented by the enmity between the two villages. Thus, we are told at the beginning of the novel, from the point of view of the young Shammas, that the Fassutans "were subject to persecutions and torture" at the hands of the Deir el-Kasi villagers in the early part of the century (11), and later during the 1936 uprising. It does not follow, however, that the novel is a document of "Arab Christian nationalism," as Feldman has argued (382), for, in the second half of the novel, it transpires that the Fassutans were not simply victims: They refused to participate in the uprising, and they subsequently escaped expulsion in 1948 because they were able to bribe the Jewish commander. The eviction order for Fassuta was duly rescinded, while the residents of Deir El-Kasi were dispersed and their village renamed Moshav Elkosh (11 and 126). Even the story of Ar-Rasad becomes part of this history: The Fassutans, already suspicious of the uprising, decide that Palestinian resistance forces are "the enemy of Ar-Rasad, who was wary of them and did not show the tip of his tail in fear they would attempt to take control of his treasures by force" (193), a reference to the Palestinian militias' commandeering of civilian food stores.

The adult Shammas is in one sense even more innocent than the child Lenny, since none of this history is the result of his own actions. Nevertheless, the implication of this narrative trajectory from innocence to awareness is that coming of age means being able to critically evaluate received history. Palestinian resistance to partition fails, this narrative suggests, not only because Palestinians are the weaker party, but also because their internal communal divisions reflect the logic of partition itself, in which group identity provides a pretext for the assertion of power. Unlike *Cracking India* where nostalgia for the pre-partition past enables a critique of the post-partition present, in *Arabesques* nostalgia takes on the more conventional cast of a dangerously dehistoricizing emotion which prevents Palestinians from taking responsibility for their own political failings, past or present.

By alternating this narrative with the story of the adult Shammas's life in "The Teller," however, and by writing the novel in Hebrew, Shammas insists that the real history of the pre-partition period—both the Shammas family history, and the history of Palestinian dispossession—is also part of Israeli history. The novel's Palestinian and Israeli narratives appear to be separate only so long as the history of Israel/Palestine is understood in terms of the "dual society thesis" which holds that Palestinian and Israeli societies developed in total isolation from one another (Piterberg 69), and only so long as Israel is defined as a Jewish state. This presentation is inherently counterfactual, since it makes it possible to envision its opposite: an Israeli state that, as Shammas argued in his famous debate with Yehoshua, "*exists in a certain territory*, [and] then everyone who is in that territory is an equal part of it, and then an Arab in Jaljulia is Israeli just like A. B. Yehoshua" (Grossman 257, original emphasis).

As a genre then the partition *Bildungsroman* might be classed as a version of what Joseph Slaughter has called the "dissensual *Bildungsroman*," which he defines as a form that protests the protagonist's exclusion from the "public realm of rights" while drawing on the norms of this realm to articulate his or her claim (181-82). In the case of the partition *Bildungsroman*, the constitutive paradox is that the form both relies on *and* resists partition's historical trajectory: It depends on its seeming inevitability for the momentum of its plot, and yet it challenges the ahistorical belief that Muslims and Hindus, or Arabs and Jews, are doomed to permanent conflict. To assert the existence of a different past, as in *Cracking India*, or the possibility of a different future, as in *Arabesques*, is to refuse this passive form of social incorporation, and to insist on the agency of individuals to promote more inclusive forms of nationality.

## 3. Fragmented Narrative

My final example, the fragmented narrative, is a stylistic rather than a plot category, defined by the use of any kind of episodic or disjunctive narration: spatial, temporal, generic, or perspectival. Narrative fragmentation is, of course, often associated with Euro/US modernism and postmodernism, and many twentieth-century partition narratives are evidently influenced by this mode. However, the use of the fragment in partition fiction can also be read as a kind of situationally specific appropriation of its Jamesonian sense, in which narrative fragmentation represents the protagonist's inability to apprehend the totality of the post-partition multi-state order. The counterfactual potential of the genre comes from the narrative impetus to reconnect the fragments; this can be read as a formal expression of the desire for reunification, or, in its more radical manifestations, as an illustration of the kind of imaginative deconstruction and reassembly that needs to be undertaken if the exclusionary forms of national identity created by partition are to be confronted and undone.

The genre can be broadly divided into two categories. On the one hand, there are the narratives that try to combat the experiential sense of fragmentation that partition has instigated by performing and then resolving it within the narrative itself. For instance, Edna O'Brien's *House of Splendid Isolation* uses non-linear chronology and postmodern changes in genre and voice to narrate an allegory of national reunification between an elderly woman from the Republic of Ireland and the IRA gunman she is compelled to shelter in her home (Harris 111-12). Deane's memoir *Reading in the Dark* offers another variation, gradually incorporating stand-alone episodes from the narrator's childhood into a coherent narrative of republican resistance and failure. In both novels, the reader's experience of piecing together the story mirrors the protagonists' experience of reconstructing the pre-partition past that governs their experiences, while the limits of the protagonists' knowledge stand in for the 'collective amnesia' of the population as a whole. The narrative's energy then derives not only from the desire for reconciliation, but also from the need to construct a more accurate and complete historical memory that will counter this mass forgetting.

By contrast, the two texts I consider below, Saadat Hasan Manto's *Mottled Dawn*[7] and Oz Shelach's *Picnic Grounds: A Novel in Fragments*, are distinguished by their refusal to connect their fragments. The two texts were published more than fifty years apart, in Urdu and English respectively, and yet their construction is remarkably similar: Each presents a series of very short narratives, often only a few sentences and rarely more than a page in length, and usually consisting of just one scene. Both texts are characterized by the extreme brevity and discreteness of these segments, which are joined not by characters, chronology, or setting, but only by their subject matter—in each case a devastating critique of the destructive consequences of partition. This thematic emphasis, underpinned by the repetition of a selection of images and tropes, counters what initially seems to be a form of anti-narrativism. Instead, the reader is encouraged to make his or her own connections between the fragments, and to seek his or her referents in the contemporary conditions they represent.

This genre, particularly in the extreme form represented by Manto and Shelach, is worthy of note in part because the 'fragment' is already a common category of analysis in Indian partition studies. This trend originates with Pandey, whose essays "The Prose of Otherness" and "In Defense of the Fragment" have become "ubiquitous citations" in studies which emphasize partition literature's disruption of dominant national narratives (Didur, *Unsettling Partition* 169, n. 6). Pandey draws on Manto, among other less well-known figures and texts, to illustrate his contention that the "fragment"—meaning literature, diaries, testimony, or other material not included in official archives, as well as the perspectives of marginalized groups more generally—"is a disturbing element, a rupture . . . in the self-representation of particular totalities and those who uncritically uphold them" (*Routine Violence* 66). Despite his reliance on literature as evidence, it must be emphasized that Pandey's definition of the fragment is not a literary one: It is directed against "totalizing" historiographical practices ranging from colonial to Marxist—he pointedly distances his definition from Gramsci's notion of the fragment (199, n. 49)—rather than describing any specific property of narrative.

However, literary critics have subsequently reversed Pandey's direction of analysis and adopted the term to read Manto's own work, particularly his iconic short stories of Partition ("Toba Tek Singh," "Cold Meat," and "Open It"), as "fragments" in both the historiographical and the narrative senses of the word. For instance, Alex Padamsee argues, following Pandey, that the short story is a popular form in narratives of the Indian partition because "it is necessarily a fragment" which "favours the narration of uncertainty" (also a term from Pandey). In his reading, Manto's stories exemplify this use of the structure in the "undecidability" of their endings, which refuses the ethical closure of the horrors of Partition offered by celebratory narratives of national independence and questions "the very possibility of narrative" after Partition (2-3). Aamir Mufti's reading is unusual in that it draws on Lukács rather than Pandey, and yet he comes to a similar conclusion, arguing that the "fragments" collected in the Urdu short story "do not merely point toward a totality [as in Lukács] . . . [but] pu[t] the terms of this totality in question" (184). Though Mufti allows that Manto's is an immanent critique of nationalism, he nevertheless concludes that in his work the fragment "disturbs the serenity in which that totality [of the modern life of the nation] is produced, pointing always to the possibility of collective ways of life that are less singular and more hospitable to individual and collective freedom" (209).

The privileged value in these readings is ambiguity, which is favorably opposed to the allegedly hegemonic forces of narrative on the one hand and nationalism on the other. Yet the fragments in Manto do not challenge the idea of totality; on the contrary, they seek to represent a new social totality in which atrocity has become the norm (Marx 623-24). For instance, in "The Benefits of Ignorance," when a sniper aims his gun at a child, he and a companion have the following exchange: "'What are you doing?' his companion asked. 'Why?' 'You are out of bullets'" (187). Here, as in many of the fragments, the impact of the episode hinges on a reversal of expectations: Under normal (pre-partition) circumstances, the murder of a child would be unthinkable, but under the new normal order this imperative no longer applies. A number of the fragments draw attention to the material economy of partition violence, which again emphasizes the ordinariness and the seeming inescapability of the new order. Violent acts are perceived in transactional terms by the perpetrators, as in "Double Cross," where the speaker complains of having been sold faulty petrol that won't burn any shops (211), and "Losing Proposition," where the protagonist is furious to discover that the girl for whom he has paid forty-two rupees is not from "the other religion," and demands a refund (198). Even the child in "Jelly" who sees congealed blood on the ground assimilates it into his own experience, saying, "Look, mummy, jelly" (192). The accumulation of such fragments points less to a skepticism or disillusionment with narrative than to a heightened narrativity, in which the reiterated banality of these acts of violence outlines the total social transformation that has taken place. For Manto the fragment is not opposed to total representation, but potentially (though never actually) productive of it.

The aggregation of analogous fragments has the further effect of constructing a public terrain whose contours are not those of either of the new nations. Manto offers few contextual details which could identify his protagonists as Hindu, Sikh, or Muslim—most characters go unnamed, for instance—and one of the recurring themes, as in "Losing Proposition," "Mistake Removed," and several other fragments, is the impossibility of identifying the group identity of any individual on the basis of his or her appearance. As Mufti points out, by refusing to label his protagonists, Manto rejects the "balance" between Hindu and Muslim acts of violence that is common to many works of Indian partition literature (206), including *Train to Pakistan*, a practice which "reduces the violence to the language of the feud" (Das and Nandy 189; Harlow 88). However, this strategy also counterfactually posits the existence of a pre-partition polity that might have become an independent nation, and which, even after partition, is still tied by a shared culture and history, which now includes the history of the partition violence. Rather than 'the nation' then Manto's critique is directed at the state order that legitimates the violence he depicts by normalizing the idea of ethnic and communal difference (Marx 624), an order that is haunted by the nation that might have been.

In marked contrast to the previous text (or indeed *Arabesques*), Shelach's *Picnic Grounds* refrains from direct representation of the violence of the Palestinian partition and its aftermath. Historical and contemporary atrocities—Deir Yassin, the torture of Palestinian prisoners, the massacre at Hebron—are alluded to in passing, but the emphasis is on the everyday acts of forgetting and willful ignorance that enable most Israelis to overlook this history of violence. While the effect of the repetition of this theme is cumulative, as in Manto, Shelach makes more deliberate use of the fragment's aporetic quality as a means of evoking the silences within hegemonic Zionist discourse. Shelach introduces this method in the first fragment of the book, "One Afternoon." The fragment opens with the line: "A professor of history from Bayit Va-Gan took his family for a picnic in a quiet pinewood near Giv'at Shaul, formerly known as Deir Yassin" (1). Though the fragment offers no comment on the massacre beyond its name, its presence at the end of the sentence reconfigures the meaning of the sentence as a whole. Both the professor's academic specialization and the stillness of the forest are given a significance which is not immediately apparent from the words "history" and "quiet" themselves, but only from the delayed revelation of the setting's relationship to this event. The reference to the Hebrew renaming of formerly Arab towns and villages repeats this act of layering, the Hebrew name obscuring the Arabic and yet continuing to gesture towards its past existence.

The professor, we are told, is careful to preserve the tranquility of the scene by refraining from dwelling on its history: "[He] did not talk of the village, origin of the stones [which they use to build a fire]. He did not talk of the village school, now a psychiatric hospital, on the other side of the hill. He imagined that he and his family were having a picnic, unrelated to the village, enjoying its grounds outside history" (1). The fragment ends on this word. By its conclusion then the "quiet" of the scene has been revealed to have a double significance: It marks both the absence of Palestinians and the Israeli protagonist's reluctance to substantiate that history by speaking it aloud. The repetition of the word "history" foregrounds the professor's putative societal role, while his desire to be "outside history" alludes to the peculiar position of historians who may be well informed about the past atrocities committed by the state, but still choose or are encouraged to narrate an ethnonationalist version of events. This presentation aligns Shelach with some of the more radical work put forward by the Israeli New Historians (Ilan Pappé, Tom Segev, Avi Shlaim), since these historians have framed their work as a revision or refutation of Zionist historiography, but Shelach's text emphasizes the act of suppression itself, not the historical record being suppressed.

Although this fragment is narrated in the third person, many others are narrated in the first person plural. This unidentified "we" acts as a witness or a party to particular acts of historical censorship, as in "Tu B'Shvat," set on the day of the tree-planting festival. In this fragment, the "we" is a group of children that shun another boy for calling the ceremonies "murderous and fascist" because, the child says, the tree-planting hides the remaining evidence of Palestinian villages (29). Like Manto's unidentified protagonists, Shelach's indistinguishable narrators function as Israeli Everymen, forming a culpable collective who are connected not because they have actually committed acts of violence—none of the fragments address this question—but because they are rational and complicit participants in the silencing of the history of Palestinian dispossession. The desire for a different social order that this representation implies is movingly voiced in the only first-person fragment in the book, "Nostalgic." It begins self-deprecatingly: "I was a nostalgic from childhood. In kindergarten I longed for my nanny. In first grade I longed for kindergarten. In high school I longed for primary school (which was a horrible experience)" (95). At the end of the fragment, however, this subjective experience is expanded to include the rest of the nation: "Having since boarded an airplane and left Israel full of bitter disillusionment and hope for the future, I now long for a time not very long ago, but which I have never known, before ever I existed, or, preferably, before we did" (95). The explicit counterfactualism of this sentiment, in which the narrator born long after partition yearns for a pre-partition past that he (or conceivably, she) has "never known," is in some respects deeply pessimistic, not least because it comes after the narrator has left the country. At the same time, however, by desiring the negation of the complicit Israeli "we," the fragment holds out a form of "nostalgia" for the future, in which the exclusionary form of that "we" will have ceased to exist, and a more egalitarian "we" might be realized.

## Conclusion

Whether or not one wants to follow Ranabir Samaddar in substituting "partitioned times" for "post-colonial times"—and I, for one, would not want the necessary connection between the two terms to be obscured—it is at least the case that the generic affinities between these otherwise disparate fictional texts are more convincingly explained as a common form of reference to partition than to the more general and variegated history of imperial rule. Taken as a group, these narratives sketch out a convergent mode of literary and political imagination, one which challenges the logic of partition by lamenting its forgotten alternatives. It is tempting, perhaps, to dismiss the kinds of counterfactuals that fiction can provide: These texts are not policy documents, and they typically only express a desire for alternative social structures rather than actually representing them. Yet the critique of partition that they offer has its own kind of power. In the closing paragraph of an essay on women's novels about the Indian partition, Ananya Jahanara Kabir tentatively suggests that if more narratives of "fratricide" (see also Francisco 372) had been produced immediately after partition, they might have enabled a cross-regional mourning within the new nations that could also have been the basis of cross-border reconciliation. This insight perhaps seems too utopian, however, and she amends it with the disclaimer: "But these are counterfactual arguments" (190). Yet the defense of partition is based on its own kind of counterfactual: The idea that partition is the 'least worst option' assumes that the violence would have been far worse if it had not been implemented, even if historical evidence suggests, particularly in the cases of India, Palestine, and Ireland, that partition has almost always produced armed conflict and not prevented it. As Bartolovich points out, if the "ubiquitous conservative counterfactualism of the right that naturalises [the] status quo" is to be countered effectively, it is imperative to develop a critical counterfactualism that makes alternatives to the present imaginable (74). The need for such a practice is particularly acute in the case of partition, since the idea that heterogeneity breeds conflict is still very much with us. Moreover, it is precisely because alternatives to partition have become so difficult to envision—especially in Palestine—that counterfactual questions need to be asked, and counterfactual scenarios need to be constructed. It may be that literature is the only arena in which this effort can be carried out in relative freedom, even if those alternatives that can be imaginatively figured are, under the current global order, always finally deferred.

### Notes

1 In what follows, references to "the Indian partition" or "Indian partition studies" are not intended to privilege the study of post-partition India over the study of Pakistan and Bangladesh; rather, I use such phrases to describe the partition of historical India, in parallel with the partitions of Palestine and Ireland. I sometimes also use the capitalized form "Partition" to refer to the Indian partition, in keeping with common practice in Indian partition scholarship.

2 Strictly speaking, of course, Palestine was not actually partitioned, since the UN partition plan of 1947 was never put into practice; the 'two-state' solution seeks to officially implement partition for the first time. Yet as Salah D. Hassan points out, the idea of partition is central both to the Palestinian "partition-to-occupation narrative," in which the partition of historic Palestine into the Jewish state and the non-sovereign Palestinian territories is synonymous with the *nakba*, and to the "narrative of a doomed peace that merely legitimates partition" (41). The idea of partition is therefore arguably even more central to Palestinian and Israeli writing than it is in writing from partition contexts such as India and Ireland, where (despite the ongoing conflict over Kashmir and the steadfastness of the Irish republican parties) partition is more commonly thought to be 'finished.'

3 I give the date to distinguish the "Great Partition" (Khan) from the partition of West and East Pakistan/Bangladesh in 1971.

4 Ayah is named once in the novel as Shanta, and some commentators refer to her by name in order to avoid objectifying her further by calling her "Ayah" as Lenny does, but I think this exaggerates her subjectivity to a degree that the novel—for different possible reasons, as contrastingly argued by Didur in *Unsettling Partition* (87-93) and Hai (398-407)—does not permit.

5 In both cases, this has much to do with the backgrounds of their authors and their language of composition. *Cracking India* was one of the earliest

and most successful Pakistani novels in English, and is arguably still the best-known, thanks in part to Deepa Mehta's film adaptation, *Earth*. *Arabesques*, meanwhile, is far and away the most acclaimed Hebrew-language novel by a Palestinian Israeli writer; Ammiel Alcalay attributes its success to its seeming confirmation ("through no fault of its own") of Israeli pluralism and multiculturalism (9-10 and 286, n. 21).

6 Sidhwa also makes this argument in an interview with Alok Bhalla (232).

7 A more recent English translation by M. Asaddudin is also available, under the title *Black Margins*.

### Works Cited


Ahmad, Aijaz. *In Theory: Classes, Nations, Literatures*. London: Verso, 1992.

Alcalay, Ammiel. *After Jews and Arabs: Remaking Levantine Culture*. Minneapolis, MN: U of Minnesota P, 1993.

Bahri, Deepika. "Telling Tales: Women and the Trauma of Partition in Sidhwa's *Cracking India*."*Interventions* 1.2 (1999): 217–34.

Bartolovich, Crystal. "History After the End of History: Critical Counterfactualism and Revolution." *New Formations* 59 (2006): 63-80.

Bhalla, Alok. *Partition Dialogues: Memories of a Lost Home*. Oxford and New Delhi: Oxford UP, 2006.

Bhatia, Nandi. "How Long Does Lahore Burn? History, Memory and Literary Representations of the Partition." *Pangs of Partition,* vol. 2. Ed. S. Settar and Indira Baptista Gupta. New Delhi: Indian Council of Historical Research, 2002. 191-208.

Bose, Sumantra. *Contested Lands: Israel-Palestine, Kashmir, Bosnia, Cyprus, and Sri Lanka*. Cambridge, MA: Harvard UP, 2007.

____________. "The Partition Evasion." *OpenDemocracy*. <http://www.opendemocracy.net/article/conflicts/india_pakistan/partition_peoples>.

Brenner, Rachel Feldhay. "In Search of Identity: The Israeli Arab Artist in Anton Shammas' *Arabesques*." *PMLA* 108.3 (1993): 431-45.

Cleary, Joe. *Literature, Partition and the Nation-State*. Cambridge: Cambridge UP, 2002.

Das, Veena, and Ashis Nandy. "Violence, Victimhood and the Language of Silence." *The Word and the World*. Ed. Veena Das. New Delhi: Sage, 1986. 177-95.

Deane, Seamus. *Reading in the Dark*. London: Vintage, 1996.

Didur, Jill. "Lifting the Veil? Reconsidering the Task of Literary Historiography." *Interventions* 3.3 (2001): 446-51.

_________. *Unsettling Partition: Literature, Gender, Memory*. Toronto: U of Toronto P, 2006.

Feldman, Yael. "Postcolonial Memory, Postmodern Intertextuality: Anton Shammas's *Arabesques* Revisited." *PMLA* 114.3 (1999): 373-89.

Francisco, Jason. "In the Heat of Fratricide: The Literature of India's Partition Burning Freshly." *Inventing Boundaries: Gender, Politics and the Partition of India*. Ed. Mushirul Hasan. Oxford and New Delhi: Oxford UP, 2000. 371-93.

Fraser, T. G. *Partition in Ireland, India and Palestine: Theory and Practice*. NY: St. Martin's P, 1984.

Ginsburg, Shai. "'The Rock of Our Very Existence': Anton Shammas's *Arabesques* and the Rhetoric of Hebrew Literature." *Comparative Literature* 58.3 (2006): 187-204.

Gopal, Priyamvada. *The Indian English Novel: Nation, History and Narration*. Oxford: Oxford UP, 2009.

Grossman, David. *Sleeping on a Wire: Conversations with Palestinians in Israel*. NY: Farrar Straus & Giroux, 1993.

Hai, Ambreen. "Border Work, Border Trouble: Postcolonial Feminism and the Ayah in Bapsi Sidhwa's *Cracking India*." *Modern Fiction Studies* 46.2 (2000): 379-426.

Harlow, Barbara. "Drawing the Line: Cultural Politics and the Legacy of Partition." *Polygraph* 5 (1992): 84-111.

Harris, Michael. "Outside History: Edna O'Brien's *House of Splendid Isolation*." *New Hibernia Review* 10.1 (2006): 111-22.

Hasan, Mushirul, ed. *Inventing Boundaries: Gender, Politics and the Partition of India*. Oxford and New Delhi: Oxford UP, 2000.

Hassan, Salah D. "Undertaking Partition: Palestine and Postcolonial Studies." *Journal X: A Journal in Culture and Criticism* 6.1 (2001): 19-45.

Hever, Hannan. *Producing the Modern Hebrew Canon: Nation Building and Minority Discourse*. NY: NYUP, 2002.

Hochberg, Gil. *In Spite of Partition: Jews, Arabs, and the Limits of Separatist Imagination*. Princeton, NJ: Princeton UP, 2007.

Horowitz, Michael C. and Alex Weisiger. "The Limits to Partition." *International Security* 33.4 (2009): 203-06.

Jameson, Fredric. *Postmodernism, or, The Cultural Logic of Late Capitalism*. Durham, NC: Duke UP, 1991.

Jassal, Smita Tewari and Eyal Ben-Ari, eds. *The Partition Motif in Contemporary Conflicts*. London: Sage, 2007.

Johnson, Carter. "Partitioning to Peace: Sovereignty, Demography, and Ethnic Civil Wars." *International Security* 32.4 (2008): 140–70.

Kabir, Ananya Jahanara. "Gender, Memory, Trauma: Women's Novels on the Partition of India." *Comparative Studies of South Asia, Africa and the Middle East* 25.1 (2005): 177-90.

Kanafani, Ghassan. *Men in the Sun and Other Palestinian Stories*. Trans. Hilary Kilpatrick. Boulder, CO: Lynne Rienner, 1999.

Karmi, Ghada. *In Search of Fatima: A Palestinian Story*. London: Verso, 2002.

Kaufmann, Chaim. "When All Else Fails: Ethnic Population Transfers and Partitions in the Twentieth Century." *International Security* 23.2 (1998): 120–56.

Kaul, Suvir, ed. *The Partitions of Memory: The Afterlife of the Division of India.* Bloomington, IN: Indiana UP, 2001.

Kesavan, Mukul. *Looking Through Glass*. London: Vintage, 1996.

Khan, Yasmin. *The Great Partition: The Making of India and Pakistan*. New Haven, CT: Yale UP, 2007.

Khanna, Ranjana. "Indignity." *Positions* 16.1 (2008): 39-77.

Kumar, Priya. "Testimonies of Loss and Memory: Partition and the Haunting of a Nation." *Interventions* 1.2 (1999): 201-15.

Kumar, Radha. "Settling Partition Hostilities: Lessons Learnt, the Options Ahead." *Divided Countries, Separated Cities: The Modern Legacy of Partition*. Eds. Ghislaine Glasson Deschaumes and Rada Ivekovic. Oxford and New Delhi: Oxford UP, 2003. 3-18.

Leonard, John. "A Tale of Love and Darkness: Motherland." *New York Times*. 12 December 2004. <http://www.nytimes.com/2004/12/12/books/review/12LEONARD.html>

Lingard, Joan. *Across the Barricades*. London: Puffin, 2003.

___________. *Kevin and Sadie: The Story Continues*. London: Puffin, 2006.

___________. *The Twelfth Day of July*. London: Puffin, 2003.

Manto, Saadat Hasan. *Black Margins*. Trans. M. Asaddudin. New Delhi: Katha, 2004.

___________________. *Mottled Dawn: Fifty Stories and Sketches of Partition*. Trans. Khalid Hasan. London: Penguin, 1997.

Marx, John. "Failed-State Fiction." *Contemporary Literature* 49.4 (2008): 597-633.

Mehta, Deepa, dir. *Earth*. Cracking the Earth Films, 1998.

Menon, Ritu. "Cartographies of Nations and Identities: A Post-Partition Predicament." *Interventions* 1.2 (1999): 157-65.

__________ and Kamla Bhasin. *Borders and Boundaries: Women in India's Partition*. New Delhi: Kali for Women, 1998.

Moretti, Franco. "Conjectures on World Literature." *New Left Review* 1 (2000). <http://www.newleftreview.org/A2094>.

_____________. *Graphs, Maps, Trees: Abstract Models for a Literary History*. London: Verso, 2005.

Mufti, Aamir. *Enlightenment in the Colony: The Jewish Question and the Crisis of Postcolonial Culture*. Princeton, NJ: Princeton UP, 2007.

Oz, Amos. *A Tale of Love and Darkness*. Trans. Nicholas de Lange. London: Chatto & Windus, 2004.

Padamsee, Alex. "Uncertain Partitions: 'Undecidability' and the Urdu Short Story." *Wasafiri* 23.1 (2008): 1-5.

Pandey, Gyanendra. "In Defense of the Fragment: Writing About Hindu-Muslim Riots in India Today." *Representations* 37 (1992): 27-55.

_______________. "The Prose of Otherness." *Subaltern Studies 8*. Eds. David Arnold and David Hardiman. Delhi: Oxford UP, 1994. 188-221.

_______________. *Remembering Partition: Violence, Nationalism, and History in India.* Cambridge: Cambridge UP, 2001.

_______________. *Routine Violence: Nations, Fragments, Histories*. Stanford, CA: Stanford UP, 2006.

Piterberg, Gabriel. *The Returns of Zionism: Myths, Politics and Scholarship in Israel*. London: Verso, 2008.

Ramras-Rauch, Gila. *The Arab in Israeli Literature.* London: I. B. Tauris, 1989.

Rastegar, Kamran. "Trauma and Maturation in Women's War Narratives: *The Eye of the Mirror* and *Cracking India.*" *Journal of Middle East Women's Studies* 2.3 (2006): 22-47.

Rushdie, Salman. *Midnight's Children*. London: Jonathan Cape, 1981.

Said, Edward. *Out of Place: A Memoir*. London: Granta, 1999.

Samaddar, Ranabir. "The Last Hurrah that Continues." *Divided Countries, Separated Cities: The Modern Legacy of Partition*. Eds. Ghislaine Glasson Deschaumes and Rada Ivekovic. Oxford and New Delhi: Oxford UP, 2003. 21-35.

Shammas, Anton. *Arabesques*. Trans. Vivian Eden. London: Penguin, 1988.

Shelach, Oz. *Picnic Grounds: A Novel in Fragments*. San Francisco: City Lights, 2003.

Sidhwa, Bapsi. *Cracking India.* Minneapolis, MN: Milkweed Editions, 1991.

Singh, Khushwant. *Train to Pakistan*. New Delhi: Ravi Dayal, 1988.

Slaughter, Joseph. *Human Rights, Inc.: The World Novel, Narrative Form, and International Law*. NY: Fordham UP, 2007.

Sommer, Doris. *Foundational Fictions: The National Romances of Latin America.* Berkeley, CA: U of California P, 1991.

Spivak, Gayatri Chakravorty. *A Critique of Postcolonial Reason: Toward a History of the Vanishing Present*. Cambridge, MA: Harvard UP, 1999.

Waterman, Stanley. "Partitioned States." *Political Geography Quarterly* 6 (1987): 151–70.

Yehoshua. A. B. *The Lover.* Trans. Philip Simpson. London: Peter Halban, 2004.

# Social Memories 'in the Flesh': War and Exile in Algerian Self-Writing

**James McDougall***

---

> One is never cured of memory. That is why one writes. . . . Today at last I have to find the words to write the narrative of my life. I have the right, after all, to choose how to narrate myself, even if I did not choose the story.[1]

'Memory' poses obvious challenges for social science, whether as an object of study or as an analytical term, despite the enormous amount of work in several disciplines that has long sought to define and elucidate it. In posing the question of how contemporary history is lived and lived with, narrated and embodied, in the formation of personal selfhood within a particular set of social conditions, therefore, some initial clearing of conceptual ground is necessary. This article makes no claim to provide a 'social psychology,' or to locate individual self-narrative within a kind of collective unconscious—a notion often implied, and much abused, in some commentary on the traumas of contemporary Algeria. I take 'social memory,' instead, as referring to social relations of *praxis* and as preferable to psychologizing and mechanistic notions like 'collective memory.'[2] The problem with this latter term, frequently resorted to in discussions of Algeria and the traumas of its modern history, is that it tends towards the abstraction of the factors of selfhood from actual social processes and relocates them, instead, in a kind of intangible, ethereal realm of collective consciousness (or repressed unconscious); at worst, such notions elide 'collective memory' into homogenizing and analytically useless categories like 'national character' or 'group psyche.' Approached in these terms, social life and meaning appear to be structured and determined by some underlying or overarching collective 'social truth' which would hold the keys to the definition of both collective and individual 'identity.' Identity here has the sense of a singular 'sameness,' (*mêmeté*), the grounds for community belonging being the mutual (self-)recognition of each in a collective unconscious, or a common narrative. (Some individuals may, of course, refuse to recognize themselves in such terms, but they will tend to be dismissed as 'alienated,' 'inauthentic,' or eccentric.) In fact, of course, no such 'collective memory' really exists: Such narratives of 'social truth' are in fact more commonly imposed by authority from above than elaborated in consensus from below—as, for example, in accounts of nationalism as 'revealing' or 'restoring' a transhistorical, pre-existing 'national identity' when in fact it fabricates a new form of cultural and symbolic authority. In the case of Algeria, recurrent outbreaks of violence have also sometimes been 'explained' by such notions of a structuring collective memory, or 'return of the repressed.'[3]

If such totalizing and mechanistic notions of collectivity are actively unhelpful, the social context of memory has nonetheless long been recognized as crucial to its operation (and indeed to its existence).[4] A more adequate way of grasping its importance, as a means of interpreting contemporary Algerian cultural production and self-fashioning—the construction of identity not as sameness but as 'selfhood' (*ipséité*)[5]—is to examine "self-writing," what Foucault called *écriture de soi*: the self-disciplinary and self-constitutive "technique of living" produced in the act of writing (of) oneself.[6] What I propose here is to consider such self-writing as a social process, as legible not in a defined corpus of literature, and even less in the official pronouncements of political rhetoric, but in the situated practices of self-constitution created and reproduced in the everyday processes of social life. In specifying the practices that constitute this object of investigation, we can also usefully add to Foucault's notion of self-disciplinary practice the work of Paul Ricoeur in narratology and the phenomenology of history, memory, and forgetting.[7] In particular, as the social sites in which self-writing, understood in this broad sense as self-constitution, most visibly takes place, we can identify the domains of *emplotment* and *enactment*. Emplotment (or narrativization) is Ricoeur's *mise-en-intrigue*. Enactment, by analogy, denotes *mise-en-scène*; the former refers to a mode of narration, the latter to its 'staging,' whether in a work of art or in public life and the built environment, in public monuments and the staking out of positions in public debate. Mise-en-scène, of course, also occurs on the most intimate level of *embodiment*, in the enactment of selfhood in one's own physicality, in personal performance, and individual self-presentation, through dress, physical deportment, relation to space, etc.—a detailed historical anthropology of such practices would reveal much more about Algerian self-constitution than is possible here.[8] To borrow a phrase from the most celebrated of contemporary Algerian novelists, Ahlam Mosteghanemi: Algerians, not, perhaps, more than other people, but perhaps sometimes more consciously so, carry their social memories in this sense 'in the flesh.'

What follows, then, is a discussion of some predominant aspects of the constitution of Algerian selfhood, focusing on the twin themes, constitutive of much of contemporary Algerian history and correlatively of much Algerian cultural production, of the experiences of exile and war. These themes are traced, eclectically but with the hope of illustrating a certain systematicity, through a variety of genres or idioms: from literary fiction and autobiography, through popular song and scholarly writing, to the languages of journalism, polemic and political humor. The question can hardly be addressed adequately in a single short article: What I propose are merely preliminary observations towards a reading of contemporary Algerian culture that might consider the practices of self-writing—of the simultaneous *emplotment* and *enactment* of social memory in a variety of 'ways of being Algerian'—through which we might discern Algerian self-constitution, not simply in terms of the imprisonment or absence of individuality, or the betrayed hopes of a 'happy' collectivity,[9] but in socially-situated and individually embodied 'techniques of living.'

## Social Bodies

Khaled, the narrator of Ahlam Mostaghanemi's *Memory in the Flesh*—the most successful Algerian novel in the Arab world and one of the most profound and original creations of contemporary Algerian culture in any language—and Hayat, the woman he loves, and hates, and of whom he writes, are perfectly allegorical figures as well as absorbing human characters. Khaled, a *mujahid* who lost an arm in the war of liberation, refuses to buy into the rentierist logic of post-revolutionary Algeria, and lives as an artist-in-exile in Paris, painting the bridges of Constantine from a window that opens onto the Seine. He carries his memory and his dreams of Algeria literally in his wounded flesh, as well as embodying them in the creative acts of painting and writing that materialize his visions of the country's landscape, the promises of its past, and their betrayal in the present. Hayat, a *fille de chahid* (the daughter of Khaled's commander in the *maquis*, who is killed in action against the French army) is a novelist, seen by Mostaghanemi's reader through the lens of Khaled's passion (in the strict sense of the term) for her. Hayat, named 'life' by her mother in the absence of the father whom the child will never meet, becomes in Khaled's (and Mostaghanemi's) portrayal, a figure first for Constantine, the lost loved home, but more broadly, also, for Algeria itself, an unfulfilled promise and an inaccessible dream, eventually to be 'sold' (in a marriage arranged by her apparatchik uncle) into the clientelist consumption of *le pouvoir*.

At one level an absorbing and tragic love story, Mostaghanemi's novel is also an exploration of a social syndrome of memory and trauma, promise and loss, individual dignity and political corruption, heroism and betrayal, self-sacrifice and depredation, that can be read as a parable of contemporary Algeria and its relation to its past. Khaled, returned to Algeria after the death of his brother (who is shot in Algiers during the disturbances of October 1988), sets down in writing his memory and his dreams in order to be rid of—or revenged upon—them. But his narrative is not simply a testimony of his own self and his own passion. On the simplest level, Mostaghanemi's novel presents a fictional Algerian (male) self-narrative created through the imaginative work of a real Algerian (female) author. From the point of view of a historical sociology, such a work can also be a window onto a much wider field of vision. At once a celebration and a denunciation, a panegyric to, and an indictment of, Algeria and its contemporary history, *Dhakirat al-jasad* possesses such powerful resonance, less because of the individual artistic achievement it undoubtedly is than because of its social situatedness, its quality as a meditation on how memory is constructed and inhabited in the indivisibly personal and societal crises of the present.

If writing itself is an act of individuation, of self-expression, indeed an act of self-construction, which is simultaneously a discovery and a performance of the individual, it is also a necessarily social act. This is true on one level because, as theorists and critics have much insisted, the poetic act of writing is never consummated except in the interpretive act of reading.[10] To envisage the writer and reader as an ideal-typical communicative couple is already to depart from a Romantic conception of individualized authorship as the site of poetic creation and to locate the significance of writing within a social relation.[11] Beyond this, though, writing is an act of social significance because, even in the case of autobiography where the distinctive self-expression of the authorial subject is most apparently primary in, and constitutive of, the text, that subject her/himself is necessarily constituted as "a moment in a social relation."[12] If an older, conservative theory of autobiography as the expression of the fully and finally self-conscious modern (implicitly Western) individual selfhood saw "the subject of autobiography as isolatable, constitutive, and self-identical,"[13] such definitions can no longer be made with the same supreme (self-)confidence. In place of the author, we have the more complex—and more interesting—subject (or even, "subject-function"[14]), no longer self-constituting (self-made) and analytically coterminous with a physical person, a lifespan, and a proper name, but a 'moment' in a system, a product, as consciousness and as agency, of social-historical circumstances, of particular discursive and social formations, generated in a specifically determined relation to others in a particular distribution of socio-economic, symbolic, and cultural power. The authorial act no longer appears as the sovereign gesture of a consciousness encompassing and narrating history from the transcendent vantage point of its end. Instead, *poiesis* occurs as the making of social meaning, located in struggles and conflicts, situated within social life with all its unforeseeable contingency, inescapable constraint, and unrealized possibility.

It may seem odd to begin a discussion of writing in—or, more precisely, of the writing of—Algeria with this observation. It might well be argued that it has been precisely the *lack* of individuation, the difficulty of establishing the legitimacy and equality of the first person singular in a society whose dominant political culture has been expressed, not in the plural, but the collective—'one hero, the people'—and whose moral and political economies have been regulated by mercilessly 'clannish'[15] networks of solidarity and exclusion, that has been a factor in many of the hardships of contemporary Algeria. Without invoking clichés about the imprisoning force of 'tradition' (since we should speak rather of the active reproduction and re-sacralization of 'traditions' than of their passive transmission), there is no doubt that a most immediate aspect of life as it is lived in contemporary Algeria has been, if anything, a surplus of the 'social' and the lack of space for individual self-expression and—precisely the paradox of this emblematic history of struggle—*self-determination*.

To say this is not to reproach an intensely rich and complex society for not delivering idealized (Western?) standards of 'freedom' (a highly dubious concept in any case); it is merely to state what many ordinary Algerians experience as the suffocation of personal life in the everyday conditions of their social and political existence.[16] The raucously brilliant singer Rachid Taha, in a reflection of the feelings of young Algerians no less accurate for being articulated by an artist *issu de l'émigration*, sums it up: In society and politics, *kull shi, kull shi maqful*, everything is locked up, locked up tight, but *ana galbi safi, nebgh el-hubb ez-zehwani,* as for me, my heart is pure, and I want joyous love.[17] From unemployment and the housing crisis, the lack of public space whether physical or political, through the lack of capacity in public transport and public utilities, to the cost of consumer goods and the routine harassment of unmarried couples (and the difficulty of acquiring money and living space to marry), it is the basic conditions of material life as much as the strict ethics of social morality that are at issue.

There are also, of course, deeper historical conditions involved in the making of this situation. The rules of adherence to, and of cohesion within, a moral community were, paradoxically, crystallized by colonial rule (in the identification of Algerians as non-citizen native subjects, bound by a religio-racial normative order, whether Islamic law or Berber custom), and simultaneously decried by colonial humanism as the inertia of tradition that stood in the way of progress and civilization. They also provided the interior space—not a refuge of national identity, inviolate from without, but a system of social discipline and moral economy, inviolable from within—in which enduring passive resistance and active armed struggle could be organized. The mobilizing effort of the revolution, the massive and indiscriminate measures of its repression, and the authoritarian military state that issued from it, all powerfully combined in the sublimation of Algerian society—an enormously varied, diverse, culturally heterogeneous society—in an inflexible ideological unanimism, the denial or suppression of individualities, particularisms, divergences, and dissidence, and, of course, in the disenfranchisement of the people from the (self-)government supposedly constituted by and for them in the achievement of independence:[18]

| | |
|---|---|
| *Qlil qlil, qlil el-haqq!* | Rights are few, |
| *Ktir, ktir, ktir ed-dolma.* | Injustice is great |
| *Fil-siyasa l-hukkam berrmu en-nas,* | The rulers have silenced the people in politics, |
| *Berrmu en-nas, kull-ha.* | Silenced them all |
| *Taqaftna hiya 'l-hizb el-wahid* | Our culture is the single party |
| *La qanun, la adaba* | With no law and no decency |
| *Qlil qlil, qlil el-haqq,* | Rights are few, |
| *Ktir ktir, ktir el-hogra!* | Arrogance is great.[19] |

To make the connection of narrative—and the problem of individual self-construction viewed through it—to the spaces of the social and political, is not, then, only a question of literary hermeneutics or of an abstract philosophy of the subject. Nor, however, is it intended to provide a diagnosis of Algeria's recent crises as characterized by a consistent refusal to recognize the individual as the rights-bearing subject of liberal sovereignty and international law (legitimate as this might be). Attending to the *social* significance of a variety of means and modes of self-writing might provide, instead, a means of reading some salient aspects of contemporary Algerian cultural and social life, not with a view to identifying exceptional expressions of the emergence of triumphant individual consciousness from the constraints of moral community and authoritarian politics, but as so many microcosms in which the social constitution of

Algerian selfhood, both within and despite these constraints, is actually enacted. Rather than being imprisoned in the context of the social, in the collective inheritance of the past as inescapable tradition or atavism, such practices also themselves constitute the tissue of social relations between past and present, in the incorporation (or, in the literal sense, embodiment) of memory, and the ritual and monumental practices of its recall (or reconstitution). "One is never cured of memory," admits Ahlam Mostaghanemi's character, but "that is why one writes."

**Poetry in Exile**

Not the least of Algeria's paradoxes is the fact that even as country descended into social crisis in the 1980s, and into increasingly terrible violence in the 1990s, and accounts of Algeria outside the country became increasingly and reiteratively obsessed with reductive, self-reproducing clichés centered on violence as constitutive and characteristic of Algerian society, history, and culture, Algerian cultural production became increasingly prolific, recognized and successful on a global scale. It is true, of course, that a great deal of such production—increasingly so with the exile of artists in the 1990s—occurred outside the country's borders. The importance of Paris as a cultural center of gravity and prestige, as the destination of the successful writer, film-maker, graphic artist, or singer, and as the place where 'success' itself (as recognition and marketability) is constituted, is arguably hardly less today than it was for the generation of Camus and Amrouche in the 1940s.

Algerian cultural production, created both within the country and abroad, particularly, perhaps, in French but also in Arabic, is often self-consciously preoccupied with the themes of separation, distance, and exile, both as contemporary realities grounded in a long history of African and Mediterranean patterns of mobility, and as idioms for reflection on the relation of past to present. This is vividly the case, for example, in texts otherwise as different as Assia Djebar's *Oran, langue morte* and Boualem Sansal's *Harraga*: the former an austere, poignant, series of sketches of extreme violence resisted by feminine courage; the latter an almost baroque narrative in which the figurative hauntings of history weigh heavily.[20] It also, especially in France, intersects with the related but distinct creations of *beur* culture and globalized counter-culture, especially in music: the neo-Kabyle music industry, *beur* and Berber radio and television created in Paris and received in Algerian cities, the French raï scene in which an older generation of established superstars, quintessentially represented by Khaled, meets younger artists like Faudel, and, more recently, in suburban rap, influenced more by African-American 'gangsta' culture than by anything of distinctly Maghribi origin.

But it is precisely in this extraversion of the physical and institutional location of cultural producers, the idioms of cultural production, and the market for cultural products, that a first—the most immediately visible—aspect of contemporary Algerian *écriture de soi* is to be seen. The production of a consciousness of oneself and one's community, of the practical and discursive location of selfhood, is no longer confined within the frontiers of the home-country (*le pays/el-bled/tmurt*), even when 'home' remains a key referent—or a key fantasm. Indeed, 'Algeria' in much of Algerian culture, musical as well as literary, is an imaginary projection, envisioned as home from a foreign horizon.[21] The evocative roll-call of cities in Cheb Mami's "Bledi" (My country) is a love-song and a lament for a land recalled from far away: *W'allah ma nsit 'Annaba l-ghalia, Qsantina wa Stif al-'aliya, Bledi narha fi galbi gadiya... Wahran zinat al-buldani, Wali ghramha rechani. Wa-la Saïda wa li rabatni...* (By God, I'll not forget dear Annaba, Constantine or high Setif. The fire of my country shines bright in my heart... Oran, most beautiful of my cities. Infatuation with her has made me weak... Or Saïda, she who raised me).[22] Mami was born Muhammad Khelifati in the high plains town of Saïda, very far from the centers of cultural cachet. But while much listened to in Algeria—"Bledi" was even used as a soundtrack in official radio announcements promoting participation in the 2007 legislative elections—before his spectacular fall from grace cut him off from the globe-trotting music scene,[23] he had perhaps become the most obviously transnational of Algerian musicians. In 2000, he recorded a phenomenally successful single with British rock star Sting and much of his 2001 album *Dellali* (whose cover art shows the singer hanging out in an American diner) was recorded and mixed in New York. The gendered and generational aspects of such an itinerary—that of the freely mobile and materially successful, enterprising young man—describe, ideologically if not in actuality, a much broader segment of Algerian society than the handful of international music stars. If young, single men recognize themselves affectively in the lyrics of Mami, Khaled, or Hasni,[24] the acquisition of some part of the style, mobility, and money that the latter so spectacularly embody is also the aim of pursuits ranging from professional education through the burgeoning informal trade economy to *trabendo* (cross-border smuggling) and *harraga* (clandestine emigration).

Moreover, although the possibility of a career such as Mami's and 'transnationalism,' as a social-scientific preoccupation, are relatively recent developments, the underlying *leitmotiv* of mobility, distance, and the longing for home in itself is not especially novel – it has arguably been central for Algerian cultural producers since the beginning of significant labor migration to France in the early 1920s. Mami's lyrical tribute to the homeland—*Bledi hiya'l-Jaza'ir, wa-'alayhu ghani khayr* (My country is Algeria; when I'm there, all is well with me) is a late, and perhaps slightly hollow, complement to the visceral sorrow of *Ya rayah*, the anthem of *el-ghurba*, the emigrant labourer's suffering in the land of exile, originally written by 'Abd al-Rahman Amrani (aka Dahmane el-Harrachi) who first arrived in France in 1949: *Ya rayah, wayn msefer taaya wa twili, Shhel nadmu l-'abad el-ghafilin qablik wa qabli, Shhel shuft el-buldan el-amirin wa'l-ber el-khali... Ya l-ghayeb fi bled el-nas shhal taaya ma tijri...* (You who leave, where are you going, growing weary, going onward? How much did they regret, the unwary ones who went before you and me? How many crowded cities have I seen, and emptied countrysides? You who are absent, in the land of others, how you'll grow weary...). It is worth noting, too, in this context that the melody of Mami's "Bledi" is itself borrowed from "Shhilet al-'ayani," a popular love song of the 1950s made famous by the great *sha'bi* (popular) singer Mohamed Zerbout (1936-1983). Zerbout moved to France in 1962, where he played in nightclubs with Dahmane el-Harrachi; making a living from wedding parties and occasional recordings, his generally impecunious career was also constituted of exilic travels between Algiers, France, and the Sahara, where he settled in the 1970s.

The long-term continuities of social history and political economy, and of the material conditions of life and the production of selfhood that emerge from them, have defied, in this respect, the most traumatic ruptures of politics. It was during. and after, the war of independence, and into the 1970s, despite the initial nationalist belief that the workers would all be able to return home with the triumph of political and industrial independence, that Algerian emigration, especially to France, reached its peak.[25] The self-constitution of the emigrant, of the ordinary, proletarian experience of being Algerian-in-exile lived out by hundreds of thousands of working men, and latterly by their families, has been one of the most crucial experiences shaping Algerian political and cultural socialization, gender dynamics, demography, and political economy since the early twentieth century. The quotidian nature of this experience, however, in no respect diminishes the acuity of the often prolonged and intense suffering which labor migration entailed. The suffering of exile, *el-ghurba*, was redoubled into what the sociologist Abdelmalek Sayad called "the double absence" of individuals invisible in the "host" society and excised from home, who curse the "narrowness" of Algeria—whose soil, especially in the Kabyle mountains from which so many emigrant laborers came, could not sustain its people—and lament the "darkness" of the metropolitan industrial cities. Sayad's sensitive presentation of the em/immigrant's own self-narrative is both methodologically astonishing and analytically acute:

> Like everyone else, I've said the same things about France, day in, day out, night after night, year after year: "Would that God would get me out of this country." The country of narrowness, the country of poverty, the country of wretchedness. . . . And we swear, we promise: "The day I get out of here . . . I will never again speak your name: I will never look back at you; I will not come back to you." . . . In reality, all that is just a lie. . . . How bitter you can be, my country, when one dreams of leaving you. And how desirable you are, oh France, before one knows you! . . . And what a France I discovered! . . . to think I'd believed France wasn't exile [*el-ghurba*]. . . . Here, you hear things being said that they never say to us back home; you hear everyone telling you: "This is no life for human beings, this is a life you cannot love; in our country, dogs have a better life than this." I will always remember this image of my arrival in France . . . you knock at a door, it opens onto a little room that smells of a mixture of things, the damp, the closed atmosphere, the sweat of sleeping men. . . . Such sadness! Such misery in their eyes, in their voices. . . . That gave me an insight into what loneliness is, what sadness is: the darkness of the room, the darkness in the room, the darkness in the streets—the darkness of the whole of France, because, in our France, there is nothing but darkness.[26]

The poetic quality of this narrative lies not only in its "opacity," to use Sayad's term, as an authentic discourse, nor in the deep textures of its imagery, but in the fact of its direct expression of socially situated and materially-imbricated, everyday individual experience. Moral and political economy are as inescapable here as the need to eat, but it is precisely therein that the subjectivity of a narrator is produced. The great achievement of Sayad's socio-ethnography 'from within' this experience—a scientific pursuit that was also, for the scholar himself, a deeply engaged and self-conscious exercise in self-understanding and self-construction—was to reveal, below the strident political rhetorics of anticolonialist independence and (neocolonialist?) dependence, the subtler, socially constructed and individually embodied *poiesis* in which ordinary Algerians in im/emigration themselves have engaged through everyday techniques of living their history.

## Testimonies at War

The construction of such self-narratives, within Algeria, has been less apparent, perhaps because they occur below the radar of social scientific studies that have focused almost exclusively on the large-scale processes of nationalism and revolution, demography and economy, Islamism, repression, and violence. Quotidian practices of self-constitution have generally passed unobserved in a country where a detailed anthropology, or sociology of behavior, of the local and the everyday, has been generally impossible for outsiders, and generally delegitimized as worthwhile scientific practice for Algerian observers themselves.[27] In the absence of much sustained investigation within Algeria into local culture, history, and the construction of relations between local, national, and transnational space, we in fact know rather little, for example, about how, in different parts of the country, the social meanings of history and selfhood are constructed. We know astonishingly little about how even the war of independence was played out and experienced on the level of locality and family—or about the ways in which this history, and the unspeakable social ruptures it occasioned, are locally managed and codified[28]—or about what 'Algeria' (*Algérie/dzair/lezayer)* actually signifies today to people. In terms of specific practices, there has been almost no sustained study of how the symbolic and physical relations between past and present (in ageing, education, commemoration, etc.) and between individual self-location and community identification (in patterns of 'internal' migration, the reception of mass media, transactions with the bureaucracy, etc.) are actually lived and understood.

In distinct contrast to this difficulty of perceiving the local and individual in general terms, there has developed, especially since the mid-1990s, an increasing mass of largely autobiographical Algerian literature claiming to articulate collective history in individual terms, framed generically as *témoignage*. The evidentiary value of such 'witnessing' is no doubt part of its importance, but as with most texts in this genre, the near-religious value of 'testifying' that is also part of its meaning always serves, too, and perhaps more interestingly, to produce such texts as acts of self-constitution rather than simply as reports of things done and seen. With the breakdown of the monolithic enunciation of Algeria's history as an epic-heroic register of legitimacy by the state,[29] individuals have begun to contribute their own voices, to construct and market their own memories, particularly of the nationalist struggle and their parts in it, but also (in a rather different set of logics) of the war of the 1990s.[30] It seems very likely that this recent visibility and marketability of 'memory' as *témoignage* within Algeria is both a reaction to the absence of sustained, critical and open historical scholarship, or of the public debate that such scholarship might ultimately inform, and a poor substitute for both.

At the same time, however, this self-writing too is evidence of a technique of living, a means of constructing oneself through narrativization, and a staging of oneself as a historical actor. If the intention is usually to partake of whatever reflected glories are still to be salvaged from the wreck of the nationalist myth, the social significance of this literature is not straightforwardly that of a by-product of breakdown, a belated scramble for recognition as fading players in a bygone heroic drama. To read, for example, the all-too-emblematically entitled *Mémoires d'un algérien* of Ahmed Taleb Ibrahimi, is, rather, to watch a painful process of self-constitution through auto-legitimation and self-defense, a fascinating lifestory tortuously and insistently reconstructed in such a way as to reveal to the reader almost nothing of the way it might in fact have been lived. The son of shaykh Bashir al-Ibrahimi, a leading figure among Algeria's reformist *'ulama* in the 1930s-1950s, Ahmed Taleb, trained in medicine and a student activist, then FLN cadre during the revolution, was imprisoned and tortured during Ben Bella's presidency. He later became Minister of Education, of Information and Culture, and of Foreign Affairs, and attempted to form an Islamist-leaning party, Wafa, in the late 1990s. A candidate for the presidency in 1999, his second attempt at running for office was disallowed on technical grounds by the Constitutional Court in 2004. His memoirs, rather than providing a self-critical reflection on this long itinerary, give a decidedly 'smoothed-out,' *événementiel* account of anticolonial struggle and state-building viewed from within a particular (relatively privileged) sphere, peppered with patriotic slogans and leading personalities, and unencumbered by any sense of history as other than unfolding in a single, predictable direction. The narrator, at every turn, seems as omniscient as any disembodied nineteenth-century authorial voice about the disappointments as well as the triumphs to come. At no point is the youth, activist, prisoner, or Minister as he was 'in the moment' visible to the reader (or, it seems likely, to the writer); each episode is reconstructed around a fairly canonical interpretation of the history of the national movement and the recovery of a national identity reducible to abstract ideals of Arabic and Islam, whose champion Ahmed Taleb was as Minister under Boumedienne and which stand in for any more subtle factors of motivation or criteria of judgment. The conditions of production of such a text—the actual political struggles and social complexities that are resolutely ignored within the narrative—dominate the book by their ostensible absence.[31] Their negative imprint is visible, at second glance, in almost everything; the economy of narration is so constrained in an unquestioned, predetermined ideological straitjacket that the central character himself, far from enlarging his own character in anything so vulgar as self-promotion, in fact appears almost anemic, suffocated by his own self-imposed rules of composition. Read as autobiography—in hopes of finding in it a critical reflection on the individual experience of a complex history—such literature is intensely disappointing. Read as *écriture de soi*, as evidence of the techniques of self-constitution by which an Algerian's memories generate a particular subjectivity within a particular social formation and political struggle, it is intensely illuminating.[32]

The production of such *témoignages* in the 1990s and in the aftermath of that decade's crisis and war has been a part, too, of a broader pattern of the construction and expression of social memory, the 'management' of the past, the construction and expression of oneself and of Algeria, in conditions of social breakdown and trauma. It is not only that such processes, in such conditions, entail political, or even ethical, stakes over the expression of truth and misinformation, important as this has been to the narration of the ongoing conflict especially since the mid-1990s.[33] There has been, within the discursive production of a memory of the unfolding drama—the fashioning of a language in which the crisis could be socially experienced and communicated—a particular economy of narration and of staging that has necessarily framed the self-constitution of the individuals involved. In, once again, the absence—which is likely to be prolonged if not permanent—of uncensored, local, and particular narratives, let alone of open, accountable public reckoning, we can nonetheless perceive something of these processes in their most overt, public expressions, in public debates over high-profile incidents in which the attribution of responsibility for violence and deaths has generated open polemic in publications and the press, and a proliferation of interpretive work by individuals all over the world in cyberspace.[34] What is at stake here is, of course, on one level the simple 'facts of the case'—who has been killing whom, and why. However, while on some analytical level, plausible causal explanations in terms of political rationality might be constructed on the basis of 'what is (thought to be) known,' it should hardly be surprising that, viewed from within the crisis itself, or from the (often obscuring) vantage point of exile, logics of explanation that can be not only plausibly constructed but also 'inhabited,' might be less straightforward. This—rather than a simple *political* opposition, let alone bad faith—might go some way towards accounting for the oppositions between analysts and intellectuals, within Algeria and abroad, over the so-called *qui-tue-qui* (who-is-killing-whom) debate, which turns on the question of the extent to which the state itself (or occult elements thereof) might have manipulated and instrumentalized the Islamist insurgency for its own ends, especially in the latter half of the 1990s. A group of 'concerned scholars' and sympathizers in France mobilized around the question with the call in 2001 for an international commission of inquiry into the role of the state security forces in human rights abuses and the alleged manipulation of Islamist terrorism;[35] others, in Algeria, declared themselves vociferously opposed to any such interference in Algerian sovereignty, which to them seemed motivated by what a counter-"declaration of Algerian intellectuals" denounced as the misguided "confusion and defeatism . . . [of] the trap of the deleterious question of '*qui tue qui*.'"[36]

The creation of an 'inhabitable' meaning, a memory that can be meaningfully emplotted in a life that can be lived—if not in comfort, at least without too much pathological dysfunction—out of the apparent chaos of events is a distinctly different operation to the idealized historiographic, or judicial, procedure of establishing the facts. An adequate examination of these dynamics both in Algeria and in various places of exile would have to do more than attribute such *prises de position*, which are also acts of self-constitution, to ill will or sensationalism, naïveté or voluntary self-deception. Nor can one simply invoke 'historical truth' as if this could be serenely decontextualized: In the making of social memory (as distinct from the professional practice of historiography, a pursuit, despite its merits, with much slighter influence on society at large), 'history' is a register of concurrent claims to legitimacy and denunciation. Hence the narration of the crisis of the 1990s, and its significance in the longer span of Algerian history, especially, of course, relative to the war of independence and its fragmented inheritances, plays out a reiterated preoccupation with (private or partisan) guarding or preserving and (publicly) proclaiming the 'truth of history,' on one hand, and simultaneously an incessant evocation of the betrayal, forgetting, or irremediable absence of historical truth, on the other. A brief sampling of the press, especially at moments of commemoration, the passing away of nationalist icons, or contested interventions in the literature of *témoignage*, produces a constantly reiterated lexicon: "the culture of forgetting"[37] and the "duty to remember,"[38] the "struggle for the truth"[39] that would "tell the truth and the whole truth"[40] against "the falsification of history,"[41] the "misappropriation of the liberation struggle,"[42] the "denial of national history,"[43] the "effacement of collective memory and the usurpation of history."[44]

If these contests over the legitimate expression of a social memory-in-the-making—especially as regards the so-called *qui-tue* debate—have been very intense, it is perhaps not simply because of the acuity of the recent crisis itself but of a desperate need for coherent and justifiable auto-legitimation and self-positioning with regard to such experiences as they are lived. It seems very likely that orchestrated disinformation, and the instrumentalization of violence to serve the ends of a regime determined at all costs to return to the *status quo ante-1991* in terms of the prevailing division of privileges and immunities, has occurred and continues to occur to some extent in Algeria, but a whole society (even less than an Islamist guerilla movement) cannot credibly be portrayed as the helpless victims, on one hand, or the mindless puppets, on the other, of a handful of general officers and intelligence operatives. The self-fashioning of journalists, policemen, writers, lawyers, workers, and ordinary people caught up in a strictly *incomprehensible* experience of atrocity are all at issue here. The staking out of positions, both in one of the several available emplotments of the recent past and in the enactment thereby of a certain self-ascribed social role, is not merely tactical, but, to the extent that people must create ways of living with themselves in conditions of trauma, processes we might almost call existential.

The intensity of this rhetorical self-fashioning, in the most recent period, also, therefore, serves to *mask* a profound insecurity, just as the official codification of nationalist memory—as 132 years of unyielding struggle, the sacrifice of one and a half million martyrs, the genocide of colonial conquest and repression, the predestined triumph of the nation not as revolutionary voluntarism but as a force of nature or the will of God—was simultaneously crushingly weighty and entirely hollow. The very strident triumphalism of the official nationalist narrative, as expressed in political rhetoric and official journalism from the 1960s through the 1980s—of the nation's recovery of its stolen sovereignty, its unshakeable 'authenticity' and perpetual solidarity in revolt, and simultaneously, its total victimization[45]—was correlative with the political impossibility of dealing with the history of colonialism and the revolution as they had actually occurred. The official coding of what happened in the 1990s as a "national tragedy"[46] of which all are victims and none perpetrators is an even hollower repetition of the same logic.

In the case of the war of independence, the official codification of Algeria's social memory as myth—as a fiction that has real social effects—

undoubtedly produced unintended effects, even automatisms, among those who, schooled in the cult of armed struggle and unanimous social authenticity, would embody the epic memory of the FLN *mujahidin* in the belief that their *jihad* to overthrow tyranny was either a continuation of the revolution of the previous generation or its sublimation in the struggle of the globalised *umma*.[47] The remedy officially prescribed for the trauma of the 1990s—amnesia and amnesty in place of transparency and justice—is an attempt to put the shattered pieces of the unanimist-nationalist edifice together again in a logic of "fraternal" reintegration, loyalty to the republic against the "Islamist International," the overcoming of a collective tragedy and the forgetting of differences along with the thousands who have "disappeared."[48] It would be surprising if some Algerians, without being either the unknowing puppets of occult forces or in the pay of the security services, were not now actively fashioning their narratives and public presentations of themselves with the symbols that this version of events offers them.

But at the same time, these official formulations have only partially disguised other and more complex ways in which Algerian history has unfolded and been experienced and remembered. The human rights movement, the organizations of families of disappeared persons or of victims of terrorism, and other constituencies, are all at work in creating their own bodies of memory in the absence, or over the remains, of the bodies of their loved ones. The doctrinaire formulations of national identity and unanimous cohesion have not precluded other practices of self-constitution, more subtle and complex techniques of self-fashioning, invisible in the realm of rhetoric but materialized on the level of everyday life. There are other ways of living with, narrating, and embodying the difficult histories of Algeria, shared with other societies (Palestine, Lebanon, etc.) in which the absurdity and atrocity of incomprehensible events can be dealt with in dignity or derision. If emigration, that central absence of contemporary Algerian history, is lived as both a dream and as *"la malédiction,"*[49] other aspects of being Algerian are equally split, in their embodiment and narration as individual experience, between these two registers. The importance of derision as an authorized space for subverting and simultaneously reinforcing collective values is vital in this case as in others, but very little explored. One might begin with the reception of the acute caricaturist, Ali Dilem, the sardonic wit of the columnist-turned-novelist Y. B., or the iconic comic Mohammed Fellag. Y. B.'s collection of "chronicles," originally published in the daily *El Watan* at the height of the terror from mid-1997 to early 1998, is prefaced by a mordant epigram that is also a definition: "Being Algerian is a dangerous profession."[50] In his stage show

*Djurdjurassique Bled*, Fellag quips: "When other people sink and touch bottom, they go up again. . . . We Algerians, when we sink and touch bottom, we start digging."[51] Such means of incorporating extremes of trauma into a collective self-mockery have become a generalized dimension of Algerian popular resilience. The statue of the anonymous *mujahid* near the waterfront at Bejaïa, dynamically poised with arm outstretched (as it happens, towards the sea) to indicate the way forward into the glorious collective future, is popularly commented upon as sending the populace a message from the authorities: '*If you don't like it, there's the way out!*'[52]

## Conclusion

Narrating, Paul Ricoeur points out, is a secondary process grafted on the primary fact of our being-entangled-in-stories; stories that are generally not of our own, individual choosing or making, but which produce us as speaking and acting subjects. The process of becoming the narrator of one's own story (not the 'author' of one's own life, but the speaker of one's own experience) is necessarily a socially-imbricated one, not because the individual is pre-determined as a participant in a collective identity, but because the practices of living in the world, through which alone it is possible to construct oneself in relation to the past, are constitutive of selfhood within, and not distinct from, social memory. This fact does not return the individual, in a society like Algeria, or anywhere else in the Middle East or Africa, to a state of perpetual and helpless entrapment in the jaws of 'tradition' or authoritarianism. It simply points to a clearer specification of the conditions within which, and the margin of maneuver with which, individual subjectivity may be embodied in actions, testimonies, and texts that are made not simply one's own, but oneself.

## Notes

* Many thanks to Kamel Chachoua, Judith Scheele, Karima Dirèche, and Karim Ouaras for conversations that helped me think about the themes of this article. None of them are responsible for any of its errors or inadequacies. Thanks also to the participants in seminars on "Language and history" (Oriel College, Oxford, 2002), "Writing the Algerian Wars" (University of California, Berkeley, 2006), "Récits de l'histoire algérienne" (MMSH, Aix-en-Provence, 2007), and the audience of a lecture at the Institut d'études politiques (Lyon, 2006), where earlier formulations of some of these ideas were aired, and to *Alif*'s anonymous readers for thoughtful and constructive comments. The first version of this article was

originally written for a different project at the invitation of Alain Roussillon, in whose memory it is respectfully and affectionately offered.

[1] Ahlam Mosteghanemi, *Dhakirat al-jasad* (Beirut: Dar al-adab, 1998), 9.

[2] See Chris Wickham and James Fentress, *Social Memory* (Oxford: Blackwell, 1992), and their criticism in particular of the earlier literature exemplified by Maurice Halbwachs, *La mémoire collective* (Paris: PUF, 1950).

[3] Such a reading of nationalism in Algeria, for example, is given in Fudayl al-Wartilani, *Al-jaza'ir al-tha'ira* (Beirut: Matba'at al-'ibad, 1956), Ali Merad, *Le réformisme musulman en Algérie de 1925 à 1940. Essai d'histoire sociale et religieuse* (Paris: Mouton, 1967), Abul-Qasim Sa'adallah, *Al-haraka al-wataniyya al-jaza'iriyya* (Beirut: Dar al-adab, 1969), and much of the subsequent literature. Similar arguments have been made more recently in respect of Islamism. For a critique of this view of national identity regarding the Maghrib, see James McDougall, "Introduction: History/Culture/Politics of the Nation," *Journal of North African Studies* 8.1 (Spring 2003): 1-13, and for broader treatments, Philip Schlesinger, "On National Identity: Some Conceptions and Misconceptions Criticized," *Social Science Information* 26.2 (1987): 219-64; Jean-François Bayart, *L'illusion identitaire* (Paris: Fayard, 1996). A fuller argument for seeing cultural authority within nationalism as a seizure of symbolic power rather than as a restoration of pre-existing social truth is developed in James McDougall, *History and the Culture of Nationalism in Algeria* (Cambridge: Cambridge UP, 2006).

[4] Jeffrey K. Olick and Joyce Robbins, "Social Memory Studies: From 'Collective Memory' to the Historical Sociology of Mnemonic Practices," *Annual Review of Sociology* 24 (1998): 105-40.

[5] I owe this distinction to Ricoeur (see note 7 below).

[6] Michel Foucault, "L'écriture de soi," *Corps écrit* 5 (1983): 3-23. The basis of Foucault's study is an examination of individual ascetic self-discipline through confessional and epistolary writing, focused on a very classical literary corpus: Augustine, Seneca, and Pliny. This might appear unsuitable as a model for a study of the contemporary, the traumatic, and the 'social,' but in fact Foucault's emphasis on writing as a constitutive disciplinary practice has two major advantages for the analysis suggested here. First, it focuses attention on *self*-writing as opposed to life-writing or autobiography in the usual sense; the self is constituted ("fashioned") synchronously with and by means of practice, rather than existing prior to and outside practice, as a transcendent authorial consciousness. It is a necessary but short step from this to the situation of such practice, extended beyond the sphere of literary activity, within a wider field of social relations. Second, we are dealing with a *disciplinary* exercise, in which, again *contra* older assumptions about autobiography as the autonomous expres-

sion of an individual's historical experience, the recounted narrative, and the embodied self are shaped, in the very form taken by their (self-)expression, by a certain set of enabling and constraining conditions; norms, expectations, forms of language, and material circumstances. This starting point is also the concluding point of Achille Mbembe's survey of (mostly) sub-Saharan African discourses of African selfhood, which ends with a call to focus on "practices of the self" in place of the historical "dead-ends" of totalizing projects of reclaiming a substantial identity. See Achille Mbembe, "African Modes of Self-writing," *Public Culture* 14.1 (2002): 239-73.

7 Paul Ricoeur, *Temps et récit* (Paris: Seuil, 1983-1985); *Soi-même comme un autre* (Paris: Seuil, 1990); and *La mémoire, l'histoire, l'oubli* (Paris: Seuil, 2000).

8 For a detailed examination of the local narration and staging of social space in funerary landscapes, for example, see Judith Scheele, "Algerian Graveyard Stories," *Journal of the Royal Anthropological Institute* 12.4 (December 2006): 859-79. Omar Carlier's work on vestimentary self-construction, visual culture, and the iconography of the *mujahid* and *shahid* in Algeria also offers excellent studies in a similar vein: see his "Le moudjahid, mort ou vif," *La guerre d'Algérie dans la mémoire et l'imaginaire*, eds. Anny Dayan-Rosenmann and Lucette Valensi (Paris: Bouchene, 2004) and "Messali et son look" *Le corps du leader: Construction et representation dans les pays du Sud*, eds. Omar Carlier and Raphaëlle Nollez-Goldbach (Paris: L'Harmattan, 2008).

9 See Assia Djebbar, *Poèmes pour l'Algérie heureuse* (Algiers: SNED, 1969).

10 Paul Ricoeur, "Life in Quest of Narrative," *On Paul Ricoeur: Narrative and Interpretation*, ed. David Wood (London: Routledge, 1991), ch. 2.

11 See Jurgen Habermas, *Theory of Communicative Action*, vol. 1 (Boston: Beacon P, 1984-1987), espeially chapter 3.

12 Michael Ryan, "Self-Evidence," *Diacritics* 10.2 (Summer 1980): 14.

13 Ryan 14. Such, for example, is the view in Philippe Lejeune's classic definition of the genre as a "retrospective prose story that a real person relates about his or her own existence, in which he or she gives emphasis to his or her individual life, and to the history of his or her personality in particular," qtd. in Robert Smith, *Derrida and Autobiography* (Cambridge: Cambridge UP, 1995), 53ff. Karl Weintraub wrote of the importance of autobiography as a defining expression of modern (by which he meant, Western) thought, "a major component of modern man's self-conception: the belief that whatever else he is, he is a unique individuality, whose life task is to be true to his very own personality." See *The Value of the Individual: Self and Circumstance in Autobiography* (Chicago: Chicago UP, 1978), xi).

14 Michel Foucault, "Qu'est-ce qu'un auteur?," *Bulletin de la société française de philosophie* 64.3 (July-September 1969): 73-95.

[15] The term 'clans,' regularly used to denote dominant networks of the distribution of goods, preferment, and influence, ought not to be understood as referring to primarily familial or 'tribal' affiliations. 'Clan' conflict in Algerian politics is factional, and obeys if anything a logic of historical and regional rather than social cleavages.

[16] See, for example, Miriem Vergès, "'I Am Living in a Foreign Country Here': A Conversation with an Algerian Hittiste," *Middle East Report* 192 (Jan.-Feb. 1995): 14-17.

[17] Rachid Taha, "Safi," *Tékitoi* (Universal, 2004).

[18] For a more detailed argument, see James McDougall, "The Fetishism of Identity: Empire, Nation and the Politics of Subjectivity in Algeria," *Counterhegemony in the Colony and Postcolony*, eds. John Chalcraft and Yaseen Noorani (London: Palgrave/Macmillan, 2007), ch. 2.

[19] Rachid Taha, "Safi."

[20] Assia Djebbar, *Oran, langue morte* (Arles: Actes Sud, 1997) and Boualem Sansal, *Harraga* (Paris: Gallimard, 2005).

[21] On transnational community-building and political imagination, especially relating to Berberism, see Paul A. Silverstein, *Algeria in France: Transpolitics, Race and Nation* (Bloomington: Indiana UP, 2004), and on the transformations of Kabyle into 'world' music, see Jane E. Goodman, *Berber Culture on the World Stage: From Village to Video* (Bloomington: Indiana UP, 2005).

[22] Cheb Mami, "Bledi," *Meli meli* (Virgin, 1999).

[23] In October 2006, Khelifati was charged with violence, sequestration, and threatening behavior, following allegations that a former girlfriend had been detained in a house in Algiers where two doctors had attempted to force her to undergo an abortion. He skipped bail in France, returning to Algeria, and an international arrest warrant was issued against him in May 2007.

[24] Marc Schade-Poulsen, *Men and Popular Music in Algeria: The Social Significance of Raï* (Austin: Texas UP, 1999) ; Angelica Maria deAngelis, "Moi aussi, je suis musulman: Rai, Islam, and Masculinity in Maghrebi Transnational Identity," *Alif: Journal of Comparative Poetics* 23 (2003): 276-308; Hadj Miliani, *Sociétaires de l'emotion: Études sur les musiques et les chants d'Algérie d'hier et d'aujourd'hui* (Oran: Dar el-gharb, 2005).

[25] From the period of World War I, when significant Algerian emigration to the metropole began, through the interwar period, there were several tens of thousands of Algerians in France. The 1954 census gave a figure of around 211,000, which almost doubled to between 350,000 (according to the census) and 436,000 (according to the Interior Ministry) in 1962, and then grew to 600,000 by the spring of 1965, reaching 884,320 at the end of 1975. Benjamin Stora, *Ils venaient d'Algérie. Histoire de l'immigration algérien-*

*ne en France, 1912-1992* (Paris: Fayard, 1992), 13, 143, and 401-02.

26 Abdelmalek Sayad, *The Suffering of the Immigrant,* trans. David Macey (Cambridge: Polity, 2004), 12, 16-17.

27 For an analysis of the "illegitimacy" of the local, particular, and fragmentary, see Fanny Colonna, "Three Intellectuals and the Culture(s) of Being Algerian," *Nation, Society and Culture in North Africa,* ed. James McDougall (London: Routledge, 2003), 155-70. For important contributions to remedying this lack, see Abderrahmane Moussaoui, *Espace et sacré au sahara: Ksour et oasis du sud-ouest algérien* (Paris: CNRS, 2002), Youssef Nacib, *Cultures oasiennes. Essai d'histoire sociale de l'oasis de Bou Saada* (Algiers: ENAL, 1986), and Judith Scheele, *Village Matters: Knowledge, Politics and Community in Kabylia, Algeria* (Oxford: James Currey, 2009). Innovative doctoral programs at the universities of Khenchela and Oran now exist that might contribute to more sustained local historical and ethnographic studies; we are also now seeing the beginnings of subtler and locally based studies of the experience of the war of independence—for veterans of Wilaya III (Kabylia), see Dalila Aït el-Djoudi, *La guerre d'Algérie vue par l'ALN, 1954-62* (Paris: Autrement, 2006).

28 On the difficulties of a local history of the war, the dynamics of remembering and forgetting, and the complex and heavily policed ways in which knowledge of its "truth" is locally perceived, see especially Scheele, *Village Matters*, ch. 5: "The Theft of History."

29 Mustafa Haddab, "Statut social de l'histoire: Éléments de réflexion," *Comment on enseigne l'histoire en Algérie*, eds. Mohamed Ghalem and Hassan Remaoun (Oran: CRASC, 1995), 15-34; Fouad Soufi, "La fabrication d'une mémoire: les médias algériens (1963-1995) et la guerre d'Algérie," *La guerre d'Algérie et les algériens, 1954-1962*, ed. Charles-Robert Ageron (Paris: Armand Colin, 1997), 289–303; Bruno Étienne, "Le vocabulaire politique de légitimité en Algérie," *Annuaire de l'Afrique du nord* 10 (1971): 69-103.

30 This literature deserves a study in its own right. Examples include Ali Kafi, *Du militant politique au dirigeant militaire (1946-1962): Mémoires* (Algiers: Casbah, 2002), Saad Dahlab, *Pour l'indépendance de l'Algérie: Mission accomplie* (Algiers: Dahlab, 1990), Mostefa Lacheraf, *Des noms et des lieux. Mémoires d'une Algérie oubliée* (Algiers: Casbah, 1998), and Ahmed Taleb Ibrahimi, *Mémoires d'un Algérien*, vols. 1 and 2 (Algiers: Casbah, 2006 and 2008). Autobiographies as such were produced parsimoniously in the 1970s and 1980s. The memoirs of Ahmad Tawfiq al-Madani, *Hayat Kifah* (Algiers: SNED,1977-1981) and Muhammed Khayr al-Din, *Mudhakkirat* (Algiers: SNED, n.d.), published in Arabic, were exceptional. Commandant Azzedine's *On nous appelait fellaghas* (Paris: Stock, 1976) and Hocine Aït Ahmad's *Mémoires d'un combattant* (Paris: Messinger, 1983) have only

more recently been reprinted in Algeria. Fadhma Aït Mansour Amrouche's *Histoire de ma vie* (Paris: Maspero, 1968), though more properly representative of everyday Algerian life than any of the above, is still an exceptional text in every respect.

31 A critical reading that gives some sense of the struggles at issue—one also pre-determined by the reviewer's unalloyed attachment to the legacy of President Boumedienne—is Ali Mebroukine's review of Ahmad Taleb's second volume, "Heurs et malheurs de la stratégie politique de Houari Boumedienne," *El Watan* (July 7, 2008).

32 More revealing as historical documents are the memoirs of Mostefa Lacheraf and Mohamed Harbi, *Une vie debout: Mémoires politiques, 1945-1962* (Paris: La Découverte, 2001).

33 See, for example, Lounis Aggoun and Jean-Baptiste Rivoire, *Françalgérie, crimes et mensonges d'états* (Paris: La Découverte, 2005), and analyses of various public debates on the website <www.algeria-watch.de>.

34 On the function of conspiracy theories—over, e.g., the 1998 assassination of the iconic Kabyle singer, Matoub Lounès, or the massacres in the Mitidja in 1997-1998—as vernacular knowledge among a transnational, internet-linked community, and their unwitting role in perpetuating the logics of power that sustain the Algerian regime, see Paul A. Silverstein, "An Excess of Truth: Violence, Conspiracy Theorizing and the Algerian Civil War," *Anthropological Quarterly* 75.4 (Fall 2002): 643-74.

35 Declaration signed by Pierre Bourdieu, Pierre Vidal-Naquet, and others: "M. Védrine et le bain de sang en Algerie," *Le Monde* (February 9, 2001), shortly before a scheduled visit of Hubert Védrine, the French Foreign Minister, to Algeria.

36 "Appel des intellectuels algériens contre la confusion et le défaitisme" in Algerian dailies *Le Matin* and *La Tribune* (March 22, 2001).

37 Obituary of Saad Dahlab, *El Watan* (December 17, 2000).

38 Celebration of anniversary of independence, *Le Matin* (July 5, 2000).

39 On the massacre of Algerians in Paris, 17 October 1961, see *El Watan* (October 19, 1999).

40 On the memoirs of Ali Kafi, ALN (Armée de libération nationale) colonel in Wilaya II, subsequently Ambassador and President of the Haut Comité d'Etat (HCE) after the assassination of Mohamed Boudiaf in 1992, see *El Watan* (November, 2, 1999). Particularly at issue in the debate over his memoirs was his criticism of the role of Abbane Ramdane, the interior FLN's principal strategist who was murdered by his comrades in 1957.

41 *El Watan* (April, 15 1999).

42 *El Watan* (April, 15 1999).

43 That is, by Islamism. See *El Watan* (April, 15 1999).

44 Interview with M'hammed Yazid on the death of Saad Dahlab. *El Watan* (December 17, 2000).

45 Both aspects are most strikingly evident in the unsubtle museography of the Museum of the Mujahid below the *maqam shahid*, the Martyr's Monument in Algiers. Algerian history from 1830 to 1962 is presented there as total victimization, and total (armed) resistance, to the exclusion of all else. The concern to construct a narrative of unremitting revolt goes so far, in a large wall-map indicating episodes of "popular resistance from 1830 to 1962" with flashing lights, as to cast the 1934 anti-Jewish riots in Constantine as an *intifada* against colonialism.

46 In the "Civil Concord" and Law on National Reconciliation that have formed the main planks of President Abd al-Aziz Bouteflika's policy of 'turning the page' on the crisis since his coming to power in 1999.

47 See Hassan Remaoun, "La question de l'histoire dans le débat sur la violence en Algérie," *Insaniyat* 10 (January-April 2000): 31–43; Benjamin Stora, "Algérie: Absence et surabondance de mémoire," *Les violences en Algérie*, eds. Mohamed Benrabah, Nabile Fares, Gilbert Grandguillaume et al. (Paris: Odile Jacob, 1998); and James McDougall, "Martyrdom and Destiny: The Inscription and Imagination of Algerian History," *Memory and Violence in the Middle East and North Africa*, eds. Ussama Makdisi and Paul Silverstein (Bloomington: Indiana UP, 2006).

48 The number of persons forcibly 'disappeared,' possibly tortured and presumed killed, by security forces in the 1990s is unknown but estimated at 7,000 by the Algerian authorities (the number of cases registered by the Presidential ad hoc Commission on Human Rights) or between 15,000 and 20,000 by various international NGOs and campaign groups. The regime's strategy has generally been to treat the issue as another aspect of the crisis about which society must simply 'forget.' In September 1999, shortly before the referendum on "national reconciliation," President Bouteflika, in a widely-reported (and much condemned) phrase, protested to families of disappeared persons that "I don't have them [the *disparus*] in my pockets."

49 Abdelmalek Sayad, "La malédiction," *La misère du monde*, ed. Pierre Bourdieu (Paris: Seuil, 1993), 823-44.

50 Y. B., *Comme il a dit lui. Chroniques (au vitriol) d'Algérie* (Paris: Lattès, 1998), 7.

51 Mahamed Fellag, *Djurdjurassique Bled* (DVD, 2001)

52 I am grateful to the friend who pointed out the statue to me, and to two students from Bejaïa in Lyon who confirmed the currency of the joke.

# The Wound that Never Heals*

**Vincent Crapanzano**

---

On March 3, 2005, Mohamed Haddouche, the president of Association Justice Information Reparation pour les Harkis France (AJIR) wrote to the president of the Conseil Régional de Haute Normandie protesting its co-production of a play, *Le nom du père* (The Father's Name), by Algerian philosopher, translator, and playwright Messaoud Benyoucef. After playing in Fécamp from February 22 to 25 without incident, the play moved to Canteleu and Louviers, also in Normandy, where—under the direction of AJIR and another Harki organization, Génération Mémoire—Harki protests were launched in which tracts were distributed demanding the cancellation of the play and its publicity.[1]

Though there was no violence, there was, as *Le Monde* put it, "considerable pressure." The Harkis tried to prevent the audience from entering the theater and Claude-Alice Peyrotte, the play's director, received a menacing telephone call. While insisting on the right of free speech, the major of Louviers tried to calm the protestors and finally managed to clear the house so that the play could be performed. In early March, the two Harki organizations brought a case for defamation against the publisher of *Le nom du père*, Les éditions de l'embarcadère, the author, and the director of the play. Protests continued. At the beginning of June, however, when I saw the play at the Théâtre de l'Epée at the Cartoucherie de Vincennes in Paris—where it had been playing for nearly a month—there were no protesters. Before the play had opened in Paris, Smaïl Boufhal, the president of Génération mémoire, told Brigitte Salino of *Le Monde* that the court case has "permitted us to act as citizens. We will not intervene when the play is performed at the L'Epée-de-Bois."

Neither Benyoucef, Peyrotte, nor Alice Yvernat, the director of the publishing house, had ever imagined *Le nom du père* would cause such an outcry. Though the protest and ensuing case are of little significance in the annals of French law, they do raise a number of questions about the Harkis. Who were the protesters? Why did they protest? What did they expect to gain from their protests? On what grounds did they base their case? On what grounds was it finally rejected by court? The text and its performance were clearly not neutral. Was the reaction they generated simply a question of content: The power or failure of representation? Or was it triggered by form, breaches of theatrical convention, or everyday etiquette? Was it a question of publicity? Of exposure? By an outsider? To me, as to many members of the audience as well as to its author, its publisher, and the director of the play, *Le nom du père* did not depict the Harkis pejoratively. Indeed, I found it sympathetic to them—to the complexities and paradoxes in which they find themselves today. (I should note that I have been doing anthropological field work among the Harkis on and off for the last several years.) Both the play itself and the Harkis' reaction raise questions of identity among a marginalized people in a modern nation-state, and to the role of memory—of a wound, pain, displaced pain, lesion—in the constitution of what I am compelled to call an ill-fitting identity. The Harki response points to the role of the possession of memory, of a wound, a trauma, in the struggle to preserve that identity, its reality and its artifice. Possession, I argue, is one of the ways in which memory resists the treachery of its historical existence—the ultimate failure, if you will, of its own memorialization. As Albert Camus observed in *L'homme revolté*, the taste of possession is just another form of the desire to last.

## The Harki

> At the end of ten years of this regime, the people in the camp saw a judge arrive: he came to see if the Harkis were ripe enough to become French. He questioned them one by one and asked them the same question: "Well, do you want to remain French?" Our fathers, they were really worthless! If not they would have answered him: "But, sir, if you ask us if we want to remain French, that means that we are already French? Well, if we are French, why haven't you treated us as French?" But all they could say was "Yes, sir, we want to remain French."
>
> -- Seif-El-Islam El Mansour in Benyoucef, *Lettres à Jeanne*

The Harkis are those Algerians, numbering between 200,000 and 260,000, who sided with the French during the Algerian war of independence. The UN puts the figure at 263,000 (Stora 80). Strictly speaking, "Harki" (from the Arabic for movement/military movement) refers to those

Algerian civilians of Arab or Berber descent who served on a contractual basis without the usual military benefits as auxiliary troops (*supplétifs*) for the French, but the term is often used loosely for any Algerian who served with the French military or police forces during the war.[2] The Harkis have been called *les oubliés de l'histoire* (history's forgotten); for, until recently, they have been ignored by both scholars and the press, and have lived, for the most part, in abject silence. Although some of the Harkis sided with the French because they believed that Algeria would be better off under them than independent, or because they and their fathers had served in the French army, most of them, poor, illiterate peasants, did so because they desperately needed what money they could earn in a war-torn country. Many had suffered at the hands of the militant and often brutal Front de libération nationale (FLN), which led Algeria to independence and, according to the Harkis and many other critics of the Algerian government, was responsible for the ensuing violence.

Despite warnings of likely bloodshed from officers who had fought alongside the Harkis, the French government ordered their demobilization after the signing of the Treaty of Evian on March 18, 1962 and sent them, unarmed, back to their villages. The treaty offered them no protection, and, in the months surrounding its ratification on July 3, 1962, some 70,000 Harkis (some claim up to 150,000) were tortured, mutilated, and killed by the Algerian population at large. I myself heard stories of Harkis whose throats were cut in front of their wives and children, and there have been reports of others who were impaled, roasted live, or even forced to eat chunks of their own flesh (Benamou 221). One man I interviewed was thrown, after being tortured, into a dry well where he was kept for eleven months and fed couscous mixed with sand and blood when he was fed at all.[3] He was never given a change of clothing nor was the well cleaned or his excrement removed.[4] Many of these deaths were instigated by the FLN or the so-called Marsiens (from the French for March: *mars*), Algerians who suddenly identified with the FLN in March 1962 when they realized that the FLN would come to power, wanting to prove their loyalty to that organization for reasons of self-interest (Jordi and Hamoumou 35-36).

Overwhelmed by the arrival in 1962 of more than a million *pieds-noirs,* or Algerians of European origin, many of whom supported the Organisation armée secrète (OAS), which had attempted a *coup* in April of the previous year, de Gaulle's government did almost nothing to halt the blood bath. As little sympathy as de Gaulle had for the *pieds-noirs*, he had even less for the Algerians themselves. On May 16, 1962, in a now famous telegram, Louis Joxe, the Minister of State for Algerian Affairs, prohibited individual efforts to settle Harkis in France, as a number of officers who had fought with them had tried to do, and, after Joxe's order was confirmed by Roger Frey, the Minister of the Interior, 55 Harki families who had tried to land in Marseilles were sent back to Algeria, where, as the Harkis I talked to insisted, many were massacred. In June, the Army Ministry acknowledged that threats to the lives of 4930 Harkis justified their settlement in France (Roux 214), and, despite the efforts of de Gaulle, Joxe, and the Army Minister Pierre Messmer, 48,625 French Muslims arrived officially in France between June 23 and September 28, 1962. It is likely that another 60,000 were able to make it to France by 1967 (Jordi and Hamoumou 49).

In France, most Harkis were incarcerated in camps—like Rivesaltes near Perpignon and Saint-Maurice-l'Ardoise near Avignon—forced to live in miserable conditions, subjected to abusive discipline and constant humiliation, and offered, if any, the lowliest of jobs. 14,000 families were eventually moved into some 75 remote villages scattered across southern France, where they worked in an enormous reforestration project. Though these villages and the camps were supposedly designed to integrate the Harkis into French society, they served to isolate them—to render them invisible, the Harkis like to say. Those who could find work outside the camps and villages, often through personal contacts, left as soon as they could. Many of those who remained, some for more than 16 years, until the last of the hamlets were closed in 1978, suffered the consequences of abjection: identity loss, depression, bouts of violence, suicide, and, among the men, alcoholism.[5] The women lived in a sort of double purdah: that imposed by tradition, and that stemming from the fear of venturing out into a 'threatening' world they could not understand. Children not only suffered discrimination at school, but lived under their fathers' silent and often violent *régime*. They neither understood why they were treated as they were, nor were they told what their fathers had done or why. Yet despite their parents' silence, the children came to know, if only indirectly, the Harkis' story, and experienced at a step removed their parents' ambivalence.

Today, though there are still concentrations of Harkis in the south of France, often near the camps where they were incarcerated, and in the industrial north, the majority of Harki families are scattered across France.[6] (Those in the North, I should add, have a somewhat different history since they were sent to work in factories after having spent only a short time in transition camps and eventually becoming part of the northern urban proletariat.) They—and to a lesser extent their children and grandchildren who retain their Harki identity—have remained a population *à part*. Though they have the rights of any French citizen, they find themselves treated as half-citizens: mistrusted, marginalized, and subjected to often virulent racism. Neither speaking up nor writing, they find themselves for the most part lost in despair. Harki writer Zahia Rahmani refers to them as "*soldatsmorts*." Yet their children have assumed the wounds they suffered, in terms of which they articulate their identity. They share, if vicariously, their parents' sense of having been betrayed, abandoned, and humiliated. Unlike most of their parents, they take an activist stance, forming political associations, like AJIR and Génération mémoire, lobbying for the recognition of the sacrifices their parents made for France, and demanding compensation for the losses their parents sustained. Paradoxically, their quest for recognition—the legal and administrative maneuvers that are required—perpetuate their marginalized status. Those bureaucrats with whom I spoke, however sympathetic they may be to the Harki cause, considered their constant demands exaggerated, a nuisance. In the last few years, they have begun publishing life histories, family memoirs, novels, and histories, all of which express their ambivalent loyalty to France.

## The Complaint

> We cannot accept this play because it puts our history in serious question.
>
> -- Smaïl Boufhal

The case for defamation was based on article 5 of the law of February 23, 2005 which prohibited "*toute injure ou diffamation commise envers une personne ou un groupe de personnes en raison de leur qualité vraie ou supposée de harki,*" (roughly translated as prohibiting all insult or defamation of a person or group of persons because of their real or supposed quality of being a Harki). The law's promulgation was the product of years of lobbying by Harki associations.[7] The French Minister of Culture and numerous writers, intellectuals, and artists opposed Harki protests against Benyoucef's play because, as they found nothing injurious or defamatory in it, they saw the charge as a breach of freedom of speech.

The position of the Harkis is best described in Mohamed Haddouche's letter to the Regional Council. He begins by stating that the author of the play is an Algerian who wants "to display the alienating surrender [*déshérence*] and rottenness [*mal être*] of Harki children."[8] The play is "a malicious and underhanded attack" on the Harkis and "casts opprobrium and discredit" on their community. By "insidiously planting clichés [*des poncifs et des clichés*]," the playwright arrives at his "hidden goal: to revive the scars of the Algerian war and to wound a community." He takes up anew the insult of treason and affirms that "it is found in the genes of the Harkis and is inherited from generation to generation" (n. pag.). He forgets that the Harkis were not against independence but against the terror imposed by the FLN. He revives the rumor that the Harkis formed battalions of Groupes islamiques armés (GIA), the most uncompromisingly militant of the Algerian Islamist groups that tried to destabilize Algeria. The rumor, it is said, was spread by the Algerian government in the 1990s to turn the Harkis into a scapegoat to justify its own failure. Haddouche argues that Benyoucef pushes "ignominy" to the point of writing that the treachery is perpetuated by blood and crime since the son "must sacrifice the father" and become treacherous in his turn. By negating the identity of the son—that is to say, the Harkis and their descendents—whom he dubs S.N.P [*sans nom patronymique,* without a patronym], he renews the idea of "the traitor always under the skin" (n. pag.).[9] Haddouche points to the paradox that though France is in the process of working through the painful memories of the Algerian war as well as its racism and anti-Semitism, it supports *Le nom du père*, and demands that the performances of he play be stopped immediately.

The language of the complaint is hyperbolic and at times falls out of grammatical constraint, but it does reveal the pain the Harkis and their children feel today. It reflects their 'exceptionalness'—and the way that exceptionalness is perpetuated by their sense of being betrayed and abandoned by the French. It is noteworthy that Haddouche begins his letter by stating that Benyoucef is an Algerian, without adding any qualification. He does not try to locate the play in the body of Benyoucef's work, as the third in a loose trilogy which deals with violent contradictions in the Algerian war of independence and its aftermath. The picture Benyoucef draws of the French, the Algerian government, the FLN, the *pieds-noirs,* and Algerians in general is hardly more flattering than that of his Harki protagonist. Haddouche fails to see the play's terrible irony, its cynicism, and the occasional relief that comes with humor—albeit vested in the cliché. He does take up the argument, which has gained currency in recent years, that the Harkis were against the FLN but not against Algerian Independence. This was certainly true of many Harkis, perhaps the majority, but there were others who were, if not opposed to Independence, then fearful of what it would bring. They were haunted, at least as they express themselves today, by what they perceived to be the incapability of the Algerian people to rule. There were many, like the Bachaga Boualam, then vice president of the French National Assembly, who wanted Algeria to remain French (see his book *Mon Pay, La France*). The fact is that the Harkis were more diversified in background, attitude, and opinion than their leaders can admit today on political grounds, but it is also true that their treatment by the French (not to mention the Algerians) has also served to unite them and give them a cohesive story.

## The Play

> And I want to make of it a literary space for memory. "Not a memory riveted to what one believes was the original reality; a memory that will only be a worn-out rehearsal of the past and a loan word for nostalgia: but an active memory that will ceaselessly reaffirm the primacy of the present—an essential condition for the correct understanding of the past—and will permit a better apprehension of the future."
>
> -- Jeanne in Benyoucef, *Lettres à Jeanne*

The works in the trilogy that concludes with *Le nom du père* all, of which treat the Algerian war of independence and its aftermath, are united by a notion of active memory. Jeanne describes the Algerian situation in the epistolary novel of Benyoucef *Lettres à Jeanne* (Letters to Jeanne) whose theatrical adaptation, *La mer blanche du milieu,* was produced by Peyrotte's company, Bagage de Sable, in 2001. *The White Sea in the Middle* is a literal translation of the Arabic for the Mediterranean, *Al-bahr al-abyad al-mutawasit*. Peyrotte's discovery of a 1955 photograph of her class in Algeria was the inspiration for the book, which consists of letters by Jeanne's French and Algerian classmates to whom she had written decades later, presumably in the 1990s, asking for news. The letters illustrate the social and cultural complexity that lay behind the Algerian struggle for independence and how that struggle affected the destiny of French and Algerians alike. Though Benyoucef is clearly critical of all the parties involved—the FLN, the Algerians, the French, the OAS, the *pieds-noirs*, and the Algerian government that followed the war—he demonstrates enormous sympathy for the individuals involved and their entrapment in history. Violence and its effects figure in each of the letters in different ways: murder, exploitation, political and moral bankruptcy, disorientation, speech, the loss of a homeland, impossible love and suicide, sex, madness, the revelation of truth, and, most terrifying of all because it has no fixed referent, pervading menace. Benyoucef notes the lack of distance between the past called up by Jeanne's letters and the present that the letters put into question. Past and present "telescope each other, they reflect in an implacable game of mirroring the grotesque effigy of that goddess who drinks the blood of her victims in their own skulls, the terrifying midwife of history, violence" (6). Can memory ever get beyond this violence, even in its active stance, toward the present and the future?

In the second play, *Dans les ténèbres gîtent les aigles* (Eagles Nest in the Shadows), from Hölderlin's poem "Patmos," the "goddess" of violence appears mysteriously as Tergou: a white woman, a woman in white, who walks on stilts and clacks the reeds that extend her long fingers, announcing the death of those she will devour. *Dans les ténèbres* is the most philosophical of the trilogy. Its two protagonists are Frantz Fanon, the Caribbean psychiatrist who became an Algerian revolutionary and wrote *The Wretched of the Earth* and other works on the psychology of colonialism, and Ramdane Abane, one of the leaders of the FLN assassinated in Morocco by his rivals in the movement. The play asks: Which should have priority in a revolution, in a struggle for independence, the political or the military? It follows the trajectory of its two protagonists during the most violent phase of the war, from January 1956 to December 1957, though it incorporates Fanon's death in Washington on July 12, 1961. Fanon, who had hoped to reform psychiatry in Algeria, which, under the influence of Antoine Porot, was deeply racist (Berthelier 71 ff), comes to recognize the futility of his project when he realizes that the delusions of one of his patients, a French-Algerian woman who believes her husband is plotting a massacre of the Algerians, is in fact true:

> If to cure a patient is to restore their ability to choose, it is still necessary not to have any illusions of freedom for a subject whose very being is denied. What is the use of returning to a deadening colonial order those who have fled it, seeking shelter in madness? (25-26)

Fanon gives up his hospital position, joins the FLN, and, among other things, edits their magazine *Moudjahid* in Tunisia. Abane, a political pragmatist with little subtlety but considerable, indeed stubborn, integrity, insists in the play and in reality on the priority of the political over the military: "A revolution cannot be led by shepherds bearing arms" (45). He recognizes that "symmetry in the use of violence does not generate an equality of political benefits for the protagonists" (50-51). He tells Fanon that "politics in arms is as dangerous and incongruous as military politics. At the limit there is no difference between them" (94). Fanon is more open to the possibility of military leadership in the struggle against colonialism (though he is troubled by Sartre's advocacy of violence in his Introduction to *The Wretched of the Earth*). His fear is the creation of a postcolonial neo-bourgeoisie. Though committed to the political, Abane, a realist, has to acknowledge the inevitable role—the temptation—of violence in the political. Indeed, it leads to his assassination, to his refusal, itself an act of perverted violence, to heed warnings of his assassination.

Although *Le nom du père* takes places decades after the end of the war, its protagonist, S.N.P, can be described by Fanon's observation in *Dans les ténèbres* that "because it is a systematic negation of the other, a fanatical decision to refuse any attributes of humanity to the other, colonialism drives a dominated people to ask continually: who am I in reality?" (89) This is the question that S.N.P constantly asks himself in word and through deed. He is caught in an intricate web of being bullied and tempted, withdrawing and engaging. The play, which is the most dramatically successful of the trilogy, begins with a song by a rapper[10] who, emerging from darkness, scrutinizes and then challenges the audience by telling them what they should not expect from the play: no hip-hop, no face-splitting clowning, no alexandrines (rather *un style malandrin,* a thug's style), no tear-jerking, no sex, no intellectuals who puff up (*se péter*) their heads, no facile psychology, no introspection, etc. It is a question of the torments of memory, of life buffeted by History: "You know that profane divinity who drinks the blood of its victim[s] from their skulls" (6). As he sings, the title of the play is projected on a screen in its several Lacanian versions: *le nom du père, le non du père, le non-dupe erre,* the name of the father, the no of the father, the unduped who wanders, who errs.[11] The Lacanian pun captures S.N.P's dilemma—and by extension that of the Harkis—for it calls attention to the question of identity as it is vested in the father's name, in his authoritative 'no' (in the Harkis' case, his refusal to talk), in the negation of having been duped, in wandering, indeed in erring, as disillusioned. Those who are not duped wander, in wandering do they err?

The play takes place in France and Algeria sometime in the 1990s when the Algerian government was caught in a violent struggle with competing Islamist and other political factions. It consists of a series of scenes that follow one another autonomously, without any necessary connection, like a picaresque tale, less in the manner of Brecht than of Büchner, figuring destiny in all its terrible absurdity and yet motivated in the instance by the insistent reality of history, its violence, its violation, ultimately by Tergou. She never actually makes her appearance, as she did in *Dans les ténèbres,* but is omnipresent in effect. At first paralyzed, if at times self-indulgently so, by his camp experiences, and more realistically by the prejudices of French society, S.N.P, like Woyzeck or the Good Soldier Švejk, is carried across, indeed forced into, multiple, conflicting, nested roles by Islamists and their warring factions; by a 'special' branch of the French army who bully him into infiltrating the Islamists; by the Algerian army which wants him to re-infiltrate the Islamists and eventually return to France to continue the war against them—that is, as it was put to him: "to take advantage of the military aid Paris gives to the apostate power in Algiers" (70)[12]—and by his love for a French school teacher named Christiane who wants him to move in with her.[13]

There is, as the rapper says, no introspection. How can there be in this whirl of identities? S.N.P can only act out, despairingly at times, with bitter irony at others, that which is prescribed, and once prescribed, inevitable. The line between inner motivation and outer coercion is never clear. Indeed, inner and outer are reflections of each other. Not only does the life space reflect the self, as Agnès, a psychologist, tells S.N.P in the first scene, but the entanglements of plot or lack thereof reflect the confusions of motivation and non-motivation, of strategy and thoughtlessness, in—for lack of a better term—S.N.P's soul space.

As the play opens, we find S.N.P in a slovenly state in a messy room with empty beer cans and a plate overflowing with cigarette butts in a Harki camp.[14] He is talking to Agnès who shakes her head in a gesture of disapproval and helplessness. He is in his thirties, immature, trapped in and by the camp. Whenever he tries to leave, he always ends up returning. In lines that are reminiscent—though less delicate and more critical of the father—of those that I heard from many of the Harki children with whom I talked, he describes his experience in the camp as follows:

> We didn't know anything but the camp, the camp school, the camp teachers, the camp guards, the camp director, the camp curfew, the glacial wind in the camp in the winter, the

> molten heat in the camp in the summer. . . . And nothing else to do but walk around the camp looking at our mothers muffled up in their covers, with their dresses on top of each other. . . . And our fathers . . . the shame of our fathers, sitting, sheltered from the wind, under the barrack walls, smoking and looking out in front. . . . But it's not the future they see, because here there is no future. It's not there for anyone. It's their past that they do not stop looking at and ruminating! Because their past, they can never swallow it [*Parce que leur passé, il ne leur est jamais passé!*]. It lies across their throats. . . . And it's their past that has prevented us from having a present and which eats up our future. (9)

S.N.P resists all of Agnès's efforts to get him to do something with his life. He says that all his effort to get the better of the camp has failed. He joined Harki associations, participated in all their protests, burned the camp at Bias, occupied Saint Laurent des Arbres, went on hunger strikes, fought with the French State Security Police (CRS), and got imprisoned. He left the camp three times looking for work, but could never find anything. "It's not that I didn't try," he tells Agnès to whom he always speaks with respectful gratitude:

> Thanks to you, I learned that I must question my thoughts and actions and try to understand what they mean [*riment*] because finally everything makes sense. And it's that way that I discovered that there's absolutely nothing in us. The camp has eaten up our insides. . . . Of course there are moments when you believe that you're free, that you can change the order of things, build a splendid future. . . . But that's a dream, delirious, not real. (11)

Does S.N.P appreciate the implication of his observation? Does Agnès? Fanon, the Fanon of *Dans les ténèbres* at least, would have appreciated the role of introspection, real or not, in displacing, indeed in eliminating, the consideration of real life impediments.

As S.N.P describes his search for work, he tells Agnès that his name was changed from Ali Lakjaa ('the lame' in Arabic) to Alain Boiteux ('the lame' in French). (Many Harki names were changed by the authorities when they filed papers in France; others changed their names voluntarily; and still others, the majority, kept their Arab or

Berber names.) But later in his conversation, S.N.P asks her not to call him Alain anymore: "I don't want to hear myself called by that name," he says excitedly. "It is not my name. It's a name [*sobriquet*] others have chosen for me. Without asking my advice." He doesn't want to be called Ali either, because his father gave him that name and he does not want to owe him anything. "It's a little late to kill the father," Agnès observes dryly before asking him what she should call him. He answers: "S.N.P." "So you have decided to become nobody," she says leaving him. "You know where to find me if you want to talk" (15).

S.N.P takes on various names as he moves from one identity to another.[15] Before asking him to choose a name, the French commander who recruits him observes that "a name is too important to leave in the hands of parents or immigration authorities. To name something is to give it life. And it's the same with human beings" (30). S.N.P names himself on this occasion "Elias" because it sounds like alias: "Up until now I was only an alias," he says as he accepts the role the commander gives him. With the Islamists, he is given no choice. He is told his new name is Abou-Chafra, Swordsman, or literally "the father of the sword" (39). The Algerian commander also gives him a name, Lieutenant Lyès, after asking him what his real name is. "The brothers finally gave you a name?," the commander asks. "I thought I could find an identity among them," S.N.P answers. "So you dumped your old name," the commander says, noting that that is perfectly understandable, especially for those (by which he means the Harkis) who had to take on a French name. "But you have rejoined your camp, the true one, the only. The camp of your blood, of your earth" (68-69). Of course, the commander misses the irony. He offers S.N.P no choice of name. It is not clear that S.N.P catches it either.

Name changes are symbolic of S.N.P's inability to assume a permanent identity. They are like the costumes he wears: Western clothes, those of an Islamist, and those of a *maquisard*, a guerilla fighter. They are also like the several languages he uses. At times he speaks near-schoolbook French; at others one argot or another (rap *beur*, army). When he mixes them, the mix is incongruous, revealing an absence of a fixed perspective. When he tells the Algerian commander that he thought he could find an identity among the Islamists, we (and, it would seem, S.N.P himself) do not know whether he means what he is saying. Does he mean he really thought he could find an Islamist identity? Or is he acting the role of a French spy? Or is he simply speaking strategically to save his neck? He is, after all, in enemy territory. Can there be any introspective certainty in such a position?

Or are there only multiple and contradictory introspective stances? Our deepest psychological assumptions that center on a fixed point, as illusory as it may be, are challenged.

Not only are the events, the roles and identities, that befall S.N.P arbitrary and autonomous, as though they are the debris of a fractured destiny, but so are many of his own acts. He need not always accept the identities offered him, but he does. In one of the most brutal scenes in the play, he kills, without any apparent need to, an old man who has been pleading for the life of a young Algerian recruit condemned by Abou-Laala, the leader of the Islamist faction S.N.P has joined. The scene, one of the longest in the play, is so filled with black humor, so grotesque in its depiction of Islamist justice, that one wonders how the Harki critiques of the play could not appreciate Benyoucef's condemnation of all sides in the Algerian war and its violent aftermath. Abou-Laala arbitrarily condemns to death one innocent villager after another—for adultery (a man and a woman who were simply seen alone together, the man turning out to be gay), for writing plays (presumably referring to the assassination of Algerian playwright Abdelkader Alloula whom Benyoucef has translated into French), for being a Westernized widow who wears pants, drives a car, and whose demographer husband Abou-Laala had had executed. At first Abou-Laala confuses "demographer" with "democrat" and then, when he is corrected, he says: "Ah, I see. Those who prescribe pills and other satanic measures to fill garbage cans with fetuses" (51). The recruit is condemned simply because he was drafted. The old man defends him. He knows the family; he saw the police carry him off to the barracks. Abou-Laala threatens the old man with death and then, in a twist worthy of the most Orientalist of tales, ends up marrying the old man's daughter. When the old man asks Abou-Laala not to announce the marriage (for, if he does, the old man and his family will be killed by his fellow villagers for siding with the Islamists), Abou-Laala says: "If I were not your son-in-law, I'd send you to Cairo [put you to death]" (56). It is at this point, in a highly stylized fashion, that S.N.P shoots the old man. Abou-Laala praises S.N.P, and the imam who has been present all along says he will issue "a post-mortem *fatwa*" (56). As a reward, About-Laala divorces the old man's daughter and gives her to S.N.P as a wife despite his protests.

Overcome by the murder he has committed, S.N.P tries to lose himself in a massive dose of opium and marijuana. Sakhr, his friend and foil, warns him that the combination will send him through the stratosphere to a meeting with Azraël, the angel of death. S.N.P ignores his friend's warning. He has a terrifying vision of a past he neither knows nor wants to acknowledge. A ghost describes how when the French executed all the young men in his village, the ghost's elder son accused his younger brother of treachery and shot him in cold blood with a revolver lent by the commanding officer. He was rewarded with a combat uniform, that is, he became a Harki. Despite S.N.P's pleas to stop talking, the ghost, who now identifies himself as S.N.P's grandfather, tells him he is now mature enough to take on the burden of his history: "A great rift in the soul [*une grande faille de l'âme*] never finds the path to forgetfulness," the ghost says. "Always identical to itself, it passes from generation to generation. All one can do is to try to live with it." The ghost goes on to tell S.N.P that only one of the two sons could have children, and that son gave a son (S.N.P) to his childless brother. When S.N.P asks the ghost who his real father is, the ghost refuses to tell him, saying: "It is a family secret sealed in iron by words pronounced over the Holy Book." "I give you at least the possibility of choice," the ghost says, and, before disappearing, adds: "Don't forget that a man is never more than the sum of his murders. How I pity you little one, *adieu*" (65).

Real or not, the ghost's revelation reinforces the failure of the father's name, his authority, his ability to name, for there is no certainty in even the father's identity. Was S.N.P's father killed by his brother? Was he, as his brother maintained, an enemy of the French? A member of the FLN? Or was S.N.P the son of the murdering brother? A Harki? Had the murdering brother himself been an FLN operative? Had either brother been involved in the war at all? Whatever his real father was, S.N.P ended up in a Harki camp because he was identified, if not with his real father, then with the father who assumed his paternity. Of course, all of these questions rest on a drug-induced vision. There is no certainty. There can, therefore, be no nominal stability.

In the following scene, after S.N.P has gone over to the Algerian side, to be sent back to the Islamists, he tells the commander, speaking more to himself than to the latter, that he had come back to Algeria to find his own people, his land, his origins: "Am I permitted to be stupid?" he asks. The commander does not trust him. He wants to know whether S.N.P has crossed over from the Islamists as a spy. S.N.P tells him he made the decision after a terrifying night and starts to tell the commander about the vision he had had, which, he says, made him conscious of his debt to Algeria. The commander tells him: "Where there is a debt, there is guilt, and that's a destructive sentiment that can be abolished by the payment of the debt. You have the historical opportunity to erase your shame which is no less than that of your father." Brushing off an objection S.N.P makes, he argues that the latter has no choice but to do as he is told, for it is only by joining the Algerian army as an operative among the Islamists in France that he will make up for his father's treason and the two betrayals he himself has committed—joining the French and joining the Islamists. S.N.P says he agrees. But does he? (72)

Trapped, back at the *maquis*, S.N.P calls Christiane in desperation to tell her of his treachery, his entrapment, his love for her, his blindness which came from pride and the desire for recognition, and the certainty that he will not escape alive. She responds with sentimental clichés about love and the need for self-compassion and at the same time takes the situation in hand. She will contact the French commander Zacherie; as S.N.P gets himself to the nearest French consulate. As he finishes his call, he is caught by his old Harki friend, Sakhr, who wants to arrest him and take him to Abou-Khadra, the leader of an Islamist group financed by American money, who opposed Abou-Laala's group and through Sakhr's treachery facilitated their destruction. S.N.P convinces Sakhr that he has an important meeting in town and will join Abou-Khadra the next day. He gives Sakhr the cell phone and a code word and tells him to have Abou-Khadra call at "eleven o'clock universal time." Abou-Khadra will be rewarded. Sakhr agrees reluctantly.

The finale of the play is an explosion that takes place the following morning when Abou-Khadra makes the call and gets the nasal voice of an American. Exalted, S.N.P cries out, "Bingo! Adieu Sakhr! Adieu Abou-Khadra!" and then hysterically adds: "A man is the sum of his murders! A man is the sum of his murders! Are my sacrifices acceptable, Babylon? Are you going to open your gates to me?" As he runs offstage, shouting "Christiane, wait for me," the rapper reappears and sings: "There you have it. We'll stop here the trials of these poor guys, but you have the right to choose another ending." A happy ending Hollywood style, with syrupy music at dawn, as in a third-rate Indian film, as a journalist's uncovering the truth of the affair. The rapper starts to leave, hesitates, returns, and, in a confidential tone, says: "Not to give you a donkey's kick, we like the Christiane ending." He winks at the audience and sends them kisses with both hands (85).

## Analysis

> That which is lived at the moment that it occurs is not History. History is that which is endlessly written and re-written. It is from this alone that you draw your legitimacy as an actor.
>
> -- Abane in Benyoucef, *Dans les ténèbres*

Despite the humor, as black as it often is, and the light ending, which some French critics took seriously as a resolution to the play (see Jaulin), *Le nom du père* is in its relentlessness a terrifying play. Though some critics saw it as *Bildungstheater*, as a growing-up play, it seems to me that it should rather be understood in terms of the picaresque—a dark, violent, cruel picaresque that puts into question the very possibility of *Bildung,* not just for the Harkis but for all Algerians who have suffered the brutality of colonialism, the violence of the war of independence, and the carnage that has ensued.[16] Despite their contingency, the events recounted and enacted are motivated by historical circumstances, and, as Benyoucef sees it, the violence that always lurks behind the movement of history. The contingency of individual life is, as it were, subsumed under ever greater contingencies which we call history and seek to understand in terms of one narrative or another, often forgetting that the understanding we have is a refraction of the narratives we have created. These narratives, particularly when they are centered on the individual, promote, if not the reality then the possibility of resolution–of an ending that makes sense. But is there ever a resolution? Is there ever an ending that makes sense? It is the picaresque, at least as I see it, that calls attention to the artifice of resolution and meaningful endings, indeed, of any endings. It plays on destiny, which, in its boldest formulation, resists the seduction of explanation. It is, as the Algerians say, *mektub* (written/fate), which Harkis, less so their children, often use. By speaking of the contingencies of their lives in terms of the "written," they avoid explaining what they cannot or do not want to explain.

Of course, they could blame de Gaulle, Louis Joxe, and Pierre Messmer for their abandonment; the Algerians for the slaughter of their people; and French racism for their subsequent treatment. It was my impression, however, that they found little satisfaction—moral, indeed metaphysical, satisfaction—in such blame. Specific in its focus, blame could not do justice to the magnitude of their change of fortune and the complexity of their own involvement in that change. However enraged they were by their treatment in Algeria and in France, they had, on some level, to recognize the consequences of their own decisions, however forced upon them, and what was no doubt even more devastating: their impotence before these forces. There lay deep within them a hurt, a wound, a lesion, what the ghost called "a great rift in the soul" (65). They were at once responsible and not responsible for that wound. They knew and did not know what they were getting into when they joined the French. Did they suffer guilt for the 'treachery' they had committed? One

Algerian psychiatrist I talked to, who had little sympathy for them, insisted that they were overwhelmed by such guilt. I did not find evidence of such guilt. If there was guilt, it was contorted by the real pressures put upon them by the war. Perhaps S.N.P expressed it better when he described the fathers of his generation: "the shame of our fathers . . . smoking and looking in front of themselves," not at the future, for they have no future, but at "a past they can never swallow." It "lies across their throats" (9). One might well add like a knife. Suicides were frequent, drunken stupors even more so, and depression was a constant. As the ghost remarked, the riven soul will never find the path to forgetfulness.

Though I distinguish between feelings of guilt and shame here, I am not invoking that simplistic dichotomy between shame and guilt cultures which anthropologists have promoted in the past, North African culture being for them a prime example of a shame culture (see Peristiany). The affective lives of individuals are far too complex for such generalizations. Rather, I am suggesting here that the Harkis, at least those I talked to, were ashamed of being duped. Though Benyoucef does not develop Lacan's third play on the name of the father, *le non-dupe-erre*, (the unduped who wanders)—and, in my reading, errs, it would seem that Lacan's formulation is not irrelevant to the Harki situation. They were duped by the French and, in suffering the consequences of their dupery, they were "unduped," and (rather more perhaps in reality than Lacan may have meant) forced to wander—to live, homeless in their new home, unable in fact and in psyche to return home. That they may have erred sounds, I believe, like a *basso continuo* in their ruminations. But here I transgress the limits of anthropological understanding.

The name situates the subject within the tissue of signification, within language, within the linguistically classified, if not constituted, world. Naming is, as the philosopher Saul Kripke observes, a baptism:

> An initial baptism takes place. . . . Here the object may be named by ostension, or the reference of the name may be fixed by a description. When the name is "passed from link to link," the receiver of the name must, I think, intend when he learns it to use it with the same reference as the man from whom he heard it. (96)

Kripke is, of course, talking about the names of objects, but he could also be talking about proper names. They too must be used as they are given, and as they are used, they, like all names, recall the initial baptismal event and the authority that lies with it. To name is a performative act, and the namer must have, therefore, the authority to name. In patriarchic societies, like Algeria at least, that authority lies, as Lacan would no doubt have stressed, with the father—in his name (for he is already incorporated within the linguistically endorsed universe), in his ability to say no, that is, in his identification with the law: "We must recognize support for the symbolic function in the *name of the father* who since the beginning [*orée*] of historical time identifies his person with the figure of the law" (Lacan 278). It is, as Lacan sees it, the name of the father, his "no" (to the boy's desire for the mother during the Oedipal phase), the law he proclaims, that fixes signification by binding signifier to signified.

In his silence, has the father lost the ability to name? It would certainly appear so in S.N.P's case. He rejects the name his father gave him. He refuses the debt imposed on him by that name: "I don't want to owe that man anything," he tells Agnès, and she understands his rejection in Oedipal terms. "It's a little late to effect the murder of the father," she says. "But if you have to follow that route . . ." She interrupts herself with a gesture of helplessness (14). She recognizes that the murderous desires of the son will not free him of the debt he owes his father. Rejected or not, the name will adhere, if only through negation. *Sans-nom-patronymique* still evokes the name S.N.P's father has given him, as well as his father's own name and all it symbolizes and demands.

In Algeria, as elsewhere in North Africa and the Middle East, the son bears not only his given name, which is confirmed in a name-day ceremony when he is a week old, but also the name of his father, for he may always be called patronymically, *bin* or *ibn* (son of) followed by his father's given name. Insofar as his father can, in turn, be called patronymically, *abu* (father of), the son is incorporated into an endless patrilineal genealogy from which he cannot escape, and to which he is obligated in various ways. The Harkis with whom I spoke and some of their sons, though by no means all of them, regretted the fact that they could not attend the funerals or even visit the graves of their fathers and grandfathers in Algeria. Their exile created a rupture in their genealogies, in their familial and social orientations, and in their relationships to the land in which they were born and their ancestors lay buried. As they talked of this rupture, I felt their pain—the pain of dislocation and misunderstanding. They told me sadly of their children's loss of ties: 'It is written,' they said, not without ambivalence; for though they were mostly a people apart, living in a foreign country, they were loyal to France, and, despite their complaints, appreciated the advantages it brought to their children. They stressed the bloodshed and misery that followed Algerian independence. 'Had we stayed. . .' always edged their conversation, but they knew better than to speculate. Their realism, the realism forced upon them, the pain that lay behind that realism, precluded such speculation. They were deprived of the optative. Yes, they were always struggling, largely through their children, to obtain as much as they could from the French government, for example, but they expected nothing until it finally came, if it ever did. It seemed to me that they guarded themselves from disappointment in ways that their children did not. I remember the crushed look of the son of a Harki who had just learned that, as his parents were dead, he would not be eligible for government compensation for the losses his family had sustained. He had hoped to use the money to buy a café.

The names S.N.P takes on during the course of the play reflect the failure of the father's authority to name him and, thereby, to stabilize his identity. Among the Harkis with whom I worked, this failure could be attributed to the fathers' silence, their incapacity to assume the paternal role after having been duped, abandoned, and, as they see it, betrayed by the French; their demeaning and unmanning life in the camps; their inability to adjust to a new country; their experience of pervasive racism and bureaucratic obstinacy; and, of course, their particular biographical circumstances—but above all, I believe, by their powerlessness to come to grips with the transcending (historical) drama in which they found themselves inadvertent actors. It can also be argued that, as products of colonial paternalism as well as the paternalism fostered by the military, they found themselves particularly dependent on the French and, therefore, suffered their abandonment and betrayal with exceptional intensity. As they described how they had been sent back to their villages unarmed with a small bonus, and the assurance that they had nothing to fear, they could barely contain their rage and give adequate expression to their disillusionment. Most refused to describe to me the horrors they had witnessed and the fears they undoubtedly felt. Their silence was perhaps the one token of masculinity they would not lose. Stoicism and silence in the face of hardship is a masculine virtue among traditional Algerians.

The failure of the father's name effects the entire family. The children, especially the sons, as they were educated in France, served as cultural brokers for their fathers. The relationship was always delicate, for they had to tell their fathers what to do without undermining their fathers' authority. Though many of them were adept at this, others were not, and spurred their fathers' rage, which was directed at them, at other family members—wife beating was frequent, I have been told—and against themselves. (Some fathers recognized with irony, if not with humor, the ploys their sons used to get their way.) Wives knew as little about what had transpired during their husbands' military service as did their children. They also kept silent to protect their children. Judging from the family memoirs and novels that Harki daughters have written in the last few years, they too suffered from their parents' silence (see Besnaci-Lancou; Kemoun; Kerchouche; and Rahmani). Their memoirs and novels are, for the most part, tales of quest to find out what exactly had happened to their parents. That S.N.P made no effort to find out the circumstances that led to his father's joining the French, that he refused, as the ghost would have it, to accept the burden of history, would not, in my experience, have been unusual among many Harki sons, but many others, perhaps the majority I talked to, were interested in finding out what had happened. They suffered their fathers' wounds without knowing exactly what these wounds were and, in consequence, an emptiness they could never fill to their satisfaction. Under these circumstances, witnessing takes on special significance.

The fact that S.N.P knew nothing about his father's fratricide (if we are to believe the ghost), that he had no idea of his father's sterility (if indeed his father was sterile), and that he would never know his father's true identity are exceptional circumstances, but they dramatically symbolize the faulted role of the father, *le père barré*, as Benyoucef expresses it, for Harki sons and their children.[17] That the information is conveyed by a ghost suggests the fantasmatic dimension of such knowledge which resists, as it insists on, the reality and the authority of the father. The paradox is mirrored not only in S.N.P's inability to escape the effect of his father's name, but in the replay of his father's paralysis in his own paralysis as he sits at the beginning of the play drinking beer and smoking in his room. Wittingly or unwittingly, he takes on the burden his father has bequeathed him. Is S.N.P destined then to repeat his father's history? When Zacharie, the French commander, explains S.N.P's mission, S.N.P stands up, pale, and says, "Ah, I understand! After the father, it's the son's turn to be used against his fellow men [*congénères,* suggesting genus, tribe, of the same birth]! (*He hits his head with his fist*) But what can I be, weak?" (32). Zacharie ignores him and continues to explain the mission.

Is the murder of the father—or father substitutes—the only means of escape? The ghost suggests this when he tells S.N.P to remember that "a man is only the sum of his murders." S.N.P repeats these words hysterically after Abou-Khadra and his friend Sakhr are blown up. Is our destiny inexorably determined by the Oedipal drama? It should be remembered that S.N.P shot an old man—a father figure—who was defending the young recruit—the son, S.N.P who seems never to have been protected by his own father. We must also remember that, for Benyoucef, violence is the midwife of history and one of the Islamists in *Le nom du père* refers to the "mother of battles" (17). Is violence then inspired by women—by the mother?

Women too, it would seem, inspire their own murders. In the penultimate scene, as S.N.P leaves for the French consulate in Algiers, the old man's daughter whom Abou-Laala gave to S.N.P as a wife suddenly appears, demands her marriage rights, informs S.N.P that she is pregnant, and, though S.N.P had never slept with her, insists that according to *shari'a* (Islamic law) he is legally the father. S.N.P kills her. It would seem that such a mechanical, indeed stereotypical, conclusion does not do justice to the complexity of the events recounted and enacted. Fanon of *Dans les ténèbres* would certainly find it unsatisfactory, for it fails to take account of the historical reality in which the drama is played out. Of course, Benyoucef tantalizes us with the possibility of escape. Two women at least, both French, and one in particular (significantly named Christiane), offer the possibility of escape from the real and psychological entanglements of history, as the rapper, with a wink and kisses blown to the audience, says he would prefer to end the play. But the play does not end that way; the rapper stops it arbitrarily: "We'll stop here the trials of these poor guys."

## Complaint Revisited

> The facts that I am going to evoke leave no place for any type of distance. . . . Impossible to be clever with them or to count on the artifices of performance [*représentation*] to hold them at a respectable distance.
>
> -- Writer in Benyoucef, *Dans les ténèbres*

Even a cursory reading of Mohamed Haddouche's letter of complaint reveals the pain the play inspired in him, and presumably other Harkis and their children who attended or read the play. It is obvious that many more joined the protest without having any first-hand knowledge of the play. The response can be understood on many levels including the political. The principal goal of associations like AJIR and Générations mémoire harkis is to advance the Harki cause. They lobby for compensation for their losses and recognition of their sacrifices for France. They are particularly sensitive to any 'slur' on the community, and do their best to call attention to its injustice in as public a manner as possible. For them, Benyoucef's play—and particularly its subvention by the government—was an insult.

There are , I have been told, more than 500 Harki associations, of which less than 80 are active. Some, like AJIR, are particularly important, and are affiliated in an informal fashion with other associations, including *rapatrié* groups (i.e. *pieds-noirs*). Others are little more than family clubs that take advantage of tiny government subventions. Though the associations share a common goal, there is, as one would expect, dissention among them. The active members of the associations are, for the most part, children of Harkis. They are often involved in local politics, and though they may and often do benefit from their membership and the contacts it provides, they are committed to advising the Harkis of their rights and helping them to work their way through French bureaucracy. Harkis themselves are less active politically, though some of them, usually the better educated, or those who have managed to adjust to French life, do participate in protests or attend political meetings as witnesses to the Harkis' plight. Of course, many of the first generation have died by now, and those who are still alive are often infirm and dependent on their children. They live retired lives, lost in themselves, in reverie, drink, and television. They symbolize, indeed incarnate for their children and grandchildren the 'wounds' Harkis have suffered. It is, I believe, these wounds, their memory, what Benyoucef refers to as history, that unites the Harkis and perpetuates a community that is now dispersed all over France and subject to social and cultural stratification that, for the moment at least, is not particularly divisive. It is these wounds—abandonment and incarceration—that constitute what Francesca Cappelletto has recently called a "mnemonic community." Under such circumstances, the possession of memory or history becomes an intensely personal affair that is, paradoxically, constantly undermined by the need to publicize that memory.

It is of significance that Haddouche starts his complaint by noting that Benyoucef is of Algerian origin. Jacques Lévêque, president of AAAAS, one of the associations of Algerian repatriates that joined the complaint, wrote explicitly in the newspaper *Paris-Normandie:* "It is absolutely intolerable that an Algerian author comes to insult on French soil the Harkis who have remained faithful to France." Though many younger Harki children are beginning to associate with Algerians living in France, the two groups do not identify with each other. Memory of the slaughter in Algeria and the violence directed toward them by Algerians living in France when they first arrived is very much alive. Both the Harkis and their children continually complain, often enough with little justification, that the immigrants are treated better than they are: 'We are traitors in the eyes of the French despite all we have done for France,' I have heard them say. Nearly everyone I talked to mentioned a speech which the president of Algeria, Abdelazziz Bouteflika, made in an official visit to France in 2001 in which he referred to the Harkis as traitors who are not welcome in Algeria.

Despite the intensity of their resentment of the Algerians, it would be a mistake to dismiss the Harkis' reaction to Benyoucef's play on the grounds of his being Algerian. They were distressed by the disparaging, cliché-filled image the play casts on the Harkis, without realizing that Benyoucef is using S.N.P and Sakhr as figures to convey the devastating effects of the war and its aftermath. Their reaction to the play is, of course, familiar in a multi-cultured world rife with one sensitivity or another.

I do not want to diminish the pain felt by one minority group or another here. Rather, I want to call attention to one important characteristic of such reactions. They are responses to a pejorative image, often intensely visual, an image so powerful that it effaces most historical circumstances. Distance—critical, esthetic distance—is near-impossible under such circumstances. Put in technical terms, the iconic power of the image is so strong, the pain that lies behind so intense, that the indexical force of the image, to call up its context, is redirected to the image itself, extinguishing or at least dramatically reducing the relevance of the image's surround. There follows a series of often stereotypical associations to the image that appear to be unconstrained by context, genre, convention, or prevailing norms. (Ironically, Haddouche speaks of Benyoucef's use of clichés and *poncifs* in his critique without recognizing that the playwright may be using these clichés intentionally.) Haddouche's protest contains the usual litany of Harki complaints: accusations of treachery, the failure to recognize that Harkis were not opposed to Algerian independence but to the terror of the FLN, the Algerian refusal to respect the Treaty of Evian, the perpetuation of the rumor that Harki sons attempted to destabilize the Algerian government by supporting militant Islamists, and the impugning of Harki loyalty to France. I am not questioning the truth of this list of complaints but are they the subject matter of Benyoucef's play? Did he intend to malign Harkis? Or did he simply portray them rhetorically to dramatize his argument, as he did the Islamists, the French secret service, the Algerian military, and even Agnès and Christiane?

So dissociated is Haddouche's litany of complaints from even the text of the play that he accuses Benyoucef of arguing that Harkis and their children possess genes for treachery. This is not the case. It is true that the ghost speaks of the passage from generation to generation of the riven soul. The Algerian commander also speaks of his camp as being the camp of S.N.P's blood (69). But these are voiced by characters in the play and have to be treated as such: figures of speech. The same claim cannot be made, however, for Haddouche's use of "genes," but his usage is, I think, a response to Benyoucef's pessimism—his emphasis on the repetition of trauma and its effects, the inevitability of the son's patricidal desires, and the role of violence as the "midwife" of history. Haddouche writes that the playwright "pushes ignominy to the point of writing that treachery is perpetuated through blood and by crime, since the son 'must sacrifice the father' and betray in turn." It is, in my view, though I speak here with caution, since I do not and can never have sufficient evidence to make this claim with certainty, that what Harkis found most disturbing about the play is the sense of their being trapped in history.

I remember discussing memory—history—with my friend Azzedine who has been campaigning for an important memorial for those Harkis who were incarcerated in the camps. We talked about the burden of history. The problem, he said, is how to be faithful to memory without becoming imprisoned by it—how to live full lives without forgetting the pain we suffered.

**Postscript**

On the country road that goes by the camp at Rivesaltes, now in ruins, there is already a small roadside memorial for those who were kept there—refugees from the Spanish civil war, Jews collected there to be sent on to Drancy and the Nazi death camps, and the Harkis. As one approaches the memorial, no doubt to distract attention from it, the government has put up a sign with an arrow pointing away from the memorial to some windmills generating electricity. *Moulins-à-vent*, it says. Of course, the windmills can be seen from just about anywhere in this flat land. It is a shoddy escape from memory—from what the French did in Algeria and what they did to Harkis as well as to Jews and Spanish refugees. As the ghost says, however, the great rift in the soul cannot find the road to forgetfulness. The soul has, of course, to recognize its rift in order for it to recognize a message from even a ghost. The history and present-day situation of the Harkis is in most ways unique, but it does bear striking resemblance to the history and plight of millions of refugees in camps around the world, and to the ever-increasing production of the socially and culturally dislocated by internecine wars and those grander ones that justify self-interest in terms of one ethnocentric value or another—like American-style democracy. For me, there is something quixotic about the juxtaposition of windmills and memorials. We see the windmills and not the memorials, but others—the refugees, the dislocated, the victims of our cultural pretense—may well see the memorials and ignore the windmills.

## Notes

[*] Sections of this article are taken from an earlier one: "Eine Wunde die nie verheilt." *Auf die Schwelle: Kunst, Risiken und Nebenwirkungen.* Eds. Erika Fischer-Lichte, Robert Sollich, Sandra Umathum, and Matthias Warstat. München: Wilhelm Fink, 2006. 207-27. My research on Harkis was supported by the Guggenheim Foundation, the National Institute of the Humanities, and the CUNY Research Foundation. All translations from French in this article are mine.

[1] They were later joined by Association des Anciens des Affaires Algériennes et Sahariennes (AAAAS).

[2] The official French definition of a Harki is "someone of Algerian origin who served in the auxiliary forces of the French army in Algeria between October 31, 1954 and July 2, 1962" (Benamou 220).

[3] Eating or drinking blood is prohibited in Islam.

[4] According to the Gaullist government and the FLN, only 10,000 were killed. It is impossible at this point to arrive at any but very approximate figures. 70,000 seems to be the figure accepted by most historians (Benamou 220).

[5] Though the camps were closed in 1978, many Harkis continued to live in forest villages, some to this day. The barracks at the Bias camp were razed in 1988 and those still living in them moved to a newly constructed housing project.

[6] It is impossible to know how many descendents of the Harkis live in France since they are not distinguished as a group in the French census. It is obvious that many lost their Harki identity as they were integrated into one sector of French society or another.

[7] Though sections of the law to which the clause protecting the Harkis from defamation was attached, have been annulled, the clause itself was retained.

[8] The word "*déshérence*" is a legal term, "escheat" in English, which refers to the reversion to the state of property when there is no legal heir. It is difficult to see what Haddouche means by it in the present context. He may have meant "*déshéritage,*" disinheritance. I have chosen to translate it as "alienating surrender."

[9] The French is awkward here: "Il poursuit sa démonstration par la negation de

l'identité du fils, c'est-à-dire des Harkis et de leurs descendents qu'il affuble du nom S.N.P, pour mieux renaître toujours dans la peau . . . 'd'un 'traître'"

10 Like the writer in *Dans les ténèbres*, the rapper speaks both from within and without the action of the play. Though he is analogous to the prologue in European theater—the barker in Brecht's *The Resistible Rise of Arturo Ui* comes to mind—he also resembles the *meddah* (storyteller) who both recounts and acts out the tales he tells, traditionally, in the marketplace and in the theater of the Algerian playwright Abdelkader Alloula. Like the rapper, the *meddah* actively engages his audience who gather around him in a *halqa* (circle). See also the beginning of *Dans les ténèbres* where Aziz, an attendant in a psychiatric hospital, describes the *halqa* and its therapeutic potential to Fanon. Benyoucef himself characterizes the rapper's songs in the manner of Brecht but with Arabo-Andalousian meter.

11 Lacan's punning here is impossible to translate into English as it plays on homophones in French. *Le non-dupe erre* puns, also, I believe, on the English "err."

12 The confusion of political factions, both secular and Islamist, violent and non-violent, in Algeria in the 1990s is reflected in S.N.P's contradictory allegiances and roles in the play. See Zaater and Roberts for a discussion of the Algerian crisis and its factionalism.

13 A French woman named Christiane helps Abane escape from Algiers in *Dans les ténèbres*.

14 Benyoucef sacrifices historical chronology for dramatic reasons. There were no longer any Harki camps in France at the time the play is set.

15 S.N.P's friend and comic foil Dahmane alias Damien also becomes Sakhr El Islam (Rock of Islam) when he joins the Islamists. S.N.P asks him if he could not find a better name than a big rock (16). Other wordplay with names include that of the French commander who recruits S.N.P: Zacharie, whose name resemble that of the Algerian commander Zakariya who recruits him later in the play.

16 I use 'picaresque' with some hesitation. The arbitrary, autonomous sequence of events and the sudden recurrence of characters and situations remind me of many stories I heard in Morocco. What seems important in them is not the denouement but the recursive convergence of chance and seemingly unrelated events and characters–much like the overlapping strands in an arabesque. The form highlights the contingency of existence—of a destiny that can neither be mastered nor explained away but always produces wonderment, fascination, humorous pleasure, and even terror.

17 In an interview with Véronique Hotte, Benyoucef explains that it is the "no" of negation of the barred father, *le père barré*, which prevents "natural genealogical transmission." It is "a metaphor for the transmission of a memory that is missing" (n. pag.).

**Works Cited**

Alloula, Abdelkader. "La representation du type non-aristotélicien dans l'activité théâtrale en Algérie." *Les Généreux*. Arles: ActesSud-Papier, 1995. 5-13.

Benamou, Georges-Marc. *Un mensonge français: Retours sur la guerre d'Algérie*. Paris: Robert Laffont, 2003.

Benyoucef, Messaoud. *Dans les ténèbres gîtent les aigles*. Nointel: Embarcadère, 2002.

__________________. *Le nom du père*. Nointel: Embarcadère, 2005.

__________________. *Lettres à Jeanne*. Nointel: Embarcadère, 2002.

Berthelier, Robert. *L'homme maghrébin dans la literature psychiatrique*. Paris: Harmattan, 1994.

Besnaci-Lancou, Fatima. *Fille de harki*. Paris: Editions d'Atelier, 2003.

Boualam, Bachaga. *Mon pays, la France*. Paris: France-Empire, 1962.

Camus, Albert. *L'homme revolté*. Paris: Gallimard, 1951.

Cappelletto, Francesca. "Long-term Memory of Extreme Events: From Autobiography to History." *Journal of the Royal Anthropological Institute* 9 (2003): 241-60.

Haddouche, Mohamed. Letter to president of the Conseil Régional de Haute Normandie. <http//www.harki.com/dernieresnouvelles 2005.htm>.

Hotte, Véronique, "Pour que la mémoire devienne histoire, en France et en Algérie." *La terrasse* 125. February, 2005. <http://www.harkis.info/portail/article.php?sid=10924068>.

Jaulin, Agnès. "L'épilogue à la Christiane." <http://www.theatreonline.com/journal/detail_article.asp?i_Production=1294&i_Spectacle=&i_TypeDoc=1&s_LibelleDetail=Archives&s_Critere=>.

Jordi, Jean-Jacques and Mohand Hamoumou. *Les harkis, une mémoire enfouie*. Paris: Autrement, 1999.

Kemoun, Hadjila. *Mohand le harki*. Paris: Anne Carrière, 2003.

Kerchouche, Dalila. *Mon père, ce Harki*. Paris:Seuil, 2003.

_______________. *Leïla, avoir dix-sept ans dans un camp de harkis*. Paris: Seuil, 2006.

Kripke, Saul. *Naming and Necessity*. Cambridge: Harvard UP, 1972.

Lacan, Jacques. *Ecrits*. Paris: Seuil, 1966.

Lévêque, Jacques. [Sans titre]. *Paris-Normandie*. March 18, 2005.

Peristiany, John George. *Honour and Shame: The Values of Mediterranean Society*. London: Weidenfeld and Nicolson, 1966.

Rahmani, Zahia. *Moze*. Paris: Sabine Wespieser, 2003.

_____________. *France, récit d'une enfance*. Paris:Sabine Wespieser, 2006.

Roberts, Hugh. *The Battlefield Algeria 1988-2002*. London: Verso, 2003.

Roux, Michel. *Les harkis, les oubliés de l'histoire*. Paris: La Découvert, 1991.

Salino, Brigitte. "La pièce 'Le Nom du père' suscite la colère des harkis." *Le Monde*. April 30, 2005.

Stora, Benjamin. *Histoire de la guerre d'Algérie*. Paris: La Découverte, 1992.

Zaater, Miloud. *L'Algérie de la guerre à la guerre (1962-2003)*. Paris: Harmattan, 2003.

# The Question of Reading Traumatic Testimony: Jones's *Corregidora* and Morrison's *Beloved*

**Abdennebi Ben Beya**

---

> Language is a place of struggle in language to recover ourselves—to rewrite, to reconcile, to renew. Our words are not without meaning. They are an action—a resistance.
>
> -- bell hooks, *Talking Back*

> All about us is noise. All about us is noise and bramble, thorn and din, each one of our ancestors on our tongues . . .
> We encounter each other in words, words spiny or smooth,
> whispered or declaimed, words to consider, reconsider . . .
> Say it plain: that many have died for this day.
> Sing the names of the dead who brought us here . . .
> Praise song for struggle, praise song for the day.
>
> -- Elizabeth Alexander, "Praise Song for the Day"

> Speaking is impossible, but so too would be silence or absence or a refusal to share one's sadness.
>
> -- Jacques Derrida, *Mémoires: For Paul de Man*

**By Way of Introduction**

Like millions of viewers, I watched and heard Elizabeth Alexander reciting her inaugural poem[1] immediately after Obama had taken the presidential oath.[2] Like Obama's, Alexander's words are sober with doses of hopeful determination. Parts of the two texts read like a 'rememory' récit, slipping within the joyful uproar that celebrates the event. Yet, without attention, one can hardly perceive the trace of an imperceptible wound through Alexander's apparently well-mastered performance. Beyond the calm of the utterance, methodically structured to build the architectural edifice of the poem, a lament is voiced. Something whispers through the verbal flow. Hardly perceivable, the muffled babble of the wound yet emerges to trace the contours of the structure. As a belated witness,

Alexander's narrative poem, like Obama's address, is uttered in the form of a hymn to the dead, as a threshold to catharsis. It is an address to an audience attending the ceremony, as well as to an absent one lurking in the poetess's mind to reach her tongue: "All about us is noise and bramble, thorn and din, each one of our ancestors on our tongues." The spirit of the dead lives on, coated with their "song for struggle," reaching out to a promising future. Note the concordant resonance between bell hooks's epigraph above and Alexander's rhythm: "We encounter each other in words, . . . words to consider, reconsider."

With the African-American traumatic saga in mind, the final emphasis in the quoted portion sounds like an insistent call for the endless repetition of an ethical performance. "To consider" is a call for attention, respect, and care; it is an ethically imperative demand for the incorporation of one another's story ("words") that should transpire and be encountered in the form of welcome. Every individual story moves beyond what is said, stated by the speaking subject, to re-emerge, naked and yet not transparent, during its reception. Each story contains its silence. Its very literal exposure is a disguise, a symptom,[3] veiling what remains untold. To "reconsider" urges the audience not to exacerbate the painful past by swiftly moving on through its enunciation in history documents. It insists on the survivors' humility by urging them to visit and to re-visit, slowly, patiently, their ancestors' narrative as a work-in-progress: "Say it plain, that many have died for this day," Alexander says. "I stand here," Obama responds, "mindful of the sacrifices borne by our ancestors." "To consider, reconsider", then, exhorts the audience against inexpedient haste or naïve, misleading speculations about the past. No time is too long when the task of memory is carried out with the unhalted rhythm of careful thought, with the impulse to abandon temporal constraints. And if survivors may have the tendency or the desire to "put the past at bay"—to borrow the words of Toni Morrison—in order to simply go on 'considering' current matters, these should be wary of the risk of contributing to deteriorate the spirit of those who "toiled [for] us in sweatshops . . . endured the lash of the whip and plowed the hard earth," as Obama put it in his Inaugural Address.

In the wake of the two addresses, this article is a work in/on memory that attempts to humbly accompany the oath by gathering and remembering testimonial fragments. Much has been written on the subject, and yet much more requires our careful attention. Billions of people in the world bear daily the burdensome trace of violence as 'a tax to pay' for their existence. Evidence is exceedingly spattered on television screens, leaving us shackled, muted by inexpressible shock and awe. Even as Maurice

Blanchot poignantly noted that the disaster always takes place after having taken place,[4] that it is excavated by the nightmarish emergence of the event through what Cathy Caruth calls "uncontrolled repetitive appearances of hallucinations,"[5] he nevertheless could not have imagined that in our current condition—in the Middle East, in Congo, in Somalia, in Sudan, etc.—the event would be exacerbated by being unspeakably turned into incident, into a swiftly-mentioned *fait divers*. But Blanchot remains right in his definition of disaster, for whatever the scale of violence, however minute the act (though no act is minute as every act is unique for every singular victim), or however cold the technologies that diffuse it, no mindless oppression is fathomable or discernible at the moment of its occurrence, nor can it be rationally articulated by the victim when it belatedly transpires, nor, accordingly, can it be coldly analyzed and comprehended by the reader when testimony is disseminated in visual or printed form.

**The Victim's Tale, the Listener**

The impossibility of comprehension, or the inability for the victim to make sense of the traumatic event, is inherently related to its overwhelming impact and the irrationality of its occurrence. The victim is so shocked that no thoughtful explanation can validate what has happened. This is actually what renders the experience more unbearable through its undesired and sudden repeated manifestations. Caruth explains the phenomenon by locating trauma not merely in the "brutal facts" which reappear unexpectedly, but more profoundly "in the way that their occurrence defies simple comprehension."[6] Consider Fred D'Aguiar's narrator's torment:

> The future is just more of the past waiting to happen. . . . I woke up one day [and realized] I had no name. I was just boy, mule, nigger, slave or whatever else anyone chose to call me. I have been called many other things besides. I don't cry anymore. . . . *I don't want to remember*. Memory hurts. Like crying. But still and deep. *Memory rises to the skin* then I can't be touched. I hurt all over, my bones ache, my teeth loosen in their gums, my nose bleeds. *Don't make me remember*. I forget as hard as I can.[7]

In his recent book, *Mémoire du mal, tentation du bien*, Tzevetan Todorov makes a list of the historical events of terror that humanity has suffered by highlighting the millions of victims that each stage in this "siècle des ténèbres" (century of darkness) has added to its records of oppression. Todorov then focuses on the question of memory and the survivors' need to forget such events. Survivors, he argues, may be rightly tempted to will to forget, for "the infinite cruelty to remember," or to be forced to remember, is sometimes as unbearable as the very experience of violence by the victim. To forget, he claims, would be a desired alternative to save oneself from the terror of memory.[8] Indeed, as D'Aguiar's testimony compellingly illustrates, the victim of trauma is actually no masochist. S/he strives to forget the traumatizing event, for s/he gets no pleasure from remembering. Yet, as the extract shows, such repression has its side-effects. The narrator has consciously attempted to displace certain intolerable moments in his life. The event, however, is not obliterated since it remains vivid in his unconscious. Memory rushes back and takes hold of the victim. It disrupts the state of normalcy and reorients him to what he attempts to forget. Memory is but a moment of fear and trembling, a moment that shakes the body, and, like an unexpected storm, shatters its wholeness, disturbs its restless quietness. It is at the difficult moment of training oneself to throw the past behind ("I forget as hard as I can") that one is awakened, hurled back to the past through the ever-persistent pain.

Considering the reader's relation to the victim's tale, Marlene Nourbese Philip recommends that we all become an integral part of the traumatic text so as to complete its story by transmitting its inexpressible messages. She goes on to question the position of the indifferent reader who remains estranged from the historical mission of the testimonial text?[9] For her, such a position is no less harmful than the literal violence exerted on the victim. So-called 'objective' criticism further silences the victim's text by imposing on it its own voice and definition. The survivor's process of coming to language is thus aborted when approached by the lashing weapon of cold interpretation. Peter Van Der Veer, in turn, warns against not considering or "not hearing the victim's story," believing that the "pomposity" of the oppressor's interpretation *is* violence, since in this case, one is simply complicit with the official "grand narrative," and is a passive participant in the cutting/erasure of the victim's tale.[10]

This is why Blanchot urges the reader to turn into that writer-to-be, a reader/writer *en devenir*, for both are witnesses of the silence beyond the traumatic discourse. Disaster precedes the word, it precedes and transcends expression. Disaster is silent. It is that silence we need to hear, read, and pass on. The reader is turned writer, as Blanchot suggests, by incorporating the victim's tale, not by analyzing its indeterminate signs so as to control its meaning. Dori Laub further comments on such a situation by stating that, albeit separate from the victim's experience, the reader turns into witness by having the event, narrated by the victim, take place and shape in her/his mind. The 'outsider-ness' of the listener as well as the 'outsidedness' of the experience with its "extreme pain" are translated into forms of 'insidedness.' As Laub explains:

> The listener to the narrative of . . . psychic trauma, faces a unique situation. . . . By extension, [he] comes to be a participant and co-owner of the traumatic event: through his very listening, he comes to experience trauma in himself. The relation of the victim to the event of the trauma, therefore, impacts on the relation of the listener to it, and the latter comes to feel the bewilderment, injury, confusion, dread and conflicts that the trauma victim feels. He has to address all these, if he is to carry out his function as a listener. . . . The listener has to feel the victim's defeats and silences, know them from within, so that they can assume the form of testimony.[11]

The victim's story is about extreme anxiety and despair. Victims are people without rescue, for hardly anything can erase the traces of violence. Even when the story is told, the latter remains intact. Cynical. Irretrievable. It reaches us and disrupts our faith in humanity and reason. Listeners and victims are brought into an apocalyptic world designed by the pen of terror. In D'Aguiar's remembered testimony above, the pain that emerges touches us profoundly, and thus shifts our critical function. One is therefore no longer a detached stranger to the text. One becomes a complicit reader, deeply involved in sharing the victim's heartbreaking experience. The reader does not interpret, s/he rewrites the story, by listening to its irrepressible logorrhoea, however indeterminate or incomprehensible. As such, one naturally turns into an ideal witness. Ideal witnessing requires a great deal of humility and patient listening. Lack of comprehension and hermeneutic indeterminacy are not deliberate manifestations of textual defiance; they should be held as inviting demands to assist victims in coming to terms with their lack of understanding.

**Revenance as Archive as Cinder**

The incipit in Toni Morrison's *Beloved* introduces readers to a scattered family, with the two sons who have run away from home, leaving their mother (Sethe), grandmother (Baby Suggs), and sister (Denver) all alone to cope with a haunting/haunted setting.[12] Immediately after, Baby

Suggs dies, while Sethe is left to her doom. It is now that memories rush in uninvited: images of the plantation, called ironically "Sweet Home," with boys that come "rolling, rolling, rolling out before her eyes," uncannily hanging from "the most beautiful sycamores in the world"; images of her dying baby's blood pulsating from its gaping throat all over her hands, alongside the sexual encounter she had to endure so as to pay for the engraving of the word "beloved" on her baby's tombstone. All this, the narrator hastens to add, Sethe "worked hard to remember as close to nothing as was safe" (*Beloved* 6). Yet memory refuses hasty burial.

In her work on trauma, Cathy Caruth relates the concept to the irresistible repeated manifestation of ghosts in the lives of trauma sufferers. These, she claims, "belatedly" undergo the persistent presence or return of a haunting past. Because the traumatic event "is not assimilated or experienced fully at the time" of its unexpected occurrence, it reappears "only belatedly, in its repeated possession of the one who experiences it." Therefore, trauma sufferers are those who are haunted, "possessed by an image or event" that they have missed. The actual trauma, then, is not the missed event; it "literally" happens for the first time through "its insistent return which thus constitutes [it]" (*Explorations* 4). Trauma victims cannot only remember what they can never forget, they also live with the unrepressed presence of that which has never left. The traumatic past in *Beloved* has never been forgotten. It is forcefully real, literally there in its concreteness, not past at all: "there it was again," Sethe tells us (*Beloved* 4). Later, she explains to her daughter, Denver:

> Some things go. Pass on. Some things just stay. I used to think it was my rememory. You know. Some things you forget. Other things you never do. . . . Someday you be walking down the road and you hear something or see something going on. So clear. And you think it's you thinking it up. A thought picture. But no. It's when you bump into a rememory that belongs to somebody else. (*Beloved* 35-36)

"There it was again" then augurs the visitation of the inarticulate, emerging from an unwished immemorial event that has been repressively buried, imprisoned within the confines of a perturbed psyche. "There it was again" is the uncalled-for memory of the survivors of hurt. In its disruptive arrival, the torrential flow of the past confounds the feigned normalcy of the present, and inhabits the inhospitable space of abuse, left unwritten out of the victims' silence, preceded by its blankness on the pages of official history, archived, as Herman Rapaport points out, by the oppressors who were determined to "liquidate [their victims'] culture . . . in order that future generations may inherit their evil as evil."[13] Indeed, all trauma narratives are released in response to the "uneven power in the production of sources, archives, and narratives,"[14] so as to recuperate what has been erased by "institutionalized regimes of forgetting."[15] This is poignantly illustrated in Gayl Jones's *Corregidora*,[16] where through Great Gram's or her mother's reminiscences, Ursa, the Blues singer, is gradually made aware of the monumental gap in her family's convoluted saga. Such lack is acutely lamented by Great Gram: "They burned all documents, Ursa, but they didn't burn all they put in their minds" she tells her (*Corregidora* 72). "They didn't want to leave no evidence of what they done—so it couldn't be held against them. . . . That's why they burned all the papers" (14).

Like Jones's *Corregidora*, Morrison's *Beloved* invites us to hear the buried voice of inexpression. Dedicated to the unarchived ''sixty million and more'' who made ''the voyage through death,'' it seeks to call us to join and reach out to the ''veil behind the veil'' (274), to the layer superimposed on the layer, which in turn masks a myriad of other layers. Repressed without, Beloved, the victim, is nevertheless housed within. She dwells in the unfathomable corners of her mother's psyche. Her intimate presence constitutes the 'heimat' (home) of the weighty silence of the survivor's old-worn memories. Her past, because unnarrated, has thus not taken place. The lack of its realization, the impossibility of its eventfulness, is contained within the folds of the unwritten book of liquidation. Her death, which resides in her mother with its unnameable authority, is the reminder of such repression. Beloved is not identifiable as she is abstracted from life and from history. It is the survivor's memory of her premature unanticipated death that is the unique *archival* remnant.

Derrida provides an interesting clarification of the concept "archive," the Greek roots of which (*arkhē*) at once suggest the ideas of *commencement* and *commandment*; and explains that the meaning of "archive" also derives "from the Greek *arkheion*: initially a house, a domicile, an address, the residence of the archons, i.e. those who command."[17] In *Beloved*, 124 is thus the house of memory that shelters the dead baby who yet still commands. 124 is the gothic threshold, the 'commencement' of the survivor's psychological voyage into a malicious history. The novel opens with: "124 was spiteful. Full of a baby's venom.'' Those who now occupy it will henceforth live under the authority of the baby-spirit who will restlessly haunt, press, and command them to keep on hunting the evil secret that still burns her annihilated limbs which have turned cinder.[18] Cinder, Derrida explains, is what remains after radical destruction. It "takes the place of everything that disappears without leaving an identifiable trace."[19] Interestingly enough, Derrida's original French title of *Cinders* is *Feu la cendre*, wherein "feu" both means "flame" and "late" followed by the proper name of someone who is dead.

Like the ghostly apparition of the traumatic moment, cinder travels from its undetermined locus—too-well-known to be fully known—to rest on the testifier's tongue, and inhabit the burning abyss of the text. The words that emerge are themselves burning remnants, split by the utterance of the living, which is itself no more than the ashy eruption of the dead: their resurrection. This nomadic process of cinder, down to its explosion, is traced through its fervent, feverish dissemination: its dispersion. Performative and fecund, it guarantees its posterity in the survivor's body which it takes as hostage. Cinder then is not an extinguished flame, or ash; it is that flame which continues to burn the survivor as long as s/he is haunted by memory, or as long as mourning has not been accomplished. It is with this cinder—the cinder of memory, or memory as cinder—that s/he lives or dies.

Henry Green, who wrote three novels on World War II,[20] perceives the traumatic past as "a threat," a fatal threat to one's "skin to wake what is left of things remembered into things to die with.'[21] What Green means here is that memory is incorporated within, sticks to the very flesh of our bodies, and accompanies us to rest in the grave. The disappearance of the missed other is recuperated in the future of our own death. Survivors never die alone. Eaten up by the hallucination of memory, they—consciously or not—seek their death as a final exit to impossible amnesia in life. It is only then that "cendre" (cinder) is transmitted to those who come after—amenable writers and readers—so as to determine all *mourning narratives* as the expression of such spectral manifestations of memory, alongside an always-already postponed, if not an impossible attempt to reach a point where the past becomes a future perfect which inaugurates the process of healing.

## Mourning, Spectrality

What is to mourn? It is to be overcome by so much grievance,[22] so much torment and torture that the body is knocked, sundered, rapped. The released words are not thought utterances; they are jabbered away, and fall like clattering pieces on the surface of silence, reaching the witness's ear in fragments—dashed, hushed, incoherent, confounded, and confusing. These are the words of the absent that will have never left. They take over the body and displace it away from the logic of the mind. They usurp the body and "rock it, shake it, rattle it, thump it so that it feels wrecked and cries without tears or movement of any kind, out of sheer exhaustion, except for that moan, groan hoarse, bass wail."[23] Alice Koller makes an overwhelming journey, tracking the diverse associative meanings of the term in various cultures and follows them, bearing their "heavy," "burdensome" impact:

> "Mourn" from Greek for "care," in turn relating to "memory," "remembering." "Pain" from Greek for "payment," "penalty"; "to pay," "to punish"; "price." "Grief" from Latin and from Greek for "heavy." "Grieve," from Middle English, Old French, Latin for "to burden," from Latin for "heavy," "grave," like Gothic, Greek, Sanskrit for "heavy." "Sorrow" from Middle English *sorow*, from Old English *sorg*. Like Old High German *sorga* "sorrow," and old Slavic *scraga* "sickness." "Anguish" from Latin for "straits," for "narrow," like Old English for "narrow." [24]

The countless massacres, coldly carried out throughout past and current human history, command the ineffability of horror. No language, no utterance is adequate to reflect the unrepresentable atrocities the world has borne: those absent-present marks of aborted life, namelessly buried without sepulcher. In these disastrous outbursts, survivors are the trace, the blurred inscription of what has been: death, not life. Something "specters in us," Derrida proclaims. Accordingly, since such new and unexpected eruption is disruptive, and since it happens inside, not outside, it is bound to be experienced in angst. The price that the living have to pay is the risk of being taken hostage by the traumatic breath of today's wounded apparitions. In the act of mourning, the survivor cedes her/his place to the dead. As mentioned earlier, even identity, *ipseity* in its conventional essence, tends to leave its narcissistic shell, its self-consciousness, as it moves away from a self-centered concern towards an unconditional concern for the other. Self-adequacy or equivalence is ruined. A scission happens from within by spectrality. Self-identity, or the long-claimed pure identification, is henceforth doomed to lose its in-dwelling assurance. Safety cedes the place to the anxious encounter with the ghost imposing itself on consciousness, and disruptively rights its presence. Derrida states:

> The conjuration, the calling forth is anxiety from the moment it calls upon death to enliven it anew. . . . This anxiety in the face of the ghost *weighs on the living brain* of the living, and if it does so, it must then have some spectral density. To *weigh*

> *is also to charge, tax, impose, indebt, accuse, assign.* And the more humiliated life there is, the graver the specter becomes, the heavier its imposition. And the more the living have to answer for it. To answer for the dead, to respond to the dead. *The specter weighs, it thinks, it intensifies and condenses itself within the grave inside of life. The latter therefore no longer has and must no longer have, in so far as it is living, a pure identity to itself or an assured inside, a living inside?*[25]

For Derrida, mourning is the debt to pay, and that debt consists in the task of the mortal living's, the dead-to-be's un-learning their secured privileges, which in fact consists in "learning to live with phantoms," with death. It is this siamese-like relationship between life and death which turns ontology into hauntology. To be is actually to be dead, not only in the past but also in the present. To be is to live in the prison-house of the dead; it is to be haunted by their presence-absence: "There is a ghost in the house," Denver warns Paul D. in *Beloved* (13). Sethe's determined will is formulated in her risky readiness to encounter the tormented spirit of her dead daughter. Hunted by the latter, relentlessly quaked from the inside, she turns into a reckless hunter herself. Dispossessed of her Beloved, Sethe becomes possessed by her weighty pressure. Being, for Sethe, is being with, connected to, the all-too-knowable unknown. Being, Derrida states, is being h(a)unted by the other; it is to be obsessed, so possessed by a phantom that one no longer distinguishes the hunted from the hunter, as the roles get confused and confusing. The angry specter never leaves those who attempt to chase it away or to push it aside. Sethe, Denver, and Baby Suggs, who are "suspended between the nastiness of life and the meanness of the dead," have had to wage in vain "a perfunctory battle against the outrageous behavior of that place; against turned-over slop jars, smacks on the behind, and gusts of sour air" (*Beloved* 4).

Beloved returns and disrupts the relative possibility of recovery. She blocks the process of the journey towards amnesia, hence, paradoxically, freezing narrative progress towards closure. Love and hatred, death and life are no longer two separate entities with the first being the negation of the second. These reach us speaking the same language as its excess, that of an imposed cruelty and annihilation. Violence of the past cannot be forgotten. It is all too present. The wound will not heal. The phantom's grip never lets go its prey, that is, its chaser.[26] As Derrida recommends:

> We should intend to understand the spirit in . . . the sense of specters, of untimely specters that one should not chase

> away but sort out, keep close by, and allow to come back. By forgetfulness (guilty or innocent, it little matters here), by closure, new ghosts will be engendered and disrupt amnesia. . . . Every revenant seems here to come from and return to the earth, to come from it as from a buried clandestinity (tomb and subterranean prison), to return to it as to the lowest, towards the humble, humiliated. (*Specters* 91-93)

With Derrida's statement in mind, Morrison's narrative comes to be read as an allegory of the trauma of a whole culture in which Beloved's murder is only partially significant: "Not a house in this country ain't packed to its rafters with some dead Negro's grief" (5). Beloved is only a small element in the whole web of the traumatic enslaved epic. Refusing to be otherized, neglected, and undesired, Beloved returns in the flesh to hear her own part, because by so doing, and only by hearing her own story, can she reach out to the stories of the sixty million and more. "Life was dead" (109) in Sweet Home. The slaves were hurled into it out of the womb of rape as mere signifiers without signification: nameless, dis-figured, objectified. The children who were born were given the name of their master: "Paul D Garner, Paul F Garner, Paul A Garner" (11). Others, "from the crew" on the ship of slavery, were simply "throw[n] away on the island. The others from more whites [were] also throw[n] away. *Without names*" (62).[27] Beloved's head was sawed off (5). She was murdered so she could be 'safe' from the white man's grip on her destiny. And now, her spirit refuses that life go on, for justice is far from having been done. The aftermath of slavocracy contains as much terror as before. The blacks' pleasure is unwelcome. The joy of carnival is saddening.[28] Therefore if "[t]o Sethe, the future was a matter of keeping the past at bay" (42), the past refuses to leave. Her recovery together with the narrative possibility have to be deferred. To the question: "Has the world learned anything?," Geoffrey Hartman gives a categorical "No". Therefore, he laments that "the call for closure, though understandable as an expression of hope that a deep wound is finally healing, remains premature,'[29] hence, impossible for the time being and has to be postponed. Spectrality's disruptive eruption resists both recovery and narrative. Thus, the ghost's return manifests itself not as a developmental feature in the process of narration, but rather as an obstruction of this process, as a blankness and shadow that blurs continuity.

**Testimony, Truth, Obligation**

All traumatic testimonies display the torn, forgotten pages of the absent on which the re-inscribed terror is made public. Humiliated, such narratives neither forcibly demand the listener's sympathy, nor request her/his empathy. They only beg the reader/interpreter/writer's humility—her/himself, perhaps, unawarely endangered, unconsciously repressive of a sense of victimhood, a survivor. All trauma literature's urgent emergence is framed around the necessity to tell, the forceful commandment to bear witness and to testify, confessing the truth of horror in what Kalí Tal calls "the halls of normalcy." To be a survivor is to be unceasingly responsible for supplying the mind with the undiminished pain of the event. "To be a survivor," notes Tal, "is to be bound to the dead, to impose upon oneself" the obligation of literally recreating "how things were, a kind of sacred historical truth,"[30] sacred because, as in the case of faith, disbelief is outrage.

Derrida's lengthy introduction to Blanchot's *Instant of My Death* is an attempt to explicate "the essence of testimony" as an exemplary instance which describes, informs, repeats an event to which testifiers have to bear witness. The testifier, Derrida says, does not actually tell a story, s/he incorporates the event, carries it, and acts as witness. In the testimonial address, by reproducing the event either graphically or physically through their body "without any technical agency,"[31] testifiers commit themselves "to speaking the truth," and therefore "to repeating the same thing" (*Demeure* 33), even if the addressee "should contest, deny, suspect, disbelieve the content of what is said." But for the addressee to begin contesting the attestation, Derrida adds, it is necessary that s/he "be certain of the distinction between a testimony and a fiction of testimony" (35). In the absence of such certainty, the addressee has no other choice but to believe in the exemplarity of the witness's testimony.

In *Corregidora,* Ursa is slapped by her Great Gram when she expresses her doubt while listening to the latter's hardly believable accounts about the ordeals her own daughter and she herself had to go through as slaves to Corregidora, the "Portuguese seaman turned plantation owner." She is slapped then is immediately urged to suspend her disbelief, tell her story, and transmit it as it is to the generations to come. When she was still a child, she recounts:

> [He] took her out of the field . . . and put her to work in the whorehouse. . . . She was to go out or he would bring the men in and the money they gave her she was to turn over to him. . . . There were other women he used like that. She was the pretty little one with almond eyes and coffee-bean skin, his favourite. "A good little piece. My best. Dorita. Little gold piece."

> "His wife was a skinny stuck little woman he got from Lisbon. . . . He wouldn't sleep with her, so she made me sleep with her, so for five years I was sleeping with her and him. . . . That was when I was from about thirteen to eighteen. . . . They had me sleep with both of them."
>
> *"You telling the truth, Great Gram?"*
>
> *She slapped me.*
>
> "When I'm telling you something don't you ever ask if I'm lying. . . . I'm leaving evidence. And you got to leave evidence too. And your children got to leave evidence. (13-14; emphasis added)

On Great Gram's raped body, torturers have stamped their marks and guiltlessly recorded their own versions. But now, through her testimony, they are pointed out, tormented in their grave, sentenced to eternal restlessness invoked by the re-apparition of assault. Great Gram's testimony is her bleeding signature. Her words are the open fresh scars containing the germs of rape. Appropriately, speaking in an interview with Evelyn Grossman about his book, *Shiboleth, for Paul Celan*, Derrida defines the latter's text as "a wound which opens, which doesn't heal, the hiatus." It is, he notes, "the mouth that speaks where something is wounded. In the space of lesion'' ("la bouche qui parle là où *c'est blessé*. Au lieu de la lésion"; emphasis in original). The reader as listener, he continues, "may attempt to explain, comment on, interpret, speak in turn," but by doing so, s/he "always runs the risk of suturing, of shutting the [testifier's] wounded mouth. The commentator's duty, then," Derrida insists, is "to countersign," that is, to write or speak in turn by yielding in, "letting the other speak or in order that the other speaks instead."[32]

Ursa's comments are shocking since her suspicion comes as disavowal, and therefore as an erasure of Great Gram's painful account. By slapping her, and by insisting that she should disseminate her "evidence" to her children as well, Great Gram wishes the instant to be repeatedly "countersigned," reproduced, multiplied, universalized. Every utterance, every singular narrative bears the trace of another, the imprint of those who suffered, and that of the would-be-sufferers, for what is being pressed out as testimony, "already a repetition, at least a repeatability; is [also] already an iterability, more than once at once, more than an instant in one instant, at the same time" (*Demeure* 41). Unique and irreplaceable as it may be, Great Gram's attested experience "allow[s] itself to be replaced," dispersed, globalized. Derrida remarks that the exemplarity of evidence resides in the fact that any other witness "could repeat exemplarily, universally, the truth of my testimony. The exemplarity of the "instant" like any exemplarity, is that it is singular *and* universal, singular *and* universalizable. The singular must be universalizable; this is the testimonial condition" (41; italics in original).

Therefore, as testimonial narrative, Great Gram's abrupt memory seeks Ursa's willingness to come to her space of trauma, meet the face of the Other, and participate in the act of a bewildered witnessing. This is perhaps what Blanchot means by ''the collapse of the subject who submits and cedes her or his place to the other'' (l'affaissement du moi qui cède et cède la place à l'autre).[33] Self-erasure does not imply complete invisibility. It is an act of humility. It simply means displacing oneself so as not to disturb the eruption of the Other. Self-erasure guarantees that the subject is not a usurper for s/he neither appropriates nor represents. S/he merely sees and listens. To testify is to repeat the truth about a past event, it is to drive it out of its secret shell, to make it happen publicly. This is not an ordinary act of substitution; it is what Blanchot calls an act of ''submission'' ("affaissement," ''effacement,'' ''céder''). This also means that the witness is being taken as a ''hostage'' by the event.

Traumatic narratives are about the failed attempt to free oneself, the impossibility of escape. In *Beloved*, Stamp Paid ''couldn't . . . save his life.'' It sounds as if, once caught in the act of witnessing, one loses every power to distance oneself. As Morrison explains, ''freeing yourself was one thing; claiming ownership of that freed self was another'' (*Beloved* 95), which means that, even if freeing oneself is achieved, the entanglement remains intact. The latter creates the ''ethical responsibility'' to tell. To witness is to hear history from the perspective of the traumatized subject, and therefore, as Felman and Laub put it, to run the risk of having "suddenly—without a warning—one's whole grip on one's experience and one's life shake[n] up." Because no testimony can transpire without witnessing, it is through their awareness of this hazard, through learning how to create a solid yet risky bond with the narrator that witnesses "allow the telling of trauma to proceed and to reach its testimonial resolution" (*Testimony* xvi-xvii).

As a fictional testimonial narrative, the victim's tale is thus effective only through its witnessing characteristic. It returns to the past, listens to the unspeakable—or unspoken—truths, in order to re-inscribe them. The act of writing is not here an artificial act of repetition. It does not merely represent or identify with someone else's trauma; it incorporates it in its entirety, in its naked yet faceless (im-)materiality. Identifying with or 'being like' leaves the gap between the subject of trauma and its representation intact.

Incorporating, in the sense of being, involves a complete immersion in another reality[34]—in the reality of the other where ipseity fades away, vanishes out of the unbearableness of the encountered condition. In this respect, through the process of repetition-compulsion, or repetition which is not one, the narrative is not only a witness to another's history, it is also a witness to its own act of witnessing. The inscription of another person's trauma becomes, accordingly, literally the transcription of one's own trauma. The haunting face of the Other, which/who is not one, becomes one's own face, which is in turn faceless, defaced.

## Traumatic Language as 'the Writing *of* the Disaster'

Erased from the grand archival historiography of knowledge, the survivors' predecessors dwell in the chaotic kingdom of anonymity, forming the un-co-opted cohort of the unnamed. Being in constant contact with loss, the survivors turn numb, incapable of articulating, let alone fathoming, the meaning of human existence. Within such lack, the traumatic scene remains active. When this is expressed, it comes out filled with holes and digressions, displaying, as Claire Kahane notes, a hysterical discourse with "excessive splittings and displacements, . . . frequent paralyses of plot, phonemic rather than semantic continuities," all suggestive of a narrative voice wherewith the subject is exposed in her struggle "to find form that will contain the confusion of [her] utterance."[35] In this case, the function of language as a communicative means fails, leaving the memory of unspeakable damage to haunt an equally damaged brain. This is so because the survivors' will to power, their desire for agency, is inappropriate since the transcendental values have proved nihilistically insignificant, empty of value and form.[36]

Living in a world without words, without signifieds to stick to the signifiers, survivors use a language which is non-language: a *parole* without *langue*. When meaning is lost; when the idea is irremediably alien, or when the concept is inadequate, the survivors' language is bound to remain on the fringe of structure. This simply, freely, explosively emerges out of too much pressure, out of a too long repression: "Some things can't be kept in" (*Corregidora* 10), Ursa says; "they [come] back whether we want it or not," Sethe echoes in *Beloved* (14).

As stated at the beginning of this article, testimonial memory emerges without will. The testifier is surprised by its sudden visitation, and resists in vain its shaking impact. For to remember is often as hard as the actual event. To remember is to relive the moment of aggression for the first time, infinitely. One is disarmed; the survivor needs only to accept and submit to the spectral revenance of the event. Survivors' days are nocturnal. They move on in feigned consciousness. The issues of narration, of how their stories are told, and authorial structural outline and plot progress are out of question. Conscious utterances have deserted them; the torrential overflow of words escapes their mastery. These are simply there—sweat-inundated flashbacks. It is starless memory that returns to re-speak its anguish:

> *It was as if the words were helping her, as if the words repeated again and again could be a substitute for memory, were somehow more than memory. As if it were only the words that kept her anger. Once when she was talking, she started rubbing my thighs with her hands, and I could feel the sweat on my legs. . . .*
>
> *"He was a big strapping man then. His hair black and straight and greasy. . . . He would take me hisself first and said he was breaking me in. Then he started bringing other men and they would give me money and I had to give it over to him. . . . I stole his [photo] because I said whenever afterward when evil come I wanted something to point to and say, 'That's what evil look like.' You know what I mean? Yeah, he did more fucking than the other men did. Naw, I don't know what he did with others."*
>
> *Sweat inside her hands. Her palms like sunburnt gold.*
>
> "Were you sleeping, Ursa?"
>
> "Naw, I was dreaming." (*Corregidora* 11-12; italics original)

The belated witness, Ursa, is thus not a plot designer, an inscriber of a planned tale. The witness does not speak when she speaks, she simply re-produces her Great Gram's hysteria. Similarly, Gayl Jones does not write when she writes. She, in turn, merely 'rememorizes' Ursa who 'rememorizes' her ancestor. This is in Maurice Blanchot's terms, the writing *of* the disaster. It writes itself. It has its own rights. It creates its own rites. What is exposed in Jones's narrative is then not a story with a beginning and closure. What is exposed is a series of suppressed impossible articulations. It is in the tension between being and its negation, between past and present, between life and death, between writing and/as absence of writing, of silence as absence of silence, that such narrative reaches our ears "where no forms hold sway, an absent meaning. Absent meaning and not the absence of meaning" (*Writing Disaster* 41).

Light is shaded. The repressed has not returned. It rather lives and grows within. What may be thought lost forever, or even consciously buried, kept at bay emerges willy-nilly. What is lost, as part and parcel of our selves, is the missing link which makes the survivors' wholeness. Without it, they are but part-objects, dismembered. "Loss," as defined by Patricia Weenolsen, "is anything that takes away [(kills)] . . . and destroys some aspect whether macroscopic or microscopic of an individual's life and/or self. . . . [It implies that] something has been cut from the self as a whole, leaving behind only a part-self"[37] with subsequent anxiety and despair, confusion and uncertainty, alienation and estrangement. What happens in the tragedy of death is but an accident. It happens abruptly, unexpectedly. It can neither be reasoned at the moment of its occurrence nor at its aftermath. Like fate, it remains inexplicable, and, because it is so, survivors remain powerless in front of its effect. Those who survive the accident of loss, those who continue to live, do not actually live in the sense of keeping on leading what one might call 'normal' life. For it is in their survival that disaster starts to have form, to actually happen. Survivors are not directly threatened by it; that is, they have not been part of the actual loss—as Maurice Blanchot puts it, they have been "spared, left aside." And yet, the survivor will feel that "it is in this way that I am threatened; it is in this way that the disaster threatens in me that which is exterior to me—an other than I who passively becomes other." (*Writing Disaster* 1) By becoming other, the survivor lives someone else's death as his own. Her/His life becomes a "deferred death: disaster" (146). With these terms, Maurice Blanchot finishes writing the disaster and begins it, for disaster starts after it has occurred. Disaster is not written about, cannot be ascribed even if we will it to.

## From Hauntology to Pure Hospitality

To *re*-write or read (a) haunted/haunting text(s) is then to be joined by an invisible thread to a dis-membered absent otherness. And even absent, are not the survivors the heirs of its shadowy presence; the text the medium and event of its revenance? Indeed, dead or alive, worldly or transcendental, palpable or enigmatic, repressed or manifest, otherness erupts and demands *receptiveness*. The literary work becomes the aesthetic site of this hauntological encounter, and so does contemporary theoretical or philosophical production. Although, Blanchot's and Caruth's works, as well as Derrida's *Specters of Marx*, *Cinders*, and *Demeure,* are used in this article to clarify, explain, and analyze Morrison's *Beloved* and Jones's *Corregidora*, I suggest that all echo one another. Philosophy and literature, for long debated as belonging to two separate realms, have radically shifted their extreme positions, and have come to share the split scene of a wholesome dialogue about an unwholesome past, always-already hauntingly present. Cultural dissonance here among, say, Derrida, Morrison, and Jones, is minimalized, if not nullified, by intellectual and ethical assonance. Their overlapping uncanny interference in one another's space fills the gap that separates them. Albeit different, the texts, nevertheless, are impressive by their intertwined communication. A-lien (a link) is therefore created despite obvious alienation. It is this bewildering uncanniness which actually produces their mutual haunting.

The production of simultaneities of this kind compacts mental spacing, blurs and even virtualizes distances. *L'espace(ment) n'existe pas ou n'existe plus* (space[ing] does not exist or no longer exists), and, with this absence, all dichotomies, separations, and differences are erased: The known and the unknowable, writer and reader, simultaneity and time lag, all are one and the same, part of one world—the world of spectrality. One is haunting the other. One is the repetition of the other. The event is simultaneously reproduced. Here is no more *like* elsewhere. Here *is* elsewhere, an echo without a difference. For Derrida, this implosion of the traditional oppositions is imperatively dictated and pressured by an imposing spectral thought, whose "virtual space" deconstructs with the promise to eliminate "the trenchant division between the real and the non-real, the effective and the non-effective, the living and the non-living, being and non-being . . . as well as the opposition between presence and absence" (*Pourquoi lire* 18).

Indeed, the mother-daughter relationship, in *Beloved*, is woven in such a way that what we witness, in our listening to the testimonial narrative, is an intertwined history between the dead and the living. But these are not conceived as polarities. Life is housed by the death it nourishes, and death is, in turn, the very expression of that life. Read in this morbid light, the novel relocates binarism and brings about new spaces where the thing and its other are disturbingly confounded.

*Beloved* and *Corregidora*, as arduous dialogues with ghosts, come into being through the manifestation of their lack. Haunted subjects have no control over their memories. These rush into their minds at a 'staccato pace.' In their extreme moments, emotions reach their peak, and, therefore, disturb the coherence of the account, or may even stop the narrative process. And, in both narratives, they seem to invade the open space of the page, leave it in order to come back again at their will—unexpectedly, however undesired or unwanted. Neglected, uncalled for, the specter invades all spaces disempowering our will. Singular, multiple, one-and-many, the ghost is all-seeing, threatening, commanding, from its unseen realm of judgment:

> Follow my gaze, I am watching the ocean and the earth and the sky, the specter seems to say with the imperturbable authority and the rock of a commandment. Let us follow its gaze. Right away we lose sight of it: it disappeared among the mob of specters, the disappeared, the departed, in the hall of mirrors where it multiplies. There is not only one spirit watching, watching you, us. Since this spirit "is" everywhere, since it comes from everywhere, it proliferates, invading all of space. Infinite number is the specter. . . . The spectral rumour now resonates, it invades everything, crosses all borders. The apparition form, the phenomenal body of the spirit, that is the definition of the specter. The ghost is the phenomenon, absolute presence. 'One hears millions of spirits speak through the mouths of people' in the middle of the night. . . . Such is created the atmosphere of anonymous threat and existence. The subject that haunts is not identifiable, one cannot see, localise, fix any form, one cannot decide between hallucination and perception, there are only displacements, one feels oneself looked at by what one cannot see. (*Specters* 135-37)

Survivors grapple with death. In their ethical act of answerability, being overwhelmed by the inarticulacy of expression, writers live on with the impossible possibility of bearing witness: impossible because the testimonial utterance is ineffable; possible because it can neither be denied nor even postponed. Re-experiencing the event through the retrospective journey of memory is then the sole means for them to come to terms with the absent-presence of death, with the haunting presence of its absence. Surviving through testifying is not only saving the faded remnants of the dead from decomposition, but also simultaneously setting for the act of mourning, as a necessary step towards healing. This is why survivors need to unconditionally welcome the unexpected manifestation of their specters, house them, face them. The process of survival, of *survivance*, cannot be achieved without response, whatever the hardship, the pain, or the anxiety that accompanies it, as in *Beloved*:

> Sethe and Denver decided to end the persecution *by calling forth the ghost that tried them so*. Perhaps a conversation, they thought, an exchange of views or something would help. So they held hands and said, "*Come on. Come on. You may as well just come on.*" (4; emphasis added)

What premature death needs, demands, from survivors is that they let it come back in, allow it a place in their minds. Survivors may continue to live, but they will not reach the state of normalcy unless they accept their outrageously erased martyrs as an integral part of what makes them be, as 'the vessel' of which they are the fragments. Return to the primal scene, through death or mournful testimony, is the indispensably necessary threshold that has to be crossed.

"124 WAS SPITEFUL. Full of baby's venom." A survivor's narrative hosts danger. The text's site—the text as site—is possessed by a devastating spirit. What it begs and demands, begs its distant readers and demands of its writer, is to prepare themselves to share its angry tale, by lending their ears to the shattered, perturbed, and disturbing lamentations of the spectral arrivant, Beloved. "Come on. . . . You may just . . . come on," is the host's call for the shadow before its manifestation. It is the host's invitation, her readiness for visitation, for what Derrida expresses, in *Of Hospitality*, as unconditionally absolute or "pure welcome" which consists in welcoming one's guests in their anonymous opacity, by letting them "come, let[ting] them arrive, and take place . . . without asking of them either reciprocity (entering into a pact) or even their names."[38] He explains that:

> In the hospitality without conditions, the host should, in principle, receive the guest even before knowing anything about him. A pure welcome consists not only in not knowing anything or acting as if one knows nothing, but also in avoiding any questions about the Other's identity, their desire, their rules, their language. . . . From the moment that [one] formulates all of these questions, and posits these conditions . . . the ideal situation of non-knowledge—*non-savoir*—is broken—*rompue*.[39]

Sethe actually knows the identity of her guest, and yet Beloved would fit in the category of the stranger that has to be welcomed with her radical difference. Sethe's "come on" sounds like "come back to me, rememory!" This call for return of the recognized other is paradoxically a call for the unknown, the vivid manifestation of the primal scene, that originary trauma of the Middle Passage and its aftermath, embodied here in the ghostly return of the little baby. Beloved, as symptom of the past that has been so far kept at bay, will not remain so if real catharsis has to occur. It is not actually Sethe who remembers. It is rather her speech that recalls those "spots of time" of displacement and dislocation: "there it was again," reproduced by the narrator, might as well be muttered by Sethe against her will, thus simultaneously combining her present reality—the persecuting memory of her little baby that "tried [her] so" (4), her sexual submission to the engraver's lust, as well as the whole experience of slavery. This is why when Beloved finally reappears, Sethe refuses to ask her any questions, for even "the what?" or "the who?" would break, eliminate, unconditional hospitality. Her pure welcome is in fact her last resort to come to terms once for all with the collective trauma—hers as integral part of her community's. It is her final act of mourning, of recognition, of belonging to an absent community, the community of the disappeared. That pure welcome does not break (*ne rompt pas*) the 'ideal' situation of hospitality. It signals instead the possibility of an ultimate communication with the other, by securing it within the protective realm of an undaunted transcendental power: *Farewell! Adieu! À-dieu! To God!* Beloved's presence then is a metaphor of absence, a metonymy for those "which were not beloved." In the act of mourning, Derrida states, there is a sense in which

> [the] Other does not present itself, but absents itself even as it presents itself, the Other is one of the disappeared [*c'est un disparu*]. When I see the Other appear, I am already weeping the Other's absence, to deplore-desire-apprehend their departure, here I am [*me voilà*] already saying: farewell, farewell, you abandon me [*adieu, adieu, tu m'abandonnes*].[40]

Host and hostage or host as hostage, the survivor's passive responsibility is gift (*Here I am! Me voilà!*). It is in the hiatus, the break between absence/presence, appearance/disappearance, death/life that the mournful survivor lives. The in-betweenness is not the either-or, it is the site of communication, of the recuperated missing link; the site of liaison and lesion, of the affective bond with the unhealed wound; it is where the moment of welcome takes place, the moment of openness to alterity, to the face of the other, which is the trace of transcendence. In the final articulation—*À-Dieu! To-God!*—the survivor does not send away, as one shuts the door at a stranger, recuperates his space; s/he rather welcomes the infinite. The other is now substituted for by the Other. Such substitution allows the survivor's readiness for the peaceful encounter with a higher spirit; allows her or his hospitality of the Other's transcendence: *À-Dieu! To-God!*.

## Notes

[1] Elizabeth Alexander, "Praise Song for the Dead," *The New York Times* (Jan. 20, 2009). I am not concerned here with a critical or political evalu-

ation of the poem. I am merely interested in selecting, from Alexander's poem, appropriate fragments that pertain to the present article, <http://www.nytimes.com/2009/01/20/us/politics/20text-poem.html>.

2 Barack Obama, "Inaugural Address," *The New York Times* (Jan. 20, 2009), <http://www.nytimes.com/2009/01/20/us/politics/20text-obama.html>.

3 Michelle Boulous Walker explains symptomatic reading as a process whereby the text's "non-vision or silence" is brought as a component of its message, and hence ends up speaking or demonstrating "its vision or voice." This, she states, "make[s] us see what the text itself says while not saying it, or does not say while saying it." See Michelle Boulous Walker, *Philosophy and the Maternal Body* (London: Routledge, 1998), 35.

4 Maurice Blanchot, *The Writing of the Disaster*, trans. Ann Smock (Lincoln and London: U of Nebraska P, 1995). Henceforth referred to as *Writing Disaster.*

5 Cathy Caruth, *Unclaimed Experience: Trauma, Narrative, and History* (Baltimore: Johns Hopkins UP, 1996), 11.

6 Cathy Caruth, ed. *Trauma: Explorations in Memory* (Baltimore: Johns Hopkins UP, 1996), 153. Henceforth referred to as *Explorations*.

7 Fred D'Aguiar, *The Longest Memory* (NY: Pantheon Books, 1994), 1-2; my emphasis.

8 Tzvetan Todorov, *Mémoire du mal, tentation du bien* (Paris: Robert Laffont, 2000), 17-18, 243, and 248.

9 Marlene Nourbese Philip, "Who's Listening: Artists, Audiences and Languages," *Fuse* 12.1&2 (September 1988): 15-24.

10 Peter Van Der Veer, "The Victim's Tale: Memory and Forgetting in the Story of Violence," *Violence, Identity and Self-Determination*, eds. Hent de Vries and Samuel Weber (Stanford: Stanford UP, 1997), 186. With reference to Emmanuel Levinas, Hent de Vries claims that "Violence is said to take place whenever the other is not welcomed or addressed as such. . . . [It] takes place wherever discourse attempts to subtract itself from the realm of interlocution . . . wherever the self relates the other to the sameness of its own horizons, the other's singularity will be effaced. . . . Violence is to be found in any action in which one acts as if one were alone to act; as if the rest of the universe were there only to receive the action; violence is consequently also any action which we endure without at every point collaborating in it. . . . Thus, violence can be found in whatever narcissistic strategy the self adopts to capture, thematize, reduce, use, and thus annul or annihilate the other" (15-16).

11 Dori Laub, "Bearing Witness, or the Vissicitudes of Listening," *Testimony: Crises of Witnessing in Literature, Psychoanalysis, and History*, eds. Shoshana Felman and Dori Laub (London: Routledge, 1992), 57-58. Henceforth referred to as *Testimony*.

12 Toni Morrison, *Beloved*, (London: Picador, 1988), 4.

13 Herman Rapaport, *Later Derrida* (NY: Routledge, 2003), 77.

14 Michel-Rolph Trouillot, *Silencing the Past: Power and the Production of History* (Boston: Beacon P, 1995), 27.

15 Azade Seyhan, *Writing Outside the Nation*, trans. Emily Apter (Princeton: Princeton UP, 2000). Seyhan maintains that "remembering is an act of lending coherence and integrity to a history interrupted, divided, or compromised by instances of loss. . . . In narrative, we may be able to redress forcibly forgotten experiences, allow the silences of history to come to word, and imagine alternative scripts of the past" (4).

16 Gayl Jones, *Corregidora* (Boston: Beacon P, 1975).

17 Jacques Derrida, "Archive Fever: A Freudian Impression." *Diacritics* 25.2 (Summer 1995): 9. Henceforth referred to as "Archive."

18 Jacques Derrida, *Cinders*, trans. Ned Luckacher (Lincoln: U of Nebrasca P, 1991).

19 Jacques Derrida, *Points ... Interviews, 1974-1994*, trans. Peggy Kamuf et al. (Stanford: Stanford UP, 1995), 391.

20 Henry Green, *Caught* (London: Hogarth, 1950); *Loving* (London: Hogarth, 1945); and *Back* (NY: New Directions, 1981).

21 Henry Green, *Pack My Bag* (London: Hogarth, 1979), 54.

22 Caroline Garland, ed., *Understanding Trauma: A Psychoanalytic Approach* (NY: Routledge, 1998). Henceforth referred to as *Understanding Trauma.*

23 Fred D'Aguiar, *The Longest Memory* (NY: Pantheon Books, 1994), 1.

24 Alice Koller, "Mourning," *The Stations of Solitude* (NY: William Morrow,1990), 308.

25 Jacques Derrida, *Specters of Marx*. trans. Peggy Kamuf (NY & London: Routledge, 1994), 109; my emphasis. Henceforth referred to as *Specters.*

26 Christian Ferrié, *Pourquoi lire Derrida* (Paris: Edition Kimé, 1998), 15; My translation. Henceforth quoted as *Pourquoi lire.*

27 The Lacanian Name and the Law of the Father, is in the African-American experience of slavery, specifically white, a logo-phallocentric ideology that has shaped the American culture, by frustrating African-American attempts at achieving subjectivity and by disallowing African-American humanity. These 'subjects' are often denied their subjecthood under the law of what Morrison calls "the definer" in *Beloved.* The African-American, initiated through language as object into the symbolic, is thus initiated as object within the dominant ideology. This is the primal Afro-American trauma: the trauma of a commodified, unnamed, and unnamable subjectivity: "Mister was allowed to be and stay what he was," Paul D. tells Sethe, "But I wasn't allowed to be and stay what I was. . . . *Schoolteacher changed me. I was something else and something was less than a chicken sitting in the sun on a tub*" (72; my emphasis).

[28] When Paul D. takes Sethe and Denver to the carnival, "[o]ne-Ton Lady spit at them, but her bulk shortened her aim and they got a big kick out of the helpless meanness in her little eyes. Arabian Nights Dancer cut her performance to three minutes instead of the usual fifteen she normally did" (48).

[29] Geoffrey Hartman, *The Longest Shadow* (Bloomington & Indianapolis: Indiana UP, 1996), 1-2.

[30] Kalí Tal, *Worlds of Hurt* (NY: Cambridge UP, 1996), 120.

[31] Jacques Derrida, *Demeure: Fiction and Testimony*, trans. Elizabeth Rottenberg (Stanford: Stanford UP, 2000), 32. Henceforth referred to as *Demeure*.

[32] Jacques Derrida, "La vérité blessante ou le corps à corps des langues," *Europe: Revue littéraire mensuelle* 901 (Mai 2004): 25; my translation.

[33] Maurice Blanchot, *Le pas au-delà* (Paris: Gallimard, 1973), 163; my translation.

[34] With reference to Freud's essays "Mourning and Melancholia" and "Beyond the pleasure Principle," Caroline Garland states that "in a world that seems irrevocably damaged . . . some survivors make an identification with the dead object . . . [with) what Freud might have called *binding*, which seems to intensify and become a kind of fusion" (*Understanding Trauma* 18-19).

[35] Claire Kahane, *Passions of the Voice: Hysteria, Narrative and the Figure of the Speaking Woman 1850-1915* (Baltimore: Johns Hopkins U P, 1995), xiv.

[36] Simon Critchley, *Very Little . . . Almost Nothing: Death, Philosophy, Literature* (London: Routledge, 1997). Quoting Nietzsche who defines nihilism as the moment when "the highest values devalue themselves, [when] the aim is lacking; the 'why' finds no answer," Simon Critchley explains it as the breakdown of the order of meaning, where all that was posited as a transcendent source of value becomes null and void, where there are no skyhooks upon which to hang a meaning for life. All transcendent claims for a meaning to life have been reduced to mere values and those values have become incredible, standing in need of what Nietzsche calls 'revaluation' (7).

[37] Patricia Weenolsen, *Transcendence of Loss over the Life Span* (NY: Hemisphere publishing Corporation, 1988), 3; 19; and 56.

[38] Jacques Derrida, *Of Hospitality* (Stanford: Stanford UP, 2000), 25.

[39] Jacques Derrida, "'Une hospitalité à l'infini': Responsabilité et hospitalité," *Autour de Jacques Derrida: Manifeste pour l'hospitalité* (Paris: Paroles de l'aube, 1999), 100; my translation.

[40] Jacques Derrida, "Fidélité à plus d'un," *Idiomes, nationalités, déconstructions. Rencontre de Rabat avec Jacques Derrida*, ed. Fethi Benslama (Paris and Casablanca: Toubkal and Intersignes, 1998), 227; my translation and emphasis.

# Extreme Realities: Naomi Shihab Nye's Essays and Poems

**Ibis Gómez-Vega**

I'm not interested in
who suffered the most.
I'm interested in
people getting over it.
-- Naomi Shihab Nye, "Jerusalem," *Red Suitcase*

Naomi Shihab Nye's work speaks of people whose lives are affected by war. She understands that "the news couldn't see into this room of glowing coals or the ones drinking tea and fluffing pillows who are invisible" (Shihab Nye, *Never in a Hurry* 253), so her essays and poems put a human face on an ancient tragedy that has only recently become the subject of daily news reports in the Western world. For Shihab Nye, the war in the Middle East is personal; the people affected are her immediate family, so her work creates a space for the forgotten, the real people who daily suffer the not-so-little indignities of attempting to live life in a world at war. That this war involves the United States and its people makes it more difficult for the Arab-American poet who is suddenly torn between two opposing sides. For Shihab Nye, Adrienne Rich's claim in "North American Time" that "Poetry never stood a chance/of standing outside history" (*Your Native Land, Your Life* 33) is an ever-present reality. Her poetry reflects the realities of her war-torn ancestral homeland and the peaceful life that she leads in the American Southwest where she lives with her husband and child in relative safety. Poems set in the Southwest reveal an almost idyllic existence where children write about lost parrots, nieces drive their aunts to buy peaches, and fathers plant fig trees. Although a war rages across the ocean in the land of her ancestors, the American Southwest provides safety, solace, peace, a space where a poet can think about the state of the world and hope to effect change. As an Arab in America, Shihab Nye is torn between two extremes, the idyllic Southwest of her Texan home and the war-torn world where her Palestinian relatives live.

In an open letter "To Any Would-Be Terrorist," written shortly after the September 11, 2001 attack, Shihab Nye addresses the issue of Arab identity in America and the concomitant connection with terrorism. She tells the "Would-Be Terrorist" that she is "sorry" to call him a terrorist because "I hate that word," but then she asks: "Do you know how hard some of us have worked to get rid of that word, to deny its instant connection to the Middle East?" (362) That a poet should "work" to disassociate the word terrorist from its connection to her ancestral land seems unfair. Why should a poet take it upon herself to explain her people, to argue as she does in "This Is Not Who We Are" that all Arabs are not terrorists? She states in this article that "because men with hard faces do violent things, because fanaticism seizes and shrinks minds, is not reason for the rest of us to abandon our song" ("This Is Not Who We Are" 84). She wants American readers to know that Arab terrorists are "men with hard faces," not the "gentle immigrants" (84) for whom life suddenly becomes more difficult as people identify them with their angry countrymen and make them the subject of scorn and mistrust in America. In this way, her poems examine contemporary American culture and values, and this examination makes her work political.

Part of Shihab Nye's political statement lies in her attempts to change the American mainstream perception of Arabs by providing readers with images of Arabs whom she knows and loves, for love lies at the core of Shihab Nye's poetry. The letter "To Any Would-Be Terrorist" speaks of her father, who "became a refugee in 1948" but "is still homesick" (362) for Palestine, and her mother who "has spent 50 years trying to convince her fellow teachers and choir mates not to believe the stereotypes about the Middle East" (363). It also speaks of "the Palestinian grocer in my Mexican-American neighborhood [who] paints pictures of the Palestinian flag on his empty cartons. He paints trees and rivers. He gives his paintings away. He says, 'Don't insult me' when I try to pay him for a lemonade" (363), evidence of a generosity that Shihab Nye recognizes as intrinsically Arab, for "Arabs have always been famous for their generosity" (363). Generosity and grace, however, are hardly the words people think of when the latest news of car bombs exploding in Jerusalem invades their homes. They think instead of the evil that men do, and the evil men in that case almost always turn out to be Arabs, which explains why Shihab Nye feels compelled to write the other side of the Arab story.

The other side of the Arab story must speak of the loss suffered by people who were unceremoniously expelled from their homeland when the Jewish State was created, people exiled from everything that gave them comfort. Edward Said describes exile as "the unhealable rift forced between a human and a native place, between the self and its true home," and he concludes that "its essential sadness can never be surmounted" (173). In "Brushing Lives," Shihab Nye writes about her father's "essential sadness," about his longing for home, and about how this longing connects him to displaced Palestinians everywhere. Waiting for her father somewhere in Alexandria, the poet states:

> Later my father appeared with a husky voice.
> In a shop so dark he had to blink twice
> an ancient man sunk low on a stool said,
> 'You talk like the men who lived in the world
> when I was young.' Wouldn't say more,
> till my father mentioned Palestine
> and the gentleman rose, both arms out, streaming
> cheeks. 'I have stopped saying it. So many years.'
> My father held him there, held Palestine, in the dark,
> at the corner of two honking streets. (*Red Suitcase* 91)

Two people displaced from the same place in the world meet as strangers in a dark shop in Alexandria, but they carry in common the pain of their displacement, the common sorrow of having lost their home. The meeting between her father and another displaced person creates for the poet a clear picture, almost a spontaneous performance, of what it means to be an exile, for the exile carries with him/her the pain of what is lost.

Although Shihab Nye is not an exile, for she has never been 'displaced,' as her father and grandmother were displaced from their homeland, she understands the magnitude of the problem. She knows that, in almost any corner of the world, she can run into an exile, someone who suffers from that strange sense of nostalgia that seems to be a constant with people who have been displaced. She asks:

> Who else? They're out there.
> The ones who could save or break us,
> the ones we're lonely for,
> the ones with an answer the size of a
> pocket handkerchief or a shovel,
> the ones who know the story before
> our own story starts,
> the ones who suffered what we most fear
> and survived. (91)

The displaced Arabs who long for home are an integral part of the Arab story, the Arab-American story. Like the poet's father, they carry home in their hearts; they do not forget. They consider themselves lucky when they encounter others who, like themselves, carry home on their backs. They are the "homeless fig" (*Words* 121) whom the poet loves, the people for whom she writes the other side of the Arab story.

In the relative safety of the American Southwest, the displaced Arab can attempt to recreate the world as he once knew it. In "My Father and the Figtree," Shihab Nye writes about her father's love for figs, a love not shared by a daughter reared in the United States. She writes that "For other fruits my father was indifferent./He'd point at the cherry tree and say,/'See those? I wish they were figs.'" When at night "he sat by my bed/weaving folktales like vivid little scarves," the tales "always involved a figtree./Even when it didn't fit, he'd stick it in." When at the age of six, the poet "ate a dried fig and shrugged," it becomes clear that the Arab-American daughter does not share her Arab father's childhood memories. Her shrug indicates that the taste of figs means little to her. For the Arab father, however, the taste of figs brings back joy, the solace of a peaceful childhood spent with family in Palestine. When the poet's father longs for a fig tree, his German American wife tells him to "Plant one!" (*Words* 20), a logical conclusion made by someone who assumes that the Arab longs for the tree or the fruit itself, not everything else which the tree and the fruit symbolize.

The poet's homesick father associates the fig tree with his childhood home, so planting his own fig tree in the United States seems like an admission, perhaps, that the world of his memories is lost forever. At the end of "My Father and the Figtree," however, the hopeful note, usually evident in Shihab Nye's poetry of the Southwest, appears when the poet states that:

> The last time he moved, I got a phone call.
> My father, in Arabic, chanting a song I'd never heard.
> 'What's that?'
> 'Wait till you see!'
> He took me out to the new yard.
> There, in the middle of Dallas, Texas,
> a tree with the largest, fattest, sweetest figs in the world.
> 'It's a figtree song!' he said,
> plucking his fruits like ripe tokens,
> emblems, assurance
> of a world that was his own. (*Words* 20-21)

The American Southwest offers the poet and her family the chance to recreate their world. Even when he does not plant his own fig tree, the poet's father can make in Dallas, Texas, a peaceful space for his family, away from the uncertainty and danger of the Middle East, while his daughter attempts to write the 'other side' of the Arab story through her poetry.

Writing the other side of the Arab story, however, does not mean that Shihab Nye does not want an independent Palestinian state, which is exactly what "men with hard faces" claim they want, but she objects to the way they go about achieving their aims. In 1991, discussing the 'liberation' of Kuwait during an interview with Bryce Milligan, Shihab Nye points out that "we are all affected by the dismal knowledge that humankind still operates on caveman principles—let's club one another if things don't work out" ("Writing to Save Our Lives" 32). She adds that she is "depressed by what Saddam Hussein has done for the already stereotyped Arabs" and "by Bush's lack of patience, by his bullying, manipulative, righteous stance. We have entered the cycle of violence in a way which will not be forgotten" (32). In 1991, Shihab Nye, as did many Americans, disagreed with President Bush's decision to use military force against Iraq. As a poet, she would rather see people solve their problems with words, not weapons, but the use of words to solve Middle Eastern problems has not proven effective. Treaties have been signed and broken, so the Arab-American poet despairs about the fate of her ancestral home, her family, her people.

In spite of evidence to the contrary, Shihab Nye believes that words can transform people. She tells the "Would-Be Terrorist" that "one of the best-selling books of poetry in the United States in recent years is the Coleman Barks translation of Rumi, a mystical Sufi poet of the 13th century, and Sufism is Islam and doesn't that make you glad?" (365). Expecting the spread of Islam in the United States to make the "Would-be Terrorist" glad seems as naïve as expecting angry men to solve their problems with words. Would a "Would-Be Terrorist" care about poetry, about the ability of words to change people's lives? Shihab Nye believes that he should care because she knows that words have a lasting impact on people. In the same letter, she writes about her "Palestinian cousins in Texas [who] have beautiful brown little boys," but those boys now "have this heavy word to carry in their backpacks along with the weight of their papers and books" (363). The word that they carry, of course, is "terrorist" because they are brown and Palestinian in America. Even though they are children in a country far removed from the chaos of their ancestral land, they now suffer the stigma of being guilty by association, by virtue of their cultural connection to an ancient grudge, regardless of how old they are or what they believe.

Shihab Nye's little cousins carry the burden of negativity and distrust created by the word "terrorist" because negative words appear to have more power than comforting, loving words, those she uses to write her poems. Gregory Orfalea claims that "poetry for Nye is powerful, but quiet supplication" because "Nye is [not] very good with evil; few poets are. The times she faces it, it is with questions, as if warding it off by verbal wolfsbane" (60). Warding off evil through supplication is not a bad thing, but it creates the sense that Shihab Nye's poetry provides an unrealistic portrait of human nature, one that addresses evil only at a slant, never directly. Orfalea's comments about Shihab Nye's inability to confront evil emanate from his own reading of "Blood," a poem in which Shihab Nye attempts to deal with evil on a personal level. Orfalea claims that the poem was written after the Sabra and Shatila massacres of more than 1,000 civilians in 1982, and he finds the poet inarticulate in the face of evil. In "Blood," Shihab Nye states that, when she calls her father, they "talk around the news" because "It is too much for him,/neither of his two languages can reach it" (*Words* 121). Her father, a prominent journalist, cannot even discuss the tragic events, and the poet herself drives "into the country to find sheep, cows,/to plead into the air:/Who calls anyone *civilized*?" (*Words* 121). Being civilized requires that people use words, not guns, to solve their differences, but in the real world angry men use guns, not words. She writes that:

> Today the headlines clot in my blood.
> A little Palestinian dangles a truck on the front page.
> Homeless fig, this tragedy with a terrible root
> Is too big for us. What flag can we wave? (*Words* 121)

The image of "headlines" that "clot" her blood suggests the poet's inability to write about the terrible events reported by the headlines. In this poem, however, the word "blood" also refers to being an Arab, to carrying the Palestinian tragedy in the blood.

Lisa Suhair Majaj argues in "Arab American Literature and the Politics of Memory" that "Blood" "offers a nuanced meditation on the notion of cultural 'blood inheritance'" (282). Majaj focuses on what she calls the "lightly humorous consideration of the possibilities of being a 'true Arab' offered by [the poet's] father's folk tales to a deeply troubled questioning of the implications and responsibilities of this identity" (282-83). She finds humor in the father's explanation that "A true Arab knows how to catch a fly in his hands" or the poet's statement that "True Arabs believed watermelon could heal fifty ways,/I changed these to fit the occasion" (*Words* 121). However, she does not stop to examine the ways in which these humorous statements humanize the Arab father who uses folk tales to explain his heritage to his American-born daughter. Majaj's statement about Shihab Nye leads immediately into the argument that "Blood" "deconstructs the naturalization of an Arab cultural 'essence,' while simultaneously foregrounding the politicized overdetermination of Palestinian identity" (282-83), her main concern.

"Blood" was published in 1986 in *Yellow Glove*, Shihab Nye's third collection of poetry. Like Orfalea, Majaj claims that the poem was written after what she calls the "Israeli and Lebanese Phalangist massacres of Palestinians during the 1982 Israeli invasion of Lebanon" (283), but she may be missing the "American" side of the poem. When Shihab Nye opens "Blood" with humorous statements about "essentialist" Arab behavior, she is juxtaposing her gentle Arab father against the "little Palestinian" who "dangles a truck on the front page" (*Words* 121). The image of the truck dangling on the front page reminds readers of the terrorist bombing of the Marine barracks in Beirut, Lebanon, on October 23, 1983. Americans were shocked to learn that 220 Marines and 21 non-military personnel lost their lives in what most Americans considered a cowardly attack on sleeping soldiers. Television reports of the attack on the barracks specifically focused on the truck driven as a weapon into the barracks. After the explosion, the truck "dangled" on the television screen and in photographs published on the front page of newspapers across America.

The image of the dangling truck resonated through the American consciousness as it reinforced the already pervasive belief that Arabs were vicious murderers who took American hostages and struck down Americans in their sleep. As happened in September 2001, the 1983 attack on the barracks gave way to a wave of angry patriotism and flag waving. When the Arab-American poet states, "this tragedy with a terrible root/is too big for us. What flag can we wave?" (121), she is very specifically referring to the fact that Arab Americans suffered a double blow on that day. An angry Palestinian drove the truck that killed American soldiers, but Arab Americans are both Arabs and Americans. They suffer a double pain. Shihab Nye's poem addresses the complicated geography of what it means to be both a Palestinian and an American who must deal with the actions of angry men—but "the headlines clot in [her] blood" (121). The best that she can offer is a humane vision of her gentle Arab father who can barely speak about the event. As an Arab and an American, he is stunned into silence. The poet, however, once again finds solace in the Southwest, a place where she can "drive into the country to find sheep, cows,/to plead with the air" (*Words* 121).

Unlike the gentle, pacifist poet who cannot read the message of violence, Orfalea reads "Blood" as if it referred to the Sabra and Shatila massacres, and he uses the poem to make a political statement. He looks at the massacre with the cold eye of a realist, not a poet; he understands the complicated political maneuverings behind the event. He claims that the massacre was perpetrated by Arabs on Arabs because "Israeli generals were smart enough to send in Arabs to carry out the killings, so-called 'Christian' Arabs" (61), so that the Israelis would not be blamed by the world. He points out that Shihab Nye's reaction to the massacre is inappropriate, for she asks at the end of the poem, "What does a true Arab do now?" (*Words* 121). For Orfalea, Shihab Nye's question rings "just plain hollow" because it "strip[s] the folk wisdom useless" (60). The folk wisdom is, as the poet states early in the poem, that the true Arab "knows how to catch a fly in his hands" (*Words* 121), but for Orfalea, the poet's question "rings with a faint note of menace and complicity" (61). He fails to explain, however, that the "complicity" lies not in the poet's act of witnessing and writing about evil but in the real evil events that took place on that fateful day in 1983. Paradoxically, he goes on to argue that "any poem that confronts evil can easily flinch—homily, sentimentality, obscurity. 'Blood' does not. Its triple-question end may not be 'poetic,' but it appropriately and movingly translates the reaction when people face horror of which they are both victim and perpetrator" (61). Although the syntax obscures the message, his point is that the massacre was perpetrated by Arabs, not that the poet is in any way complicit in the crime.

The issue of complicity seems important to Orfalea. He writes in the same essay that Shihab Nye "has been asked and often asked herself: What is my responsibility in this tragedy as a writer with a gift? How is the gift deployed?" (60), but the poet's response to such a question seems more appropriate than Orfalea's complicated notion of complicity. During her interview with Milligan, Shihab Nye's statement about the irrational behavior of political leaders ends with an anecdote about Palestinian writers who once "discussed with me the difficulty of writing personal poems in the shadow of larger communal issues" (32). The statement addresses the disappointment that some people feel when they find that her poetry is not strong enough in its condemnation of political leaders when she writes personal poems instead of anti-war diatribes. The answer goes back to the poet's belief in the power of poetry to transform. When journalists asked her after September 11, "Why do you suppose that people are finding strength in poetry now?" she tells them:

> As a direct line to human feeling, emphatic experience, genuine language and detail, poetry is everything that headline news is not. It takes us inside situations, helps us imagine life from more than one perspective, honors imagery and metaphor—those great tools of thought—and deepens our confidence in a meaningful world. ("This Is Not Who We Are" 86)

Poetry provides people with the tools to recreate experience. It does not change the experience, but it makes empathy possible. It allows people to understand their feelings and those of others, which is why, in her poetry, Shihab Nye continues to write about the Arabs she knows and loves, not the ones who blow up buildings.

Writing "A Comment on the State of the Art: Poetry in 2004," Jeanne Murray Walker states that "To sit with great poetry is to reflect on love and death, to open the window to mystery, to ask childlike questions again, to find a path that is not the broad way" (95), which is exactly what Naomi Shihab Nye provides for her readers in her poems. Although she finds it hard to face the evil that men do, she does not deceive herself or her readers about the destructive power of evil, a fact that she acknowledges in "Lunch in Nablus City Park" when she asks "What makes a man with a gun seem bigger/than a man with almonds?" (*Words*122-23). The man with the gun may only "seem" bigger, but he receives more recognition than the man with almonds. In her letter "To Any Would-Be Terrorist," Shihab Nye attempts to reach the terrorist with words by telling him that "Our hearts are broken, as yours may also feel broken in some ways we can't understand, unless you tell us in words. Killing people won't tell us. We can't read that message" (366). The problem, however, is that violent men know that we can, in fact, read the message perpetrated by violence because the man with the gun can accomplish things that the man with almonds cannot accomplish. He can force people to fear him; he can impose his will on a terrified population.

In a world where men with guns loom large, Shihab Nye's unapologetic optimism and faith in human kindness and compassion seem naïve. To explain her optimism, she reports that she grew up in a special home where her Palestinian American father and German American mother created a world in which music and love made her feel safe. As a child at home:

> The world rang rich counterpoint, mixed melodies, fragrances, textures: crushed mint and garlic in the kitchen, cardamom brewing in coffee, fabulously embroidered Palestinian pillows plumped on the couch. And always, a thrumming underchord, a hovering, hopeful note: Things had been bad, but they would get better. Our dad had lost his home, but he would make another one. People suffered everywhere, but life would improve. I refuse to let that hope go. ("This Is Not Who We Are" 84)

The message that she received through the example of her parents was that people could recover from whatever happened and "life would improve." This "hovering, hopeful note" resonates through her life and renders her unable to understand that people could choose violence, even though she knows that violence often permeates people's lives.

In "Lunch in Nablus City Park," Shihab Nye addresses her optimistic view of life and rebukes herself. She writes about a group of people who have lunch in a park shortly after the fighting has stopped. The poem opens with a clear sense of place, a strong statement that the poet is speaking of a world at war:

> When you lunch in a town which has recently known war
> under a calm slate sky mirroring none of it,
> certain words feel impossible in the mouth.
> Casualty: too casual, it must be changed.

Even in a world damaged by war, life goes on as "a short man stacks mounds of pita bread/on each end of the table" and "Plump birds landing on park benches/surely had their eyes closed recently,/must have seen nothing of weapons or blockades." People, however, have been affected by the recent war because a man tells her that "the University of Texas seems remote to him/as Mars, and last month he stayed in his house/for 26 days. He will not leave, he refuses to leave." The safety of the Southwest represented by the University of Texas "seems remote" to the man affected by war. Likewise,

> When the woman across from you whispers
> I don't think we can take it anymore
> and you say there are people praying for her
> in the mountains of Himalaya and she says
> Lady, it is not enough, then what? (*Words* 122-23)

People praying for peace cannot stop the war; they cannot make the woman feel better about the fact that she is caught in something beyond her control. When the woman tells the poet, "Lady, it is not enough," the poet is once again left wondering, "then what?" The poet's statement speaks to the sense of impotence that so many people feel when they are faced with violent men who seem bigger than the ones who carry almonds simply because they carry guns. The statement rebukes Shihab Nye's optimism as she faces the fact that innocent people are trapped in a violent world in which even prayers are not enough to stop the violence.

Lorraine Mercer and Linda Strom read "Lunch in Nablus City Park" as a poem in which "the friends [who] share a meal" manage to "temporarily [forget] the war" (37) by virtue of their comraderie, their sitting together to share a few moments of peace. They argue that Shihab Nye's "reccurring themes of cooperation, generosity, and gratitude" (34) are evident in this poem when "food provides nourishment for war-torn souls and unites friends who seek a temporary respite from the violent conflict" (37). They point to the fact that Shihab Nye brings together a group of people who choose to sit and talk in a park "in a town which has recently known war" as if in fact the war had not affected them, and they argue that the characters in the poem "toast each other in the 'languages of grace,' and their words are full of love, faith, and hope for the future" (37-38). Like the poet, Strom and Mercer focus on the positive aspect of the poem, on the fact that these characters do something incongruous with war, suggesting that "the contrast between their words and the reality of their situation transform [sic] the toasts into a prayer for peace" (38).

Gregory Orfalea, however, does not see the positive side of having lunch "in a town which has recently known war," and he does not share Shihab Nye's optimism that life will get better, that the war will end and people will return to sharing communal meals in parks where there once existed the fear of war. He calls "Lunch in Nablus City Park" a "political poetry quite muted, unconfrontational" (62). He objects most of all to the poem's ending, where the poet asks:

> How can there be war
> and the next day eating, a man stacking plates
> on the curl of his arm, a table of people
> toasting one another in languages of grace:
> For you who came so far;
> For you who held out, wearing a black scarf

to signify grief;
For you who believe that true love can find you
amidst this atlas of tears linking one town
to its own memory of mortar,
when it was still a dream to be built
and people moved here, believing,
and someone with sky and birds in his heart
said this would be a good place for a park. (*Words* 122-23)

The town's memory of its own beginning speaks of the possibilities that once existed. At one point, there was nothing but a dream of a town, but people moved in and someone thought it a good idea to build a park. The poem ends on the hopeful note that maybe some day, when the war ends, this town can return to the original dream of being a town with a park where people enjoy each other's company during lunch. Orfalea, however, finds in this poem "a strong element of American pragmatism, an ornery attachment to the land, a statement of love so unadorned and solid it is resistant to all that is not love" (62). The poem's resistance "to all that is not love" reads like an indictment of Shihab Nye's relentless optimism, of her faith that things will improve, but it is also reminiscent of Wallace Stevens's message at the end of "Sunday Morning" that people should value what they have.

Shihab Nye's faith in the power of positive thinking is once again evident in "The Grieving Ring," a poem written "In Memory of Izzat Shihab I. Al-Zer," a family member. In this poem, Shihab Nye focuses on the grieving family members' reaction to their loved one's death. She states that "When word of his death arrived/we sat in a circle for days/crying or not crying," and instead of focusing on the negative,

it felt fine to say nothing
about him
or something small

the way he carried
oranges and falafel
in his pockets

the way he was always
slightly mad

what he said to each

the last time we saw him
hurt the worst. (50)

The memories of the loved one make him real for both the grieving family and the reader. Izzat Shihab becomes simply a man who carried oranges in his pockets and was always slightly mad, not one of the men with hard faces whom Shihab Nye addresses as "terrorists." The personal information about Izzat Shihab provides him with characteristics with which readers can identify. When they read the poem, they understand that this man, an Arab, could also be a good man, a man who, for some reason, carried oranges in his pockets.

Writing personal poems in the shadow of larger communal issues has become Shihab Nye's life work. She rewrites the negative stereotypes of Arabs without losing track of the political turmoil that caused their grief and displacement in the first place. This is clear when she speaks of her grandmother, Sitti Khadra (my grandmother Khadra), who in 1948 "lost her home in the Old City of Jerusalem to Israeli occupiers" (*Never in a Hurry* 52) with the expulsion of Palestinians from Israel. Khadra Shihab symbolizes the Arab community missing in the poet's life. In 1966, when she was only thirteen years old, Shihab Nye spent a year in the West Bank with her grandmother, crying relentlessly. She was too young to recognize the importance of living amidst family, of learning Arabic, a language she did not know. The teenage poet missed her life in the United States so much that her parents decided to return. The choice became more important when rumors of war spread. By the Six-Day War of 1967, the poet, her parents, and her younger brother had returned to the United States to settle in Texas, but by then:

> *Home* had grown different forever. *Home* had doubled. Back *home* again in my own country, it seemed impossible to forget the place we had just left: the piercing call of the muezzin from the mosque at prayer time, the sharp, cold air that smelled as deep and old as my grandmother's white sheets flapping from the line on her roof. (*Never in a Hurry* 46-47)

The year spent with family in the West Bank provides the poet with a new sense of being an Arab in America. While she feels safe at home in the United States, she is also suddenly aware of the random violence that threatens the lives of her family in the West Bank. Her sense of home is therefore forever altered by the time spent with the

Palestinian side of the family. She becomes an Arab in America, specifically an Arab in Texas, where, as the poet writes in "Blood":

> Years before, a girl knocked,
> wanted to see the Arab,
> I said we didn't have one.
> After that, my father told me who he was,
> "Shihab"—"shooting star"—
> a good name, borrowed from the sky.
> Once I said, "When we die, we give it back?"
> He said that's what a true Arab would say. (*Words* 121)

Ironically, the poet's sense of belonging in the United States is undermined by the suggestion of otherness in the question made by the girl who asks for the Arab, as if being an Arab in Texas were somehow incongruous with being Texan. This point is subtly made by Jan Epton Seale in her essay in *Texas Women Writers*. According to Seale, when a group of Texans from the Central Texas school district gathered to decide which artists to invite to Texan classrooms, someone opposed the idea of inviting Shihab Nye "because she wore funny socks," what Seale calls "part of the rich-textured clothes that are [Shihab Nye's] predilection" (312). Whether the objection to Shihab Nye's socks hid a deeper, more insidious fear of the Other is not even addressed by Seale, who remarks instead that Shihab Nye's "track record worldwide in those socks has given her an enviable national reputation as a poet, and Texans, even those in the outback, have come to accept and admire her" (312).

Almost as if she has to prove Shihab Nye's worthiness as a Texan, Seale promptly points out that Shihab Nye "has paid her dues to Texas literature" (313) by listing the many things done by Shihab Nye in Texas, the state where the poet has lived since she was fourteen years old. The few pages dedicated to Shihab Nye in *Texas Women Writers* belie the "enviable national reputation" mentioned by the writer and lead one to think that the people who edited this volume did not know what to do with an Arab poet who lives and writes in Texas. Seale compounds the problem when, in her attempt to explain Shihab Nye's poetry, she states that "one of the charms of Nye's gift is her wisdom rising out of the disjointedness which—the reader comes to realize—she has taken pains to create" (312). A reader who is surprised by a poet's wisdom or by the magical way in which poets weave words together to create complex statements that simultaneously appear simple may need to reconsider the definition of poetry. That a critic should refer to a poet's skill as her "charm" points out that far too many critics have no idea what to do with Shihab Nye's work. Although they seem to understand that she is an American poet and a Texan by choice, they do not know what to do with the extreme realities evident in her work. Seale in fact does not even mention the theme of violence evident in Shihab Nye's work which lies at the core of her message.

The threat of violence worries Shihab Nye to such an extent that it has become a recurring theme in her poetry. Over and over, the poet uses words to remind her readers of the pervasiveness of violence in contemporary life. In "Our Nation's Capital," she writes about the night that she spends in a hotel in Washington, where "All night emergency vehicles race by outside, wailing and blinking. In the morning a newspaper rich with disasters will be resting outside each door. We brush our teeth. We feel at home" (*Mint Snowball* 39). Life goes on even as emergency vehicles alert people to everyday disasters. "We brush our teeth" because people have learned to "feel at home" living in such conditions. In "The Garden of Abu Mahmoud," she writes about an Arab man who looks across the valley from his home in the West Bank:

> Across his valley the military
> settlement gleamed white.
> He said, That's where the guns live,
> as simply as saying, it needs sun,
> a plant needs sun. (*Words* 124)

Across the valley lives the potential for violence. When Abu Mahmoud comes out to his garden, he looks across the valley and sees guns, not trees. For him, the awareness of the evil that lives across the valley is a constant, a fact of his life, something he cannot change. The poet seems amazed that, for him, the recognition that guns live across the valley appears to be as natural as saying that "a plant needs sun."

Violence, however, makes the headline news, which explains why the men with hard faces choose violence over words. In *Fuel*, Shihab Nye is still stunned by the violence of everyday life in the Middle East, but she also becomes a conscious and articulate witness to that violence as she chooses to write about it in detail so that it is never forgotten. Carolyn Forché points out that "poetry of witness reclaims the social from the political and in so doing defends the individual against illegitimate forms of coercion" (45). Shihab Nye may not be able to protect or "defend" her family from "other forms of coercion," such as the coercion they suffer under the occupation and the constant fear of attack, but she can nevertheless document what is happening to her family and her people through her poetry. Forché sees this kind of writing as an act of resistance, which is exactly what Shihab Nye does when she specifically targets what is said/unsaid about the war in the Middle East.

By focusing on what newspaper and television reporters say or do not say about the war in the Middle East, Shihab Nye points out that the war is personal, that it affects real people, and that far too often the news reports miss the historical context of what is actually happening. This is common knowledge to most people in the United States who realize, as Alisa Solomon articulates, that "the news media—and especially television newscasts, the primary news source for more than eighty percent of Americans—shape public understanding of and attitudes toward systematic human rights" (1586). Solomon points to something as simple as the statement used by a reporter when s/he "signs off" at the end of his/her report from the Middle East. She reminds the reader of the sign off from "Dean Reynolds, ABC News, in the Israeli occupied West Bank" (1589) in 1989, a statement that at least mentions the fact of the Israeli occupation in the West Bank. Solomon argues, however, that more recent news reports from the Middle East ignore the history of the area and focus instead on the most recent events. This emphasis on the most recent acts of violence creates what she calls a "frame" that "erases the occupation":

> the humanity of Palestinians is thrown into question. They appear as incorrigible, unaccountably violent, preternatural Jew haters. The Palestinian escalation of suicide bombings of civilian targets inside Israel during this period is, then, seen through this frame not as a desperate weapon of resistance, morally reprehensible as it may be, but as motiveless malignancy, proof of innate Palestinian barbarism. (1589)

She points out that a historically-challenged recent report

> seeking to contextualize a skirmish in, say, Jenin, would comment, "This latest outbreak comes two years into the Palestinian uprising that followed the breakdown of peace talks at Camp David in 2000." It would not say, "This latest outbreak comes two years into the Palestinian uprising that followed thirty-three years of Israeli occupation." (1589)

Solomon's point is that the news reports influence the way in which Americans perceive the struggle in the Middle East, by removing its historical context.

In "The Small Vases from Hebron," Shihab Nye uses the vases, fragile glass containers, as a metaphor for the many fragile lives damaged by the violence in the Middle East, and she also challenges what the news reports say about what is happening in her ancestral homeland. After documenting an attack, the poet asks: "And what do the headlines say?" Her point is that the headlines will say "Nothing of the smaller petal/perfectly arranged inside the larger petal/or the way tinted glass filters light." The beauty of the flowers in the small vases will not make the headlines, not because beauty is lost on the people who write headlines but because the headlines focus on the more striking message created by violence. The headlines may point out that the dead and wounded are "Men and boys, praying when they died," but they miss

> The whole alphabet of living,
> heads and tails of words,
> sentences, the way they said,
> 'Ya'Allah!' when astonished,
> or 'ya'ani' for 'I mean'—
> a crushed glass under the feet
> still shines.
> But the child of Hebron sleeps
> with the thud of her brothers falling
> and the long sorrow of the color red. (*Fuel* 27-28)

The headlines focus on the big picture that attracts attention. Recording the sound of the brothers falling and the pain caused by bleeding children is what the poet who bears witness does, the poet whose task it is to flesh out the subject, to make the dead children human for her audience. Shihab Nye becomes, through her poetry, a witness to the evil that takes place in her ancestral land.

Violence also takes the lives of innocent people, a fact that Shihab Nye not only finds hard to accept but even harder to witness. In "Darling," a poem that begins with the celebratory line spoken at a gathering of friends, "I break this toast for the ghost of bread in Lebanon," continues with the violent threat that "Someone's kettle has been crushed./Someone's sister has a gash above her right eye" (*Fuel* 29). The poet follows with the acknowledgement that

> Someone was there. Someone not there now
> was standing. In the wrong place
> with a small moon-shaped scar on his cheek

and a boy by the hand.
Who had just drunk water, sharing the glass.
Not thinking about it deeply
though they might have, had they known.
Someone grown and someone not-grown.
Who imagined they had different amounts of time left.
This guessing-game ends with our hands in the air,
becoming air.
One who was there is not there, for no reason.
Two who were there.

It was almost too big to see. (*Fuel* 29-30)

This pain that is "almost too big" for the poet, as the news of the headlines once clotted her words, refers to the random violence that kills children, "someone not-grown," as it kills adults, people with "different amounts of time left." Even though the poetry still focuses on the small details of daily life, like sharing a glass of water, it also documents the horror of what happens. Shihab Nye, through her work, has now become a witness to the killings.

Becoming a witness and, thereby, writing poetry as an act of resistance leads Shihab Nye to name names. In "For the 500th Dead Palestinian, Ibtisam Bozieh," Shihab Nye no longer lacks the words to say exactly what she thinks about the death of a child who was in the wrong place at the wrong time in history. She writes:

Little sister Ibtisam,
our sleep flounders, our sleep tugs
the cord of your name.
Dead at 13, for staring through
the window into a gun barrel
which did not know you wanted to be
a doctor. (*Red Suitcase* 97)

Shihab Nye does not acknowledge that an angry man from Israel pulls the trigger that sends the bullet out of the barrel. The poem focuses on the girl whose life is cut short, not the war or the warring men.

True to her generous spirit, the poet tells Ibtisam, "I would smooth your life in my hands,/pull you back" (*Red Suitcase* 97), but she cannot bring the child back from the dead. In fact, the poet acknowledges that she could have become a victim too if she had not lived elsewhere, in the relative safety provided by America:

> Had I stayed in your land,
> I might have been dead too,
> for something simple like staring
> or shouting what was true
> and getting kicked out of school. (97)

The shock provided by such knowledge leads the poet to ask: "How do we carry the endless surprise/of all our deaths?" The answer speaks of reconciliation, of "Becoming doctors/for one another, Arab, Jew,/instead of guarding tumors of pain/as if they hold us upright?" (97). Ever optimistic, Shihab Nye hopes that Arabs and Jews can live together in peace "instead of guarding tumors of pain," but the death of another Palestinian child adds to the problem, makes the tumor of pain grow. The poem serves as a reminder of the random acts of violence killing innocent people, particularly Arab children whose only crime is living in a world at war.

Shihab Nye indirectly addresses the pain suffered by Arabs in "Arabic," where the poet reports that "the man with laughing eyes stopped smiling/to say, 'Until you speak Arabic—/—you will not understand pain.'" The man explains that his meaning has

> Something to do with the back of the head,
> an Arab carries sorrow in the back of the head
> that only language cracks, the thrum of stones
>
> weeping, grating hinge on an old metal gate.
> 'Once you know,' he whispered, 'you can enter the room
> whenever you need to. Music you heard from a distance,
>
> the slapped drum of a stranger's wedding,
> wells up inside your skin, inside rain, a thousand
> pulsing tongues. You are changed.' (19)

Despite thinking "pain had no tongue," the poet feels bad that she "live[s] on the brink of Arabic, tugging/its rich threads without understanding/how to weave the rug. . . . I have no gift./The sound, but not the sense." Still:

I touched his arm, held it hard,
which sometimes you don't do in the Middle East, and said,
*I'll work on it*, feeling sad
For his good strict heart, but later in the slick street
hailed a taxi by shouting *Pain*! and it stopped
in every language and opened its doors. (19-20)

Pain has no tongue; it is a shared moment, a feeling recorded forever by the poet's words. Words create the image of an Arab with a "good strict heart" for whom the poet still feels enough compassion to break cultural taboos and hold his arm tightly in empathy. However, when she hails a taxi by screaming "Pain," the poet seems to argue that Arabs are not the only ones who know pain; pain is universally understood.

In "Palestinians Have Given Up Parties," Shihab Nye remembers life as it was before the occupation and resettlements, before the war.

Once singing would rise
in sweet sirens over the hills
and even if you were working
with your trees or books
or cooking something simple
for your own family,
you washed your hands,
combed water through your hair.
Mountains of rice, shiny shoes,
a hurricane of dancing.
Children wearing little suitcoats
and velvet dresses fell asleep in circles
after eating 47 Jordan almonds.

*Who's getting married? Who's come home*
*from the far place over the seas?*

Sometimes you didn't even know.
You ate all that food without knowing.
Kissed both cheeks of anybody who passed,
slapping the drum, reddening your palm.
Later you were full, rich,
with a party in your skin.

*Where does fighting*
*come into this story?*

Fighting got lost from somewhere else.
It is not what we like: to eat, to drink, *to fight*.

Now when the students gather quietly
inside their own classroom
to celebrate the last day of school,
the door to the building
gets blasted off.
Empty chairs where laughter used to sit.
Laughter lived here
jingling its pocket of thin coins
and now it is hiding.
. . . .
*They have told us we are not here*
*when we were always here.*
*Their eraser does not work.* (*Fuel* 57-58)

This last statement refers to the often-quoted Israeli assertion that Palestinians have no claim to the land, bringing the poet squarely into the quarrel. She adds: "the bombs break everyone's/sentences in half" (58), a reference to the Israeli leaders' refusal to hold peace talks after terrorist attacks.

In this poem, the poet becomes a more active participant than she was before. She asks a taxi driver about the bombs: "*Who made them? Do you know anyone/who makes them?*" Her question speaks to the issue of complicity. When the Israeli leaders walk out of the peace talks, they claim to do so because the Palestinian government cannot guarantee that the terrorist bombings will stop. The Israeli leaders do not seem to understand that the terrorist bombers are beyond anyone's control, for they are often isolated individuals who have taken it upon themselves to disrupt the peace process. When the Israeli leaders assume that any Arab could be a suicide bomber, the implication is that all Arabs are somehow complicit in terrorist activities. Even in what should be their own land, Palestinians find themselves suspected of terrorist activities. When Shihab Nye questions the taxi driver, an Arab 'Everyman,' he "shakes his head back and forth/from Jerusalem to Jericho" to deny knowing who makes the bombs, but he does explain the futility of peace talks when he tells the poet:

They will not see, he says slowly,
the story behind the story,
they are always looking for the story after the story
which means they will never understand the story.

Which means it will go on and on.

*How can we stand it if it goes on and on?*
*It is too long already*. (*Fuel* 58)

The war goes on, but the poet once again points out that some of what happens is never revealed:

No one hears the soldiers come at night
to pluck the olive tree from its cool sleep.

Ripping up roots. This is not a headline
in your country or mine.
No one hears the tiny sobbing
of the velvet in the drawer. (58-59)

The little indignities that never make the headlines are the subject of Shihab Nye's poems as she bears witness to what happens and puts a human face on the terrible tragedy taking place in the Middle East.

While she often worries about American perception of Arabs, Shihab Nye herself becomes suspect when she travels through the Middle East. After one of her trips to the West Bank to see her grandmother, the poet reports:

> In the airport at Tel Aviv, we begged my uncle to leave us, go on back. But he had to stride ahead, turning faces with his red and white *keffiyah*, repeatedly comparing his watch and the clock on the wall. When they put us in the slow line, the line for trouble that we earned without even trying, he shook his massive head. He could see he wasn't helping. Said his favorite little English, 'Okay,' and turned away.
>
> I heaved my suitcase onto the table. A young Israeli flipped the pages of my passport, exaggerating names. 'Syria, E-gypt, Jor-dan, *Saudi Arabia*—why you want to go there? For what reason you go there and then come here?'

> Each time I was asked to explain to an official how a human being might love a grandmother, a village, my tongue knotted up. Blood swelling inside my veins.
>
> 'Did you talk to Arabs? Did any Arab enter the room where your suitcase lay?'
>
> Their wild fluttering when I answered, 'Every hour. Every day.' So they X-rayed my socks. They X-rayed my white nightgown, my toothbrush, my extra shoes. Each item lifted onto a cart, separately, and wheeled away to another place. The shame of what we had become, marks against one another, though the olive tinted his skin as it tinted mine. (*Never in a Hurry* 216-17)

Israelis cannot tell the difference between one Arab and another, between the one who is a law-abiding citizen and the one who is willing to break the law in order to defy the rule of the occupying army. Traveling to the West Bank to visit her grandmother becomes a humiliating experience simply because she is an Arab at a time when all Arabs carry the burden of the work done by "men with hard faces" ("This Is Not Who We Are" 84).

Being treated as a criminal at the airport is only one example of the many indignities suffered by people whose only crime is sharing a cultural history with 'terrorists.' At home, in Texas, the poet can think and write about these things, about the common assumption that people who come from Arab countries are all the same. While "idling in the drive-through line at a fast-food franchise in Texas" waiting to purchase her son a hamburger, Shihab Nye weeps at the sound of Simon Shaheen's violin music coming from the radio. She knows the violinist as "the Arab-American virtuoso violinist, an elegant man who wears starched white shirts and black suits and plays like an angel" ("This Is Not Who We Are" 83). To her son's accusation that she is "*so weird!*" for crying at the sound of music, the poet states that she is "simply an Arab-American in deep need of cultural uplift to balance the ugliness that has cast a deep shadow over our days" (83-84). All Arabs are not the same: some are violinists; some are poets; some are resistance fighters; and some are terrorists. When she hears the voice of her grandmother telling her to "'Say this is not who we are'" (86), to explain that all Arabs are not terrorists, the poet sits down to write the essay. The behavior of men with hard faces causes an Arab American poet to defend herself and her people against the suggestion that she is one of those with hard faces who choose violence over words.

For Shihab Nye, writing about being an Arab in America serves the dual purpose of disassociating herself from the men who commit acts of violence and of explaining to other Americans, Arabs and non-Arabs alike, that blaming all Arabs for the behavior of the few is unfair. She tells the story of "a gentle man I don't know [who] approaches me in a crowd at a literary conference to say, 'I am afraid for my daughter to admit she is half-Arab now. What should we do?'" As is so often the case when she is confronted with an unpleasant reality, the poet finds herself "momentarily tongue-tied." Later, however, after much reflection, she finds her voice:

> Later I wish I had told him, 'Tell her never deny it. Maybe Arab-Americans must say we are twice as sad as other people. But we are still proud, of everything peaceful and beautiful that endures. Then speak beauty if we can—the beauty of culture, poetry, tradition, memory, family, daily life. Each day, live in honor of the ones who didn't have this luxury of time. We are not alone.' (86)

Shihab Nye's poetry speaks beauty but the poet never forgets the fate of people who suffer the daily indignities of living in a world at war, of enduring the pain created by men with hard faces. Written from the relative safety of the American Southwest, from her home in San Antonio, Texas, Shihab Nye's poetry speaks for the ones whose stories never make headline news. From Texas to Palestine, Shihab Nye's poems bridge the challenging geography of two very different countries with the very human voices of people who suffer.

**Works Cited**

Forché, Carolyn. Introduction. *Against Forgetting: Twentieth Century Poetry of Witness*. Ed. Carolyn Forché. NY: W. W. Norton & Co., 1993.

Majaj, Lisa Suhair. "Arab American Literature and the Politics of Memory." *Memory and Cultural Politics*. Eds. Amritjit Singh, Joseph T. Skerrett, Jr., and Robert E. Hogan. Boston: Northeastern UP, 1996. 266-90.

Mercer, Lorraine and Linda Strom. "Counter Narratives: Cooking Up Stories of Love and Loss in Naomi Shihab Nye's Poetry and Diana Abu-Jaber's *Crescent*." *MELUS* 32.4 (Winter 2007): 33-46.

Milligan, Bryce. "Writing to Save Our Lives: An Interview with Naomi Shihab Nye." *Paintbrush* 18.35 (Spring 1991): 31-49.

Orfalea, Gregory. "Doomed by Our Blood to Care: The Poetry of Naomi Shihab Nye." *Paintbrush* 18.35 (Spring 1991): 56-66.

Rich, Adrienne. "North American Time." *Your Native Land, Your Life: Poems*. NY: W. W. Norton & Co., 1986. 33-40.

Said, Edward. *Reflections on Exile and Other Literary and Cultural Essays*. Cambridge, MA: Harvard UP, 2002.

Seale, Jan Epton. "Three Contemporary Poets: Naomi Shihab Nye, Pattiann Rogers, and Betsy Feagan Colquitt." *Texas Women Writers: A Tradition of Their Own*. Eds. Sylvia Ann Grider and Lou Halsell Redenberger. College Station: Texas A & M UP, 1997. 310-13.

Shihab Nye, Naomi. *Fuel*. NY: BOA Editions, 1998.

________________. "The Grieving Ring." *Paintbrush* 18.35 (Spring 1991): 50.

________________. *Never in a Hurry: Essays on People and Places*. Columbia, South Carolina: U of South Carolina P, 1996.

________________. "Our Nation's Capital." *Mint Snowball*. Tallahassee, Florida: Anhinga P, 2001. 39.

________________. *Red Suitcase*. NY: BOA Editions, 1994.

________________. "This Is Not Who We Are." *O* (April 2002): 83-86.

________________. "To Any Would-Be Terrorist." *75 Readings: An Anthology*. Eds. Santi V. Buscemi and Charlotte Smith. Boston: McGraw Hill, 2004. 362-66.

________________. *Words under the Words*. Portland, Oregon: A Far Corner Book, 1995.

________________.*Yellow Glove*. Portland, OR: Breitenbush Books, 1986.

Solomon, Alisa. "Who Gets to Be Human on the Evening News?" *PMLA* 121.5 (2006): 1585-92.

Walker, Jeanne Murray. "A Comment on the State of the Art: Poetry in 2004." *Christianity and Literature* 54.1 (Autumn 2004): 93-110.

# Aristophanes's Response to the Peloponnesian War and the Defeat of the Comic Hero

**Vassiliki Kotini**

---

Our knowledge of Old Comedy is shaped mainly by Aristophanes, if only because eleven of his comic plays have survived, providing an almost exclusive representation of the literary genre.[1] Aristophanic comedy is political comedy[2] because it revolves around, and stages, the life of the *polis* (city), tackling contemporary political, social, literary, as well as philosophical issues. The time span of his plays ranges from 425 BCE (*Acharnians*) to 388 BCE (*Wealth*)—a period which roughly coincides with the Peloponnesian war (431-404 BCE).

The reality of the war between Athens and Sparta provides a constant background against which Aristophanes's plays are projected and performed; more than just a recurrent motif, the war-peace idea becomes the main topic in three of his comedies: *Acharnians*, *Peace* and *Lysistrata*. Focusing on these plays, as well as on *Frogs*, which was staged only a year before the defeat of Athens (405 BCE), the present article discusses the significance of the war as a catalyst for the changes that take place in the Aristophanic plays, and argues that the war trauma defines the fate of the literary genre[3] because it damages irreparably the model of the comic hero.

Aristophanes's "peace plays" reflect the war as experienced contemporaneously in Athens.[4] Whether as a true pacifist, or simply for the sake of his audience (or for the first prize in the dramatic festival), the playwright creates comic heroes who support peace.[5] In each play, the comic hero's peace-plan reflects the contemporary war situation while Athens's actual strength in the war defines the character's conciliatory tone and his desire (or lack thereof) to negotiate with the enemy.

The progress and final outcome of the war, however, does not simply affect the negotiation strategies of the comic hero. From *Acharnians* to *Peace, Lysistrata*, and *Frogs*, one follows the gradual changes in the genre as depicted through the development of the comic protagonist. I do not intend to "bring owls to Athens" by arguing that *Assemblywomen* (*Ecclesiazusae,* 392/391 BCE) and *Wealth* (*Ploutos*, 388 BCE) introduce new elements which do not conform to the principal model of Old Comedy; rather they anticipate the poetic practices of Middle Comedy.[6] Old Comedy is broadly accepted as coming to an end with *Frogs* whose production almost coincides with the end of the Peloponnesian war.[7]

I shall argue that the war necessitates such modifications in the identity of the comic hero that gradually bring Old Comedy (as formed in Aristophanes's plays, from *Acharnians* to *Frogs*) to an end. Accordingly, Aristophanic comedy 'photographs' the birth and growth of the war trauma in Athenian society, but does not overcome it; the war experience disrupts the genre in a way from which Aristophanes's (Old) Comedy never recovers.

## Acharnians, Peace, Lysistrata: Ceasefire!

*Acharnians* is the earliest extant Aristophanic play[8] about the quest for peace in Athens at a time when the city feels victorious and powerful (even arrogant) enough to turn down any peace offer. Dicaeopolis, the main hero, is an Athenian farmer who longs for peace and all the luxuries that come with it. He is firm in his decision to sign peace with the enemy, but since his countrymen, belligerent Acharnians, do not share his view, Dicaeopolis acquires his personal peace treaty and declares the yard of his house a non-war zone. In his 'yard of peace,' he proceeds to trade freely with all, including the enemies of Athens. Dicaeopolis embodies the ideal Aristophanic hero, who, despite his humble origins, overcomes all problems and is powerful enough to achieve all he wants; he is omnipotent, powerful like the gods, and ruler of the comic war-free cosmos which he has established on his own.[9]

Not only does the war uproot Dicaeopolis from his village and confine him within the walls of the city, it also forces the Aristophanic hero to perform horrendous acts: the acquisition of peace involves "a fearful and mighty deed" (*deinon ergon kai mega*; l. 128). Dicaeopolis is now willing to *buy* the peace treaty (l. 130), although back in his village he was not familiar with any "buy" practice (*oud' ēidei 'priō'*; l. 35).[10] Faced with the new reality, he compromises and adopts the tactics of the city against his own desire in order to secure peace. Dicaeopolis's diversion is conscious, and foreshadows a series of changes which derive from the war and oblige the comic hero to critically modify his behavior.

Apart from any psychological strain, the war experience and the new way of life in Athens cause Dicaeopolis physical pain, a fact which he communicates to the audience from the beginning of the play. The vocabulary of pain marks the entrance of the comic hero. In his opening monologue, he extensively describes overwhelming feelings of stress, pain, as well as joy: *dedēgmai tēn emautou kardian* ("I have bitten my own heart"; l. 1); *hēsthēn* ("I was delighted"; ll. 2, 4, and 13); *ōdunēthēn* ("I have suffered"; ll. 3 and 9); *chairēdonos* ("delectation"; l. 4); *ēuphranthēn idōn* ("I was rejoiced at seeing"; l. 5); *eganōthēn* ("I exulted"; l. 7); and *eseise tēn kardian* ("It shook my heart"; l. 12).

Surprisingly enough, Dicaeopolis's pain, discomfort, and relief emanate mainly from his theatrical experience and not the war raging around Athens.[11] It is as if the war, which started only recently, has not yet seriously threatened the city and, therefore, peace is not treated as an urgent or even necessary matter by the Prytaneis: *eirēnē d' hopōs estai protimōs' ouden* ("but about peace they do not care at all"; ll. 26-27). Dicaeopolis is exasperated: *ō polis polis* ("oh city, my city!"; l. 27); it is soon revealed, though, that his exasperation is not for the sake and fate of the *polis*—which he actually hates (*stugōn men astu*; l. 33)—but for his village which he longs for (*ton d'emon dēmon pothōn;* l. 33).[12]

Dicaeopolis is a farmer[13] who has not managed to integrate into city life. He is the collective voice of Athenian farmers whose land was the first to endure the enemy's attacks at the outskirts of Athens.[14] He represents people who suffered most, having to leave their villages and move into the city, becoming refugees in their own country. In the city, he feels alienated, and is treated as a parasite and inferior: *kathēso, siga* ("sit down, be quiet"; l. 59) and, again, *siga* ("silence!"; l. 64). Dicaeopolis dreams of his village and longs to return to it. The unaccomplished *nostos* (return) turns into *nosos* (illness), and displacement develops into war trauma for the comic hero.

Six years after *Acharnians,* and only a fortnight before the actual peace treaty of Nicias was signed,[15] Aristophanes presented *Peace*. The protagonist, Trygaeus, rides a gigantic beetle and flies to heaven to claim Eirēnē (Peace) back from the gods, for the sake and benefit of all Greeks. Longing for peace, the comic hero suffers more than Dicaeopolis: Dicaeopolis's physical pain (*nosos*) caused by the war is now replaced by Trygaeus's *mania* (madness, frenzy): *mainetai* ("he is mad"; l. 54); *tōn maniōn* ("insanities"; l. 65).

As equally omnipotent as Dicaeopolis but more generous, Trygaeus is willing to share peace with all Greeks from the beginning (ll. 105-08 and 435-38). In real non-dramatic time, the forthcoming peace treaty, although not satisfactory for all, is highly anticipated.[16] Trygaeus's magnanimous act of sharing peace preemptively celebrates the peace agreement soon to be signed.

The optimism reflected in *Peace* could hardly be repeated in the next comic play which treats the subject of war. In *Lysistrata*,[17] staged after the Sicilian expedition and the ensuing catastrophe of the Athenian fleet, peace is replaced by reconciliation (*diallagē*), as the result of the women's sex strike and their seizing of the Acropolis. Their actions lead men to despair because of sexual frustration and deprivation of the city's war funds.

Like Dicaeopolis and Trygaeus, Lysistrata suffers because of the war, but she succeeds in achieving her goal. And yet, she is different from Dicaeopolis and Trygaeus. The first and most obvious modification in the comic hero is, of course, the change of sex. In this third peace comedy, the omnipotent male comic hero who can fly to heaven and have all his wishes fulfilled, mightier than any mythological model,[18] has now been replaced by a woman who, by classical Greek standards and law, is inferior to man.[19]

While Dicaeopolis declares that women are not responsible for the war (l. 1062),[20] Lysistrata emerges as the leader of an "army" of women who decide the fate of war and men alike, and claims that the war is "a woman's affair too" (ll. 506-614).[21] It is not only that Lysistrata impresses us with her "serious" personality,[22] as compared to Trygaeus and Dicaeopolis. After all, the impossibility of a woman leader in classical Greece equals Trygaeus's wondrous flight to heaven, and must have been received as hilarious because it would have been considered absolutely unrealistic. For the Athenian audience at the time, *Lysistrata* is no less an escapist comedy than *Birds*; Lysistrata's peace scheme is not 'doable,' although it may seem so compared to Trygaeus's act. Women were generally invisible in public—especially in public offices. Lysistrata's deed lies purely in the sphere of imagination, and this is why it is considered laughing matter; with the power of a dream, comedy actualizes the impossible.[23]

Lysistrata is not a unique example of the female comic protagonist. Aristophanes started investigating the possibilities of women playing main roles in 411 BCE when he presented *Thesmo-phoriazusae*, a comedy where women dominate the stage, although the protagonist is a man.[24] With the war still raging and Athens having received a severe blow after the failure of the Sicilian expedition, Athenian men do not seem able to provide a solution, whether in real or dramatic life. The war experience now urges the poet to modify his heroic model, look into new material, and explore alternatives.[25] Lysistrata is successful, of course, and her plan brings peace but not without a price for Aristophanic comedy which has substituted the all-powerful male hero with a heroine. *Lysistrata*, one of the most commonly staged Aristophanic plays, marks the poet's subtle compromise in modifying the model of the city's savior.

The kind of peace achieved in each of the three plays gives a clear indication of the power of the war in defining the comic hero's plans and defying his omnipotence. From Dicaeopolis to Lysistrata, there is a gradual regression regarding the hero's peace plan and his ability to achieve it. Dicaeopolis does not really ask for peace but for truce (*spondai*) which comes in the form of wine.[26] Selectively, he chooses the thirty-year truce as compared to the five-year or the ten-year truce options.[27] He then simply declares his yard a peace-zone. Dicaeopolis acts on his own while his fellow Acharnians (the chorus) oppose him, initially reject his plan, and consider him a traitor: *prodota tēs patridos* ("traitor of the homeland"; l. 290). The hero risks his life and in the end manages to win them over. Reflecting Athens's success at war, the play presents Dicaeopolis having more trouble convincing the hot-tempered Acharnians to accept the truce than to obtain it in the first place. The peace treaty comes almost leisurely; it is actually Amphitheos, a semi-divine figure that brings the *spondai* for Dikaiopolis. The enemy is nowhere to be seen and poses no threat; on the contrary, once Dicaeopolis has established his personal peace, the enemy befriends him quickly and starts trading with him. He is now able to enjoy all the luxuries and delicacies he was deprived of thus far because of the war. Furthermore, the comic hero applies his own peace criteria and is willing to share his treasure with some, but not with all.

In *Peace*, Trygaeus needs to try harder than Dicaeopolis to reach his goal; half the play is about retrieving Eirēnē while it is announced from the beginning that Trygaeus wants peace for the sake and benefit of all Greeks. Trygaeus faces the threat of Polemos, the personification of war itself, who is visible on stage; he has, however, the support of all Greeks—collectively represented by the chorus—who soon appear in heaven to assist him. Eventually, Trygaeus's mission is accomplished and the hero returns not only with Eirēnē, but also with Opōra (Fullfruit) and Theōria (Showtime).[28] After ten years of war, the Athenians have been deprived of a lot more than just Dicaeopolis's delicacies; accordingly, the personification of abundance (Opōra) is a fitting image for their increasing desires.

By the time *Lysistrata* is presented, the war progress obliges Aristophanes to offer even more help to his heroine, and consequently reduce her independence. Like Trygaeus, Lysistrata wants peace for all Greece; unlike Trygaeus, however, Lysistrata cannot perform miracles. Instead, she needs the help of others to see her plan through. For the realization of her plan and its success she relies on the women's chorus and even on the enemy represented mainly by Lampito, the Spartan, who is invited to collaborate in the peace scheme. Moreover, Lysistrata's plan is fought from within,[29] and when the goal is reached, peace is achieved through reconciliation. The peace agreement involves mutual understanding and takes place on stage.

Aristophanes's work does not advocate peace at any cost. If in *Lysistrata* the Spartans agree to withdrawals and concessions in order to achieve peace, it is because the Athenians have to do so first.[30] Whereas Trygaeus offered peace to all Greeks without any negotiations, Lysistrata's peace, and, accordingly, the heroine's power, cannot be unconditional anymore; the war has traumatized her omnipotence and independence and forced both the comic protagonist and the playwright into reconciliation.

From *Acharnians* to *Peace* to *Lysistrata*, one can detect the subtle, yet significant, change in the power and performance of the comic hero. Between *Lysistrata* and the following extant play, *Frogs*, there are only few surviving fragments which do not allow us to form a clear idea of further changes (if any) which take place in Aristophanes's writing. *Frogs*, however, is a revelation. Presented one year before the end of the war and Athens's defeat, *Frogs* is about the god of drama, Dionysus, who descends to the underworld in his quest for Euripides but ends up with Aeschylus after having judged a literary contest between the two tragedians. It is not a play about peace; nonetheless, contemporary war politics is of extreme importance to the play: the idea of salvation of Athens and the proposed solution become the main criteria for the declaration of the winner of the tragic contest. The most striking presence is that of Dionysus, an established religious figure, in the role of the comic hero on Athenian stage. Regardless of any comic horseplay, divine Dionysus is undoubtedly omnipotent, matching the previous comic heroes. As if reversing Trygaeus's ascension to heaven, Dionysus performs a descent to the underworld (*katabasis*), and by the end of the play is about to return to Athens with a long-dead poet who can hardly be compared to Trygaeus's trophy.

Despite the brilliant victory of the Athenian fleet at Arginusae the year before (406 BCE),[31] many could see that disaster was a matter of time. *Frogs* is performed with Athens's defeat looming over the city. It attempts to offer relief, employing a god in the main role, as if to guarantee success. At the same time, this choice reveals the magnitude of the trauma in comedy itself. From a male hero to a female character and then a god, each choice appears more fantastic than the previous one. Closer to the end, no (human) comic character can offer encouragement and inspiration; no Dicaeopolis or Trygaeus or Lysistrata can secure peace or safety for Athens. It seems that only a divinity can perform the ultimate miracle: the salvation of the city. The god appears to be Aristophanes's last resort for Athens and drama itself. Nevertheless, Dionysus's presence underscores the deterioration of the comic hero, and, consequently, of Aristophanic comedy, not because he is rendered as cowardly and un-heroic but because his presence proves the human comic protagonist—who has so far sustained the poet's work—inadequate.[32] Dionysus's achievement leaves much to be desired. The actual resurrection of Aeschylus does not take place on stage. This is in sharp contrast to Trygaeus's return with Eirēnē. In dramatic time, Aeschylus never leaves Hades and does not reach Athens; Dionysus's plan never comes to success, and the god becomes the dying echo of the once-powerful comic hero. The end of the play is far from happy or exhilarating; it is a 'memorial service' to a *polis*, an era, a political institution, and a literary genre.

From the male comic hero to a woman to a god, Aristophanes gradually dissociates the comic hero from the audience, while adjusting the hero's plan for peace. With Lysistrata's plan in particular, the poet leaves behind Trygaeus's heaven and looks for peace on earth, in the acropolis of Athens. The dramatic actualization of Lysistrata's plan, however, would be likely to leave a bitter aftertaste; whereas Trygaeus's deed enhances the audience's fantasy (e.g., man flying to heaven, or man as powerful as the gods), Lysistrata's stratagem plays on men's actual fear of women rebelling in a society which acknowledges male supremacy by law. Obviously, the comic play does not advocate women's emancipation and rights; nonetheless, the image of women who overturn the established order is likely to arouse real fears and phobias in the male audience.[33] What makes it even more 'dangerous' is that Lysistrata is successful in her plan; men in the play have been defeated. In times of need, the 'enemy' becomes an ally, and comedy uses all possible means to fight the war even at its own expense.

Reaching *Lysistrata*, the war does not only destabilize the social order of comedy, it also threatens the comic hero's sexual prowess. Dicaeopolis and Trygaeus are rejuvenated by the end of the play and celebrate their victory with sexual indulgence; sex confirms peace and the fulfillment of their plan,[34] while the female body (*Opōra, Diallagē*) heals the trauma of the war. In *Lysistrata,* though, sex is the bait well before it becomes the award, and the female body symbolizes the battlefield, as well as the desired and divided land. Despite the playful and amusing stance, sex in *Lysistrata* appears problematic and is initially forbidden to both men and women. What is taken for granted in previous comedies now has to be claimed and fought for.

The worst is yet to come. Sex, which so far has celebrated life, hope, and the victory of the comic hero, disappears in *Frogs*, and not only because Aeschylus is not sexually rejuvenated in the end of the play—after all Aeschylus is *not* the comic hero. Even for Dionysus, sex is unattainable. In the more farcical first part of the play, while still at the threshold of Hades, the divine comic protagonist has to "compete" with his slave for the enjoyment of the young dance girls who are waiting inside (ll. 513-14). Once in Hades, Dionysus does not pursue this further and the episode is forgotten. Of course, sex equals life and, as such, would have no place in the world of the dead.[35] Taking it a step further, *Frogs* condemns sex altogether and makes it unavailable for the comic hero: even the tragic heroines who are mentioned in the literary contest (Phaedra and Stheneboia, ll. 1043, 1049, and 1052) are condemned on the grounds of their sexual licentiousness.[36]

In addition to sex, the degree of theatrical knowledge and experience is another indicator of the degradation of the comic hero model. In his opening monologue, Dicaeopolis comments on plays, poets, and comic actors (ll. 5-16 and 139-40) and reveals his engagement with theater as an active theater-goer.[37] Furthermore, in his attempt to win over the chorus, he dresses up and performs the role of Telephus (ll. 393-556) as it had been presented by Euripides. In his metatheatrical presence, Dicaeopolis offers a parody/criticism of the tragedian's work. In *Peace*, Trygaeus appears aware of Bellerophon's flight and fall as staged by Euripides (ll. 126-79), but stays away from the tragic hero model and reaches Olympus in his comic gear. As for Eirēnē's concern about Athens, she starts with the politicians but ends up asking about the dramatic festivals, underlining the necessity and priority of drama in the life of the *polis* (ll. 670-705). While theater embellishes Trygaeus's peace plan, it has no place in *Lysistrata* where women are not concerned with theater at all. Regarding Dionysus's association with theater and dramatic poetry in *Frogs*, the god exhibits inconsistent behavior, confirming a significant aspect of the comic character.[38] On his way to Hades, he seems aware of the contemporary theatrical stage in Athens and appears determined to retrieve Euripides (ll. 66-82). Once in Hades, though, faced with the literary contest, not only does he change his mind regarding Euripides, he also seems to lose any critical ability he previously exhibited. Ignorant, silly, gullible, and confused, Dionysus ends up choosing Aeschylus whose victory is as arbitrary as Dionysus's final decision. The divine patron of drama is the last Aristophanic character concerned with theater, and it is the god who draws the final curtain.

Along with his theatrical knowledge, the comic hero's participation in politics and war decreases as well. Dicaeopolis is aware of the war situation and comments that both sides are responsible (ll. 309-10), and even offers a (comedic) explanation of the cause of the war blaming it on Pericles (ll. 526-34). He introduces himself as "a good citizen . . . a combatant" (*politēs chrēstos . . . stratōnidēs*; l. 595). Both Trygaeus and Lysistrata are aware of the political status quo but the first is too old to fight and the second cannot. Nonetheless, Lysistrata underlines women's participation in the war by means of giving birth and providing men for the war, albeit involuntarily. In *Frogs*, Aristophanes takes advantage of an existing image to bid farewell to the model of the politically engaged comic hero. Dionysus, a proverbial coward in comedy,[39] appears idle and soft (ll. 203-04); even Xanthias, the slave, refuses to fight, wasting his chance for freedom (ll. 191-92). So from Dicaeopolis, an active soldier (*hoplitēs*), to Trygaeus, a veteran old citizen (*politēs*), to a woman (with no political rights), to a lazy god, to a selfish slave, the comic plays resonate with the outcome of the war and the courage of the comic hero regresses. It is as if the loss of men at war affects comedy directly, and the male comic hero has become scarce.

## A Pyrrhic Victory

*Frogs* does not focus on peace although peace was more desired than ever in Athens at the time of production; aptly *Frogs* discusses salvation instead. The play reflects the instability of contemporary politics and abounds with 'inconsistencies': it is a comedy which discusses tragedy; the divine judge wishes to retrieve Euripides but chooses Aeschylus; the god refuses to justify his choice and remains silent. The patron god of drama has nothing to say regarding Aeschylus's victory, as if he has regretted his decision already.

Indeed, tragedy as established by Aeschylus is now retrieved but is not the same. Aeschylus's style in *Frogs* is full of rhetoric and makes use of Euripidean techniques against Euripides himself, brags about his pure and wise characters—purity and wisdom (sōphrosynē) being main concerns of Euripidean dramaturgy[40]—and attempts to prove his literary superiority by 'usurping' the style of his competitor.[41] The final straw comes with his last comment: his warning to Sophocles to guard the throne of tragedy and protect it from Euripides is far from reminiscent of his grandiose tragic style (ll.1515-23) and suggests that any prospects of return to the heroic era of Marathon and Salamis has irrevocably vanished.

By rescuing tragedy, comedy attempts to rescue itself.[42] Aristophanes's work is interwoven with Euripidean tragedy in particular, and the poet's literary relation with Euripides was already known and attacked by his rivals.[43] Contrary to expectations, Dionysus does not save Euripides but Aeschylus, who had fought against the Persians in Marathon and whose plays are imbued with Athens's heroic past (ll. 1015-17). Euripides and all that his tragedy stands for have no place in Athens any more. The era of democracy and political debate seems to have reached an end. The war calls for a state of emergency and needs military rather than freely roaming, intellectual, and independent minds; it requires few leaders, many soldiers, and no objections. Dionysus acknowledges the urgency of the situation and acts accordingly. Aeschylus, with his long silences and pompous adjectives inspiring 'awe and terror,' is considered more appropriate to save Athens, but this choice dictated by war backfires on comedy; the poet whose work unfolds the heroic past and glory of Athens is not compatible with comedy. Euripides's metaphoric loss in *Frogs* sheds light on a growing trauma which comedy cannot heal and to which it eventually succumbs.

*Frogs* is a tragic omen for Aristophanic comedy, "a tragedy in comic form."[44] The final scene in *Frogs* is a reversal of *Peace* where Hermes, Trygaeus, and Eirēnē discuss the political and literary situation in Athens (ll. 670-705). Eirēnē, although a divinity, is not aware of the recent changes in the political scene in Athens, and is briefly informed by Trygaeus while the god is only the mediator. The differences between the two plays are striking. It is not surprising that Trygaeus has the answers to Eirēnē's questions; he is the powerful comic hero; he even knows the cause of conflict between the Athenians and the Spartans which Eirēnē is ignorant of.[45] In *Frogs*, the *agon* between the two poets, although literary, is determined by a question that concerns the politics and the city; nevertheless, it is not the comic hero—and judge of the contest—who has the answers but Aeschylus whose sibylline response contrasts with Trygaeus's clarity. Aeschylus's attitude clashes with, and annihilates, a vital characteristic of Aristophanic comedy:

Comedy is by definition incompatible with loss, and the comic plays have so far offered positive answers and instant gratification; there have been no uncertainties for the comic hero who does not negotiate success and whose plan always proves right. In *Frogs*, however, the war keeps the city's problems pending and does not allow for quick fixes. The invincible Athenian hegemony has now been defeated; so has Aristophanic comedy that reflected this power in the stories of comic heroes with incredible and unlimited powers. The Aristophanic plays produced after *Frogs* are more concerned with the *oikos* (the house) rather than the *polis*. The comic world leaves the open air and the agora and becomes domesticated, almost introverted.[46] The imaginary extravaganza and its exuberant protagonist have become a memory; worse than that, the magic is lost.

## Notes

* All translations from Greek in this article are mine unless otherwise stated.

1 For a concise discussion of the conventional division of Greek comedy into Old, Middle, and New, see A. H. Sommerstein, *Acharnians* (Warminster, Wilts.: Aris and Philips, Ltd., 1992), 8-13. On the interrelation of the three periods and the transition from one period to the other, see K. Sidwell, "From Old to Middle to New? Aristotle's *Poetics* and the History of Athenian Comedy," *The Rivals of Aristophanes: Studies in Athenian Old Comedy*, eds. D. Harvey and J. Wilkins (London: Duckworth and The Classical P of Wales, 2000), 247-58.

2 See A. Lesky, *A History of Greek Literature*, trans. James Willis and Cornelis de Heer (NY: Crowell, 1966), 418. "'Political' comedy is not meant as comedy dealing with current politics, although Old Comedy does take much of its material from that source: the epithet rather refers to the intimate association of the genre with the common life of the polis, an association which in its closeness is unequalled anywhere else in Greek literature." On the relation of Old Comedy and the *polis*, and on the influence of the comic poets on the civic ideology, see J. Henderson, "The Dēmos and Comic Competition," *Nothing to Do with Dionysos?: Athenian Drama in its Social Context*, eds. J. Winkler and F. I. Zeitlin (Princeton, NJ: Princeton UP, 1992), 271-313.

3 For the purpose of this article, Aristophanic comedy from *Acharnians* to *Frogs* is taken as synonymous to Old Comedy, since Aristophanes is the only representative of Old Comedy whose plays survive intact (albeit a quarter of the poet's total production) and whose development we can follow with relevant consistency.

4 Old Comedy often depicted the role of Athens in the war before Aristophanes treated the subject. In *Dionysalexandros,* Cratinus apparently attacks Pericles's decisions and opposes his war policy as early as 430 BCE (probable date of production of the play); see J. McGlew, *Citizens on Stage: Comedy and Political Culture in the Athenian Democracy* (Michigan, MI: U of Michigan P, 2002), 25-56. Pericles dies in 429 BCE, two years before Aristophanes presents his first comedy.

5 Aristophanes's political beliefs and personal views regarding the war have been extensively discussed. See A. W. Gomme, "Aristophanes and Politics," *Oxford Readings in Aristophanes*, ed. E. Segal (Oxford: Oxford UP, 1996), 29-41 and G. E. M. de Ste Croix, "The Political Outlook of Aristophanes," *Oxford Readings in Aristophanes*, 42-64. On Aristophanes's possible influence outside the theater, M. Heath argues that "Aristophanic comedy is . . . political, in the sense that contemporary political life is its point of departure. . . . But the product of the fantasising process did not and was not intended to have a reciprocal effect on political reality; comedy had no designs on the political life from which it departed, and in that sense was not political. Politics was the material of comedy, but comedy did not in turn aspire to be a political force." See *Political Comedy in Aristophanes* (Göttingen: Vandenhoeck & Ruprecht, 1987), 28. On pacifism, patriotism, and Aristophanic comedy, see Newiger, "War and Peace in the Comedy of Aristophanes," *Oxford Readings in Aristophanes*, 143-61. More recently, discussing Aristophanes's objection to the civil war, Segal notes that the poet "is on the side that will get him the most laughs." See Segal, *The Death of Comedy* (Cambridge, MA: Harvard UP, 2001), 45.

6 Most scholars agree that *Assemblywomen* and *Wealth* are more or less specimens of Middle Comedy; see H. G. Nesselrath, *Die Attische Mittlere Komödie* (Berlin and NY: Walter de Gruyter, 1990); D. Olson, "Aristophanes and Athenian Old Comedy," *Greek and Roman Comedy: Translations and Interpretations of Four Representative Plays*, ed. S. O'Bryhim (Austin, TX: U of Texas P, 2001), 3-13. For Segal, the change in style has already started with *Frogs* which "is no longer Aristophanes as we have come to know him" (*The Death of Comedy* 102). For an opposite view regarding *Assemblywomen* in particular see K. Reckford who classifies it as Old Comedy in *Aristophanes' Old-and-New Comedy. Volume 1: Six Essays in Perspective* (Chapel Hill, NC and London: North Carolina UP, 1987), 32. On the originality of the last two Aristophanic plays and their diversion from the standards of Old Comedy, see H. Flashar, "The Originality of Aristophanes' Last Plays," *Oxford Readings in Aristophanes*, 314-28.

[7] Throughout the present article, the term *Aristophanic comedy* refers to the Old Comedy period of Aristophanes, from *Acharnians* to *Frogs*.

[8] Presented at the Lenaia festival in 425 BCE, it won the first prize.

[9] The wondrous deeds and divine-like qualities of the comic hero are best exemplified in *Birds*, where Peisetairos founds Nephelokokkygia, a city in the clouds, lives in the sky and establishes a comic cosmos where he is the absolute and unparalleled archon. On Peisetairos's comic cosmos and the unlimited power of the comic hero, see V. Kotini, *The Dialectics of Myth in Aristophanic Comedy,* Ph.D. diss. University of London, 2005, 179-258.

[10] For a detailed discussion of the financial problems and complaints of Dicaeopolis, see Olson, "Dicaeopolis' Motivations in Aristophanes' *Acharnians*," *JHS* 111 (1991): 200-03.

[11] I agree with N. W. Slater who notes that the reference to Cleon (*Ach.* 6) is not related to real-life politics but to a theatrical performance which satirized the politician causing Dicaeopolis overwhelming joy. See *Spectator Politics, Metatheatre and Performance in Aristophanes* (Philadelphia, PA: U of Pennsylvania P, 2002), 44-45.

[12] G. Compton-Engle argues that this picture changes as Dicaeopolis moves from a country persona in the beginning of the play to an urban one in the second part, where he even establishes his own market. See "From Country to City: The Persona of Dicaeopolis in Aristophanes' *Acharnians*," *CJ* 94.4 (1999): 359-73.

[13] Old Comedy praises life in the country; both Trygaeus in *Peace* and Strepsiades in *Clouds* are farmers.

[14] Thucydides, *The Peloponnesian War*, II.19.2.

[15] Thucydides, *The Peloponnesian War*, V.19.1.

[16] On the problems of the peace of Nicias, see D. Kagan, *The Peace of Nicias and the Sicilian Expedition* (Ithaca, NY: Cornell UP, 1991), 19-32.

[17] Staged (probably) at the Lenaia festival in 411 BCE. For the date of production, see Sommerstein, "Aristophanes and the Events of 411," *JHS* 97 (1977): 112-26 and Sommerstein, *Lysistrata* (Warminster, Wilts.: Aris and Philips, Ltd., 1990), 7-15.

[18] Note how Trygaeus flies to heaven and succeeds where Bellerophon failed. For a detailed discussion of the omnipotent comic hero and his unlimited power as compared to any mythological heroic figure, see Kotini.

[19] See S. Blundell, *Women in Ancient Greece* (Cambridge, MA: Harvard UP, 1995), 113-29 for a thorough analysis of the position of women in classical Athens.

[20] *Hotiē gunē 'sti tou polemou t'ouk aitia* ("because she is a woman and she is not responsible for the war"; *Ach.* l. 1062).

[21] For a discussion of the impact of the Peloponnesian war on women as depicted in contemporary art and literature, see L. Tritle, *The Peloponnesian War* (Westport, CT: Greenwood P, 2004), 79-94.

[22] Lysistrata does not comply with the standard representation of women in Aristophanic comedy as drunken, deceitful, and lustful. See, for example, how women are rendered in *Thesmophoriazusae,* ll. 383-519. On Lysistrata's masculinity, see L. Taaffe, *Aristophanes and Women* (London and NY: Routledge, 1994), 72ff.

[23] Segal discusses the dream-like characteristics of comedy (*The Death of Comedy* 1-9), noting that "in both dream and comedy, the impossible wish comes true" (2).

[24] Aristophanes's 'female' extant plays include *Lysistrata* (411 BCE), *Thesmophoriazusae* (411 BCE), and *Assemblywomen* (392/391 BCE) and explore the possibility of female characters in main and male roles. Women also feature in a number of Aristophanic fragments but no safe conclusions can be reached regarding the role of women in these plays due to the nature of the evidence. On the presence of women in comic fragments, see Olson, *Broken Laughter: Select Fragments of Greek Comedy* (Oxford: Oxford UP, 2007), 321-51.

[25] In changing the identity of the comic hero, Aristophanes could have also been influenced by Euripides who extensively uses female characters in his war plays: *Hecuba, Trojan Women,* and *Andromache* expose the cruelty of the Trojan War, the horrible fate of the city of Troy and its people. Euripides also discusses civil war in his *Suppliants* and *Phoenician Women* whose theme is borrowed from Theban myth. The war theme in Euripides's tragedies is discussed by D. Konstan, "War and Reconciliation in Greek Literature," *War and Peace in the Ancient World,* ed. K. A. Raaflaub (Oxford: Wiley-Blackwell, 2007), 191-205.

[26] With a double entendre on the term for truce (*spondai*) and for libation (*spondē*); therefore, Dicaeopolis's peace is a 'wine-peace.'

[27] Slater underlines the relation between the five-, ten-, and thirty-year peace treaties and the geography of Athens. The longer the peace treaty, the farther away from the city it takes the comic hero, until it reaches the countryside where "the fantasy space finally breaks free and becomes self-sufficient" (45).

[28] The translation of the names Opōra and Theōria follows Sommerstein, ed., *Peace* (Warminster, Wilts.: Aris and Philips, Ltd., 1990).

[29] The women in *Lysistrata* find it increasingly difficult to keep their oath and abstain from sex (*Lys.* ll. 717-68).

[30] Heath notes that "Given Athens' highly unfavourable military situation in 411, no one could have expected Sparta to open negotiations or, if Athens

took the initiative, to offer tolerable terms" (6). On negotiations in *Lysistrata*, see Sommerstein, *Talking about Laughter: And Other Studies in Greek Comedy* (Oxford: Oxford UP, 2009), 223-36.

31 Discussing the aftermath of the sea-battle at Arginusae, R. A. Bauman notes that "the Athenians were presumably pleased with the victory . . . but their elation is buried under an avalanche of accusations and counter-accusations." See *Political Trials in Ancient Greece* (London: Routledge, 1990), 69-70.

32 Dionysus is the only divine protagonist in extant Aristophanic comedy; other plays feature gods on stage, like Hermes in *Peace* or Poseidon in *Birds*, but not in the main role. Names of gods feature in a few more comedies of which only the titles and/or a few fragments survive. Divine presence in Old Comedy, though, is not necessarily limited to the plays which feature a god in their title, as the case of *Frogs* indicates.

33 See J. F. Gardner, "Aristophanes and Male Anxiety—the Defence of the Oikos," *G&R* 36.1 (1989): 51-62.

34 On the (revived) sexuality of Dicaeopolis and Trygaeus, see Segal, *The Death of Comedy* 44-67 and 68-84, respectively.

35 Sex and fertility are far from being the dominant theme in *Frogs*. On the contrary, "the imagery of death pervades all" (Segal, *The Death of Comedy* 102). Aeschylus is revived but not rejuvenated; he actually seems to detest anything related to sexuality and sexual pleasure and proudly announces that he does not allow it in his tragic work (*Frogs* ll. 1043-45).

36 Aristophanes attempts to return to the theme of sex in *Assemblywomen*, the first extant comedy after *Frogs*; nonetheless, sex appears rather problematic and becomes even punishment instead of joy. In addition, the play lacks the powerful comic hero who enjoys sex unconditionally. As for *Wealth*, sex is non-existent, and the model of the comic hero who identifies his victory with sexual indulgence has been abandoned.

37 In addition, Dicaeopolis's comments on Euripides's works and props reveal solid knowledge of the Euripidean tragedy (*Ach.* ll. 415-78).

38 On inconsistency as a main characteristic of the Aristophanic hero, see M. S. Silk, *Aristophanes and the Definition of Comedy* (Oxford: Oxford UP, 2002), 207-55.

39 Dionysus features in two more Aristophanic plays of which only the titles survive: *Babylonians* and *Dionysos Shipwrecked*. According to the *Vita Aristophanis*, *Dionysos Shipwrecked* was spurious (*test.* 1. 59, K-A, vol. 3.2, p. 1, in R. Kassel and C. Austin, eds., *Poetae Comici Graeci* [Berlin: Walter de Gruyter, 1989]). From the Scholia in *Peace* (741) we learn that the "cowardly Dionysos" was a familiar feature of the plays of Eupolis and Cratinus.

40 See P. Neils Boulter, "'Sophia' and 'Sophrosyne' in Euripides' *Andromache," Phoenix* 20.1 (1966): 51-58; C. Segal, "Shame and Purity in Euripides' *Hippolytus*," *Hermes* 98.3 (1970): 278-99.

41 This line of thought has been stimulated by S. Halliwell's inspiring talk "Aristophanes' *Frogs* and the Failure of Poetics" at the conference "Comic Interactions: Comedy across Genres and Genres in Comedy' in University College London, 2009.

42 Slater notes that "The *Frogs* presents itself initially as such a literary comedy: the god of theater goes to get a poet from Hades to save his choruses and keep them singing. In the play's second half, however, we discover that the frame of view is more encompassing—the choruses can be saved only if the city is saved, and that means saved in the war" (181).

43 On the relation between Aristophanic comedy and Euripidean tragedy, see Silk 42-97.

44 C. Whitman, *Aristophanes and the Comic Hero* (Cambridge, MA: Harvard UP, 1964), 231.

45 Dicaeopolis claims to know the reason of the war and proceeds to explain it to the chorus (*Ach.* ll. 496-556).

46 Segal writes: "This growing tendency toward domestication and financialization culminates in the *Plutus* (288 BC) and then in middle comedy" (*The Death of Comedy* 114). Middle comedy is concerned with private and not public business; it flourishes on stock scenes (rapes and recognitions, etc.) and stock characters (the cook, the parasite, the doctor, the slave, the soldier, etc.) and employs predictable plots which are based on variations of a known theme.

# Epistolary Memory: Revisiting Traumas in Women's Writing

Walid El Hamamsy

## Introduction

The epistolary form is one that has been employed by writers throughout the history of world literature, and not surprisingly, since letters are intimate and immediate modes of expression and communication (Singer 1). Books written in letter form, whether one letter or a series/exchange of letters, can be found among the works of historically varied writers such as Ibn Hazm (994-1064), Fanny Burney (1752-1840), and Oscar Wilde (1854-1900). This article deals with two contemporary novels written in letter form, depicting traumatic contexts—the legacy of slavery in the first, and civil war in the second: *The Color Purple* by Alice Walker; and *Beirut Blues* by Hanan al-Shaykh.[1]

The events of *The Color Purple* take place in the American South, in Georgia, in 1909. The novel is written entirely in the epistolary form—mainly by Celie, the main protagonist. The first two thirds of the novel comprise letters that Celie writes to God giving Him a sketch of her miserable life, first as subject of torture by an alleged father who rapes her and gets rid of her two children and then as the sex object and servant of a husband to whom she is almost sold off. It is in this section that Celie shows the patriarchal oppression she and other women are exposed to. The remaining third of the novel is a set of letters written by/to Celie and her sister, Nettie, who now lives in Africa with the missionary couple she works with and to whom her sister's children were given. Even though the sisters write to one another, there is no communication between them as the letters either never arrive, or do arrive but too late. This part of the novel demonstrates Celie's transformation and liberation through the help of other women like Shug, the Blues singer she is in love with, and Nettie. The novel ends with a letter addressed to no one in particular that shows Celie at her happiest with the final family reunion—her sister and children having come back from Africa.

*Beirut Blues*, also written in letter form, centers on wartime Beirut in 1985. Asmahan, the protagonist, writes ten letters to people, some of whom she knows and others she only knows of; she also writes letters to places and entities that show the impact of the civil war. Her first letter is addressed to her best friend, Hayat, who lives in Belgium, telling her about herself and her bitter feelings toward the war. The second letter is addressed to Jill Morrell, the friend of a war hostage Asmahan has never met, in an attempt to identify with the hostage and find refuge somewhere. This is followed by a letter to Naser, the protagonist's Palestinian ex-lover, in which Asmahan recollects some of their memories together and admits to having had other amorous adventures. The fourth letter is written to her Land in frustrated nostalgia and an attempt to find security in the past, embodied in her village. The following letter is addressed to the Blues singer, Billie Holiday, Asmahan's song idol, also reminiscent of a happy past. This is followed by an apologetic letter to Asmahan's grandmother whom she has let down by standing witness to her grandfather's love affairs. A letter then follows that is addressed to the Lebanese *émigré*, Jawad, the man Asmahan is sexually attracted to, and who symbolically embodies her hope of escape from Beirut. The eighth letter is written to War itself, showing Asmahan's ambivalent feelings towards it, wavering between hate, blame, and indifference. This is followed by her letter to Beirut, lamenting its past and showing how hard it is to recognize the city because of the war. It is in the tenth and final letter that Asmahan writes to Hayat—rounding up the novel—that a final reconciliation with the war is reached, and Asmahan gets to accept her situation.

This introduction explores theoretical positions on the epistolary novel and letter writing, showing the various reasons why the letter has frequently been employed as a form of expression in fictional writing and why it has been claimed to be suited to certain types of confessional writing. Lorna Martens defines letter-journals as "novels . . . addressed to a recipient who is usually also a confidant" (75). They are forms of "writing to the moment" and as such "lay the foundation for an uninhibited confession of intimate feelings and for an unmediated expression of thoughts" (79). The literary epistle came to existence as the natural development of the formal letter writing impulse that Singer proposes mankind has always possessed. The letter writing tradition had already been established as a means of written communication, and one breaking away from oral tradition, by the time of Cicero (Martens 1). Singer cites Hughes discussing four types of letters that had been written before the development of the fictional epistle. These are: the "rifled" post-bag, the "letters of travel", the "friendly correspondence," and the "correspondence of lovers" (40).

It was with the writing of Richardson's *Pamela* that the letter form came into existence as a literary fictional form *per se* in the English-speaking world. The epistle has since been used by different creative writers as a mode of narration. Looking at the reasons why this particular form emerged at the time of Richardson might provide some insight into its popularity. One of these reasons is that the tendency toward realism had already started by 1660: "At this time the desire for some sort of realism began to become strong in the fictional output of the day and the romances were superseded by more realistic stories developed from the French and Spanish *novella*" (Singer 60). The letter thus provided authors with a chance to write realistically, being one of the most credible narrative media due to the first-hand experience it encompasses. This is coupled with another advantage of letter writing, namely, immediacy. Letters are written "to the *moment*, while the heart is agitated by hopes and fears, on events undecided" (Singer 79). It is this *undecidedness* that gives the reader the feeling that s/he is taking part in the writing process, a feeling that naturally appeals to her/him, thus making the form become even more popular.

This intimacy attracts both the reader and the writer of the epistle. The reader feels privileged to be able to partake in the thoughts and feelings of the writer which are expressed to her/him and the fictional reader(s) alone. The letter writer, on the other hand, is given a chance to voice feelings and thoughts that s/he might not otherwise have been able to do due to social conventions and the nature of public discourse.

One final advantage of the letter as a form is the insight it provides into the writer's psyche. Letter writing is one of the sophisticated modes of writing that gives the author the chance to probe certain feelings and emotions that s/he would not be equally able to express in the case of first-/third-person method of narration. The time one takes to write about her/his feelings allows the space needed to discover how one is really feeling at a given moment.

Interestingly in our context, letter writing has almost always been a mode chosen by women writers throughout the history of English literature. Although there have always been men writers resorting to the epistolary form, the genre remains associated with women (Salsini 352-53). Martens goes as far as saying that "some contemporary women writers see fragmentary, open forms like the diary as the readiest possibility for finding a new women's voice" (182). She accounts for the appeal of that particular form to women by the fact that "as a flexible, open, and non-teleological structure, it complements the nonautobiographical quality of women's lives and the traditionally dependent, accommodating female role. A diary can be written in snatches and with little concentration; it is adaptable to the housewife's interrupted day" (182). Martens maintains that women are assigned a role subservient to that of men, which conditions the forms and genres used for literary expression. Having started off writing journals "for wholly traditional reasons, which go back to diary keeping as a religious exercise," women moved on to using the form in expressing the inner feelings and thoughts that society would not otherwise have allowed them to vent (173).

Rebecca Hogan holds similar ideas on the nature of letter writing, while offering different reasons why more women than men writers resort to the epistolary form. The first factor she mentions is the detailedness of the letter form, one based on "inclusion" rather than exclusion (103). This detailedness is often "gendered and doubly gendered as feminine" (98). Like Martens, Hogan believes that this idea is one propagated by men, especially as the use of too many details supposedly leads to "anarchy" in a text (98).

Another reason why the diary form has always been associated with women is one that relates to the nature of the letter form itself:

> [The diary is] private, secret, locked—the paradoxical idea of a writing which will remain unread, a sort of "silent" text. If we see "feminine" as a cultural signifier, standing for the historically determined social construction of feminine behavior, psychological characteristics, and the like, then the diary is a feminine form. (Hogan 99)

In this view, the diary form becomes one where women find a medium of expression that they can identify with, one that is most readily accessible. Hogan's concept of the process of identification is telling:

> Like *l'écriture féminine* . . . diary-writing can perhaps be seen as a potentially subversive form of writing because it tends to cross and blur the boundaries between things traditionally kept separate. . . . [I]t crosses the boundaries between self and other . . . between author and reader . . . between text and experience, art and life. (100)

The letter thus suits "new feminine writing" which Hogan characterizes as "open, non-linear, unfinished, fluid, exploded, fragmented, polysemic" (100).[2] Letter writing becomes a question of identity that has to do with a whole gender's choice to speak, instead of being silent, and to subvert, instead of being subservient.

**Epistolary Presences**

To turn to an application of the above views on both texts, it is interesting to note that both protagonists, Celie in *The Color Purple* and Asmahan in *Beirut Blues*, are exposed to involuntary circumstances that lead to a state of psychological, if not physical, isolation. Naturally wanting to keep contact with the outside world, they resort to letter writing, a process that keeps them alive.

Celie in *The Color Purple* is initially portrayed as a fourteen-year-old girl who is physically/sexually abused by her father—who turns out later to be her step-father. Being a barely literate southern woman, and forsaken by those she loves—her mother dead; her two children taken away from her; and her sister forced by oppressive circumstances to leave the country with a missionary group seeking a better life—Celie finds no way out of her dilemma but writing letters which, isolated and desperate, she initially addresses to God. This becomes Celie's readiest solution when she is advised by her step-father to keep silent about it: "*you better not never tell nobody but God. It'd kill your mammy*" (1). The letter becomes Celie's first step towards getting out of the vortex of silence into which the step-father forces her.

The state of isolation suffered by Celie is doubled later by the forced marriage she has to go through to the unnamed Mr.____, a man who originally wanted to marry her sister. In an attempt to get rid of Celie, both "ugly" and not "fresh" (having already given birth), the step-father convinces Albert to marry Celie, instead of her sister, and entices him with a cow that will leave the house together with Celie. The same patriarchal oppression that dehumanizes and objectifies Celie, putting her on the same level as a cow, is later demonstrated more brutally in Mr.____'s treatment. In Mr.___'s house, Celie acts as maid, baby-sitter, object of sexual gratification, and target for sadistic tendencies: "He beat me like he beat the children. Cept he don't never hardly beat them. He say, Celie, git the belt. The children be outside the room peeking through the cracks. It all I can do not to cry. I make myself wood. I say to myself, Celie, you a tree. That's how come I know trees fear men" (23). Being objectified once again, she finds no way out of her plight except by writing letters.

The letter acts as a medium through which Celie can voice her thoughts and feelings which no one else would be interested to know about. Her only solace becomes the pen and paper she uses to write her letters. They thus provide her with an interlocutor and an outlet. However, she is totally alone even during the process of letter writing: "There is no description of Celie with pen in hand, no discussion of where and when she writes. She must remain invisible so as not to expose this essential contradiction—that as dehumanized object she projects a self in the act of writing even as she records her inability to be self-defining" (hooks 293). Celie does, however, become self-defining through the only medium of contact available to her, namely, the letter.

Letter writing assumes a different role later in the course of the novel. As Celie starts to accept her circumstances submissively, Shug—the Blues singer Mr.____ has always been in love with—appears in her life. Celie's fascination with Shug since she saw her photograph by accident prepares the reader for the homoerotic attraction Celie develops for her. Although Celie's love for Shug performs the redemptive role of making her a whole person, and though she admits that she does not hate Mr.____ partly because he loved Shug and partly because Shug loved him—Celie's feelings are so complicated and difficult to grasp that she feels burdened by them. Celie's inability to understand why she does not enjoy her marital/sexual relationship, or why she feels sexually aroused by Shug, is what motivates her to find a companion to share these feelings with, an area where she can feel secure. Letters thus become her way of combating her traumatizing situation.

It is important to examine how Celie's relation to the letters themselves changes from one stage to another. Celie, who initially starts writing a letter to God to let *someone* know what had happened to her, later gets emotionally attached to the letters in which she finds *acceptance*—of her blackness, womanness, ugliness, and sexuality. Celie's letters, while providing an addressee, do not provide an interlocutor who responds to them; rather it is Celie writing and responding to herself, reflecting on her own situation. Thus, letter writing starts assuming a different role, becoming an end in itself.

This phenomenon is first demonstrated in the (f)act of ceasing to write letters to God, and writing to Nettie instead:

> I don't write to God no more, I write to you.
> What happen to God? Ast Shug.
> Who that? I say.
> She look at me serious. (199)

This development shows the change in attitude that Celie undergoes towards her letter-companions. Celie's main aim in writing to God was not really to write to *God* but rather to *write*. It is the need to write that makes Celie compose her letters and that makes her substitute Nettie for God. This is only possible through Nettie's appearance in her life and the realization that God is not the only available addressee. This is shown more clearly when she eventually addresses her last letter to "Dear God. Dear stars, dear trees, dear sky, dear peoples. Dear Everything. Dear God" (292). Celie is willing to talk to anyone/anything that will listen to her. This desperate need is more openly expressed when she finds out that her sister does not receive her letters, and still goes on writing them. The response does not matter any longer; it is the process of writing itself that counts.

Hanan al-Shaykh's protagonist, Asmahan, is portrayed as a woman at odds with her situation and reality. She starts writing from the midst of chaos forced upon her and others by the civil war taking place between political and religious sects, tearing the country apart. Her fragmented letters reflect "the war-weary life in Lebanon. Asmahan's voice, alternating passion and cynicism, despair and exultation, is that of a woman unwilling and unable to surrender" (Hussein 20). In addition to Asmahan's psychological/emotional isolation due to the war, she experiences a state of physical isolation.

The novel opens with Asmahan writing a letter to her friend, Hayat, telling her how impossible it has become to maintain contact with the outside world even on the level of telecommunication:

> I know you're trying to contact me now, since our telephone's been dead for a month. . . . You're trying to contact me, for the battles between Hizbullah and Amal must be all over the front pages in Belgium. Instead of feeling—as I normally do—that I don't want you constantly worrying about me during the fighting, I must admit that this time I'm comforted by the thought. (5-6 [6])[3]

Living among her grandmother, maid, and neighbors, Asmahan still feels lonely. She is unable to find a companion among people who have always been familiar and close. Each of the individuals Asmahan encounters during the war period has her/his own fears and worries. No one cares any more how others feel, or what they are suffering. It is this fact that makes Asmahan identify with the hostage to whose friend she writes her second letter. Like him, she feels like a hostage in a land that no more resembles the old Beirut she had always known. She is a "stranger here" and even the language that people speak "has different meanings which are unfamiliar to me" (34-35 [31-32]). It is this estrangement and unfamiliarity that makes Asmahan unable to recognize her city:

> How can I recognize a city which only lets me hear a faint echo of what it thinks as it dances and fights, fights and dances? I hear the sound of its breathing mingled with Arabic and Western music. . . . I've grown used to the dark and I no longer see shadows or reflections. . . . I've made friends with the darkness since there's no escaping it. (36 [32-33])

Naturally, Asmahan seeks refuge from her loneliness, her sense of exile and loss, in letter writing.[4] Letters also seem the most suitable medium of communication she has, simply since she has no other option. The letters Asmahan writes thus act as a space where she can feel secure, finding something that is still familiar, something she can identify with. In addition to this, what al-Shaykh herself says about her reasons for the letter writing technique is illuminating: "I wanted Beirut to become a place cut off from everything: from communications such as telephones, telegrams, planes, etc. . . . completely removed from reality so that only Asmahan's voice, the writer of these letters, is heard" (Sunderman 302).

Asmahan thus replaces the missing company of her friends and familiar land with that of the letter. This is most explicitly shown when she visits her grandfather's village, her last remaining hope, and the object of her nostalgia until this point. When she actually sees her land, Asmahan is devastated by the degree of deterioration. The land is no longer owned by her family—like Beirut is no longer owned by its people—and, instead of the familiar beautiful green, all she can see is the opium and hashish sticks all over the place—an observation that is both realistic, as people were growing grass, and symbolic, of the state of unconsciousness prevalent in wartime Lebanon. Asmahan's frustrated expectations, as well as being forsaken by all and cut off from all, lead her to take full refuge in letter writing. Her letters are "at pains to record these political obstructions and historical disruptions if only to chart an itinerary through to their other side" (Harlow 894). It is partly the need to express these traumatizing "obstructions" and "disruptions" that motivates Asmahan to write. Letter writing thus becomes a mode of resistance against despair.

Asmahan's letters now assume an existence of their own. She reaches a point where she writes letters for the sake of letter writing itself. It does not matter then who reads her letters or whether they are read at all. Like Celie's, hers are one-sided letters, and she does not get a single letter in response—hearing only "their own resounding echoes" ("Beirut Blues" 1). Asmahan's lament becomes an end in itself.

Asmahan is not just content to write without getting an answer; she even seeks to erase the act of writing itself. Towards the end of the novel, the reader is shocked to find out that even the one-sided letters that she gets no answer to are not written (296 [349]). Asmahan *thinks* her letters rather than writes them: "That's what I needed in this country, to receive letters, to sit down and write letters and get replies instead of composing them in my mind. Like a heroine in a novel, I'd tell . . . about what went on in the atmosphere of war and cease-fires, I would be a martyr or a witness" (296 [349]).

Though neither protagonist writes for a reader, the difference is that, whereas Celie does have hopes of being read and responded to, Asmahan knows from the start she is not going to get a reaction, since no action is taken to start with. However, neither Celie's frustration nor Asmahan's knowledge stops them from writing. Both novels "celebrate the resilience of the human spirit and . . . [its] dogged determination" (Milani 2). Asmahan's letters "bear witness and celebrate writing as a record of memory and desire," and that is precisely what sets her apart from "victimized, submissive women in other Arab fictions" (Hussein 20). Celie, likewise, writes a narrative that becomes "the space where the voice of an oppressed black female can be heard" (hooks 293). In writing letters to tell addressees what they already know, Celie and Asmahan (read Walker and al-Shaykh) mainly subvert, deconstruct, and—consequently—*re*construct the patriarchal/canonized narrative system that has excluded them for so long.

## Confessional Therapies

Having examined the motives of both characters for writing their letters, it remains now to look into the function these letters perform and the sense of emotional/psychological gratification they provide both protagonists with, exploring the therapeutic, cathartic role that the letters play in the two women's lives. This relates closely to the confessional nature of the letters themselves. For in writing letters, both Celie and Asmahan confess feelings and thoughts that they are otherwise unable to tell anyone.

Confession is often connected with an act of deviance from the normal that leads to feelings of guilt. The deviance norm is seen as "one which treats forms of social control as a system of rituals of exclusion and which explains social order in terms of the consensual imposition of deviant labels on actions or persons threatening the existing moral order"

(Hepworth and Turner 17). Confession is thus a "private act of contrition for wrong-doing" during the space and period of which "an individual accepts responsibility for his offense," thus being able to share a sense of conscience and moral status with fellow human beings (145). It is an act of ridding oneself of feelings of guilt, obtaining forgiveness, and regaining self-image—in short, a form of liberation.

On different levels, Celie's and Asmahan's letters can be seen as forms of confession. *The Color Purple* has been labeled by some critics a "narrative of sexual confession" because of the graphic, detailed language that it uses in describing sexual acts (hooks 284)—a fact that explains the controversy that attended the publication of the novel (George 357). Descriptions such as "he grab hold of my titties" and "he push his thing inside my pussy" are not uncommon in the novel (1). It must be noted, however, that Celie's main aim in initially writing to God is to confess the sense of guilt that she experiences after being raped by her so-called father. As a fourteen-year-old, Celie can hardly cope with her feelings and thus needs an outlet.

Another major component of Celie's confessional narrative is her sexuality, yet another form of 'deviance' that the protagonist needs to confess and for which epistolarity is most suited (Garlinger). Puzzled and intrigued by her homosexual love for Shug, Celie has a need to confess that feeling, better understood within the context of seeing lesbianism as a stigmatized and offensive act against society's imposed heterosexuality. The "bias of compulsory heterosexuality" makes lesbianism an "experience perceived on a scale ranging from deviant to abhorrent, or simply rendered invisible" and, consequently, establishes it as a "taboo" or "rejection of a compulsory way of life" (Rich 22-23).

It is the sense of wrong-doing and tabooed action, on the levels of both incest and sexual orientation, that leads to Celie's confessional act. Celie's need to confess is even doubled later with the new understanding that she reaches, with the help of Shug, of God—one that deviates from the normal concept that most people adopt. Shug helps Celie deconstruct the original image she had of God as a "graybearded" "white" "man" with "blue eyes" (201). It is Shug who shows her that God is not to be found in churches, but is more a pantheistic concept: "[God] don't look like nothing. . . . It ain't something you can look at apart from anything else, including yourself. I believe God is everything. . . . Everything that is or ever was or ever will be. And when you can feel that, and be happy to feel that, you've found it" (202-03).

As sophisticated as Asmahan is compared to naïve Celie, guilt takes up a vast area of her conscience, too. Asmahan's first letter is a confession of guilt to Hayat, guilt at begrudging her friend the life of peace and security she is having in Belgium: "Can I really be irritated with Hayat, whose name was so closely linked with mine that our two names were spoken as one?" (3-4 [7]). Unable to cope with the guilt, Asmahan chooses to vent it. This is coupled with other feelings of guilt that she has for Naser, her former lover who joined the Palestinian resistance (69 [71]). In 'voicing' her feelings of guilt to Naser for having been sexually and emotionally attracted to other men, Asmahan performs a similar act of confession, on a deeper level, to the reader, as women's sexuality is often seen as a tabooed subject in Arab culture. This is the reason why "daring" has been the term most commonly used by critics to describe al-Shaykh's work.[5] Among other things, Asmahan feels guilty for having watched her grandfather flirt with other women without protesting.

In examining Celie's and Asmahan's 'confessions,' one should bear in mind that there is one factor that sets them out as different from standard confessions, that is, neither Celie nor Asmahan has the free will to decide whether or not they should confess what they do, or whether they should do it to begin with. Both protagonists are portrayed as objects, rather than subjects, succumbing rather than *doing*, except towards the end. Celie is raped and married off by her step-father, left by her sister, and abandoned by Shug. Asmahan too, has to wait for the war to end, for something to happen, having been forsaken by her best friend and her lover.

This is reflected on the linguistic level as well. Hardly ever does the reader see Celie or Asmahan occupying the space of subject in the sentences that constitute their letters. On the first page of the novel, Celie wants God "to give me a sign letting me know what is happening to me"; her mother "left [her] to see after the others"; her father "never had a kine word to say to [her]" (1). She naturally sees herself as the object of other people's actions, never taking the initiative to *do* things herself. Asmahan is also a linguistic object in her letters; one example is when she *waits* for Naser: "I waited for him in Tunis, burning like a hot coal with the sun and longing. My craving for him made a fool of me, and I kept lying there, deluding myself that he was watching me from a distance, enjoying the sight of me waiting for him" (41 [36]). Waiting is symptomatic of Asmahan's writing; "lying there" being the only thing she can do, for the war has made it impossible for anything else to be done. This linguistic representation of Celie and Asmahan is highly in keeping with the portrayal they are given in the two novels as oppressed, silenced individuals. Celie's silence makes her unable to react to Shug's decision to leave her for a man, except by getting a scrap of paper and writing her a note (257), while Asmahan's sense of oppression makes her feel "like a big soap bubble, rolling along, not touching anything around me until I meet up with other bubbles" (35 [32]).

Letter writing also becomes a medium through which the two protagonists avoid resorting to darker thoughts of destruction. The sense of isolation and futility that they experience can lead to feelings of hopelessness and helplessness, which in turn may cause suicidal feelings:

> At the beginning of life the common emotion is probably randomised general excitement. In the suicidal state it is a pervasive feeling of helplessness-hopelessness . . . [associated with] shame, guilt, frustrated dependency. But underlying all of these is that emotion of active, impotent ennui, the feeling of helplessness-hopelessness. (Varah 75)

The distinction between guilt and shame is quite an important one, and particularly relevant in the cases of the two protagonists. Celie is primarily troubled by the feeling of guilt she experiences after her rape and at similar moments, when she reaches her new understanding of God or when she asks her step-son Harpo to beat his wife Sofia.[6] Her conscience carries the entire burden. Asmahan's main concern, on the other hand, is to remain hidden; she feels more ashamed of herself than guilty. For instance, it is not Asmahan's guilt that causes the awkwardness in dealing with her grandmother, having stood as witness to her grandfather's flirtations, but rather the fear of being found out. This difference between the nature of the two feelings may be explained culturally: Celie's American culture is one that places much emphasis on the individual and her/his feelings, whereas Asmahan's Arab culture is one that marginalizes individuals for the sake of the community/society.

Both protagonists experience some of the feelings cited as danger signs of acute suicide risk.[7] Among these are the feelings of "isolation, loneliness and uprooting" (Varah 111). Although all three are felt by both protagonists, the sense of uprootedness is one that is especially felt by Asmahan due to the state of devastation that the war has led to. Both experience the severe feeling of "having to live with few human contacts" (Varah 111). Even though the two protagonists have people around them, there is hardly any *real* contact or communication, a factor that leads to a worse state of emotional/psychological isolation. Finally, lacking "a philosophy of life such as a comforting type of religious faith" is a factor that enhances the potential for developing suicidal feelings (Varah 111). An implied sense of disbelief lies at the heart of *Beirut Blues*, the war having made it impossible for one to maintain belief in anything. Celie, on the other hand, breaks away from the conventional view of God, a sign of disbelief in orthodox faith which leads to a feeling of uprootedness, even though it is replaced by another quasi-mystical belief.

Both protagonists express ideas related to self/other destruction more than once in the course of their letters. For instance, Celie's anger at discovering that Mr.____ has been hiding her sister's letters from her—which, together with her feelings of guilt, could have led to self destruction—makes her initially want to kill her husband: "I watch him so close, I begin to feel a lightening in the head. Fore I know anything I'm standing hind his chair with his razor open. . . . All day long . . . I stutter. I mutter to myself. I stumble bout the house crazy for Mr.____ blood" (125). Yet letter writing gives vent to these feelings and thus purges Celie of them. Because she is able to write these feelings down, she no longer wants to enact them in reality.

Asmahan mentions suicide more explicitly in *Beirut Blues* when she remembers Naser saying that he wanted at many points to commit suicide but could not, simply because "it is a gesture of pride which I'm not fit to make" (79 [84]). Suicide is thus established as part of Asmahan's subconscious, a factor that increases the potential for developing suicidal thoughts (Varah 111). This is echoed in the novel by Asmahan's own thoughts about death. The nothingness, futility, and loss of identity that Asmahan experiences lead her to think of death as a solution: "All the same, I'm always thinking about death. It's there, and sometimes it's coming towards me. I open my eyes or keep them closed, depending on whether I'm interested in seeing and eating and staying alive or indifferent and without hope" (38 [34]). Indifference towards life and loss of hope are factors indicative of a sense of withdrawal that a suicidal person must experience. Like in Celie's case, the letters Asmahan writes play the role of the emotional sponge that absorbs her suicidal feelings and thus rids her of them. Again, the letter performs a cathartic function.

Both characters seek therapy in letter writing. Finding no one to share one's feelings with except a piece of paper that is not even replied to, sometimes never sent, reveals the state of despair the two characters go through. Lindberg-Seyersted mentions this "desperate need" in reference to Nettie's letters to Celie: "Nettie has a desperate need to maintain even an imaginary contact with her sister. Her correspondence functions as the same kind of therapy against loneliness that drives Celie to maintain her correspondence to God although he, as far as she can tell, never answers by act or vision" (82). The same could be said about Asmahan who knows from the start that her letters are not going to be answered. Walker herself mentions in an interview that she is able to imagine Celie's thoughts and feelings while writing to God: "Celie is able to write, 'Dear God, this has happened to me and I have to tell somebody and so I write to you'" (Wilson 325). "*Having*" to tell somebody and finding nobody to tell, either because no one cares or because others are too busy healing their own wounds, the two protagonists set out to write letters that eventually assume the role of companion—a process that saves their sanity.

**Writing Identities**

In light of the therapeutic view of letter writing, it is worth considering how these letters help their writers gain a better understanding of themselves. In both novels, letter writing becomes a process of self-discovery, ending in a better understanding of oneself as well as one's surroundings and situations. The one-sidedness of the letter writing process allows for more space within which the two characters can reflect on their lives. The usual interaction that takes place in letter writing, between addresser and addressee, is replaced by another kind of interaction between the addresser and herself, a dialogue of a monologic nature that eventually leads to the protagonists' liberation from their oppressive circumstances. As Hogan notes, what happens to the self in letter writing is a process of "reflection and self-discovery," similar to that of retreating from the world or the public sphere into a letter (97-99).

In *The Color Purple*, Celie's letters to both God and her sister help her find out more about herself and about life in a variety of ways. First, on the cognitive level, the letters Celie receives from Nettie constitute a learning experience that makes up for the education she was deprived of. What Celie asks for at the beginning of her letter sequence is a sign from God letting her know what is happening to her and that indeed is what she gets. Nettie's letters from Africa, which Celie tellingly obtains with Shug's help, perform the role of widening Celie's horizons by telling her about places she has never visited, probably never heard of. Nettie's role as instructor/informant had already been established earlier in the course of the novel. It is Nettie who teaches Celie that "the way you know who discover America . . . is think bout cucumbers. That what Columbus sound like. I learned all about Columbus in first grade, but look like he the first thing I forgot. She say Columbus come here in boats called the Neater, the Peter, and the Sanomareater" (10). The reader is thus prepared for Nettie's role as teacher.

Nettie's letters also perform a more practical function. Apart from learning about other ways of life, Celie is also able to use the knowledge she receives through the letters in her everyday life. When Henrietta falls sick with the blood disease, Celie's mind goes back to one of the letters that Nettie had sent her: "Then I think back to one of Nettie's letters bout the sickness children have where she at in Africa. Seem like to me she mention something bout blood clots. I try to remember what she say African peoples do" (230). Celie is not only taught the lesson but learns it *and* tries to use it. This in itself is a sign of the change in personality that she undergoes. This is a far cry from the representation of the fourteen-year-old Celie that the reader gets at the opening of the book. At school, Celie cannot remember the name of the person who discovered America, and cannot be bothered; now she is willing to exert effort and remember things Nettie teaches her. Obviously, Celie is developing a taste for knowledge.

On a more abstract level, the letter writing process gives Celie the chance to find out more about herself by comparison. Nettie's letters about Africa, the Olinka tribe, and such people as Tashi and her parents subconsciously sink into Celie's psychology, and in a sense reform her. The Olinka tribe's traditions are the objective correlative of the patriarchal oppression that Celie and other black women are exposed to. Being immersed in her oppressive circumstances, Celie cannot theorize about her state and decide she needs to change. It is only when she finds out about other women like Olivia and her love of learning that she changes. Only when she is made aware of the existence of other women living under oppressive circumstances and fighting against them does she take responsibility for her actions. It is these letters that make Celie reflect on her own circumstances and reach the final stage of tranquility. In this way, letter writing becomes a process of self-discovery, learning, and liberation. It is through her letters that Celie manages to regain her identity, an identity crushed by a society which rejects all that is black, then crushed further by a patriarchy that dominates women and their existence.

It would be interesting to consider Celie's change within the context of Walker's views of black women. Walker's protagonists are often seen in relation to her historical division of all black women into three cycles. The women of the first cycle are those "suspended" women, of the eighteenth, nineteenth, and early twentieth centuries, who were not given the ability to express their creativity in any way and thus ended up being crushed and silenced (Washington 39). Following these are the women of the second cycle of the 1940s and 1950s. This cycle is characterized by the break away from values of ethnicity, propagated and advocated by whites, that made the women experience a sense of uprootedness and non-belonging (44). Celie belongs to the third cycle: women of the 1960s who were given the chance for the first time to become creative and take part in the process of change African-Americans went through. What characterizes these women is that "although they are more fully conscious of their political and psychological oppression and more capable of creating new options for themselves, they must undergo a harsh initiation before they are ready to occupy and claim a new territory" (Washington 46).

Celie does indeed go through such a process of "harsh initiation." It is one exemplified in a society that feeds Celie misrepresentations of her body, teaching her that she has less right to live due to her ugliness; a society that suppresses her sexuality in favor of an imposed heterosexuality that she does not/cannot identify with; a society that teaches her to take what is there and be content. What the letters do to Celie is teach her that other modes of life exist. Through writing and receiving letters, Celie gets a better chance to think and find out for herself what she wants out of life. The letter becomes a mediator enhancing Celie's process of liberation. Having liberated her, the letter also gives Celie an identity.

Asmahan goes through a similar process of liberation and self-discovery in *Beirut Blues*. Living in a war-torn city, Asmahan's identity is, consequently, fragmented.[8] The protagonist experiences a state of alienation, living like a hostage in her own country, as she writes in her letter to Jill Morrell. Asmahan's identity is torn between the two parts of the city, between the Palestinians and the Israelis, between the different political parties and the opposing religious sects. Al-Shaykh herself, in an interview, describes the state of Beirut during the war as follows:

> The war was still going on and continuing to affect the people in the streets. The city became a city of hostages, whether they were foreigners or Lebanese; it was torn into two sections: East and West. Other militias emerged and became powerful. . . . In addition, the military from Syria, Israel and Iran invaded Lebanon. (Sunderman 305)

It is almost impossible to expect one to have a sense of identity, or even to preserve one, amidst all this chaos. For Asmahan sees the war "dragging a Persian carpet from under my feet thread by thread and then weaving it together again from one moment to the next" (230 [274]). She is unable to understand what is going on, and she has lost her sense of security. What Asmahan tries to do is make sense of her life and find an identity where she can feel secure through letter writing.

And indeed she does. Asmahan's letters constitute a learning process, at the end of which the protagonist is liberated and given a better understanding of herself, even though she follows a different route than the one Celie takes. For there is a basic difference between the two cases. Whereas Celie's letter writing process allows her the psychological space needed to retreat from the world and think about herself and her situation, Asmahan's letters represent an attempt to belong and be part of the outside world she has been cut off from because of the war. It is the state of retreat from the world that Asmahan is trying to escape by writing her letters. She has already realized that the war has made individuals atomized, unable to partake in the existence of others; sharing a state of "separatedness" (230 [274]). In the letters, she can enjoy human relations which have been denied to her by her environment. Unlike Celie, she does not seek her identity within, for that is an area that has already proved frustrating. There is only a vacuum inside, a self on the verge of madness.

Asmahan is aware that a fragmented, distorted self can only be restored through a fragmented, distorted search. As Hussein puts it, "Asmahan defines herself . . . through her feelings for those who receive her letters. . . . As she addresses them in turn, relentlessly and lyrically, Asmahan analyses her own emotions, past and present; the written word is her record and her weapon of sanity" (20). One has to imagine the kind of devastated identity that would lead one to define oneself in reference to how one feels about others, this being the only means available of reaching self-understanding.

Asmahan does not only define herself by how she *feels* about others, but by also comparing herself to them. In writing to Hayat, she tries to see how similar to/different than her friend she is, thinking what choices she would have made, had she been in her place. In writing to her grandmother, she tries to put her finger on the things that she has inherited from her. In writing to the land, Asmahan tries to identify with it in terms of how the war has affected both of them. In writing to Jill Morrell, she tries to discover the relation between her friend's situation and her own. Asmahan is constantly and desperately seeking a space where she can feel secure, an area where she can find echoes of herself. This despair is nowhere more explicitly shown than in her attempt to identify even with her mother, a mother who had left her and the whole country to get married to another man, without even thinking about what would happen to her daughter.

From the beginning of the novel, Asmahan is shown as more concerned with her own feelings than those of the people she writes to.

She does not really *address* her letters to others; she, rather, *looks for herself* in others. She writes to people to tell them how she feels about them and how she would have (not) liked to react to things they did, and, in so doing, gains a degree of understanding of the nature of her own feelings. Asmahan is portrayed as a woman holding a mirror to the outside world, craving to be part of it, bent over it, looking at reflections of herself as they appear in the objects of the smashed pieces of glass making that mirror. In doing that, she pieces together the jigsaw puzzle of the shattered and fragmented self she is.

As Nelson notes, Asmahan's letters "humanize the non-humanity of the war in ways that international media, academic thinkers in study centers and ideologists are not capable of" (19). This is the only way that Asmahan can cope with this 'non-human' war. Her letters become the only way of preserving what is left of old familiar Beirut, for the

> epistolary exercise importantly challenges genre conventions and political processes and keeps Beirut on the contemporary map as both cultural capital and literary topos. It represents neither a sniper's perspective nor the coercions of factions, but the necessary message from out of the disorder and disarray of postresistance writing that new directions are still an imperative. (Harlow 896)

In challenging these conventions, Asmahan also challenges the war itself. Nostalgic to the past, Asmahan rediscovers herself through rediscovering her historical heritage (Al-ʿAbdallah 50).[9]

Letter writing thus becomes the two protagonists' only way out of their dilemmas. Both are faced with incredible forces of oppression. However, each of the two characters calls upon some force deep inside herself that guides her out of her trauma, using the letter as a reliable medium of expression. Both write letters in order to reach knowledge, understanding, and identity—the quest itself becoming a celebration of the powers of resistance and of the resilience to which their letters stand as witness. Letters provide Celie and Asmahan with a number of abilities, but, above all, they endow them with insight and 'clairvoyance' that make them see who they really are, and how they can become who they want to be. As Walker puts it:

> This . . . is the only hope. Because it's as if this world is constructed almost entirely of lies, and so we can't help but be lost. We are . . . trying to find the path, and they have delib-

erately said East where it's West, North where it's South, up where it's down, green where it's blue. And all the time they are wrong. These signposts have been deliberately put on the path to send us off somewhere else. So clear seeing, clear speaking—that is our responsibility. (qtd. in McLeod 4)

Both Celie and Asmahan try to find the truth about what has been misrepresented while *speaking* up to express *them*selves. Each follows her own path, but both eventually reach what they set out to reach.

**Conclusion**

Having examined the letters' roles as companion and therapist in the traumatic situations of the two protagonists' lives and the way they help them attain a better understanding of self, it is worthwhile now to try and see the letters Celie and Asmahan write within the context of their character development. The letters written by the two protagonists act as mirror-images of their final reconciliations with the world on several levels. The letters that Celie writes, patching together her own self, reflect on a deeper level the process of quilting that brings women characters in the novel together.[10] Throughout, the female characters of the novel are seen at different points making quilts. One could almost argue that quilting becomes the most solid act that unifies all of them and brings them together. Quilting and letter writing become synonymous acts, both based on a process of piecing together cloth and words. Just like quilting and sewing give meaning to Celie's life, the letters give her an identity and understanding with which to grasp this meaning. Interestingly, this act of quilting that Walker's characters resort to has been used to describe her own work. Walker's writing itself has often been seen by a number of critics as a quilt where she puts together parts of herself, her heritage, and *her*story: "Alice Walker's works are quilts—bits and pieces of used material rescued from oblivion for everyday use. She takes seemingly ragged edges and arranges them into works of functional though terrifying beauty" (Christian 180). Quilting itself as it appears in the novel is a reflection of another process that takes place among the female characters, namely, that of female bonding, a phenomenon that Walker uses to bring her women—all exposed to involuntarily severe and oppressive circumstances—together: "*The Color Purple* is about the struggle between redemption and revenge. And the chief agency of redemption, Walker is saying, is the strength of the relationships between women: their friendship, their love, their shared oppression" (Smith 20). This act of female bonding is a crucial factor in Walker's "womanist" philosophy. It is *womanist* because it is essentially and primarily based on women coming together, sharing their experiences, reaching out for one another and, in doing so, guiding each other toward the light of liberation and self-understanding.[11]

Celie's letters reflect and enhance the acts of quilting and female bonding in the novel, for part of her awareness that something has to be done comes from the understanding she gains through writing her letters. It is these letters that cause Celie's final crescendo of forgiveness and her ultimate reconciliation with the world. She is back in Mr.____'s house, a different person, however, sitting out on his porch, writing a letter to "Dear Everything" (292) and feeling "the youngest us ever felt" (295).

Asmahan's letters celebrate a similar process of reconciliation with the world, reflecting the sense of transformation that she experiences. Asmahan changes from a shattered, isolated, confused woman to one who knows she wants to stay in Beirut with all its wars and cease-fires and contradictions. Her struggle with the war ends, as the novel ends, with the realization that she has "become addicted to this war" (367 [424]). Surprisingly, it is a realization that she can *now* easily cope with, having come to terms with the war, her letters having already made the war understandable. It is precisely this realization and this acceptance that give Asmahan the courage to utter her last statement: "I went to *confront* the city which has made its war die of weariness" (370 [427]; emphasis added). Confrontation is made possible through writing letters.

What the letters do, among other things, is give Beirut, the only remaining subject Asmahan can identify with in her surroundings, a voice. Beirut becomes as important a character in *Beirut Blues* as Asmahan. The strength that Asmahan gets from giving the war-torn city that voice, as well as from humanizing the people involved in civil strife, helps her eventually realize that the war is an entity that she can react to, rather than a scary incomprehensible happening. Together with this realization comes another: Asmahan knows by the end of the novel that "success and asylum sought elsewhere is illusory. Fulfillment and identity can only be achieved in Lebanon, and especially during this war. The war has recuperated the women's escape. Their loneliness and alienation in Beirut is as nothing compared with the greater alienation of the emigrants" (Cooke 160). Only when Asmahan reaches that realization is she able to let go of Jawad, her *émigré* friend, and to stay in Lebanon. It is her letters that make Asmahan reach this state of reconciliation with the world and this understanding of the war.

The letters Celie and Asmahan write constitute a liberating process by restoring both characters to the state of healthy human beings and pulling them out of the abyss of insanity as they confront their traumas of rape and civil war. The sets of letters become much more peaceful in tone by the end. The two novels end on cheerful optimistic notes, giving one hope that the protagonists will then start teaching others what they had been taught. One has great expectations of Celie going on with the act of quilting and showing other women the light of truth and self-respect. One also hopes that Asmahan, having preserved her sanity, will help others out of their dilemmas. For it is in times of crisis that the individual submerges her/himself in others and becomes one with them, assuming "responsibility for the maintenance of public as well as private orders" (Cooke 150).

The letters become catalysts that help both protagonists reach an understanding of life and of themselves that they would probably have never been able to gain otherwise. Writing letters is moved from the sphere of the physical act of holding a pen and writing on a piece of paper into that of human projection and mediated reflection. It is moved from the realm of realism and immediacy to that of self-expression and subversiveness that Hogan refers to, shedding a new light on the epistolary form and the reasons why it has been used throughout history. In subverting their realities, the writers also subvert the whole genre and its rules, for the letters both characters write become not only a narrative mode but a life-giving force, a *raison d'être*. They constitute a psychological and emotional experience that turns the protagonists' written words into voices they use to rebel against the legacy of dispossession and the confusion of war. The ability to *articulate* restores both protagonists to life. It is no wonder they both identify with singers: Shug Avery and Squeak in *The Color Purple*; Billie Holiday, Ruhyyia, and Asmahan (after whom the protagonist was named) in *Beirut Blues*, for it is their sad experiences that these singers express in their Blues and lament songs. The same happens with Celie and Asmahan who are "speaking on behalf of other individuals, probing a private existential problem" (Cooke 162). In addition to their roles of caring and healing, the letters the two protagonists write have an ultimate effect on them that is quite similar to that of the story-telling of Shahrazad who is not freed, and does not manage to free other women, until she is given a voice with which to express herself and to be heard.

## Notes

[1] I would like to express my deepest thanks to Hanan al-Shaykh and Catherine Cobham for their encouragement and support during the material collecting stage for this research.

2 For more on these qualities in relation to feminist writing, see Christiane Makward's "To Be or Not to Be … A Feminist Speaker."

3 All references to *Beirut Blues* are from Catherine Cobham's English translation. The corresponding page number(s) in the original Arabic will be given between square brackets throughout.

4 In a telephone interview (August 8, 1997), Hanan al-Shaykh explained to the author the reasons why she chose the epistolary form as a medium of expression in this novel. Having written the first draft of *Beirut Blues* in a more traditional narrative form, and while revising it, al-Shaykh did not feel comfortable with its "artificiality." In her words: "I wanted to create a distance between me—living in London—and the war in Lebanon." She wanted the letter to act as "mediator" between her and Lebanon, as well as between Asmahan and her fictional/real readers. She added: "There is always correspondence at war times." Letters, in her opinion, are what connects people. She gave an example of her communication with a close friend who was in Beirut during the war, and how phone calls meant nothing compared to their written contact: "The eye takes the written word more seriously than the ear does the spoken."

5 Labeling al-Shaykh's work "daring" can be noted in most criticism written on her work. Most critics refer to al-Shaykh primarily as a non-conformist, breaking the taboos of politics, sex, and religion—so firmly ingrained in the Arab world. The writer herself refers to this attitude, saying that it is typical of "us, Arabs, to overreact to things, especially when it comes to these deep human relations that we do not fully understand yet" (al-Shaykh, "Al-riwa'iyya al-libnaniyya" 11). For more on the subject, see Hanan al-Shaykh's interview in *Ros Al Youssef*, "Katiba 'arabiyya jadida". Interesting in this respect is how Richard Jacquemond places this attitude within the context of Arab women writers flouting norms typically associated with the East, and refusing to adhere to a male voyeuristic attitude: "les oeuvres des romancières arabes les plus traduites et les plus populaires sont aussi celles qui sont le plus marquées par l'opposition entre les valeurs modernes (associées à l'Occident) d'émancipation et de liberté défendues par ces auteurs, et l'oppression sexuelle du 'mâle oriental' qu'elles dénoncent—à quoi s'ajoute . . . le plaisir voyeur d'accéder aux 'secrets d'alcôve' du harem (29). Aghacy's assertion that "[Lebanese] women's fiction fastens on city life as a way to counter stereotypes that align them with the restrictive past with more liberating images of women's experience within the unchartered urban space" (505) is particularly relevant to our discussion of *Beirut Blues* in this article.

[6] For an interesting discussion on Celie's reasons for advising Harpo to beat Sofia, thus enacting "horizontal violence," see Floyd-Thomas and Gillman, pp. 536-37.

[7] For a detailed analytical study of the psychology of the suicidal person and the way s/he does (not) relate to social factors and surroundings, see Emile Durkheim's *Suicide*.

[8] "Fragmented" is a term frequently used to describe most of al-Shaykh's work. It has been noted that her work verges more on the psychological than the realistic, especially in *Beirut Blues* and *The Story of Zahra*. For a detailed analysis of this aspect of al-Shaykh's writing, see al-Ra'iy's article and al-Shaykh's interview with Liana Badr. Ann Marie Adams sees this fragmentation as dictated by al-Shaykh's representation of space: "Asmahan's country is both real and imagined, personal and communal, at war and at peace, eastern and western, hurtling toward destruction and on the brink of rebirth. Mapped, charted, and signified in so many contradictory ways, it necessarily defies coherent representation" (210).

[9] Rediscovering Lebanon's heritage and rewriting history are two factors that critics refer to when discussing the work of Hanan al-Shaykh. For more analysis of these two phenomena, see Ghandour's article which particularly analyzes al-Shaykh's novel *The Story of Zahra*.

[10] For an interesting analysis of the processes of quilting and sewing as factors that move Celie toward agency, and their relations to traditional black gender roles, see Grobman, pp. 85-86. For more on this point in relation to rape vs. empowerment, see Cutter's "Philomela Speaks" and her assertion that "Celie's sewing functions as an alternative methodology of language that moves her away from violence and victimization and into self-empowerment and subjectivity. . . . In Walker's text rape leads not to erasure, but rather to the start of a prolonged struggle toward subjectivity and voice" (163-67).

[11] For a detailed discussion of Walker's womanist philosophy and its four-part definition, see Donald McCrary's "Womanist Theology and Its Efficacy for the Writing Classroom," especially pp. 528-29. For more on how Walker's womanist philosophy has come to represent a paradigm of resistance and can be seen in the larger context of Walker's attempt to write a multicultural text, see Marilyn Edelstein's "Multiculturalisms Past, Present, and Future." Relevant in this context is E. Shelly Reid's "Looking Good and Looking Forward in Contemporary Black Women's Stories" which traces the influence of Walker's work in shaping the consciousness of a new generation of black writers.

## Works Cited


Adams, Ann Marie. "Writing Self, Writing Nation: Imagined Geographies in the Fiction of Hanan al-Shaykh." *Tulsa Studies in Women's Literature* 20.2 (Autumn 2001): 201-16.

Aghacy, Samira. "Lebanese Women's Fiction: Urban Identity and the Tyranny of the Past." *International Journal of Middle East Studies* 33.4 (November 2001): 503-23.

Al-ʿAbdallah, ʿImad. "Al-zikrayat al-maskuna." *Al Naqid* 63 (1993): 48-50.

Badr, Liana. "Hanan al-Shaykh li-*dafatir thaqafiyya*" (Interview). *Dafatir thaqafiyya* (July 1996): 18-19.

"Beirut Blues." <http://www.randomhouse.com/acmart/catalog/display.pperl?isbn=9780385473828>.

Christian, Barbara. "Novels for Everyday Use: The Novels of Alice Walker." *Black Women Novelists: The Development of a Tradition, 1892-1976.* London: Greenwood P, 1980. 180-238.

Cooke, Miriam. *War's Other Voices: Women Writers on the Lebanese Civil War.* Cambridge: Cambridge UP, 1988.

Cutter, Martha J. "Philomela Speaks: Alice Walker's Revisioning of Rape Archetypes in *The Color Purple.*" *MELUS* 25.3/4 (Autumn-Winter 2000): 161-80.

Durkheim, Emile. *Suicide: A Study in Sociology*. Trans. and ed. John A. Spaulding and George Simpson. Glencoe: The Free P, 1951.

Edelstein, Marilyn. "Multiculturalisms Past, Present, and Future." *College English* 68.1 (September 2005): 14-41.

Floyd-Thomas, Stacey M. and Laura Gillman. "Subverting Forced Identities, Violent Acts, and the Narrativity of Race: A Diasporic Analysis of Black Women's Radical Subjectivity in Three Novel Acts." *Journal of Black Studies* 32.5 (May 2002): 528-56.

Garlinger, Patrick Paul. *Confessions of the Letter Closet: Epistolary Fiction and Queer Desire in Modern Spain.* Minneapolis: U of Minnesota P, 2005.

George, Olakunle. "Alice Walker's Africa: Globalization and the Province of Fiction." *Comparative Literature* 53.4 (Autumn 2001): 354-72.

Ghandour, Sabah. "*Hikayat Zahra*: Al-riwaya al-mudadda—al-tarikh al-mudadd." *Fusul* 12 (1993): 213-23.

Grobman, Laurie. "The Value and Valuable Work of Multi-Ethnic Literature." *MELUS* 29.3/4 (Autumn-Winter 2004): 81-90.

Harlow, Barbara. "City of Flight." *The Nation* (June 19, 1995): 894-96.

Hepworth, Mike and Bryan S. Turner. *Confession: Studies in Deviance and Religion*. London: Routledge and Kegan Paul, 1982.

Hogan, Rebecca. "Engendered Autobiographies: The Diary as a Feminine Form." *Autobiography and the Question of Gender*. Ed. Shirley Neuman. London: Frank Cass, 1991. 95-107.

hooks, bell. "Reading and Resistance: *The Color Purple*." *Alice Walker: Critical Perspectives Past and Present*. Eds. Henry Louis Gates, Jr. and K. A. Appiah. NY: Amistad, 1993. 284-95.

Hussein, Aamer. "A Local Lament." *TLS* (March 31, 1995): 20.

Jacquemond, Richard. "Langues étrangères et traduction dans le champ littéraire égyptien." *Alif* 20 (2000): 8-38.

Lindberg-Seyersted, Brita. "Who Is Nettie? And What Is She Doing in Alice Walker's *The Color Purple*?" *Black and Female: Essays on Writings by Black Women in the Diaspora*. Copenhagen: Scandinavian UP, 1994. 79-94.

Martens, Lorna. *The Diary Novel*. Cambridge: Cambridge UP, 1985.

Makward, Christiane. "To Be or Not to Be ... A Feminist Speaker." Trans. Marline Barsoum et al. *The Future of Difference*. Eds. Hester Eisenstein et al. NJ: Rutgers UP, 1985. 95-105.

McCrary, Donald. "Womanist Theology and Its Efficacy for the Writing Classroom." *College Composition and Communication* 52.4 (June 2001): 521-52.

McLeod, Melvin. "A Wind through the Heart: A Conversation with Alice Walker and Sharon Salzberg on Loving Kindness in a Painful World." <http://www.purifymind.com/WindHeart.htm>.

Milani, Abbas. "A Warm, Sad Blues Riff on Life in Beirut: Novel's Letters Patch Together Haunting View of a Fractured City." <http://alumni.eecs.berkeley.edu/~dany/lebanon/Articles/sad_blues.html>.

Nelson, Cynthia. "Barid Bayrut." *Nour* 5 (1995): 17-19.

Al-Ra'iy, 'Ali. *Al-riwaya fi-l-'alam al-'arabi*. Cairo: Dar al-mustaqbal al'arabi, 1991.

Reid, E. Shelley. "Looking Good and Looking Forward in Contemporary Black Women's Stories." *African American Review* 34.2 (Summer 2000): 313-28.

Rich, Adrienne. "Compulsory Heterosexuality and Lesbian Existence." *Feminist Literary Theory: A Reader*. Ed. Mary Eagleton. Oxford: Blackwell, 1992. 22-27.

Salsini, Laura A. "Maraini Addresses Tamaro: Revising the Epistolary Novel." *Italica* 78.3 (Autumn 2001): 351-66.

Al-Shaykh, Hanan. *Barid Bayrut*. Cairo: Dar al-hilal, 1992.

_______________. *Beirut Blues*. Trans. Catherine Cobham. NY: Anchor Books, 1995.

_______________. "Katiba 'arabiyya jadida" (Interview). *Ros Al Youssef* (January 19, 1976): 42-44.

_______________. Personal Interview. August 8, 1997.

_______________. "Al-riwa'iyya al-libnaniyya Hanan al-Shaykh l-il-*watan*" (Interview). *Al-watan* (May 15, 1993): 11.

Singer, Godfrey Frank. *The Epistolary Novel: Its Origin, Development, Decline, and Residuary Influence*. NY: Russel & Russel, 1963.

Smith, Dinita. "*The Color Purple*." *Alice Walker: Critical Perspectives Past and Present*. Eds. Henry Louis Gates, Jr. and K. A. Appiah. NY: Amistad, 1993. 19-21.

Sunderman, Paula W. "Between Two Worlds: An Interview with Hanan al-Shaykh." *The Literary Review* 40 (1997): 297-308.

Varah, Chad. *The Samaritans: Befriending the Suicidal*. London: Constable, 1988.

Walker, Alice. *The Color Purple*. NY: Pocket Books, 1982.

Washington, Mary Helen. "An Essay on Alice Walker." *Alice Walker: Critical Perspectives Past and Present*. Eds. Henry Louis Gates, Jr. and K. A. Appiah. NY: Amistad, 1993. 37-49.

Wilson, Sharon. "A Conversation with Alice Walker." *Alice Walker: Critical Perspectives Past and Present*. Eds. Henry Louis Gates, Jr. and K. A. Appiah. NY: Amistad, 1993. 319-25.

# Catastrophic Subjectivity: Representing Lebanon's Undead

**Mark Westmoreland**

> I don't have a homeland to say I live in exile. . . .
> I live in postmortem . . . daily life, daily death.
>
> — Elia Suleiman

> On the one hand, this invitation to meet the corpse should not be mistaken for a call to embrace materiality, a return to hard facts and familiar corporeality. For a corpse is precisely that which sheds its own name, becomes unfamiliar. Unnamable, the corpse is unrecognizable and yet tangibly available. On the other hand, it would be equally mistaken to consider the work an invitation to side with a subversive historical narrative written from the point of view of the defeated. Rather, a corpse is governed by a downward-spiraling dialectic coursing endlessly toward ruination; it is incapable of safeguarding a memory.
>
> — Walid Sadek

## Introduction

Many contemporary Lebanese artists and filmmakers subversively engage visual media in an effort to disrupt the expectations of official and objective 'truth telling.' This body of experimental media provides a critical historiography of Lebanon's recent past, particularly in regards to the country's fifteen-year civil war. The intent is not to replace one 'false' history with another 'true' one, but to go against the grain of sanctioned forgetfulness, commonly referred to as "official amnesia." This cadre of experimentalists who dominate the public culture of art, documentary, and cinema have engendered a mission to challenge the dominant political and social discourses implicated by the Lebanese wars.[1] In a manner of speaking, this particular constellation of artists has kidnapped the historical record in an act of urgent sabotage. This provides a distinctly different approach to the spectacular and sensational reporting provided by

Western media. Critical of naturalized notions of cultural predispositions toward violence, this work embeds everyday anxieties within historical and political contexts which have been inscribed with temporal and spatial catastrophe (Chakar, *Catastrophic Space*). Indeed, much Lebanese experimental documentary produced during the last decade explores the everyday violence that permeates the social landscape and perpetuates a tyranny of uncertainty about the future.

This mode of critique is all the more significant considering its emergence during Lebanon's so-called "postwar era." While the usage of "post" engenders a periodization by marking moments of significant transition, the notion of a period of postwar peace has been rendered oxymoronic in the return of widespread bloodshed during recent years. Although not explicitly prophetic, the themes of unresolved trauma prefigure the political turmoil that has been unfolding since the 2005 assassination of former Prime Minister Rafiq Hariri and the 2006 Israeli invasion intended, albeit unsuccessfully, to dismantle Hezbollah's military apparatus. Indeed, Hezbollah has become more influential in domestic politics, partly by renewing 'wartime' political violence against opposition parties in May 2008. Even before these recent episodes, however, Lebanon's peace can better be characterized as a state of emergency kept in check by two occupying forces: Israel and Syria.

I should note that although I continue to use the term "postwar," I remain suspicious and antagonistic to the falsely forwarded premise that postwar means the end of violence. I retain this terminology precisely for its contentious ramifications, contradictory claims, and tired insufficiencies. Thus, my use of "post" is always issued as a critical prefix. When the Lebanese are celebrated as resourceful people, resilient in the face of despair, and playful despite bombardments, this "postwar" tendency bypasses the draining depression, horrific hopelessness, and virtual violence that Lebanese resilience must endure on a daily routine. Furthermore, as Beirut-based journalist Robert Fisk notes, the mythology of Lebanon's history is premised on a recurrent destiny of destruction and revival. North of Beirut at *Nahr al-Kelb* ("Dog River"), "inscriptions, steles, cuniform reliefs and plaques" commemorate 2500 years of conquesting armies, from Nebuchadnezzar II to the British army in 1941 (53). The Lebanese spirit of rejuvenation that is quick to say "Beirut will rise again" fails to mention that by the same premise it will likely fall again, too.

Indeed, the erasure of people in Lebanon is pervasive and multifaceted—from the 75-year-old census that has ossified the political demographics, to the half-million resident Palestinians refused citizenship and attending rights, to the 150,000 deaths during the civil wars, to the 18,000 disappearances, to the detainment of prisoners without legal recourse, to the occupation by foreign armies, to the millions of Lebanese living in exile, to those assassinated by bombings, to those massacres of mass victimization. Given such parameters, how does one write a history of recurrent violence? What are the connections between the historical discourses and the mundane lived experience of those who witness the demise of their social fabric? Can mimetic media resurrect the martyrs of the Lebanese wars? And can the representation of monstrous specters elucidate the invisible, unsayable, and unrepresentable postwar subjectivity?

By way of answer, this article examines the types of mediated subjectivities engendered by these experimental historiographies of unresolved trauma. I suggest that within Lebanon's catastrophic time and space, governed by selective amnesia, reproductive media has enabled the articulation of an imaginary world.[2] This is not a false or pretend world, nor is it an objective and factual one. Rather, this mediated world opens up vantage points for seeing parallel realities inhabited by phantoms and monstrous subjects. Faced with all these violent forms of disappearance, Lebanese experimental documentary has endeavored to reincarnate these latent bodies in order to break the official silence and collective amnesia that keeps the Lebanese distracted from collectively engaging the trauma of the past.

## Latent Pyromaniacs

Abdallah Farah is an imaginary photographer whose career begins during Lebanon's 'Golden Age' and extends into the recent postwar period. A creation of Joana Hadjithomas & Khalil Joreige[3] in their *Wonder Beirut: The Story of a Pyromaniac Photographer* installation series (1998-2006), audiences learn that Abdallah Farah began working in his father's photography studio in the mid-1960s. Located in downtown Beirut, Studio Wahed received an order from the Lebanese Tourism Agency to produce three-dozen images of Beirut for the official calendar and a series of postcards. These photographs were meant "to reveal the most beautiful tourist sites in Beirut" (*Homepage* n. pag.). In this case, the most beautiful sites are deemed to be the cinemas, souks, hotels, avenues, beaches, and banking district. In other words, "the city's modernity, its diversity and its richness" provide an iconography of photographic idealism (n. pag.). We are told that these same postcards can be found for sale today, "despite the fact that majority [sic] of the sites they represent were destroyed by armed conflicts and the Lebanese wars," thus implicating a postwar nostalgia for a bygone era (Chouteau, n. pag.).

During the Golden Era of the 1960s, the Lebanese Riviera had become a globalizing site of exchange through petroleum, finance, and leisure, described by Khalaf as "a nation of services [and] middlemen" (307). Inheriting the hybrid sensibilities of a colonized nation, plus the amalgamated identity of Muslim, Christian, and Jewish confessions, a modernizing and mediating Lebanon could accommodate both Arab customs and European exoticism. Often remembered as the "Paris of the Middle East" amid the "Switzerland of the Orient," Beirut's cosmopolitan history is deeply entangled in a decadent and violent past that precedes the civil war and implicates the duplicity of an 'other' Paris existing in ruins. Although the bikini-clad tourists and multicultural modernity of these images highlight an ideal Lebanon, this "prewar" period already bears the markings of a contrary political climate. In the wake of the 1967 six-day war between Israel and several surrounding Arab states (not including Lebanon), in which Israel occupied Gaza, Sinai, the West Bank, and the Golan Heights, political violence loomed large on the southern frontier. Sarah Rogers points out that in 1968 "the Israeli Army destroyed thirteen planes of Middle East Airlines (the Lebanese civilian airline) as they sat on the tarmac in retaliation for the activities of Palestinian commandos operating on the border" (12).

As for Studio Wahed, we are told that a fire destroyed it after the civil war broke out in 1975. However, Abdallah Farah did succeed in rescuing some of his negatives and hundreds of virgin film rolls, unshot and unexposed. "For an unexplained reason," Hadjithomas and Joreige say, "Farah kept quiet about embarking on a new venture. Three years after the start of the war, and a few months after his father's death, he began to damage his postcard negatives . . . as if seeking a way to have their states conform to his present" (*Homepage* n. pag.). On these images of Beirut, Farah would trace the destruction of the city by methodically burning the negatives "in accordance with the street battles and bombardments which were then in progress" (Chouteau, n. pag.). Farah's act of burning the negatives (systematic exposure) corresponds to the burning of the city. As described by Rogers, "The boils incurred on the surface of the photographs are at once symptomatic of the tensions underlying the city's image of modernity and parasitic of such representational coherency" (13). Furthermore, by burning the image it takes on textured qualities that ground the representation in its materiality and evoke an affective ephemerality, in which the image becomes stuck in the representational gap, neither allowed to stand for what it indexes, nor be fully available in its object form. This is further manifested in the way Hadjithomas and Joreige reproduce and distribute these altered postcards for sale at their exhibitions.

Chouteau remarks that the narrative about Farah's photographic experiments provides a coherency to the visual fragments. She says: "this commentary confers a documentary status upon the images," which in turn supports the believability of this "reasoned fiction" (Chouteau, n. pag.). Hadjithomas and Joreige expand the Farah narrative to examine the prospects of image-making under conditions of mass civil violence. Farah remains largely confined to his house throughout the war. Using the virgin film rolls salvaged from Studio Wahed, Farah takes photos of his neighbors and neighborhood. Without lab chemicals, Farah's photos remain undeveloped, waiting for a safer day to be printed. After the war he keeps the habit, satisfied just to shoot the photos—well, almost satisfied. Without a need to see these images again, "He nonetheless precisely documents each photograph he takes in a small notebook, describing it thoroughly. . . leaving an immense space for the imagination." Based on this propensity for written description, Farah calls his unexposed work the "image in the text" or the "invisible image" (*Homepage* n. pag.).

Cited on their website, the "critic" Pierre Ménard [sic] speaks admiringly of Farah's work, as "a subterranean body of work, endlessly heroic, unequaled, and, certainly, perpetually unaccomplished, a sublime attempt to capture each passing minute" (*Homepage* n. pag.). This intertextual reference to Jorge Luis Borges's "review" of a fictional author named Pierre Menard helps elaborate the Farah fantasy. According to Borges's fabulation, Pierre Menard is re-writing Cervantes's *Don Quixote* word for word, but from the vantage point of the twentieth century. This is not a mere copy according to Borges, but a work more "astounding" than the original. Indeed, in a comparison between Cervantes's and Menard's versions, it is the relationship between history and truth that Borges chooses to most closely analyze. "Historical truth," for Menard, like the Lebanese artists, "is not what took place; it is what we think took place" (Borges 49). Borges's review of Menard's *Don Quixote* thus challenges the authority of the text as well as the author, and grants more agency to the reader (or the reviewer as the case may be). This homage to Borges evokes an important interplay between fictional and non-fictional discourses, which is a central esthetic in Lebanese documentary artwork.[4]

Furthermore, the potential of unexplored narratives (whether fictional or not) relates to Hadjithomas and Joreige's notion of a latent image. Hadjithomas and Joreige provide this definition: "Latency is the state of what exists in a non-apparent manner, but which can manifest itself at any given moment. . . . Latency is the introduction to the possible, to the state of becoming" ("Latency" 40). In photography, a latent image is literally an image on an exposed film or print that has not yet been made visible by developing, so a "fundamental question remains" about "the revelation of these images." Hadjithomas and Joreige ask: "At what moment, and to what purpose, would Abdallah Farah choose to develop his films?" (*Homepage* n. pag.). Remarking on the fastidious notation by which Farah documents his unexposed images, Jalal Toufic considers this "a contribution to the resurrection of what has been withdrawn by the disaster" (*The Withdrawal of Tradition* n. pag.). Hélène Chouteau identifies this latent image, with force enough "to transform violence into critical freedom," as an "incarnate image." She says:

> To incarnate is not to imitate, reproduce, or simulate. The image is fundamentally unreal. To incarnate is to give flesh, not to give body. The image which gives body, which incorporates, is that which includes the other, without leaving the other space for thought. The incarnate image, however, contains three entities that are indispensable to each other: the visible, the invisible, and the gaze, which brings them into relation. (n. pag.)

**Mediated Subjectivity**

These postwar (or post-orientalist) esthetics[5] not only foster an awareness of constructedness, but also an affective experience of embodying the dislocation between the historical record and the sites of memory's acquisition. The contemporaneity, virtuality, and psychological qualities of this imaginary archival record suspend subjectivity within a mist of pixels and particles. This mediated suspension focalizes a viewer's perspective, not in the world of car bombs, snipers, and assassinations, but within a world of photography, filmmaking, and archival research—an imaginary world of documentary acquisition as the site of interpretation where history becomes fact. By giving attention to the medium rather than the representation, the archive and the historical record become the site of experimental historiography. This does not imply a corrective or a mission of telling the actual 'truth' of political violence. Instead, it endeavors to disenchant viewers' expectations about how to understand history and reenchant them with a way of mourning the present.

As articulated by Bazin several decades ago, photography "embalms time" in a way that reminds us of "the disturbing presence of lives halted at a set moment in their duration" (8). This metaphysical dislocation between sign and referent evokes the traumatic postwar experience. In other words, this artwork elucidates a mediated subjectivity that exists in chronological and geographical dislocation, in which the rupture of time and place approximates an experience of exile within one's own nation. The subsequent longing for "home" typically becomes contingent on an idealized nostalgia for the past, but it can also articulate the imagination of impossible futures. In the context of war and displacement, the temporal imaginary can have very different political underpinnings.[6] While experimental Lebanese documentary endeavors to critique the representational frameworks inherited by rational modes of objectivity, it also engenders new modalities for documenting the dislocation of Lebanon. Whether in exile or in residence, Lebanon exists as much as an idea, or an imaginary image, as it does in bodies, buildings, rubble, and dirt. So the creativity of these impossible narratives endeavors to rethink the relationship between the imaginary and the physical.

In the case of the pyromaniac photographer, Abdallah Farah, these representational moments exist in the time of an unstable archive rather than the time of the historical event. The archival object, displayed with annotation, asserts its authority as evidence, but the fictive narration accompanying the visual representation gives it a subversive pulse.[7] Like other fictive characters concocted in the Lebanese art world, Abdallah Farah's archival "documents" narrate and show an observational subjectivity, one obsessed with looking. This self-reflexive dimension implicates the production of historical content as culturally constructed instead of 'real.' If this were merely a critique of rep resentational veracity, then many other examples could be given from other contexts. Instead, we must also consider the way that these 'false' elements have the potential to reveal something taken for granted.

By affectively implicating the viewer in the contemporaneity of the media object rather than the indexical representation (i.e., a photograph or film negative rather than the image it bears), the viewer is drawn into the subject position of the author rather than into the contemporaneity of the historical moment. For in any documentary image, the immutable realness of the mimetic artifact hides an invisible author somewhere behind the lens. In another time, this image appeared for the first time in a viewfinder of a camera. So to put one's face in the 'same' image, to look through the screen, maintains the traces of the face behind the camera. This secondary viewing can evoke the gap between the witness and the document, a position exemplified by the archivist endeavoring to make sense of a fleeting moment recorded in the blink of a camera shutter. Giving attention to the archive of images shifts the authorial perspective from photographer to collector. In between these subject positions exists a liminal space where the differences between documented and undocumented remain undetermined. By subverting the promise of realism, this image also engenders an intersubjective experience of dislocation. The (absent) presence of these authors invites the viewer to witness an imaginary world where the disappeared can be mediated, but not necessarily imaged or rendered visible.

Like vampires, the phantoms of Lebanon's wars bear no reflection and they cannot be imaged directly. Indeed, the concept of mortality has emerged as an imperative issue in Lebanese experimental documentary and narrative film and video. For instance, Jalal Toufic's notion of the "undead," developed around his reading of vampire cinema, has taken literal formation in Ghassan Salhab's *The Last Man/Atlal* (2006), in which a city coroner is mysteriously linked to a series of nocturnal murders. And as we have begun to see, Joana Hadjithomas and Khalil Joreige have together written and produced films, videos, and installations around the concept of latency, evocative of an absent presence in both undeveloped film and postwar subjectivity. The phantom subjectivity of Hadjithomas and Joreige's latent themes, Ghassan Salhab's nocturnal world, and Jalal Toufic's ruinous anytime all mark a withdrawn subjectivity—both present and absent—embedded in the mediated object but never fully available. Accordingly, this article traces the mediation of latent subject positions in the work of these artists and filmmakers in an effort to reconsider the significance of postwar experimental media as a site for the incarnation of monstrous subjectivities. These mediated subjectivities have emerged in a context of horrifying violence and are not based on identities that correspond to victims or victimizers, but instead they have become phantasmic emblems of both the irrecoverability of objective traumatic experience and the nation's refusal to reconcile its past.

**Perfect Day**

In Joana Hadjithomas and Khalil Joreige's second feature film, *The Perfect Day/Yawmun akhar* (2005), the members of a Lebanese family each exist in some state of latency. Malek is a handsome, young professional with a sleeping disorder. Whenever he stops moving, Malek instantly falls asleep. He must stay distracted in order not to fall into a latent state of slumbering. Throughout the film, Malek is trying to contact his ex-girlfriend in a desperate desire for one "perfect day," but his nostalgia lulls him into sleep and she escapes as he slumbers. It is not slumber that distracts him in this case, but rather wakefulness. Although referencing the American film, *Groundhog Day* with Bill Murray, Toufic's notion of a "perfect day"—in a comment on the film—elucidates an anti-nostalgic temporality: "The perfect does not induce nostalgia" (*Forthcoming* 77). Toufic explains: "A man stuck in the same day tries to get released from it as it repeats itself a stupendous number of times, and he manages to do so only when at last he wills its eternal recurrence" (76). In other words, the non-subject does not desire delivery from the mundane or the recurrence of trauma, but accepts the state of limbo. In this sense, the perfect day for Malek does not mean obtaining some impossible future with his girlfriend, but rather the acceptance of her imminent departure. For Malek, willing the eternal return of the same day would also mean relinquishing his desire to be awake and instead to will the eternal return of sleep. Indeed, we never know what sort of promises the ritual of sleep provides for him; however, it is important to note that Malek's distracted state also enables him to fleetingly forget the unacknowledged death of his father who disappeared during the war. Or, perhaps, instead it is only in slumber, a state approximating death, that he is able to reunite with his father.

For Malek's mother, the perfect day is held at abeyance because she has not mourned her husband. She refuses to leave the house in case he might return. If mourning is the acceptance of loss, then not to mourn is a futile attempt to refuse the eternal return of trauma. This inevitable repetition only ends once the desire for this eternal loss is appropriated. But the distraction of Malek and his mother hint at a broader condition of postwar latency, a subjectivity that refuses the future because it has not accepted the past. It is Malek's father, however, who, having disappeared years earlier, (dis)embodies the state of latency as an absent presence—being one of 18,000 people who disappeared during the war and did not receive proper burial. For this reason he is not of the dead, but of the undead: a state of latency that exists in "a diffused state, uncontrollable, underground, as if lurking, as if all could resurface anew" (Hadjithomas and Joreige "Latency" 40).

The notion of the missing corpse is central to Hadjithomas and Joreige's short film, *Ashes/Ramad* (2003), which depicts the struggles of Nabil (played by Rabih Mroué) to honor his father's cremation request, while also orchestrating a façade to appease his extended family's expectation to have an open-casket viewing and burial. While poignantly presenting the struggle with social customs, *Ashes* evokes a powerful metaphor about the war's disappeared and society's inability to mourn without accounting for those missing corpses. This obsession with latency in Abdallah Farah's photography, Malek's sleeping condition, and the war's missing corpses, stems from the fact that Khalil Joreige's uncle disappeared during the war. Neither he nor his body was ever recovered: "He is still reported missing; and, the circumstances of his disappearance remain a mystery" (Hadjithomas and Joreige "Latency" 47). In 1995, a law was issued that defines the status of these disappeared people as "kidnapped," but after four years the family can petition to have the missing person declared deceased. Joreige points out that families in this situation face a difficult choice: "To declare someone dead without a trace, without the physical presence of a body, a corpse" (47).

Khalil's sister, Lamia Joreige, has also explored this traumatic site. Her documentary video, *Here and Perhaps Elsewhere* (2003), probes the social memory of kidnappings during the civil war, by confronting people along the "green line" and probing their memories.[8] Rather than an investigative journalism approach in search of the true story, her video reveals the multiplicity of reactions, not the least of which is the refusal to remember. Furthermore, those who choose to remember and talk with her do not provide coherent accounts, and her provocation confronts both the official amnesia and sectarian animosities that have persisted during the "postwar era," not to mention the harrowing traumas experienced by people on both sides of the green line.

Like Lamia's latent-witness accounts, Khalil warns that with latency and indeterminacy comes a "risk of loss . . . it constitutes the hope of something that will be revealed; the confrontation with a real that can be potentially disappointing" (Hadjithomas and Joreige "Latency" 47). He discusses the difficulty he faced when uncovering a latent 8mm film reel that his uncle had never developed. Khalil's uncle enjoyed amateur photography and filmmaking. This errant reel that lay dormant for fifteen years might have contained his last images; however, Khalil ponders for a long time whether to develop it, knowing "that this 'latent' image may reveal nothing, causing a disappointment, which would be impossible to compensate" (47). When he decides to develop it, the film comes out mostly blank, with a few shadowy images. But like the mourning for the dead, latency presupposes "the acceptance of being revealed and the risk of loss" (48). This acceptance means living with one's ghosts and longing for them. Hadjithomas and Joreige say that by being haunted they "do not succumb to cynicism in the acceptance of images and of realities in a continuous present" (48). Instead, their work explores questions about the convergence of the self, the social body, and the individual body "in a communitarian society . . . where it is difficult to pose oneself as an individual . . . a singular subject" (48).

**Monstrous Subjectivity**

As indicated by Hadjithomas and Joreige, it is necessary to problematize the idea of a singular subject in the context of Lebanon. In order to understand the manifestation of catastrophic subjectivity, it is useful to trace how the fragmentation of the singular subject stands in direct contradiction to the Liberal notion of subjectivity advanced by Enlightenment thinkers, in which "individuals are viewed as naturally free, rational, and equal and are assumed to have an interest in their preservation, their liberty, and their property" (Mehta 80). Under this framework, the pursuit of these interests requires "a superintending authority" to prevent a "*state of war*" (80). Given these parameters, Lebanon would seem to lack the authority necessary to ensure the liberty, rationality, and equality of Lebanese subjectivity. Considering the integral importance of institutions and technologies to mold and transform "the individual with strange passions, with a frenzied imagination, with undisciplined and chaotic urges . . . to be rational and self-interested (85); do we suppose a state of war would have the opposite effect: making unmolded and untransformed individuals? Or perhaps catastrophic space and time (e.g. a state of war) would produces subjects with strange passions, frenzied imaginations, and undisciplined urges instead? That is to say, subjects full of feelings.

In other words, liberalizing "institutions and technologies" are not capable of replacing the "strange" individual with a "rational" one, because this dualistic pairing at once assumes the exclusion of all others and confers onto subjects an either/or status established by a 'superintending authority.' To be sure, institutions and technologies may also mold and transform individuals in ways not deemed rational and self-interested. In the absence of a superintending authority during a state of war, what promise do institutions and technologies offer? In an age marked by the disintegration of the state and the rational subject, the intensified globalizing flows of media, capital, ideologies, and weapons, how have these affected people, institutions, and authority? This relationship can be traced in a variety of ways. In Lebanon's postwar era, several "institutions" have emerged as facilitators of Beirut's nascent bohemian culture. Largely dependent on funding from international foundations, the main contribution they provide is the creation of sites where the public can engage contemporary cultural production of Lebanese art, cinema, and scholarship. I participated in/attended several festivals and events sponsored by these institutions during the fall of 2005 and summer of 2009. However, in this article I am more concerned with the "technology" used for mediating between contested publics and divergent subjectivities.

I suggest that tracing the characteristics of mediated subjects in Lebanese experimental film and video may reveal a withdrawn subjectivity, one enacted by the virtuality of the medium and suggestive of the subject's ultimate absence. In fact, the mediation of latent subjects must assume a new model of subjectivity that does not presuppose the existence of a superintending authority, but instead grapples more directly with the state of war (catastrophic time and space) which produces types of subjectivities different than those articulated by liberal rationality. Since, in the context of Lebanon, the state of war is perpetually recurring even when not marked as such (e.g. civil war versus postwar); the strange and the violent exist with the rational and self-interested, how might we theorize the mediation of catastrophic subjectivity? One possible line of inquiry can be traced through the postmodern premise that the individual is a construct of capitalism, framed as the "death of the subject." Accordingly, the death of individualism also means the death of originality (as explained by Jameson). James Heartfield asks: "What if the free subjectivity at the core of our social order is all used up?" (10). In the context of western literature, Heartfield implies that "we" (European progeny) have exhausted our narratives. And even in "our" poaching from other cultures, we burden these elements of cultural difference by making them adhere to our tired ossified structures of telling and feeling. If the nineteenth century witnessed the emergence of the literary heroic human subject, then Heartfield declares its marginality and erasure in the twentieth century. This trend flows in the opposite direction to documentary films, in which Renov notes the increasing prevalence of autobiographical documentaries as an assertion of documentary subjectivity. This disparity makes one wonder if we are witnessing the transference of subjectivity from a primarily written medium to a primarily visual one, if not also from fictive embodiment to lived experience. Lebanese media art evokes both these trends, first, in the withdrawal of subjectivity and, second, in the reassertion of the personal in the face of social and political machinations.

In order to understand the ramifications of this trend, it is necessary to further trace the contemporary formations of morbid subjectivity. Rei Terada attempts to reclaim the self-divided subject as a norm by resisting a philosophy that might be nostalgic for the lost singular subject. In fact, she argues that there never were any subjects, that subjectivity in the rational self-knowing sense was a fiction (3-4). In American cold-war culture, this fiction manifests itself as the perfect consumer, that is, a zombie. Steven Shaviro shows that George Romero's "living dead" films, often with extended scenes in shopping malls, demonstrate that "the zombie is a nearly perfect allegory for the inner logic of capitalism" (84). In other words, "Capitalist expropriation involves a putting to death, and a subsequent extraction of movement and value—or simulated life—from the bowels of that death" (84). Devoid of affective intensities, the zombie is a consumer of intensities who even when attacked exhibits zero change in disposition, or as Terada puts it:

> The living dead emblematize postmodern subjectivity: everyone knows that if there's one thing dead subjects don't have, it's emotion. Actually things are the other way around. Romero's living dead are notably undivided about their desires . . . they are mere needs and compulsions . . . they are pure intentionality. (156)

The zombies with their pure intentionality are directional in only one direction at a time, whereas the non-subject as a "living system" is multi-directional, self-differential, and self-divided. "When critics literalize the 'death of the subject'" says Terada, "[t]he persistence of monstrous metaphors suggests that the non-subject—the functional but self-differential being—needs to be seen as someone else" (154).

This morbid subjectivity relates to Jalal Toufic's work on the (vampiric) "undead," but must be differentiated from Romero's (zombie) "living-dead."[9] Toufic's undead are tragically displaced phantoms caught in a cycle of abject violence, whereas "Romero's zombies seem almost natural in a society in which the material comforts of the middle class coexist with repressive conformism, mind-numbing media manipulation, and the more blatant violence of poverty, sexism, racism, and militarism" (Shaviro 83). Interestingly, the catastrophic context of postwar Lebanon produces both senseless zombies and sensitive vampires. Although both these monstrous figures can be characterized as parasitic consumers, the difference has more to do with the emotional state of each. The absence of emotion in the death-time of the zombie-subject is contrasted with the heightened emotional state of the vampire/non-subject.

Whether in a monstrous or deathly state, or mediated between documentary veracity and esthetics, anthropologists Veena Das and Arthur Kleinman provide an apt definition of subjectivity: "the felt interior experience of the person that includes his or her positions in a field of relational power" (1). In other words, the focus on affective qualities and power relations helps to situate the disaffected, but intensely-feeling, catastrophic subjects within a history of recurrent violence. Das and Kleinman argue that the occurrence of state pathologies happening every day requires a closer examination of the ordinary: "Is the ordinary a site of the uneventful, or does it have the nature of something *recovered* in the face of terrible tragedies?" (7; emphasis in original).

This relationship between affect and ordinary violence has significant implications for the manifestation of both zombies and vampires. The zombies, in a state of distraction, have "no conscious knowledge of the history from whence they come, are unable to mourn past wars, and are haunted by the images of the dead whom they have outlived" (Chouteau, n. pag.). Like Malek with the sleeping disorder in *A Perfect Day*, zombies live half-asleep in ever-recurring "imperfect" days, holding emotion in abeyance. In contrast, Terada evokes Philip K. Dick's treatment of "replicants," one of whom cries as she discovers she is not human, which indicates, "destroying the illusion of subjectivity does not destroy emotion . . . on the contrary, emotion is the sign of the absence of that illusion" (156-57). Since emotion is often experienced as an uncontrollable and unknowable eruption, an irrational state, the presence of emotion produces non-subjects, as subjects do not have emotions. As explained by Terada:

> Romero's zombies have no feelings *because they* are *subjects*. They do not represent the poststructuralist post-human; they represent the "death of the subject" in the strongly gen-

itive sense, the sense in which if there were subjects, they would have to be dead. (156; emphasis in original)

In other words, zombies are *non-feeling subjects*, while those who experience what Toufic calls a "surpassing disaster" are *feeling non-subjects*.

The antithesis of the zombie is then the unmaking of the subject, what Deleuze and Guattari would call a "body without organs." As Brian Massumi writes: "Think of the body without organs as the body outside any determinate state, poised for any action in its repertory; this is the body from the point of view of its potential, or virtuality" (70). In an inorganic and undetermined state of becoming, the non-subject is an intensely feeling body without organs. And yet, when building a body without organs but full of virtuality, one must be cautious of self-destruction. As Massumi says, the process of becoming-other engenders "the madness of the imagination" (108). Thus, Toufic's advancement of "undeath" ushers in unimaginable potentials—becoming a non-subject, becoming latent, becoming monstrous—before enabling the resurrection of imaginary memories that may or may not have occurred in the past, as a way to mourn the invisible and disappeared, if only by witnessing it askance (*(Vampires)* 169). After all, the disappeared, the undead, can never be imaged directly. So if the recovery of the ordinary within catastrophe, as advanced by Das and Kleinman, cannot be ascertained directly, then does the entrancement of peripheral vision (looking askance) allow viewers to see the ghosts in the walls of ruinous catastrophe? In order to represent the ordinary as something recovered from catastrophic conditions, must one strategically employ a narrative of uneventfulness to show the latent trauma even when it appears that 'nothing happens'?

**Ruins**

Originally included in Toufic's dissertation-turned-book, *(Vampires) An Uneasy Essay on the Undead in Film* (1993), his essay on "Ruins" has recurrently been reprinted in expanded form in various volumes on Lebanese experimental visual culture in 2002 and 2006 (twice).[10] In this essay, we learn how Toufic and his family deserted their apartment when fleeing the war. Toufic says that the act of desertion, rather than physical destruction, is what makes a place ruinous.[11] Neither its destruction nor its reconstruction affects its state of ruin. Ruins can be identified as "places haunted by the living who inhabit them," be they refugees or squatters inhabiting the damaged buildings or the vacant houses of dead owners ("Ruins," *We Can Make Rain* 8). As described by Hadjithomas and Joreige, ruins exist as both "[o]ccupied uninhabitable areas, and deserted habitable areas" (qtd. in "Ruins," *We Can Make Rain* 8). In contrast to the living haunting those ruins, the undead vampire does not inhabit the houses that s/he haunts, evidenced by his failure to appear in a mirror.

The "labyrinthine space-time" of these ruins, Toufic says, "undoes the date- and site-specific" ("Ruins," *We Can Make Rain* 9). He recounts the story of a woman who visited downtown Beirut on an architectural tour just after the war. On hearing the names of streets and buildings, the decimated city scene could not accommodate the mental map created from memories her parents had told. After the tour she had difficulty recalling the destroyed city, and it was only after several visits and noticing the presence of refugees living in the buildings that "she really felt that the destroyed city center was the reality" ("Ruins," *We Can Make Rain* 10). Commenting on the massive reconstruction of Beirut's Central District and its prerequisite bulldozing of much of downtown, Toufic calls this destruction "sacrilegious because of the brutal unawareness it betrays of the different space and time ruins contain" ("Ruins," *We Can Make Rain* 11). In fact, he suggests that this reconstruction exhibits the brutality of the war: "the war on the traces of the war is part of the traces of the war, hence signals that the war is continuing" ("Ruins," *We Can Make Rain* 11).

Several filmmakers and video artists have endeavored to address the current state of post-war recovery and dire economic recession, which filmmaker Ghassan Salhab describes in a personal interview as a crevice: "Beirut *is* a crack," one in which daily life cannot escape from a perpetual present; the past is irretrievable, the future unavailable. Every moment contains the potential for "radical closure," which denies access to temporal escape for the victims of history.[12] Under such conditions, the disappeared face a radical closure if they are forgotten (Toufic, *Forthcoming* 67). This is not a preservation of the past, but a recognition of its violence on the present. In other words, if it is accurate to say that the desire for the preservation of 'tradition' indicates that it is already withdrawn, then, according to Toufic, it is imperative to document the withdrawal rather than reconstruct a nostalgic vision of tradition. Furthermore, the withdrawn can be lost in a moment of radical closure if not acknowledged and documented. Toufic's work on the threat of a radical closure of memory represents the "irruptions" of withdrawn entities as a declaration that "they are not party to their desertion by the rest of the world" (*Forthcoming* 98).

Toufic uses the term "irruption" instead of "eruption" in order "to describe the sudden appearance of unworldly entities in radical closures," because the latter could be misunderstood as the breaking out of a rash or as a "return of the repressed" (*Forthcoming* 250, n. 49). Toufic argues that in the threat of a radical closure of memory, characters more accurately "irrupt" inside the images even while remaining withdrawn (69). The representation of withdrawn memory as an irruption in the image, in contrast, "does not do what memory otherwise often does: falsify, beautify, interpret; it does not even fool one into believing/feeling that the event happened an original time" (*(Vampies)* 10). Rather, the irruption of unworldly entities in Lebanese experimental film and video puts the authenticity of the image in doubt. To show the images as inaccessible would instead acknowledge the impossible referentiality that results in the wake of a disastrous ordeal, what Toufic calls a "surpassing disaster."[13]

For Toufic, the "undead" serve a critical purpose in the mediation of postwar society, they "come to prevent the world's desertion of those suffering a surpassing disaster from turning into a radical closure" (*Forthcoming* 70). The "undead," as an allegory for postwar subjectivity, builds its constitution in opposition to a particular fantasy about memory. This fantasy presents an imagined idea of how memory works without reliance on accuracy. Toufic writes: "To think and write about the dead as they were when still alive is already a forgetfulness of them—as undead" (*Forthcoming* 61). In other words, to remember them as alive is to forget that they are not. Re-*membering* these bodies, as if reconstituting a whole from its parts, suggests a false hope that they can be resurrected to a living state. This is the presumption which objective documentary theories make about evidence—that what is indexed is still available and actually exists. This is why the mediation of the undead is of critical concern to Lebanese documentary experimentalists faced with representing erased history and disappeared bodies. Toufic believes that artists who have experienced a "surpassing disaster" must acknowledge the "withdrawal of tradition" that occurs therein, that tradition "has effectively disappeared even in cases where it seems to have survived" (Colla 308). The resurrection of the undead in films is not a preservationist compulsion, but a desire to acknowledge the passing of traditional subjectivity. As such, Toufic connects the withdrawal of the referent (not as real but as another image) to the withdrawal of postwar subjectivity, which, as the result of witnessing a surpassing disaster, has had tradition withdrawn. In circumstances where one has suffered a surpassing disaster, Toufic warns: "one must be sensitive to the eventuality of the withdrawal, and, in the absence or failure of the resurrection of tradition, of the obligation to suspend transmission, so as not to hand down counterfeit culture" (*Forthcoming* 75).

Sensitive to this eventuality and the bad taste of "counterfeit culture," these experimentalist documentarians do not claim to depict reality, which would be invariably mis-represented and artificial; yet, the usage of fictive elements remains as 'real' as facts, documents, and historical archives for both the effects and affects they produce. In this regard, the undead enable Toufic to trace the process of depersonalization and disrupt the transmission of counterfeit culture. In such conditions threatened by radical closure, Toufic calls for a "relay between documentary and fiction" in order to address the withdrawal of a surpassing disaster. In settings that have experienced such a disaster, he warns: "fiction is too serious a matter to be left to 'imaginative' people" ("Ruins," *We Can Make Rain* 13). The ghost or vampire is fiction, not because it is an imaginative creation, but because fiction provides the "main loci for his appearance" (13). Toufic considers the absence of specters in the fiction of a postwar society to be a dangerous sign of collective amnesia.

In Lebanon, Ghassan Salhab provides the exception. Salhab's films explore the disaffected subjectivity of postwar Beirut haunted by phantoms, ghosts, and vampires. *Beyrouth fantôme/Ashbah Beyroot* (aka *Phantom Beirut*; 1998) tells the story of Khalil's mysterious return after disappearing during the war. Presumed dead for ten years, his old friends briefly sight Khalil (played by Aouni Kawas) coming from the airport, symbol of departure and return. Apparently, Khalil had faked his death to escape the war and now that the war is ending he tries to return to Beirut to reclaim his life, but the postwar moment does not provide the possibility of renewal he had hoped for. Furthermore, his friends resent him since they stayed and toiled through the senseless war. His sudden phantom-like appearance disrupts the fabric of their existence, and they begin to question their reality as well. When they confront him about the truth of his disappearance, his withdrawn emotional state provokes an intensified self-examination of their existentiality. While the non-subject is intensely emotional, its affect is withdrawn and seemingly dispassionate. Like Toufic's "vampire" subjectivity, he never reveals the violence of her/his emotions. These undead entities have been rendered mute, and yet their 'invisible' presence is evoked in the image, revealing their withdrawn absent presence.

As this experimental thriller unfolds, Salhab intercuts interview segments with the cast commenting on the film's narrative, creating a multi-diegetic approach for reacting to the war. These self-referential 'documentary' moments bear witness to the experience of war and survival characterized by fleeting encounters with phantoms from the past and ever-present uncertainty about the future. In effect, we have stepped outside the story of Khalil and into the history of postwar Lebanon. Nearing the end of the film, "in a symptomatic structural mistake," Khalil is mistaken for someone else and kidnapped, which reveals him as a phantom of "objective chance" ("Ruins," *We Can Make Rain* 15, n. 9). In other words, his return to the world of the living was a fluke; his fate had already been determined, so his abduction also serves as a rescue mission if it delivers him from the immortality of never ending undeath.

Salhab again actualizes Toufic's vampiric vision in his latest feature film, *The Last Man* (*Atlal*: "ruins"). Khalil Shams (Carlos Chahine) is a physician participating in the autopsies of a recent number of victims drained of their blood. Shams begins to connect himself to the victims, and suspects that he is responsible for their deaths, but this process happens slowly, and he seems unaware of the violence that he has been enacting on the city's residents until late in the film. Meanwhile, periodic news blurbs announce fatalities in Palestine and Iraq, thus linking Shams's vampiric violence to colonial occupation and guerrilla resistance. Furthermore, his traversal between the sterile environment of the hospital, juxtaposed with the dank streets, suggests the rupture of false boundaries. Intertextual boundaries are also traversed with the inclusion of cameo appearances. Jalal Toufic appears as a psychiatrist Shams is supposed to consult about his malaise and Aouni Kawas (the Khalil from *Beyrouth fantôme*) serves as the Lestat-figure (Quilty n. pag.), i.e., the vampire responsible for Shams's affliction.

Khalil Shams, literally "the companion of the sun," is an ironic name for a character who becomes a nocturnal vampire and feels repulsed by the sun. Engulfed by the darkness of the night, Salhab's film reveals a "concealed space that slowly swallows [Khalil Shams]" (Chakar, "F**k the Sun," 71). Shams enters a new world, suffocating and underworldly, in which he becomes increasingly withdrawn. Disinterested in his friends and avoiding his lover, he finds solace in the recurrent scuba dives into the coastal city's underworld. Above ground, rain, darkness, and loneliness increasingly engulf his world. Retreating from the light and the distracted people living in the sun, the vampire becomes "a metaphor for the extreme isolation of individuals, and their perpetual fight to remain individuals" (Chakar 71). The way Salhab's film traverses catastrophic space and time actually bears witness to the process of depersonalization in postwar Lebanon.

Indeed, Toufic's use of vampires—the undead—is not reducible to mere literalization (see Colla). Likewise, the fragmented existence of postwar survival is a notion Toufic would consider oxymoronic. To experience an event as a surpassing disaster does not allow for escape. The notion of escaping with one's life means of course to experience one's ultimate death. As such, according to Colla:

> [Jalal Toufic] would insist that he is not using a metaphor in describing the experience in that way since what has happened is an actual change in experience: a different state of mind has come into place, one which is not unlike how vampires would be if they existed or as (for Toufic) they do exist in the survivors of the [Lebanese] Civil War or other disasters. (315, n.8)

Toufic sees communities as defined by the disasters they have survived. As Colla comments: "Toufic suggests paradoxically that the heart of community and culture is a recognition of loss. . . . It may appear that some people and objects actually survive a catastrophe. The fact is they do not, because what survives the catastrophe is no longer what was before the event" (308). Furthermore, witnessing the process of becoming a non-subject, a body without organs, reveals a double violence: first, having to bear witness to an originary violence; second, withdrawing from the violence by the repetition of its representational occurrence. Acknowledging the withdrawn requires one to confront the deep violence of mourning for one's vampires.

**Entranced By Toufic**

Despite the latent violence of the vampire, Toufic seems principally concerned with those who have witnessed a surpassing disaster without necessarily perpetrating it, but he would insist that even a perpetrator must be revealed as withdrawn by his own violence. Unlike the zombie, the undead subjectivity is conditioned on the repetition of loss in martyrdom. Accordingly, the mediation of withdrawn subjectivity must provide an examination of the mundane rhythms of violence and the ordeal of the ordinary. This type of examination engenders the sites of everyday lifeworlds with the vitality of self-mediation and the empowerment of the incarnate image.

As pointed out by Boris Groys, Toufic's videos lead the viewer to feel like a witness of a ritual. This is literally the case with Toufic's pieces on the Shi'a tradition of *'Ashura*, which commemorates the mourning of Imam Hussein ibn 'Ali.[14] Groys notes the more private rituals mediated in *The Sleep of Reason*, which uses long extended takes of sleep followed by the slaughtering of cattle. Groys writes: "The ability to reveal the inner complicity between ritual and the medium of video is one of the reasons Toufic's videos so powerfully capture the imagination of the viewer" (83). These rituals are neither true nor false, neither sacred nor profane; they are rituals of the mundane. While characterizations of war are typically spectacular or traumatic, catastrophic time and space is more often filled with the tedium of the mundane. And it is here that the certainty of monotony interacts with the anxiety of uncertainty.

Toufic's 2005 short video, *The Lamentations Series: The Ninth Night and Day*, subverts time to enact a feeling of eternity. For "sixty minutes,"[15] we watch a continuous shot of a *'Ashura* rite of self-flagellation. In endless repetition, the men swing their arms up to beat their chests in "a ritualized striking of one's body in grief"--known as *latm* (Deeb 131).[16] After about a minute, the video slows to a fraction of its normal speed as we watch the same ritual scene unfold. Several minutes later, the viewer cannot help but become entranced by a single man staring directly at the camera. The rhythm of this commemorative self-flagellation at extremely slow speeds gives way to a slower, more latent rhythm of entrancement. While his compatriots remain entranced by the mourning ritual, this transfixed man, entranced by the camera, looks into the eyes of the audience, captivating them in the entrancement of a staring contest. Noting the acknowledgements to Shi'a Imams who had given Toufic permission to film, one Lebanese artist commented to me that the man was probably instructed to keep an eye on Toufic. Since his eyes never leave Toufic, does suspicion arise? If so, in what way does Toufic's video camera mediate this trance to viewers? While the man on screen is forced to repeat this entrancement regardless of audience, the audience can try to refuse the hypnotic trance. In fact, it is common to see people walk out of Toufic's screenings in frustration, exclaiming, 'Nothing happens!' The reader should recall the earlier discussion about affect and ordinary violence, that it is precisely this sense of uneventfulness that enables the audience to see catastrophic subjectivities.

But what is the Shi'a man really looking at in his gaze? Is he looking at Toufic? Is he looking at us? No, he is looking at the camera. Of course, the camera is also looking at him and Toufic is looking at him through the camera. The camera is an object that engenders a nexus of gazes all transfixed by the mimetic magic of the reproduction machine. Indeed, as Toufic asks: "In what state may I feel that an object is gazing at me? Vice versa in trance, when an object gazes at me, either I enter into trance or this indicates that I am already entranced" ("Saving Face" 9). In a much different context, the anthropological filmmaker Jean Rouch has described his work on spirit possession as a choreography of entranced participation: "it is the 'film-trance' (ciné-transe) of the one filming the 'real trance' of the other" (DeBouzek 304-05). Given the parameters of the spirit world with "fragile mirrors," Rouch asserts: "the observer's presence can never be neutral" (7). While Rouch's ethnography is characterized as a collaborative and shared anthropology, Toufic's recording of the *'Ashura* mortuary rite suggests a more detached state that activates an entranced state of suspicion.[17] This entranced intersubjectivity implicates the viewer in the realm of suspicious complicity.

The magical ability of the image to captivate audiences is inextricably implicated in the 'soul'-stealing modernity of the nineteenth and twentieth centuries; however, these artists of a post-orientalist digital age draw on multiple registers of mimetic layering to participate in the revoicing, or remediation, of these 'captivity' narratives. As Groys indicates, the repetitive reproducibility of video enables Toufic to reveal the ritual protagonists "in a state of ecstasy, or in sleep, or in a mood of deep mourning. . . . The video image is the moving icon of the unmoving and invisible digital code," so foregrounding a deep connection between mediation and ritual enables video's hidden digital data to visualize the invisible, to render visible the "invisible God" (83). The mechanical reproduction of the dead image and its loss of aura constitute, to borrow the terms of Benjamin, "the most radical religious experience under the conditions of modernity" (Groys 84). For Toufic who has become *entranced* by postwar esthetics, the repetition of ritual and video provides the possibility of rearticulating the deferral of the loss.

## Shahīd Subjectivity

Consider the representations of martyrdom made by militia groups before their suicidal missions in the context of repetition and withdrawn subjectivity. Performance artist Rabih Mroué and novelist Elias Khoury addressed this issue in their video-performance entitled *Three Posters*

(2000). Mroué explains how the practice of videotaping martyr testimonials would be screened on the evening news after they had executed their missions. Because government-run Tele-Liban was the only operating TV station in Lebanon, the majority of Lebanese remember this as a singular element in the finality of death. Mroué and Khoury obtained the "uncut rushes" of a fourteen-year-old testimony made by Jamal El Sati, a combatant for the National Resistance Front in Lebanon. Disguised as a local sheikh, El Sati loaded a donkey with explosives, and detonated it at the headquarters of the Israeli military governor in Hasbayya.

In the rushes of El Sati's martyr testimonial, he repeats his testimony three times, making slight changes in each version. Although the differences between the versions may be inconsequential, the repetition of the rehearsal signals an awareness that the testimony had more significance than the actual mission, as a final statement of his manhood and humanity before leaping into the void of radical closure. Yet these televised testimonials recurring on the nightly news engulfed individual identity in the seriality of forgetting—in which case, the official celebration of collective death in the name of ideological slogans quickly slips into amnesia. By recouping this repeated testimony, the artists obstruct the commemoration of heroic death and reveal the human being, who, even in the preparation for death, has accepted the responsibility of representation. This footage reveals the space-time of the undead, the liminal state between El Sati's testimonial rehearsal and the explosion. This deferred testimony must bear the weight of a corpse, because, as Mroué reminds us: "We know the body of the fighter will never be found. He has disappeared" (117).

This example can be used to reconsider the notion of withdrawn subjectivity under the slightly different terminology of shahīd subjectivity. *Shahīd* is Arabic for martyr. My use of this term is meant to disabuse the understanding of the term "martyr" which often exoticizes the Islamic "orient," conflating it with *jihad* terrorism. It is also meant for precision of meaning: A martyr is one who dies for his/her cause, but a *shahīd* is a witness, one who bears witness. In the context of Toufic's theoretical terrain, I mean "shahīd subjectivity" to imply a martyr who has 'witnessed' a surpassing disaster and must confront the repetition of loss. Here I am drawing upon Chris Harker's critical engagement with Jayce Salloum's video *untitled part 1: everything and nothing* (2001), which features an extended conversation with Soha Bechara, imprisoned after a failed assassination attempt on Antoine Lahad, the leader of the South Lebanon Army, which served as Israel's proxy force during its occupation of Lebanon 1982-2000. After her release from 10 years of imprisonment, Bechara emerged as a spokesperson for the Lebanese resistance against Israeli occupation. Her status as a spokesperson of the resistance is partly based on her status as a 'living martyr,' someone who was held in captivity and tortured, but who did not ultimately perish. Drawing on Giorgio Agamben's thesis on witnessing, Harker connects Bechara's experience to that of a Holocaust survivor who can recount the horrors witnessed on the brink of death. Bechara "speaks for those who 'touched the bottom' and therefore cannot bear witness to what they went through" (55).

In Toufic's parlance, Bechara is not a postwar survivor, but among the undead. Her subjectivity has been withdrawn. Her awareness of this marks the intense affective quality of her non-subject status. Of course, as a living martyr, she has 'witnessed' her own death as a surpassing disaster, but remains among the living as a withdrawn subject and thus a spokesperson for the dead. Since there is no language to describe the horror of touching bottom, a non-survivor can only experience it mediated through the undead. Based on deep intimacy with withdrawn subjects, Lebanese video experimentalists establish a fleeting bond between the undead and the viewer in an intersubjective space of witnessing personal and collective violence (Harker 52).

Laleh Khalili convincingly argues that choosing to use "*shahīd*" over "martyr" privileges the status of victim while downplaying the martyr as a self-sacrificing fighter (141). Nevertheless, it is not my intention to privilege either the role of witness or perpetrator of injustice. On the contrary, the double nature is crucially important for understanding the monstrosity of the undead, particularly in the context of Lebanon, where postwar amnesty has let killers and ghosts roam the streets together. Indeed, the evil of this violence requires that we do not give in to an urge to valorize the undead, rather the undead require both mourning and public trial. It is unclear what a public trial of Bechara would achieve as she is locally valorized as a hero. Nevertheless, regardless of my political agenda, I cannot deny that Bechara transformed herself into a (potential) killer. I am not interested in analyzing motives, but rather understanding the effects of becoming ensnared in a cycle of abject violence. My interest here is not to make claims about the relationship between martyrdom and suicide bombing (see Asad), martyrdom and national commemoration (see Khalili), martyrdom and lamentation rituals (see Deeb), or even martyrdom and *sumud*, steadfastness, and *zahaq,* weariness (see

Allen). While these vectors certainly intersect with any reference to Islamic martyrdom (even though the Greek Orthodox Bechara was a member of a secular party), my interest here is one of representation, or more precisely mediation, of death and mortality.

I am explicitly interested in how these monstrous subjectivities become mediated by Lebanese artists and what these figures mean for an emergent but precarious public culture faced with a traumatic past, residual violence, and political erasure. Although there is a strong trend in Lebanese visual culture that attempts to elucidate loss, this is not an effort to make visible what is invisible, nor to recover what has been lost. Rather, it is an attempt to recognize the loss that has been denied. In this way, it is a process of mourning, a lamentation enacted through video and photography. Mediation is the ritual, the camera is the fetish object, and the images are the ghosts and phantoms of the witnesses and martyrs ensnared in the cycle of violence haunting Lebanon and the broader region for several decades. These artists employ postwar esthetics of withdrawal and latency to engender representations of unacknowledged specters forcibly silenced by the state apparatus and social prohibitions. Although the engineers of distraction banish these afflicted phantoms to invisibility, the undead secretly spread their affliction throughout society. These subjectivities irrupt in Lebanese experimental film and video in ways that remark on the latent violence still invisibly walking the streets of Beirut. In other words, among the undead are militiamen whose amnesty has not provided them with redemption, confining them to stalking darkened avenues and government buildings. Based on the definitions of witnessing provided earlier, mass murderers and militiaman are the ultimate witnesses of suffering, able to kill *and* live to tell about it. But if the undead cannot name the dead , we must ask how the guilty bears witness against himself or herself and what evidence the murderous body provides besides a confession.

This issue arose in the controversial screening of *Massaker* (2005), featuring several Maronite Phalangist militiamen who recount the way they perpetrated the massacre of Palestinian refugees in Sabra and Shatila in 1982. Their stories tell of friends bonding in times of crisis in an effort to humanize these killers. The claustrophobic space of their interview locations emulates the simplistic emptiness of an interrogation room, but these men refuse to be hated, and regret is largely absent from their testimonies. Through one stretch of interviews, the filmmakers show the militiamen photographs taken of corpses strewn in the streets after the massacre. The decision to include this evidentiary device was no doubt made to provoke the men's emotions for the camera. Remarkably, these horrific images hold little emotive intensity for these men, or at least not visibly so. According to Toufic's criteria, *Massaker* fails to acknowledge the withdrawal of these killers' affect. Showing them photographs of their victims reveals a false expectation that the images will provoke an irruption.

These men are victims too—of lost innocence—fallen to sectarian distraction and desire for killing. Perhaps the undead thirst for resurrection because they have not been mourned. Perhaps they thirst for judicial closure because their crimes have been ignored. Perhaps the threat of radical closure compels them to thirst for life, to thirst for blood, because they are not regarded as withdrawn by popular discourse. Until the undead can be put to rest, they will further compel violence. My reading of subjectivity and non-subjectivity, juxtaposing zombies/living-dead with vampires/undead, should not delimit the range of other possible postwar subjectivities. Such categories are both slippery and contradictory, and their assigning becomes tenuous in the dislocated space/time of catastrophe. Nevertheless, these representations provide a generative effort to talk about the various forms of violence conjured in the act of bearing witness in postwar societies.

**Vitality of Mediation**

For Jalal Toufic, the unconscious acceptance of the ontological link between model and image remains powerfully in play. He attributes this belief not to its realism, but to the laws of magic, particularly "contiguity and similarity" (see Mauss). Images have a very important relationship to the ghostly figure of the undead as the magic of mimetic technology provides the only means for revealing evidence of these ghostly figures. The evidence produced does not adhere to a 'realist' paradigm, but rather this medium engenders the incarnation of a latent imaginary. Put another way, if one is distracted by dominant discourse of 'official amnesia,' s/he will not be able to see the ghosts roaming the streets. The incarnate images provide media with a vitality capable of resurrecting the dead even at the risk of grave disappointment, as discussed earlier in the context of undeveloped film rolls.

Hamid Naficy suggests: "For such a person [a deterritorialized filmmaker] mediation is somehow life itself" (217). By intimating at the vitality of media, Naficy identifies an affective relationship between filmmakers and their tools of mediation. Unfortunately, Naficy does not elaborate on the way mediated vitality informs larger social conditions of displacement, violence, and politicized forms of othering. In the context of Lebanese experimental documentary, I offer five possible explanations for why Naficy ascribes this 'vital' attribute to 'accented' esthetics. First, the micro-ritualization of the moment provides simple joy in its experience, like a tourist, while answering the "demand to activate all the senses" (Löfgren 98). Second, one is compelled by a sense of duty to bear witness to the disappeared and occupied. Third, there is a desire to replace tired and ossified narratives with alternative imaginary ones. Fourth, one maintains belief in resurrection or hope in psychoanalytic recovery. Finally, fifth, one becomes entranced by mediation.

If we consider how "media are not merely conduits for social forces, or expressive of social realities, but possess logics and power that are constitutive of thought, identity, and action" (McLagan 605), then the vitality of mediation should translate to audiences in particularly significant ways. The circulation of these sensibilities through 'new media' and 'small media' and their ability to embody, act upon, and think through contemporary forms of social disempowerment present an important context for understanding connections between personal agency and public expression.

The vitality of mediation signals the latent images of Hadjithomas and Joreige's unexposed rolls of film, the incarnate image of nocturnal ruins of the undead, and the repetition of video ritual; but one is compelled to ask why take a photograph of an image if never to develop it? This freezes the image before it becomes a representation; it cannot be represented but by the material reference to drawers full of film spools—media objects in a latent state. Representation is revealed, not as the mimetic image, but by the materiality of its mediation, not as a photograph, but as a spool of latent images. Trapping the magic of mimesis in invisibility corresponds to both the virtuality of digital information and the invisibility of undead subjectivity.

By mediating subjectivity, demarcating thresholds of referentiality, these works invite the viewer into an embodied experience of contemporaneity and intersubjectivity. The documentary experimentalist invites the viewer to see, not through her/his eyes, but through the camera-eye. The urge to collect, archive, and comment upon the constructed nature of media is pervasive in Lebanese postwar esthetics. The impulse to record and collect one's social, cultural, and political experience represents a strange sort of vitality in the act of resistance to radical closure, a vitality based not on life *per se* but on the deferral of loss in order to reclaim it without denying its inherent absence.[18] As stipulated by Walid

Sadek's words in the opening epigraph, "this invitation to meet the corpse" is not about embracing materiality, or a return to familiar corporeality, but it is about embracing virtuality, the ephemerality of digital media which is tangibly available, but still nameless and unrecognizable as virtual data. This invitation does not narrate the legacy of the defeated and victimized, but marks the endless ruination and constant risk of historical withdrawal. Thus, the commitment to reproductive media, albeit critical and suspect, provides a practice for reincarnating the disappeared and engendering a vitality in the face of incessant destruction.

## Notes

[1] The political violence that mired Lebanon from 1975 to 1990 is typically referred to as the Lebanese civil war. Following the critique of many Lebanese intellectuals and artists, I find this phrasing problematic. First, the hostilities involved both regional and international players, which greatly challenges the Muslim vs. Christian framing that this war usually elicits. Second, the shifting alliances and periods of intensity and lull in addition to another civil war in 1958 and the continued hostilities since the 1990s challenge this clean packaging.

[2] Here, I am engaging recent work on the 'imaginary' (see Taylor) to apprehend aspects of identity construction, community formation, and expressions of trauma in emergent public culture. As a generative means for negotiating personal agency and realms of possibility, I also draw upon Appadurai's usage of imagination. Combining three concepts of image, he elucidates the imagination in social life: "the mechanically produced images (in the Frankfurt School sense); the idea of the imagined community (in Anderson's sense); and the French idea of the imaginary (imagnaire), as a constructed landscape of collective aspiration" (31).

[3] In this article, I engage with several members of Beirut's cultural scene. Joana Hadjithomas and Khalil Joreige work as a team on narrative, documentary, and experimental films and videos as well as produce art installations. They taught film at Université Saint Joseph in Beirut and inspired many younger filmmakers. They are now based between Beirut and Paris. Lamia Joreige is a documentary and experimental video artist. She trained at the Rhode Island School of Design, before returning to Beirut. She recently opened the Beirut Art Center as a premiere exhibition space in Beirut. Rabih Mroué has acted in many Lebanese films and videos, but is best known for his work that incorporates both photography and video into performance pieces. Jalal Toufic has both Palestinian and Iraqi parent-

age. During the civil war, his family fled Lebanon to the United States where he studied and taught film theory before returning to Beirut. A prolific writer and artist, he now teaches in Istanbul. Born in Senegal, Ghassan Salhab moved to Lebanon in 1970, where he spent much of the war years. Working in both narrative and experimental film, his work gives expression to the postwar milieu. Jayce Salloum is not part of this same scene. This Canadian-Lebanese artist is based in Vancouver, but much of his work has engaged with Lebanon and Palestine. After the end of the civil war, he stayed in Lebanon for a year to work on projects and offer workshops for a recovering art scene. Monika Borgmann is a German woman with a background in journalism who runs the UMAM Documentation and Research Center with her Lebanese husband, Lokman Slim. In addition to creating an archive about the wars in Lebanon, they have conducted several interviews with people involved in the war, which they use as the basis for documentary film projects.

[4] There are other interesting connections between Borges's piece and the story of Farah, such as the connection between the burning of photographic negatives and the burning of manuscript drafts. Menard assiduously burned his failed versions, "not one page of a rough draft remain to bear witness to this work of years" (Borges 46).

[5] I have argued that the poetics and politics of documentary and narrative cinema in postwar Lebanon articulate a Post-Orientalist esthetics that pushes Said's critique of orientalism and of historical representation into new domains (see Westmoreland).

[6] While contemporary artists engender practices of mourning for a present trauma, the Lebanese context is not easily recouped by recent reassessments of nostalgia. For instance, where Nauman Naqvi critiques the "critique of nostalgia" for supporting an ideology of progress, he too easily generalizes this to scenarios of postcolonial resistance. The idea that indigenous resistance can draw upon precolonial memories is a point well taken, but nostalgic discourses in Lebanon are not reducible to a colonial context, and they often obfuscate the national problems that existed previously and remain unaddressed. Nostalgia is not necessarily a critique of progress as Naqvi suggests. Instead, nostalgia may be the progenitor of particular discourses of progress. For instance, while many Lebanese may 'innocently' long for times since past, nostalgic discourses have also been appropriated by neoliberal reconstruction projects and amnesiac political elites. Nevertheless, the importance of mourning in Lebanon is palpable as is envisioning futures that break from ossified narratives.

In this regard, Peter Fritzsche's important work on the French Revolution, which convincingly articulates a relationship between melancholy and modernity, provides a useful way to recoup the sense of loss in the transition to modernity. This model, however, cannot be haphazardly applied to twentieth-century Lebanon. Whereas Fritzsche suggests that the eighteenth century produced a new sense of the individual partaking in the drama of a linear history, if anything, Lebanese artists discussed here articulate the way the individual has become subsumed within the circularity of history.

7 For more on the interplay between image and text, particularly the tensions generated in the genre of ekphrasis (the verbal representation of visual representation), see W. J. T. Mitchell's *Picture Theory*.

8 The "green line," which divided the city during the civil war, runs from the city center eastward down Damascus Road.

9 In a jab at the ivory tower, Toufic has said that he "has more affinities with the 'un-dead' and the vampires of cinema than with the 'living-dead' who populate much of academia" (Bensmaïa and Toufic 15).

10 The 2006 versions are accompanied by French and German translations.

11 Toufic's ideas about ruins can be partially linked to Riegl's work on the "monument," particularly the deserted age-value monument. While Riegl defines these monuments based on "the passage of a considerable period of time," Toufic expands this usage to account for modern ruins in which age does not account for their ruinous quality (Riegl 24). Nevertheless, Riegl already recognized in 1902 (when the article was originally published) that "all artifacts of the past are irrecoverable" (22).

12 Toufic's concepts and understanding of catastrophe relates to the post-traumatic, postwar existence in Lebanon in which he grew up, before leaving with his mother and siblings during the 1982 Israeli invasion. This also points to the larger catastrophes experienced by the Palestinians as well as many others in the region.

13 Although not developed here, one should note the way that Toufic's nuanced terminology relates to particularly charged socio-political registers, like the Palestinian *Nakba* (the catastrophe of 1948) and Shi'a occultation. For instance, the abstract use of "surpassing disaster" to generalize social trauma can be read as a refusal to privilege either Lebanese or Palestinian suffering and discourses of national victimization. As for his use of a "withdrawn" status, this alludes to the occultation of the vanished Imam, the Mahdi, in Shi'a tradition. It is believed that this messianic figure will remain hidden until he returns to bring

justice to the world. One could make an interesting connection to Walter Benjamin's messianic materialism, in which the proletariat masses lead a cataclysmic revolution to end history (see Benjamin). I thank *Alif*'s anonymous peer-reviewer for elucidating these points.

14 Hussein, the grandson of Prophet Muhammad and the third Imam in the Shi'a tradition, was killed in battle after challenging the Umayyad caliphate as a corrupt entity. In the Battle of Karbala (680 CE), a large army ambushed Hussein ibn 'Ali and his followers, beheading all the men and imprisoning the women and children. Shi'a Muslims commemorate Hussein's martyrdom on the tenth day of the Islamic month of Muharram, known as *'Ashura*.

15 The movie only lasts about half an hour, but several listings accessed by the author erroneously say sixty minutes. I suspect that this is intended to challenge people's expectations of cinematic time.

16 The *'Ashura* ritual has faced various attempts for reform. As recounted by Lara Deeb, this commemoration practiced in Nabatieh in southern Lebanon is attended by many men with blood flowing down their faces from self-afflicted wounds; in the suburbs of Beirut *fatwas* (religious decrees) have discouraged bloodletting (129-64).

17 The differences between the Songhay spirit possession and the Shi'a ritual of lamentation are important and cannot be categorized solely on the comparison between Toufic and Rouch. Nevertheless, the differences and similarities between the filmic practices of Toufic and Rouch are ripe for comparative analysis. Rouch is the only anthropological filmmaker I know of who has discussed the intersubjective relationship between filming and ritual.

18 By way of comparison with artists cited in this article, Group Tuesday—an informal Lebanese think tank consisting of Walid Sadek, Bilal Khbeiz, and Fadi Abdallah—also considers the image suspect, but the potentiality of mimetic tools nevertheless sustains their critical commitment to the visual. Critical of the image and its representational presumptions, these artists prefer to write their witness accounts. Sadek says: "What we try to do when we write is slow images down. We try to give them weight. We experience, we who live in the third world, that to be in an image, to be photographed, is almost like a death warrant. But we are equally uneasy about standing behind the lens. We work and live somewhere between the lens and the photograph" (qtd. in Wilson-Goldie 27).

**Works Cited**

**A. Texts Cited**


Agamben, Giorgio. *Remnants of Auschwitz: The Witness and the Archive.* NY: Zone P, 1999.

Allen, Lori A. "The Polyvalent Politics of Martyr Commemorations in the Palestinian *Intifada*." *History and Memory* 18 (2006): 107-38.

Appadurai, Arjun. "Disjuncture and Difference in the Global Cultural Economy." *Public Culture* 2 (1990): 1-24.

Asad, Talal. *On Suicide Bombing*. NY: Columbia UP, 2007.

Bazin, Andre. "The Ontology of the Photographic Image." *Film Quarterly* 13 (1960): 4-9.

Benjamin, Walter. "The Work of Art in the Age of Mechanical Reproduction." *Illuminations: Essays by Walter Benjamin*. NY: Schocken, 1969. 217-51.

Bensmaïa, Réda and Jalal Toufic. "Recommending Deleuze—in 1998!" *Discourse* 20.3 (1998): 4-16.

Borges, Jorge Luis. "Pierre Menard, Author of *Don Quixote*." *Ficciones*. Ed. Anthony Kerrigan. NY: Grove P, 1962. 42-51.

Chakar, Tony. "Catastrophic Space: An Audio Tour through East Beirut." <http://www.partizanpublik.nl/catastrophicspace/site.html>.

__________. "F**k the Sun: A Journey into Beirut's Dark Side." *Bidoun: Arts and Culture from the Middle East 9* (2007): 71.

Chouteau, Hélène. "Ah, Les belles images! … Imagining and Describing War." *Les belles images*. Clermont-Ferrand: La Tôlerie, espace d'art contemporain, 2006. <ecoledumagasin.com/IMG/pdf/ah_les_belles_image_-cdp.pdf>.

Colla, Elliott. "The Image of Loss: Jalal Toufic's Filmic Beirut." *Visual Anthropology* 10 (198): 305-17.

Das, Veena and Arthur Kleinman. Introduction. *Violence and Subjectivity*. Ed. Veena Das et al. Berkeley, Los Angeles, & London: U of California P, 1997. 1-18.

DeBouzek, Jeanette. "The 'Ethnographic Surrealism' of Jean Rouch." *Visual Anthropology* 2.3-4 (1989): 301-15.

Deeb, Lara. *An Enchanted Modern: Gender and Public Piety in Shi'i Lebanon*. Princeton and Oxford: Princeton UP, 2006.

Fisk, Robert. *Pity the Nation: Lebanon at War*. Oxford: Oxford UP, 1992.

Fritzsche, Peter. *Stranded in the Present*. Cambridge, MA: Harvard UP, 2004.

Groys, Boris. "Ritualizing Life: Videos of Jalal Toufic." *Art Journal* 66 (2007): 83-84.

Hadjithomas, Joana, and Khalil Joreige. *Joana Hadjithomas and Khalil Joreige Homepage*. <http://www.hadjithomasjoreige.com>.

______________________________. "Latency." *Home Works: A Forum on Cultural Practices*. Ed. Christine Tohme and M. Abu Rayyan. Beirut: Ashkal Alwan, 2002. 40-49.

Harker, Christopher. "'A Close and Unbreachable Distance': Witnessing Everything and Nothing." *ACME: An International E-Journal for Critical Geographies* 6.1 (2007). <http://www.acme-journal.org/vol6/ CH.pdf>.

Heartfield, James. *The 'Death of the Subject' Explained.* Sheffield: Sheffield Hallam U, 2006.

Jameson, Fredric. "Postmodernism and Consumer Society." *The Continental Aesthetics Reader*. Ed. C. Cazeoux. NY: Routledge, 2000. 282-94.

Khalaf, Samir. *Cultural Resistance*. London: Saqi Books, 2001.

Khalili, Laleh. *Heroes and Martyrs of Palestine: The Politics of National Commemoration*. Cambridge: Cambridge UP, 2007.

Löfgren, Orvar. *On Holiday: A History of Vacationing*. Berkeley, LA and London: U of California P, 1999.

Massumi, Brian. *A User's Guide to Capitalism and Schizophrenia: Deviations from Deleuze and Guattari*. Cambridge, MA and London: MIT P, 1992.

Mauss, Marcel. *A General Theory of Magic*. NY and London: Routledge, 2001.

McLagan, Meg. "Principles, Publicity, and Politics: Notes on Human Rights Media." *American Anthropologist* 105 (2003): 605-12.

Mehta, Uday. "Curiosity, Imagination, and Madness." *The Anxiety of Freedom*. Ithaca: Cornell UP, 1992. 80-118.

Mitchell, W. J. T. *Picture Theory*. Chicago: U of Chicago P, 1994.

Mroué, Rabih. "The Fabrication of Truth." *Tamass: Contemporary Arab Representations* 1 (2002): 114-17.

Naficy, Hamid. "The Accented Style of the Independent Transnational Cinema: A Conversation with Atom Egoyan." *Cultural Producers in Perilous States*. Chicago: U of Chicago P, 1996. 179-231.

Naqvi, Nauman. *The Nostalgic Subject: A Genealogy of the 'Critique of Nostalgia'*. Messina: CIRSDIG, 2007.

Quinty, Jim. "The Last Man: Becoming a Ghost of Himself." *The Daily Star*. September 26, 2006. <http://www.1stjordan.net/actuuk/ archivesuk/ resultat.php? id=1149&debut=0>.

Riegl, Alois. "The Modern Cult of Monuments: Its Character and Its Origin." *Oppositions* 25 (1982): 21-50.

Rogers, Sarah. "Out of History: Postwar Art in Beirut." *Art Journal* 66 (2007): 8-20.

Salhab, Ghassan. Personal interview. July, 11, 2001.

Sadek, Walid. "Place at Last." *Art Journal* 66 (2007): 34-47.

Shaviro, Steven. *the Cinematic Body*. Minneapolis and London: U of Minnesota P, 1993.

Taylor, Charles. "Modern Social Imaginaries." *Public Culture* 14 (2002): 91-124.

Terada, Rei. *Feeling Theory: Emotion after the 'Death of the Subject'*. Cambridge, MA and London: Harvard UP, 2001.

Toufic, Jalal. *Forthcoming*. Berkeley: Atelos, 2000.

__________. "Ruins." *Tamass: Contemporary Arab Representations* 1 (August 2002): 19-25.

__________. "Ruins." *We Can Make Rain But No One Came To Ask*. Ed. Jalal Toufic. Montreal: The Atlas Group with the Ellen Art Gallery of Concordia U, 2006. 7-16.

__________. "Ruins." *The Atlas Group (1989-2004): A Project by Walid Raad*. Ed. K. Nakas and B. Schmitz. Koln: Verlag der Buchhandlung Walther Konig, 2006. 55-60.

__________. "Saving Face." *Review of Photographic Memory*. Ed. Jalal Toufic. Beirut: Arab Image Foundation, 2004. 6-27.

__________. *(Vampires) An Uneasy Essay on the Undead in Film*. NY: Station Hill, 1993.

__________. *The Withdrawal of Tradition Past a Surpassing Disaster.* Berkeley: Forthcoming Books, 2009. <http://www.jalaltoufic.com>.

Westmoreland, Mark R. "Post-Orientalist Aesthetics: Experimental Films and Video in Lebanon." *Invisible Culture: An Electronic Journal for Visual Studies* 13 (2009): 37-57.

Wilson-Goldie, Kaelen. "Witness to Loss: Group Tuesday." *Bidoun: Arts and Culture from the Middle East* 11 (Summer 2007): 27.

Yakir, Dan. "Ciné-transe: The Vision of Jean Rouch." *Film Quarterly* 31 (1978): 2-10.

## B. Films Cited

Borgmann, Monika, Lokman Slim, and Hermann Theissen, dir. *Massaker*. 2005. Available from monika.borgmann@gmail.com.

Hadjthomas, Joannna and Khalil Joreige, dir. *Ashes/Ramad*. 2003. Available from http://www.hadjithomasjoreige.com.

____________________________________. *The Perfect Day/Yawmun akhar*. 2005. Available from http://www.celluloid-dreams.com/library/m_r/perfect_day.

____________________________________. *Wonder Beirut: The Story of a Pyromaniac Photographer* (installation series). 1998-2006.

Joreige, Lamia, dir. *Here and Perhaps Elsewhere/Houna wa roubbama hounak*. 2003. Available from http://www.lamiajoreige.com/films/films_houna.php.

Mroué, Rabih and Elias Khoury, dir. *Three Posters* (video-performance). 2000.

Salhab, Ghassan, dir. *Beyrouth fantôme/Ashbah Bayrut*. 1998. Available from ghfilms@hotmail.com.

________________. *The Last Man/Atlal*. 2006. Available from ghfilms@hotmail.com.

Salloum, Jayce, dir. *untitled part 1: everything and nothing*. 1999-2000. Available from http://www.vdb.org/smackn.acgi$misc?clips/UNTITLEDPA.mov.

Toufic, Jalal, dir. *The Lamentations Series: The Ninth Night and Day*. 2005. Available from http://www.jalaltoufic.com.

______________. *The Sleep of Reason: This Blood Spilled in My Veins*. 2002. Available from http://www.jalaltoufic.com.

# Trauma and Testimony: Heather Raffo's *9 Parts of Desire*

**Magda Romanska**

---

Although I am not very fond of personal inserts into one's theoretical writings, I feel the need to provide the reader with some information about my own cultural background to explain my interest in Raffo's play. I have lived in the US for the last fourteen years, but I grew up in Poland, a country shaped by centuries of serendipitous historical forces and fickle geopolitical circumstances: three hundred years of partitions, two wars, years of Nazi occupation and Soviet regime. What attracted me to Raffo's play was the odd similarity of Polish and Iraqi history: the long lack of stability, years of internal violence, external occupations, and their cumulative generational effects. The profound sadness of Raffo's women, the sense of having been broken down, the sense of time frozen in the moment of one's trauma seemed eerily familiar. It reminded me of my grandmother who survived the German labor camp. There was something in my grandmother's eyes that stayed there through years of turmoil: the merciless endless sediments of history passed on from her mother to her daughter, without beginning or end.

What also attracted me to Raffo's play was her painful attempt to bridge the gap between her two identities: American and Iraqi. Although born in the US, Raffo found herself in a situation all too familiar to emigrants and refugees: the need to balance and reconcile two separate, often antagonistic, social, political, and cultural paradigms. As Brecht famously put it:

> The best school of dialectics is emigration. The most acute dialecticians are refugees. They are refugees as a result of changes, and they study nothing but changes. Out of the tiniest signs they conclude the greatest events. When their opponent wins, they calculate how much the victory cost, and for contradictions they have a refined eye. Dialectics, here's to you![1]

Thrust between the American-Iraq conflict, Raffo struggles to build a viable narrative that would reconcile her alliances. But to what degree is the dialectics of her experience translatable into the political or cultural sphere of either country? After all, to what degree is it possible to communicate such an experience to either American or Iraqi audiences, and, to use Paul de Man's rhetorical question: What's the difference?[2] To which audience is she speaking? Although Raffo's play focuses on Iraqi women, it also tells a larger story of Raffo's liminal dialectic: a delicate art of negotiating impossible social and political alliances. In her own words, she felt compelled to "soften" some of her women to make them accessible to American audiences.[3] What does such "softening" imply and how does it function on the esthetic, literary, and dramatic level *vis-à-vis* the genuine trauma she attempts to capture? And to what extent is this "softening" and exoticization aimed at 'domesticating' a complex situation to suit an audience? These were the questions that drew me to her play. For some of them, I have found answers; for others, I am still searching.

* * *

Based on a series of interviews with nine Iraqi women, Heather Raffo's one-woman show *Nine Parts of Desire* chronicles, through the prism of their lives, the successive stages of Iraq's troubled history since 1963 and up to the late 1990s. Years of ethnic conflicts, Saddam's regime, and American invasions created a mosaic of shared and shattered national experience, starting with the professional mourner whose lyrical wailing opens the show, and ending with the female artist, Layal, who tells the horrific story of her friend's suffering and death. With Raffo performing all nine parts, the show premiered in 2003 at the Edinburgh Fringe Festival, where it was immediately noticed. Hugh Rorrison, writing for *Plays International,* called it "a very moving insider's view of [Iraqi] women's lives . . . [and] riveting performance by the author."[4] From there it moved to other theaters and cities, and was performed by Raffo as well as others.[5]

Despite the general enthusiasm for the play, it is important to note that its performance (though not writing) came after the American invasion of Iraq in 2003. There was curiosity about Iraq and Iraqis in the US, at the same time as the invasion was presented to American people as if it were meant to 'liberate' Iraq, and particularly oppressed Iraqi women. Thus, the depiction of dispossessed Iraqi women in the play corresponds at times—in terms of dress and monologue—to Orientalist visual images and presentations, which came to be interpreted by some as confirming, rather than dislodging, stereotypes, with an ideological axe to grind.

Heather Raffo grew up in Okeno, Michigan in the 1970s. Her father is an Iraqi civil engineer and her mother is American. She holds a BA from the University of Michigan and an MFA from the University of San Diego. She also studied at the Royal Academy of Dramatic Art in London. As a young child, Raffo visited Iraq with her family in 1974, and then returned there in her early twenties in 1993, right after the first American invasion. Around that time, Raffo came to a painful realization. She recalls:

> I am an American, but I became aware of myself as an Iraqi—had a sense of myself as "the other"—for the first time during the Gulf War. . . . I'd walk down the street and overhear people saying, "Let's go fuck the Iraqis." I realized from that point on that my cousins in Iraq—family whom I loved—would be viewed by many Americans as dark and dirty. I also realized that the only difference between my cousins and myself was the accident of where we were born.[6]

In another interview, she adds:

> Oh, I am not just from Michigan—I'm living in Michigan with a big family in Iraq. I'm not on one side of this war. I can't sit in a bar with people cheering as bombs are going off. My body, my blood and my psyche want my family to live. What if I never see them again? What if they're just in the wrong place in the wrong time?[7]

It was at this point that Raffo had an epiphany. Rather than struggle with herself, she decided to bridge the gap that put both of her identities at odds with each other. She began recording the experiences and tales of various Iraqi women—relatives and strangers—she met while in Iraq. As she puts it: "The memories of the country and of my family rooted deep in me and continued to tug at me as something I needed to share with the world. . . . I did not do formal interviews with people. I went and lived with them and loved them and collected their stories."[8] In this endeavor, ironically, her double sense of belonging put her in a privileged position. As she writes: "[being an Iraqi] got me in the door, and being an American . . . oddly enough made it possible for the women to trust me. They felt that they could say things to me, as an American, that they wouldn't allow themselves to say to another Iraqi."[9] In 1998, the project was turned into Raffo's MFA thesis and, eventually, into a play (2003). By then, it also included Iraqi women living outside of Iraq: a sixty-year-old expatriate living in London, and a young New Yorker worrying about her Iraqi family, Raffo's alter ego.

The title of the show refers to Geraldine Brooks's *Nine Parts of Desire: The Hidden World of Islamic Women* (1996).[10] During the late 1980s and early 1990s, Brooks was a foreign correspondent for *The Wall Street Journal* covering the Middle East. Traveling throughout the Middle East with her freelance-journalist husband, Brooks found herself able to access a world unavailable to male Western journalists: the world of Muslim women. Narrating their stories, Brooks created a first-of-a-kind travel journal, one that gave readers a glimpse into a previously inaccessible domain, dispelling many Western stereotypes. The title of Brooks's book and, in turn, the title of Raffo's play, is derived from a statement by 'Ali Ibn Abu Talib, the cousin of Prophet Mohammed and the husband of his daughter Fatima,[11] and the fourth and final Rightly Guided Caliph: "God created sexual desire in ten parts; then he gave nine parts to women and one to men."[12] The statement, enigmatically expresses fundamental ambivalence toward women: The nine parts of desire can make women superior but also dangerous. In Raffo's play, the dark irony of this sentiment emerges slowly from the bits and pieces of the stories: The lives of Raffo's women are warped by the one part of male desire that, as John Lahr notes, turns "men into savages—brutes, betrayers, rapists."[13]

The nine women are, respectively, Mulaya, a hired mourner; Layal, an artist; Amal, a middle-aged Bedouin woman; Huda, an elderly expatriate living in London; a young British-educated Iraqi doctor; a nine-year-old Iraqi girl; Umm Ghada, a mother who lost her children in an American bombing raid; the American, a young New Yorker of Iraqi descent; and Nanna, an old, rugged street woman who sells everything she can find in the ruins of Baghdad. Although they are very different in age and character, what all nine women in Raffo's play share is the common experience of history, one that has left all of them with post-traumatic stress disorder (PTSD).

Trauma (from the Greek word meaning "wound") is defined as a violent rupture in the social and psychological order that fundamentally alters an individual's concept of self and world. The origins of contemporary trauma studies date back to 1980, when PTSD "was first included in the diagnostic canon of the medical and psychiatric professions."[14] Experts in the field of trauma studies, including psychologists, psychiatrists, as well as those who specialize in contemporary critical theory, disagree about the precise definition of PTSD; but

> most descriptions generally agree that there is a response, sometimes delayed, to an overwhelming event or events, which takes the form of repeated, intrusive hallucinations, dreams, thoughts or behaviors stemming from the event, along with numbing that may have begun during or after the experience, and possibly also increased arousal to (and avoidance of) stimuli recalling the event.[15]

A way out of the closed circuit of one's psyche is to be able to tell one's story: "a therapeutic process—a process of constructing a narrative, of reconstructing a history and essentially, of re-externalizing the event—has to be set in motion."[16] By interviewing the women, allowing them to speak, and recording their memories and fantasies, Raffo set in motion the process of constructing a narrative with therapeutic potential, but by eventually performing the episodes as testimonies as in the form of documentary theater, she also inevitably posed ethical questions about the role of writing and performance in registering, representing, and imagining the details of violent traumatic events.

As many critics have pointed out, "postmodern art has an interest in probing the wound and exploring the effects of the repetition of the trauma."[17] Heir to the psychoanalytical search for the 'primal scream,' postmodern art, especially writing, thrives on trauma, both personal and collective, often blurring the line between art and trauma theory. Consequently, analyzing postmodern work via the prism of trauma theory can throw "a light on figurative or poetic language, and perhaps symbolic process in general, as something other than an enhanced imaging or vicarious repetition of a prior (non)experience."[18] Such an approach to the literary, poetic, or dramatic language of trauma inevitably examines

> how knowledge of extreme experiences is possible [as it] moves from epistemological battles to an underconsciousness deeply involved in story, speech act, and symbolic process. This shift does not leave the cognitive behind but puts us in a different relation to it. It leads to an unsentimental acknowledgment of the human condition, and a view of art as at once testimony and representation.[19]

Framing, contextualizing, and narrating one's trauma is a necessary step in the healing process, but having someone else frame, contextualize, and narrate it in the poetic language of metaphors and symbols can have both a liberating and numbing experience. As Whitehead points out, "if trauma comprises an event or experience which overwhelms the individual and resists language or representation, how then can it be narrativised in fiction?"[20] How can it be narrativized in performance? Who can/cannot narrativize it? And to what ends? This article analyzes the relationship between trauma, testimony, and performance, as constructed, represented, and performed in Raffo's play, with particular attention to the interface between the survivors, the performer, and the audience.

Negotiating her own bi-cultural identity, Raffo's play struggles with esthetic, political, and ethical questions. Although the play was widely seen in the US, its primary audience was still fairly limited to urban, liberal groups which tended to condemn the two American invasions of Iraq. Historically, Iraqi women's perspectives towards Saddam's regime have varied and depended on many factors:

> Many secular, apolitical middle-class Shia, Sunni, Kurdish and Christian women appreciated the achievements of the early Ba'th period in education, modernisation of infrastructures and welfare provisions. While those who actively opposed the regime remember political repression, mass arrests, torture and executions.[21]

The fact that Raffo chose to focus on the second group, portraying Saddam Hussein as the ultimate villain of Iraqi history, and generally avoiding passing any moral judgment on the American army (American bombings are represented as almost a necessary evil brought on by Saddam), begs the question: Why did she choose this approach, thus going against the political mantra of her potential audience? Ironically, for many liberal audience members, the graphic description of Saddam's crimes came as a surprise. Nested in their own ideological comfort zone of anti-American rhetoric, the audience's moral dissonance demanded erasing any knowledge of Saddam's crimes for the outrage at American government's action to be ethically coherent.

Showing the other side of the story, Raffo unwittingly plays into what Gayatri Spivak calls "axioms of imperialism,"[22] a paradigm of conscious and unconscious normativization of Western claims, stirring uncomfortable, if reductive, questions: Whose 'side' is she on, in terms of both American politics and American-Iraqi conflict? Which American agenda is she catering to: liberal or conservative? Which viewpoint is she assuming: American or Iraqi? Who, in this play, to cite Spivak again, has the "dominant subject-position" and who has "objectified" subject-position? In other words, who is "the other"?[23] Spivak argues that the "the 'correction' of a performative deconstruction" can only be successful if, instead of drawing sweeping generalizations, "you grant the thoroughly stratified larger theatre of the Third World, the stage of so-called de-colonization, equal rights of historical, geographical, linguistic specificity and theoretical sophistication."[24] What Spivak asks is a critical and representational recognition of the complexity and specificity of the colonized nations. The fact that Raffo's play is difficult to pin down ideologically suggests that her own internal dialectics lead her towards the space of political ambiguity–Raffo's characters are complex, self-aware, and, most of all, torn by contradictory impulses; they occupy the space of what Spivak calls 'human'-ness and thus, in what follows, they are beyond ideology. As Raffo put it in one of her interviews:

> These women just aren't in the world. There are no images of Iraqi women out there that aren't flat, one-dimensional and somewhat victimized. The real Iraqi woman does not exist in western culture. . . . That's when I knew I had to tell the stories I'd heard because they're funny, sexy, radical and deeply emotional.[25]

Ironically, it is this complex position that makes Raffo's characters, as representations, vulnerable to ideological interpretations in the same way that their real-life counterparts are vulnerable to violent currents of history.

### Mulaya the Mourner

The play starts with Mulaya, who enters the stage singing "Che Mali Wali," a traditional Iraqi song whose title translates ambiguously as "Because I Have No Guardian [Protector/Master]." Mulaya "carries a great bundle on her head. She empties her load of shoes into the river" (3). She mumbles metaphorical verses about lost souls/soles. In Arabic cultures the name "Mulaya" indicates "professional mourner." As Raffo explains in her stage directions, Mulaya "is a woman in Arabic culture hired to lead call-and-response with women mourning at funerals. She is considered very good if she can bring the women to a crying frenzy with her improvised heartbreaking verses about the dead" (3). From the Western perspective, the fact that Raffo chooses to open her show with the verses of the hired mourner is already startling. Sigmund Freud writes that mourning can be healthy and unhealthy.[26] Healthy mourning resolves itself in time and eventually finds closure; unhealthy mourning, either prolonged, resisted, or sublimated, turns into a melancholia and can manifest itself through a variety of symptoms of PTSD. Mourning and trauma are inevitably connected: When the subject fails to mourn properly, the event that caused the mourning is designated as traumatic. But in Raffo's play, mourning is a commodity; it is staged and performed as required by cultural standards. How, then, can such mourning, for which one pays and performs, be designated as either healthy or unhealthy? How does it work itself out in individuals and in culture?

The play does not state for whom Mulaya is mourning or who has hired her. In a way, she is more symbolic figuration than character, and her wailing is directed at no one in particular and for no one in particular. In fact, what she mourns is the nation as a whole: its past, history, and culture. She closes her speech with a melancholic and bitter tribute:

> and now the river has developed an appetite for us
> its current runs back
> beneath Iraq.
> . . .
> underneath my country
> there is no paradise of martyrs
> only water
> a great dark sea
> of desire. (5)

The river here is a peculiar image of *panta rei*, an inevitable turn of history that is not supposed to repeat itself, yet which is repeated, each time with bloodier outcomes. Rich in natural resources, Iraq, the "land between the rivers," has been ravaged by centuries of conflict: from the Ottoman Empire to British rule, from Saddam's regime, the Iraq-Iran war, and Shi'ite and Sunni conflicts to the first American invasion and international sanctions.[27] Mourning in Raffo's play has a much broader context, and it encompasses trauma as a shared national experience, one that is as much a response to the breakdown of the nation as it is a source of national identity.[28] Mourning here is a response to the trauma of the loss of what Benedict Anderson would call an "imagined community" of the nation-state that transforms "fatality into continuity, contingency into meaning."[29] It is a trauma of the nation that has lost its sense of history besides the traumatic experience itself, and that has no other source of identity but the prolonged state, not of mourning, but of trauma. As John Lahr notes: "For more than a generation under Saddam, Iraqis lived in a state of permanent paranoia, which left them passive and mute."[30] Cathy Caruth calls PTSD a pathological symptom, not a symptom of the unconscious, but "a symptom of history." She writes: "The traumatized, we might say, carry an impossible history within them, or they become themselves the symptom of a history that they cannot entirely possess."[31] By narrating the life stories of women with varied ages and backgrounds who share a common nationality, Raffo narrates a traumatic experience that goes beyond any limited geographic or historical framework: "a collective trauma transcends the contingent relationships between individual persons and forges them into a collective identity."[32] It is a shared sense of national belonging, tragically rooted in one's awareness of its loss.

**Layal the Artist**

The second heroine of the play is Layal: "a painter for the Saddam regime. She is sexy and elegant, a resilient and fragile woman. She is a daredevil with a killer smile" (6). She is also perhaps the most complex and paradoxical of all nine women. The character of Layal, whose name translates loosely as "all the nights," might have been based on a real-life artist, Layla al-Attar, who was director of the Iraqi Art Center and a leading Arab artist, one of the few who survived and thrived during Saddam's regime.[33] Raffo describes her first encounter with Layla's work in the Saddam Art Centre in Baghdad vividly:

> It was like being in the Museum of Modern Art in New York—if you can imagine that filled with floor-to-ceiling portraits of Saddam Hussein. Then I went upstairs into this little back room and there was a wonderful nude of a woman, standing with her back towards the viewer amid a thicket of bare trees. I was transfixed because I thought, "It's a painting of me." It spoke to me of femininity and of sorrow, everything I had felt in

> Iraq. . . . I found so much of myself in that painting. I immediately photographed it. When I got the film back it was the only picture that had come out on that roll of film. I've lived with that image ever since. I knew Layla had to be a character in my play, so I asked everyone if they knew her or her work. I tried so hard to meet someone that had met her but she kept slipping through my fingers like a shadow.[34]

Layla allegedly created the mosaic doormat with the face of George Bush Sr. that used to adorn the Rashid hotel entrance in Baghdad.[35] The story goes that she made it from the pieces of her home destroyed during the American bombings in 1991. In 2002, *The Wall Street Journal* published a short editorial about Layla, trying to account for all the stories about her:

> Streaking in from US warships in the Persian Gulf, 23 Tomahawk cruise missiles hit this city in the early hours of June 27, 1993. One killed Leila al-Attar, who was a painter and the head of Iraq's state institute for the arts. The Iraqi government was enraged. It described the 48-year-old Ms. Attar and at least five other civilians killed that night as innocent victims of the US air strike on President Saddam Hussein's foreign-intelligence headquarters nearby. Today many Iraqis espouse a more sinister view of Ms. Attar's death: She was assassinated by the US because of an unflattering portrait of George Bush Sr. on the floor of a Baghdad hotel lobby.[36]

The fictional character of Layal that Raffo created in her play is warped with contradictions: Layal is both a sympathizer and subtly subversive critic of the regime. She is represented as the only artist allowed to paint female nudes with a respectable career and access to more resources than anyone else. She silently witnesses one of her friends being stripped, covered in honey, and eaten by Dobermans. Though she never speaks a word about it, she quips that "Iraqis know not to open their mouth not even for the dentist"; she pays tribute to her friend in one of her paintings, portraying her as "the branch's blossom leaning over the barking dogs they cannot reach no matter how hungry they are" (7). Layal identifies and absorbs all of the stories: "These stories are living inside of me/each woman I meet her or I hear about her/and I cannot separate myself from them" (9). In a way, Layal has been so traumatized and horrified by the regime that she is unable to function on any other level but that of pure survival: "Isn't everything in this country a matter of survival?" she asks rhetorically (10).

Trapped between her concepts of herself as collaborator, critic, and victim of the regime, and unable to come to terms with any of these, Layal struggles to maintain a coherent self-image. Since women are *a priori* marked by patriarchal norms, to survive they are often forced to negotiate their gendered position *vis-à-vis* the oppressor, and this experience can in itself be traumatizing.[37] Retelling her story, Layal does not try to justify herself as much as she places herself in a position from which she can view herself as a free agent, regardless of the ethical consequences it would entail.[38] She cannot conceive of herself as a helpless, passive object "passed around from one man to another" (51). She asks with bravado: "You tell me about freedom, about choice and possibilities. . . . But what are you creating with your freedom?/I am more free than you" (50). To hammer her point home, or perhaps to convince herself as much as her audience, she resorts to a larger, global scheme of gender relations. For women everywhere, she says, freedom is an elusive concept, and her particular collaboration with this particular regime makes her choice morally irrelevant:

> so many women have done the same as me
> everywhere they have to do the same.
> If I did the same in your England or America
> wouldn't they call me a whore there too?
> Your western culture, sister, will not free me
> from being called a whore
> not my sex
> women are not free. (61-62)

Like many survivors, Layal might be in denial, afraid "of hearing, or of witnessing oneself," and hoping "to bury the dead witness inside oneself."[39] To quote Culbertson:

> The survivor most often, nearly invariably, becomes silent about his victimization, though the experience nevertheless in every case remains somehow fundamental to his existence, and to his unfolding or enfolded conception of himself. This silence is an internal one in which the victim attempts to suppress what is recalled (so as not to relive the victimization countless times), or finds it repressed by some part of himself which functions as a stranger, hiding self from the self's experience according to unfathomable criteria and requirements.[40]

Confounded by the contradictions, Layal's fractured self is stuck in the post-traumatic moment of misrecognition. But underneath her casual tone and philosophical detachment, Layal seems to be torn by a sense of masochistic guilt. Though she wants to survive, she cannot imagine herself fully free and happy. She refuses to leave Iraq, despite having the means to do so: "I don't know/maybe I feel guilty/all of us here/it's a shame if all the artists leave too," she says (6). This guilt is a burden that she bears with tragically profound self-awareness, and she is—as if on the sly—constantly waiting for a sign of universal justice to contradict the morally ambivalent world that surrounds her, even if it means that it would strike her as well, that her luck would run out: "I am aware that I will die./I am complicit," she says, resigned (51). The production notes specify: "At the end of the play, when Layal is closest to death, she willfully explodes under the weight of the many women she has taken on. Her psyche fractures, and she speaks using fragments of lines we have heard throughout the play in the other characters' language" (69).[41] Layal's self dissolves metaphorically in the history that surrounds her, as the flesh of those who died in the bombings dissolves into thin air in the heat of the blasts.

**Amal the Bedouin**

The third heroine is Amal, a Bedouin: "Bright, festive and robust, Amal is a woman of thirty-eight who looks intently at whomever she is talking to that you would swear her eyes never blinked. She asks many questions; she really thinks there is an answer out there for her" (11). Amal's character keeps wavering and searching: She leaves Iraq and goes to London with her husband and two children, but decides to come back when she finds her husband in bed with one of her friends. The play never specifies whether she divorces him; it only states that she left: "I left/ I never told him why I left" (15). Not wanting to live in her small town anymore, she moves to Israel where she meets a friend of her father's, an Arab Israeli tribesman, and becomes his second wife. Since the first wife would leave for months at a time, Amal was entrusted with the responsibility of raising the woman's eight children. The tribesman promises Amal they would leave the Middle East and go to Canada, but they do not, so Amal, once again, decides to leave: "I am looking for this freedom/and he says 'No, we are not going to Canada.'/So I care very much for him, but again/I left" (15). She goes back to Baghdad, where she begins a phone relationship with a friend of her ex-husband's. Their phone conversations span over a year, but when they finally meet, he rejects her. Too ashamed to face her family, Amal returns to London to her first husband. "I will have my freedom there," she says, "but not my peace/maybe freedom is better than peace?" (18). Amal's hapless love life is a journey toward some metaphorical sense of freedom and peace that she cannot name: "I do, I very much feel this void/I have no peace/Always I am looking for peace" (11).

The movement from silence to words is difficult because, as Cathy Caruth argues: "To cure oneself—whether by drugs or the telling of one's story or both—seems to many survivors to imply the giving-up of an important reality, or the dilution of a special truth into the reassuring terms of therapy."[42] For that reason, out of fear of curing oneself, or perhaps out of fear of the freedom one may experience after telling one's story, many survivors cannot bring themselves to tell their story. In Amal's case, however, we ask whether she indeed cannot speak of her life or, more tragically, whether she simply has no one who would listen.

Amal's choices may seem incomprehensible; her decisions erratic and somewhat as if made outside of herself. In search of something she cannot name—she calls it peace—she goes back and forth between West and East, running away from one man toward the phantom of another. She does all of this to fill the void inside her, trusting naïvely that once she finds the man, the void will be gone. But the more she persists in her search, the emptier she feels, unable to see the absurd futility of her plight. It is only when she finds someone who listens to her story, when she can finally find her own voice, that she discovers, to her surprise, that the peace she has been so desperately searching for is nowhere else but within her.

**Huda the Emigré**

The fourth woman is Huda, a seventy-year-old "whiskey drinker with fifty years as a smoker" (18). She is an émigré living in London who drowns her nostalgia in alcohol and political discourse. Next to Layal, Huda is perhaps the most complex of the nine characters. She left Iraq a long time ago, and by now should have adjusted to her new life, but Huda lives in her past, reliving traumatic memories from the old country. In 1963 when Saddam's Ba'th Party came to power, Huda was a member of the opposition and was rounded up with 18,000 other members of the resistance and thrown into prison:

> We could hear things, all night, always rape
> or rape with electronic instruments.
> But their way, I promise you, their way
> was to torture the people close to you
> that is how they'd do it. (52)

These brutal memories play in Huda's head repeatedly, a near-compulsion. She both fights them and somehow grows numb to them. In part, Huda's alcoholism is an escape, not only from memories but also from herself and the contradictions within her that she must reconcile. She has always been politically engaged—she marched for peace in Vietnam, and she walked for Chile—so the US war against Iraq is against all her beliefs. Yet, as she says, she wants it: "Because Saddam/Saddam was the greater enemy than, I mean,/imperialism. . . . we all can say/congratulations/the regime is gone/Saddam is gone" (20). As she says: "I prefer chaos to permanent repression and cruelty" (19)—which overlaps with statements made by the US government (Condoleezza Rice) about "creative chaos." Like all immigrants, Huda is also frozen in time, remembering her country for what it was and what it was not, misplacing her nostalgia and converting absence into loss and *vice versa*.[43]

For Huda, the possibility of reconciling her past with her present and her future, just like the possibility of reconciling her love for her country and her hate for Saddam Hussein *vis-à-vis* the American invasion, is forever foreclosed. She says: "I am in a period of disheartenment everywhere./Maybe I should be there./I don't know what to do with myself now, I have doubts, yeah, well/About my whole life" (39). Huda cannot come to terms with herself; a prisoner of historical circumstances, all she can do is make herself numb with alcohol and random discourse: "Myself, too, it takes a lifetime to be liberated," she says sadly (53).

**Unnamed Woman Doctor**

The next woman is a British-educated doctor. She chooses to return to Iraq out of a sense of obligation for her country and its people. But instead of treating children's colds and chicken pox, she finds herself delivering mutant babies: "Here, it is your first son, I am sorry he has two heads?" she says, "six babies no head, four abnormally large heads, now today another one with two heads" (20-21). Throughout the play, she is "pondering with nausea the growing number of malformed babies being born in a country she fears is contaminated with uranium depletion."[44] But children are not the only victims of the war; men are victims, too: "My husband he sits at home without his legs" (22). She is surrounded by death and deformity, trying to survive. Raffo does not give her a name, calling her only the Doctor. Nausea becomes the singular characteristic of this young woman, and, indeed, when the lights come up on her scene, the audience sees her throwing up. She blames it on the smell from nearby sewage, then on the flashing memories of the mutant babies she has just delivered, but at the very end of her scene, when again she becomes nauseated, she says simply: "No I'm fine, I'm fine/I'm pregnant" (22). The statement comes as a shock to the audience, as they realize by now that she too might give birth to a double-headed child. What is more heartbreaking is the knowledge of her knowledge. Unlike most Iraqi women, this one knows first-hand the potential consequences of radiation, and she knows what it may mean to her fetus.

**Unnamed Girl**

The youngest of Raffo's nine women is nine-year-old Iraqi Girl. After a couple of American soldiers visit the Girl's school and make the girls laugh, her mother—afraid that her laughter would make her vulnerable to both cultures, American and Iraqi—stops sending her to school.[45] To justify her fears, the mother tells the girl she is stupid and should not attend school. It is only her father, who disappeared after the war broke out, who used to tell her she was smart, and she cherishes this memory with childish zealousness. Casually, she "tells us of the fates of her various family members; she vows she will study hard so that when her father . . . returns, she will be smarter than he is."[46] The girl talks also about her mother, who could disappear as well; she relates this possibility matter-of-factly, so used to the twisted reality around her that she appears unaware of its horror. In one of the play's few bitter-comic moments, she convinces herself that her mother will not be kidnapped after all because "her hair is not that nice." She says:

[My mother] is afraid of getting stolen by gangs—
now they steal women for money
or to sell them.
I try to tell momma she won't get stolen
her hair is not that nice. (24)

Since, ironically, the Girl does have TV and satellite access, she watches American programs almost compulsively, enamored of pop-culture icons like any other child her age. In a subtle moment of self-awareness, she contemplates dreamily: "maybe I should get stolen/so I could leave my country" (25).

Although the disappearance of her father and the constant fear of losing her mother is sufficient to traumatize the girl, what is even more disturbing to us, the audience, is the fact that out of boredom she has learned to distinguish between different kinds of weapons by listening to the shots outside her bedroom windows. She is proud of this skill and brags about it with a blasé attitude, on the same emotional scale with which she chats about Justin Timberlake and Oprah:

I am not stupid
I count bombs even
I count between the
hissing when it is high
until the sound becomes low
then two seconds—and it explodes!
If I hear the hissing I know it's in our neighborhood
like in a few blocks
then I hear glass breaking for 4 seconds
after the hit.
I can tell if it is RPG's or American,
tank or armor vehicle,
Kalashnikov or M16. (26)

The girl's apparent numbness to the events that surround her is typical of trauma survivors: "Trauma emerges as that which, at the very moment of its reception, registers as a non-experience, causing conventional epistemologies to falter."[47] A person who lives through a traumatic event cannot judge it as such at the moment when it happens, or else one would not be able to survive it. The awareness 'what-is-happening-to-me' has to be muted if the individual is to be able to psychologically withstand the onslaught of fear and terror. Awareness comes with time, long after the event has passed, but then it comes full force, gripping the individual in a vicious circle of traumatic repetition:

> Insufficiently grasped at the time of its occurrence, trauma does not lie in the possession of the individual, to be recounted at will, but rather acts as a haunting or possessive influence which not only insistently and intrusively returns but is, moreover, experienced for the first time only in its belated repetition.[48]

Watching Raffo's nine-year-old girl narrating her story with calm and oblivion is painful for us, the audience. We are aware of what is happening to her, and we are aware of what will happen to her years after this war is over. If she survives, she'll suffer from PTSD, forever trapped by her memories, reliving in her mind the Kalashnikov nights with the stubborn persistency of a DVD player with a broken replay button.

**Umm Ghada**

Perhaps the most tragic of all nine women is the one who renamed herself Umm Ghada, "the mother of Ghada," after her daughter, who perished during the American raid on the 'Amiriyya bomb shelter, which Umm Ghada miraculously survived, and in which 408 civilians, including her nine children, evaporated, "fused" together, in one instant.[49] Based on an actual person, Umm Ghada is described as "a woman of great stillness and pride, peaceful and dispassionate" (28). Since 1991, she has lived in a yellow trailer outside of the shelter, keeping vigil. Like a textbook trauma victim, Umm Ghada relives the experience:

> everything is fire
> I couldn't find my children
> I couldn't find my way out
> But somehow I did.
>
> In the whole day later
> I am searching, searching charred bodies
> bodies they were fused together
> the only body I did recognize
> is my daughter Ghada
> so I did take her name

(*with so much pride*)
I am Umm Ghada, Mother of Ghada. (28)

The event is so traumatizing that it leaves Umm Ghada in a permanent state of suspension. Her life never returns to normal, as she is unable to function outside of the shelter. Like many survivors of traumatic events, Umm Ghada makes it her life's mission to make the world aware of what happened at the shelter. Although there is no tribunal, no court, and no judges, Umm Ghada considers her trailer to be her "witness stand"; she believes she has a responsibility to tell the story, as this is the only way she can honor all of those who perished:

This trailer is my witness stand.
All photos on this wall—and here—are me
with emissaries from the world
who come to Amiraya shelter to look
what really happen here
not what they read in papers
or see in the CNN.
Here is guest-book they all sign. (29)

Umm Ghada gives a tour of the shelter as if it were a museum, describing in detail the evidence of the genocide:

And here a silhouette of a woman
vaporized from heat.
This huge room became an oven,
and they pressed to the walls to escape from the flames.
. . .
*La*, *la*, I do not want to show you there
it is too much
the walls are stuck with hairs and skin. (29-30)

Umm Ghada's "imperative to tell and to be heard can become itself an all-consuming task. Yet no amount of telling seems ever to do justice to this inner compulsion . . . never enough . . . to articulate the story that cannot be fully captured in *thought, memory* and *speech*."[50] In the symbolic erasure of her own identity, renaming herself so as to designate her relationship to her daughter but nothing else, Umm Ghada, though alive, ceases to exist on the same night her daughter died:

"Ghada means tomorrow . . ./so I am Umm Ghada, Mother of Tomorrow./My full name is dead with them," she says (31).[51] She has a guest-book that she gives everyone willing to listen to her story, tangible proof that they heard and understood her, that they are witnesses, too. She tells the audience: "Now you sign the witness book/Your name will be witness, too" (31, 29).[52]

Fixated on the horrific images of destruction, Umm Ghada exemplifies what Hartman calls the traumatic "rupture of the symbolic."[53] Relinquishing her individual identity, Umm Ghada loses herself in the symbolic order of communal memorial, but guarding the memory of the dead does not necessarily bring her relief. On the contrary, the repetitions of memory trap her in the moment of the event, or as Hartman puts it:

> Repairing the breach between the symbolic order and the individual seems to be an endless task. . . . The repetitions, too, though cathartic, suggest an unresolved shock: a rhythmic or temporal stutter, they leave the storyteller in purgatory, awaiting the next assault, the next instance of hyperarousal. Concerning such repetitions Yeats said that a personal demon always brings us back to the place of encounter—to make it final.[54]

Umm Ghada is frozen in her mourning, testifying to the events with compulsive sorrow, and, like many survivors, she too feels guilty that she survives: "I am hard to understand/why I survive/and my children dead" (29).

**Iraqi-American Woman**

The eighth woman in Raffo's play is the one most familiar to American audiences; she is the American, or more accurately, the Iraqi-American, Raffo's alter ego. The American is a young woman who "hasn't left her studio apartment in New York City for days" (35). Since her family still lives in Iraq, she is "transfixed in front of the TV, watching the progress of the Iraq war and caught in a frenzy of worry over relatives there."[55] She narrates:

> I watch TV
> looking for
> faces
> of our family
> so all I do is cry.

. . .
I'm on my knees usually
in the middle of my apartment
with my mom
we're on the phone
I'm watching
I'm holding a rosary
watching
CNN
I want to pray
but I don't have
words. (36-37)

Watching the bombs come down on her family neighborhood, the American is stunned by her own sense of alienation: She has grown to identify herself as an American, and now, she is asked to view herself as the other, the enemy. At the same time, ingrained in the American lifestyle, she is shell-shocked at the realization that it can be so easily numbing:

a woman actually turned to me
and said that
she said
"The war it's all so heartbreaking."
She was getting a pedicure.
I was getting a fucking pedicure (44).

Getting a pedicure while a TV blasts images of war becomes a symbol of the twentieth and the twenty-first century. Raffo's American is forever marked by her own growing numbness to what surrounds her. In order not to drive herself crazy, she must engage in all the frivolities of life, but living itself becomes a burden. She cannot escape the memories of what she has seen because escape means betrayal.

Ironically, the American actually mentions the notion of trauma, describing the gap between what she sees as the narcissistic self-indulgence of the American talk-show 'trauma circuit' and the horrors of war-torn Iraq:

Here
there's space
we throw our arms wide
amber alerts and

seven men get trapped underground
and we stop everything
we fly in engineers
to save
everything
we make a movie
we go on Oprah, we talk about it
like we are moving on
or maybe
we can't move on
but just one trauma we say
ok
this can change you
possibly
your psychology, for the rest of your life
ok
But there's no one saying—
when their parents get
blown apart
in front of their eyes. (44-45)

Recent postmodern culture's fascination with "trauma drama" seems to construct what Mark Seltzer calls "a pathological public sphere" of spectatorship that

> is everywhere crossed by the vague and shifting lines between the singularity or privacy of the subject, on the one side, and collective forms of representation, exhibition, and witnessing, on the other. Along these lines, the trauma has surfaced as a sort of crossing-point of the "psycho-social."[56]

Thanks to historical distance, this phenomenon eventually allowed not only for "the entry of Holocaust representations into the circuits of the public sphere and commodity culture"[57] but also for the glorification, commodification, and 'traumafication' of potentially trivial matters. Thus, the talk-show circuit of trauma discourse can encompass a range of issues, from the distant memory of a grandfather's death in Auschwitz, to the recent death of a family pet, to one's childhood struggles with obesity, bad breath, or freckles.[58] Everything can be equally traumatizing. Surviving, overcoming, and discussing one's trauma has somehow become an essential element of the American *bildung* (as entangled in the weave of modern identity politics as it is in the myths of the American frontier and the nation's revolutionary origins). What is missing from the "pathological public sphere" of collective discussion is the trauma of the concurrent historical moment. Juxtaposing pedicure, Oprah, and TV images of bodies blown apart by American bombs, Raffo touches on the impossibility of speaking about the 'now' of trauma and what follows "the need for new forms of representation capable of registering the traumatic shock of modern genocide and for new forms of publicity that will translate knowledge of extremity to a mass audience."[59] The challenges are many: How is one to break through the numbness (and blindness) of the present moment?

**Old Nanna**

The last of the nine women is Nanna: "She wears the abaya traditionally over her head so only her face and hands remain showing. [She is] an old, old woman, scrappy and shrewd; she has seen it all" (41):

> I have too much existence
> I have lived through twenty-three revolutions
> my life has been spared—
> if my life has been spared
> to whom do I owe my debt?
> I have so much to repay.
> To whom do I owe my debt? (42)

Like many survivors, Nanna feels a sense of debt and guilt. Both numb and necessarily pragmatic, she sells anything she can on the street corner. Nanna is a true survivor; she does not pass judgments or show outrage. She takes things as they are, trying to live day by day, by whatever means she can. She calmly narrates the destruction of her culture and Iraqi identity:

> I saw
> Iraqi peoples
> bringing petrol,
> shhh
> and
> burning
> all
> National Archives,

Qur'anic Library
all—
. . .
Our history is finished.
Sunni, Shi'a, Kurd,
Christian even, Jew—
if they take what we share
it is easier
to finish. (43)

To survive chaos, Nanna sells whatever bits and pieces of Iraqi history she can find in the ruins of plundered museums and archives: books, carpets, shoes, paintings, "very old" things.[60] The last item she tries to sell is Layal's painting *Savagery*. It is from Nanna that we learn that Layal is now dead: a bomb fell on her house. In the production notes that accompanied a published version of the play, Raffo explains: "Nanna's selling of the painting *Savagery* functions then as an epilogue to remind us finally that everything we have witnessed has a price."[61] It depicts "a nude woman clinging to a barren tree. Her head was hanging bowed, and there was a golden light behind her, like a sun."[62] Whose savagery has Layal depicted? Saddam's, the Americans', or, simply, men's?

* * *

The nine women in Raffo's play give an incomplete and complex picture of the Iraqi-American relationship contextualized by Iraqi history in the last 50 years. In one of her interviews, Raffo says she wanted "American audiences to . . . understand how difficult it is to grasp the psyche of people who have lived under Saddam for 30 years with American support, then had a war with Iran, resulting in 1.5 million deaths, followed by 13 years of sanctions and two wars under American firepower."[63]

Since Raffo's play deals with trauma that has been partially perpetrated by the United States, introducing the victims' experience to American audiences is difficult. Asked which lines were the most difficult to perform, Lanna Joffrey, who acted all nine parts on Lyric Stage in Boston in 2006, replied: "The lines which were directed at the audience. Once you say something like 'you Americans,' people kind of shut out. There is a resistance to listen to what others think you are."[64] Unable to identify with the 'other,' the audience inevitably turns inward, precluding any attempt at communication: "For an audience to be traumatized by an experience that they themselves do not directly share, symbolic extension and psychological identification are required, which is equally true for Iraqi or Arab audiences attending the play though in an inverse way."[65] On the other hand, "the possibility that reference is indirect, and that consequently we may not have direct access to others', or even our own, histories, seems to imply the impossibility of any access to other cultures, and hence of any means of making political or ethical judgments."[66] What then are the ethical implications of altering the image of the 'other' for artistic purposes? Does it indeed foster communication and the possibility of reconciliation, or does it only breed more misconception, misperception, and misinformation? At which point does an attempt to create an image that fosters identification turn into an impossibility of identification with reality that is not being artistically redrawn? To what degree must 'the other' be more like us or less like us? Does it matter? Does it have to matter? Can empathy be possible without identification? Raffo's play and particularly its performance and interpretation make us reflect on such issues as representation and cultural interaction.

## Notes

1 Bertolt Brecht, "On Hegelian Dialectics," trans. Charles Senger, *Denmark or Humor* (1940–41): *Flüchtlingsgespräche* [Refugee Conversations], 1459–63, <http://www. autodidactproject.org/other/hegel-brecht.html>

2 Paul de Man writes an account of Derrida's famous philosophical/grammatological question: "Jacques Derrida—who asks the question 'What is the difference'—and we cannot even tell from his grammar whether he 'really' wants to know 'what' difference is or is just telling us that we shouldn't even try to find out. Confronted with the question of the difference between grammar and rhetoric, grammar allows us to ask the question, but the sentence by means of which we ask it may deny the very possibility of asking. See "Semiology and Rhetoric," *Diacritics 3* 3 (Fall 1973): 27–33.

3 Qtd. in Simi Horwitz, "Face to Face: Heather Raffo: Exploring the Complexity of Identity," *Back Stage—The Performing Arts Weekly* 45. 44 (October 29-November 4, 2004): 7. All citations from the play are based on Heather Raffo's *9 Parts of Desire* (Chicago, IL: Northwestern UP, 2006).

4 Hugh Rorrison, "Edinburgh-03: Hugh Rorrison at the Festival Fringe," *Plays International* 18.12 (September-October 2003): 20.

5 The same year, the show was brought to London and performed at the Bush Theatre, under the direction of Eva Breneman. The show was heralded by *The Times* as the best show in London, and by *The Independent* as one of the five best plays in London in 2003. From there it went to New York for a reading

at the Public Theater. After seeing it there, David Fishelson, Artistic Director of the Manhattan Ensemble Theater, optioned it, and in 2004 it was performed at the MET under the direction of Joanna Settle. The same year it won the Lucille Lortel Award for Outstanding Solo Show, garnering critical accolades in *The New Yorker*, *The New York Times,* and *The Wall Street Journal,* among others. Raffo then took the show on the road and performed it subsequently at the Geffen Playhouse in Los Angeles (2005) and at Arena Stage in Washington, DC (2006). Around that time, through word of mouth, the play gained an independent existence and began to be produced across the United States, with actresses other than Raffo assuming the nine parts. Mozhan Marno performed it at Berkeley Rep with Joanna Settle as the director (2006); Jacqueline Antaramian performed it at the Wilma Theatre in Philadelphia under Kate Saxon's direction (2006); Najla Said performed it at Seattle Rep, again under the direction of Joanna Settle (2006); Lanna Joffrey did a Boston show at the Lyric Stage Company under the direction of Carmen O'Reilly (2006); Aysan Celik played it at Actors Theater of Louisville under K. J. Sanchez's direction (2007); and Carolyn Cook, Suehyla El-Attar, and Marianne Fraulo shared the roles between them in a Horizon Theater production directed by Lisa Adler (May 2007). It was also performed (March 2008) at Gutherie Theater, under the direction of Joel Sass, and at the Kennedy Center in Washington DC (March 2009) as part of the Arabesque Festival. The performances, needless to say, vary in their interpretation of the play.

6 Qtd. in Horwitz, 7.

7 Qtd. in Pamela Renner, "Iraq Through the Eyes of Its Women," *American Theater* 22.4 (April 2005): 20.

8 Raffo, qtd. in Canary Promo, "The Wilma Theater Presents Heather Raffo's 'Nine Parts of Desire.'" *Philly Future* (January 17, 2006), <http://www.phillyfuture.org/node/2463>.

9 Qtd. in Horwitz, 44.

10 Geraldine Brooks, *Nine Parts of Desire: The Hidden World of Islamic Women* (NY: Anchor Books, 1995).

11 Fatima was the only child of the Prophet who propagated his lineage. Thus, the roots of Islam are as much matriarchal as they are patriarchal. 'Ali Ibn Abi Talib did not have any wives besides Fatima (until after her death, when he remarried, and had many other children). Their marriage is regarded by many Muslims as one between the most saintly and revered figures within the Prophet's immediate circle.

12 Brooks, 1.

13 John Lahr, "The Critics: The Theater: The Fury and the Jury: Women, and Men, Make Themselves Heard," *The New Yorker* 80.34 (November 8, 2004): 136.

[14] Anne Whitehead, *Trauma Fiction* (Edinburgh: Edinburgh UP, 2004), 4.

[15] Cathy Caruth, *Trauma: Explorations in Memory* (Baltimore: The Johns Hopkins UP, 1995), 4. In extreme circumstances, the function of memory is tied to survival. The body remembers violence and learns to avoid it. PTSD, with its panoply of symptoms that are essentially expressions of the inability to forget, such as flashbacks or nightmares, can be then thought of as the mind's survival strategy: To remember means to avoid, and to avoid means to survive. As Roberta Culbertson writes: "[S]uch slivered memories [of traumatic events] take on various lives of their own, perhaps altering behavior, working out as templates for response to current life circumstances. Violence is about survival, and the body is designed to take the lessons of violence seriously. To do so, it need not, perhaps best not, recall the violence itself, but rather must merely arrange to avoid it in the future, using whatever cues can be stored and maintained from before. This is not memory to be told, not memory to be analyzed, but memory to be used for purposes of survival." See Roberta Culbertson, "Embodied Memory, Transcendence, and Telling: Trauma, Re-Establishing the Self," *New Literary History* 26.1 (Winter 1995): 175.

[16] Dori Laub, "Bearing Witness, or the Vicissitudes of Listening," *Testimony: Crisis of Witnessing in Literature, Psychoanalysis, and History*, ed. Shoshana Felman and Dori Laub (NY: Routledge, 1992), 69.

[17] Susan Stewart, *Crimes of Writing* (NY: Oxford UP, 1991), 280.

[18] Geoffrey H. Hartman, "On Traumatic Knowledge and Literary Studies," *New Literary History* 26.3 (Summer 1995): 540.

[19] Hartman, 545.

[20] Whitehead, 3. See also Juliet Mitchell, "Trauma, Recognition, and the Place of Language," *Diacritics* 28.4 (Winter 1998): 121-33.

[21] Nadje Sadig Al-Ali, "Iraq's Women Under Pressure," *Le Monde* (May 5, 2007),<http://mondediplo.com/2007/05/05iraqwomen>. The situation is quite similar in Eastern Europe. In Russia, for example, there are those who clearly condemn Soviet atrocities, and those who are nostalgic and openly mourn the dissolution of communism.

[22] Gayatri Chakravorty Spivak, "Three Women's Texts and a Critique of Imperialism," *Literary Theory: An Anthology*, eds. Julie Rivkin and Michael Ryan (Malden, MA: Blackwell, 1998), 838.

[23] Gayatri Chakravorty Spivak, "Imperialism and Sexual Difference," *Oxford Literary Review* 8.1-2 (1986): 229.

[24] Spivak, "Imperialism and Sexual Difference," 238.

[25] Raffo, qtd. in Jackie McGlone, "Looking for Layla," *News Scotsman* (July 24, 2003), <http://news.scotsman.com/ViewArticle.aspx?articleid=2446194>.

26 Sigmund Freud, "Trauer und Melancholie," *Sigmund Freud: Gesammelte Werke*, eds. Marie Bonaparte et al. (Frankfurt: Fischer Taschenbuch Verlag, 1999).

27 See Thabit A. J. Abdullah, *A Short History of Iraq: From 636 to the Present* (NY: Pearson/Longman, 2003); Marion Farouk-Sluglett and Peter Sluglett, *Iraq Since 1958: From Revolution to Dictatorship* (London: I. B. Tauris Publishers, 2001); and Christoph Bangert and Jon Lee Anderson, *Iraq: The Space Between* (NY: PowerHouseBooks. 2007).

28 Eric L. Santner, *Stranded Objects: Mourning, Memory, and Film in Postwar Germany* (Ithaca/London: Cornell UP, 1990).

29 Benedict Anderson, *Imagined Communities: Reflections on the Origin and Spread of Nationalism* (London: Verso, 1983), 19.

30 Lahr, 136.

31 Caruth, *Trauma: Explorations in Memory*, 5.

32 Bernhard Giesen, "The Trauma of Perpetrators: The Holocaust as the Traumatic Reference of German National Identity," *Cultural Trauma and Collective Identity*, eds. Jeffrey Alexander et al. (Berkeley: U of California P, 2004), 113.

33 See also "Iraqi Artist Layla Al-Attar" Video report from *Democracy Now!,* February 20, 1998, <http://www.youtube.com/watch?v=AgF914EHmeg>.

34 Raffo, qtd. in Jackie McGlone, n. pag.

35 Al-Rashid Hotel is a prominent establishment where foreign dignitaries often stay. See "Bush Doormat in Baghdad Hotel Dismantled," *First Coast News, April 11, 2003,* <www.firstcoastnews.com>; Nic Robertson, "A Return to Baghdad's Al-Rashid Hotel," *CNN*, October 14, 2002, <www.cnn.com>.

36 Hugh Pope, "Artist's rendering: After Painter Dies, A Myth is Born in Insular Iraq—Baghdadis Believe Ms. Attar Was Target of US Missiles," *Asian Wall Street Journal* (June 3, 2002), retrieved from ProQuest Newsstand <http://www.proquest.com/en-US/catalogs/databases/detail/newsstand.shtml>, document ID: 122139921.

37 Anne Cubilié writes: "Gender, in its regulation through patriarchal cultural norms, is a category to which all women are subject. . . . Thus the vantage of already inhabiting categories of gender difference may encourage some women to negotiate their positions as survivors in ways that more readily acknowledge difference, fragmentation, and the negation of multiple identity categories. Such gender difference does not uniformly suggest a 'female' relationship to atrocity but it does suggest that some women approach their positions as survivors from a certain critical location that is more open to instability and flux than negotiations of difference suggest." See Anne Cubilié, *Women Witnessing Terror* (NY: Fordham UP, 2005), 90.

[38] After all, *violenti non fit injura*: to one willing, no harm is done.

[39] Shoshona Felman, "The Return of the Voice: Claude Lanzmann's *Shoah*," *Testimony: Crisis of Witnessing in Literature*, 225.

[40] Culbertson, 169. Culbertson argues that the survivor's silence is partially based on the "paradox of the distance of one's experience" (170).

[41] The play's dialogue (particularly that of certain characters) includes grammatical errors and stylistic awkwardness, reflecting foreign speech, and specifically Iraqi speech, in English.

[42] Caruth, *Trauma: Explorations in Memory*, vii.

[43] Dominick LaCapra writes about nostalgia: "When absence is converted into loss, one increases the likelihood of misplaced nostalgia or utopian politics in quest of a new totality or fully unified community. When loss is converted into (or encrypted in an indiscriminately generalized rhetoric of) absence, one faces the impasse of endless melancholy, impossible mourning, and interminable aporia in which any process or working through the past and its historical losses is foreclosed or prematurely aborted." See Dominick LaCapra, "Trauma, Absence, Loss," *Critical Inquiry* 25.4 (Summer 1999): 698.

[44] Ron Cohen, "Reviews: Theatre: '9 Parts of Desire,'" *Back Stage—The Performing Arts Weekly* 45 (November 26-December 2, 2004): 48. See also Sajjad S. Essa et al., "Cancer Mortality in Basrah," *The Medical Journal of Basrah University* 25.1 (2007): 56-60.

[45] In Huda's words, the young Iraqi girls like her "are shell shocked, all these girls/they're going backwards/ they abandon their education now, since the occupation/ now they are wearing the veils./Their grandmothers are more liberated than them" (39).

[46] Cohen, 48.

[47] Whitehead, 5.

[48] Whitehead, 5.

[49] Two USAF laser-guided "smart bombs" destroyed the Baghdad 'Amiriyya bomb shelter ("Public shelter no. 25") on the night of February 13-14, 1991. The US intelligence community claimed that the shelter was one of Saddam's command centers. During the raid, over 400 civilians, most of them women and children, were killed.

[50] Dori Laub, "An Event Without Witness: Truth, Testimony and Survival," in *Testimony: Crisis of Witnessing*, 78.

[51] According to *kunya* tradition, parents would refer to themselves in relation to their first-born son. This tradition is rarely practiced in relation to daughters. Having Umm Ghada rename herself in relation to her daughter reinforces the matriarchal bond that underlies Raffo's play. The

Arabic word for "tomorrow" resembles "Ghada" but differs in vocalization; it is a near homonym.

52 Writing about the weight of testimony, Laub points out that: "It is a dialogical process of exploration and reconciliation of two worlds—the one that was brutally destroyed and the one that is—that are different and will remain so. The testimony is inherently a process of facing loss—of going through the pain of the act of witnessing, and of the ending of the act of witnessing—which entails yet another repetition of the experience of separation and loss. It reenacts the passage through difference in such a way, however, that it allows perhaps a certain repossession of it" ("An Event Without Witness," 91).

53 Hartman, 543.

54 Hartman, 543.

55 Cohen, 48.

56 Mark Seltzer, "Wound Culture: Trauma in the Pathological Public Sphere," *October* 80 (Spring 1997): 4-5.

57 Michael Rothberg, *Traumatic Realism: The Demands of Holocaust Representation* (Minneapolis: U of Minnesota P, 2000), 27.

58 A similar theme appears in the segment of Iraqi Girl, who says: "On TVs, on *Oprah*, I saw people/they have so many hard lives, at first we feel bad for them/but always by some miracles their things get better!" (25). Her oblivion to the true hardship of her own life is heartbreaking.

59 Rothberg, 58. See also Monica Bohm-Duchen, ed., *After Auschwitz: Responses to the Holocaust in Contemporary Art* (London: Lund Humphries Publishers, 1995).

60 See Patrick Cockburn, "Book Market Fire Piles on the Misery for Broken Baghdad," *The Independent* (November 1, 2003), <http://www. independent.co.uk/news/world/middle-east/book-market-fire-piles-on-the-misery-for-broken-baghdad-737593.html>; Milbry Polk and Angela M. H. Schuster, *The Looting of the Iraq Museum: Baghdad, the Lost Legacy of Mesopotamia* (NY: Harry N. Abrams, 2005).

61 Raffo, 70.

62 Raffo, "Introduction," x.

63 Qtd. in Horwitz, 7.

64 Personal Interview,November 16, 2006.

65 Jeffrey Alexander, "On the Social Construction of Moral Universals: The 'Holocaust' from War Crime to Trauma Drama," *Cultural Trauma and Collective Identity*, eds. Jeffrey Alexander et al. (Berkeley: U of California P, 2004), 199.

66 Cathy Caruth, "Unclaimed Experience: Trauma and the Possibility of History," *Yale French Studies* 79 (1991): 181.

# Child of the Revolution: Sara Dolatabadi and the Esthetics of Memory (An Interview)

**Amy Motlagh**

---

## Introduction

To invoke the phrase "modern art" is to bring to mind images like Picasso's *Guernica*, or the iconic splatter paintings of Jackson Pollock. "Modern Iran," on the other hand, conjures grainy televised news images of Ayatollah Khomeini waving to throngs of admirers, or perhaps, more recently, the crowds of green-swathed Iranians who flooded the streets to protest the outcome of the June 2009 presidential elections. But bring these two phrases together to say "modern Iranian art" and there is generally a blank. If the words "Iran" and "art" are associated at all, it is in terms of the stunning reliefs that embellish the walls of ancient Persepolis; or perhaps the vivid miniatures that decorated manuscripts of the Safavid period and spread into the larger world of Persianate influence, including the Mughal, Tajik, and Ottoman cultural spheres. It is unlikely that they would address some of the works Iranians are most proud of: Mahmoud Tanavoli's sculptures; the paintings of Parviz Kalantari; or the photographs of 'Abbas. For most Westerners, the perception that Iran's modernity came at the cost of its cultural and artistic integrity—an impression amplified by the 1979 Revolution and the Islamic regime's censorship of all artistic production—prevails. Even if they have seen the colorful, lurid, government-sponsored murals sometimes pictured in popular news magazines like *Time* or *Newsweek*—the paintings that decorate Tehran's buildings, expressing Iranian defiance of US imperialism or honoring martyrs of the Iran-Iraq War—these typically do not register as art at all, but as a manifestation of the religious zealotry that many believe created the revolution in the first place.

To some extent, these strong associations—of modern Iran with ideological rigidity, and pre-modern Iran with vanished cultural splendor—have prevented those outside Iran from seeing the rich tradition of visual art that has developed in modern Iran during the last hundred years. At best, those living in the metropolitan centers of the West may be familiar with the work of Iranians living or born in the diaspora, whose work often incorporates Iranian themes, but which may reflect primary training in the host country's artistic traditions rather than Iran's. The work of Shirin Neshat and Marjane Satrapi—two Iranian-born artists—is perhaps the most famous example of this phenomenon. Both women have distinguished themselves through their Iran-related art: Neshat, the noted visual artist who has lived and worked in New York for the last twenty years, creates work that directly engages Western stereotypes about veiling and Islam that the West brings to any encounter with Iran; Satrapi's graphic novel *Persepolis* tells the story of the Iranian Revolution of 1979 through the personal lens of autobiography. Yet at the same time, both artists' work is undeniably cast in the Western traditions with which they are most familiar: Neshat's photographs and short films owe an obvious debt not only to Iranian cinema, but also to the critique of Orientalism expressed by US-based cultural critics like Edward Said, while Satrapi, whose illustrations occasionally nod toward an Iranian art form like the miniature, is most firmly grounded in the French *bande-desinée* tradition.[1]

Like Neshat and Satrapi, artist Sara Dolatabadi (1978-) was born in Iran, but now lives and works abroad. The comparison between Dolatabadi and these diasporic peers is perhaps inevitable, yet what distinguishes the Tokyo-based Dolatabadi from Neshat and Satrapi is not only that she received her artistic training in Iranian institutions, but that her work is not so easily defined as theirs—there are no overt references towards veiled women or religious symbols in her work, and her imaginative and changing style will not allow her nationality to define or limit its range of interpretations. At the same time, Japan—unlike the US or France, where Neshat and Satrapi live—is not typically counted among the primary sites of the Iranian diaspora. Unlike Los Angeles, London, Paris, or even Washington, DC, it does not have an active and defined culture or society of Iranian expatriates. Yet through Dolatabadi's work, Tokyo—where she moved for personal reasons—is insinuating itself into ideations of both Iran and the diaspora.

Though Dolatabadi acknowledges the influence of both Iranian and non-Iranian artists on her style, her exhibitions, discussed below, do not only show a keen attention to the artistic, social, and political concerns of Iran and Japan, but also to the dehumanization and sense of statelessness that seem to plague a world that is increasingly considered successfully "globalized"—connected by myriad forms of media and transportation that make the distances between geographic spaces long isolated from one another seem easily traversable—both physically and imaginatively—in a matter of seconds; or at most, hours. Dolatabadi's work examines the consequences of this ease, and imagines ways of bridging the new psychic distances among individuals that globalization has ironically seemed to create.

This brief introduction makes no claim to comprehensively define Dolatabadi or to offer a comprehensive survey of modern Iranian art. However, it does aim to suggest some possible contexts for understanding Dolatabadi's oeuvre to date, and in the process, to shed light on a wider tradition too often relegated to the margins of modern art. I had the privilege of interviewing Dolatabadi in a series of written exchanges during the summer and fall of 2009. Though I came to the interviews with questions about diaspora and her relationship to an Iran from which she is currently separated (by choice, she reminds us), her replies helped reshape my understanding of her work, which both demonstrates the continuity of Iran's unique contribution to modernism and expresses a familiarity with the artistic traditions of the world beyond Iran. Conceptualized in a variety of media—wire sculpture, different paint media, photography, and installation pieces—Dolatabadi's work offers a counter to the stereotypical views of modern Iranian art, which tend to conceptualize it as an absence; or as derivative of Western styles; or else formed entirely in the crucible of the 1979 Revolution.

The palette of works like *Simple Blue* suggests the influence of Japanese art and society on Dolatabadi's work. Dolatabadi explains that the collection was inspired by the government-issued blue plastic tents used by the homeless for shelter in Japan. Yet, as she points out, she sees this blue as a symbol of a broader metaphorical "homelessness" that afflicts many in today's society: "Homelessness can apply to people who have been uprooted from their social or cultural identity. . . . Maybe because of [the] general wandering [in our time]."[2] The dominance of this vivid blue against black comprises the defining contrast of the work, and while these colors suggest Japanese color preferences (especially those of the *ukiyo-e* woodblock prints and paintings so admired and reproduced in the West), the largeness of the style evokes David Hockney and Mark Rothko, both artists whose influence Dolatabadi acknowledges.

*Seat*, an installation piece inspired by her father, noted Iranian novelist Mahmoud Dolatabadi (born 1940), suggests the influence of Iranian forms. In a corner beneath a curving stair, Dolatabadi creates a place for thought: A simple white cushion is placed on the floor, and writing in Persian decorates the corner—as though someone sitting there were working out his thoughts on the wall. The connection between word and image is an important and enduring one in Iranian art and letters, on multiple levels. As art historian Lynn Gumpert points out, Persian calligraphy embodies a unique connection between word and image, combining the two in a unique form of visual representation that appeals simultaneously to our figurative and linguistic capacities.[3] In her work, Dolatabadi recognizes the influence of artists who have embodied this complicated relationship in their work, such as Mahmoud Tanavoli; she particularly admires what may be his best-known sculpture, *Hich* (Nothing). *Hich* brings the esteemed art of Persian calligraphy into three dimensions by casting the word *hich* as a piece of sculpture. In doing so, Tanavoli establishes a conflict between the literal meaning of the word—"nothing"—and the sculpture's palpable materiality. Similarly, works like *Seat* challenge us to imagine what is implied, but not there: the father whose seat and writing this commemorative work recalls.

*Ordinary Fruits* depicts a series of cocoon-like figures hanging suspended from a single line. Its title is taken from the poem "Strange Fruits" by Jewish writer and teacher Abel Meeropol (who wrote under the pseudonym Lewis Allan) that condemned lynching in the American South. (Most Americans know it through Nina Simone's hauntingly beautiful performance of the poem as a song by the same name.) Rendered in wire figure installations as well as in mixed media canvas works, these figures suggest the hybridity of Dolatabadi's art, both in terms of her choice of materials and in her style of representation.[4] The impulse of the collection is itself an act of what Gayatri Spivak (evoking an idea from Jacques Derrida's *Politics of Friendship*) has called "teleopoiesis": the "cutting and pasting" of one kind of cultural rhetoric into a foreign context, the consequence of which is a demonstrable affinity across cultural boundaries of language and artistic practice.[5] Here,

Dolatabadi practices teleopoiesis in an effort to bring the critique of a barbaric practice in the American South to an analysis of, and protest against, the public executions reinstituted by the Islamic Republic upon taking power in 1979. Public hangings, discontinued by Reza Pahlavi in the 1920s, were re-initiated by the new regime as an exercise of power and instillation of fear.[6]

Dolatabadi asserts that in spite of the non-figurative nature of many of her series, "People are the main subject in most of my work. The displacement, confusion, and feeling[s of] loss in today's life . . . [are what] I try to communicate . . . to the viewer [to] provoke empathy."[7] With its abstracted images of cocoon-like bodies, *Ordinary Fruits* is a kind of bridge between Dolatabadi's figurative and non-figurative works. *Breaking the Habits*, which depicts human figures in various modes of reflection, expression, and exchange, may be her most explicitly figurative collection. Many of the paintings show a recognizably female figure (possibly the artist herself) communing with herself in a mirror. Oftentimes, as in *Breaking the Habits* 9, the canvas is divided into two or three frames in which the figure (and her reflection) are seen from different positions. In *Breaking the Habits* 1, a figure whose head and shoulders alone are pictured in the frame twists its head to one side as though in pain, its features effaced by patterned scratches of grey. In *Breaking the Habits* 11, a bride is pictured at the center of the canvas in a portrait-style pose, while another figure, perhaps the bride at another moment, has her back to the viewer, and looks over one shoulder towards the bride. *Breaking the Habits* 14 shows what may or may not be a human folded into itself in a painful expression of grief. Viewing the collection as a whole, the pattern emerges to focus on one feminine figure. Are the habits to be broken those of the woman, or those of humankind at large? Dolatabadi does not offer clear answers, leaving it to the viewer to determine whether we are to understand the series as a process of "breaking the habits," or of the inability of humans, individually or collectively, to ever fully do so.

In her most recent solo exhibition, *Pejvak (God is Great)* (*pejvak* means "echo" in Persian), Dolatabadi created a space in which green fluorescent lights lit up a darkened room where the phrase "Allahu Akbar" ("God is great"—a Muslim proclamation of faith) was repeated over and over again. In Tehran—both during the 1979 Revolution and this summer's "Green Wave"—dissidents chanted this phrase both at protests and every night from urban rooftops in a nonviolent protest against injustices being perpetrated by the regime. In 1979, the regime of Mohammad Reza Pahlavi was being censured; today, it is the Islamic Republic of Iran, whose behavior in last summer's presidential elections led to widespread public protest and prolonged unrest. *Pejvak* explicitly engages the ongoing "Green Wave" in Iran, known in Persian as *Moj-e Sabz*—the opposition movement that supported Mir-Hossein Moussavi, the reformist candidate, in the contested June elections, and which has continued to protest the outcome of those elections in spite of violent persecution by the state. The work's title is suggestive on a number of levels, drawing our attention not only to the echoed "Allahu Akbar" which ironically draws together dissidents of the regime, but also the way in which the "Green Wave" is an echo of the 1979 Revolution—a movement that began with broad-based opposition to the dictatorial nature of Pahlavi rule.[8]

Works like *Pejvak (God is Great)* demonstrate that in spite of her geographical distance from Iran, Dolatabadi clearly remains emotionally close to its trials and traumas, even if that relationship is often recreated through memory rather than direct experience. Are artists like Dolatabadi, Neshat, and Satrapi, who center Iran in the work they produce and show abroad, best understood as Iranian artists or diasporic ones? We must ask at what point an artist ceases to be most appropriately associated with the nation of her/his birth, and belong instead to the nation to which s/he has immigrated. And perhaps more importantly still, we must ask what influence and relationship Iranian artists living abroad have on those living at home. Dolatabadi herself feels some ambivalence about being termed a "diasporic" artist, and wonders whether the term can be appropriately used to describe her. Pointing out that she left Iran voluntarily, and believes she will one day return, Dolatabadi echoes the sentiments of many of those who live outside of Iran but feel connected to it by birth or heritage. At the same time, it is tempting to view Dolatabadi, born in the year of the revolutionary fervor that changed Iran and its relationship with the outside world, as the child of that same revolution and the intellectual forces that helped create it.

## Notes

[1] See Lindsey Moore's "Frayed Connections, Fraught Projections: The Troubling Work of Shirin Neshat," *Women: A Cultural Review* 13.1 (2002): 2-17 and Iftikhar Dadi's "Shirin Neshat's Photographs as Postcolonial Allegories," *Signs: Journal of Women in Culture and Society* 34.1 (2008): 125-50 for further discussion of Neshat's relationship to Iranian cinema. On Satrapi's visual references to the miniature tradition, see, for example, p. 77 of *Persepolis* (NY: Pantheon, 2003). The film version of Satrapi's memoir (Vincent Parronaud, dir., *Persepolis* ([Sony Pictures Classics, 2007]) develops and heightens many of these references to earlier Persian art forms.

[2] See <http://www.sara-dolatabadi.com/gallery/simple-blue/01.html>.

[3] Lynn Gumpert, "Introduction," *Picturing Iran: Art, Society and Revolution,* eds. Shiva Balaghi and Lynn Gumpert (London & NY: I. B. Tauris, 2002), 14-15.

[4] Though she does not mention any influence, this collection may be compared to Japanese artist Akiyama Yo's cocoon-like ceramic sculptures in his exhibition *Oscillation.*

[5] Gayatri Spivak, *Death of a Discipline* (NY: Columbia UP, 2003), 45-47.

[6] Dolatabadi mistakenly suggests that public executions were practiced by the Pahlavi regime. Though the Pahlavis did not outlaw the death sentence, Reza Shah forbade public executions. Crimes punishable by death today in Iran include adultery and treason.

[7] See <http://www.sara-dolatabadi.com/gallery/breaking-the-habbits/01.html>.

[8] Although the 1979 Revolution was supported by populations comprising a variety of ideological positions on what kind of government should succeed the Pahlavi regime, the movement was rapidly overtaken by the religious faction that supported Khomeini's vision of a *vilayat-e faqih*, or "rule by the jurisconsult," that remains the articulating ideology of the regime today. Khomeini's idea, controversial even among Shi'ites, is wrongly regarded by many in the West as a "conservative" or "fundamentalist" interpretation of Islamic ideologies of temporal rule. In fact, it is quite radical, in the sense of being innovative in Shi'i thought. See, among others, Said Arjomand, *Turban for the Crown* (NY and Oxford: Oxford UP, 1988), 104-05.

## Interview

**Amy Motlagh**: Tell me about *Ordinary Fruits*—the series that evokes the memory of the public hangings that have taken place in Iran since the 1979 Revolution. You say in the description: "They can be as simple or as complicated as we are." Can you elaborate on this? And perhaps also say a bit about the conflation of an everyday ("ordinary") object for consumption—fruit—with the bodies of the executed?
**Sara Dolatabadi**: Capital punishment still exists in many countries. In Iran this takes the form of hanging, and as far as I know it also existed in Iran prior to the 1979 revolution as well.

The project of *Ordinary Fruits* in my mind does not apply to Iran only, but of course I have been affected more by news of hangings in my country recently. Unfortunately, capital punishment is still practiced in many countries, and I hope my work encompasses this topic as a whole and is really not subject to borders. For example Japan, where I am currently living, also exercises the death penalty by hanging. Sadly though, capital punishment is still carried out in many countries and, regrettably, Iran had over 300 executions in 2008 second only to China. In Japan, less than ten people were executed the same year. I feel very strongly about this and I hope one day Iran will not be among the top three vengeful countries in the world.

The name *Ordinary Fruits* which I have used was derived from a song which Billie Holiday performed many times titled "Strange Fruit." This was originally a poem written by Abel Meerapol in 1939 to express his horror of the lynching of blacks at the time. I took this title and changed "Strange" to "Ordinary," to express the fact that now these executions have become more "ordinary" in Iran, which is very sad. The first sketches I did for this series, the hanging objects, looked like bags of potatoes, which are worthless and maybe thrown out in real life. But these objects were complicated people and this is really a form of irony in my work.

**AM**: Your birth date coincides with that of the revolution. In what ways do you feel that your life and work have been influenced by the memory of this event, which you cannot remember but must nonetheless be an important effect on your life and on your family's life. Many people view this national trauma as the effect of earlier violence committed against Iran's sovereignty. Does your art reflect this view—or any view—on the revolution?

**SD**: The revolution did not have a direct effect on my life as I was very young when it happened and grew up in post-revolutionary Iran. But I would see the effects of the revolution indirectly in my extended family and friends. When I was young, for example, my uncle suddenly left Iran, leaving his wife and children behind. They, in turn, tried to reunite with my uncle a few times before they finally succeeded. I would hear about acquaintances fleeing Iran by wearing animal skins to disguise themselves and risking their lives while doing so. I heard of others held in prison due to their political views. So I could feel the disruptions in families and friends around me. And of course, I knew that I should never speak in public about these troubling situations. These things certainly affected me indirectly, but fortunately I had a relatively normal childhood and upbringing in Iran. I guess my experiences affect my work, but I feel I am more concerned about current social and political situations, which may not directly be related to the revolution

**AM**: To what extent has the engaged position of the artists and writers that precede you—including, perhaps, your father, the distinguished Iranian author Mahmoud Dolatabadi—influenced your view of art and its role in redressing the wounds of a society? Do you feel a sense of responsibility specifically as an Iranian artist—rather than just an artist?
**SD**: Of course my father's work and companionship have also inspired me, but I think more in terms of outlook and content than technique.

I remember confiding in my father that I had lost my concentration in work, my father advised me to start and the process itself would bring focus and concentration back. And it did. It is my hope to become a bit more patient and consistent, as he was, in my career.

Every artist is affected by other artists in their career. I think I was affected by my professor, Hossein Maher, initially, as I worked with him for a few years at the start of my career and also Manouchehr Motabar. They influenced me mostly in a technical sense, as they were both painters too.

I think to a certain extent I do sense some responsibility, yes. Of course issues in Iranian society affect me and I feel a need to communicate them to my audience.

**AM**: In June 2009, I visited an exhibition called *Iran Inside/Out* at the Chelsea Museum in New York City. The exhibition showed the work of Iranian and Iranian diasporic artists. Many of the works—especially those by diasporic artists—were concerned with representations of

Iran in Western media, which they feel are inaccurate. How concerned are you with this issue? Further, how would you categorize yourself: Do you consider yourself, living in Japan, to be primarily an "Iranian," or have you moved into what might be called the post-national state of "diaspora"? If these categories of identity are not relevant to you, which are? If they are relevant to you, what do you think the difference between these categories is?

**SD**: Of course I too am concerned with the representation of Iran in the world. I think most Iranians would be, especially the ones living abroad.

I do not really consider myself part of the diaspora, as I left Iran at the age of 27. I was given an opportunity to move to Japan and I might have the chance to move back again. But I have returned to Iran twice a year to keep contact with my country and cannot imagine that I would never live there again, I am pretty sure I will one day return.

But I think that leaving Iran and being in Japan for about 3 years now has affected me. I think living in Japan has affected me in very positive ways, personally and in the progression of my work. However, I sometimes felt lost and lonely since I had left my home and country for the first time. But I think this is a very natural feeling.

**AM**: You say of the series *Simple Blue* that the "blue packages represent dispersed homelessness in Japan." Can you elaborate on what you mean by "dispersed" here? Also you say that "homelessness can apply to people who have been uprooted from their social or cultural identity. These are the ones who have lost their link with their familiarity and society. Maybe because of a general wandering this exists in the time that we are all part of." How did you become preoccupied with this idea of homelessness or the displacement of the modern world?

**SD**: By "dispersed" I simply mean scattered, as the homeless in Japan can be seen to be in various parts of the country. In and around Tokyo, you do not only see them in central locations like Shibuya, or in a very manicured park near the Tokyo Metropolitan Tower in Shinjuku, but also in the outskirts of the city along Tamagawa river, for example. These are all very interesting places in Tokyo, all are places that a tourist would visit; the homeless have very good taste in choosing their location. The reason I was attracted to the homeless is that, unlike most in other countries, they seem very clean and tidy and seem to be content. They all used the blue waterproof fabrics for shelter, and I love that color.

I may have related to the homeless in Tokyo, as I also felt a degree of "homelessness" in Japan when I just moved. I felt secluded from the Japanese society as a foreigner. Even though I live in a central area in Tokyo, I felt apart from the general public at first. This may be mostly because Japan is indeed a unique country and has a very distinctive culture. People are very comfortable maintaining distance from each other. This isolation gives them privacy, and the Japanese seem very much at ease with it. But initially this was bothering me, and I was not used to it. In public areas like the subways or in the streets, I felt invisible because people do not smile at one another to acknowledge each other or avoid eye contact completely. But I gradually adjusted to my new home, and now I am used to it and I like it.

Also in this series I have taken the idea of homelessness in general to include having to move away from your home for some reason. Just as the homeless in Japan had to move to the streets from their home, many people move away from their country and leave their home in search of a better life in other countries. Of course, these two issues are different but in both situations people are uprooted from what is familiar and move to a place that is unknown and unpredictable.

**AM**: Tell me about the differences between the palettes of the Iran and Japan series. What differences do you see between the two cultures, and how do you try to convey these through your colors and materials?
**SD**: The main difference between my work in Japan and Iran is that the projects in Japan included various installations and some of my work has become more abstract. Japan and Iran differ greatly in culture; this is a very broad question. I think Japan is unique and this would be the case if we compare Japan with many countries. But what I wanted to mention about my work is that it became more and more social and political in Japan. I think I brushed on social issues in both countries in my work which I completed in Tokyo.

**AM**: Many of your series and installations, especially *Seat*, which you acknowledge is a tribute to your father, seem influenced by memory. How would you characterize the role that memory plays in your work?
**SD**: My memories have a major part in my art work, and particularly since I left Iran, this fact has become more and more evident.

Memory was in play in my series *Ordinary Fruits*, for example. I remember vividly one day when my friends told me that someone was hanged in a big square near our school in Iran. They occasionally hanged people in public then. Fortunately, I was not witness to this act, but I recall being deeply affected and saddened. And, even though I did not see this terrible incident, it influenced me greatly and this memory definitely played an important role in this project.

And of course *Seat* is a clear example of one of my works that is solely based on memories I had of my father working through the night. Maybe I was thinking more of memories of my family since I was away from them while in Tokyo?

**AM**: Could you say a bit more about how your life in Japan has influenced your art? How has the Japanese art world influenced you, if at all?
**SD**: From a superficial point of view, my work has become more general, simpler—which of course may be said to be an effect of this Japanese environment. But something important that has happened to my work while living abroad is that more and more, the work portrays the issues and disturbances occurring in Iran. I do not know whether the reason for this is my homesickness or being far from Iran, but whatever the reason, it allows me to see the problems in Iran more clearly and to better portray them. I see this new perspective as an important development in my work. Perhaps I am not truly a part of the diaspora, but, at the same time, I really feel that I have experienced this aspect of the experience for it to be true. It is also true that, although I grew up in Iran, I left Iran of my own accord. In spite of this, the experience has been a challenge for me.

**AM**: Could you tell us more about your training as an artist—both institutional and non-institutional? Have other artists (Iranian or otherwise) been important influences on you?
**SD**: I studied art in the Academy of Graphic Arts—meaning I went to the academy for the four years of high school and at that time, I began to work seriously with Hossein Maher in his atelier. I became familiar with sketching, printing, and photography to a good extent, and then when I went on to university, I chose to study painting. I cannot say that university was particularly useful to me because there were not many opportunities at the college of arts but, on the other hand, it did have good teachers. In any case, my serious training was not at university, but in the additional classes that I took outside of the university.

It is not easy to say which painters or artists have influenced me most. Many and no one! At each stage of my training, I was drawn to different artists. For example, when I was in high school, I really liked Modigliani and, when I began university, I was a fan of David Hockney, and I am always amazed by Mark Rothko. In my view, some of Rothko's works must be viewed from up close. Among Iranian artists, I particularly admire the sculpture of Tanavoli, especially his piece *Hich*.

**AM**: Do you see any continuity between your art and classical/traditional forms of Iranian art (miniatures, carpet design, etc.)?
**SD**: I can say that I regularly study books of Persian miniatures. Whether or not there is a direct influence from this on my work, I cannot say. However, in some of my figurative works, there is emotional and lyrical content that may be viewed as akin to that of the miniatures.

Of course, now, I am in the process of setting up an installation piece where I hope to make use of the spirit of miniatures. But, well, since this work has not been completed yet, I cannot comment on it.

## Illustrations: Sara Dolatabdi

*Breaking the Habits* 5, mixed media, 120 cm x 210 cm

*Breaking the Habits* 9, mixed media, 60 cm x 260 cm

*Breaking the Habits* 10, mixed media, 26 cm x 60 cm

*Ordinary Fruits* 9, mixed media, 50 cm x 70 cm

*Breaking the Habits* 14, mixed media, 20 cm x 30 cm

*Simple Blue* 10, monoprint 30 cm x 40 cm

*Breaking the Habits* 8, mixed media, 26 cm x 60 cm

*Ordinary Fruits*, wire installation

*Breaking the Habits* 11, mixed media, 24 cm x 54 cm

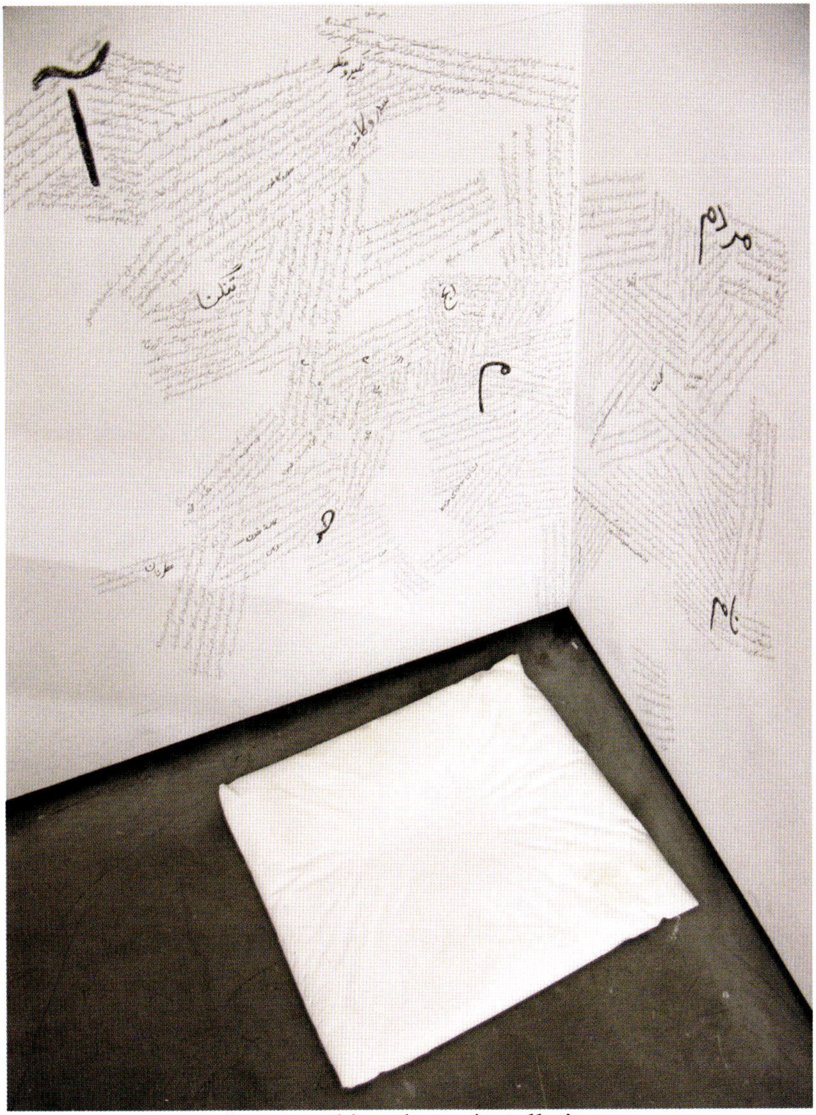


*Seat*, graphite-plaster installation

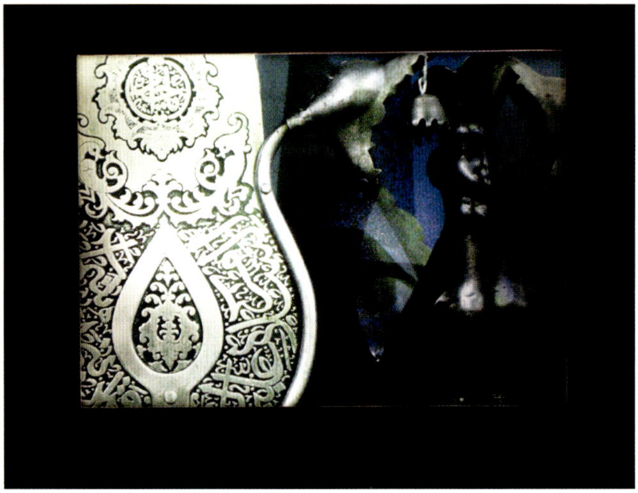

Detail from *Pejvak (God is Great)*, photograph

Detail from *Pejvak (God is Great)*, photograph

# Abstracts of Articles
# (Alphabetically by last name)

---

## Nasser's Resignation Speech and the Memory of Defeat: A Rhetorical Introduction to Political Discourse Analysis

**Emad Abdel Latif**

This article analyzes Nasser's resignation speech after the 1967 defeat from a rhetorical perspective, arguing that its rhetorical construction has played a major role in producing subsequent reactions, culminating in mass anti-resignation and defeat demonstrations. The article examines prominent rhetorical features in the speech such as euphemism, personal pronouns, conceptual metaphors, and non-verbal signs (vocal performance, body language, etc.). The article combines formal analysis of linguistic and rhetorical phenomena with an analysis of the problematic socio-textual relationships.

## Return to Half-Ruins: Memory, Postmemory, and Living History in Palestine

**Lila Abu-Lughod**
**(Translated by Hosam Nayil)**

This essay is about Ibrahim Abu-Lughod's return to live, and then to die, in Palestine after forty years in exile in the US. His return to Palestine changed his experience of the cataclysmic and defining event known as the *Nakba*. He inserted his memories of Palestine and Jaffa directly into the present and into a living history. His insertion of memory into the historical present made possible a different knowledge and identification for his daughter, who interweaves his stories with her experiences in her essay, underlining how postmemory of the daughter works when the Palestinian trauma is not over and persists in everyday life in Palestine.

## The Question of Reading Traumatic Testimony: Jones's *Corregidora* and Morrison's *Beloved*

**Abdennebi Ben Beya**

Contemporary writing is haunted by the manifestation of the repressed. This is why the beginning of this new millennium may appropriately be coined 'the era of monstrological revenance': disruptive, angry, and vengeful. The act of writing is henceforth dispossessed, powerless, and unauthoritative. This article is mainly concerned with the question of reading today's ghostly literary productions, focusing on the limits of interpretation, understanding, and comprehension as containment. This is illustrated via an ethical re-evaluation of Toni Morrison's *Beloved* and Gayl Jones's *Corregidora* in their encounter with trauma theorists, but mainly with Jacques Derrida's overwhelming reflections on mourning, spectrality, and testimony.

## Hearts Exhausted by Diaspora: A Reading of Kamal Ruhayyim's Novels

**Mohammed Birairi**

This article examines Kamal Ruhayyam's novels from a formalistic and thematic point of view, in an attempt to explore the underlying ideology behind the narrative. The author reaches the conclusion that religion, despite its significance, is but one component of culture as anthropologically defined—a living language and daily practices and rituals that collectively shape a certain society's individual identity. The trauma of estrangement suffered by the Jewish Egyptian protagonists of the novels in France is derived from their sense of nostalgia for Egypt as their cultural identity is strongly linked with the country which they had to leave. The article examines in detail the dilemma of a hybrid identity where the national and cultural affiliations manifest themselves, overpowering narrow religiosity.

## Forms of Memory: Partition as a Literary Paradigm

**Anna Bernard**

This article speculatively proposes a method for comparing works of "partition literature," with reference to narratives of the partitions of India, Palestine, and Ireland. It contends that it is possible to identify distinct genres, plotlines, and esthetic modes within the category of partition literature, specifically the romance, the Bildungsroman, and the fragmented narrative. It argues that each of the genres considered has an inherent propensity towards counterfactualism. These forms contest the current order by evoking a yearning for what might have been, and they seek to make alternatives to partition thinkable once again.

## The Wound that Never Heals

**Vincent Crapanzano**

This article discusses the Harki reaction to Masaoud Benyoucef's play *Le nom du père*. Harkis are Algerians who sided with the French during the Algerian War of Independence, tens of thousands of whom were massacred at the war's end by their compatriots. Those who managed to escape to France were incarcerated in camps, some for sixteen years. They considered the play a slur on their identity and attempted, unsuccessfully, to stop its performance. They objected to the portrayal of the protagonist, the son of a Harki, who, entrapped by his father's fateful decision, has lost his bearings and is manipulated by the Algerian military, the Islamists, and the French.

## Death of the Self in Modern and Contemporary Arabic Poetry

**Amr Elsherif**

This article examines the relation between text and society. If the individual can be defined through the relation to the whole of which he is a part, being separated from it leads to a state of self-division which leads to its death or loss of direction. The article traces this phenomenon in modern and contemporary Arabic poetry. Unlike the symbol which predominates in poetry produced in organic societies, and in which the signified is supposedly immanent in the signifier, the distance between the signifier and the signified in allegory and the contradiction in irony recreate the distance between the individual and society.

## Extreme Realities:
## Naomi Shihab Nye's Essays and Poems

**Ibis Gómez-Vega**

This article explores the connection between Naomi Shihab Nye's life as a writer who lives in the relative safety of the American Southwest and her emotional and familial connection to Palestine, a land torn by war. For Shihab Nye, the war in Palestine is personal because this is her ancestral homeland. Many of her poems deal with events that most Americans only see on the television news, but the Arab-American poet also writes about a world far removed from the war in Palestine. These poems offer evidence of life in a safer environment, but an environment where the poet nevertheless feels the stigma of being an Arab in America at a time when every Arab is suspect, including a poet. Through her poetry and essays, Naomi Shihab Nye navigates the two very extreme realities of her life.

## Epistolary Memory:
## Revisiting Traumas in Women's Writing

**Walid El Hamamsy**

This article deals with two epistolary novels: Alice Walker's *The Color Purple* and Hanan al-Shaykh's *Beirut Blues*, showing the similarities between the two works from the formal/structural point of view as well as pointing out the function of the letter form and its symbolic significance in each. It tackles the confessional nature of the letters and the way they help the two protagonists in achieving a better understanding of their positions, even though the letters written by both protagonists are for the most part one-sided, and do not receive responses as in regular correspondence.

## Absence as Trauma and Familiarity:
## The Theme of Death in the Egyptian Novel

**Hussein Hamouda**

This article explores the theme of death in a number of selected Egyptian novels by such writers as Naguib Mahfouz, Gamal al-Ghitany,

Bahaa Taher, Ni'mat al-Bihairy, and others. The article analyzes the trauma of absence in the fact of death and the way in which it manifests itself in these novels, both through their preset events and their protagonists' recollections which seek to keep the memory of the dead alive.

## Hazina's Agonies

**Abdel Hamid Hawas**

This article explores folk culture as a reservoir of the collective memory of the people. It tackles the mechanisms through which traumatic collective memories figure and how they express collective worldviews. The article foregrounds the protagonist of a novella by Yahya Taher Abdullah, *The Collar and the Bracelet*. Her proper name, Hazina, which also means "sorrowful woman" is used as a key to unlock the sorrows of the people. The article analyzes examples of traumatic events as recalled in different verbal genres: folk epics, work songs, women's solo chants, narrative *mawwals* and tales.

## Aristophanes's Response to the Peloponnesian War and the Defeat of the Comic Hero

**Vassiliki Kotini**

This article discusses the experience of the Peloponnesian war through the plays of Aristophanes, tracing the writer's career and examining the way the civil conflict is reflected in his work. It underlines how the experience and outcome of the war was progressively shaped into trauma not only for the Athenians but also for Aristophanic comedy itself. It focuses on three Aristophanic comedies: *Acharnians*, *Peace*, and *Lysistrata*. It also examines *Frogs*, Aristophanes's comedy which discusses the salvation of his city. Language, motifs, the comic hero, and the (impossibility of the) solution provided becomes the indicator of the political and military condition.

## A Wartime Cinematic Testimony

**Arab Lotfi**

The author of this essay depicts in a personal tone her cinematic experience as a citizen in a country that was central in the unfolding of a regional history beset with traumas. Her roots in South Lebanon, bordering on Palestine, have marked her life as she witnessed the ongoing political struggles in her own country and in the Arab World. She underlines how geography shaped her own personal history from childhood and how she in turn was inspired by that history in her filmmaking. She points out how her individual traits as a director are interwoven with collective concerns to memorialize and analyze events.

**Social Memories 'in the Flesh':**
**War and Exile in Algerian Self-Writing**

**James McDougall**

This article proposes an interpretive reading of contemporary Algerian cultural practice as providing 'techniques of living' in which social memories of traumatic experiences are encoded. Working across several genres—literary fiction, popular music, scholarship, autobiography, political humor, and journalism—the essay seeks to delineate the economy of narration through which intensely disruptive experiences of exile and war, and competing ways of accounting for them, are internalized and expressed in the social production of self-narratives.

**Reflections on Trauma and Memory**
**in Youssef Chahine's Films**

**Dalia Said Mostafa**

This article focuses on Youssef Chahine's films *September 11* and *Alexandria .. New York* in order to engage critically with some theoretical, political, and cinematic issues in relation to collective and personal memory and trauma. The films reflect Chahine's viewpoint on the relationship between the US and the Arab world at the present time. They are among the very few in the context of Arab cinema which have addressed the September 11 attacks. The author discusses some of the cinematic motifs and techniques which Chahine uses. She argues that the importance of Chahine's two films arises from the political issues they engage with, which are rarely addressed in Egyptian cinema in general.

**Child of the Revolution:**
**Sara Dolatabadi and the Esthetics of Memory**
**(An Interview)**

**Amy Motlagh**

The perception that modern Iran's cultural production is characterized, like its politics, by revolution and ideological rigidity has prevented those outside Iran from seeing the rich tradition of visual art that has developed in modern Iran during the last hundred years. In this interview, Amy Motlagh discusses the work of the talented young Iranian artist Sara Dolatabadi (1978-), who was born and educated in Iran, but now lives and works in Tokyo. Dolatabadi's art and life offer an exceptional—yet at the same time, oddly representative—example of the plight of the modern Iranian artist.

**Trauma and Testimony:**
**Heather Raffo's *9 Parts of Desire***

**Magda Romanska**

This article analyzes a recent play, *9 Parts of Desire* (2003) by Heather Raffo—an Iraqi American—which deals with the tragic conditions of Iraq as expressed by nine Iraqi women of different backgrounds and age groups. The performance of the play, often featuring one actress playing the nine roles, was successful in the US. The author finds parallelism between Iraqi trauma marked by repression, sanctions, and wars, and narrated by women, and other catastrophic events and testimonies. She links staged discourse with traumatic syndromes and dramatic theory. The article raises issues related to representation of the Other and identification.

**Anxiety of Erasure: Arab Women Writers**
**between Shahrazad's Memory and the Nightmare of Infanticide**

**Hanadi Al-Samman**

This article examines the literature of Arab women writers of the European and North American diaspora, showing how they use their engagement with Western societies to reclaim their voice not as exiles, but as continuing participants in their homelands' intellectual life. The article traces their double obsession with the motifs of the medieval Shahrazad and the pre-Islamic *wa'd al-banat* (female infanticide) as a fascinating, productive, and creative force in their writings. This article proposes a theory of Arab women's authorship and creates a paradigm for understanding the narrative strategies of Arab diaspora women writers. It shows how the writers move beyond the negative, haunting trauma of the *wa'd*, and into the positive awakening of the Arab female writer.

## Catastrophic Subjectivity: Representing Lebanon's Undead

**Mark Westmoreland**

This article engages with several artists and filmmakers working in Lebanon's postwar period and the way they use experimental media in order to envision the experience of social catastrophe. Advancing the idea of a withdrawn subjectivity, likened to a state of "undeath," these projects accentuate the gap between sign and signified in order to mediate the phantoms of war without necessarily rendering them visible. Like vampires, the phantoms of Lebanon's wars bear no reflection and cannot be imaged directly. This article asks if the representation of monstrous specters can elucidate the invisible, unsayable, and unrepresentable under conditions of "official amnesia."

# Notes on Contributors
## (Alphabetically by last name)

---

**Emad Abdel Latif** teaches rhetorics and discourse analysis at the Faculty of Arts, Cairo University. He is on the editorial Board of *Al-lugha* magazine. He studied at Lancaster and Cairo Universities. His research focuses on contemporary rhetorical studies, political and religious discourses, and inter-cultural relationships. He has recently published two books on mass manipulation in arts and politics and Sadat's political speeches.

**Lila Abu-Lughod** is the Joseph L. Buttenwieser Professor of Anthropology and Gender Studies at Columbia University. A Palestinian-American anthropologist who has done extensive fieldwork in Egypt on women, gender politics, and expressive culture, including media, she is the author of three ethnographies: *Veiled Sentiments: Honor and Poetry in a Bedouin Society*, *Writing Women's Worlds: Bedouin Stories*, and *Dramas of Nationhood: The Politics of Television in Egypt*. She has edited a number of other books, including *Nakba: Palestine, 1948 and the Claims of Memory*.

**Abdennebi Ben Beya** is Assistant Professor of English and Comparative Literature at the Faculty of Human and Social Sciences, University of Tunis, Tunisia. He has published articles on postcolonial literatures and ethics, and is now writing a book on Anglophone and Francophone migrant aesthetics.

**Mohammed Birairi** teaches classical and modern Arabic literature at the American University in Cairo and Beni Suef University. He has published a book on classical poetry and has another forthcoming on pre-Islamic poetry. He has published a number of articles and translations on classical and modern Arabic poetry and prose.

**Anna Bernard** is Lecturer in Postcolonial Studies in the Department of English and Related Literature at the University of York. Her work has previously appeared in *Textual Practice* and *Amerasia*. She is completing a monograph on narrative form and national allegory in contemporary Palestinian and Israeli writing.

**Vincent Crapanzano** is Distinguished Professor of Comparative Literature and Anthropology at the Graduate Center of the City University of New York. He is the author of several books, including: *Imaginative Horizons, Hermes' Dilemma and Hamlet's Desire* and *The Hamadsha: A Study of Moroccan Ethnopsychiatry*. He is currently working on a book on the *harkis*.

**Sara Dolatabadi** is an Iranian artist who lives and works in Tokyo. She received her BA in Fine Arts at Azad University Faculty of Arts in Tehran, Iran, and has exhibited her work in Tehran, Tokyo, and New York, among other places.

**Amr Elsherif** received his MA in English literature and is currently working on a PhD in literary criticism. He studied in Egypt and the US. He has published articles in literary and philosophical periodicals concentrating mostly on the relation between esthetics and literature.

**Ibis Gómez-Vega** is Associate Professor at Northern Illinois University where she teaches twentieth-century American literature, including drama, with an emphasis on ethnic literature as well as Gay and Lesbian literature. She has published scholarly articles, a novel, *Send My Roots Rain*, and several short stories.

**Walid El Hamamsy** is Assistant Lecturer in the Department of English, Cairo University. He received his MA in comparative literature from the American University in Cairo. He is currently working on a PhD thesis on film adaptations of fictional works. He has published articles and translations on film, postcolonial literature, and gender studies.

**Hussein Hamouda** is Associate Professor in the Deptartment of Arabic, Cairo University. He specializes in modern literary criticism. He is Associate Editor of the *Naguib Mahfouz Periodical* and member of the literary book committee at the Egyptian Supreme Council of Culture.

**Abdel Hamid Hawas** Professor Emeritus at the Academy of Arts. He is former director of the Center of Folklore Studies. He received the

State Award in social science, 2005. He has taught in Egypt, the Arab world, and the US. He has published numerous books and articles on popular culture and participated in various literary conferences.

**Vassiliki Kotini** is Assistant Professor in the Department of English and Comparative Literature at the American University in Cairo. She specialized in Greek language and literature in Greece and England, receiving her PhD from the University of London. Her research focuses on ancient Greek literature, mythology, and classical drama (tragedy and comedy in literature and performance) and their influence and continuity in modern literature.

**Arab Lotfi** is a filmmaker. She teaches film production at the American University in Cairo. She studied film and specialized in documentary cinema at the Higher Film Institute in Cairo. She has released a number of documentary films related to Middle Eastern struggles.

**James McDougall** is Fellow and Tutor in History at Trinity College, Oxford. He previously taught at SOAS, London and at Princeton. His research focuses on the cultural, political, and intellectual history of North Africa, French colonialism, and nationalism and revolution in Africa and the Middle East.

**Dalia Said Mostafa** is Postdoctoral Research Fellow in Modern Arab Cultural History, the University of Manchester where she teaches Middle Eastern literature and cinema. She received her PhD from the University of Manchester and her MA from the American University in Cairo. She has published in Arabic on cinema and popular culture; and her recent publications in English focus on Lebanese fiction and gender relations in contemporary Egypt. Her current research revolves around the image and transformation of the city in literature and cinema, with a focus on the cities of Cairo and Beirut.

**Amy Motlagh** is Assistant Professor in the Department of English and Comparative Literature at the American University in Cairo and a creative writer. She received her PhD from Princeton University. Her research focuses on modern Iranian literature and culture produced in Iran and abroad.

**Hosam Nayil** is an Egyptian researcher and translator. He received his MA in contemporary criticism and rhetorics. He has written, co-authored, edited, and translated a number of books on Jacques Derrida and deconstruction. He is currently working on a book on mysticism and deconstruction.

**Magda Romanska** is Assistant Professor at Emerson College (Boston, USA) where she is the head of Theater Studies. She is also a research associate at Harvard University (Center for Russian and Eurasian Studies). She has published several articles and contributed to *Columbia Encyclopedia of Modern Drama*.

**Hanadi Al-Samman** is Assistant Professor of Arabic Language and Literature in the Middle Eastern and South Asian Languages and Cultures Department at the University of Virginia. Her research focuses on Middle Eastern and Arab women's studies, transnational and Islamic feminism(s), postcolonial and identity formation theories, as well as on literature of the Arab diaspora. She has published in scholarly journals and in edited collections. She is currently working on a book entitled *Anxiety of Erasure: Trauma, Authorship, and the Diaspora in Arab Women's Narrative*.

**Mark Westmoreland** is a visual anthropologist and documentary filmmaker. He is an Assistant Professor of Anthropology at the American University in Cairo. He earned his PhD from the University of Texas at Austin in Anthropology and Public Culture. He has worked on projects in India, Ethiopia, and Texas, where he co-founded the SEED Documentary Collective in order to facilitate opportunities for scholars and artists to develop public history projects by working closely with under-represented communities.

أَلِف

مجلة البلاغة المقارنة
العدد الثلاثون، ٢٠١٠

# الفجيعة والذاكرة

صورة الغلاف: «كسر العادات ٨» لسارا دولات آبادي.



توزيع قسم النشر بالجامعة الأمريكية بالقاهرة.
رقم الإيداع بدار الكتب: ٣٤٦٤/١٠
الترقيم الدولي: ٩٧٨-٩٧٧-٤١٦-٤٠٧-١
الرقم الدولي الموحد للدوريات: ١١١٠-٨٦٧٣

أعداد **ألف** السابقة ناقشت المحاور الآتية (الأعداد السابقة متوفرة بالسعر المذكور):

**ألف ١**: الفلسفة والأسلوبية
**ألف ٢**: النقد والطليعة الأدبية
**ألف ٣**: الذات والآخر: مواجهة
**ألف ٤**: التناص: تفاعلية النصوص
**ألف ٥**: البعد الصوفي في الأدب
**ألف ٦**: جماليات المكان
**ألف ٧**: العالم الثالث: الأدب والوعي
**ألف ٨**: الهرمنيوطيقا والتأويل
**ألف ٩**: إشكاليات الزمان
**ألف ١٠**: الماركسية والخطاب النقدي
**ألف ١١**: التجريب الشعري في مصر منذ السبعينيات
**ألف ١٢**: المجاز والتمثيل في العصور الوسطى
**ألف ١٣**: حقوق الإنسان والشعوب في الأدب والعلوم الإنسانية
**ألف ١٤**: الجنون والحضارة
**ألف ١٥**: السينمائية العربية: نحو الجديد والبديل
**ألف ١٦**: ابن رشد والتراث العقلاني في الشرق والغرب
**ألف ١٧**: الأدب والأنثروبولوجيا في أفريقيا
**ألف ١٨**: خطاب ما بعد الكولونيالية في جنوب آسيا
**ألف ١٩**: الجنوسة والمعرفة: صياغة المعارف بين التأنيث والتذكير
**ألف ٢٠**: النص الإبداعي ذو الهوية المزدوجة: مبدعون عرب يكتبون بلغات أجنبية
**ألف ٢١**: الظاهرة الشعرية
**ألف ٢٢**: لغة الذات: السير الذاتية والشهادات
**ألف ٢٣**: الأدب والمقدس
**ألف ٢٤**: حفريات الأدب: اقتفاء أثر القديم في الجديد
**ألف ٢٥**: إدوارد سعيد والتقويض النقدي للاستعمار
**ألف ٢٦**: شهوة الترحال: أدب الرحلة في مصر والشرق الأوسط
**ألف ٢٧**: الطفولة: بين الإبداع والتلقي
**ألف ٢٨**: الاقتباس الفني: مقاربات تطبيقية ومفاهيم نظرية
**ألف ٢٩**: الجامعة وهمومها: محلياً وعالمياً

**الطباعة**: دار إلياس العصرية بالقاهرة

**سعر العدد**: في جمهورية مصر العربية: عشرون جنيهاً؛ في البلاد الأخرى:
الأفراد: عشرون دولاراً أمريكياً، المؤسسات: أربعون دولاراً أمريكياً.

**النسخة الإلكترونية**: الأعداد ١–٢٦ متوفرة على
http://www.jstor.org

**المراسلة والاشتراك على العنوان الآتي:**
مجلة **ألف**، قسم الأدب الإنجليزي والمقارن،
الجامعة الأمريكية بالقاهرة،
ص. ب ٢٥١١، القاهرة ١١٥١١،
جمهورية مصر العربية.
هاتف: ٢٧٩٧٥١٠٧-٠٢-٢ فاكس: ٢٧٩٥٧٥٦٥-٠٢-٢.
البريد الإلكتروني: alifecl@aucegypt.edu
الموقع الإلكتروني:
www.aucegypt.edu/academics/dept/eclt/alif

المحتويات

## القسم العربي

## القسم الإنجليزي

. . . وللذكرى روائح زهرة
ليلية تبكي وتوقظ في دم المنفيِّ
حاجته إلى الإنشاد . . .

– محمود درويش

المكان الذي لم نعد نراه يكفّ عن كونه مكاناً. فالمنفي كفيف بدون أرضه . . . يتبع طريقين متوازيين: أحدهما ذاكرته والآخر خطواته. وقد تخونه خطواته، أما ذاكرته فلن تخونه أبداً.

– إدمون جابيس

# ذاكرة الفجيعة

يتمحور هذا العدد من **ألف** حول الصدمة والفاجعة وحضورهما في الذاكرة الفردية والجماعية. وقد تم التركيز على الأحداث الكارثية وأثرها في علم النفس وفي التحليل النفسي وفي الأدب، لكن الدراسات والبحوث كانت تدور حول المآسي التي وقعت في الغرب: الحرب العالمية الأولى والثانية والمحرقة. يسعى هذا العدد إلى توسيع حقل دراسات الذاكرة المفجوعة لتحتوي تجارب في مناطق أخرى من العالم: الجزائر ومصر والعراق وإيران والهند وإيرلندا ولبنان وفلسطين وباكستان، وأمريكا بتعددها الإثني، والعالم القديم. وسواء كانت الحرب الأهلية الحديثة في لبنان أو الحرب الأهلية القديمة في اليونان، نكبة ١٩٤٨ أو نكسة ١٩٦٧، فالمقالات الأكاديمية والشهادات الشخصية في هذا العدد تتحرى التعريف بانعكاسات الكوارث والصدمات على الجنس الأدبي والسينما والرواية والثقافة الشعبية والشعر والمسرح والفن التشكيلي.

و**ألف** مجلة سنوية (تصدر في الربيع) وتنشر مقالات مكتوبة باللغة العربية والإنجليزية (والفرنسية أحياناً)، وهي تتبع نظام التحكيم التخصصي المتعارف عليه في الدوريات الأكاديمية. وكل عدد يرحّب بمقالات نقدية أصيلة، نظرية أو تطبيقية أو مقارنة، تلقي ضوءاً على أدبيات وبلاغيات محور محدد. وستدور محاور الأعداد القادمة حول:

**ألف ٣١**: أمريكا الأخرى.
**ألف ٣٢**: التخييلي والوثائقي: دراسات ثقافية في الأدب والتاريخ والفنون.
**ألف ٣٣**: الصحراء: الجغرافيا الإنسانية والاقتصاد الرمزي.

# تباريح «حزينة»

عبد الحميد حواس

---

## ما وراء حزينة

تطالعنا شخصية حَزِينة بعد السطور الثلاثة الأولى من رواية يحيى الطاهر عبد الله **الطوق والإسورة**. ثم تظل شخصية حَزِينة ملازمة لنا طوال الرواية حتى السطور الأخيرة. وهذا الاسم، حَزِينة، لا يتوافق مع الشخصية الروائية فحسب، ولا مع عالم الرواية فقط، إنما هو – أصلاً – من الأسماء الواردة في المحيط الاجتماعي الذي تُمثل له الرواية.

ونحن نعرف أن نُسُغ الثقافة الشعبية المتواترة في ذلك المحيط الاجتماعي يسري في إنتاج يحيى الطاهر عبد الله، وأنه مُغَذٍّ رئيس يُكسب هذا الإنتاج تدفقاً في الصياغة وحيوية في التخييل الفني. ورواية **الطوق والإسورة** من أكثر أعمال يحيى الطاهرعبد الله تجلية لسريان نُسغ الثقافة الشعبية في نسيجها، وخاصة مع تحديداتها الزمانية والمكانية، حيث تجري الوقائع ما بين ثلاثينيات القرن العشرين وخمسينياته، في مجتمع شعبي تقليدي في أحواز الأقصر.

إذن، فإطلاق اسم حَزِينة اسماً لعلم ليس دخيلاً على عالم الرواية، وإنما هو تسمية واردة في البيئة الاجتماعية التي مَثَّلت لها الرواية. والاسم في الثقافة الشعبية لا يوجد بالصيغة المؤنثة فقط، إنما يوجد – أيضاً – في صيغة المذكر: حَزِين، وإن كان تصغيره: حُزَيِّن، أكثر شيوعاً.

وفي الآن ذاته، فإن إطلاق اسم حزينة على هذه الشخصية الروائية إنما هو نعت لها وتحديدٌ لسمتها الغالبة مع توالي المحن والأرزاء عليها. وكأن أهلها – حين اختاروا لها هذا الاسم – كانوا يتحسبون لما ستعانيه من ابتلاءات وآلام. ولا ننسى أن من وظائف اختيار اسم بعينه للمولود في الثقافة الشعبية قد يكون للتوقي ودفع الضُر، كما يكون بقصد التَيمُن واستجلاب الخير.

والحال، أنه قد تحالف على حَزِينة **الطوق والإسورة** ألوان من المُتعسات والمحبطات ما سلبها مُقومات الحياة الكريمة، وتآزرت عليها الرزايا العائلية مع تردي الأحوال العامة في المجتمع الكبير، مما جعلها تفقد إمكانات الوقاية من مسببات الحزن، وصار الاسم نعتاً دقيقاً لشخصيتها.

غير أن حَزِينة لم تكن مُنفردة بمعاناتها وآلامها التي سببت حزنها، وإنما كانت المعاناة تُطوق أمثالها من المستضعفين، قبل وجود حَزِينة وبعد وجودها، مما أورث الجماعة الشعبية مخزوناً هائلاً من مشاعر القهر والإحباط جعل الحزن حالة شائعة وأمراً معتاداً. وأصبح الحُزن حالة متوقعة إلى درجة أن تجري - كما رأينا - ممارسات لوقاية الوليد من مسبباتها، وتسميته باسمها عساه يدفع الحزن بعيداً عنه.

وأحسب أن ميل بعض الطرق الصوفية إلى إيلاء الحزن مكانة مُحبذة، واعتباره حالة ضمن تدرجات أحوال مقاماتهم، قد عزز من تقبُل الحزن اجتماعياً، وخفف من وقع المفردة المؤلم، كما زكّى من استخدام الكلمة اسماً للأعلام. وقد شاع من بين سِمات بعض المتصوفة ملازمة الحزن، بل وعكوف بعضهم على البكاء. ويبدو أن أحد مسببات هذه الحالة هو معايشتهم الظرف البشري المتردي الذي يحياه أبناء مجتمعهم. وهكذا صار من الألقاب المميزة التي اكتسبها بعض المتصوفة: البكّاء والحَزِين وحُزَيِّن.

وهذه الرابطة التي ربطت أحوال المتصوفة بحالة الحزن لم تُؤد إلى التخفيف من وقع مُفردة حزن واشتقاقها فقط، ولا إلى تزكية إطلاق اسم حزينة على المواليد فحسب، وإنما أضاف - أيضاً - إلى المفردة ظلاً من معنى المَسْكنة. ونحن نعرف مكانة المَسْكنة في المصطلح الصوفي، ومدى شيوع اتخاذ الصوفية صفة مِسكين، كما صارت لقباً لبعضهم، وتابعهم في هذا بعض من احتذى بهم تواضعاً. وقد ظهر أثر هذا الظل المعنوي - أيضاً - عند التنادي بها، وخاصة عندما تتبطن بالشعور بالشفقة، كأن تلوم الأم ولدها: "لماذا فعلتَ هذا الأمر؟ يا حزين!"

وفي الوقت نفسه، يبدو أن بعض الاستعمالات قد أكسبت كلمة حزين ظلاً يشير إلى مَهمُوم، أي الذي يتحمل المسئولية ويشغل باله بالتفكير والتدبر في شأنها. وهذا المعنى الأخير هو الذي يسوّغ أن يصيح خليفة الزناتي، بعد أن قصت عليه ابنته حلمها المنذر بمصرعه، في رواية من روايات **السيرة الهلالية** المتواترة في الإقليم الذي تنتمي إليه حزينة **الطوق والإسورة**:

جَضّ الزَّناتي قال: آخ!
حَزِين ما نَصَفَني زماني
لا لِقِيت لي ابن ولا أخ
في الحرب يِسْند قُبَالي!(١)

وقد وسعت هذه الظلال من الدائرة الدلالية لكلمة حزين، بحيث أضافت إلى معناها الأساس، الذي يتمركز حول الغم والكدر، معاني تشف عن الأسى. وقد أضيف هذا المزيد لاستساغة الثقافة الشعبية استعمال الكلمة في التسمية وفي النعت.

ومن جهة أخرى، فإن اشتمال الدائرة الدلالية للكلمة على هذه الظلال أكسبها طاقة امتدت بها إلى الإنتاج الأدبي الرسمي، الذي أضفى عليها مزيداً من الجلال. وهكذا وجدنا صورة البطل الحزين تتجسم في القصص الأوروبي، منذ الفترة الملحمية في العصور الوسطى حتى عصر الازدهار الرومانسي الحديث. والشواهد البارزة على ذلك تظهر من تسمية تريستان (التي تعني «حزين») في ملحمة **تريستان وإيزولد**، وانتحال دون كيخوته لقب الفارس الحزين، واعتزاز أبطال الأدب الرومانسي – عموماً – بسمة الحزن واتخاذها شعاراً.

**الصرخة المحبوسة**

غير أن اللافت في حالة حَزِينة **الطوق والإسورة** عدم إفصاحها عن معاناتها، وإنما كانت تلجأ إلى الصمت والكتمان. وقد أشارت الرواية إلى رد فعلها عندما توفى زوجها بين يديها هي وابنتها: «فما قدرت البنت على كتمان الصرخة العالية، أما الأم المجربة فقد حبست صرختها وأطلقت دموعها».(٢) وهذا الصمت والكتمان لا تقدر عليه الثقافة الشعبية. فإذا كان للفرد خياره في أن يصمت أو يبوح، وأن ينسى أو يتذكر تجاربه المؤلمة، فإن الثقافة الشعبية، بوصفها مَوئل وعي الجماعة بذاتها ورؤيتها لعلاقاتها وتواصلها مع الماضي والحاضر، ملتزمة بإيجاد الوسائل للمحافظة على تجارب الجماعة الشعبية – السار منها وغير السار – وضمها إلى رصيدها مَعِيناً تستقي منه وتعود إليه عند الحاجة وتستحضره للتأمل والتفكير فيه والاعتبار به. والتجارب التي يحويها رصيد الجماعة تخص كل الجماعة، وإن كانت التجارب – في البداية – تحدث للأفراد كل على حدة. فالجماعة الشعبية لم تكن تتعامل مع أفرادها بحسبانهم كينونات مستقلة بذواتها، وإنما هم – بالنسبة لها – مجرد أعضاء متكاثرة من الذات الجمعية، أفراحهم تصير أفراحها وأتراحهم تصير أتراحها.

واستجابة لهذا، صاغت الجماعة الشعبية أنساقاً من التصورات والممارسات والأعراف التي تدمج التجربة الفردية في الخبرة الجماعية، وتكفل تنادي الجماعة الشعبية للتعامل معها. فما بالك – إذن – مع الابتلاءات العامة، بدءاً من الكوارث الطبيعية والأوبئة والحروب، واستمراراً مع الحكم الجائر وما ينتج عنه من قهر وانتهاك واستلاب عام. إنها ليست مجرد مصائب تقع على الأفراد، وإنما هي – أصلاً – مهددات لكيان الجماعة الشعبية ووجودها ذاته.

وهذا ما يدعونا إلى الوقوف عند هذه التصورات والأعراف التي تعبر عن الخبرة الجماعية لنرى كيف جرى التعبير عنها بواسطة أساليب ووسائل متنوعة تُبَيِّن فعل الذاكرة واستدعاءاتها في تجسيدها للشعور بالفجيعة مما يعانيه البشر.

غير أن هذا الوقوف عند تفاعل استدعاء الذاكرة مع مظاهر الفجيعة، وما ينتج عن ذلك من تجليات للمشاعر الحزينة والأسيانة، لا يعني أن الخبرة الجمعية، ولا الذاكرة الجمعية، ولا الثقافة الشعبية طابعها هو الحزن أو الابتئاس فقط. فالثقافة الشعبية، وما تنضح عنه من خبرة جمعية، إنما هي ديوان جامع شامل تذخر بكل ما يُحَصِّله أبناء الجماعة من خبرات سارة وغير سارة.

وبالتالي، فإن ظهور تجليات للشعور بالفجيعة إنما هو وجه من وجوه الثقافة الشعبية التي تتعدد بتعدد وجوه الوجود البشري ذاته. ولا محل هنا لتلك الإطلاقات والأقوال المُرْسَلة حول الطابع القومي الحزين أو المرح، ولا للفتاوى عن الشخصية المصرية بأنها كئيبة أو مِهزارة! وإنما القصد هو بيان كيف وعت الثقافة الشعبية شعورها بالفجيعة وكثفتها في ذاكرتها.

## بيت الأحزان

ومن أبرز الوسائل والأساليب التي ابتدعتها الثقافة الشعبية لحفظ خبرتها واستدعائها عند الحاجة أشكال التعبير الفنية التي تتكثف في فن القول. وهنا يقوم فن القول بتحقيق عدة أغراض، منها: التفكر في التجربة والإفادة من دراستها، ومنها: التنفيس والاصطبار بما يعين على المقاومة ومواصلة الصمود، ومنها: صقل الأداء الجمالي للغة وتجلية قدراتها الإبلاغية. وكل هذا يؤدي إلى تكثيف حصيلة التجارب وبلورتها بحيث يساعد على احتفاظ الذاكرة بها ويُيَسّر استدعاءها عند الحاجة إليها.

وتعد أشكال السرد القصصي أكثر أشكال فن القول شيوعاً. وفي الكثير منها يكون الفقد والانتزاع والاغتراب، والموت بوصفه الفقد الأكبر، مكونات رئيسية لحبكات هذه القصص الشعبية. وكأن الإبداعية الشعبية توظفها لاستحضار هذه الخبرات المكثفة فى الذاكرة الجمعية وطرحها للتأمل والتفكير.

ولكي لا أستطرد إلى حكي شواهد قصصية مفصلة، أحيل إلى مجموعة **ألف ليلة وليلة** فهي حافلة بالشواهد. وألمح إلى قصة موجودة في أول سردها، وهي قصة «الصياد والعفريت». وينبثق منها حكاية فرعية عن سمكات مُلونة مسحورة.(٣) وكان السمك سُكان مدينة مسحورة أصبحت بحيرة. وفي الحكاية ينشق الحائط عن صبية تسأل السمك في المقلاة: "هل أنت على العهد مُقيم؟"

والسؤال مطروح علينا - نحن مستمعي الحكاية وقرائها المسحورين أيضاً - مثلما هو مطروح على سمك الحكاية. ومع السمك، تجيب عنا الذاكرة الجمعية: ″نعم، نحن على العهد باقون!″ وتحافظ الذاكرة الشعبية على هذا التعهد الجمعي من خلال المحافظة على الروابط مع الأسلاف والراحلين وتجاربهم، وتأكيد استمرارية الانتماء إليهم، والتشديد على أن تراثهم ومآثرهم مصونة ولم تذهب أدراج الزمن. ويتم هذا بواسطة الأعراف، والممارسات الجمعية، والتقاليد المرعية، وأشكال التعبير الفني.

ويكثف التصور الشعبي مجال استدعاء الأحزان وتذكرها بأن خصها بمكان أسمته الحكايات «بيت الأحزان»، ينعزل فيه المرء مع أحزانه. وكأن بيت الأحزان محراب مُكرسِ لاسترضاء أرواح المفقودين، أو نُصُب مجسد لحضورهم في الذاكرة. وذِكر بيت الأحزان مُتكاثر في **ألف ليلة وليلة**، بل إنه مذكور في حكاية السمكات الملونةِ المسحورة نفسها. فقد طلبت الملكة، المفجوعةِ على عشيقها، من الملك: «أريد أن تبني لي في قصرك مدفناً مثل القبة، وأفرده للحزن، وأسَميه بيت الأحزان». وذلك قبل أن تنتقم لمصرع عشيقها بأن عَمَدت إلى سحر الملك ومدينته.(٤)

ويظهر أثر هذا التصوير لبيت الأحزان في الأدب الدارج، كما يظهر في نص أورده رشدي صالح من مرثية لأحد أعيان المنيا في منتصف القرن العشرين:

وعَلَشان إيه يا قصر الأحزان
وكم مِنْ مَقادِم أتُولَك
وكم من حواليك لآحْ زَان
بِفرْسَان والعِزّ جُولَك.(٥)

## غِناء العَناء

كانت طرق اكتساب العيش في الجماعة الشعبية التقليدية، وخاصة مع أسلوب الإنتاج ما قبل الصناعي، تعتمد عمل البدن البشري نفسه، أو أدوات ووسائط يدوية. وكان يصحب أداء معظم هذه الأعمال أنماط من الغناء أسماها الدارسون «أغاني العمل». ولأن مُعظم هذه الأعمال كان يتطلب جهداً بدنياً شاقاً، وكان إنجازها يحتاج - عادة - إلى مُدة زمنية طويلة، كما كان أداؤها يقوم على التكرار، تكرار الحركة وإيقاعها؛ لذا توافقت أغاني العمل مع السمات السابقة واستفادت منها في تكوين خصائصها. ومن أبرز هذه الخصائص: التكوين القائم على القِطع القصيرة، بمعنى اعتماد الأغنية تلاحُق شطرات ثنائية أو ثلاثية قصيرة تكّون قطعة قصيرة ولكن تامة النظم والمعنى، ثم تتلاحق هذه

القطع حسب إيقاع العمل وفترته الزمنية. ولا نستنتج من هذه الخصيصة أن الأغنية سائبة، حيث إن لها تكوينها الذي يشبه تكوين المسبحة أو العِقد الذي يتألف من حَبّات تبدو مُستقلة ولكنها تنتظم – في النهاية – في هيئة محددة لتؤدي وظائف مبتغاة.

وبذا، أفسحت هذه الخصائص لآلية التداعي الحُر أن تعمل بفاعلية في المتح من رصيد ذاكرة المغني–العامل أو ذاكرة جماعته. ولهذا تحفل هذه الأغاني بالأحلام والأماني، كما تحفل بالشكوى والحسرة ورثاء الذات والآخرين، واستدعاء الغائبين والمفقودين، من مثل:

لَوْ كان دَمع العِين يِجِيب الغَايْبِ
كُنَّا مَلِينَا الطُّرق والمَسَارْبِ.(٦)

وقد وردت هذه القطعة ضمن أغنية تُغنى على الساقية في كتاب ماسبيرو **الأغاني الشعبية في مصر**، الذي جمع مادته في بدايات القرن العشرين. وهذه القطعة تثير عدداً من الملاحظات يحسن أن أورد أربعاً منها الآن. أولى هذه الملاحظات: أن تنويعات القطعة ما زالت تتواتر؛ ولقد سجلت – في نهايات القرن العشرين – تنويعة على القطعة نفسها من منطقة سوهاج، وكانت على النحو الآتي:

إنْ كان دَمع العِين يِجِيب حَبَايِبِي
كُنَّا مَلِينَا الطُّرق والمَسَارْبِ.(٧)

وثانية هذه الملاحظات، أن هذه القطعة ترد في أغانٍ مصاحبة لأعمال أخرى، مثل دِراس المحصول أو حرث التربة. وثالثةً هذه الملاحظات، أن القطعة وردت أيضاً ضمن نصوص البكائيات، وهي بذلك تماثل عدداً آخر من قطع أغاني العمل. ورابعة هذه الملاحظات، اتسام التصوير في القطعة بالعمومية، حالها حال سائر نصوص أغاني العمل والأنواع القولية القريبة. إذ هي ترسم صورة تُشير إلى العموم وتبتعد عن التخصيص، أو تحديد حالة بعينها، بحيث يمكن استعمال القطعة في الحالات المتماثلة ولا تقصر نفسها على حالة مفردة.

ومن الموضوعات المتواترة في أغاني العمل استدعاء الأبطال والشخصيات الأسطورية، شكوىً إليهم أو اعتباراً بمآلهم. وتحفل النصوص المسجلة من الصعيد الأعلى بالشخصيات التي وردت في **السيرة الهلالية**. وها هو جزء من أُغنية تُغنى أثناء العمل على العُود (أي الشادوف، وهو أداة يدوية لرفع الماء والري):

«حَسَن» يقُول:
يا «جَبْر» مَالَك بَاكي؟
: – باعوا النخيل،
وقسِّموا الأملاكِ.
ودمْعَها دَمْعِينِ
تِبْكي «عَزِيزَة»
ودمْعَها دَمْعِينِ
تِبْكي عَلَى «يُونِس»
غرَيب يا عِين!(٨)

وفي أغنية أخرى أداها العامل نفسه، وهو يشتغل على الطنبور (وهو أنبوب يُدار لرفع الماء والري)، ينادي الجازية الهلالية، ولكن باسمها المُرَخّم:

قَصْرِك يا «جَان»
مَبْنِي بجزاز
والصَّبَّة بجزاز
وِتْقُول وِتْطُول!(٩)

أما استدعاء الأولياء والاستنجاد بهم، فإن ذكرهم يكثر ويتعدد بتعدد الجهات والنواحي التي يعتقد أهاليها في أي منهم. ولكنا سنمثل بالقطعة الآتية التي تلوذ بأبي الأولياء الإمام علي بن أبي طالب بعد أن استعانت بالولي المحلي، الذي يعتقد فيه صيادو الأسماك من بحيرة قارون بالفيوم.

وِعَشَمْنَا فِي «عَلي مِيزَار»
بِعُون الله يِعَدِّينا
وإنْ حَصَّلَك ضِيم
نَادِي «الإمَامُ عَلِي».(١٠)

## بوح المواجد

في المجتمع الشعبي التقليدي، ومع أسلوب الإنتاج ما قبل الصناعي السائد فيه، كانت الأعمال تنقسم إلى مهن وحرف متمايزة. ولكن انقسامها الأكبر كان بين العمل النسائي والعمل الذكوري. فبالإضافة إلى الأعمال المشتركة، خصصت أعمال للمرأة ومن في حكمها، وأعمال أخرى للرجل ومن في حكمه. وقد امتد هذا الانقسام الجنوسي إلى الأعمال التي تُؤَدَّى في المجال الواحد، بل

وفي الموقع الواحد. فعند شتل فسائل الأرز، مثلاً، كانت النساء تقوم بعملية الشتل نفسها؛ بينما كان على الرجال تسوية حوض الشتل وغمره بالماء ونقل كتل الفسائل إلى داخله في متناول الشاتلات. وفي بعض الجهات كان على الرجل تشغيل المواشي في الأعمال الزراعية، كحراثة التربة وما إلى ذلك؛ بينما كان على المرأة حلب الماشية وإعداد منتجات ألبانها.

ثم زاد على هذا سيادة الاعتقاد باختصاص المرأة بأعمال بعينها، يُستنكف أداء الرجل لأي منها. فبالإضافة إلى أعمالها المنزلية والعناية بالصغار، كان عليها الخبز وإعداد الطعام والملابس ونحوها، كما كانت تختص بتخزين الحبوب وتجهيزها وطحنها. وكانت المرأة تؤدي معظم هذه الأشغال منفردة، اللهم في حالات المناسبات الاحتفالية حيث كانت تتجمع النسوة وتتعاون في إنجاز أشغال الإعداد الواجبة. وكان يصاحب هذه الأشغال الفردية والجماعية، ألوان غنائية اختصت بها المرأة. ولأن هذه الأغاني كانت تصاحب أعمالاً مكرورة الحركة والإيقاع، فضلاً عن أن إنجازها يستغرق زمناً طويلاً عادةً، لذا نجد أداء هذه الأغاني يكتسب خصيصة التكرار والتكوين القِطَعي القائم على توالي وحدات قصيرة. يعتمد تواليها التداعي الحر، حيث تنشط آليات التذكر. ومن ثم، تميزت أغاني النساء المصاحبة لأعمالهن بتدفق ذكريات آلامهن، كما يرشح في صور هذه الأغاني تمثيلات لتذمرهن المكبوت. يشهد على ذلك هذا الجزء من أغنية كانت تُغنى مع إدارة الرحا لطحن الحبوب:

رَكبُّوني الرَّحَا، وقالوا: شَدِيدَة!
ياكْلُم بِالهَنَا، واللَّيالِي السَّعيدة
طِحِين الرَّحَا عَلَى الشَّبَاب قَاسِي
وانا عَجُوزة مِنْ عُقَاب نَاسِي!
...
يا ناس لاجِيتُوا وشِفْتُوني
لُولا لُغَات الِحِسّ تِغْبُوني.(١١)

وعموماً تنهض النساء بدور رئيس في الحفاظ على المأثور الشعبي وإعادة إنتاجه، فأبدعن إنتاجاً حافلاً في مختلف جوانب الثقافة الشعبية. وانفردن بإنتاج أشكال مُتعددة من الإبداعات أتاحت إمكان تمايز الصوت النسوي عن الصوت الذكوري المهيمن.

ولكن انفرادهن الأكبر يظهر في شكلين من فنون القول، هما: الحنون والنواح. ومع هذا، لم يحظيا بالانتباه من معظم الباحثين.

ويبدو أن قرابتهما من أشكال أخرى أخفتهما عن الانتباه. كما أن أداءهما يتميز بقدر من الخصوصية والحميمية، يجعلهما يتواريان عن انتباه الغرباء. وفي الوقت نفسه يتطلب أداء – أي منهما – قدراً من الموهبة تجعلهما غير ميسورين لمجرد حاملات المحفوظ.

فعادة ما ينصرف الانتباه إلى العديد عند تناول ما يتصل بالألم أو الفجيعة أو رثاء الراحلين، حتى أصبح العديد شكلاً جامعاً يحوي كل ما ينتمي إلى تلك المشاعر. غير أني أميز فى البكائيات بين ثلاثة أشكال من فنون القول. يؤدى كل من هذه الأشكال في مرحلة مختلفة من الشعائر الحزينة. فقد كان يجري أداء الندب إثر الإعلان عن وفاة المتوفي إلى حين تشييع جنازته، وكان يصحب أداء الندب القولي أداء حركي إيقاعي. بينما كان العديد يستغرق أداؤه فترة العزاء التي تمتد ثلاثة أيام على الأقل. وارتبط شكل كل من الندب والعديد وموضوعاتهما بالوظيفة التي يؤديها كل منهما في هاتين المرحلتين، فضلاً عن ورود شواهد تفيد أداء بعض الرجال لشيء منهما.

أما النواح فلم يكن مرتبطاً ارتباطاً مباشراً بمناسبة الوفاة، بل كانت المرأة تؤديه – عادة – وهي مُنفردة بنفسها، أو وهي تعمل أعمالاً منزلية رتيبة، بحيث تستغرق المرأة في خواطرها الداخلية حيث تتداعى عليها تجاربها غير السارة، ويغلبها شعورها بالغبن والانتقاص أو فقدانها السند الذي يدعمها برحيل الأعزاء المفتقدين. وكما عبرت بعضهن: أنها تِنَوَّح عندما يِطُوف بها.(١٢)

ولهذا يؤدى النواح بصوت قريب من الخفوت، وتنغيم ممدود، وطابع شجي يرشح بالحزن والأسى. وها هي نائحة تنعي حظها:

قالُوا: حَزِينَة      قُلْت: مِنْ يُومِي
لَمّا قَسِّمُوا النَّوايِب طِلِع الكبير كُومِي.(١٣)

أما النائحة الأخرى فترتكز إلى الصورة التقليدية للمهمومة أو الحزينة التي تعمد إلى التخطيط في التراب بعود في يدها، وكأن التخطيط يُساعدها فى تحديد خواطرها الموّارة:

يامَا التُّراب لمَّام
لَمّ الصَّبَايا والجِدَع عَمُود الزَّان
إبْكي عَلِيه وخَطَّطِي بالْعُودِ
إبْكي عَلى الزَّمَان اللِّي مَضَى ما يْعُودِ.(١٤)

وهذه الثالثة تستحضر فقيدها الغالي وتتحسر على مشروعه الذي لم يكتمل:

يا وَرْد في الفِنْجَان
يا قَصرْ عَالي مَاكَمِّلُوش بُنْيَان
يا وَرْد ونْشِمَّك
حَاجَة مَلِيحَة واسْتَخْسَرُه في أُمَّك
. . .
يا وَرْد ونْشِمُّوك
حَاجَة مَلِيحَة واسْتَخسَرُه في أبُوك
. . .
والمُوت صَحِيح، بَس الفُراق صَعْبَان
حِزْنِي عَلِيك ياللِّي انْطَرَدْت بعِيد.(١٥)

أما الشكل الثاني الذي ينفردن به، وهو الحِنُون، فيرتبط بمناسبات أوسع، وخاصة مناسبات التَجَمُّع الفرحة. وقد تتغير تسميته في بعض الأقاليم، كأن يُسميه البعض حنين أو مشتقات أُخرى؛ كما توجد منه تنويعات أخرى قريبة، مثل النجريح والسومير، ونحوها. وقد آثرت أن أتعرض للحنون، مع ارتباطه بمناسبات يغلب عليها التجمع الفرح، لاعتماده آليات الذاكرة في إنتاجه وحميمية أدائه مما ينتج عنه اتساع عمليات الاستدعاء، من ناحية، وإمكانات المساراة والنجوى والمكاشفة، من ناحية أخرى.

والحِنُون – بوصفه أداءً – شكل غنائي تؤديه النساء كبيرات السن نسبياً، ولا تشارك في أدائه حديثات السن غير المتزوجات. وقد تؤديه المرأة مُنفردة، ولكن الأشيع أن تتشارك في أدائه مجموعة من النساء المتجمعات، إما في أداء جماعي أو تنقسمن إلي مجموعتين تتبادلان الرد.

والحنون لايُؤدى إلا في مناسبة احتفالية، ولكن في وقت سابق على موعد الاحتفال الرئيسي بأيام. ذلك أن نساء الأُسرة واللاتي عليهن واجب المجاملة، يتجمعن للتعاون في إعداد متطلبات الاحتفال المنزلية، مثل: نقش الكعك وخبزه بكميات كافية للعرس، أو تجهيز زوادة سفر الحاج أو مستلزمات استقباله، وما أشبه. ويتميز أداء الحنون بالرقة والتنغيم اللحني الممدود ومط الأصوات وتطويلها زمنياً؛ كما يعتمد – نظماً – على قِصر العبارات وتكرارها. ويتخذ نموه شكلاً أسميه الشكل الحلزوني بحيث يتوافق مع السياق الأدائي. والنموذج التالي يُردد إبان انتظار عودة الحاج، ويُقال على لسان الحاج نفسه،

من قبيل استدعاء حضوره من ناحية، ومن ناحية أخرى للتيمن والاستبشار بعودته سالماً:

يا رَايح بلَدْنا
يا بشير الهنا
يا رَايح بلَدْنا
قوُل لِوَلدِي الكبير
يبَيَّض عتَبْنا
يا رَايح بلَدْنا
يا بَشِير الهَنَا
يا رَايح يا رَايح
قوُل لِوَلدِي يَكتَّر الدَّبَايِح.(١٦)

والمناسبة الفرحة تسمح بدخول أغاني الغزل. والملاحظ أنها تتخذ صياغة تميل إلى العتاقة، من مثل:

والله زمَان يا جذُور الوَرْد ما بنْتُوا
انْتُو عَلى عَهدْكم واللاَّ انْتُو غيَّرْتُوا
احْنَا عَلى عَهدِنا مَا غير إلاَّ انْتُو.(١٧)

ويظهر هذا النحو من التصوير والتركيب بشكل أجْلى في الشاهد الآتي من محافظة الشرقية:

يا بنْت يا أُمُّ القُلِيلَة حوِّدِي اسْقِينِي
مِطشْطِشْ أنَا مِن الْعَطش والحرّ كاوِيني
وإنْ كان شعْرك طويل حِلّيه وعَدِّينِي
شعْرِي قُصيَّر وفِي اطْرَافُه المنَادِيلي
وكُلّ قلِّة عَليها أرْبَع منَادِيلي
وكُلّ منْدِيل يِسَافِر مَصْر ويِجِيلي.(١٨)

وللشاهد بقايا تنويعة موجودة في محافظة أسوان، يحسن إيرادها:

عَلَى كُلّ سِكِّين تِقَشَّر مُوزَة وتِدِّينِي
عَلَى كُلّ قُلة عَليها أرْبَع قُلل صِيني
عَلَى كُلّ بُسْتَان تِسَافِر مَصر وتْجِينِي

يا مِين يِبلَّغ سَلامي في الوَابُور اللِّي فَات
يا بُو عِيُون كَحِيلَة وحَاجْبُه يا قَلَم ضُبَّاط.(١٩)

كما أن المناسبة المفرحة وتجمع الكبيرات يُبيح الدعابة، بل والتلميحات الجنسية. فقد تنفلت واحدة في الغناء، بينما تتردد الأخريات ويتضاحكن مجاوبات:

إفْرَحُوا يا بَنَات!
مَرْكِب مَوْسُوقَة صَعَايْدَة
رِسِيِتْ في مُورْدِتْنَا اللِّيلَة.(٢٠)

**نفوس مُهدرة**

يندرج ضمن فنون القول في الثقافة الشعبية عدد مُتجدد من طرز القصص المُغنى. وقد اصطلح الدارسون على تسمية طراز من هذا القصص المُغنى باسم «الموال القصصي»، لأن الإنتاج التقليدي منه كان أداؤه الغنائي يتبع طريقة الغناء الموّالي، وكان نظمه الشعري يتبع شكل الموال الشعري. وقد شاع، في النصف الثاني من القرن العشرين، ثلاثة من بين هذا الإنتاج التقليدي للموال القصصي، وهي: موال أدهم الشرقاوي، وموال شفيقة ومتولي، وموال حسن ونعيمة، وألحق بها أغنية ياسين وبهية، وعلى نحو أقل موال دنشواي.

وما أن عُرفت هذه المواويل على مستوى أجهزة الإعلام، حتى طفقت الإنتلجنسيا تتناول هذه المواويل بشتى وسائط الاتصال: الإذاعة والتلفزيون والسينما والمسرح والطباعة. وشُغِل الجميع بإسقاط مشاغلهم السياسية والاجتماعية على المادة القصصية لتلك المواويل، ومن ثم أباحوا توجيه تلك المادة حيث شاءوا.

غير أن تلك المواويل القصصية في سياقها المعيش كانت عملاً فنياً يتجادل مع قيم جماعته الشعبية جمالياً وفكرياً. والملاحظ ميدانياً أن جمهور تلك المواويل كان يستقبلها على أنها عمل مُركب يُحقق عِدة مقاصد. وكان من أبرز تلك المقاصد رثاء أبطال هذه المواويل والتفجع على حيواتهم المُهدرة. وما موال أدهم الشرقاوي إلا بكائية على مصرع متمرد جسور بواسطة خيانة رخيصة. وما موال شفيقة ومتولي إلا مرثية لشفيقة وحسرة على قدرها الذي مزقها بين ما ابتلاها به من وعد وبين وطأة مفهوم بعينه للعار وغسله. وما موال حسن ونعيمة إلا تفجع على الحب المغدور نتيجة التعصب للفوارق الاجتماعية. إن كل واحد من هذه المواويل هو تمثيل وأمثولة، وهو تذكار دائم لمُسببات الفجيعة، وهو باثٌ مستمرٌ أسىً على اضطراب مصائر البشر.

يستهل موال أدهم الشرقاوي إنشاده بحفز المُستمع كي يتحرى الدلالة الكامنة فيما سيرويه:

مِنِين أجِيب نَاس لمَعْنَاة الكَلَام يِتْلُوه؟
شِبْه المُؤَيَّد إذا حَفَظ العِلُوم وِتَلُوه
الحَادثَة اللِّي جَرَت عَلى سَبْع شَرْقَاوِي
الاسم أدهم لكن النقب شرقاوي.(٢١)

لقد تصدى أدهم الموال للإدارة الاستعمارية، وينجح في الانتقام لمقتل عمه، ويُحبِط مُحاولات السلطات القبض عليه، ولكن الفاجع أن يتم مصرعه على يد صاحب خائن. ولهذا ينصحنا وهو يحتضر:

أمَانَة يا مِنْ عِشْت بَعْدِي مَا تْأَمِنْش لصَاحِب
مافِيش وَلاَ صَاحِب إلاَّ يِجيلَك الأَذَى بإيدِيه.(٢٢)

ويدعو أسرته إلى التوقف عن تبادل الانتقام والثأر:

أمَانة يا عِيلةِ الشَّرْقَاوِي مَا حَدّ بَعْديِّة
لا أخ ليِّة، ولا عَمّ ياخُد التَّار بَعْدِيِّة.

و ينبهنا مُغني الموال، وهو يُطلقنا من أسر الموال:

يا قاعْدِين كُلُّكم: وَحِّدُوا الإله يا هُوه!
دي الحَادثَة اللِّي جَرَت عَلَى سَبْع شَمْلَول
داسُوا عَلِيه الرِّجَال قَتلُوه
ومِنين أجَيب نَاس لِمَعْنَاةِ الكَلاَم يِتْلُوه.(٢٣)

وبالمثل يستهل موال شفيقة ومتولي مرثيته بدعوتنا إلى التأمل والتفكير. ثم يأخذ في تعريفنا بشفيقة، حريصاً على إثارة تعاطفنا معها وبيان قهر المقدر والمكتوب لها:

يا اللَي قَريت الكُتُب شوُف فعَال جِرْجا
واسمع لحَادِثَة صَبيِّة مِنْ نِسَا جرجا
الوَعَد جَالها غَصْب عَنْها مِنْ جرجا
فاتِت بِلدها وطِلِعت تِوفي ما عَلِيها.(٢٤)

حتى القوادة التي ساقتها إلى مصيرها الفاجع تُشفق عليها مُتسائلة: «عَلَى فِين رايحة يا عَديمِة البَخْت؟!» وها هو متولي شقيقها وقاتلها يرثيها باكياً:

يا شَفِيقَة نَصِيبِك كِدِه في كِتاب الله
والدَّم غَالِي بَسّ الشْرَف له حَدّ
ويا عِين هاتي دِموعِك ما اتْخِرِب دَارِي
والدَّم غَالِي بَسّ الشَّرَف لِلّه!(٢٥)

وفي دراسة سابقة نُشرت سنة ١٩٩٦، أشرْتُ إلى صور وتنويعات أخرى من الموال تم الترويج الجماهيري لها في العقد الواقع بين منتصف سبعينيات القرن العشرين ومنتصف ثمانينياته. وفي تلك التنويعات المستحدثة من الموال نجد بؤرة الموال تتغير ليصبح التركيز على متولي غاسل العار، بل إن بعضها يُصوره جزاراً يتشفى بتقطيع أعضاء أخته وإلقائها من البلكونة على جمهور سوق أسيوط. وعندما يسأله القاضي في المحكمة لم مَثَّل بأخته، يجيبه باستعارة قُدمت على أنها إجابة مفحمة:

أنا عِندي شَجرة بُرَتُكَان
لكن مَالِت في كل مَكان
وأكل مِنِّيها كل مِنْ كَان
وأنا قُلتْ أحسن أما نِتْخَلَّص مِنْ:
الجِرْجَاوِيَّة (جواب المرددين مع المغني).(٢٦)

ويجد القاضي في هذا التبرير الكفاية فيحكم عليه بالسجن ستة أشهر مع إيقاف التنفيذ!

أما استهلال موال حسن ونعيمة، فإنه يضعنا مباشرة أمام الفجيعة، بحيث لا ننخدع من بساطة نمو الأحداث الموالية، والتي تبدو وكأنها مجرد واقعة حب:

لَوْ كُنْت أعْلَم بأنّ الوَعْد مِدَّارى
لا كُنْت أطْلَع ولاَ أخْطر قَطَّ مِنْ داري
وارْضَى بِقَلِيلُه، واقُول للقَلْب ما تْدَارِي
داري عَلَى بَلْوِتَك ياللِّي ابْتَلِيتْ دَارِي.(٢٧)

وبعد أن يُمني والدا الفتاة الشاب بقبولهما زواجه من ابنتهما، يقومان باستدراجه حيث يتم قتله. ولكي يقوي الموال شعورنا

بالفجيعة يجعل الفتاة تحتفظ برأسه المفصول تبكيه إلي أن تقدمها إلى السلطات بَيِّنة على فعل والديها الغادر.

أما غناء بهية وياسين فهو في واقع الثقافة الشعبية المعيش لم يكن موالاً قصصياً. وما وصل إلى الجيل الماضي، الذي عاصر خمسينيات وسيتينيات القرن العشرين، أغنية تحوي شذرات وأبياتاً تومىء إلى قصة مأساوية يفوتنا الكثير من تفاصيلها. ولكن الباقي منها كان مؤثراً وحاز انتشاراً حتى بين الشباب المديني في ذلك العهد، الذين كانوا يرددونها بشكل جماعي، وخاصة لازمتها ذات اللحن المميز:

عطشان يا صبايا دِلّوني على السبيل
يا بابور الساعة اتناشر يا مِقَبِّل على الصعيد

وكان البعض يكمل:

يا بابُور السَّاعَة اتَنَاشر
يا بو عَجَل حَدِيد
سَلِّم لي على السِّت بَهيَّة
اللِّي حَبَّت ياسِين.(٢٨)

وهكذا ندخل إلى إلماحات تشير إلى مقتل ياسين بواسطة جنود السلطة، ثم لجوء بهية إلى المحاكم، التي يحكم قاضيها بالسجن أربع سنوات. وخلال هذه التفاصيل القصصية تظهر لازمة أخرى أثيرة:

وأنا كُلّ ما أقُول التُّوبة،
تِرْمينِي المَقَادِير!
وَعْدِ ومَكْتُوب عَلَيَّ
ومِسَطَّر عَلى الجِبِين.(٢٩)

وقريب من الحالة التي وصلتنا بها بهية وياسين كانت حالة موال دنشواي، بل كان أكثر تشظياً. ولكن الكثيرين كانوا يذكرون مطلعه المؤثر: «يوم شنق زهران كان صعب وقفاته». ثم يلجأون إلى السرد القصصي الذي يتفجع على زهران بوصفه رمزاً لتصدي أهالي قرية دنشواي لعدوان جنود الاحتلال البريطاني سنة ١٩٠٦. وقد كان رد المعتمد البريطاني لورد كرومر باطشاً على النحو المعروف تاريخياً. وقد وردت رواية تُقدم صورة متغيرة للموال قام بها أحد

مؤلفي المواويل الذين كانوا موجودين في منتصف القرن العشرين. وتستثير الرواية نخوة المستمع – منذ البداية – بأن تجعل رصاصة أحد الإنجليز تصيب إحدى عجائز القرية:

سَبَب القَضِيِّة وِلِيِّة فِي الجُرْن عَرَبِيِّة
واحِد مِن الإنْجِلِيز عَمَّر بَارُود وضَرَب
مِن أجْل صِيد الحَمَام مَرْصُود عَرَبِيِّة
حَرَق الوِلِيِّة حتَّى جُرِّتْهَا انْضَرَب

ويتفاقم الأمر ويحضر كرومر بنفسه يقود حملة التأديب:

إتلمم عليه (عاجز ومسن) بعزوتهم قوام قتلوه
والظلم دا شين ما يرضاه إنس ولا جِنّ

ثم تنتهي مهزلة محاكمة الأهالي:

حَكَم عَلى أرْبَعَة بالشَّنق والإعْدَام
واللِّي مَا انْشَنَق مِنْ ضَرْب الجَلْد إعْدَام
ودِه شيء كَمان يِبكِي أهْل الوَطَن ونَجِيب.(٣٠)

## جرّ السيرة

منذ أربعينيات القرن العشرين، نشطت حركة واسعة، قام بها المُثقفون الديموقراطيون الوطنيون. وكان من بين ما أسهموا فيه، إثارة الاهتمام الواسع بالمأثورات الشعبية في الحياة الثقافية، وإقرار أن منتجات الثقافة الشعبية جديرة بالنظر والاعتبار، بل إن منها ما يمكن إدماجه في مُكونات الثقافة الوطنية الناهضة. وحظيت السيرة الشعبية بمكانة مميزة نسبياً في مجرى حركة الاهتمام العامة هذه. وكان لاكتشاف العدد الكبير من السير الشعبية التي تحويها ذخيرة الثقافة الشعبية أثره في التوفر على التعريف بها ودرسها وإعادة إنتاجها في أعمال أدبية وفنية متعددة. وكان لارتباط هذا النشاط بالحركة الوطنية أثره في طريقة التعامل مع هذه السير الشعبية، حيث جرى التركيز على وجهها القتالي وتم إبراز أحداثها وشخوصها في حالات صدام وصراع مع خصوم خارجيين أو أتباعهم في الداخل. واستمر هذا التوجه حتى عندما انتقل الاهتمام من السير الشعبية المكتوبة والمطبوعة إلى السير التي ما زالت تُؤَدَّى شفهياً، وخاصة الذي ما زال يُؤَدَّى من فصول **السيرة الهلالية**.

غير أن السيرة الشعبية في سياق أدائها المعيش هي عمل قصصي جامع ذو وجوه وجوانب متعددة. وتتركب السيرة الشعبية – أية سيرة – من عديد من القصص الفرعية متباينة المحاور والمقاصد. ولهذا سنجد في السيرة الشعبية – أية سيرة – تمثيلات وتصاوير لمواقف وأحوال متباينة؛ حيث سنجد قصص الحب بأنواعه، كما سنجد قصص الخيانة والخديعة، كما سنجد قصص البحث والاكتشاف وتحصيل المعارف، بالإضافة إلى قصص الحرب ومجالدة الخصوم.

والراجح عندي أن معظم السير الشعبية التي ظلت تحظى بإقبال من جمهورها الشعبي حتى النصف الثاني من القرن العشرين كانت تحفل بالمواقف المؤسية، بل والفاجعة. وكانت تلك المواقف جزءاً متكاملاً بنائياً مع سائر أجزاء السيرة، مما يدل على أنها ليست أجزاء زائدة أو مُلصقة. وأغلب الظن أن وجود الأجزاء المؤسية والحزينة، بالإضافة إلى دورها في البناء القصصي، كان ينهض بوظيفة الحفاظ على الأحداث والمواقف التي سببتها، في الذاكرة الجمعية، وتجديد الاعتبار من نواتجها الفاجعة في كل مرة تؤدى فيها.

وتتعدد الأجزاء الحزينة وتتنوع بحيث يصعب حصرها في مقامنا هذا. وقد يكون إلماح كاف إذا نبهنا إلى أن أية شخصية من الشخصيات الرئيسية في السيرة لم تُستثن من المعاناة والوقوف من حين لآخر نادبة حالها؛ بل ووجد من الشخصيات غير الرئيسية من وُسم بالحزن. وفي **السيرة الهلالية**، اشتهرت شمَّة (شيماء) ببكائها على فقدها أولادها الثلاثة دفعة واحدة، وكانت جارية السفيرة عزيزة تُدعى مي الحزينة.

وهناك من الشواهد ما يجعلني أستنتج أن نهايات أبطال السير الشعبية رُسمت على أن تكون نهاية مأساوية. ودعك من **سيرة سيف بن ذي يزن** و**سيرة الظاهر بيبرس**، فكل منهما لها ظرفها الخاص. ولكنا لو تأملنا نهايات شخصيات مثل عنتر بن شداد، أو عامر الخفاجي، أو خليفة الزناتي، أو أبو زيد الهلالي، سنجد سيرهم تتفنن في تصوير مصرعهم المؤسي.

درج عنتر بن شداد في مراحل سيرته بوصفه البطل شديد البأس الذى لم يقف سيفه عند حد حل مشكلته الشخصية والانتقال من فئة العبيد إلى مستوى الأحرار، ولا تحقيق حلمه بالزواج من عبلة، بل إنه تدرج من وضع حامي قبيلته بني عبس إلى حامي الجزيرة العربية ونصير الممالك المجاورة. ولم يكن عنتر يتمتع بالقوة القتالية فقط، وإنما كان يمتلك قوة جسدية خارقة أيضاً. وتُصوِّرالسيرة مظهراً من مظاهر هذه القوة البدنية: «وكان الأمير عنتر إذا أراد أن يُريق الماء تسمع له صوت وهدير كدوي الرحا في البئر، لأن هذا الأمر من قوة همته وشدة عزيمته. وكان إذا بال على حجر ثقبه من شدة حيله وقواه الذي ركبه فيه

الإله».(٣١) غير أن السيرة لا تورد هذا الوصف لمجرد بيان مِقدار قوته الجسدية فقط، وإنما أوردته لكي تبني منه، ومن قوة عنتر المُفرطة، مفارقتها الفنية الكُبرى. فقد أصبحت هذه القوة المُفرطة، ومظهرها في التبول، هما مكمن ضعفه ومثار هلاكه. لقد تَعَقَّب عنتر – طلباً للانتقام – أحد ضحايا قوته المفرطة، واسمه الأسد الرهيص. ولم يكن عنتر قد اكتفى، في معركة سابقة، بهزيمة الأسد الرهيص، وإنما قام – أيضاً – بسمل عينيه. وبهذا الفعل تتعزز المفارقة وتزداد تركيباً، ذلك أن هذا المهزوم الأعمى هو الذي يصرع عنتر، عندما يُسدد سهماً مسموماً نحو عنتر فيصيبه إصابة مُصْمِية.

لقد كمن الأسد الرهيص إلى أن سمع «حس دوي إراقة الماء»، فأطلق سهمه في اتجاه مصدر الصوت، «فلم يشعر الأمير عنتر إلا وتلك النبلة قد وقعت في وسط مخصاه، وقد دخلت وغاصت في وسط أمعاه».(٣٢) ومع تزايد آلام الإصابة، يُدرك عنتر أن النهاية وشيكة، ولذا يشرع في ترتيب أوضاع جماعته، وخاصة عبلة.

ولكي تُقوي السيرة مشاعر الفجيعة، تخصص لمشاهد مصرع عنتر حوالي خمس وعشرين صفحة، تُورد فيها عدداً من قصائد الرثاء، كما تحكي قصة فرعية عن حماية عنتر لقافلة عبلة وجماعته وهو يحتضر، ويبقى شاخصاً على ظهر حصانه يُرْهِب أعداءه بعد أن مات. ولا يعرف أعداؤه بموته إلا بعد أن يطفر حصانه فيسقط الجسمان. وهي طريقة في التعرف على موته قريبة مما ترويه القصص عن كيفية معرفة الجن بموت النبي سليمان كُلي البأس، ولكن هذا موضوع آخر.

أما عامر الخفاجي، فقد صورته **السيرة الهلالية** أميراً على إمارة في بلاد العراق، وفارساً في السلوك وفي الحرب، وشهماً عفيفاً لذا كان حامياً للصبايا. وذكرت بعض الروايات أنه رحل مصاحباً بني هلال في تغريبتهم نحو شمال أفريقية متابعةً لحبه العفيف للجازية، ولكن أغلب الروايات تنسب حبه إلى وطفاء بنت دياب. غير أن الموقف الرئيس الذي تتلبث عنده السيرة، بالنسبة إلى عامر الخفاجي، هو مصرعه ومرثيته لنفسه. وهو موقف أثير عند رواة السيرة وجمهورها، وكان يُطلب وحده مراراً، ولذا حظي أداء هذة المرثية بتجويد ملحوظ، شعرياً وموسيقياً، سواء لدى مؤدي الدلتا أو مؤدي الصعيد.

ولكي نقترب من هذه المرثية سأجتزئ القطعة الآتية من بين اثنين وستين بيتاً شعرياً تُغنيها رواية من روايات الوجه البحري:

يِقُول الفَتَى مَلِك العِرَاق العَامِر
سَهم المَنِية عَلى الرِّجَال بِيْدُور

شبَّهتِ نَفْسِي كسَفينِة صُغَيَّرة
فِي بَحْر طَامِي ومَاؤُه عَكُور
مُوجَة تِعَلِّى بِي وِمُوجَة تِحُطّ بِي
وبَحر النِّيَا ظُلْمَة وماؤه عَكُور

وبينما هو في رقدته، يعبر السماء سرب من البجع الذي يُسمى الوز العراقي فيلتفت إليه مُنادياً:

طَاطِي لِي يا وِزّ العِرَاق لَمَّا أقُول لَك
ياللِّي عَلَى الغُرْبَة تِبَان صَبُور
...
يا وِزّ أدِلَّك عَنْ أمَايِر بِلادِي
مَدِينَة، وِمِن خِلْفِ المَدِينَة سُور
يا وِزّ سَلِم يَمّ أمِّي، وقّل لِها:
جَمَلِك وَقَع، ولا عَادْش قَطّ يِثُور
سَلِّم عَلَى ابُويا الحَزِين، وقُل لُه:
اللِّي انْكَتَب ما مَنَّع المَقْدُور!(٣٣)

وتمضي المرثية في تفصيل تجربته المؤسية، وتعزز تأثيرها الحزين بالإشارة إلى غربته وتركه ابنته غريبة في وسط غرباء قد ينتهبونها، ثم يذكر غدر خصمه في المبارزة، ثم ينتقل إلى وصيته لأبي زيد بالعناية بشعائر دفنه الجنائزية، مُفصلاً في بيان الكتابة والنقوش التي تُثْبَت على مقبرته.

أما بالنسبة إلى شخصية خليفة الزناتي، فقد أخذت دوراً مركزياً في حلقتي الريادة والتغريبة من حلقات **السيرة الهلالية**. وصورته السيرة بطلاً مطلقاً لبلاد المغارب، وصمد للغزوة الهلالية أربع عشرة سنة. وكانت الأحوال حوله أقرب إلى التفكك، وكأنه المدافع الأخير، رغم أنه قد بلغ الثمانين من عمره وفقد الكثير من قواه.

ويقودني استقرائي الميداني إلى ملاحظة أن غير قليل من الروايات الموجودة في أقطار المشرق العربي لا تكتفي بدور خليفة الزناتي الكبير، وإنما تتوقف طويلاً مع مواقفه مصورة إياها من زاويته، لا من زاوية خصومه الهلاليين. ولا تحظى شخصية خليفة الزناتي بالقدر نفسه من المكانة في روايات أقطار المغرب العربي التي اطلعت عليها. وقد توفرت بعض الروايات المتواترة في مصر على تنمية الشخصية القصصية لخليفة الزناتي لتصبح في طريقها إلى التحول من الصورة الملحمية لتتخذ السمت التراجيدي.

إنه رغم كبر سنه وفقده لقوى صباه وشبابه، ورغم إدراكه لوحدته في معسكر زناتة وخيانة بعضهم وعمل الآخرين ضد إرادته، ورغم النبوءات التي توالت تخبر عن مصرعه وخراب دياره، بل حددت النبوءة أن مقتله الوشيك سيكون بواسطة طعنة حربة من دياب؛ رغم كل هذا يمضي خليفة شامخاً لمواجهة قدره.

لذا أصبح فصل مقتل خليفة الزناتي من الفصول الأثيرة لدى قسم كبير من جمهور **سيرة بني هلال**. ويزدحم مشهد مبارزته الأخيرة بالتفاصيل المؤسية، وخاصة بعد سقوطه عن فرسه إثر طعنة الحربة في عينه:

رِكِز عليها أبو غانم، حَواليه وِدَار
وهُو مَرْمِي عَلى الثَّرَى والحَرْبَة فِي عِينيُه
ولَفَّ حَواليه يمِين ويسَار
عَلى الأرض بِينُه وبِينُه
جَرُّو بالحَرْبَة وَرَاه
وِهيّ الحَرْبَة خَاشَّة في عِيُونُه
لَمَّا دَخلُوا خِيَامُه حَدَاه.(٣٤)

مما أثار استياء أبو زيد فتوجه لإيقاف دياب:

والاسْمَر جَرَّد زَنَاتُه
وقال لُه شيء لا يِرْضِي الرَّحْمَن!
اِخْلَعْ الْحَرْبَة مِنْ عِينْ الزَّنَاتِي
دِه رَاجِل مَلْو عِينْ الأعَادِي.(٣٥)

وعندما يقوم حسن الهلالي، قائد الخصوم، بإسناد خليفة مبدياً الإشفاق، يتحسر خليفة على مآله:

والله كلامَك زِين يا أمير بُوعلي
يا حِيفْ مَاهُوش مِنْ لِسَان حَبِيب
فَمِن قِلِّة الحِنِّة وَقَعْنَا فِي الجَفَا
وأَخَذْنا مِنْ دَارِ العَدِوّ حَبِيب.(٣٦)

ولا يجد ملجأ إلا أن يوصي أبو زيد على ابنته سعدى:

يا أبو زيد اسْمَع كَلامي
يامَا الزَّمَان يِوَرِّي عَجِيب
وِصَايْتَك يا بوزيد سِعْدِه
إِوعى تِدِّيها للأمير الدِّيب.(٣٧)

أما أبو زيد، فقد أطلقت عليه كثير من روايات **السيرة الهلالية** المشرقية: «عامود هلال». فقد اعتبرته فارس بني هلال وحكيمهم، كما كان صاحب الحيلة والمفاوضة. وتُضيف الروايات الميدانية إلى هذه الصورة الرسمية وجوهاً وسمات أخرى تجعل شخصية أبو زيد أكثر غنىً من الزاوية القصصية. ففي هذه الروايات تجد شخصاً عملياً لا يجد غضاضة في التنازل عن مُثل الفارس ومثاليته. وما فعله مع أولاد أخته الثلاثة، رفقائه في الريادة، إلا مثال واحد ولكنه كان فعلاً مكروراً، حتى أنه اكتسب المثل المأثور: «أبو زيد مالوش رفيق!» وتحولت صفة صاحب الرأي إلى صاحب مراوغة، مما جعله يكتسب – أيضاً – المثل المأثور: «سكة أبو زيد كلها مسالك». كما اكتسب المثل الأكثر تواتراً: «كأنك يا بو زيد ما غزيت»، وله تنويعة أخرى: «يا ريتك يا بو زيد ما غزيت». ويُضرب المثل للجهد المُبدد، والسعي الذي يُحبط ويرتد على نفسه. وفي هذا، تكاد الحلقة الأخيرة من السيرة أن تكون تجسيداً لهذه الفكرة. فقد تحولت الغزوة الهلالية لشمال أفريقية وصدامهم مع الزناتة إلى صراع داخلي بين أطراف الحلف الهلالي تفانى فيه أبطال كل الأطراف، حتى جيل الأيتام. وهكذا يفقد الهلالية ما حاربوا من أجله هذه الحرب الطويلة المدمرة؛ بل إن من لم يفر منهم من الشمال الأفريقي انضوى تحت قيادة زناتة!

ومن زاوية التفجع على الجهد البشري المُهدر، والحسرة على قدرة البشر على تبديد ما ينجزونه، نتيجة التعصب الأحمق وضيق الأفق والأثرة، التي تُورِث عماء البصر والبصيرة، وتجعل البشر قادرين على العدوان على الآخرين واستلابهم، وتُطلق طاقات الشر والتدمير وتخريب حتى ما بنوه بأيديهم؛ في هذا تُعد **السيرة الهلالية** أمثولة مشخصة، وتغدو مرثية مؤسية للوضع الإنساني. وتصبح وقائع السيرة وشخصياتها مثاراً للتفكير والاعتبار لمن يسمع القول وهو شهيد.

في ظلال هذه المعاني نفهم اختيار السيرة للكيفية التي صُورت بها نهاية أبو زيد وموته. فهناك رواية تقول بأن دياب صحب أبو زيد إلى الصيد في البرية، إعلاناً عن التصافي بينهما وعودة علاقاتهما

الرفاقية. ولكن دياب كان عازماً على الغدر بأبو زيد والتخلص من وجوده بقتله غيلة. ولهذا يتظاهر دياب بأنه يلعب معه لعبة المطاردة، إلى أن وجد منه تخلياً عن حذره المعهود، ويطعنه من الخلف بحربته المشهورة بأنها «لا تخرج إلا بدم».(٣٨) ولكن هناك رواية أخرى محبوكة قصصياً، على نحو آخر، مع نسيج السيرة الفني. تستفيد الرواية مما ذكر في بدايات السيرة عن الحمل بأبو زيد وميلاده. وقد تمنت والدته أن تحمل بصبي يكون مشابهاً لطائر أسود ذي بأس رأته مع صاحباتها عند نبع الماء. وبالفعل، يولد لها أبو زيد الذي شابه الطائر، لا في شدة البأس فقط ، بل – أيضاً – في لونه الأسود.

وفي مفارقة بليغة، يظهر الطائر الأسود في مشهد موت أبو زيد في هيئة غراب، ويكون السبب في فقده الحياة عطشاً. ذلك أن أبو زيد كان قد غادر تونس، مُشرقاً هذه المرة، لأداء فريضة الحج. وفي طريقه يمر بالعلمين حيث ضرب حربته، ويقال إن مكانها موجود حتى الآن تتفجر منه المياه العذبة. وعندما يمر بصحراء غزة يتسلط غراب على قربته حتى يثقبها وتهدر ماؤها، دون أن يدري أبو زيد. وهكذا، يموت أبو زيد وحيداً عطشاً في الصحراء التي أتى منها بصحبة الجحافل الهلالية. وتستنزف الرواية أسى المستمع بالوقوف عند تفصيلات المشهد:

ونِزِل عن الهَجِينِة ونَخِّها أبو زيد
وجَنْبِيها رَيَّح بسِيفُه
رَاجِل وِعُمْرُه عَن الحَقّ مَا يِزِيد
ويُومْهاَ سِكِر مِن كِيفُه
قَال: يَا غَزَّة غَزِّك البين
ما فِيكِي مَاء عَلَى الأَرْض جَارِي
وجَرْحِي فِي جُوفِي مِعِين
ورَبِّي ما عِنْدُه خِيَارِي
قَال أبو زيد: يِبْقَّى الأَمْر لله
آدِي الطِير فَضَّى قِرَابِي
والعلم دِه عِند الله
مولايا عِنْدِه عِلْم جَهْرِي وغِيَابي
وسَبِّل أمُورُه إلى الله
فِي غَزَّةِ ونِزِل الهلالي
قَال: اللِّي جَعَلُه رَبي سَوَّاه
أجَلَه لمَوْلَى المَوَالي.(٣٩)

## الصوت الجامع

نقرأ في نهاية رواية **الطوق والأسورة** آخر تصوير لحزينة في سطور الفقرة الآتية: «الدمع جف في المحجرين، والضوء انطفأ في العينين منذ زمان، وها أنت يا حزينة بعد مرور الزمان مع الابن المقعد داخل المكان، رحل الزوج ورحلت البنت وهلكت بنت البنت، وحولك المشفقون والحدادة الشامتة، ولا ضوء ولا نار بموقد، وما الحاجة للنار والموقد؟!».(٤٠) تجلس حزينة مكلومة تتأمل حصاد الرماد لعمرها بطوله، تتحسر على خلاء دارها، كأن لم تَعْمُر بالأحلام والرغبات وتدافع التواصل! مستغرقة في بُحرانها، متلفعة بصمتها. وماذا تقول؟ أو بالأحرى، تقول ماذا، وتترك ماذا؟ آنئذ، تقول الثقافة الشعبية. فالثقافة الشعبية، مستودع أصوات الجميع، تطلق صوتاً جمعياً ينفث قدراً من تباريح حزينة وكل الحزينات والحزانى من أبناء الجماعة الشعبية. وقد تنوّع هذا الصوت الجمعي من مساحاته وطبقاته وألوانه، وعدد أساليبه ووسائله، ساعياً إلى التعبير عن شمول تجارب الجماعة، عساها تفيد منها في إقامة حياة أقل حزناً وأوفر بهجة.

## الهوامش

(١) عبد الحميد حواس، «حُلم سُعدى المُنذِر»، **مجلة الثقافة الجديدة**، العدد الأول (مايو ١٩٨٠)، ص ص ٥٩-٦٣. جض = صاح ألماً، الأغلب أنه قلب مكاني لأصوات حروف الفعل ضج. قُبالي = معي، وقد أتت الصورة من عملية الحمل المُشترك التي يرفع فيها اثنان ثُقلاً، كل واحد منهما مُقابل الآخر. وبمناسبة تدوين النصوص، أود أن أنوه إلى أن مذهبي في تدوين النصوص المنطوقة يتأسس على التمييز بين مستويين من التدوين. أولهما هو ما نُلزم به طلابنا في الجمع الميداني من وجوب تحري الدقة بالنقل الصوتي الأمين لما يتلفظ به الرواة، نظراً للضرورة الحيوية لهذه الدقة في عمليات التوثيق والدرس اللهجي والمقارنة الفيلولوجية. ويُساعد في هذا النقل الأمين تيسُر استخدام أجهزة التسجيل الصوتي والمرئي المتطورة. أما المستوى الثاني لتدوين النصوص ورسم حروفها، فهو الذى يتم عند نشر هذه النصوص لأغراض أدبية أو ثقافية وتكون موجهة للقارئ العام. إذ ذاك يكون يُسر مقروئية النصوص من القارئ العربي وحُسن فهمه هو المطلب الرئيس. لذا يجب مراعاة أن تكون الفصحى هي المرجعية لرسم الأصوات وصرف كلمات النصوص الواردة في هذا المقال بالمبادئ التي يقوم عليها المستوى الثاني، مع تنبيهي للقاريء بمراعاة اختلاف نطق حرف القاف – مثلاً – وتحولاته إلى الهمزة أو الجيم حسب اللهجة المحلية، وهكذا.

(٢) يحيى الطاهر عبد الله، **الطوق والإسورة** (القاهرة: دار المستقبل العربى، ١٩٩٤)، ص ٣٥٥.

(٣) مجهول، **ألف ليلة وليلة**، طبعة مصورة عن طبعة بولاق ١٢٥٢هـ، الجزء الأول (بيروت: دار صادر، د. ت.)، ص ١٩.

(٤) **المرجع السابق**، ص ٢٤.

(٥) أحمد رشدي صالح، **الأدب الشعبي** (القاهرة: مكتبة النهضة المصرية، ١٩٧١)، ص ٣٦٢.

(٦) جاستون ماسبيرو، **الأغاني الشعبية في مصر**، إعداد أحمد مُرسي ومحمود الهندي (القاهرة: الهيئة المصرية العامة للكتاب، ٢٠٠٠)، ص ١٧٦.

(٧) عبد الحميد حواس، **أوراق في الثقافة الشعبية** (القاهرة: الهيئة المصرية العامة للكتاب، ٢٠٠٦)، ص ٣٦٦.

(٨) **المرجع السابق**، ص ٣٦٤.

(٩) **المرجع السابق**، ص ٣٦٧.

(١٠) «نصوص ميدانية»، نُشرت في دورية **الفنون الشعبية**، العدد الأول (أبريل ١٩٥٩)، ص ص ٥٦–٥٧.

(١١) جاستون ماسبيرو، ص ٢٣٤. عُقاب = جمع عُقب. والعقب آخر كل شيء وخاتمته، والكلمة هنا بمعنى أن العجوز أصبحت من البقية الأخيرة من أهلها. لاجيتوا = عندما تجيئون. لولا لغات الحس تغيبوني = لولا صوت كلامي لن تعرفوني.

(١٢) كما يتذكرها كاتب المقالة من صباه. يطوف بها: أي تتوالى عليها أطياف فيكون الفعل من طواف الأطياف، أو أن يكون بمعنى فيض الكيل بها، وبذا تكون الكلمة مشتقة من الجذر المُشترك مع الطوفان.

(١٣) أحمد الليثي ومحمد عبد الرحمن، **جابر أبو حسين شاعر الهلالية** (سوهاج: نشر المؤلف نفسه، ٢٠٠٦)، ص ٢٦٩. النوايب: ما يخص كل فرد عند الاقتسام، كما أنها تلمح إلى معنى النوائب. كوم = المقدار الذي خصها.

(١٤) جاستون ماسبيرو، ص ٢٠٣. لَمَّ = جَمَع. الجدع = الشاب ذو الهمة. عمود الزَّان = مستقيم القامة مثل قضيب من الخشب الزَّان المرن.

(١٥) **المرجع السابق**، ص ١٠٤.

(١٦) أحمد الليثي ومحمد عبد الرحمن، ص ٢٦٤. يبيض عتبنا: المقصود هنا دهان واجهة المنزل باللون الأبيض. يكتَّر الدبايح: أن ينحر عدداً كبيراً من الذبائح لأن الوليمة ستكون كثيرة الضيوف.

(١٧) حامد أنور، **أشكال الغناء الشعبي في الشرقية** (القاهرة: الهيئة العامة لقصور الثقافة، ٢٠٠٨)، ص ١٣٧.

(١٨) **المرجع السابق**، ص ١٣١. حوِّدي: أن تميل تجاهه أو أن تَمرّ به. مطشطش = ارتفعت درجة حرارته. كاويني = من الكي بالنار.

(١٩) محمود أحمد فضل، **الأغنية الفولكلورية للمرأة المصرية** (القاهرة: الهيئة العامة لقصور الثقافة، ٢٠٠٢)، ص ١٩٨. الوابور يُقصد به في المنطقة - عند الجيل القديم - سفينة الركاب البخارية. حاجبه يا قلم ضباط: أي أنه مستقيم الحاجب منتظمه كهيئة قوام الضابط الممشوق.

(٢٠) كما يتذكرها كاتب المقالة من طفولته. والمركب الموسوقة هي السفينة المشحونة المليئة. ورسّو المركب في الموردة: أي استقرار المركب عند مكان ورود الماء على شاطىء النيل. ومعروف أن المُورَدة مكان تردد البنات لجلب الماء للاحتياجات المنزلية.

(٢١) أحمد علي مُرسي، **الأغنية الشعبية** (القاهرة: دار المعارف، ١٩٨٣)، ص ٢٩١. شبه المؤيد: كلام الموال موثوق به مثل صحيفة **المؤيد**.

(٢٢) **المرجع السابق**، ص ٢٩٧.

(٢٣) **المرجع نفسه**.

(٢٤) أحمد رشدي صالح، **فنون الأدب الشعبي**، الجزء الأول (القاهرة: دار الفكر العربي، ١٩٥٦)، ص ١١٢. الوعد: مفهوم مُرَكَّب، ويُستعمل هنا بمعنى إلزامها بالوفاء لما نذرها القدر له. وطلعت تِوفِّي ماعليها: أي خرجت استجابة لنداء قدرها لتفي بما ألزمها به.

(٢٥) **المرجع السابق**، ص ١١٣.

(٢٦) عبد الحميد حواس، **أوراق في الثقافة الشعبية**، ص ٣٣. برتكان = برتقال، الجرجاوية: إشارة إلى شفيقة والمولودة بجرجا.

(٢٧) أحمد علي مُرسي، ص ٣٣٤.

(٢٨) صفوت كمال، **من فنون الغناء الشعبي المصري، مواويل وقصص غنائية شعبية** (القاهرة: الهيئة المصرية العامة للكتاب، ١٩٩٤)، ص ٢٠. مِقَبِّل = مُتجه جنوباً نحو الوجه القبلي.

(٢٩) **المرجع السابق**، ص ٢٢.

(٣٠) **المرجع السابق**، ص ٩٣. الجُرة = الأثر.

(٣١) مجهول، **سيرة عنترة بن شداد**، المجلد الثامن، طبعة جديدة منسقة ومنقحة (بيروت: المكتبة الثقافية، ١٩٧٩)، ص ٢٦٥.

(٣٢) **المرجع نفسه**.

(٣٣) سعد محمد الحداد المشهور باسم سعد الشاعر، تسجيل صوتي من تسجيلات مركز الفنون الشعبية سنة ١٩٦٢. قمت بالتدوين المكتوب للجزء الخاص بمرثية عامر الخفاجي لنفسه في منتصف الثمانينيات، واستخدمته في بعض الدروس منذ ذلك الوقت. النِّيَا = البُعد والرحيل والافتراق. تِبَان = تبدو. يَمّ أمي = في تجاه أمي. يِثُور (يثور) = ينهض.

(٣٤) أحمد شمس الدين الحجاجي، «الزناتي خليفة: بطل المغارب والراوي الشعبي» **مجلة الفنون الشعبية**، العددين ٣٠/٣١ (يناير/يوليو ١٩٩٠)، ص ص ٧٦–٨٨. خَاشَّة = في داخل. حداه = عنده.

(٣٥) **المرجع نفسه**. زناته = الزانة الخاصة به، وتتجانس مع زناتة الأخرى التي تشير إلى القبيلة المعروفة.

(٣٦) **المرجع السابق**، ص ٨٧.

(٣٧) **المرجع نفسه**. تِدِّيها = تُعطيها، تتركها لدياب.

(٣٨) مجهول، **تغريبة بني هلال ورحيلهم إلى بلاد الغرب**، نُسِّقت هذه الطبعة وضُبطت وصُححت بإشراف الناشر (بيروت: مؤسسة المعارف، د. ت.)، ص ص ٢١٤–٢١٥.

(٣٩) أحمد الليثي ومحمد عبد الرحمن، ص ص ١٦٢–١٦٥. وقد أُثبتت ملاحظة أسفل الصفحة ١٦٥ تقول بأن النص من رواية عز الدين نصر الدين التي سجلها في برنامج «الفن الشعبي»، الثلاثاء ١٩٩٥/٩/٥ بالتلفزيون المصري تقديم الدكتور أحمد شمس الدين الحجاجي وإخراج شوقي جمعة.

(٤٠) يحيى الطاهر عبد الله، ص ٤٠.

# فجيعة الغياب، ألفة الغياب:
# تناولات الموت في نماذج من الرواية المصرية

حسين حمودة

لم يكن المصريون بدعة بين شعوب الأرض في تعاملهم مع ظاهرة الموت. لكن هذه الحقيقة لا تنفي، ربما، إمكان المجادلة في الحيز الكبير، اللافت، من الاهتمام الذي نالته هذه التجربة في الحياة المصرية القديمة ثم في امتداد هذا الاهتمام إلى زمننا الراهن، كما لا تنفي هذه الحقيقة إمكان ملاحظة خصوصية ما، كانت ولا تزال ماثلة، في تعامل المصريين مع تجربة الموت.

لم ير المصريون القدماء في الموت «حدثاً» تنتهي الحياة بانتهائه؛ «بل كان المرء يواصل حياته فيه».(١) وتأسيساً على هذا، لاح الموت بمثابة «انفصال العنصر الجسماني عن العناصر الروحية»، أو بدا محض «انتقال من حالة إلى حالة أخرى».(٢) وقد حفلت المعتقدات المصرية القديمة بأفكار شتى حول العالم السفلي والحساب، ومن ثم الراحة المطلقة أو العذاب الدائم في «الحياة الأخرى» (وتتناثر هذه الأفكار في أدبيات الموروث المصري القديم المتنوعة، ومنها **كتاب الموتى** على سبيل المثال). من هذه الرؤية انبثقت وتبلورت، في الحياة المصرية، صيغة خاصة للعلاقة بين الأحياء والموتى، اقترنت بطقوس وشعائر بعينها في التعامل مع الموت نفسه، وواقعته نفسها.(٣) وامتدت هذه الصيغة، بشكل أو بآخر، عبر مسار اجتاز فترات تاريخية طويلة. وليس بعيداً عن هذا السياق، المتصل بما يبقى وبما يندثر من تصورات وممارسات، ما طرحه جمال حمدان حول مفهوم التراكب بين تاريخ مصر القديم والوسيط والحديث، فيما وصّفه بجدل «الاستمرارية» و«الانقطاع»، وليس بعيداً أيضاً عن هذا السياق نفسه تناولات سيد عويس لظاهرة «الموت» وطقوسه، ولفكرة «الخلود»، ووقفاته عند هذه الظاهرة وتلك الفكرة وامتدادهما من الحياة المصرية القديمة إلى الحياة المعاصرة.

فيما يلاحظ جمال حمدان، ثمة كثير «من العادات والتقاليد والممارسات والطقوس، وكذلك من المعتقدات والأفكار حتى الخرافات والأساطير... فضلاً عن الاحتفالات والأعياد.. إلخ، انحدر إلينا من مصر القديمة وظل حياً لآلاف السنين دون تغيير أو تحوير أو إضافة».(٤)

واقترانا بهذه الملاحظة، تلوح الاستمرارية واضحة «في كثير من التقاليد الشعبية في . . . عادات الزواج والولادة والأفراح . . . ثم المآتم والدفن وزيارة المقابر (خميس الميت، فطير الرحمة، الأربعين.. إلخ)».(٥) وبهذا المعنى، يبدو التاريخ المصري، رغم الانتقالات التي ينطوي عليها، مستمراً متصلاً «بلا انقطاع كالنيل في جريان مائه».(٦) وتتراءى الحقب في هذا التاريخ متراكبة، متداخلة، لا تزيح إحداها الأخريات ولا تنفيها، وكأن تاريخ مصر كله، بل مصر كلها، أشبه بـ«وثيقة من جلد الرق، الإنجيل فيها مكتوب فوق هيرودوت، وفوق ذلك القرآن، وخلف الجميع لا تزال الكتابة القديمة مقروءة جلية».(٧)

في مجال هذه الاستمرارية، وفي سياق هذا التراكب، يتأكد امتداد الظواهر الثقافية في المجتمع المصرى، «خصوصاً فيما يتصل بعاداته وتقاليده»، كما يلاحظ سيد عويس في أكثر من سياق.(٨) ولعل تجربة الموت واحدة من أوضح تلك الظواهر التى استمر الكثير من معالمها عبر العصور، واتصل عدد غير قليل من التصورات حولها، والممارسات والشعائر المتعلقة بها، منذ زمن الفراعنة حتى الآن،(٩) وهذا ملمح ملحوظ في القرى المصرية، ومنها قرى صعيد مصر، حيث – مثلاً – بعض طقوس البكاء على الميت لا تزال قائمة، حية، مستعيدة ومستدعية صوراً قديمة مبكرة، ومنها ما يسمى نظام «البكوة» الشائع في الصعيد، رغم تحريم الإسلام – فيما يؤكد عويس – النواحة والنواح.(١٠)

وقد اقترن حضور الموت والموتى، في تلك الممارسات والشعائر والطقوس الممتدة، عابرة الأزمنة – إن صح التعبير – برغبة ظلت، دائماً، تناوئ الموت من حيث هو تلاش وغياب نهائي، وسعت دائماً سعياً واضحاً إلى أن تتلمس نوعاً من الألفة في تجربة مؤلمة. وفي هذه الوجهة، ثمة تعبيرات مصرية «ملطّفة» كانت – ولا تزال – تستخدم في الحديث عن الموت والموتى؛ فالموت في الموروث المصري القديم «يعني حرفياً الرحيل»،(١١) وكان يشار إلى الموتى على أنهم «الذين ذهبوا إلى هناك»،(١٢) وكأن الموت، بهذين التعبيرين، ليس سوى محض انتقال من مكان إلى مكان، وإن ظل التشبث بالمكان الأول ماثلاً في رغبة «الخلود» التي تم التعبير عنها بطرائق شتى، وظل التوق إلى «الأجل الخالد» أو إلى «الوجود السرمدي الدائم»(١٣) مطلاً في كثير من الأدبيات المصرية، وأيضاً وإن ظلت فكرة «الحياة الأخرى» مسلماً بها، غير مطروحة للتساؤل، ساعية إلى التخفيف من وطأة الوحشة المتخيلة في ذلك المكان الآخر.

ثمة «تكوين» ما، إذن، جعل تجربة الموت – التي استوقفت البشر جميعاً، عبر الأزمنة المتباينة، وفي الحضارات المختلفة، وخلال المعتقدات والديانات المتعددة(١٤) – هاجساً ملحاً في كثير من المعتقدات،

والتصورات، والتناولات الإبداعية المصرية، وجعل مناوأة الموت – المتواشجة وفكرة «الخلود» – عنصراً أساسياً، قاراً وثابتاً، في «التكوين» المصري، عبر فترات عدة من التاريخ، كامناً في المعتقد والفكرة، متحققاً في الطقس والشعيرة، ومتجسداً في الأواصر الممتدة بين الأحياء والراحلين، بما يجعل هؤلاء الأخيرين، حتى بعد رحيلهم – الذي لم يُتصوَّر أبداً على أنه نهائي – يظلون «مقيمين» بين الأحياء، على نحو ما.

ولعل جزءاً من هذه الخصوصية، في رؤية المصريين للموت، ماثلٌ في عدد من الروايات التي نتوقف، هنا، عند نماذج سبعة منها، كان لتجربة الموت فيها جميعاً «حضور» واضح، إن لم يكن الحضور الأساسي: **بداية ونهاية** (١٩٤٩) لنجيب محفوظ، **كتاب التجليات** (١٩٩٠) لجمال الغيطاني، **خالتي صفية والدير** (١٩٩١) لبهاء طاهر، **يوميات امرأة مشعة** (٢٠٠٦) لنعمات البحيري، **تغريدة البجعة** (٢٠٠٦) لمكاوي سعيد، **شجرة أمي** (٢٠٠٧) لسيد البحراوي، **جروح الأصابع الطويلة** (٢٠٠٨) لسهى زكي. وفضلاً عن انتماء هذه الروايات إلى فترات متغايرة على مستوى تواريخ كتابتها وصدورها، وإلى توجهات فنية متباينة على مستوى صياغاتها الفنية، فإنها تقدم تمثيلات متنوعة الزوايا لتجربة الموت، بما يكشف عن أبعاد عدة لهذه التجربة.

### الموت اختباراً، الموت اختياراً

في رواية نجيب محفوظ **بداية ونهاية**(١٥) يدخل الموت طرفاً أساسياً في تناول مركزي كان ماثلاً في القلب من عالمه خلال رواياته التي كتبها فترة الأربعينيات: العلاقة بين البدايات والنهايات، أو الآصرة التي تربط، بنوع من الحتم، بين اختيارات الشخصيات ومصائرها، أو تصل بين منطلقها الأول ومآلها الأخير. في الفصل الأول من فصول الرواية – المشيدة على نوع من التسلسل والتعاقب الزمني – يقف التلميذان، حسين وحسنين، أمام ناظر مدرستهما فينقل لهما الخبر الفاجع: «أرجو أن تكونا رجلين كما ينبغي. **لقد توفي والدكما** كما أبلغني أخوكما الأكبر **والبقية في حياتكما**» (ص ٥، وهذا التشديد وكل التشديدات التالية في نصوص الروايات من عندنا). ورجاء الناظر أن يكون التلميذان «رجلين كما ينبغي»، وأمنيته لهما بـ«حياة باقية» – حتى وإن قفزنا عليهما أو عبرناهما بسرعة، أو إن أدرجناهما ضمن سياق عبارات العزاء التي قد لا تعني حقاً ما تشير إليه مفرداتها – سوف يمثلان لهذين التلميذين ما يشبه «الاختبار» الذي سيتأسس عليه، ويتعلق به، مصير كل منهما في «الزمن المحتمل» القادم: أن يكونا رجلين «كما ينبغي» أو ألا يكونا، وأن تمضي حياتهما في بقية ممتدة أو تنتهي عند نقطة ما.

وأياً كانت قراءة صيغة الموت في **بداية ونهاية**؛(١٦) حدثاً اجتماعياً مقروناً بغياب الأب/العائل - ومن ثم نقطة تحول في حياة الأسرة التي كان يعولها - في بداية الرواية، أو مصيراً أشبه بحكم أخلاقي، يطال بالفعل، في نهاية الرواية، مَن اجترحا المواضعات الأخلاقية والاجتماعية: الأخت نفيسة وأخاها حسنين، فإن الموت يظل مطروحاً خلال الوقائع الروائية عبر علاقته بسياق أكبر، وفي الحالين يظل مرتبطاً بما يحيط به من تجارب أحياء لم يتهددهم الموت وإن رجّتهم تجربته رجّاً عنيفاً. في البداية - خلال الصفحات الأولى من الرواية - نحن إزاء مشاهد ما بعد رحيل الغائب الأول، الأب. ولكننا أيضاً، في المشاهد ذاتها، إزاء تفاصيل تشي بـ«وجود» هذا الأب، حاضراً ممتداً على نحو ما في أسرته: نتاجه المثمر؛ ثلاثة شباب ذكور وفتاة شابة (فضلاً عن أمهم/زوجته). وسوف يظل هذا النتاج الحي، في مشاهد أخرى متنوعة تالية، يدافع الذبول والتلاشي ويتشبث بأسباب الحياة، بل ويتطلع - بطرائق شتى - إلى تجاوز المحنة ثم إلى التحقق والتنامي. وفي النهاية - خلال الصفحات الأخيرة من الرواية - سوف يخطّ الموت، بإرادة صارمة وبما يشبه الحكم الذي لا راد له، مصائر من «يستحقون» أن يطالهم: يطال، أولاً، الفتاة التي انقادت لغريزتها واستسلمت، أو أجبرت كالمختارة - إن صح هذا التعبير - على الاستسلام للضغوط من حولها، مجترحة أخلاقيات ومواضعات غير قابلة للاجتراح، ثم يشرع في أن يطال، ثانياً، الابن الذي ظل يتطلع دائماً إلى الصعود الفردي، وإن كان على أنقاض الآخرين.

يضعنا هذا الموت الأخير المزدوج، الفعلي أو الوشيك، إزاء تساؤلات شتى حول إمكانات استمرار «حياة» بقية «النبت». وإذا كان الموت قد غيّب عائل الأسرة في أول الرواية، وإذا كان سيغيّب اثنين آخرين من أبناء هذه الأسرة في آخرها، تاركاً إيانا نتأمل - للمرة الأخيرة - لعبة البداية والمآل، فإننا فيما بين الموتين، فيما بين البدء والختام، خلال أكثر من تسعين فصلاً، نتحرك في عالم يتدفق عبر مساحات كبيرة من «الحياة»، محتفياً بما يمور فيها من مساع وصراعات؛ حيث نشهد وقائع تمثل تعبيرات عن الآمال والطموحات، والبحث عن المتع الصغيرة والانقياد أحياناً لها، والانكفاء على عمل مضن للحصول على نقود قليلة تخفف من وطأة الفقر الذي أطبق دفعة واحدة عقب موت العائل، والسعي الدائب من أجل إعادة التوازن إلى ميزان كان قد اختل برجّةٍ مفاجئة مدوية، وتلمّس السبل نحو شكل من أشكال الارتقاء الطبقي، إلخ. وفي ذلك كله، نكون إزاء أجساد وأرواح حية، تستعيد أحياناً صور «الأب» الذي تحول من حي حاضر إلى

«مرحوم» غائب، وتناوئ دائماً ذلك النذير بالتهاوي، متسلحة بإيمان – يكاد يكون «فطرة» – بأن «الحي **أبقى** من الميت». وخلال ذلك كله، تتماس هذه الأجساد والأرواح وتتفاعل مع أجساد آخرين وأخريات وأرواحهم، جيران وجارات وأقارب وأصدقاء ورفيقات ورفقاء وزملاء، إلخ، لا يفكرون ولا يفكرن في الموت إلا كما يفكر فيه أغلب الأحياء: جزء من سنّة الحياة نفسها، آتٍ لا ريب فيه، ولا مدافع له حين يحوم ثم يحط، ولكنه ليس قريباً بما يجعله هاجساً ملحاً أو تهديداً ماثلاً.

في المسافة بين الموت المطروح بوصفه «قدراً اجتماعياً» في الفصل الأول من **بداية ونهاية**، والموت المفروض بوصفه «حكماً أخلاقياً» في فصلها الأخير، ثمة مسار متصاعد، عبر فصول الرواية الاثنين والتسعين، المرقمة المتصلة تعبيراً عن تسلسل الأحداث وتعاقبها، مما يجعل أغلب هذه الفصول تبدأ بـ«واو» تعطف الوقائع الجديدة على وقائع سابقة:(١٧) «**وغادرا** المدرسة إلى الشارع» (ص ٦)، «**وغادر** الشقيقان الشقة» (ص ٩)، «**وعند** اقتراب موعد الجنازة بلغ الاضطراب بحسنين مداه» (ص ١٣)، إلخ. وإذا كان هذا التعاقب يفصح عن تصاعد تدريجي في مجابهة صدمة موت «البداية»، ثم في السعي إلى النأي عن وطأة هذا الموت وتأثيراته بعد ذلك، فإنه يمثل – في الوقت نفسه – تسلسلاً في اتجاه آخر، تدريجي أيضاً، هو بمثابة اقتراب من موت «النهاية». كأن وقائع الرواية جميعاً محاطة بقوسين كبيرين وضعهما الموت، تجتاز مسافتها محكومة بحدّيهما؛ في نصف المسافة الأول ثمة توغل للابتعاد عن القوس الأول، ولكن في نصفها الثاني خروجاً يقترب، شيئاً فشيئاً، من القوس الأخير.

النزوع الأخلاقي في صياغة المصير الختامي لكل من نفيسة وحسنين، حيث الثمرة المسمومة لخطيئة الجسد (والروح؟) بالنسبة إلى الأولى، وعقاب التطلع على حساب معاناة الآخرين بالنسبة إلى الثاني – هذا النزوع يتحقق خلال مسحة بنائية واضحة تتخلل السرد الروائي، تكاد تنتمي إلى مفاهيم الحكي الشعبي القديم ووظائفه. يتمثل هذا المعنى في المغزى الذي يضعه إزاءنا، ويضعنا إزاءه، نجيب محفوظ: «الاختيارات» (ونستطيع أن نقول أيضاً «الاختبارات»)، ثم مآل الثواب والعقاب. ولا ينفصل تجسيد هذا المغزى عن تسلسل «الحكاية» التي لها، دائماً، «بداية» و«نهاية». ولذلك، ينهض سرد الرواية على مداخل زمنية تصاغ بالصيغة الحكائية المتوارثة نفسها، وتتوقف عند ما هو استثنائي، أو غير متوقع، في سلسلة الوقائع المعتادة المتواترة. وعلى سبيل المثال، يبدأ الفصل الثاني والأربعون بعبارة تمثل هذا المنحى: «**وذات ليلة زار** حسن الأسرة **زيارة غير متوقعة**» (ص ١٧٠). والموت الأخير، الحدث الاستثنائي الأكبر، في سياق تنامي وقائع

الرواية، موصول بنهاية الـ«طريق» الذي تم عبور الخطوة الأولى فيه، ثم المرور بكل خطواته، بما يخفف قليلاً من «فجائية» أو «استثنائية» هذا الحدث، وبما يدرجه – بيسر مشهود – في لعبة البدايات والنهايات. لقد اختارت نفيسة طريقاً، أو أجبرت على اختياره، واختار حسنين طريقاً يمكن المجادلة في مدى حريته أو مدى إجباره في/على اختياره، ولكن في كل من الطريقين قادت الخطوة الأولى، دائماً، إلى الخطوة الأخيرة.

ما بداية الطريق (الانحراف، ثم الموت) بالنسبة إلى نفيسة؟ لم تكن خطوة نفيسة الأولى في هذا الطريق قاصرة على تلبية نداء جسدها أو إشباع شهوتها مع ابن البقال، جابر، الذي أغواها وانقادت – كالراغبة – إلى غوايته. لقد ذهبت معه إلى بيته حيث لا أحد هناك: «كان قلبها يدق بعنف يكاد تصدع له الضلوع»، ولكنه عندما «فتح لها الباب وهمس في أذنها "تفضلي" دخلت بعد أن قالت بتوسل كلمة واحدة: "لنعد". لم تكن خطوتها هذه مترنحة تماماً. لقد دخلت ودخل وراءها وأغلق الباب» (ص ١٠٣). سوف يضايقها الظلام حقاً، ولكنها ستألفه، وسوف تستسلم في النهاية وهي ترى كل شيء من حولها. أما الخطوة الأولى في طريق سوف ينتهي بها إلى الموت، فقد بدأت من التكسب بإشباع شهوات الآخرين، مع صاحب الجراج محمد الفل. لقد ذهبت إلى الفل بعد «صراع عنيف نشب في نفسها في غير ما رحمة ولا هوادة طوال الأسابيع الماضية. . . . ومع أنها كانت قد انتهت من ترددها المعذب إلى نهاية، إلا **أن الخوف ركبها وهي تخطو الخطوات الأخيرة**» (ص ١٦٤). وعلى أية حال، سوف تخطو خطوتها الأولى هذه، في طريق تحولها إلى داعرة، مجتازة عتبة ترددها،(١٨) بعد تفكير قصير: «ألا يحسن بى أن أستزيد من التفكير؟ كلا، كلا، لن أجني من التفكير إلا وجع الدماغ . . . **فات أوان التراجع**» (ص ١٦٤).

بالروح نفسها، تقريباً، التي تسلم بفوات أوان التراجع، سوف تمضى نفيسة إلى نهايتها؛ موتها الذي سوف ترى فيه عقاباً عادلاً، بل وخلاصاً مما هو أسوأ منه: «إن ما ورائي في الحياة **أفظع من الموت**» (ص ٣٦٤). هاهي الآن قد تقطعت الأسباب التي تربطها بالحياة التي «هانت عليها»؛ «هانت **الهوان الذي يجعل من الموت نجاة**» (ص ٣٦٤)، وهاهي الآن تحدق في الموت بعينين ثابتتين بعد أن «اقتلعت الجذور التي تشدها للبقاء، ووجدت مع هذا اليأس راحة زحزحت عن كاهلها الأعباء، فلم تعد تفكر في شيء ذى بال، **ورمقت الموت الذي تنهب الأرض إليه باستسلام** كأنه التخدير». لقد اجتازت عتبة الموت حتى قبل أن يلفها ظلامه؛ «هذه هي **النهاية الوحيدة** . . . **إني ميتة**» (ص ٣٦٤).

تجربة حسنين، وإن اختلفت ملابساتها، ليست نائية تماماً عن هذا الاختيار/الاختبار نفسه، ولا عن صيغته ولا عن مغزاه. تخلى حسنين –

منصاعاً لتطلعه – عن خطيبته الأولى بهية، وعن أسرتها التي ساعدت أسرته؛ لأنه رأى في فتاة أخرى، ابنة أحد أقربائه الأثرياء، سلماً للصعود الطبقي. وكان حسنين، من بين أخوته جميعاً، الساعي الأول إلى الانتقال من الحارة المتواضعة التي تربى فيها إلى شقة بمصر الجديدة تليق بـ«مقامه» الجديد. وإذن، كان هناك من ضحايا طموحه، بمعنى ما، خطيبته الأولى، ثم كانت أخته التي أمدته كثيراً بنقود لم يتساءل عن مصدرها، وأيضاً كان – إلى حد ما – أخواه حسين وحسن. وسوف يقود حسنينَ خبرُ القبض على أخته نفيسة بتهمة الدعارة إلى السقوط من حالق، بعد أن كان قد صعد درجات عدة على سلم طموحه/تطلعه الذي لم يلتفت وهو يصعده إلى أحد من حوله. سوف تنزاح عن عينيه الغشاوة – أو قل «العمى» – في وقت متأخر جداً، بعد شهوده مصرع أخته الذي شارك فيه. لقد حدق في «جثتها الراقدة غير بعيد عن قدميه. جرى بصره عليها وقد تبعثر شعرها وتلصقت خصلات منه بخدها وجبينها، وران على الوجه جمود صامت لا يبشر بيقظة وعلته زرقة مروعة» (ص ٣٧١)، وسوف يسأل نفسه: «لماذا أضطرب هكذا؟ ألم أقتنع حقاً بأن هذه هي خير نهاية! **ألم أسقها إلى الموت بنفسي**؟ ينبغي أن تطمئن نفسي» (ص ٣٧١). ولكن نفسه لم تطمئن، لقد بدأت الآن تساؤلاته ليس عن الموت بوصفه نهاية طبيعية لما فعلته أخته، ولكن عما يستحق هو أيضاً من نهاية. طريق تساؤلات حسنين، المكثف القصير، يتخلل سرد الراوي الموازي له، ليرسم ما يشبه محاكمة أخلاقية عاجلة لنفسه ولأخته ولكل من حوله (ص ٣٧٢)، وسوف ينتهي من تساؤلاته هذه إلى التوجه نحو الموضع ذاته من النهر الذي ألقت أخته منه بنفسها في الماء، وسوف يرتفق السور ذاته أيضاً، ويطلب الشجاعة لنفسه، ويطلب – لمن؟! لنفسه؟ لأخته؟ لأهله؟ لنا جميعاً؟ – الرحمة: «ليرحمنا الله». وهي العبارة التي تنتهي بها الرواية، لتنغلق معها دائرة الموت التي بدأت بها.

## الموت نسياناً، النسيان موتاً

تحلق رواية جمال الغيطاني **كتاب التجليات**(١٩) في فضاءات شاسعة، تجاوز تخوم الأزمنة والأماكن، الشخصيات والمشاهد، التجارب والمعارف، وتنوس بين عالم التجليات والرؤى والإشراقات الداخلية، الصوفية، وعالم المشاهد والوقائع والأسماء المرجعية، وتخلق من ذلك كله كياناً يتجاور فيه ما لا يتجاور عادة. وفي مركز هذه الحركة الواسعة، ثمة حضور لافت وأساسي للموت والموتى: للشهداء والراحلين – ممن يتماسون مع تجارب الراوي، المسمى «جمال»، الذي يتقاطع صوته في غير موضع مع صوت المؤلف – سواء ممن ينتمون إلى التاريخ العام أو إلى السيرة الشخصية، حيث تمحي المسافات بين عبد الناصر والحسين وابن عربي وابن إياس، ووالد

الراوي وأمه وأخيه. وفضلاً عن ذلك، ثمة تأملات في تجربة الموت نفسه، في كينونته وتعريفه وكنهه الغامض، وفي مراوحته بين الحضور والغياب، وفي موضعه على متصل الذاكرة/النسيان.

تترامى تجارب الراوي المتكلم عبر أسفار الكتاب الثلاثة، التي تنبني – متمثلة بعض الكتابات التراثية العربية القديمة – بعناوين إجمالية خارجية وأخرى فرعية داخلية، تجاوز جميعاً محض كونها «حليات» لتصبح مكوناً أساسياً من مكونات العالم الروائي؛ إذ تمثل جزءاً من الأحداث أو اختزالاً لها أو تعليقاً عليها أو انتقالاً فيما بينها. تتحرك الأسفار الثلاثة من الـ«تجليات» والـ«مواقف» إلى الـ«مقامات» والـ«أحوال». يمضي السفر الأول بين تجليات الفراق، والتجليات الديوانية، وتجليات الأسفار ومنها تجليات الغربة، ثم «المواقف» (التأهب، الظمأ، الحنين، اللقاء والتلقي، كان وسيكون، الندم، النجم، الشدة، الجمع). ويتنقل السفر الثاني، بعد «مدرج» البداية، بين مقام الاغتراب، ومقام الضنا، ومقام القربى، ومقام الحزن، وسريان بين مقامين، ومقام الجوى، ثم «منتهى». والسفر الثالث، بعد «مفتتح»، ينوس بين حال الوداد، وحال الفوت، وحال الجهات الأربع، وحال الوداع. وعبر هذه الأسفار، وعبر انتقالاتها بين التجارب والمشاهدات والتأملات، تتمثل ارتحالات تجاوز المألوف، ويتجاور فيها الأحياء والموتى، وتجوب مساحات تقع فيما وراء حدود الحياة وحدود الموت.

ويسمح منطق «التجلي» – الذي يتأسس عليه عالم هذه الرواية ويفصح عن مغامرتها الأساسية – بإمكانات لا تتيح الارتحال عبر تخوم الأزمنة والأماكن فحسب، وإنما أيضاً تفتح مجالات رحبة لرؤية ما لا يرى، وبإمساك ما لا يمسك، عادة، استناداً إلى «طاقة» استثنائية، تتماس وبصيرة الراوي الداخلية ثم تفارقه وقد دخل في حال غير الحال، وأصبح كائناً غير الكائن، ممتلكاً قدرة غير القدرة، نافياً المسافة بين ذاته وما يراه، أو بين عالمه الداخلي، الباطني، والعالم الماثل خارجه. في موقف «التأهب»، مثلاً، يقول الراوي:

> أوقفني في موقف التأهب، ثم فارقني، هجرني ونأى عني فصرت إلى غربة وفقر بعد أنس وألفة . . . صرت بمفردي، غريباً في غربتي، نائياً في نأيي، بعيداً في بعدي، لكنني أشبه بمن يستجمع كافة قواه تأهباً لانطلاق عظيم، كنت قادراً على رؤية ما أمامي وما ورائي، فوقي وتحتي بدون حركة من عيني أو رأسي، صرت بصراً كلي، كأني الناظر والمنظور إليه كأني الرائي والمرئي. (ص ١٤٦)

وانطلاقاً من هذه الطاقة، ينزع الراوي - الذي أصبح صاحب قدرة على استبصار ما لا يُستبصَر - عن الغامض غموضه، وعن المستتر أستاره، وعن الظلام ظلمته، فتتكشف له إجابات عن أسئلة محيرة، ويتاح له علم بكل ما هو مجهول. ومن ضمن هذا الغامض المستتر، المظلم المجهول، المستثير للأسئلة والتساؤلات، تجربة الموت: تجارب من ماتوا وتجربة الموت ذاته.

وجوه النائين بفعل الموت تستعاد مع وجوه البعيدين بفعل السفر والغربة، كما تستعاد وجوه المشرفين على هذا النأي المزدوج قبل تمامه. كذلك تبتعث، مع الجميع الذين قطعوا بعض الرحلة، فاجتازوا مسافات من مسيرة، وجوه القادمين إليها ولما يبدأوا خطواتهم الأولى فيها: «رأيت وجوهاً مثقلة بالغربة، بالوحدة، بالعزلة . . . رأيت وجوهاً قادمة إلى الدنيا لتوها وأخرى ماضية إلى مجهول غامض . . . رأيت وجوهاً في وجوه. مبحرة عبر الشظايا، تغوص، تطفو» (ص ٧٥). لا تنفصل هذه الاستعادة، ولا ذلك الابتعاث، عن «تأمل» ما يتوارى وراء ملامح الوجوه، في الأزمنة المنقضية وفي الأزمنة الراهنة وفي الأزمنة التالية، استكناه تفاصيل حياتها وموتها، واستبطان الموت ذاته بعد التحديق فيه.

في مجال تأملات الموت ما يستكشف أبعاداً متنوعة لحدوده ومعناه ولبه وامتداداته. من هذه التأملات ما يصل الموت بالميلاد؛ حيث تتجاور أسفار كل منهما (ص ٥٩). ويسري هذا المعنى على الكون كله؛ فالنهاية دائماً «متصلة بالبداية، لابد من نهاية وإلا ما كان ثم بداية» (ص ٦٨). ومن هذه التأملات، أيضاً، ما يجعل الموت الواحد يتكشّف عن موتين: «موت أعظم وموت أصغر، **أما الموت الأعظم** فيتمثل في السكوت على الجور، والتغاضي عن الزيف، وإخماد الضمائر . . . **أما الموت الأصغر** فهو بطلان الحواس، وتوقف الأنفاس، وهجوع القلب» (ص ١٣٥)، وبذلك ينسحب معنى الموت على كثيرين يتحركون حول الراوي أو يتحرك هو بينهم. ومن هذه التأملات، كذلك، ما يسعى إلى الإحاطة بمعنى الموت؛ فيتصوره بمثابة «الهول الأكبر» (ص ٤٩٤)، أو «اكتمال الدائرة الكبرى» (ص ٣٦٠)، أو الانتقال إلى «أبد الأبد» (ص ٨٠١)، أو يرى أنه «نزع» و«جهل» و«غيبة» و«فراق» (ص ٨٠٥؛ واقترانات الموت والفراق تتكرر في مواضع شتى بالرواية، انظر ص ص ١٥، ٢٨٩، ٤٦٠، ٤٧٤، ٥١٣، ٧٩١)، أو ينظر إليه على أنه «القطع» في ثنائية «الوصل والقطع»: «الوصل حياة والقطع موت . . . الوجود مبني على وصل، الأنفاس المتصلة تعني استمرار الحياة فإذا انقطعت الوصلة بين النفسين مات الإنسان» (ص ١١٢)، أو يجسده في استرداد «صاحب الأمانة وديعته» (ص ٧٧٩)، أو يتخيله في «الوحدة» المطبقة، حيث الجيران الموتى «رقود يجهل كل منهم الآخر، جيران لكن لا يتزاورون» (ص ٢٦٥)، أو يؤكد أنه - فيما يستعيد

الراوي كلمات شيخه ابن عربي – عودة بالجسم إلى أصله: «الجسم خلق من تراب، وعاد بالموت إلى أصله، فلا فرق بينه، في حال انفصاله وبروزه، كونه على وجه الأرض أو حصوله تحت التراب، فهو منها» (ص ٤٩٥). ومن هذه التأملات يلوح «العالم الدنيوي الذي نحن فيه الآن له انتهاء يؤول إليه لأنه محدث، وحكم المحدث أن ينقضي» (ص ٧٩). وهكذا، يقترن الموت – في تصور ابن عربي أيضاً – بلحظات فارقة، هي جزء من مواجهة النتائج التي انبنت على أسباب، أو المصائر المتباينة التي ترتبت على أعمال مختلفة: «الموت فزع للمؤمن لما قدم من إساءة، وفزع للعارف لحيائه من الخالق عند القدوم إليه، وندم للكافر لفقد المألوفات» (ص ٨٠٥). لكن، مع كل ما تمنحه هذه التأملات من مقاربات لحقيقة الموت، واستكشافات كنهه، فإنه يظل محاطاً بتساؤلات أخرى عصية على الإجابة؛ منها ما يتوقف عند موقع لحظة الموت من الزمن المعدود (ص ١٢٩)، وما يتصل بتوقيته وكيفيته (ص ٧٩٩)، وما يحدد الفارق بين صورته أو صوره بعد أن يحل، عند إغماضة العينين، ثم بعد عام أو عامين أو مائة (ص ٨٠٥).

يُطرح النسيان في الرواية كأنه الامتداد الأوضح للموت، أو التمثيل الأظهر له. وفي الرواية حشد من العبارات والمواقف التي تؤكد هذا المعنى، بصيغ تستند أحياناً إلى نبرة من نبرات اليقين، وتصاغ أحياناً بإيحاءات لا تخلو من تساؤل. فالموت تارة هو النهاية حيث يلوح الإنسان نسياً منسياً (ص ص ٢٩ و٤٨٠)، والموت تارة ثانية هو التلاشي «**في منزل النسيان**» (ص ٨٥)، والموت تارة ثالثة هو المحاق أو النسيان (ص ٩٧). وإذا كان النسيان بهذا المعنى هو الموت الحقيقي، حيث يتأمل الراوي بصوت الشهيد: «**إذا تم النسيان .. يكون الموت**» (ص ٤٥٦)، فإن الموت يظل غير منفصل عن فعل الزمن الذي يمضي بالحضور، ثم بالذكرى، إلى غياهب النسيان، شيئاً فشيئاً، أو عبر رحلة تبدأ متريثة الإيقاع ثم تتسارع. وبذلك، يتم الانتقال من نسيان ملتبس إلى نسيان تام مكتمل. يجسد الراوي اكتمال موت من ماتوا بتمام نسيانهم الذي يتحقق عبر درجات متصاعدة؛ موت الأب، مثلاً، يبدأ بعد اختفاء لفظ «أبي» من قاموس الراوي، ثم مع انقضاء عام كامل باعتياده القسم بـ«رحمة أبيه» (ص ص٢٦٥ و٧٦٩)، وعبد الناصر، أيضاً، يكتمل موته عبر مراحل النسيان الذي يتم بمرور السنوات، من نهاية العام الأول حيث بدت الطرق المؤدية إلى ضريحه «مزدحمة غاصة. الوفود تترى، والجماعات تتوالى والخلق كثير، والممر وبهو المسجد يفيض بالورود. في العام الثاني لم يعد الجمع هو الجمع، وفي الثالث قل المدد، وفي الرابع اتسعت المسافات وصار الضريح وجهة المخلصين الأشداء المحبين» (ص ٢٦٦). كذلك، يلوح متصل الموت/النسيان قائماً مع أخ يفقده الراوي، كمال الذي اختطفه الموت ثم

رسّخ النسيان فقدانه (ص ص ٦٥١ و٦٥٤). يبدأ النسيان بالأصوات: «أول ما يستسلم للنسيان، ثم تتبعها العادات الصغيرة، كطريقة النظر إلى الموجودات وحركة الأيدي عند الحديث . . . وهيئة الضحك والإطراق عند التفكير وجوهر الحضور. يندغم هذا، وتبهت الفواصل» (ص ٢٦٨).

في مواجهة الموت/النسيان، يمثل «التذكر» وسيلة مدافعة الغياب. في عبارات «الشهيد» الراحل، كما تصل إلى الراوي، تأكيد لهذا المعنى: «لا تنس. إذا استمر ذكر الإنسان، أو اللفظ باسمه بعد موته، أو اجترار سيرته مع من أحبوه وعرفوه، فإنه يصبح في اعتبار الحي» (ص ٤٥٦). كذلك، في نصائح الأم للراوي ما يبدو سعياً إلى مدافعة نسيان موت الابن/الأخ كمال: «لا تنس كمال أخاك، اطلب له الرحمة واقرأ الفاتحة» (ص ٦٥١)، «اذكر شيئاً عن أخيك كمال» (ص ٦٥٣)، ثم يطل من نصائح الأم لوم واضح: «يعني ما من ذكر لكمال»، ثم تفصح عباراتها، في زمن لاحق، عن عتاب وتقريع: «نسيته [أنت] كما نسيت سورة يس» (ص ٦٥٤). وفي هذا المنحى، تمثل زيارات الراوي لقبر أبيه وسيلة لمدافعة نسيانه ولمناوأة التسليم بحقيقة غيابه (ص ٢٦٤). وهكذا، يغدو التذكر نفياً للنسيان الذي يجلبه الزمن، فيما يجلب من تحول وتبدل، فلا يثبت العالم قط على حالة واحدة (ص ص ٢٨٣ و١٠٣). ومن هنا، تقترن مدافعة الموت/النسيان بمغالبة الزمن، أو بمغالبة ما يأتي به من تغير. وتندرج في هذا زيارات أهل الراوي للأضرحة التي تضم «مراقد البيت»: «سيدنا الحسين، والسيدة زينب، والسيدة نفيسة، والسيدة رقية» (ص ص ١٧٦ و٣١١)، كما يندرج في هذا رصد الراوي زيارته لقبر أبيه، وحواره معه كأنه حي: «وعندما طلع صباح الواقعة كان الأربعاء يقابل الثلاثاء، عقدت الهمة وقصدت زيارة المثوى . . . وقعدت فوق حجر عند موضع قدميه . . . حدثت أبي بكلام كثير بددت به صمتي، عللت النفس أنه ربما يصغي» (ص ٢٦٤).

ارتباطاً بهذا المعنى، يغدو منطق «التجلي» عطية في مدافعة الموت/النسيان. وبجانب قدرة الراوي، الآن، في زمن خارج الأزمنة، على أن يرى – بالتفصيل – وجوهاً معروفة لمن ماتوا عبر بعض فترات التاريخ، فوق تراب كربلاء أو فوق رمال سيناء (ص ص ٧٤–٧٥ و٨٨)، فإنه أيضاً في زمن خارج الأزمنة يستحضر شهداء وغير شهداء، مجهولين، ممن غيّبهم الموت في عصور عدة، وفي بقاع متعددة من الأرض: بعضهم كان قادماً من الريف إلى المدينة في الزمن المملوكي (ص ٩٤)، وبعضهم كان يلتف حول علي بن أبي طالب (ص ٧٣)، وبعضهم كان حول الحسين الشهيد (ص ص ١١٦ و٧٧)، وبعضهم كان من شهداء حرب أكتوبر «التي قيل إنها آخر الحروب» (ص ٢١). ومن

هؤلاء جميعاً، وبعضهم قد توارت ملامحه، تبرز في تجليات الراوي، في سعيه إلى مناوأة النسيان/الموت، شخصيات بأعيانها يتكافأ – على مستوى ما – حضورها الراهن بعد موتها وحضورها القديم حين كانت بين الأحياء: الأب (انظر الرواية صفحات ١٠، ١١، ٢٨، ٤٧٧، ٤٧٩)، الحسين (صفحات ٣٨، ٣٩، ٨٣، ٨٥)، عبد الناصر (ص ص ١٢ و١٥)، «الأم» (صفحات ٧٩٤، ٧٩٥، ٨١١)، ابن عربي (ص ٨٤)، الجدة (ص ص ٨٠–٨١)، الشهيد مازن (ص ٧٧)، مع كل من كمال وإسماعيل، أخوي الراوي (ص ص ٥٤٥–٥٤٧، ثم ص ٧٨٥ وص ٧٨٧). ومع هؤلاء جميعاً، يتجلى مشهد شخصيات «الديوان»، الأقطاب الراحلين الذين تترأسهم السيدة زينب، تتصدرهم هي وتُجلِس إلى يسارها الحسين وإلى يمينها الحسن (ص ٣٧)، وتتجلى هذه الشخصيات جميعاً بهيئات مفعمة بالحياة. هؤلاء الراحلون، المبتعَثون، يطلون على الراوي – أو يطل هو عليهم – أحياناً في اللامكان، وأحياناً في أمكنة بعينها؛ تتداخل أزمنتهم أحياناً مع زمنه، وتجاربهم مع تجربته، وهم في هذا كله يبرحون غيابهم فيكون لهم حضور كبير، وربما الحضور الأظهر، داخل الرواية.

كما تُمحى فواصل الأزمنة والأماكن في حضور هؤلاء جميعاً، تتلاشى أيضاً المسافات بين أصواتهم المتنوعة، أو بين شخصيات بعضهم وبعض؛ فيتحاور الراوي مع واحد منهم يتراءى له بهيئة واحد آخر أو يتكلم بلسانه. يتكلم عبد الناصر، مثلاً، بصوت الأب: «رأيت عبد الناصر، مكشوفاً، حاسراً، مبهدلاً، أقبلت عليه وعندما تكلم، تكلم بصوت أبي» (ص ٢٠)، ويتحدث صاحبه الشهيد أيضاً بصوت أبيه: «سمعته يقول بصوت أبي» (ص ٩٧)، كما تتراءى له ملامح أبيه «في جسم عبد الناصر» (ص ١١٢).

حضور الموتى في حياة الراوي لا ينفصل عن حضور الهاجس المراود بموته هو. يقول: «ثقل قلبي حتى موتي» (ص ١٨)، ويعذبه «ما فات»، «ما انقضى وما ينقضي» (ص ٢٧). إنه موقن من موته، أو من موت وجوده المادي الذي «يهوي في قرار سحيق. . . . اليقين عندي أنني راحل بعد ثوان، **الموت سيتم في اللحظات التالية، سأغمض عيني ولن أفتحها قط**، ماض إلى مجهول» (ص ٤٨٠). قد يعتريه أسى ما على نهايته التي يقول عنها: «لا أدري متى ستحين؟ فأرثي ذاتي لحظة ميلادي، **وأبكي على رحيلي بعد سفري**» (ص ٥١٣)، وقد يتساءل عما سيتبقى منه، وعمن سيتذكره بعد رحيله: «ما الذي سيبقى مني، ومنذا سيتطلع إلى رسمي؟ إلى ظلي بعد اندثاري؟ ومن سيخلو إلى نفسه ويتطلع إلى صوري التي ستمسي قديمة بالية؟ من سيجيء ومن سيتذكر نبرة صوتي؟» (ص ٥٧٩). ولكنه مع ذلك يسلم بمنطق جمعي متوارث عن الموت، كانت جدته قد أشارت إليه، فيه يغدو الموت محض

استرداد «وديعة لابد أن ترد» (ص ٥٠٧)، ومعه يكون الموت، كل موت، نهاية طبيعية لكل حي؛ إنه فقط يظل يخشى أن يموت بعيداً عن أهله: «**تنتابني خشية موت الفجأة، فلا أرى الأهل والصحب**» (ص ٢٩١)، كما يظل يخشى أن يموت ميتة تتشوه معها هيأته؛ فيغدو رأساً بلا بدن، أو بدناً بلا رأس، فجمال «الجسم البشري وكماله في اتصاله» (ص ٢١٨). إنه، في النهاية، موقن من أنه سيغمض عينيه يوماً ولن يفتحهما قط، كما أغمض عينيه – بكلماته – «أبي، وجمال عبد الناصر، ومازن، وإبراهيم، وخالد، وكل صحبي الذين راحوا»، ولكنه أيضاً يتمنى أن تتم مناوأة الغياب خلال الذكرى، خلال عدم نسيان هؤلاء الراحلين وعدم نسيانه هو؛ يظل يأمل، «أن يتأخر مغيب شمسهم، وألا تنطوي ظلالهم، كما أدعو وأرنو إلى بقاء شمسي، ونأي ليلي» (ص ٣٦٠).

## الموت حباً، وثأراً، وخلاصاً

على كثرة إمكانات قراءة رواية بهاء طاهر **خالتي صفية والدير**،(٢٠) من زوايا متنوعة، يظل الموت تيمة أساسية ينهض عليها عالمها، ومصيراً يطارد شخصياتها الرئيسة، ومحوراً من محاور تجربتها، وعنصراً ملحاً يهيمن على بنائها وسردها كله، وإن دخل الموت طرفاً في أكثر من متصل: متصل الموت/الحب، متصل الموت/الثأر، متصل الموت/الخلاص،(٢١) بل أيضاً متصل الموت/الحياة. الموت ماثل في هذه الرواية عبر صور شتى، وعبر توقف عند دلالاته وطقوسه ومراسيمه وشعائره في المكان المرجعي للرواية – جنوب مصر، قرب الأقصر – وخلال عدد من شخصيات الرواية تبدو قادمة من موت وذاهبة إلى موت آخر، في رحلة أقرب – بتعبير المقدس بشاي، إحدى شخصيات الرواية – إلى نوع من «العيش للألم» (ص ١٢٠).

تعبير المقدس بشاي يتصل، سياقياً، بموت حربي، الذي يقدم في الثلث الأول من الرواية صورة الفتى الوسيم القوي، «الجميل بين الرجال»، (ص ٤٨)، المرشح للزواج بمثيلته المكافئة؛ صفية «الجميلة بين النساء»، «صاحبة العينين اللتين كان جمالهما فريداً» (ص ٤٨). لم يكن الجمال وحده الذي وضع كلاً منهما نصفاً متوقعاً للآخر، مترعاً بسيماء «الحياة»؛ فهناك أسباب وملابسات أخرى جعلت كلاً منهما مثيلاً ونداً وزوجاً مرتقباً. صفية – التي تدخل طرفاً في عنوان الرواية، مع «الدير» الذي يمثل حضوراً كبيراً في عالمها – المتدفقة بالحياة، بزغت وترعرعت بعد موتين؛ أبوين غيبهما الموت في واحد من أوبئة الملاريا التي «كانت تضرب بلدنا كل حين» (ص ٤٧)، كذلك كان حربي «يتيم الأب والأم هو الآخر» (ص ص ٤٨ و٥٨). بدأت صفية، وهي لا

تزال صغيرة السن، تمثل غواية للرجال، وقد تكشفت عن جمال آسر لا قبل لأحد بمقاومته، فشرع خطّابها يتوافدون على والد الراوي، «الذي كانت تعيش معه كابنة من بناته»، «منذ كانت في العاشرة تقريباً» (ص ٤٨). وبموازاة هذه الفتنة الأنثوية المبكرة، كان «الرجل» حربي «أمهر مزارع في البلد»، المغنّي صاحب الصوت الجميل، اختزالاً لصورة الشاب الوسيم القوي، وقد وقعت أكثر من امرأة مصروعة بحبه (انظر الرواية ص ٥٠ مثلاً). لذلك كله، فيما يقول الراوي: «كان هناك . . . إحساس في بيتنا وخارج بيتنا بأن صفية لحربي» (ص ٤٩). ورغم أن الراوي يتساءل، بعد إشارته إلى تفوق حربي في ميدان العشق: «ولكن هل كانت صفية تحب حربي؟» (ص ٥٠)، ثم يؤكد: «لا أستطيع الجزم» – فإنه يقدم لنا ما يجعلنا قادرين على الوصول إلى إجابة لم يستطع هو أن يقولها صراحة. سوف نشهده يلحظ صفية تغني، سراً، الأغنية التي شاعت عن حربي بعد أن غنتها الغجرية أمونة التي كانت تعشقه (انظر الرواية ص ٥٠)، ثم في سياق متأخر من الرواية؛ إذ تحتضر صفية وتعتصرها قبضة الهذيان، قبل أن تدخل «في غيبوبتها الأخيرة» ثم في غيابها الأخير، سوف تقول لوالد الراوي إنها موافقة على الزواج من حربي، و«موافقة على أي مهر يدفعه حربي» (ص ١٢٢).

لكن حربي لم يتقدم للزواج من صفية وقت أن كان ذلك ممكناً ومتوقعاً ومرتقباً، بل أسوأ من ذلك كان مشاركاً في خطبتها إلى «آخر»: «القنصل» أو «البك». وعندما تأكدت صفية من موافقته على زواجها من رجل آخر سواه، قالت – كالمطعونة – إنها قبلت هذا الزواج. على أية حال، ستمضي الوقائع – وهذه رواية وقائع، فضلاً عن كونها رواية شخصيات، بامتياز – إلى حيث تصوغ فراق الحبيبين اللذين تباعدا، ثم تمضي لتجعلهما أشبه بعدوين – من طرف صفية على الأقل – بعد تعذيب القنصل، الذي أصبح زوج صفية، لحربي، ثم اضطرار حربي إلى قتله، وعزم صفية، وإمعانها في تصميم، يشارف حد العناد، على قتل حربي ثأراً لزوجها (هل دافعها هو الثأر لزوجها فقط؟!)، وتربيتها ولدها حسان كأنها ستدخر حياته كلها للقيام بهذه المهمة. وهكذا، من موتين مزدوجين قديمين، في «زمن وقائع» غابر، جعلا كلاً من صفية وحربي يتيمين، إلى سلسلة من الموت، أحاطت بهما أو طاردتهما ثم طالتهما معاً، في زمن الرواية الحاضر، تكتمل هيمنة الموت على عالم هذه الرواية.

ترسم الرواية الموت في كل مراحل حياة صفية مصيراً يكاد يكون قدراً ملحاً مطارداً. فبالإضافة إلى أنه في زمن الوقائع القديم توفي أبواها، ثم في زمن الحاضر الروائي مات زوجها، فإنها إذ تعلم بوفاة هذا الزوج تضم إليها ابنها حسان، وتظل «صامتة فترة طويلة قبل أن تقول:

ياحزنك يا صفية، أمك وأبوك ورجلك **وابنك**. ثم قبّلت حسان وهي تقول: مكتوب علينا يا ولدي» (ص ٧٠). وصفية، بهذه العبارات، تضم إلى من ماتوا في الماضي والحاضر من سيموت في «الزمن المحتمل»؛ ابنها الذي – رغم كونه طفلاً – أصبح منذوراً للموت، فغدت حياته كلها مبذولة من أجل الثأر لأبيه. وفي زمن لاحق، سوف تلقي صفية ابنها الطفل، «بعزم قوتها»، نحو الحائط، حين تعلم بموت حربي، صارخة: «مات ميتة ربنا؟ مات ميتة ربنا؟»، ثم تدخل بعد ذلك «إلى غرفتها ولم تنطق بعدها ولم تذق طعاماً أو شراباً»، (ص ١٢١)، لتمضي في رحلة قصيرة نحو موتها هي. لقد قالت عنها أم الراوي، بينما كانت طفلة لا تزال: «مسكينة صفية، ما زال عيدها بعيداً» (ص ٤٧). وسوف تنتهي حياة صفية وعيدها لم يأت؛ لم يأت بعد ولن يأتى أبداً.

أما حربي، اليتيم بدوره، فيبدو بطلاً تراجيدياً مدفوعاً نحو مصيره أيضاً. لن يكون بمقدورنا الوصول إلى إجابة واحدة قاطعة عن السؤال عن السبب الذي دفع به إلى المشاركة في خطبة صفية للبك. ولكن كل حياته بعد هذه المشاركة سوف تسير في مسار الألم والعذاب ثم الموت. ستكون هناك وشاية به يصدقها البك، وسيعذبه رجال البك، بعد ربط جسده العاري بشجرة، عذاباً لا قبل لبشر بتحمله (انظر الرواية ص ٦٦ وما بعدها)، وسينجح في أن يفك وثاقه ويقتل البك، ويمضي مطارداً ثم مسجوناً ثم مفرجاً عنه لأسباب صحية، ثم مريضاً يعيش داخل أسوار الدير حياة أشبه بحياة السجين، إلى أن يتسلل الموت إلى داخله ويستشعره هو بوضوح. يسأله الراوي: «– ماذا بك يا حربي؟ ما هو مرضك؟»، فيقول «وصوته لا يكاد يبين: – أنا يا ولدي مثل النخلة العويل التي لا تطرح البلح ولا ترمي الظل، أنا انتهيت من زمن **ولكن الموت يعاندني**» (ص ص ١١١–١١٢). وفي مشهد موته الختامي سوف يطلب السماح من والد الراوي، وسوف يرد عليه والد الراوي راجياً أن «يسامحهم» هو (ص ١٢٠)، وسوف يتلاشى حربي، موغلاً في غيابه النهائي، تاركاً إيانا متخبطين في متاهة التخمينات حول من ذا الذي يستحق – بالفعل – أن يسامح من، وعلى من يمكن أن تصدر أحكام الإدانة أو الغفران.

ليس للموت في **خالتي صفية والدير** بعد واحد. الموت الذي قد يلوح عذاباً، في حلوله أو في ترقبه، قد يمثل راحة في أدائه بوصفه «واجباً». وثنائية الراحة والعذاب التي تتصل بما قبل الموت تمتد فيما بعده أيضاً. بعد أن مات القنصل تظل صفية تؤمن بأنه لن يلقى الراحة في موته حتى يتم الأخذ بثأره. تتمنى أن تحظى بطول العمر حتى يكبر ابنها ويأخذ بثأر أبيه كي يرتاح في موته (ص ٨١)، وعند فشل محاولة لها لدفع أحد «المطاريد» إلى قتل حربي تنشج وهي تقول: «اشهد يا بك أني حاولت . . .

واشهد يا بك أني سأحاول حتى **ترتاح في نومتك**» (ص ١١٧). وهذا الإيمان، بأن ميتة البك هي محض «نومة» تنقصها الراحة، يمتد إلى أم الراوي نفسها، التي تسلّم بأن من حق صفية أن «تأخذ ثأرها». تجلس الأم أحياناً وتبكي، وتقول للراوي [ابنها] وكأنها تواصل كلاماً لنفسها: «سيظل البك على رأسك حتى يوم الدين **ولن يرتاح في نومته**» (ص ٩٠).

بجانب هذا التسليم بأن الموت محض نوم قلق، ثمة حضور للموتى، وكأنهم في غياب مؤقت. وما أكثر السياقات التي تخاطب فيها صفية زوجها الراحل كأنه لا يزال حياً. لقد ظلت صفية – بعبارات الراوي – «تتحدث عن القنصل دائماً باستخدام الزمن الحاضر، كأنه لم يقتل ولم يغب عنها»، «فحين تؤنب الخدم في البيت تقول إن هذه الفوضى **لا تعجب البك**، أو **ماذا يقول البك لو رأى ذلك؟** . . . وكانت تقول هذه الأشياء بهدوء وثقة حتى أن الغريب كان يعتقد أنها تتكلم عن **شخص موجود في الغرفة الأخرى**» (ص ٧٢). كانت تتحدث كثيراً و«تتطلع نحو السماء **مخاطبة البك** الذي تراه وحدها» (ص ٧٨). وهي إذ تعطي الراوي جنيهاً على سبيل الـ«عيدية» تقول له: «خذه، وحياتي عندك **لا تغضب البك**» (ص ٨١). وحين تصلها أخبار عن مرض حربي تلطم خديها صارخة: «يامصيبتي لو مات حربي . . . **ماذا أقول للبك؟** قولوا لي ياناس **ماذا أقول للبك؟** تركناه يموت **قبل أن نأخذ ثأرك ونطفئ نارك**» (ص ١١٢). ثم عندما يصلها خبر موت حربي تجلس على الأرض وتقول هامسة: «مات ميتة ربنا؟ **أترى يا بك؟** لماذا فعلت بي هذا؟» (ص ١٢١). ولم يكن هذا التصور ضرباً من الخيال لدى صفية وحدها، فقد كان هناك – فيما يشير الراوي – اعتقاد شائع في البلد «أن صفية مكشوف عنها الحجاب.. وأن البك يأتيها في المنام كل ليلة **ليحدثها بما كان وبما سيكون**» (ص ٧٣).

فضلاً عن حضور الموت بوصفه واقعة مفصلية في بناء الرواية، تترتب على وقائع سابقة وتقود إلى وقائع تالية، بحيث يمكن قراءة هذه الرواية على أساس من تراتب أو ترابط حلقات سلسلة الموت فيها، فإن أبعاداً أخرى للموت تتناثر أيضاً على مستويات عدة في الرواية، من هذه الأبعاد ما يجعل الموت وسيلة للتعبير في عبارات تُقْسِمُ بها الشخصيات: «قال، **أقسم** [حربي]، **إنه مستعد أن يموت** فداء تراب حذاء القنصل» (ص ٥٨)، ومنها ما يجعل الموت وسيلة للتهديد، أو للراحة من عذاب، فيقول القنصل لحربي: «لا تخف يا حربي ولا تتعجل الموت، **سأجعلك تتمنى الموت** دون أن تراه» (ص ٦٥)، ومنها ما يتصل بتوقف السرد طويلاً عند طقوس مأتم عزاء النساء؛ حيث «طوال أسابيع يتحول المأتم إلى جلسات هادئة تستمر طول النهار وتضم كل قريبات الميت، أي كل نساء القرية، ويحمل الطعام كل يوم من بيت أو من أكثر من بيت . . . وربما بعد إغفاءة

قصيرة تقوم واحدة من النساء بالواجب وتقول بصوت ممطوط "يا حبيبي" أو "يا حبيبتي" فيبدأ النشيج والتعديد بصوت مرتفع إلى أن يخمد بعد قليل في نهنهات من البكاء» (ص ٧٥). وعن هذا الطقس الممتد، يؤكد الراوي: «ولما كانت المآتم تستمر أربعين يوماً، فقد كانت تشغل النساء طوال العام تقريباً متنقلة من بيت إلى بيت» (ص ٧٦).

هذه الطقوس، التي تجعل حياة النساء تذكراً ممتداً للموت، ليست كلها حزناً فيما يشير الراوي (ص ٧٥). لكن الحزن الحقيقي، مع ذلك، تجرّعته شخصيات محورية عدة في هذه الرواية، وعرفت فيه آلاماً وقاست منه أهوالاً صار معها الموت نفسه أملاً مرتجى.

## الموت كشفاً، الموت اكتشافاً

يتأسس نص نعمات البحيري **يوميات امرأة مشعة**(٢٢) على تجسيد تجربتي المرض والألم، بوصفهما مدخلين إلى موت لا نشهده. وخلال هذه التجربة يغدو المرض وسيلة لاكتشاف العالم من منظور جديد، ولاقتراح شكل آخر لعلاقة «الذات» الراوية بنفسها، وبمن حولها، وبما حولها، فضلاً عن أن هذه التجربة، بما تفرضه على المستوى الإنساني والجسدي والنفسي جميعاً، من التحرك في أماكن بعينها، ومن السعي إلى الائتناس بدفء رفيقات ورفاق جدد ممن يشاركن ويشاركون معاناة الآلام ذاتها، ومن التعرض لضروب من الإحساس بالجسد الإنساني في حالات غير معتادة له. تفتح – هذه التجربة – عينيّ الراوية على آفاق جديدة لم تشهدها في ماضيها الذي تستعيد بعض ملامحه في غير موضع، كما تهبها القدرة على اكتشاف عوالم غامضة لم يكن بمقدورها التوصل إليها إلا عبر معاناتها الراهنة التي تعايشها وتتعايش معها، وتدافعها وتسعى إلى الانتصار عليها، في آن.

المرض، المشرع على الموت، يمثل إذن التناول الأساسي في هذا النص، كما يمثل النبع الذي تستقي منه الكاتبة تقنياتها وجمالياتها، فضلاً عن أنه يهبها مفتاح الخروج من أسر دائرة الذات الضيقة إلى ذات أكبر تشمل أخريات وآخرين، يكتشفن ويكتشفون «جماعية» جديدة في مواجهة «توحد» خانق مطبق، شائع ومتفش، رازح عند كثيرين وكثيرات منذ زمن بعيد ممتد، سابق على تجربة المرض. كأن الكاتبة، بذلك كله، تصوغ عالمها الفني عبر ما يفرضه وما يتيحه الألم من حالة غير مألوفة، على مستوى الخبرة والمعايشة، وعلى مستوى المشاعر والمعاناة، وأيضاً على مستوى الوعي والإبداع.

العبارات التي تسوقها الكاتبة–الساردة في مفتتح نصها لمحمود درويش: «في كل كتابة إبداعية نصر صغير على الموت» (ص١١)، ولفرانز

كافكا: «إننا نمضي سنوات من حياتنا ونحن نرقص من الألم» (ص ١١)، ولنفسها: «الإبداع أهم طريق للمقاومة» (ص١٥)، ثم العبارة التي تسوقها خارج هذا المفتتح لسعدي يوسف: «أن تكون فناناً يعني أن تكون مسئولاً بذاتك أولاً، عن تناول الحياة كما تتناول فاكهة ذات مذاق» (ص ٢٩) - كلها عبارات تمثل شارات متنوعة على معنى ربط الإبداع بمناوأة الألم ومدافعة الموت، فضلاً عن أن هذه العبارات تقدم لنا - نحن القراء - ما يشبه «التعاقد» الأوليّ حول الوجهة التي سوف نسير فيها خلال تلقينا هذا النص: سنشارك، عن طيب خاطر، من يتألمون بعض آلامهم، وسنتقاسم معهم شيئاً من مكابداتهم، ولكننا أيضاً، فيما يومئ هذا التعاقد كذلك، سوف ننعم ببعض مذاق طيب ينعمون به، وسوف ننتشي ببعض الفرح القليل الذي به ينتشون.

ينبني نص **يوميات امرأة مشعة** على تقاطع السرد الروائي، بجمالياته المتعارفة، مع سرد السيرة الذاتية، بتقنياته الشائعة. والإشارة إلى هذا التقاطع ماثلة خلال قول الراوية المتكلمة، بعبارة دالة: «نزلت وسرت في ردهات مركز الأورام متجاهلة أنه **أنا نعمات البحيري** بلحمها ودمها، زاعمة لنفسي **أنني شخص آخر** خارج دائرة الورم والخبث» (ص ٢٤). وفي هذه الكلمات القليلة والواضحة، معاً، ما يشي بحركة مراوحة، سوف تظل مستمرة ومتصلة ودائبة، بين «**أنا نعمات البحيري**» و«**أنني شخص آخر**»؛ بين المرجعي وغير المرجعي، أو بين ما هو شخصي ذاتي، موصول بصوت الكاتبة المتعينة، وبين ما يجاوز ذلك.

البعد المرجعي سوف يتدعم بإحالات الكاتبة/الراوية، خلال مواضع عدة تالية في النص، إلى صديقاتها المبدعات، المحددات بالاسم: هالة البدري، سهام بيومي، شعبان يوسف، صفاء عبدالمنعم، محمد مستجاب الابن، أحمد الخميسي، سمية رمضان (انظر الرواية ص ٩٨)، كما يتدعم هذا البعد بما يشبه الرصد التوثيقي لملامح وعلاقات بعينها ترتبط ببعض الأماكن المسماة، في فترة زمنية مشار إليها بجلاء. أما البعد غير المرجعي، فسوف يتجسد خلال تصعيد تجربة الألم إلى آفاق رحبة، مفتوحة على التساؤلات وعلى التخيلات وعلى التأمل في جوهر المعاناة التي تتعالى على حدود التعين. وتتأكد هذه المراوحة بين المرجعي وغير المرجعي، أيضاً، خلال ربط الرواية بين ما هو شخصي وما هو عام (انظر الرواية ص ١١٢)، ثم خلال موازاتها بين نطاق الأماكن التي تفرض وتحصر تجربةُ المرض والتحركَ فيها، من جهة، والدنيا الواسعة، الضيقة في الوقت نفسه، خارج عالم المرض والمرضى، من جهة أخرى.

في هذا المنحى، تشير الراوية المتكلمة إلى بعض تفاصيل تلقّيها العلاج وتصلها بسياق محيط أرحب؛ فتطال إشارتها - وهي تحس بالسائل الكيماوي يغزو جسدها - «العالم المائع» و«الدنيا الشاحبة»

والجسد المريض والوجود كله، في آن (ص ٦٦). وفي هذا المنحى أيضاً، لا يتوقف رصد هذه الراوية عن نقلنا من دائرة تجربة المرض إلى ما يحيط بها في العالم القائم، المقرون بوضع تاريخي ومكاني بعينه. وفي هذا المنحى كذلك، نلمح ما يشبه متصلاً يربط بين موضعين للمعاناة، أو بين مجالين من مجالاتها، يقعان في زمن واحد، أحدهما محدود والآخر غير محدود؛ إذ يضاهي السرد بين مباني المستشفيات التي تحاول احتواء المرضى الذين تتزايد أعدادهم باستمرار، من جانب، ومباني «المولات الكبيرة التي **انتشرت هذه الأيام**.. متاهة كبيرة تشبه بيت جحا لكن **بشروط العصر**»، من جانب آخر (ص ٢٠).

يجاوز نص **يوميات امرأة مشعة**، إذن، خلال تعامله مع تجربة «المرض–الموت»، ما هو فردي شخصي، ذاتي ومحدود، إلى ما ليس كذلك؛ يتخطى ما هو خاص إلى ما هو عام، شامل وممتد. وفي هذا السياق، يحتشد سرد الرواية برصد – مشبع بحس هجائي – لأوضاع المستشفيات في مصر؛ حيث يجلد المريض «بسلسلة الإجراءات والأوراق الرسمية واللف على المكاتب ونظرات جامدة للسأم والضجر، يصعد مبنى وآخر ويسير طرقات [كذا] وممرات وردهات طويلة يلاحقه فيها الوهن والموت في الوجوه وعلى الجدران» (ص١٦٣)، كما تتردد في السرد عبارات واضحة تقرن بين تفشي الأمراض الخطيرة في فترة بعينها والقوى الشريرة التي «عكفت عبر أربعين عاماً أو خمسين على الفتك بالجهاز المناعي للمصريين» (ص١٥١)، كذلك تضع تأملات الراوية المتكلمة مرضها في موقعه من خريطة «توزيع الأمراض» على مجتمعها كله: «ديموقراطية المرض وهم كبير. كل أنواع المرض تنحاز للأغنياء فتتجنبهم وتتحاشاهم» (ص ٢٢). ولأن ذلك كله غير منفصل عن الاحتفاء – الذي تنطلق منه الرواية – بالوقائع المسماة، والمعلومات شبه الموثقة، وبالطبع غير منفصل عن صوت الراوية المحدد بالاسم، الذي يشير – كما لاحظنا – إلى الكاتبة بوضوح، فإن سرد هذه الرواية، وعالمها كله، يتحركان بين رصد عالم الألم الفردي الذي يمكن ألا يكون مرتبطاً بزمن أو بمكان محددين، وعالم آخر، جماعي شامل، يحتوي ذات الراوية مثلما يحتوي حشوداً من ذوات أخرى، ويتعين في فترة تنتمي إلى «زمن إطار» بعينه. تهتم الراوية المتكلمة بتجسيد بعض معالم هذه الفترة، وترصدها بصوت مثقل بأحكام قيمية، فتؤكد مثلاً أن المدارس قد تحولت إلى «**مؤامرة على الروح**» (ص ٥٤)، وترى أن التلفزيون – الذي تشاهده في قاعة الانتظار بالمستشفى – «**حليف متواطئ** مع كل أشكال القرف» (ص٢٢)، وتقول إن بعض المسؤولين الحكوميين يطلون على الناس «بوجوه ذات **ملامح حادة وعيون متقدة بالكذب**»، «يتحدثون عن النصر بأصوات جهورة.. أو عن أمجاد غابرة ويوهمون الناس بأنها ما زالت قائمة» (ص ٢٧)، وتتوقف

لتصوغ التقاطاً مكثفاً لمظاهر الحياة في بعض المدن الجديدة (ص ٨٦)، ولممارسات الانتقال عبر سيارات «الميكروباص» من هذه المدن وإليها، و«شرائط النحيب والعويل» التي يبثها السائقون في تلك السيارات، إذ إن هذه الشرائط – بعبارتها – «**تهيمن بضراوة على كاسيتات الموت** والعقاب والآخرة والثعبان الأقرع وفتاوى فايف ستارز» (ص ١١٠).

تقود تجربة المرض العضال إلى ما تقود إليه من إحساس خاص بالعالم؛ بالزمن وبالأشياء وبالناس،(٢٣) وتتيح إمكانات جديدة لإعادة رؤية التاريخ الشخصي والجماعي. وفي هذا السياق، تعيد الراوية المتكلمة استكشاف عالمها القديم خلال الإطلال عليه من منظور لم تطل عليه خلاله من قبل؛ فترى – كأنما من ضفة أخرى – العشرين عاماً الماضية، وبعض ذكرياتها مع أمها ومع النوم والأرق (ص ١٧)، وتصل بين وقائع جزئية وأخرى غير جزئية؛ بين أحداث شخصية وأخرى عامة، وربما ذات طابع تاريخي: «أصدر رئيس الجمهورية قراره بقطع العلاقات مع العراق **بعد غزو صدام حسين للكويت**، فسقطت كل القضايا **وحصلت على الطلاق**» (ص ١١٢).

تهب تجربة المرض – السرطان – في الكتابة عنها، هنا، مجموعة من التقنيات السردية التي تمثل تعبيراً موازياً عن مراحل المرض، وتأثيراته، وتفاصيله، وخباياه وأسراره التي ربما يجهلها الأصحاء. ومن هنا، تمثل تقنيات هذا النص استجابة ملائمة للتناول المحوري فيه، ويحتشد السرد بصياغة تتأسس على مجموعة من الانتقالات الزمنية والمكانية، ويبرز فيه استخدام خاص لعلاقات «المدة» و«التواتر»، أثناء الأوقات الطويلة والمتعددة، المتشابهة والمتباينة معاً – إن صح هذا التعبير – من مراحل الخضوع لتلقي العلاج تحت أجهزة معقدة، تفرض على صياغة هذا السرد وعلى حركته إيقاعها الخاص.

يكشف المرض لصاحبته، ولنا، أبعاداً جديدة في لعبة الحياة والموت، وآفاقاً مغايرة فيما يتعلق بالإحساس بالعمر أو بانقضاء الزمن، فتستعاد التجارب السابقة بنظرة ترنو إلى رحلة العمر كله بمنظور اختزالي واضح، ينطلق من هاجس بقصر فترة الحياة المتبقية؛ فيقتنص من تفاصيل تلك التجارب الماضية ما يستحق أن يدوم وأن يبقى وأن يستعاد، ويقفز قفزاً على كل ما يغاير ذلك، ويتم تلخيص مسيرة الحياة السابقة كلها في معالم أساسية، قليلة ومختزلة ولكنها دالة على الـ«تكوين» كله، تلخيصاً يصفيها من شوائبها ويستخلص بعض قسماتها الجوهرية، كما يحل بعض طلاسمها التي ظلت مستغلقة غامضة لفترات طويلة، سواء ارتبطت هذه التجارب بالعلاقات الإنسانية الطبيعية: «بعد انفصالي عن سليم خشيت أن يدخل حياتي رجل تدهشني معه البدايات البراقة والأغنيات والأحلام والأوهام كما حدث من قبل،

ثم اكتشفت [أكتشف؟] عند أول محك أنه جامد أو ضعيف»، «**شغل هذا حيزاً كبيراً من حياتي** ولم يكن هناك متسعاً [متسع] لأي رجل في غير حدود الصداقة والود البسيط» (ص ٢٩)، أو ارتبطت هذه التجارب ببعض الوجوه التي مرت عليها أو مرت بها الراوية المتكلمة: «المشهد كاملاً تحتفظ به ذاكرتي وأستدعيه دائماً ثم أتراجع.. **آن الأوان لفك سره**، هناك ضرورة ملحة ليكون ماثلاً أمامي مثل **ذكرى فاضت رائحتها في الخريف**.. ووجه فيفي.. بنت عبد العزيز بائع اللبن الذي يتحرك في شوارع العباسية البحرية كل صباح» (ص ٥٠)، أو تعلقت هذه التجارب بالقراءة والتعرف: «**ما قرأته طيلة حياتي أصبح ذاكرة محفورة في عقلي وروحي** ونفسي مثل مدينة كاملة . . . كنت عبر القراءة أجدني دون أدنى شك أفك قيودي واحدة فواحدة [كذا] وأعمل على حل العقد التي تسبب فيها غيري» (ص ٤٧). وباختصار، يتيح المرض إمكاناً جديداً لتعامل مغاير، كأنه انعطاف عن التعامل القديم المألوف الذي لازم حياة الراوية المتكلمة كلها، مع كل شيء وكل أحد؛ مع النقاط الفاصلة التي تمثل مراحل أساسية في التكوين والحياة، ومع العلاقة بالذات، ومع الصلات بالبشر القريبين وغير القريبين، ويتحقق ذلك كله انطلاقاً من إحساس جديد بالزمن؛ سواء الزمن الذي مر وانقضى، أو الزمن القادم، الباقي، القصير، الذي يجب التشبث به: «**صرت أعد اليوم الواحد خلية حية، أو وحدة زمنية لحياة كاملة** . . . **أرى فيه كل الأزمنة** وكل الفصول . . . **وأعيش كل الحالات** . . . البهجة والحزن والفرح والبكاء . . . أرى المخلصين والشرفاء كما أرى الغادرين والخونة والفاسدين» (ص ٩٣).

«التوحد والتواصل» ثنائية قائمة في هذه الرواية (وقائمة في أعمال أخرى لنعمات البحيري)، يستثيرها ويحدد أطرافها تناول تجربة المرض. فهنا، تمثل الصداقة نعمة وقيمة كبرى حقيقية: «أحببت أصدقائي ربما أكثر من نفسي» (ص ٤١). والرواية، في هذا السياق، تحتفي بإشارات عدة إلى مواقف المساندة من صديقات وأصدقاء في مواجهة المرض، وإشارات أخرى إلى عكس ذلك.

يمثل المرض المهدِّد بالموت سبيلاً لـ«تنقية» العلاقات الإنسانية بين الراوية المتكلمة وكل من حولها من الصديقات والأصدقاء والأهل والأقرباء، ويمثل في الوقت نفسه «اختباراً» لهذه العلاقات؛ فبعض العلاقات يقوى الآن، في زمن الوقائع الراهن، وبعضها يذوي ويتلاشى، وبعضها يُخلق من عدم (انظر ص ٧٠ – ولاحظ قول الراوية: «انفض من حولي أصدقاء **كانوا** أعمدة خرسانية **في حياتي**» ص ١٨٠). وفي مقابل ذلك، أو بالأدق في مواجهته، تعيد الراوية اكتشاف نوع من «جماعية» جديدة تدافع بها وحدتها المطبقة.

لقد ظلت الوحدة، السابق وجودها، بالطبع، على تجربة المرض، جزءاً من وضع مألوف كانت الراوية المتكلمة قد اعتادته في صلاتها

بكثيرين وكثيرات من حولها. وأصبحت الوحدة، مع المرض، مهيأة للتضاعف والتكاثر: «في ذلك النهار **لم أجد أحداً** أبكي على صدره فبكيت على صدري» (ص ٧٨)، «باستثناء صوت أمي وصوت أختي **لا يحدثني أحد**» (ص ٨٢). وقريباً من هذا المعنى إشارات الراوية المتكلمة إلى الإحساس بـ«اغتراب لا حدود له» تكابده، فيما تكابد، داخل عالم المدينة التي تسكنها من بين المدن الجديدة (ص ١٣١). لكن خارج هذا التوحد، وبعيداً عن ذلك الاغتراب، قبل المرض ثم بعده، تستكشف الراوية أواصر أخرى تصلها برفقة جديدة تلوح عطية أتت على غير توقع، وتصهر ذاتها ضمن ضمير جمعي يشملها ورفيقاتها اللاتي تنهشهن أنياب متماثلة لوحش واحد، غامض ومروع؛ فتتحدث بصوت يشملهن جميعاً: «نحن النساء المُشعّات» (ص ١٦٨)، أو «نحن نساء الثدي الواحد» (ص ٥٩)، ومع هؤلاء ممن يتقاسمن تجربة الألم والعلاج، يظل هناك «الأحباء والأصدقاء رفقاء الحلم الواحد»، الذين تهدي إليهم الكاتبة روايتها.

بهذا الإحساس الجديد بالزمن وبالعلاقات وبالمحيطات وبالمحيطين بها، وبما يصل ذلك كله وهؤلاء جميعاً بسياق عام، واسع ممتد، تصوغ الراوية المتكلمة معالم تجربتها الماثلة، المؤلمة، في الحاضر الراهن. وبهذه الجماعية الجديدة التي تكتشفها، تناهض هذه الراوية ألمها وتوحدها. وبهذا كله، وبغيره، تمثل هذه الرواية كتابة عن الألم ضد الألم، أو كتابة عن ما قبل الموت، تدافع كل موت.

## الموت غناءً، الموت استشرافاً

تنهض رواية مكاوي سعيد **تغريدة البجعة**(٢٤) على ما يشبه المرثية الأخيرة، غنائية النبرة، لمن غيّبهم الموت وإن ظلوا أحياء داخل الراوي المتكلم، بل وتجسد ما يشبه مرثية ذاتية له هو أيضاً؛ إذ يكابد موته المجازي ويستشعر موته الفعلي القادم. عنوان الرواية، الذي يشار إليه في موقع متأخر من فصولها (الفصل الحادي والثلاثين، من ثلاثة وثلاثين فصلاً)، يختزل تجربة ما قبل الموت، عبر إحالة إلى عالم يتصادى مع – أو تتصادى معه – ممارسة كائن آخر؛ البجعة التي تشبه – أو يشبهها – عصام صديق الراوي المتكلم: «كنت أراه **كالبجعة في أيامها الأخيرة حين تستشرف الموت** فتتجه إلى شاطئ المحيط وتنطلق في رقصتها الأخيرة **وتغرد تغريدتها الوحيدة الشجية**» (ص ٢٦٥). وبموازاة تجربة عصام، سوف تلوح أيضاً تجربة الراوي المتكلم، وتجارب كل أولئك الذين أحاط بهم الموت أو لاحقهم بطرائق وبأشكال شتى.

هذه الإحالة إلى «تغريدة البجعة»، قبيل موتها، تثير تساؤلات شتى حول متصل الغناء/الرقص/الموت: لماذا ترقص أو تغني بعض الكائنات إذ تستشرف موتها؟ هل تودع الحياة مستمسكة بأهدابها، خلال شعيرة

الرقص والغناء اللذين ينتميان إلى تلك الحياة، أم أنها تواجه مواجهة الختام – بفعلين من أكثر أفعال الحركة والتعبير وضوحاً – عالمها القادم المجهول حيث لا قدرة على الحركة ولا إمكان للتعبير؟ هل هو نوع من احتفال الوداع قبل أن يحل الظلام المطبق، ويجثم عالم ليس فيه احتفال؟ كل هذه التساؤلات، وغيرها، مطروحة على مستويات متنوعة بطول الرواية، قبل أن تثار في ذلك الموضع المتأخر، وكل هذه التساؤلات تظل تحوم حول تجربة – أو تجارب – الموت الذي يطل، بين آن وآن، بأشكاله وأبعاده ودلالاته، عبر فصول الرواية جميعاً تقريباً، بما يجعل منه الملمح الملحوظ، وربما المعلم الرئيس، من ملامح تجربة الراوي المتكلم ومعالمها، وتجارب كثيرين ممن يتحرك في مجالهم ويتحركون في مجاله.

نعم! ما أكثر الموتى، وما أوضح حضور الموت، في هذه الرواية. هناك، من الموتى، هند، حبيبة الراوي المتكلم مصطفى، وزميلته في كلية الهندسة، التي اختطفها الموت بطريقة فاجعة، مدوية، انفجار «دانة تذكارية» في الكلية، بقيت ملقاة هناك طيلة خمسة عشر عاماً، وكان قد حصل عليها طلبة الجوالة من «معرض للغنائم» عقب حرب أكتوبر ١٩٧٣ (انظر الرواية ص ١٣٤). لقد ظل الطلاب لزمن طويل يلهون بها ويتقاذفونها، وسقطت على الأرض عشرات المرات، قبل أن تختار ضحاياها في ذلك اليوم الدامي. كان هناك ذعر الطالبات والطلاب، وكان هناك جرحى ودماء كثيرة رآها الراوي المتكلم تنزف بغزارة، ثم في المساء، في المستشفى، نقل إليه الخبر الفاجع: أن «هنداً قد ماتت». وسوف يقول الراوي إنه، تقريباً، مات أيضاً معها: «**كأنني مت مع هند**» (ص ١٣٣).

وهناك، من الموتى أيضاً، يوسف حلمي، وابنه الشهيد، وأم الراوي المتكلم، وسامنثا، ومع هؤلاء هناك موت عصام الوشيك، الذي أشرنا إليه، ثم هناك أخيراً تهاوي الراوي المتكلم في منحدر الموت، خلال سطور الرواية الأخيرة، بعد أن «تذوق» و«استحلب» الكثير من الأدوية والعقاقير، وبعد أن أفرغ «كل الحبوب [أمامه]. الصفراء.. الزرقاء.. والحمراء.. والكحلي الفاتح والبرتقالي.. والزهري والقرمزي.. والأخضر والأبيض.. وسن الفيل.. الكبسولات والأقراص المستديرة والمربعة والمثلثة والأسطوانية» (ص ٢٨٩)، ثم بكلماته:

> لم أعد أرى غير شارع ممتد بلا نهاية. بلا سحب في الأفق ولا غيوم لا سيارات ولا زحام مركبات . . . الشارع ممتد على مدى البصر، يلفظ جوفه الناس والحيوانات والجماد . . . ثم بدأت أرى خلفهم مساحة بيضاء تماماً منزوعة الهواء.. ريحها ساكن.. ثم رأيت خلقاً كثيراً يلوحون لى من خلف هذه المسافة

يوسف حلمي وابنه الشهيد.. أمي وجوليا.. هند وسامنثا.. وعندما دخلت هذه المساحة **توقف كل شيء فلم أعد أسمع أو أرى إلا محض فراغ.** (السطور الأخيرة من الرواية، ص ٢٩٠).

لم تكن تلك الخاتمة سوى انتقال بالراوي المتكلم من «الموات» إلى «الموت». لقد عانى الموات، وكابده، في الزمن الماضي، فيما عانى وكابد خلال تجربته/تجاربه المثقلة بدموع حبيسة لا تخرج أبداً. لقد جعل فقدان الحبيبة، هند، هذا الراوي ينقسم على ذاته، ويتحول - في الزمن الراهن - إلى «شخصيات» عدة، لم يعد يعرف عددها، يتخبط فيما بينها، بما جعل أيام الدراسة، التي باتت نائية عن هذا الزمن الراهن، نعيماً عاشه وبات يتحسر على انقضائه، رغم أنه كان آنذاك، بعبارته: «أعيش بشخصيتين فقط» (ص ١٢٨). الآن، لا يجديه العلاج عند طبيب نفسي (انظر ص ٩١)؛ إذ يعيش موزعاً غير قادر على «اتخاذ قرار صائب واحد» (ص ١٨١)، يحاكم ذاته ويؤكد: «لم أفعل شيئاً صائباً في حياتي... وتمسكت بإصرار وعن عمد وبغباء شديد بمشاريع حياتية كانت نتائجها الحتمية فشلاً» (ص ٢٧). ومن قلب هذه الحالة، يختزل مسيرته كلها في كلمات دالة: «لم أكن سيداً في حياتي.. كنت خادماً ملعوناً لوسائل الرزق» (ص ٢٨٧). إنه لم يعد يملك يقيناً ما حول أي شيء، بما في ذلك ذاته التي تصدعت وانشطرت (انظر ص ١٨٣)، يعاني السأم والملل (انظر ص ٢١٥)، ويرى أيامه تتدحرج بلا معنى، يخوض علاقات مبتورة مع صديقات وأصدقاء، بمن فيهم صديقه الأقرب عصام، وصديقته (حبيبته، افتراضاً) مارشا التي تربطه بها علاقة جسدية. ويمتد هذا الملمح خلال تجاربه مع النساء جميعاً؛ كلها مرتبك وكلها غير عميق. يشير - بكلماته - إلى: «قدري مع مارشا، وأوهامي مع ياسمين . . . وذكرياتي مع هند» (ص ١٤٣)، ويؤكد، في «رؤيا» يرى فيها ذاته كأنما من موقع آخر: «الدنيا تكاد تأفل عليّ.. أجلس على قطعة فلين في متاهة محيط ضخم.. لا أعرف أين سترسي بى مارشا؟ ولا أين سيأخذني كريم ووردة وصحبتهما؟.. ولا نهاية لطريقي مع ياسمين.. ولا متى سيتركني عصام؟» (ص ١٦٤). لا صداقة دامت من صداقات الراوي المتكلم، ولا حب بقي أيضاً. كان عصام بالنسبة له، في وقت ما، فيما يقول: «الشخص الوحيد الباقي لي في هذا العالم» (ص ١٤٠)، وسوف يتلاشى مع من تلاشوا؛ سيرحل الجميع ويغيبون عن حياته بأشكال الغياب المتعددة: «ستغادرني زينب كما غادرني الآخرون بلا عودة» (ص ١٩٠).

وكل علاقات الحب، لدى هذا الراوي، بعد موت الحبيبة الأولى، كانت شائهة وغير حقيقية ومحكومة بفقدان وشيك: «كل نماذج المرأة بداخلي مشوهة»، وكل هذه العلاقات أيضاً جزء من طريق طويل، «محفوف بالمخاطر»، يخوضه «عالقاً بين شتى العوالم بلا حب

حقيقي» (ص ١٦٧). باختصار، لا شيء حميم أو مستقر في علاقات هذا الراوي جميعاً (ص ٢١). إنه يرى عدم التحقق وكأنه بات قانون علاقات الحب في هذا العالم، ويشير إلى «حبيبات» بعض أصدقائه أو رفاقه، القدامى والجدد، إشارات لا تخلو من حكم قيمي مشبع بنبرة هجاء؛ فشاهيناز – حبيبة أحمد الحلو ثم زوجته – «متطرفة» (ص ١٠٤)، ووردة حبيبة كريم هي «البنت الجربانة»، «المقشفة» (ص ٢٦٧)، وسامنثا، حبيبة عصام هي مرة «ضرة»، ومرة «الغراب المهاجر»، ومرة «المستنسخة»، ومرة «الحرباء»، ومرة «العاهرة» (صفحات ٤٨، ٨٤، ٨٥، ٨٦، ٢٢٠، على التوالي).

تمزق الأواصر، إذن، بين الراوي والأخريات والآخرين، يمثل جزءاً من معالم علاقاته جميعاً. وشكوكه العميقة، إذن، في كل رفقة يراها من حوله، وربما يحسد أصحابها، ملمح أساسي من رؤيته لكل علاقة قائمة. يتصل بهذا إحساسه بالفقدان، القديم أو الماثل أو الوشيك، بما يجعل كل رابطة حب تنطوي على بذرة أفولها أو دمارها. ينبني هذا الإحساس على تجربته السابقة مع هند؛ إذ بترت هذه العلاقة، التي كانت محتشدة بالآمال، بالموت الذي وأد كل الأحلام. كما سوف تؤكد هذا الإحساس تلك النهايات التي تلاحق علاقات الحب بين الكثيرين والكثيرات من حول الراوي. تنتهي علاقة عصام وسامنثا بموتها بعد مرض عضال، وتنتهي علاقته هو بزينب بسفرها، وتلوح علاقته بمارشا معلقة في فراغ، وتنتهي علاقة كريم ووردة بانفصالها عنه، وتنتهي – في جهة أخرى من هذا العالم – علاقة الرسام المكسيكي دييجو ريڤيرا بعد مرض زوجته، وتنتهي علاقة جوليا وحبيبها بمصرعها أو بهجرتها «إلى الآخرة» (ص ٢٧٧)، وتلوح علاقة ديانا وشريف غير مستندة إلى شيء يدعم إمكان استمرارها. وباستثناء علاقة عوض (إيڤالد) وعائشة، وعلاقة شاهيناز وأحمد الحلو، يبدو الفقدان، أو الموت تتويجاً للفقدان، مآل كل علاقة خاضها الراوي، وكل علاقة شهدها.

في مدافعة الغياب القريب والبعيد، الذي يلاحق الذات والآخرين والأخريات، يلوذ الراوي المتكلم بلعبة من ألعاب المخايلة التي تتداخل معها الهويات والأزمنة؛ يرى من فُقِدَ من قبل فيمن لم يُفْقَدْ بعد، ويحاول أن يستعيد الزمن الماضي – محال الاستعادة – في الحاضر القائم. هكذا، تتخايل له حبيبته التي ارتحلت، هند، في هيأة ياسمين،(٢٥) تمتزج ملامحهما وتختلط صورهما بين عقل وغيب، بين مثول واختفاء، بين طيف وجسد، بين عقل باطن وعقل يوشك أن يصير باطناً، في مساحة تمّحي فيها المسافة بين الذكرى والحدث المشهود، أو بين الرغبة الموءودة والإحساس المراود، أو بين معالم الموت ومعالم الحياة: «انتبهت إلى أن صوتها منذ بداية الجلسة هو

صوت ياسمين. ولم يكن صوت هند الذي توهمته.. ثم بدأ الشك يراودني في وجود ياسمين أساساً وعقلي الباطن المراوغ يحرضني على ملامستها لأتأكد إن كانت طيفاً أم جسداً» (ص ٢٤١)، «كانت هند أو ياسمين أو أي من الأسماء الدنيوية المجردة تنظر إليّ برعب» (ص ٢٨١)، «رأيت البشارة ومسستها وتأكدت أنها [ياسمين] هند. كانت العجوز [جدتها] تضرب على ظهري بضربات قوية بعظام ذراعيها. وكان جسد الفتاة تحول بالكامل إلى جسد هند» (ص ٢٨٣)، «لكني فجأة رأيت تلون الملامح. ظهرت لي نظرة هند قوية جلية بقسمات وجهها الصلبة إذا ما أرادت شيئاً. استحضرت هند ياسمين وجعلتها تهتف وتصرخ» (ص ٢٨٣)، «كنت حائراً بين ظل عقلي يشدني إلى ياسمين وغيب يشدني إلى هند» (ص ٢٨٢).

هذا التخبط، المستدعى من «وعي شقيّ» لذات منقسمة على نفسها، غير منفصل عن سياق عام يحيط بالراوي، وغير مبتور الصلة بعالم يتصادى فيه ما هو داخلي وما هو خارجي. يتساءل الراوي، الذي يدرك عمق مأساة حَبَكَ الموت أطرافها، عن فصامه وفصام المجتمع من حوله: «ما زال يشغلني من منا مريض الشيزوفرينيا. أنا أم المجتمع؟» (ص ٩٧)، ويربط الراوي بين ما حدث له من تحول (ص ٢٧١) وتحولات - أشبه بانقلابات - طالت كل شيء وكل أحد من حوله. الشخصيات تحولت، تحول أحمد «مائة وثمانين درجة» (ص ١٠٢)، وما حدث لأحمد «أفضل بكثير من بعض تحولات الإخوة اليساريين» (ص ١٣٩)، كذلك تحول عصام تحولات متعددة: «خرجت وكلي يقين أن هذا ليس عصام الذي عرفته» (ص ٢٧٣). والراوي المتكلم نفسه تحول أيضاً (انظر ص ٢٧١)، وأسماء الشوارع تغيرت: شارع «آمون» بالهرم أصبح شارع «المساعي الحميدة»، وشارع «خوفو» أصبح شارع «خاتم المرسلين» (ص ص ٧٣ و١٠٠، على التوالي)، والوطن كله تغير بعد ما أسماه الراوي «الغزو الوهابي»: «تغيرت أنماط الحياة بمصر كثيراً» (ص ٩٣). لقد فعلت تغيرات الزمن فعلها في صياغة مصائر الجميع تقريباً، انتقل من موقعه من انتقل، وتبدل من تبدل، واختفى من - وما - اختفى. وإذا كان جزء من هذا التغير ينطوي على «قيمة» ما يحمد الراوي الله عليها: «حمداً لله على أننا لم نظل بنفس الخندق لتطيح بنا الرؤى المغايرة وتحولات العالم التي جاءت بما لم يخطر على قلب بشر» (ص ٢٨٨)، فإن هناك أبعاداً أخرى من هذا التغير جعلت الراوي غير قادر على العيش في الحاضر المتقلب، قابعاً مقيماً - على المستوى الداخلي - في ماض ولَّى وانقضى؛ ففي الماضي كانت هند، وفي الماضي كانت الأحلام، وفي كل زمن آخر، لاحق، غابت هند وآلت الأحلام إلى كابوس ممتد.

في هذه الوجهة، تلوح وقائع ومشاهد جزئية تنتمي إلى الماضي وكأنها باتت تحكم حياة الراوي إلى الأبد، تهيمن على حاضره وعلى زمنه المحتمل جميعاً، تلازمه في رحلة موته المجازي حتى موته الفعلي الأخير. وفي هذه الوجهة أيضاً، يصوغ الراوي ما يشبه القانون الذي على أساس منه لا تستطيع لحظات الحاضر أن تنسل من جذب الماضي، بعبارات تجسد مشاهد قديمة تلوح كأنها أبدية، عابرة للأزمنة: «فابتسمت [هند] **ستظل** هذه الابتسامة **تأسرني حتى مماتي**» (ص ١٢٠)، «**ستحلم** ليلاً بمدرّستك فردوس ذات الجمال الآسر الذي **لن تجده في امرأة أبداً في المستقبل**» (ص ٢٤)، «هو [خليل] قاتلك في الصغر بسكين **سيظل يقطر بالدم إلى الأبد**» (ص ٣٤)، «يبيع [الراوي] عمره الآن مقابل الحصول على مظروف بللته بلسانها» (ص ١٢٤)، «**لن** أحصل على مثل هذه المكافأة **مرة ثانية حتى ولا في حياة أخرى**» (ص ١٢٥). هكذا، تترى الأزمنة يلاحقها سلوك قديم، ماثل أبداً. والراوي الذي حلم في زمن ما أصبح يواجه موته في كل الأزمنة؛ لم يحصل على تلك «الحياة الأخرى» التي يشير إليها مثلما لم تحصل هند على تلك الحياة. غيّبها الموت في الزمن الماضي كما يغيّبه الموات في الزمن الحاضر الذي لا يكف عن صيرورته وتحوله وانقضائه أيضاً. ومرور الزمن، على إطلاقه، يلوح مرهوباً أكثر من أي أحد ومن أي شيء: «فلم يعد باقياً لديّ شيء أخافه عدا الزمن» (ص ١٨٨).

هيمنة الماضي على الحاضر وعلى الزمن المحتمل، تجاوز محض الحنين أو النوستالجيا Nostalgia إلى نوع من «المصادرة» الحقيقية – إن صح هذا التعبير – وإن كانت هناك إشارات تشي بهذا الحنين، منها ما يتصل بتوقف الراوي، بكلماته، عند «تلك اللحظات التي كانت تعيدني إلى سنوات موغلة في الماضي السحيق.. إلى حياتي التي كانت مبهجة ومبشرة بشيء آخر غير ما أنا موحول به الآن» (ص ٢٨)، ومنها ما يكاد يرتبط بموضوعة «البيت القديم»، بالمعنى الحرفي،(٢٦) حيث يتوقف الراوي عند البيت الذي تربى فيه، محاولاً – محاولة مقضياً عليها بالإخفاق – أن يستعيده: «عندما أدخله أستنشق رائحة أمي رحمها الله أتذكر ضعفها ورقتها ومؤازرتها لي.. وأستحضر لمّة الأسرة حول منضدة الطعام ... ذكرياتي المخبوءة في أركانه وبين ثناياه ... بلاط الصالة الرخيص ممسوح النقوش بفعل لهونا ولعبنا ومشينا ونحن صغار» (ص ٧٧). ولكن هذا كله ليس سوى محض استعادة للذكرى فحسب، لا للعبق الفعلي؛ فلا الزمن القديم يمكن استعادته، ولا الطفولة النائية قابلة للتكرار، وليس من الممكن أن تعود الأم – كما لا يمكن أن تعود هند – مرة أخرى إلى الحياة.

لقد غيّب الموت من غيّب في زمن قديم، ولكن من «غابـ/ـت» «ظلـ/ـت» من الأحياء داخل الراوي المتكلم، تتخايل «ملامحهـ/ـا» –

بصور شتى – مع ملامح شخصيات الزمن الحاضر. كان الموت في الماضي هو الفجيعة الكبرى، وظل الموت في أزمنة تالية شاخصاً رازحاً، جاعلاً من كل حياة محض استشراف لموت جديد، محض أغنية أو رقصة أخيرة قبل أن يطبق الظلام.

### الموت «حسابات» وصراعاً

تنهض رواية سيد البحراوي **شجرة أمي**(٢٧) على رصد تجربة الموت؛ على التحديق فيه والتعبير عن وجعه، وأيضاً على التوقف عند معالم الحياة التي تتصل به وتمور من حوله وتستمر من بعده. ويرتبط بهذا مثول الموتى في حياة الأحياء وإطلالاتهم عليها وتأثيراتهم فيها. وحضور الموت – موت أمّ الراوي المتكلم – الذي يتم تناوله في الوقائع الأولى بالرواية بوصفه حدثاً أساسياً كبيراً، وإن كان متوقعاً، يمثل بؤرة مركزية تستقطب كل التفاصيل وتجعلها تدور في مدارها، ثم بانقضاء الزمن تتحول هذه البؤرة إلى جزء من مجال لبؤرة، وربما لبؤر أخرى تدور في مدارها تجارب الموت وتجارب الحياة معاً. هاهنا، نوع من «كتابة الوجع»، فيما تشير الصفحة الأخيرة من صفحات الرواية (ص ٩٥)، ولكن هاهنا أيضاً حشد من مشاغل الحياة وشواغلها التي تقيم مسافة ما مع ذلك الوجع، ومن ثم مع مصدره؛ أي مع الموت.. وهذه المسافة في مواجهة الموت، ثم في كيفية استدعائه وتذكره، تتأكد بمرور الزمن، وتتدعم بالسعي إلى النظر «المحايد»، في واقعة لم يكن هناك – في تاريخ الإنسانية – حد لغموضها والتباسها وتأثيرها، ومن ثم لم يكن هناك مجال لنظرة محايدة في التعامل معها. بهذا المعنى، فعالم هذه الرواية الذي يتمحور حول موت الأم، يتركز أيضاً حول ذات الراوي التي تتلقى هذا الموت، تتفهمه وتستوعبه وتتكيف معه؛ تواجهه أو تحاوره أو تتلقى تبعاته، وأيضاً تتخذه نقطة فاصلة بين ما سبقه وما سوف يتلوه، فتسعى – خلال وطأة تجربته وعقبها – إلى أن تعيد صياغة العلاقة بنفسها وبالآخرين وبالعالم.

عنوان الرواية، **شجرة أمي**، يشار إليه، حرفياً، مرتين فحسب طوال الرواية (ص ص ٤٧ و٥٥)، وترتبط هاتان الإشارتان بشجرة تنسب مرة إلى «الأم»، محور تجربة الموت: «شجرة أمي»، ومرة إلى ضمير جمعي، ربما يعبر عن أسرة الراوي المتكلم: «شجرتنا»، وتأتي الصيغتان متجاورتين في سياق واحد متصل: «فوجئت – وأنا جالس – بأن أحد أبنائهم [الجيران] يعتلي **شجرتنا** – **شجرة أمي** – ليعلق عليها فرع كهربة» (ص ٤٧). وإذا كانت هذه الشجرة سوف تظل باقية حية بعد انقضاء حياة الأم، بمعنى مطروح منذ الحكايات الشعبية وغير الشعبية القديمة – ومنها قصص الشعراء العشاق/العذريين – بما يومئ إلى

حياة، حتى وإن كانت لنبتةٍ، تمتد فيما بعد الموت، فإن عالم الرواية كله يؤكد هذا المعنى وإن بطرائق أخرى بعيدة عن هذا المنحى؛ إذ يتوقف وقفات مطولة عند تفاصيل حياة البشر؛ حساباتهم وصراعاتهم الصغيرة – وقد تبدو كبيرة من وجهة نظر مغايرة – التي لا تعقب الموت فحسب، بل توازيه وتقترن به حتى في ذروة حدوثه.

الحسابات والصراعات حول تفاصيل واقعة الموت في الرواية تبدأ من قبل دفن الجثمان المسجى. ثمة صراع يتم صوغه – وكأنه «معركة» – بين الشيخ يونس، ابن عم الراوي المتكلم، والشيخ عبدالمعطي، حول عدد «أدراج الكفن» الذي سيلف به الجثمان (انظر ص ٣٢)، وثمة «مفاوضات» حول من يؤم الصلاة على الجثمان قبل دفنه (انظر ص ٣٣)، وثمة نزاع «يصل إلى قمته بين الفقهاء وجماعة التبليغ والدعوة»؛ إذ «كان كل فريق يحرص على أن يتولى الدعاء للميت» (ص ٣٣)، وثمة حسابات معقدة، أشبه بمؤامرة، بين الشيخين اللذين يقرآن القرآن في العزاء: «القارئ الأول أطال أكثر مما ينبغي، فأخذ بعض وقت القارئ الثاني، فقرر الانتقام منه بأن يختم هو.. العادة أن يختم القارئ الأول» (ص ٣٤)، وكان قد تم اختيار هذين القارئين على أساس من حسابات سابقة: «كان لابد من اختيار اثنين من أربعة استبعد أحدهم لأنه قريب لنا ومن ثم سوف يكون محرجاً في أخذ الأجر واستبعد آخر لثقل دمه أو بمعنى أدق فضل عليه الثالث لأنه فقير» (ص ١٩)، كذلك كانت هناك حسابات أخرى حول مكان الدفن؛ في «مقابر الضعفا» الذين تنتمي الأم إليهم أم في مقابر العائلة (انظر ص ١٧)، وحول الدوار الذي سيتم فيه تلقي العزاء، وحول من يقدم القهوة إلى المعزين (انظر ص ١٩).(٢٨)

بجانب معنى استمرار الحياة، بمشاغلها الدنيوية، بعد الموت، هناك ما يبدو حضوراً للأم نفسها التي ماتت، على الأقل فيما يرى ويشعر ابنها الراوي المتكلم. عقب وفاتها، وقبيل دفن جثمانها، يسلك الراوي وكأنه يراها لا تزال تحس بجسدها، يشهدها مسجاة فوق السرير، تنام بعرضه «ورأسها تكاد تكون على الحافة»، فيشعر بأن هذه النومة «**غير مريحة بالنسبة لها**»، ويحاول أن «يعدل رأسها قليلاً ليبتعد عن حافة السرير» (ص ١٨). والأمر نفسه يتكرر مع طريقة حمل نعشها: «لاحظت أن طريقة حمل النعش **غير مريحة للجثمان**» (ص ٣٣). ويتصل بهذا إحساس الراوي بحركة الأم من حوله بعد وفاتها بثلاثة أيام: «عندما خرجت من الحمام خيل إلي أنني سمعت صوتها تتحدث مع ابنتها في الدور الأول لكني بعد وقت انتبهت إلى أنه ليس صوتها» (ص ٣٩). كما يتصل بهذا توقف الراوي عند مهام كانت تقوم بها، وكأنه يتوقع أنها سوف تظل تقوم بها: «وجدت الأثاث في غير ترتيبه ولمحت آثار ماء على الكراسي.. المطر بللها ولم يكن هناك من يضعها تحت الشمس. كانت تفعل ذلك» (ص ٤٢). كذلك يتشمم

الراوي رائحة ملابسها في دولاب يجد نفسه مدفوعاً إلى فتحه: «فتحته ففاحت رائحة ملابسها فسالت دموعي» (ص ٤٤). إن عالمه الآن، بعد وفاتها، لا يزال موصولاً بعالمها؛ يصحو من نومه «على ذكراها» (ص ٦٥)، ويحلم في قيلولته بها، يراها «**نشيطة، تعجن وتخبز**» (ص ٦٥)، يزور مقبرتها وتلح عليه حاجة إلى «سيجارة **يدخنها معها**» (ص ٥٤). وبعد مضيّ فترة من الزمن، إذ تفتح مقبرتها لدفن زوجة ابن عمه، يتشمم رائحة ما ويطمئن، ويسأل رشدي: «**إيه أخبار ستك** [الأم] قال: زيّ الفل. ما فيش أي ريحة» (ص ٦٦)، كما يستمر في زياراته المعتادة للبلد، كل أسبوعين، وكأن هذه الزيارات – في جانب منها – زيارات لها.

اتصال عالم ما بعد موت الأم بعالم ما قبل موتها – بما يعني استمرار وجودها – لا ينفي أن موتها كان – في حياة الراوي – نقطة زمنية فاصلة؛ تلوح – مثلها مثل «أيام العرب»، فترة الجاهلية – حدثاً يتم اتخاذه سبيلاً للتأريخ، والتمييز بين ما سبقه وما تلاه. في هذا المنحى نلحظ عبارات متعددة: «**قبل عام من موتها**» (ص ١٣)، «**قبل أسبوعين من موتها**» (ص ١٩)، «**بعد ثلاثة أيام** [من وفاتها]» (ص ٣٩)، «ها أنا ذا **بعد أقل من شهرين**، أجلس نفس الجلسة، في نفس المكان» (ص ٥٨)، «**ثلاثة أشهر بعد الوفاة** تقريباً. أيقظتني عفاف» (ص ٥٩). وفي هذا المنحى أيضاً، يشير الراوي إلى اختلاف ما قد طرأ على حياته ابتداء من تلك النقطة الفاصلة؛ عودته إلى الكتابة: «اليوم أعود إلى الكتابة. توقفت عدة أشهر. شغلتني أيضاً أمور الحياة. اليوم أعود إلى الكتابة لمجرد التمرين» (ص ٢٩)، وهو، إذ يعود إلى الكتابة، فيما سيقول لصديقة له، فإنه يعود إليها بطريقة مختلفة، إذ كان موت أمه هو «أهم حدث» «أثر عليّ وعلى كتابتي، حتى قبل أن يحدث . . . هو وراء تضامني مع كل النساء المقهورات» (ص ٣٠).

بمرور الزمن، يتحول الحضور المهيمن إلى محض «ذكرى»، لكنها ذكرى مؤثرة، خلالها يتحول فعل التذكر نفسه إلى إعادة استكشاف عالم الأم، وإعادة تقييم العلاقة – التي لم يعد بالإمكان تغييرها – بها، عبر إشارات كثيرة تحيل إلى ذلك العالم، وتستدعيه، وتتأمله. ومن هذه الوجهة، تحتشد فصول الرواية بمفردات التذكر التي تستحضر الأم من غيابها، وتضعها في قلب مشاهد الحياة: «**وأمام البحر . . . تذكرتها**. كلما رأيت البحر تذكرت أنها رأت البحر معي» (ص ٤٨)، «**الذكريات التي ظلت تعودني طوال شهر هي أساساً اللحظات المؤلمة في حياتها**» (ص ٤٩)، «**ذكرتني السجادة بخشونة ملمسها**»، «**تذكرت أنها** كانت قليلة الطلبات» (ص ٥٧). يتصل بهذا توقف الراوي وقفة مطولة، خلال الفصل التاسع عشر، عند ثلاثة أكياس مليئة بأوراق، «عقود بيع وشراء. عقود ملكية. مراسلات. إيصالات. شهادات»، كانت الأم تطلعه عليها «كلما احتاجت إلى شيء» (ص ٧٦). الآن،

في حضرة تلك الأوراق، بات بإمكان الراوي أن يتحرك عبر مراحل شتى وتجارب عدة من مراحل حياة أمه وتجاربها، موثقة بالتواريخ الدقيقة: سفرها لتأدية العمرة للمرة الأولى سنة ١٩٩١، استقباله لها في السويس عند عودتها، تاريخ ميلادها المدون وتاريخ ميلادها الحقيقي، عقد زواجها من أبيه، بتاريخه الذي يكشف أنها لم تكن أصغر سناً منه بكثير كما كانت تدعي، رسائله إليها في أزمنة متعددة غير مؤرخة (انظر ص ص ٧٧-٨٢). وخلال الحركة عبر رحلة الحياة التي تسترجعها تلك الأوراق - ولم تكن تخلو من «صور» فوتوغرافية - يعيد الراوي المتكلم من خلالها رؤية عالم أمه، ورؤية عوالم آخرين وأخريات، ورؤية عالمه هو نفسه.

لكن فعل تذكر الأم، واستدعاء حضورها، يخفتان تدريجياً عبر فصول الرواية المرقمة القائمة على نوع من التصاعد الزمني. واللافت، هنا، أن هذا الخفوت التدريجي يؤول في الفصل الثالث والعشرين، الأخير، إلى نقيض التذكر، بالمعنى الحرفي: «بعد عيدين من وفاتها، كنت حريصاً على الذهاب إلى المقبرة يوم الوقفة . . . **لم أتذكرها جسداً، عادت ذكرى غامضة**» (ص ٩٣)، «بالأمس كانت ذكرى وفاة أمي. **لم أتذكر ذلك سوى الآن. ولست أدرى بالضبط ما الذي ذكرني به»**، «**الآن أحاول أن أتذكر كم مر من السنين على وفاتها**» (ص ٩٤). لقد انتصرت مشاغل الحياة على ذكرى الموت الذي لم يعد سوى تجربة مطروحة للكتابة. يسترجع الراوي أمه خلال هذه الكتابة، ويشير إلى نقطة زمنية أخيرة في تجربة موتها، إذ اتخذها موضوعاً لروايته. وبذلك، فإن الموت الذي كان مؤلماً خلال حضوره الفعلي بات الآن موجعاً في الكتابة عنه فحسب. ورغم كل الزمن الذي مر، ورغم التذكر الذي بات شحيحاً إلى حد النسيان، فإن دائرة موت الأم لم تغلق بعد. يقول الراوي في عبارة مختزلة دالة: «رغم مرور السنوات **لم يكتمل موت أمي** بعد». (ص ٩٤). وهل من سبيل إلى اكتمال الموت؟!

**الموت نذيراً**

تنهض رواية سهى زكي **جروح الأصابع الطويلة**(٢٩) على ما يشبه البكائية لموت الحبيب/الزوج، عبر أحد عشر فصلاً معنونة، متراتبة: «الأصبع الأول»، «الأصبع الثاني»، إلخ.، والفصل الحادي عشر، الأخير - «أصبع واحد جديد: سكن هناك ولن تصيبه الشيخوخة» - يتأسى بكون الزوج الذي رحل شاباً قد توقف انحداره إلى ما بعد الشباب، وتأبت ملامحه - من ثم - على كل ذبول واضمحلال تفرضهما حركة الزمن في خطوه الثقيل. تتنوع رواية الفصول ما بين راوية خارجية، وأخرى تتحدث بصوت المتكلم، وتتحدث في الفصول الأخيرة بلسان الزوجة المسماة سهى، التي يلتقي صوتها وصوت

الكاتبة (انظر ص ١٠٦). وخلال هذا التنوع نشهد، بأكثر من منظور، رؤى متعددة للموت، متمثلة في رحلة حياة ثم موت عمر عبد العزيز الكردي، الطفل المتسائل، ثم الشاب المحلق وراء أحلامه، ثم الكاتب، ثم الزوج/الأب، وعبر هذه الرحلة القصيرة اللاهثة يلوح عمر محاطاً بالموت، وتقريباً منذوراً له، منذ طفولته حتى رحيله الأخير.

في حياة عمر، على قصرها، تترى ترديدات الموت. مات والده بينما كان صغيراً وأورثه مرض الصدر فكانت تنتابه «أزمات» متلاحقة (انظر ص ٤٣). وسوف تموت أخته أيضاً؛ فيتأمل هو – وقد دخل عالم القراءة – ما يربط بين موتها وموت الشاعر أمل دنقل (انظر ص ٥٠)، كما سوف تموت أمٌّ تبنته فيما بعد، إذ التهمها ذلك «الغول الشهير» نفسه (انظر ص ٥٢)، كذلك تموت جدته، أم كردي (ص ٦٣). مثل هذا الموت المتلاحق، في حياة تلوح مختزلة وملاحقة بهاجس النهاية، يجعل الموت نذيراً قريباً على المستويين الداخلي والخارجي معاً، ويرسم صورته شاملة ومطبقة وكلية القدرة، ممتدة ومتكررة أيضاً. وقد أومأ أحد عناوين الفصول إلى شيء من هذا الملمح: «الإصبع الرابع»: «للمرة الثانية، **للموت نفس اللون والطعم والرائحة**». لكن، مع حصار الموت، الذي يلاحق عمر، ثم تنهشه مخالبه، فإنه يظل يدافعه، مثقلاً بهاجسه القريب الملح.

يتمثل هاجس الموت بطرائق شتى بما يجعله «يقيناً» ثابتاً يحمله عمر بداخله. يقول لحبيبته، زوجته فيما بعد: «أنا عمري قصير، ولو عايزا حد عمره طويل مش أنا» (ص ٩٣)، وإذ يتحول عمر إلى كاتب، يكتب قصصاً قصيرة ويشرع في كتابة رواية، تسأله: «حاتخلصها إمتى»، يجيب: «قبل ما أموت حاكون مخلصها» (ص ٩٦). وتشير زوجته/الراوية إلى أنها عندما أنجبت ابنته قال لها: «أنا مش عايز أشوفها خالص، كل ما باشوفها بافتكر إني هاموت وأنا مقدرتش أعملها أي حاجة، خلي بالك منها» (ص ٩٩)، وإذ يصاب صوته بـ«بحة» يقول لها: «إظاهر أن أول حاجة تموت فيّ صوتي» (ص ١٠٠). وكما ربط عمر بين موت أخته وموت أمل دنقل، سوف يربط بين موته هو وموت يحيي الطاهر عبد الله (ص ١٠٧).

في مقابل يقين عمر بالموت، ثمة محاولات عدة – خارجه – لنفيه. لقد كانت زوجته تكذب كلامه عن الموت وتعده «جنون عبقري مهموم بالإنسانية الجافة». كانت تعتقد أنه «كلام فيلسوف مرعوب من المرض فيقاومه بهجوم عنيف» (ص ٩٩). لكن فضلاً عن هذا «التكذيب»، الهادئ المتعقل، وربما المنطقي، كان هناك موقف غريب من أم عمر تجاه موت كل الذين يموتون من حولها وتجاه الموت ذاته؛ كانت ترفض أن يقترب من بيتها أي ميت. تموت حماتها التي تعيش

فوق سطح البيت الذي تسكنه فلا تصعد إليها، وتنادي «على أحد الجيران ليأخذها إلى بناتها وأولادهم، فهي **لا تحب الميتين ولا سيرتهم** لأنه فأل سيئ» (ص ٨٣)، وتموت ابنتها بالمستشفى ويذهب ابنها ليأتي بجثمانها فتصيح فيه: «جاتك داهية أنا قلت لاخواتك ميجوباهاش البيت **أنا مش هادخل ميتين عندي**» (ص ٥١).

خارج الهاجس بقرب الموت، وخارج التوجس الذي يلقي به – أو يحاول أن يلقي به – بعيداً، ثمة تجسيدات عدة للموت نفسه في **جروح الأصابع الطويلة**، منها إشارات لعلاماته، ولوطأته، ولطقوسه، ولمجابهاته المؤلمة. وفي هذه الوجهة، يتجاور الرصد الخارجي لمشهد الموت مع التعبير الداخلي عن الإحساس بفجيعته. يتوقف سرد الراوية/الزوجة، بكلمات محايدة، عند مشهد جثمان عمر المسجى بالمستشفى: «بشريط شاش أبيض عريض قطعه الممرض من شريط الشاش اللاصق وكتب عليه "عمر عبد العزيز الكردي غرفة ٣٢–٧٤٣ سنة [كذا، ولعل الصواب: غرفة ٧٤٣–٣٢ سنة] أ. د. مختار جمعة" ثم لصقه على جبهته»، ويبرح السرد حياده، متسائلاً: «أهكذا انتهت مأساته»؟ (ص ١٠٦)، ثم يمضي السرد نائياً عن كل حياد: «لم يكن بوسعي أن أمنع عنه **هذا الزائر الثقيل المفاجئ**.. رغماً عني اقتحم غرفته التي كرهها جداً جداً.. رغماً عني وعنه.. **انتزع منه تلك الروح الشفافة الطموحة**» (ص ١٠٦). وسوف يمتزج المستويان، الخارجي الراصد المحايد والداخلي المثقل بوطأة التجربة، مرة أخرى، مع طقوس «تغسيل» الزوج الراحل، فيتوقف السرد عند معالم المشهد: «التفوا حوله يحممونه ويلبسونه زيه الجديد، فاخراً، كما كان يحب دائماً أن يرتدي أفخر الثياب، حملوه ليضعوه في التابوت الطويل . . . كان يتمنى أن يهتموا به طوال الـ٣٢ عاماً.. ولكنهم اهتموا به الآن!» (ص ١١١). لقد أتى الموت، في النهاية، دون مبالاة، ثم مضى بعد أن خلّف وراءه الكثير من المبالاة.

## تعدد الموت.. تحولات الموت

هكذا يتحول الموت، في أغلب هذه الروايات السبع، من «كارثة» أو فجيعة مطبقة إلى محض «ذكرى»، قريبة أو نائية. وإذا كان في كل ذكرى قدر من مدافعة النسيان، فإن «الراحلين» – الموتى أيضاً في أغلب هذه الروايات – يظلون مع الأحياء، «مقيمين» على نحو ما، حتى وإن لم يتوقف بعض هذه الروايات عند كيفية هذه «الإقامة»، أو يصور معالمها، وأيضاً حتى وإن بهتت، بمرور الزمن، ملامح هؤلاء الراحلين أو أحاطت بذكراهم غلالات من ضباب.

فيما بعد الرحلة التي تقطعها **بداية ونهاية**، من «الموت/الكارثة» في مفتتحها، إلى «الموت/العقاب» في خاتمتها، تمكث الذكرى معنا - نحن القراء - بعد السطور الأخيرة من الفصل الأخير.

وفي **كتاب التجليات**، ثمة تحليق بذكرى الراحلين إلى آفاق وذرى تتراجع معها وطأة كل رحيل، بل يؤول الرحيل إلى أوبة حقيقية. وأيضاً ثمة نظرة - تستعير من تجربة الصوفية القدرة على مجاوزة تخوم الأزمنة والأماكن - ترنو إلى فضاء يتكافأ فيه حضور الأحياء وحضور الموتى، بما يجعل الموت واقعة تنأى - رغم إيلامها - عن معاني الغياب الفعلي.

وفي **خالتي صفية والدير** يتم تناول تجربة الموت خلال أكثر من متصل: متصل الموت/الحب، متصل الموت/الثأر، متصل الموت/الخلاص، وأيضاً متصل الموت/الحياة، ويقود طريق الآلام - كما قاد السيد المسيح من قبل - إلى الختام الأخير، المشرع على مصير مأمول، أبهى وأجمل، فيغدو الموت نفسه محض تذكرة بالحياة، ماثلة واضحة، لا تتضاءل، ولا تتلاشى، ولا تنقضي.

وتتحول الذكرى في **يوميات امرأة مشعة** إلى فعل قصدي يسبق واقعة الموت، يناوئ التلاشي/الموت بالكتابة، أو يحول الذكرى التي لم يأت زمنها بعد إلى سعي راهن/مسبق - إن صح القول - للمقاومة؛ فتدافع الموشكة على الموت رحيلها المحتوم، وتطمح إلى أن تقدم - من قلب تجربة الاحتضار - ما يدافع الموت القادم.

وتؤول الذكرى في **تغريدة البجعة** إلى مرثية لموت سابق، وأنشودة تستشرف موتاً قادماً، بما يجعل الموت يلتف على كل الأزمنة، ويحيط بكل التجارب.

وتطل الحياة في **شجرة أمي** من طقوس الموت نفسها/نفسه، بصراعاتها وحساباتها، فينحصر الموت في ظل واحد من ظلال الحياة، ثم تغدو ذكرى الموت - وإن بهتت - وسيلة لإعادة استكشاف الذات والعالم.

وفي **جروح الأصابع الطويلة** يتحدد الموت في نقطة ماثلة على مسار زمن لا يتوقف، يحتفظ خلالها الراحل بسيماء البهاء والتأبي على كل تغير واضمحلال يفرضهما الزمن عبر حركته، فيأتي الموت - الذي كان الحدس به نوعاً من اليقين - في موعده، ولكنه - إذ يأتي ويمضي - يترك وراءه ما يدافع وطأة عالم موغل في بلادته ولا مبالاته.

يطل الموت، في هذه الروايات، بوجوه شتى، ويظل يحتفظ بوجهه الكارثي أيضاً. من الموت بوصفه «قدراً غاشماً» في أول رواية **بداية ونهاية**، ثم الموت بوصفه حكماً أخلاقياً في نهايتها، إلى الموت بوصفه محض غياب جسدي، تؤوب خلاله الروح إلى مصدرها، ويتراءى معه عالم محلق عبر الأزمنة والأماكن، يتجاور به - في وجود متكافئ - حضور

الموتى وحضور الأحياء في **كتاب التجليات**، إلى الموت بوصفه «عقاباً» ثم «ثأراً»، ثم «أملاً مرتجىً»، ثم «خلاصاً» في **خالتي صفية والدير**، إلى الموت بوصفه «تهديداً»، ثم «حافزاً» للتشبث بالبقاء، في **يوميات امرأة مشعة**، إلى الموت بوصفه مصيراً مرتقباً يدفع إلى أنشودة أخيرة، تصله بالحياة أو تصل الحياة به في **تغريدة البجعة**، إلى الموت بوصفه سبيلاً للتوصل إلى علاقة جديدة مع الراحلين وإلى اكتشاف جديد لعالم/عوالم الأحياء في **شجرة أمي**، إلى الموت بوصفه «قدراً منذوراً»، ووسيلة لكشف لامبالاة العالم في **جروح الأصابع الطويلة**.. رحلة تقطعها تناولات الموت، في هذه الروايات السبع، لتجسد رؤى بعينها له – وهي جزء من رؤى أخرى كثيرة، مطروحة في روايات غير هذه الروايات – كلها يرقب في الموت وجهه الأوليّ القريب، ويرنو مع هذا الوجه إلى وجوه أخرى مغايرة.

تتنوع، إذن، تناولات الموت في هذه الروايات السبع، لكنها – جميعاً، تقريباً – تجسد المسعى نحو استكشاف سبل وطرائق لاستئناس ذلك الموت، ولإقامة جسور ممتدة بين الأحياء والموتى، بما يشي بتصور جمعيّ مشترك، سابق على هذه الكتابة، محيط بها، وأيضاً ملازم لها وماثل فيها، يؤمن – لا يزال – بعدم انفصال الموتى، بموتهم، عن حياة الأحياء، ويطمح إلى أن يحول «كارثة» الموت – فجيعته ووطأته وغيابه المفاجئ أو المتوقع – إلى ألفة مقيمة، تناوئ كل فجيعة وتدافع كل وطأة وكل غياب.

### الهوامش

(١) جيمس ب. كارس، **الموت والوجود – دراسة لتصورات الفناء الإنساني في الفكر الديني والفلسفي العالمي**، ترجمة بدر الديب (القاهرة: المجلس الأعلى للثقافة، ١٩٩٨)، ص ٣٦٢.

(٢) أحمد على مرسي، **في الأدب الشعبي – كل يبكي على حاله، دراسة في العديد** (القاهرة: عين للدرسات والبحوث الإنسانية والاجتماعية، ١٩٩٩)، ص ٣١.

(٣) عن طقوس الموت في مصر القديمة، انظر **المرجع السابق**، ص ٢٤.

(٤) جمال حمدان، **شخصية مصر – دراسة في عبقرية المكان** (القاهرة: دار الهلال، ١٩٩٥)، الجزء الرابع، ص ٥٥٢.

(٥) **المرجع السابق**، ص ٥٨٠.

(٦) **المرجع السابق**، ص ٥٨٢.

(٧) **المرجع السابق**، ص ٥٨٥. والعبارة الأخيرة منسوبة إلى بي.إي. بري، فيما يشير جمال حمدان. وقد استخدمت لوسي دف جوردون العبارة نفسها في زمن أسبق. انظر أحمد خاكي، **رسائل من مصر – حياة لوسي دف جوردون في مصر ١٨٦٢–١٨٦٩** (القاهرة: الهيئة المصرية العامة للكتاب، ١٩٧٦)، ص ٦٥.

(٨) سيد عويس، **نظرات باحث اجتماعي مصري** (القاهرة: الكتاب الذهبي، ١٩٨٨)، ص ٦٤.

(٩) سيد عويس، **الخلود في حياة المصريين المعاصرين – نظرة القادة الثقافيين المصريين نحو ظاهرة الموت والموتى** (القاهرة: الهيئة المصرية العامة للكتاب، ١٩٧٢).

(١٠) «البكوة» من «البكاء». وتبعاً لهذا النظام، تجتمع النساء يومي الخميس والسبت من كل أسبوع، لتبكين من ماتوا لديهن بكاء مستمراً. انظر سيد عويس، **حديث عن المرأة المصرية – دراسة ثقافية اجتماعية** (القاهرة: مطبعة أطلس، ١٩٧٧)، ص ص ٩٧–١٠٠. وانظر أيضاً كتابه **حديث عن الثقافة – بعض الحقائق الثقافية المعاصرة** (القاهرة: مكتبة الأنجلو المصرية، ١٩٧٠)، ص ص ١٢٦–١٣١.

(١١) أيمن عبدالفتاح حسن وزيري، **مفهوم ومظاهر الخلود في مصر القديمة حتى نهاية عصر الدولة الحديثة**، رسالة دكتوراه، كلية الآثار، قسم الآثار المصرية، جامعة القاهرة، ٢٠٠٩، ص ١٨.

(١٢) **المرجع السابق**، ص ١٩. ومن التعبيرات المصرية الشائعة، الراهنة، عن الموت، القول عمن مات بأن «فلان ربنا افتكره»، ونقل خبر الموت بمنحى يتداخل والدعاء: «فلان تعيش انت». والتعبيرات الفصحى عن حدث الوفاة لا تبتعد كثيراً عن مثل هذه الصياغة: «انتقل إلى الرفيق الأعلى»، «انتقل إلى جوار ربه»، أو «إلى الأمجاد السماوية».

(١٣) في هذا السياق، ثمة تعبيرات عدة عن رغبة الخلود في **كتاب الموتى**، كما ورد في أيمن عبدالفتاح حسن وزيري، ص ٦٨.

(١٤) عن تناولات الموت في الحضارات والثقافات المتعددة، يمكن الرجوع إلى: خزعل الماجدي، **ميثولوجيا الخلود – دراسة في أسطورة الخلود قبل الموت وبعده في الحضارات القديمة** (عمّان: الأهلية للنشر والتوزيع، ٢٠٠٢)؛ عبد السلام المساوي، «الموت بين الأسطورة والفلسفة»، مجلة **عمان**، العدد ١٠٣ (فبراير ٢٠٠٤)؛ مجموعة مؤلفين، **ديوان الأساطير**، الكتاب الرابع: **الموت والبعث والحياة الأبدية**، ترجمة قاسم الشواف، تقديم أدونيس (لندن: دار الساقي للطباعة والنشر، ٢٠٠٠)؛ سامي أحمد الموصلي، **مفهوم الموت في الإسلام** (بيروت: دار النفائس للطباعة والنشر والتوزيع، ٢٠٠٤)؛ مصطفى بنحمزة، «فلسفة الموت عند بديع الزمان سعيد النورسي»، مجلة **حراء**، العدد ٢ (يناير–مارس ٢٠٠٦)؛ الأب أوغسطين دوبره لاتور، **دراسة في الإسكاتولوجيا**، ترجمة صبحي حموي، (بيروت: دار المشرق، ١٩٩٩).

(١٥) نجيب محفوظ، **بداية ونهاية** (القاهرة: مكتبة مصر، ١٩٨٤).

(١٦) كتب عن هذه الرواية نقاد كثيرون، وكتاباتهم تعكس هذه التناولات متنوعة الزوايا. من هؤلاء النقاد: عبد العظيم أنيس ومحمود أمين العالم، **في الثقافة المصرية** (القاهرة: دار الفكر الجديد، ١٩٥٥)؛ غالي شكري، **أزمة الجنس في القصة العربية** (بيروت: دار الآداب، ١٩٦٢)؛ رجاء النقاش، «عندما يموت الأب»، جريدة **الأخبار** (١٧/٣/١٩٦٣)؛ أنور المعداوي، **كلمات في الأدب** (صيدا: المكتبة العصرية، ١٩٦٦)؛ سامي خشبة، «نجيب محفوظ والبحث عن الإنسان المفقود»، جريدة **المساء** (٣/٦/١٩٧١)؛ فاطمة موسى، **نجيب محفوظ وتطور فن الرواية العربية** (القاهرة: مكتبة الأنجلو المصرية، ١٩٧٢)؛ طه وادي، **صورة المرأة في الرواية المعاصرة** (القاهرة: مركز كتب الشرق الأوسط، ١٩٧٣)؛ عبد المحسن طه بدر، **نجيب محفوظ – الرؤية والأداة** (القاهرة: دار الثقافة للطباعة والنشر، ١٩٧٨)؛ محمد حسن عبدالله، **الإسلامية والروحية في أدب نجيب محفوظ** (القاهرة: مكتبة مصر، ١٩٧٨)؛ لطيفة الزيات (إعداد)، **صوت المرأة في القصص والروايات العربية** (بغداد: اللجنة الاقتصادية والاجتماعية لغرب آسيا، الأمم المتحدة، ١٩٨٥)؛ إبراهيم فتحي، **العالم الروائي عند نجيب محفوظ** (القاهرة: الهيئة المصرية العامة للكتاب، ١٩٨٨)؛ علي شلش، **نجيب محفوظ – الطريق والصدى**، (بيروت: دار الآداب، ١٩٩٠)؛ محمد دكروب، «دراسة عن صراع اليمين واليسار في شخصيات نجيب محفوظ»، مجلة **أدب ونقد**، العدد ٣ (١٩٩١). وللمزيد من الدراسات الأخرى لهذه الرواية، راجع حمدي السكوت، **نجيب محفوظ – ببليوجرافيا تجريبية وسيرة حياة ومدخل نقدي** (القاهرة: الهيئة المصرية العامة للكتاب، ٢٠٠٧)، ص ١٠٨ وما بعدها.

(١٧) في هذا المنحى، يمكن قراءة الرواية على أساس من تسلسل وقائعها – حسب تصور جريماس – بما يجعل كل واقعة تترتب على واقعة سابقة وتؤدى إلى وقائع جديدة.

(١٨) تجربة اجتياز العتبة، في هذا السياق، وبهذه الملابسات، تندرج في تصور ميخائيل باختين حول «زمكان العتبة» الذى يمثل جزءاً من «زمكان الطريق». راجع كتابه **أشكال الزمان والمكان في الرواية**، ترجمة يوسف حلاق (دمشق: منشورات وزارة الثقافة، ١٩٩٠)، ص ٥٣ وما بعدها، ص ٢٢١ وما بعدها.

(١٩) جمال الغيطاني، **كتاب التجليات** (القاهرة: دار الشروق، ٢٠٠٧).

(٢٠) بهاء طاهر، **خالتي صفية والدير** (القاهرة: دار الشروق، ٢٠٠٨).

(٢١) من هذه الزاوية، تلتقى وهذا الطرح للموت رواية إدوار الخراط **صخور السماء** (القاهرة: مركز الحضارة العربية، ٢٠٠١)، وإن لم يكن الموت هو التجربة الأساسية فيها.

(٢٢) نعمات البحيري، **يوميات امرأة مشعة** (القاهرة: الهيئة المصرية العامة للكتاب، ٢٠٠٦) . وتفيد هذه الفقرة، إفادة أساسية تماماً، من مقالي «الكتابة الترياق»، مجلة **الثقافة الجديدة** (سبتمبر ٢٠٠٨).

(٢٣) قريباً من هذا التناول، يمكن أيضاً قراءة رواية بدر الديب **أوراق زمردة أيوب – الأعمال الكاملة لبدر الديب** (القاهرة: المجلس الأعلى للثقافة، ٢٠٠٩).

(٢٤) مكاوي سعيد، **تغريدة البجعة** (القاهرة: الدار للنشر والتوزيع، ديسمبر ٢٠٠٦).

(٢٥) لعل هذه المخايلة بين محبوبة ماتت وفتاة أخرى تقيم نوعاً من الحوار مع موقف كمال في **ثلاثية** نجيب محفوظ الذي – رغم يقينه برحيل محبوبته، من طرف واحد، عايدة – تختلط عليه ملامحها وملامح أختها الصغرى التي يلتقيها صدفة.

(٢٦) حسين حمودة، **في غياب الحديقة – حول متصل الزمان/المكان في روايات نجيب محفوظ** (القاهرة: مكتبة مدبولي، ٢٠٠٦)، وبخاصة الفصل الثاني: «الحنين إلى البيت القديم»، ص ص ٤٥–٦٤.

(٢٧) سيد البحراوي، **شجرة أمي** (القاهرة: آفاق للنشر والتوزيع، ٢٠٠٧).

(٢٨) لعل هذه «الحسابات» في طقوس الدفن والعزاء تتصل بنوع من تقوية الروابط الاجتماعية، وتدعيم البنية الاجتماعية للجماعة، حسب ملاحظة دوركايم، كما ورد في: أحمد على مرسي، ص ٣٣.

(٢٩) سهى زكي، **جروح الأصابع الطويلة** (القاهرة: الدار، ٢٠٠٨).

# قلق الاندثار:
# الكاتبة العربية بين ذكرى شهرزاد وكابوس الموءودة

هنادي السمان*

تلقي هذه الدراسة الضوء على الإنتاج الأدبي لبعض كاتباتنا العربيات المعاصرات في المهجر الأوروبي أو الأمريكي، كما تهدف إلى التركيز على رمزين أدبيين يثير تواجدهما المستمر والمُلح الدهشة والتساؤلات عن ماهية دورهما الأدبي في الأدب النسوي المهاجر. إني أتكلم – بالتحديد – عن شهرزاد التي يُصرّ طيفها، دائماً وأبداً، على الظهور في الأدب النسوي بين حين وآخر، وشبح الموءودة الذي يقضُّ مضاجع الذاكرة الفردية والجماعية لدى الأديبات، فيتحول إلى كابوس أزلي يذكرنا بتاريخ الوأد والصدمة النفسية الناتجة عن هذه الذكرى الأليمة عند كاتباتنا العربيات. ومن خلال هذه المقالة، أودُّ أن أطرح منطلقاً نظرياً خاصاً بكاتبات المهجر العربيات، على وجه التحديد، وقد يمكن تطبيقه على نتاج بعض الكاتبات العربيات الأخريات أيضاً، مفاده أن الكاتبة العربية تكتب، دائماً، بدافع من قلق المحو anxiety of erasure الذي يتولد في عقلها الباطن، والذي يتراسل – مجازياً – مع أدب شهرزاد الشفهي الذي اغتصبه الرجل، ومع مجاز الوأد بوصفه هاجساً يهدد جسدها الفعلي والأدبي بالدفن والاندثار. ومن الجدير بالذكر أن استرجاع أدب شهرزاد الشفهي وصدمة الموءودة يشكلان عاملين أساسيين لتخطي خوف المحو الأدبي وتجاوز الصدمة؛ مما يخلق نتائج إيجابية عن ماض سلبي، يمكن معها معالجة هذه الصدمة الفردية والجماعية؛ من أجل خلق مجتمع قادر على الاعتراف بالدور المهم الذي يلعبه العنصر الأنثوي في خلق الأمة والوطن وإعادة بنائهما.(١)

وعلى الرغم من تركيزي على القصة بشكل خاص في هذه المقالة، فإني أستعين أيضاً بآراء أعربت عنها أديباتنا المعنيات، فيما يتعلق بمفهوم الكتابة وهاجسها بالنسبة إليهن، سواء في مقابلات شخصية، أو في سير ذاتية روائية تكوّن جُزءاً من أدبهن، مثل: سيرة غادة السمان الروائية **الرواية المستحيلة: فسيفساء دمشقية (١٩٩٧)**، وسيرة نوال السعداوي الذاتية **أوراقي.. حياتي** (٢٠٠٠). وقد علّمنا النقد

الأدبي المعاصر أن كل تاريخ يُكتب، أو حادثة تُروى، تكتسب نوعاً من الأسلوب السردي الذي يمثل وجهة نظر الكاتبـ/ـة السياسية والاجتماعية الخاصة. ولذلك، من النادر أن نجد نوعاً من الكتابة التاريخية، أو التقريرية، يخلو من عنصر السردية.

ولعله من الضروري تعريف مفهوم المهجر ومعيار استخدامه عند تلك الكاتبات، فهذه المقالة تُعنى بفحص نتاج الأديبات العربيات اللواتي يَقْطُنَّ في المهجر الأوروبي أو الأمريكي، ولكنهن ما زلن ينشرن مؤلفاتهن الأدبية باللغة العربية، وأحياناً بلغة المهجر الفرنسية أو الإنجليزية. وقد تعددت أسباب هجرة كل منهن حسب الظروف السياسية والاجتماعية في بلادهن، وحسب ظروفهن الشخصية أيضاً. وعلى سبيل المثال، كانت هجرة غادة السمان، وإيڤلين عقاد، وإيتل عدنان – في الستينيات وأوائل السبعينيات – إلى لندن وأمريكا الشمالية بسبب التحصيل العلمي في بداية الأمر، ثم اضطررن إلى البقاء في المنفى لأسباب شخصية وسياسية. فمثلاً، بعد وفاة والد غادة السمان، الذي كان يشغل منصب وزير التعليم العالي ورئيس الجامعة السورية آنذاك، خسرت الكاتبة الدعم المادي والمعنوي الذي يعينها على تحصيلها العلمي. وأمام إصرار عائلة والدها الدمشقية المحافظة على تركها برنامج الدكتوراه والعودة إلى دمشق، بالإضافة إلى الحكم عليها غيابياً بتهمة ترك العمل في جامعة دمشق وحرمانها من الحصول على جواز سفر من جرّاء ذلك، وجدت السمان أن المنفى الإنجليزي أو اللبناني أو الفرنسي (بعد الحرب الأهلية اللبنانية) أصبح موطنها الدائم.(٢) وقد أدَّتْ أسباب سياسية معينة إلى نفي حميدة نعنع عام ١٩٧٠ من وطنها الأم – سوريا – إلى الجزائر أولاً، وبعدها إلى باريس حيث استقرت هناك حتى الآن.(٣) كما كانت هجرة الأخريات، من أمثال هدى بركات وحنان الشيخ، نتيجة اندلاع الحرب الأهلية اللبنانية التي دامت خمسة عشر عاماً (١٩٧٥–١٩٩٠). أما عالية ممدوح، فأجبرها نظام صدام حسين، ومن بعده الاحتلال الأمريكي للعراق، على الهجرة من العراق إلى فرنسا أيضاً. لقد كان واقع المهجر حالة دائمة بالنسبة إلى الأديبات المذكورات حتى الآن، ما عدا نوال السعداوي التي كان واقع الغربة بالنسبة لها مؤقتاً، لا يتعدى النفي المؤقت، أو الهرب من بلدها مصر بدافع الخوف على حياتها، حين وضعت بعض الأحزاب الإسلامية اسمها على اللائحة السوداء بعد نشر كتابها **سقوط الإمام** (١٩٨٧)، ثم تفاقم إحساسها بالخطر بعد أن اغتيل الكاتب اليساري فرج فودة عام ١٩٩٢، فوضعت الحكومة المصرية حراسة دائمة لها؛ مما أشعرها بأنها تحت الإقامة الجبرية.(٤)

وبسبب ذلك، غادرت مصر لتقيم على مدى أربعة أعوام في الولايات المتحدة الأمريكية تدرّس فيها مادة الإبداع الأدبي في جامعة ديوك في ولاية نورث كارولينا، وهناك كتبت سيرتها الذاتية **أوراقي.. حياتي**. وبعدئذٍ، أقامت لمدة عام في أوروبا قبل أن تعود إلى مصر، ثم تركت مصر مرة أخرى. ولعل ما يميز هؤلاء الأديبات، بشكل عام، أن صلتهن لم تنقطع مع الوطن الأم قط، بل استمرت عن طريق قيامهن برحلات مكوكية من المهجر إلى الوطن بشكل متواصل؛ مما أدى إلى تعميق إحساسهن بهموم الوطن الاجتماعية والاقتصادية والسياسية، وإلى شعورهن بضرورة إيجاد حلول جذرية لها.

**داء شهرزاد الشفهي**

من الضروري هنا توضيح ما أعنيه بعبارة داء شهرزاد الشفهي حتى يتسنى لنا فهم الدور المزدوج الذي تلعبه بوصفها رمزاً في ذاكرة حفيداتها: كاتبات المهجر. تلعب شهرزاد – بوصفها سيدة السرد القصصي التى استطاعت بذكائها وحنكتها أن تنقذ نفسها وبقية عذارى المملكة من بطش السلطان شهريار – دور الملهمة الروحية للكاتبات العربيات، ولكن سيطرة راوي **ألف ليلة وليلة** على قصصها وتحويلها من ملكة القص إلى مجرد شخصية من شخصيات الكتاب حين كُتبت القصص بأمر من السلطان، بعد شفائه من داء قتل زوجاته، جعلها حبيسةٍ السرد الشفهي إلى الأبد؛ إذ منعها من أن تخط لياليها بقلمها، وأُسند هذا الدور إلى راوي الإطار الخارجي في **ألف ليلة وليلة**، وقد كان إسناد دور الراوي العام لهذا القاص الخارجي، كما في مقدمة **ألف ليلة وليلة** ونهايتها، في النسخة المكتوبة، يُجرّد شهرزاد من دورها الأصلي بوصفها قاصَّة الكتاب الحقيقية، ويحولها إلى مجرد زوجة وأم، بعد الحكم على مخطوطتها بأن تظل حبيسة خزانة السلطان، وكأنه محا دورها بوصفها راويةً، وسيطر عليها أدبياً وجسدياً.(٥)

إن كاتبات المهجر اللائي نحن بصددهن (غادة السمان، وإيڤلين عقاد، وإيتل عدنان، وحنان الشيخ، وحميدة نعنع، ونوال السعداوي) يقمن بدور شهرزاد – ملكة الرواية – الأدبي، ولكنهن يَريْن ضرورة الخروج من سجن الأدب الشفهي وكتابة قصصهن بأنفسهن حتى لا يتمكن أي رجل من محو أدبهن أو الاستيلاء عليه فيما بعد. فعلى الرغم من أنهن يحترمن براعتها القصصية، وذكاءها، وتضحيتها بنفسها، من أجل شفاء السلطان شهريار من غيرته القاتلة، مما يترتب عليه تخليص الأمة بأجمعها من الهلاك، فإنهن يرفضن

تمثل دور «الممرضات/ملائكة الرحمة»(٦) اللائي يمحون أنفسهن من أجل الآخرين، فيصررن على كتابة ذاتهن الأنثوية بأنفسهن في نصوصهن المنشورة. لذلك، عليهن الخروج من عالم السرد الشفهي الخاص إلى عالم السرد المكتوب العام، وأن يثبتن وجودهن على صعيد الكلمة المكتوبة. وهنا، يجدر بي أن أتطرق إلى مفهوم الأدب الشفهي وطريقة تدوينه. وإن كان من الصحيح أن ما وصلنا من هذا الأدب قد نُقل بيد ذكورية وحوّر ليتلاءم مع معتقدات المفهوم الأبوي وانحيازاته، فإن جُلَّ ما يستطيع الناقد/ة فعله هو تنظير كيفية نقل هذا الأدب الشفهي لنا وتأطيره، فنحن لا نستطيع العودة في التاريخ إلى اللحظة الأدبية الدقيقة التي نُطق بهذا الأدب أو خُلق فيها، أو استعادة العنصر الأنثوي فيه قبل أن يدخل عليه التحرير الذكوري. لهذا السبب بالتحديد، يصبح من الضروري تسليط عدسة النقد الأدبي على مواضع التناقض في تمثيل هذا الأدب الذي ينوه عن اختلاف صوت الراوي وبالتالي جنوسته. فمثلاً، يدعونا تحويل دور شهرزاد من القاصة الذكيَّة إلى زوجة وأم وشخصية من شخوص روايتها الأصلية، إلى تخمين أن تشويهاً ما، أو محواً لدورها الأصلي، قد حدث، وأننا يجب أن نعود، ولو حتى بمخيلتنا الأدبية، إلى دورها بوصفها قاصة محنكة، وإلى شخصيتها الأصلية التي ظهرت في إطار الليالي الخارجي، والتي قدمتها لنا بوصفها أديبة ومؤرخة ومُخلّصة لبنات جنسها من بطش شهريار الغاشم.

لقد حققت هؤلاء النساء ما لم تستطع شهرزاد أن تحققه زمن عالم **ألف ليلة وليلة** التقليدي في القرن التاسع؛ إذ أصررن على إحياء ذكراها عن طريق البعد عن داء الشفهية، وعن طريق ترك أثر أدبي مكتوب وملموس يبعد عنهن شبح الاندثار والمحو من تاريخ الأدب. ولذلك، فإن وجود طيف شهرزاد في طيات قصصهن إنما هو تذكير دائم بدورها بوصفها ملهمة لهن، وإنذار لما يمكن أن يتعرضن له من استيلاء الرجال على أدبهن، تمهيداً لنفيهن إلى عالم النساء الخاص، ومحو بصماتهن الجسدية والأدبية من ذاكرة الأجيال القادمة.

## الكتابة لتجاوز صدمة الوأد

> أنا أعرابية عمرها ٢٠٠٠ سنة، حاولوا وأدي في الصحراء وفشلوا. قتلوني عدة مراتٍ، وكنتُ دوماً أنهض من رمادي لأطير.. وأكتب. (دي كابوا، ص ١٠٣)

هكذا، قدمت غادة السمان نفسها إلى القارئ الإيطالي في مقابلة أجرتها معها باولا دي كابوا، أستاذة الأدب العربي الحديث في جامعة نابولي. وكما نرى من مداخلتها، تتكرر صورة وأد البنات لتشكل رمزاً أدبياً في أدبها بشكل خاص، وفي معظم كتابات أديبات المهجر المعاصرات بشكل عام. إن صورة الوأد تشكل هاجساً مخيفاً، وترمز إلى المحو البيولوجي المتعمد للذات الأنثوية المتمثل في دفنها. وحين نضيف رمز الوأد إلى رمز المحو الأدبي لآثار شهرزاد، كما أشرنا سابقاً، تتولد لدينا صورة مرعبة عن الخطر الذي يحدق بالكاتبة العربية التي تتجرأ وتمسك القلم لتخط اسمها وأثرها في التاريخ. ويتمثل هذا الخطر في دفن جسدها الملموس كما حصل للموءودة، أو دفن أعمالها الأدبية وسجنها في خزائن السلطة الأبوية كما حصل لرواية شهرزاد. ويثير هاجس الوأد سؤالاً مهماً، ألا وهو: لماذا يسيطر كابوس الوأد على عقول أديباتنا العربيات على الرغم من أن ممارسة هذا التقليد الجاهلي قد حرّمه الرسول في بداية عهد الإسلام في القرن السابع الميلادي؟

ربما كان الرجوع إلى تاريخ الوأد وأسبابه عند عرب الجاهلية مفتاح الإجابة عن هذا السؤال. لقد انتشر وأد البنات عند عرب الجاهلية لأسباب عدة، أهمها الخوف من العار والفقر. إن طبيعة الغارات القبلية وحياة الصحراء العسيرة كانت تضطر القبائل إلى ترشيد إمكاناتها الاقتصادية المحدودة واستثمارها في تربية الذكور الذين سينضمون إلى جيوشها مقاتلين في المستقبل. أما الإناث، فإذا وقعن ضحية السبي والاغتصاب في إحدى الغارات، فسيجلبن العار إلى رأس القبيلة حين يلدن أطفالاً من نسل العدو (الآخر). وبالفعل، يشكل هذا الاعتقاد الخلفية التاريخية لأول حادثة وأد حصلت قبل الإسلام، إذ تروي إحدى القصص أن قيس بن عاصم التميمي، من قبيلة تميم، كان أول أب مارس عملية الوأد في تاريخ العرب، إذ سُبيتْ إحدى بناته حين أغار جيش النعمان بن المنذر (ملك الحيرة) عليهم. وعندما حصلت الهدنة بين الأطراف المتحاربة بعد ذلك، خَيَّرَ النعمان السَّبايا إما أن يعدن إلى أهلهن أو يبقين مع خاطفيهن. وحين اختارت ابنة قيس أن تبقى عند خاطفها، ولم تعد إلى بيت زوجها، أقسم قيس أن يدفن في الرمال أية ابنة تولد له حتى يتجنب هذا العار في المستقبل. وتوجد قصة أخرى تنسب أول حادثة وأد إلى قبيلة ربيعة. والقصتان متشابهتان تماماً حيث تختار الفتاة المَسبيَّة البقاء مع خاطفها وعدم الرجوع إلى أبيها (فضل الله، د. ص.).

يتولد عامل العار من رغبة المرأة في ترك بيت أهلها، فتضرب بقوانين الزمان والمكان عرض الحائط، حين تذهب إلى عوالم أخرى

وتنشئ علاقات محرمة: عاطفية وجنسية مع العدو أو الآخر. وبهذا العنصر الدخيل تتدنس سلالة القبيلة العريقة. إن فكرة العار تأتي أيضاً من الأصول اللغوية لكلمة «عار» القريبة من كلمة «عورة» التي تعني النقص، والشيء المعيب، والمنطقة الجنسية. و«عَارَ» بمعنى دَفن عين الماء. وتأتي كل هذه المصطلحات اللغوية من جذر الفعل الثلاثي «عور» الذي يشمل معاني العيب والنقص والدفن. إن جسد المولودة الأنثى يمثل كل معاني هذه الثلاثية غير المقدسة؛ حيث إن «عورتها» ترمز إلى أنوثتها الناقصة، التي ستجلب بدورها العار إلى القبيلة، ولذلك تستحق أن تُعَارَ، أيْ تُدفن في الرمال. ويظهر هذا الخوف القَبلي من الخطر الذي تشكله المولودة الأنثى على ديمومة المجتمع الأبوي واستقراره، بشكل جلي، مثلاً، في الأساطير الشعبية التي استقرت في ذاكرة الكاتبة السورية حميدة نعنع وخيالها منذ طفولتها، حيث كانت نعنع تسمع عن سعدى، بنت الزناتي خليفة حاكم تونس، التي أحبت شاباً من قبيلة بني هلال، وترتب على ذلك خيانتها لعائلتها ووطنها حين فتحت أسوار المدينة التي لا تُهزم لجيوش العدو. وتروي نعنع، حين تتذكر هذه القصة، أن حاضري الجلسة «قد لعنوا سعدى أشد لعنة»، وتضيف قائلة إن «قصتها هي قد بدأت بالطريقة نفسها» (Na‘na‘، ص ص ٩٤-٩٥).

وعلى الرغم من مضي ثلاثة عشر قرناً منذ أن حَرَّمَ الإسلام وأد البنات تحريماً قاطعاً، فإن بعض النساء العربيات يَعِشن بوصفهن مواطنات من الدرجة الثانية في مجتمعاتهن، ويتحملن أنواعاً مختلفة من الرفض الأسري والاجتماعي لمحاولات تأكيد ذاتهن؛ فهن مجازياً موءودات. ولذلك، فإنه من غير المستغرب أن تحمل كاتباتنا العربيات ذكرى الوأد في عقلهن الباطن بوصفها ذكرى صدمة trauma بعيدة تتمثل في أدبهن بأشكال مختلفة تدل على استمرارية حدوثها في مخيلتهن حتى بعد انتهاء الصدمة، وبعد مرور هذه الأجيال المتعاقبة على حادثة الوأد الأولى. فمثلاً، تصور كل من غادة السمان ونوال السعداوي وحميدة نعنع وإيڤلين عقاد هذا الكابوس التاريخي في رواياتهن، فيظهر هذا القلق على سطح القصة أو العقل الواعي حتى يسهم بتعجيل مشروع الشفاء من هذه الصدمة والتركيز على الحياة لا على الموت. ولذلك، فإن الكتابة عند الأديبات العربيات ليست محاكاة لنظرية هارولد بلوم الذي يؤكد أن الكتَّاب الغربيين من الذكور يكتبون بدافع «قلق التأثر» المتمثل في عقدة النقص الأوديبية التي يشعر بها الكاتب تجاه هؤلاء الذين سبقوه على درب الإبداع (انظر Bloom). كما أن هذه الكتابة مختلفة تمام الاختلاف عن تصوير جيلبرت وجوبار

لإبداع الكاتبات الغربيات، وبخاصة في العصر الڤيكتوري، المتأثر بما أسمتاه «قلق الكتابة» المتولد عن عدم وجود كاتبات سابقات يلعبن دور الملهمات الأدبيات لهن (انظر Gilbert and Gubar). إن الكاتبة العربية محظوظة جداً؛ لأن لها ملهمات وأديبات قد سبقنها على طريق الإبداع، مثل شخصية شهرزاد، وجداتنا اللواتي نقلن الموروث الشعبي الشفهي. ولكن المشكلة تتمثل في أن هذا الموروث قد سرقه – وحجبه – المجتمع الذكوري حتى اندثر أثره. ولذلك، حين تنظر أديبة اليوم إلى تراث شهرزاد المندثر، وإلى تاريخ صدمة الموءودة، فإنها تدخل إلى الكتابة بهاجس المحو وقلقه؛ فهي – دائماً وأبداً – تكتب لتقاوم شبح الموت الأدبي، أو الفعلي، المتمثل في شخص شهرزاد وكابوس الموءودة. ولذلك، فإن كتابتها تَعِدُ بحلم البعث والحياة لا للنساء وحدهن بل للأمة بأجمعها.

**مفهوم الصدمة بين النظرية والتطبيق**

يُعرف محللو علم النفس الصدمة بأنها حدث مفاجئ وعنيف يشكل خطراً على حياة الشخص المعني بالأمر أو الأشخاص المحيطين به، وتُهدد بالموت الفعلي، أو بأذى جسدي، الشخص الذي يعاني من هذه الصدمة (Vees-Gulani، ص ص ٢٦–٢٧ وHerman، ص ٣٣). إن معاناة الفرد من صدمة من هذا النوع تولد ضغطاً غير عادي على العقل الواعي الذي يقرر أن ينسلخ عن الوعي ليحمي عضوية الشخص المصدوم، فيلجأ إلى تقنيات دفاعية تحمي الإنسان من عواقب الصدمة، مثل: انفصام الشخصية ونكران ذكرى حدوث الصدمة dissociation؛ مما يؤدي إلى عودة تلك الذكريات بشكل قوي وملح عن طريق تطفل الأحلام أو التهيؤات intrusion على عالم الشخص المصدوم بشكل يومي؛ مما يؤدي بالتالي إلى محاولة ابتعاده عن كل شيء يذكره بالصدمة، ومن ثم تشنجه وقلقه المفرط hyperarousal (انظر Vees-Gulani).

وقد تطور مفهوم الصدمة منذ بدايات تشخيصه على يد عالم الأعصاب الفرنسي جان مارتن شاركو Jean-Martin Charcot وخليفته في السوربون جوزيف بابينسكي Joseph Babinski اللذين درسا الصدمة من الناحية العضوية، وربطا مفهوم الصدمة بالهستيريا وعصاب الحرب في غضون عقد الثمانينيات من القرن التاسع عشر، ليشمل الناحية النفسية بعد الدراسات التي قام بها كل من جوزيف بروير Josef Breuer وسيجموند فرويد Sigmund Freud في عام ١٨٩٠؛ حيث صرح فرويد في هذا الوقت أن الهستيريا لها مسبب

نفسي ناتج عن ذكرى صدمة جنسية معينة حدثت في الطفولة. لكنه تخلى بعد فترة عن هذه النظرية، وعن فكرة أن للمسبب – دائماً – أصلاً حقيقياً يعود إلى مرحلة الطفولة، واستعاض عنها بفكرة أن الصدمة يمكن أن تكون ناجمة عن رغبات وهمية في نفس المريض وخياله. وفي فترة ما بين عامي ١٩٠٧–١٩١٣، تأثر حقل دراسة الصدمة بنظرية كارل يونج الذي عاصر فرويد وأيده بفكرة أن العصاب له أصول كامنة في عالم الأحلام والخيال، ولكنه اختلف معه بشدة حول ماهية تفسير رموز هذه الأحلام. فبينما يُرجع فرويد هذه الأحلام إلى رموز لها علاقة بعالم الفرد الشخصي، يعزو يونج تفسير هذه الأحلام إلى عالم اللاوعي الجماعي الذي يتخطى حدود الفرد إلى حضارته وأساطيرها على نحو شامل (انظر Jung).

وبينما يبقى مفهوم العصاب – حسب تعريف فرويد – مكبلاً بقيود التجربة الشخصية حيث يشل حركة الإنسان المصاب به، فإن ربط يونج هذا العصاب باللاوعي الجماعي له نتائج إيجابية؛ لأنها تدفع الشخص المصاب بالعصاب/الصدمة إلى الإبداع الأدبي، فيثري بذلك أساطير حضارته. وعلى غرار يونج، فإن المفهوم الذي أطبق به صدمة الوأد – في هذه المقالة – يتخطى الصعيد الشخصي ليشمل الصعيد الجماعي للحضارة العربية نفسها وتأثيرها على كاتباتنا بشكل عام. لقد تخطت أديبات المهجر مفهوم الصدمة بوصفه تجربة شخصية تشل الإبداع وتعطله إلى مفهوم الصدمة الجماعية التي تحمل مبدأ فهم ذلك الحدث المروع وتخطيه.

إن اكتشاف اضطراب توتر ما بعد الصدمة post-traumatic stress disorder في عام ١٩٨٠ بعد الاستماع إلى معاناة الأفراد الذين عانوا من تجربة إبادة اليهود في المحرقة، إبان الحرب العالمية الثانية، وفي حروب ڤيتنام وهيروشيما، وكذلك الاستماع إلى حوادث اغتصاب النساء، قد أعان على تعميم مبدأ انتقال الصدمة من الفرد الذي تلقى الصدمة إلى أفراد آخرين شهدوا الصدمة، بحكم أنهم ينتمون إلى الأقلية المسحوقة نفسها، أو سمعوا عنها عن طريق توارث الأجيال. وفي نطاق هذا التطبيق الجديد لمفهوم الصدمة، تخرج الصدمة من داخل عالم الفرد الشخصي لتقطن خارجه؛ أي في الوسط الحضاري بأكمله. ومن ثم، لم نعد بحاجة إلى أن نكون ضحايا مباشرين للصدمة حتى نشعر بها؛ إذ يكفي الآن أن نكون شاهدين على حدوثها، أو حتى سامعين لخبر تناقلها بين الأجيال في حضارتنا العامة. ومن أعلام مؤيدي هذا التطبيق الجديد لنظرية الصدمة شوشانا فيلمان – التي صرحت بأننا جميعاً نعيش في عصر ثقافة ما بعد الصدمة post-traumatic culture –

ودوري لوب Dori Laub وكاثي كاروث (Felman and Laub، ص ١). وعلى حد تعبير كاروث: «نحن – جميعاً – متأثرون بصدمةٍ ما حدثت في الماضي، ونحن مجرد شهود على حدوثها» (Caruth, *Unclaimed Experience*، ص ٢٤ وVees-Gulani، ص ١٩). وفي هذا السياق، يمكننا أن نتكلم، إذن، عن صدمة في اللاوعي التاريخي؛ حيث لا يرمز تأريخ الصدمة إلى حادثة حصلت للفرد فقط، ولكن إلى تيار غير ملموس يتخللنا نحن وحضارتنا على حد سواء.

إن تأثير صدمة الأجيال السابقة في الجيل المعاصر يتجلى، مثلاً، في مقدمة إيڤلين عقاد لكتابها الفرنسي والمترجم إلى الإنجليزية بعنوان *The Excised* (المختونة)؛ حيث تتكلم عن قراءتها لحوادث الختان في أفريقيا وبعض البلاد العربية، وعن مشاعر الألم والغثيان والصدمة التي عانتها، حتى بعد مضي فترة على وقوع هذه العمليات، بسبب معرفتها لهذه الحوادث؛ الأمر الذي دفعها إلى كتابة *The Excised* (ص ١). وبالمثل، فإن دافع الشهادة والتبليغ عن هذه الجرائم، من خلال توثيقها بالكتابة، هو الدافع نفسه الذي حدا بكاتبات المهجر إلى الاستماع إلى قصة الموءودة التي نُقلت لنا على لسان النظام الأبوي الجاهلي ومن بعده الإسلامي. وفي كلتا الحالتين، يبقى صوت الموءودة التي عانت صدمة الوأد مدفوناً في الرمال، ينتظر أنامل حفيدات هذا الموروث ليسمعن قصتها، ويدوّنها بأقلامهن المعاصرة ليبعثن فيها الحياة من جديد.

## صدمة الوأد

لم يكن مجتمع عرب الجاهلية المجتمع الوحيد الذي مارس وأد الأطفال. فمثلاً، عند الإغريق والرومان القدماء، كان يمارس الوأد استناداً إلى التشريع حتى العصر الرابع بعد الميلاد (Giladi، ص ١٨٥). كما انتشرت هذه العادة عند الصينيين والهنود القدماء. ولا يزال الوأد منتشراً في بعض أرجاء الهند حتى يومنا هذا بمساعدة التقنيات الطبية الحديثة التي تكشف عن جنس المولود قبل ولادته، أو حتى قبل تلقيح البويضة، مما يسرع بإجهاضها إن كانت أنثى.

وحتى عند قبائل العرب القدماء، كانت عادة الوأد منتشرة بين بني تميم وبني كندة وبني ربيعة فقط. وكانت المولودة الأنثى تُدفن بعد الولادة مباشرة، حيث كان يجهز لها قبر، غير عميق، قرب المرأة الوالدة؛ فإذا كان المولود ذكراً سُمح له بأن يعيش، وإذا كان أنثى دُفنت في القبر مباشرة، أو تُدفن في عمر السادسة، أو في وقت المراهقة. وكانت حالات الوأد في عمر السادسة أو في عمر المراهقة المتقدمة

نادرة جداً، وترتبط في الغالب بطقوس التضحية البشرية للآلهة مثلاً، أو لتهدئة غضب وحميَّة الآباء الذين يلجأون إلى الوأد، حتى لا تتزوج بناتهم من رجل ينتمي إلى قبيلة غريبة. كان الآباء – عادةً – هم الذين يقومون بتنفيذ الوأد، ويمكن أن تقوم به الأمهات أيضاً لتهدئة حفيظة الرجال، وحتى لا يتركهن أزواجهن.

يروي التاريخ أيضاً أن الخليفة عمر بن الخطاب تذكر باكياً مرة أنه قبل إسلامه قد وأد ابنة كان عمرها كبيراً نسبياً، إلى درجة أنها نَفَضت الرمال عن لحيته وهو يحاول دفنها. كما أن هناك حادثتين ترويان عن دفن ابنتين في سن المراهقة وهما: ابنة قيس بن عاصم التميمي وابنة رجل من الأنصار؛ إذ اعترف والدا كل من البنتين للرسول أن الابنتين أفلتتا من مصير الوأد عند الولادة بسبب حيلة والدتيهما، فقد كان قيس مسافراً خارج مضاربه عندما ولدت امرأته بنتاً فأرسلتها لتعيش عند أهلها، وادّعت أن المولودة قد ماتت عند الولادة. ويحكي الرجل الثاني أنه جَنَّبَ ابنته الوليدة مصير الوأد استجابة لتوسلات أمها العديدة. وحين أصبحت الفتاتان في سن الزواج كان من الضروري أن يتعرف قيس على ابنته حتى تُخطب منه شخصياً، بينما تضرب الحميَّة رأس الأب الثاني فيرفض تزويجها لخاطبيها. ويدَّعي والدا كل من البنتين أنهما سيأخذان الفتاتين في رحلة لزيارة ذويهما، وفي الطريق يحفران بئراً في الصحراء ويرميان الفتاتين فيه، ثم ينتظران ملياً حتى تنقطع أصواتهن المطالبة بإنقاذهن وعدم قتلهن. ويروي قيس أن ابنته سألته محتجة: «يا أبتِ أتغطيني بالتراب!» أما الابنة الثانية فتمسك أباها طالبة الرحمة، ويحتار هو بين إنقاذها أو رميها في البئر، وعندما يُنفذ عملية الوأد تصرخ الفتاة: «لقد قتلتني يا أبتِ»(٧)، وحين سمع الرسول هذه القصص، بكى من التأثر، وقال لقيس: «إن الذي لا يَرحم لا يُرحمِ». وفي رواية أخرى قال للأب الثاني: «لو أمرت أن أعاقب أحداً بما فعل في الجاهلية لعاقبتك» (القرطبي، ص ص ٩٦-٩٧).

إن تفحصاً دقيقاً لروايات الوأد التي حدثت في عهد الجاهلية يدلنا على أن هذه القصص قد نُقلت لنا في العهد الإسلامي لتبرز سماحة الدين الجديد وتعاطفه مع الموءودات بخاصة، والنساء على وجه العموم. وعليه، بإمكاننا التمييز بين نوعين من السلطة الأبوية: السلطة الجاهلية التي ارتكبت جريمة الوأد، والسلطة الإسلامية التي شجبته ودونته في كتب التاريخ. ومن الجدير بالذكر أننا في كلتا الحالتين لم نسمع صوت النساء الموءودات أنفسهن، أو الأخريات اللواتي فقدن بناتهن أو عايشن هذا التقليد المُجحف. ولهذا، تمثل

عملية إعادة بعث صوت الموءودة في أدب كاتبات المهجر رمزاً مهماً يدل على المحاولة الأنثوية لإعادة الأمور إلى نصابها وكتابة قصة الوأد بشكل مستوحى من صوت الضحية ويدها. وتبين لنا روايات الوأد هذه أمرين مهمين، ألا وهما: صوت الفتاة الموءودة الذي يتخطى حدود القبر ليطارد أباها كي يصر على إثبات وجوده، وآثار صدمة أو كارثة الوأد التي لا تتوقف حدودها عند البنت الموءودة فقط، ولكن تظل تلاحق الآباء بعقدة الذنب؛ وبخاصة بعد أن أعلنوا إسلامهم واكتشفوا فجأة جُرْمَ ما فعلوه في أيام الجاهلية. إن هؤلاء الآباء يستعيدون حادثة الوأد، ويعانون من جَرَّاءِ آثار ما بعد الصدمة post-traumatic syndrome، فهم يستأنفون البكاء ويخافون من عقوبة الله لهم في الآخرة، ويلاحقهم شبح صوت بناتهن الموءودات دائماً وأبداً. وفي الحقيقة، فإن صوت الموءودة الذي أراد هؤلاء الآباء أن يخنقوه ويدفنوه هو الذي يتصدر الساحة في الآية القرآنية الوحيدة التي تذكر الوأد، وتُحرمه بوصفه كبيرة من الكبائر التي يعاقب الله مرتكبيها في الآخرة. ومع أن وأد الأطفال يُشار إليه في أربع آيات أخرى في القرآن الكريم: (سورة الأنعام وسورة النحل وسورة الإسراء وسورة الممتحنة)، فإن الآيتين الثامنة والتاسعة من سورة التكوير تُشكلان الموضع الوحيد الذي يذكر الله – عز جلاله – كلمة الوأد فيها على النحو الآتي: «وإذا الموءودة سُئلتْ، بأي ذَنب قُتِلت» (التكوير: ٨ و٩). وتُركز هاتان الآيتان على اللحظة الحاسمة حين تُبعث الموءودة، وتُسأل عن طبيعة الجريمة التي ارتُكبتْ ضدها في السر والخفاء. إن صوتها المكتوم وجسدها المدفون يمثلان الأثر، أو الدليل القاطع على الجريمة التي اقترفت في حقها. ولذلك، ستستطيع الموءودة عندها أن تُبرز جسدها المدفون بوصفه دليل اتهام للآباء، مما يعطي معنىً جديداً مؤنباً لعبارة «لقد قتلتني يا أبتِ». فهل من الغريب، إذن، أن نجد الآباء يعانون من آثار ما بعد صدمة الوأد، بعد أن اكتشفوا طبيعة جرائمهم المرتكبة في الجاهلية؟ وهذا يفسر أيضاً، فيما أرى، سبب التلازم الأكيد بين جسد المرأة وصوتها في كتابات أديباتنا العربيات. في ذلك السياق، تصبح كاتباتنا شاهدات على ذكرى الوأد وعلى وعي/يقظة المجتمع لهذا الموروث الرهيب الذي نستطيع استعادته على هيئة صور في الذاكرة فقط، وسرد شفهي يجب أن يوثق بعدها بالكتابة حتى نستوعب الصدمة ونتخطاها.

تُؤكدُ كاثي كاروث في سياق تعليقها على كتابات فرويد عن الصدمة، أن «الصدمة هي دائماً قصة جرح يصرخ ليحاول إخبارنا بحقيقة أو واقع غير حاضر في ذاكرتنا مباشرة. وهذه الحقيقة التي

تظهر بشكل لاحق لا ترتبط فقط بما هو معروف، ولكن أيضاً بما هو غير معروف في أعمالنا ولغتنا» (Caruth, *Unclaimed Experience*، ص ٤). فإذا كانت تلك هي الطريقة التي نستعيد بها ذاكرة الصدمة، على حد زعم كاروث، فإن صوت الموءودة سيُذكّر الآباء الذين أسلموا الآن بحقيقة ما ارتكبوه في الجاهلية، فكيف يمكن لهذا الصوت أن يُسمَع إذن، وكيف يمكن للنساء العربيات المعاصرات اللواتي لم يَعشن تجربة الوأد مباشرة أن يكتشفن جرح الصدمة؟

إن للإجابة عن هذا السؤال شقين: أولاً، تظهر آثار الصدمة دائماً، فيما يرى فرويد، بشكل كامن أو متأخر latent بعد فترة من كبت الحدث/الصدمة ورجوعه مرة أخرى إلى العقل الواعي. وهذا ما يسميه فرويد «فترة الحضانة latency» (Freud، ص ٨٤). ثانياً، إن النساء المعاصرات يعشن ما أسمته المعالجتان النفسيتان ماريا روت Maria Root ولورا براون بـ«الصدمة التسَلليَّة» insidious trauma التي تنتقل من جيل إلى جيل، بين النساء اللواتي يعرفن تاريخ الوأد وطبيعته السرية. هذا ما يسمونه «صدمة ما بين الأجيال» intergenerational trauma (كما ورد في Brown، ص ١٠٧). فالكاتبات العربيات المعاصرات يعشن صدمة الوأد من جديد، على صعيد الأجيال وعلى صعيد جانبي lateral أيضاً، لأن الصدمة تنتقل من الجدات إلى الأمهات إلى البنات، فتذكرهن بالتقاليد البالية التي تصر على مسح آثار أجسادهن، وعلى دفن أصواتهن في قبر الموءودة والأدب الشفهي.

إن الأدب الشفهي أو الشعري غير كافٍ لنقل أبعاد الصدمة إلى الأجيال القادمة؛ إذ أثبتت دراسات بين عدد من مرضى الصدمة أن المرضى يتذكرون الصدمة عن طريق ومضات أو صور فكرية يصعب التعبير عنها بشكل شفهي، ولذلك تشكل الكتابة الطريقة المُثلى لتدوين ذكرياتهم عن الصدمة (Vees-Gulani، ص ٢٧). وبالرغم من أن التعبير الشفهي يُشكل، أحياناً، المرحلة الأولى من استيعاب الصدمة وإيداعها أدراج الماضي (Herman، ص ص ١٧٦–١٨١)، فإنه غير كاف؛ حيث تُشكل الكتابة، وبالأخص القصة الأدبية بعد ذلك، الطريقة المثلى لتدوين ذكريات الصدمة (Vees-Gulani، ص ٣٥). ففي القصة مثلاً، على حد تعبير ڤيز–جولاني، يستطيع المرء أن يتخطى الصدمة عن طريق رؤيتها مجسدة في شخوص الروايات، وبالتالي يساعده هذا على دفعها عن نفسه وتخطيها (ص ٣٥). هذه العملية لا يمكن أن تحصل في حقل الشعر مثلاً، حيث يبقى الشاعر مرتبطاً بشكل شخصي بعالم القصيدة. يمكن لهذه الحقيقة أن تُفسر لنا عدم تأثر كاتبات المهجر بشاعرتي الجاهلية وصدر العصر الأموي المرموقتين: الخنساء وليلى

الأخيلية مثلاً؛ لأن هاتين الشاعرتين برعتا في نظم شعر شخصي يتماشى مع قوالب القصيدة الجاهلية الذكورية وأغراضها، وقد كان جُلّ همهما، فيما ترى باحثة الأدب الجاهلي سوزان ستيتكيڤيتش، توثيق نضج الفتيان إلى محاربين شجعان (Stetkevych، ص ١٦٤). ولهذا السبب، كانت مجمل قصائدهما رثاء الأخوة أو الأحباء الذين قُتلوا في المعارك. ومع أن ليلى الأخيلية قد تطرقت في موضوعات قصائدها إلى المديح (كمدحها مروان بن الحكم والحجاج) وتغزلها العذري في ابن عمها توبة بن الحمير، فإنها لم تكسر قوالب القصيدة التقليدية التي ظلت تدور في فلك الرجل. وعلى العكس، إن تبني أديبات المهجر القصة بوصفها وسيلة تعبير عن كارثة الوأد وصدمته يعطيهن الحيز الملائم لخلق أنواع أدبية جديدة، تعترف ببصماتهن الأنثوية، بمنأى عن سيطرة الأدب الذكوري، حيث تتاح لهن الفرصة، عن طريق توالف الأصوات وغياب الشخصيات وظهورها، للتعبير بشكل أدق عن زئبقيَّة صدمة الوأد، وبالتالي ضرورة تخطيها. ولهذا السبب، فإن تخليد أشعار الخنساء وليلى الأخيلية في دواوين الشعر الجاهلي أو الأموي لا يغير شيئاً من حقيقة محو آثار شهرزاد التي تشعر كاتباتنا أنها اندثرت مع صوت الموءودة.

### كوابيس الوأد

تظهر صورة الوأد في أدب بعض كاتباتنا بشكل فعلي ورمزي عبر صور السجن والكبت والخوف من الأذى الجسدي. فمثلاً، تعيش زين، بطلة غادة السمان في **الرواية المستحيلة** (١٩٩٧)، هذا الكابوس بشكل يومي؛ إذ تشعر أنها تختنق لأن أحداً ما يدفنها حيَّة في الرمال؛ فهي تعترف للقارئ بمدى خوفها، وتُرجح أن أمها وجَدَّتَها قد عانيتا مسبقاً من هذا الكابوس أيضاً: «ثمة من يدفنني حية في الرمال، ولا أرى وجهه، أو لا أريد أن أراه. ثم ينهال الرمل داخل حنجرتي، فأشهق رملاً، وأتنفس رملاً حتى تمتلئ رئتاي وأختنق، ويتضاعف ذعري حين أرى الكابوس بصورة أخرى، حين أفتش في أوراق أمي وأقرأ في دفتر مذكراتها أنها كانت ترى الكابوس ذاته! هل كانت تراه، أيضاً، جدتي وجدتها وجدة جدتها من قبلها... ومن قبلها إلى آخره... إلى آخره!» (ص ص ٣٨١-٣٨٢). إن صدمة الوأد التسللية التي تتوارث عبر الأجيال تظهر في تكرار هذا الكابوس المخيف الذي تراه زين كل ليلة، والذي يهدد بتدمير أنوثتها ومستقبلها بوصفها كاتبة. وحين تشرع زين في الكتابة، فهي تحاول أن تعود بالذاكرة إلى مكان الوأد الفعلي والرمزي حتى تُشفى من نتائجه المدمرة عن طريق إعادة سرد قصة الوأد.

وبشكل مماثل، فإن صورة الوأد تسيطر على خلفية التجليات التي تراها ريم، بطلة قصة «ثلاثون عاماً من النحل» في **القمر المربع** (١٩٩٤) لغادة السمان؛ حيث تتصور البطلة أنها تُخنَق في خزانة، وأن أحداً ما يدفنها حيَّة في تابوت ما (ص ص ١٤٨-١٤٩). وتُحيي نوال السعداوي ذاكرة الوأد في بداية مذكراتها **أوراقي.. حياتي** حين تصور محاولة إغراق طفلة حديثة الولادة، تمثلها هي، في الماء (ص ص ٥-٨). كما تشير، في موضع آخر من الرواية، إلى أنها «كان يمكن أن [تكون] ضمن هؤلاء الموءودات لو [أنها] ولدت في ذلك الزمان» (ص ص ٥-٨ وص ١١). إن تكرار صورة الوأد في أدب كاتباتنا العربيات يمثل وعداً قطعنه على أنفسهن بأن لا يسمحن للسلطة الأبوية، ولا لحظة ضعف مؤقتة، بأن تدمر الذات الأنثويَّة. ويؤكد جاك لاكان Jacques Lacan أن عملية التكرار «تخلق الجِدَّة»، وتنبه الذات الأنثوية إلى ماضي الوأد الأليم، بل وإلى مسؤوليتها بأن تكون «الشاهدة الأخلاقية»، وأن تعين على «إيقاظ الآخرين وتوعيتهم» بهذا التاريخ المرير من خلال إعادة سرد قصة الوأد حتى «يَضعن الماضي خلفهن، ويركزن على المستقبل المشترك» الذي يربط سليلات الموءودة الأحياء بوثاق من نوع خاص (كما ورد في Caruth, *Unclaimed Experience*، ص ص ١١٠-١١٢). عندئذ، وبهذه الطريقة، يمكن أن تتحول تجارب صدمة الوأد الفردية، المؤدية إلى الموت، إلى لحظات بعث جماعية تهدف إلى خلق تاريخ أنثوي جديد مفاده استمرارية الحياة والبقاء.

## هاجس الأذى الجسدي

إن خطر الوأد الذي يهدد البطلات بالموت وأهمية نزعة البقاء المناهضة له يخلقان هاجساً بالأذى الجسدي الذي تتخيل الشخصيات أنه موجه إلى ذاتهن الأنثوية، وبالتحديد إلى منعهن من كتابة تاريخهن الأنثوي بأنفسهن. فعلى سبيل المثال، زين بطلة **الرواية المستحيلة**، التي أرادت أن تَبعَثَ روح أمها وتاريخ أدبها المدفون بتقمصها شخصيتها بوصفها كاتبة، هي على يقين جازم من أن الرصاصة التي أطلقها عليها أولاد عمومتها - خطأً - كان المقصود بها إصابتها بالعمى لكي يمنعوها من الرؤية ومن الكتابة في المستقبل (ص ٤٨٩). بالإضافة إلى ذلك، فإن شخصية الراوية نوال في **أوراقي.. حياتي** تدل على أنها متأكدة تماماً من أن طريقة ناظرة المدرسة في تعنيفها بضربها بالمسطرة على يديها حتى تدميا، يُقصد بها شلّ يديها ومنعها من كتابة أدب معارض للسلطة الأبوية (ص ص ٥-٧ وص ٢٤). وفي الحقيقة، فإن هذا الهاجس له مُبرراته؛ إذ إن

معظم بطلات الروايات موضع الدراسة يتعرضن للأذى الجسدي على يد ممثلي النظام الأبوي. وعلى سبيل المثال لا الحصر، نذكر ختان الإناث المذكور في مذكرات نوال السعداوي، وبنات الواحة المذكورات في رواية *The Excised* لإيڤلين عقاد (ص ص ٥٨–٧١)، كما تعزو زين بطلة السمان وجود جرح مبهم قديم في كتفها إلى محاولة مُسنّات العائلة قص جناحيها لمنعها من التحليق. هذا التعنيف الجسدي يلحق أيضاً جارات زين مثل مُعزز، التي دفعها والدها إلى السقوط من سطح المنزل، وبدرية التي ألهب الجمر لسانها حين أجبرتها والدتها على وضعه في فمها بعد أن اعترفت بحبها لابن الجيران (ص ١١٤ وص ١٩٣).

علاوة على ذلك، تشكل روايات الحرب مسرحاً جديداً لتمثيل العنف الأبوي على جسد المرأة أيضاً، فنرى أن بطلة حنان الشيخ، زهرة، في **حكاية زهرة** (١٩٨٦) تعاني من سلسلة من الاغتصابات والإجهاضات حتى القتل، في النهاية، على يد قناص الحي الذي يلعب دور أداة النظام الأبوي. كما تُعذّب ماري روز، بطلة رواية *Sitt Marie Rose* التي كتبتها إيتل عدنان أصلاً بالفرنسية (وترجمت إلى الإنجليزية والعربية فيما بعد)، من قبل فصائل الميليشا المسيحيَّة، ثم تُقتَل، بتهمة ترك طائفتها ومساعدة الفلسطينيين المسلمين. وأخيراً، فإننا نشهد إجراء عملية تجميل قسرية لناديا، بطلة حميدة نعنع، في **الوطن في العينين** (١٩٨٩)؛ من أجل أن يُمَوِّهَ حزب المقاومة – الذي كانت تنتسب إليه – تاريخ نضالها الثوري، ويمنع العدو من التعرف عليها. وفي الحقيقة، ترسم أديباتنا صورة مروعة للجسد الأنثوي الذي يُشَوَّه، ويُغتصب، ويُسجن، وتُقطع أوصاله، ثم يُعاد تركيبه في عمليات تجميل جبرية، ويُلتَهم رمزياً من قبل النظام الأبوي والضغوطات الاجتماعية والسياسية والاقتصادية والاستعمارية التي تسيطر على محيطه، ومن ثم يُدفن على قيد الحياة. وكما ذكر جاك لاكان، فإن استعادة هذه الصورة المرعبة تساعد على التذكير بتاريخ الصدمات الفردية ونقل هذه الذاكرة من الجدات إلى الحفيدات؛ حتى تتحول إلى ذاكرة جماعية؛ وحتى تسهم الحفيدات في حركة البعث الجماعي من غفوة التاريخ الذي يُصرّ على تغييبهن. إن التركيز على رمزية الجسد، والرجوع بالذاكرة إلى موقع الوأد، إنما هو تأكيد ضرورة الاعتراف بهذا الجرح التاريخي عند نساء العرب، كما أنه وسيلة لتحويل كابوس الماضي الأليم إلى حاضر جديد ومستقبل واعد. وفي هذا السياق، يمثل تكرار حضور هذا الجسد الأنثوي في أدب كاتباتنا بعثاً أو يقظة حقيقية ورمزية لشبح الموءودة، فلعل إعادة تطبيع علاقتنا مع الجسد الأنثوي تؤدي إلى تحسين علاقة المواطن العربي، ذكراً كان أم أنثى، بحضارتنا وأمتنا بشكل عام.

## الخوف من السجن

نلحظ أن صور الخنق المتكررة في كوابيس الوأد تتطور إلى صور أدبية جديدة تعبر عن السجن الحقيقي أو الرمزي، مما يعكس في الغالب حبس جسد المرأة الشخصي وحقيقة القسر الجنسي والسياسي الذي يحيق بالنساء ككل، وببعض الرجال أيضاً. فنوال السعداوي، مثلاً، عانت مرارة السجن الفعلي على يد نظام أنور السادات عام ١٩٨٠، بينما عانت أديبات أخريات، مثل غادة السمان وحميدة نعنع، تجربة السجن الرمزي حين مُنعتا من التنقل ومن العودة إلى بلدهما، سوريا، بسبب عدم تجديد جواز سفرهن! وأيضاً مُنعت أخريات من العودة إلى أوطانهن بسبب الحرب الأهلية، أو الاستعمار الأجنبي، مثل: هدى بركات، وإيڤلين عقاد، وإيتل عدنان، وعالية ممدوح. ولذلك، فإن إحساس الحصار الداخلي هذا يُتَرجَم إلى صور سجن حقيقية أو رمزية في أدبهن؛ فنجد ناديا، مثلاً، بطلة **الوطن في العينين** مسجونة في زنزانة، في ألمانيا الغربية، بعد فشل محاولة اختطاف الطائرة التي أجبرها الحزب الثوري على القيام بها. وتروي لنا حميدة نعنع تجربة سجن شخصية في بيت أهلها، عن عمر يناهز الرابعة عشرة، بعد أن اكتشف أخوها أن أحد الشبان قد أرسل لها رسائل حب. تقول نعنع:

> لقد حبسوني في غرفة مظلمة لمدة خمسة عشر يوماً، وقدموا لي الخبز اليابس فقط، وما استطاعت أختي التي كانت تكبرني بسنتين، والتي لم تدرس في المدرسة، أن تُهرِّبَ لي من الطعام سراً. حرقوا كتبي وأقلامي ودفاتري كلها، ومنعوني من مغادرة الغرفة. منذ ذلك الوقت، أصبح العالم كله سجناً كبيراً. وبالرغم من أني سافرت بعدها في أرجاء القارات الأربع، فلا زلت أحمل ذكرى السجن داخلي. وحتى عندما وقفت في منتصف حقول الألبناوس الكولومبية الشاسعة، شعرت أني سجينة وانتحبت. ولم يفهم زوجي الفرنسي عندها لماذا بكيت وأنا أشرف على أوسع واد في العالم. (Na‘na‘، ص ص ٩٥–٩٦)

إن حالة الحصار التي تعيشها نعنع تؤكد لنا الاضطهادات الأدبية والجسدية التي تعيشها المرأة بسبب جنوستها؛ فهي تُثبت لنا، على حد زعم جوليا كريستيڤا، أن تحقيق استمتاع المرأة الجسدي jouissance يعد دائماً نوعاً من الانتهاك وتخطياً للحدود الأبوية (Kristeva، ص ٢٠٣)، أو أنها موضع يذكرنا بالصدمة الأولية فيما يرى سلافوج

زازيك (Žižek، ص ٤٩). فكما رأينا من المقطع السابق، يعد بوح نعنع برغباتها الأدبية والجنسية انتهاكاً لقواعد المجتمع الأبوي. ومن الغريب أن غياب السجن الفعلي في المهجر يثير في نفس الكاتبة مشاعر السجن الرمزي الذي يكمن بداخلها دائماً وأبداً. ويشكل السجن، هنا، صدمة من الناحية المجازية؛ لأنه يرمز إلى النقطة التي تدرك فيها الكاتبة تقييد حريتها الأدبية والشخصية، وهو ما يشبه وأداً رمزياً لصوتها وحرية جسدها في التنقل. إن البعدين المكاني والزمني اللذين يوفرهما المهجر للكاتبة هما عنصران مهمان جداً، ويلعبان دوراً أساسياً في تذكر تجربة الصدمة وتخطيها مهما كانت.

إن مشاعر الحصار هذه تقض مضاجع بطلات أخريات مثل زهرة التي تحبس نفسها في حمامات مختلفة، طوال القصة، حتى تعبر عن إحساسها الداخلي بالسجن، ومثل بطلة إيڤلين عقاد E التي يسجنها أبوها القس، ثم زوجها المسلم الذي يفرض عليها الحجاب فتتخيل أنه سيخنقها (*The Excised*، ص ص ٣٠–٣١ وص ٥٠). وعلاوة على ذلك، فإن ذاكرة زين الطفلة، عند غادة السمان، مليئة بحوادث الحبس في خزائن مظلمة تمثل عقاباً لها على ذنوب طفولية طفيفة. وفي تلك الروايات، يتطور الإحساس بالسجن الداخلي في الغالب إلى سجن حقيقي حين تمنع الأسرة أو الدولة البطلة من الحركة أو السفر، كما حدث لبطلة أسفار نوال السعداوي في **رحلاتي في العالم** (١٩٨٦)؛ فكَادَ يحرمها من السفر موظف المطار الذي كان يصر على موافقة زوجها، أو وليّ أمرها، على سفرها. إن تكرار صورة السجن هذه في الأدب النسوي يدل على مدى حرمان المرأة من الحريات الشخصية والسياسية، وعلى مدى صدمة الحصار والحبس التي تحملها في نفسها أينما ذهبت.

## أحلام الطيران

ليس بالغريب، إذن، أن تولّد مشاعر الخوف من الأذى الجسدي والحصار والسجن رغبةً في الهروب من هذا الواقع المرير حتى تحلق الذات الأنثوية، ولو بشكل رمزي، فوق مواقع الآلام والصدمات. ويشكل موضوع التحليق رمزاً متكرراً في الأدب الأنثوي، يعبر عن نهاية واعدة بالأمل في أغلب قصصهن. فعلى سبيل المثال، تنتهي روايتا السمان **الرواية المستحيلة** ونعنع **الوطن في العينين** بتحليق البطلتين زين وناديا لتبشرا بالخلاص والشفاء من صدمات الماضي. كما أن سيرة السعداوي الذاتية مليئة بأحلام الطيران التي راودتها منذ طفولتها الأولى. إن رمزية التحليق وتعدد الأسفار يشكلان العامل الحافز للتغير على صعيد الكاتبة الشخصي، وعلى

الصعيد الجماعي أيضاً. وعلى سبيل المثال، أدب الأسفار عند السمان والسعداوي ومقالات عقاد ونعنع في الموضوع نفسه يؤكدان أهمية مغادرة أرض الوطن ومواجهة الأجنبي الغريب. هذه المجابهة الثقافية تسمح، فيما ترى العقاد، بـ«رؤية المشاكل من زوايا متعددة»، وتدفع الكاتبات إلى العودة إلى الوطن في حال شعورهن بـإمكان الإسهام في تغيير الأوضاع الاجتماعية والسياسية في مجتمعاتهن» (*The Excised*، ص ١٣). وفوق كل شيء، فإن السفر يساعدهن على تخطي قلق الاندثار والمحو؛ وبخاصة عند مزاولة الكتابة. حول هذا الموضوع، تقول السعداوي في نسخة مذكراتها المترجمة إلى الإنجليزية بعنوان *A Daughter of Isis* (والمختلفة قليلاً عن الأصل العربي): «كان يجب أن تكون هناك آلاف الأميال بيني وبين وطني، أن أنفصل نهائياً عن الماضي والحاضر والمستقبل، ألا يكون لي أية احتياجات، وأن أشعر بأن الحواجز والأربطة التي أثقلتني بوصفها قيوداً غير مرئية سقطت كلها، وأن لأصابعي حرية أن تحرك قلمي في أي اتجاه قبل أن تبدأ ذاكرتي بالتذكر. فقط عندها، بدأت الأشياء المحجوبة خلف غيمة الذاكرة السوداء في الظهور» (*A Daughter of Isis*، ص ١٠). إن مغادرة موقع الصدمة عامل أساسي في فهمها، كما أن البعد المكاني يساعدنا على فهم «ما ليس معروفاً» و«لا يمكن استيعابه» من عوامل هذه الصدمة (Caruth, *Trauma*، ص ١٥٣). ولذلك فإن البعد الزماني والمكاني اللذين تكسبهما الكاتبة يعينان على تحوير الصدمات الفردية وخلق جسر منها لفهم صدمات التراث الجماعية (Caruth, *Unclaimed Experience*، ص ص ٦٦–٦٧). وفي الحقيقة، لا يحرر السفر الكاتبة من القيود الجسدية فقط، بل اللغوية أيضاً؛ فبعض القيود المتعلقة بالكتابة باللغة العربية ومحرماتها اللغوية والحضارية تنكسر حين تعبر الكاتبة عن نفسها بلغة أخرى. وفي هذا السياق، تقول نعنع: «عندما بدأت أكتب بالفرنسية تحررت فجأة من المحظورات اللغوية، وبخاصة أن لغتي الأم هي لغة المحرمات» (Na'na'، ص ١٠١). وكما نوهت في المقطع المأخوذ من مذكرات السعداوي المترجمة إلى الإنجليزية سابقاً، فإن النسخة الإنجليزية تحوي فصلاً بعنوان «الهدية» يتضمن تفاصيل عن اعتداءات جنسية حدثت للقَاصَّة في سن الطفولة لم يأت ذكرها طبعاً في النسخة العربية (*Saadawi, A Daughter of Isis*، ص ص ١٠–١١). إن رمز التحليق إذن مسيطر على نهايات الروايات الأنثوية، ويقطن دائماً في أحلام سيرهن الذاتية، وبالطبع، يسيطر على أدب أسفارهن أيضاً.

**شهرزاد في مرآة المهجر**

حين تحلق الذات الأنثوية بعيداً عن أرض الوطن فإنها تجبر على رؤية نفسها في مرآة المهجر المزدوجة التي تلعب دور المركبة السحرية التي تنقل الشخصيات في رحلات خيالية مكوكية من الشرق والغرب وإليهما. إن رحلة الشخصية إلى العالم الغربي تجبرها على القيام برحلة أخرى داخلية إلى الشرق؛ من أجل المقارنة بين نظرة الغرب إلينا ونظرتنا إلى أنفسنا. فمرآة المهجر هذه، كما تظهر في كتابات السمان والسعداوي ونعنع، تفكك نظرة الإنسان المسبقة إلى نفسه بوصفه وحدة متكاملة، وتثبط أية اعتقادات خاطئة بالية بخصوص أهمية النفس الشرقية وعظمتها، وأخيراً تعكس لنا ما يراه الآخر الغربي فينا لتتيح لنا فرصة إعادة النظر إلى أنفسنا وإلى هويتنا العربية. فمثلاً، رحلة فاطمة المرنيسي إلى الغرب في كتابها *Scheherazade Goes West* (شهرزاد تسافر إلى الغرب؛ ٢٠٠١) أثبتت لها أن هناك نوعين من الحريم: الشرقي والغربي، وأن شهرزاد تخسر الكثير من ذكائها وبراعة سردها القصصي حين تتحول في لوحات إنجريه Ingres وماتيس Matisse إلى جارية وأداة جنس فقط، في عالم الحريم الغربي، على عكس الاحترام الذي تتمتع به في الشرق بوصفها ملكة القص. إن هذه المرآة تفتح الحوار بين الذات والآخر، وتجبر الكاتبات على التخلي عن أفكارهن السابقة عن الهوية والوطن، فلا يبقى الوطن ممثلاً في وجهة نظر واحدة تعبر عن طائفة معينة، ولكن ممثلاً في وجهات نظر مختلفة ومتنوعة تشمل كل من ينتمي إليه. ولا يعود الوطن ملك اتجاه فكري أو سياسي معين، بل متفاعلاً ومتناغماً مع كل المواطنين المَنفيين عنه، وفيما يرى إدوارد سعيد فإن جسد المهاجر يعيش «مع الأرض وليس عليها» (Said، ص ٥٩).

وبالمثل، تحمل كاتباتنا في المهجر الوطن في أجسادهن، فتقول السمان: «إن الوطن الحقيقي الذي تقطنه هو جسدها» (**تسكع داخل جرح**، ص ٣٧). وهكذا، يتجسد الوطن في الجسد المهاجر، كما رأينا في روايات الحرب مثلاً، ومع تنقل مواطنيه من مكان إلى مكان نبتعد عن النظرة الأحادية القسرية للوطن، فننظر إليه من منظور متعدد وشمولي. وهكذا، فإن مفهوم الوطن والمواطنة يُعاد تشكيله، من مواقع المهجر المختلفة، من قبل أديباتنا، حتى يبتعد عن النظرية الذكورية الثابتة التي تعتمد الحرب لتدعم هذا المنطلق، فينتقل إلى وطن يبتعد عن الظلم والقسرية، ويفتح ذراعيه ليستوعب كل مشاركات أبنائه مهما اختلفت خلفياتهم السياسية والاجتماعية والجنوسية. وهكذا، فإن أثر كاتبة المهجر في اكتشاف أدوار جديدة للهوية العربية ينعكس بالنفع

على الحضارة العربية التي تعيد النظر إلى نفسها، وتعيد تقييم واقعها حسب المعطيات الحديثة. فعندما تمثل الكاتبة تفكك جسد الوطن من خلال سرد أحداث العنف الذي ارتكب على جسدها، يدرك الجميع ضرورة رفض الأوضاع السياسية المسببة لهذا التفكك والدمار، وأهمية الحوار في الحثِّ على اتباع فلسفة سلمية تعكس مبادئ التعددية، وتواصل الوطن مع كل أبنائه حتى ينتهي شتاتهم، وحتى تكتب السيرة الوطنية للمرة الأولى بأقلام أنثوية.

## إحياء تاريخ الأم الأدبي

وبما أن إعادة تركيب الوطن ومفهوم المواطنة يتطلب الإصرار على تواجد العامل الأنثوي في السير الأدبية والقومية، فإن البحث عن أدب الأم المنسية وإحيائه يعد الرمز الأهم في أدب كاتبات المهجر المعاصرات. لقد تعلمت كاتبات المهجر درساً مهماً من جدتهن الراوية شهرزاد – ملكة السرد القصصي – التي يدل وجودها الدائم في قصصهن على غيابها عن الساحة الأدبية العامة. إن طيفها يحذرهن من السماح للرجل بأن يسرق صوتهن وقلمهن، فيئدهن أدبياً وفعلياً كما حصل للموءودة فيما قبل عصور الإسلام. ويظهر دور الأم الأدبية هذا في سيرة السعداوي الذاتية، مثلاً، فتقول: «اسم أمي ذهب معها إلى العدم. . . لم أحمل اسم أمي، دفن اسمها مع جسدها في القبر، واندثرت في التاريخ» (**أوراقي.. حياتي**، ص ٢٠). هذا وتعترف السعداوي بأنها تعلمت القراءة والكتابة من أمها التي أعطتها هدية اللغة التي مكّنتها من تحويل الكلمة إلى «فعل ثوري» فيما بعد، وإلى مرآة ووسيلة «لدحض أشياء كثيرة قبلناها منذ آلاف السنين» (*A Daughter of Isis*، ص ٢٩٢). وفي موضع آخر، وعن ربط فعل الكتابة بفعل الإثم الذي تستحق الذات الأنثوية العقاب عليه، تقول أيضاً: «منذ بدأت أكتب وأنا أدرك الإثم، إثم التفكير أو الإحساس أو مجرد التفكير. لكن الكتابة عندي كانت ضرورية مثل التنفس. أحاول عن طريق الكلمات أن أستعيد وجه أمي، فملامحها تضيع من ذاكرتي كأن لم يكن لي أم. وأحياناً، تتجسد أمامي قبل أن أتعلم النطق» (**أوراقي.. حياتي**، ص ٤٩).

وبالمثل، فإن زين بطلة السمان تستعيد صوتها بوصفها كاتبة، فقط، حين تكتشف سيرة أمها الذاتية وكتاباتها غير المنشورة المنسية في صندوق أبيها. إن الرغبة الدفينة في التعرف على تاريخ الأم الأدبي، المنسي والمدفون بين طيّات التاريخ وحصونه المنيعة التي تمنع البنات من إحياء ذكرى الأم ومتابعة الكتابة، تدفع البنات إلى التنصت من خلال هذه القبور المنيعة على أصوات شهرزاد والموءودة.

وحسب اعتقاد بعض منظري نظرية الصدمة trauma theory، مثل فرويد وكاروث، فإن عدم القدرة على العودة إلى النقطة المحددة التي حدثت فيها الصدمة يمنعنا من فهم الحقيقة التاريخية لها. فالصدمة، على حد قولهم، تجعل الحدث المسبب لها غائباً عن وعينا، فيستعصي على الذاكرة، ولا نستطيع استعادته بشكل كامل. وإذا كان هذا التحليل صحيحاً، فكيف تتمكن كاتباتنا من استعادة ما لا يُدرك وتمثيله في أدبهن؟ تكمن الإجابة عن هذا السؤال في مقولة كلود لنزمان Claude Lanzman، مخرج فيلم *Shoah* عن تجربة المحرقة وإبادة اليهود إبّان الحرب العالمية الثانية، حيث يؤكد أنه يمكننا أن نفتح أقفال الصدمات التاريخية المغلقة عن طريق رفض «إطار ثابت ووحيد نفهم من خلاله الصدمة. إن هذا الرفض يشكل بداية تجربة التنصت على التاريخ الإبداعية» (كما ورد في Caruth, *Trauma*، ص ١٥٤).

وباتباع هذه الطريقة فقط، يمكن للأماكن غير المطروقة من سير النساء أن تفتح نفسها لإدراكنا المعاصر حتى نفهم ما لم نكن نعرف كنهه عن ماهية الصدمة التاريخية في روايات الأديبات العربيات، وحتى تتمكن حفيدات شهرزاد والموءودات من تمثل ما في هذه الصدمة وإدراكها في رواياتهن الحديثة؛(٨) حيث يمكن أن يتجلى ماضي هذه الصدمات الأدبية والجسدية، بشكل كامل، في ذاكرتنا المعاصرة فقط، حين نسترجع – ونعيد – كتابة تجربة هذه الصدمات في أدبنا؛ لنغير واقع الموت وسيرته إلى سيرة حياة وبعث. إن سماعنا قصص شهرزاد الشفهية وصوت الموءودة المكتوم يشكلان البذرة التي ستُبنى حولها القصة المعاصرة لتجربة الكتابة لدى المرأة العربية. ويشكل إحياء تراث الأم الأدبي تجسيداً لكيانها الممحو، كما يقدم علاجاً لصدمة الوأد التي تتوارثها بناتها. إنها قصة بعث بعد الموت، وقصة كتابة أثرها بعد المحو الشفهي، وإعادة تأطيرها من أماكن المنفى المختلفة ومراكزه حتى تشمل كل الأصوات المنبوذة والمسحوقة. إنها يقظة/صحوة يجب أن تتوارث من جيل إلى آخر حتى تمحو، إلى الأبد، تاريخ تغييب أدب المرأة. وفي الحقيقة، كل أديباتنا يشعرن بالامتنان لأدب أمهاتهن اللواتي دفعنهن إلى إعادة كتابة تاريخ الصدمة حتى يتمكن من كتابة أنفسهن في مستقبل الأدب والأمة. وهكذا، فإننا حين نفتح هذه المساحات اللغوية والسردية في الأدب النسوي المهاجر، نفسح مساحة أكبر للعناصر الاجتماعية والقومية أيضاً. ولذلك، فإن هذه الروايات المهجرية لا تحرر الذات الأنثوية فقط، ولكنها تعد ببناء الأمة والمجتمع العربي من خلال دعوتها إلى إعادة النظر في

مفاهيم الهوية العربية والنظريات السياسية القومية السائدة من أجل تحرير الشخصية العربية العامة، رجلاً كانت أم امرأة، وإعادة بنائها بأسلوب تكافلي وشمولي جديد.

**الهوامش**

* أود أن أتوجه بجزيل الشكر للأستاذ مدحت كريدي، مدرس اللغة العربية في جامعة نيويورك، على تنقيحه لهذه المقالة. كما أشكر محكمي **ألف: مجلة البلاغة المقارنة** اللذين أسهمت تعليقاتهما النقدية في إثراء هذه المقالة.

(١) يشكل هذا البحث مقدمة عامة لموضوع كتابي الذي سينشر باللغة الإنجليزية في العام القادم بعنوان **قلق المحو: الصدمة وفن الكتابة والمهجر في السرد النسوي العربي**. ويتطرق الكتاب إلى دراسة مفصلة لبعض مؤلفات ثماني كاتبات عربيات (غادة السمان، وإيڤلين عقاد، وإيتل عدنان، وحميدة نعنع، وحنان الشيخ، وهدى بركات، وعالية ممدوح، ونوال السعداوي) ناهزت العشرين مؤلفاً أدبياً ما بين رواية وسير ومقابلات صحفية، كما شملت أنواعاً متعددة من الأدب القصصي منها: أدب السيرة الذاتية، والأسفار، والحرب، والخيال. وبالتالي، فإن معظم التنظير الذي أطرحه عن مفهوم صدمة الوأد والدور الذي يلعبه أدب شهرزاد الشفهي في مؤلفات أديبات المهجر المعاصرة يلقى تفنيداً وتوثيقاً مطولاً في كتابي. وبما أن المقالة الحالية لا تتسع لتعداد شامل لكل إثبات نصي يدعم نظرية قلق المحو، فلقد ارتأيت أن أدرج نماذج مقتضبة من هذه الإثباتات هنا، أما تفصيلها فسيجده القارئ في كتابي المنوه عنه.

(٢) غادة السمان، **القبيلة تستجوب القتيلة** ، ص ٣٣.

(٣) Na‘na'، ص ص ٩٩–١٠٠.

(٤) Malti-Douglas, *Men, Women, and God(s)*، ص ١.

(٥) راجع: Burton، ٥٨ –٦٠: ١٠. ولشرح مفصل ونقدي لهذا الفصل الأخير من الليالي، راجع Malti--Douglas, *Woman's Body, Woman's Word*، ص ص ٢٦–٢٨.

(٦) أما عن دور نساء العصر الڤيكتوري والقرن التاسع عشر بوصفهن ملائكة رحمة، فراجع Gilbert and Gubar، ص ص ٤٥–٩٢.

(٧) يوجد تشابه غريب بين اتهام صوت الموءودة لأبيها «لقد قتلتني يا أبتِ»، وبين ذكر فرويد لاتهامات مماثلة وجهها شبح صبي محترق لأبيه في المنام، حيث قال الولد: «ألا ترى أني أحترق يا أبتِ؟». وعند

تفسيره هذا الحلم، يربط فرويد تقنية الصدمة بنظريته عن الأحلام، فيراه وسيلة لتحقيق الرغبات؛ إذ يقول إن مجيء الطفل إلى أبيه في الحلم يدل على رغبة الأب في عدم موت الطفل، الذي كان قد مات نتيجة حريق اندلع بسبب اشتعال شمعة في غرفة نومه ذلك اليوم. ولكن جاك لاكان يؤكد في تحليله الحلم نفسه أن الطفل يريد إيقاظ الأب وتنبيهه إلى حادثة وفاته، ليلزمه بمسؤولية نقل مُلابساتِ هذه الصدمة/الكارثة إلى الآخرين حتى لا يحدث هذا في المستقبل لأي شخص آخر. راجع Caruth, *Unclaimed Experience*، ص ص ٩١–١١٢.

(٨) أدين بهذه الفكرة لليزا وولفورك وبحثها المماثل عن استرجاع صدمة العبودية لدى الكتاب الأمريكيين من أصل أفريقي. راجع *Embodying American Slavery*.

## المراجع العربية


السعداوي، نوال. **أوراقي..حياتي**. بيروت: دار الآداب، ٢٠٠٠.

———. **رحلاتي في العالم**. القاهرة: دار الهلال، ١٩٨٦.

السمان، غادة. **تسكع داخل جرح**. بيروت: منشورات غادة السمان، ١٩٨٨.

———. **الجسد حقيبة سفر**. بيروت: منشورات غادة السمان، ١٩٨٠.

———. **الرواية المستحيلة: فسيفساء دمشقية**. بيروت: منشورات غادة السمان، ١٩٩٧.

———. **شهوة الأجنحة**. بيروت: منشورات غادة السمان، ١٩٩٥.

———. **غربة تحت الصفر**. بيروت: منشورات غادة السمان، ١٩٨٦.

———. **القبيلة تستجوب القتيلة**. بيروت: منشورات غادة السمان، ١٩٨١.

———. **القمر المربع: قصص غرائبية**. بيروت: منشورات غادة السمان، ١٩٩٤.

الشيخ، حنان. **حكاية زهرة**. بيروت: دار الآداب، ٢٠٠٤.

القرطبي، محمد ابن أحمد. **مختار تفسير القرطبي: الجامع لأحكام القرآن**، جـ ٧ ( القاهرة: الهيئة المصرية العامة للكتاب، ١٩٧٧).

دي كابوا، باولا. **التمرد و الالتزام في أدب غادة السمان**. بيروت: دار الطليعة، ١٩٩٢.

فضل الله، مريم. «وأد البنات في العصر الجاهلي». **حواء** (١١ تشرين الثاني، ٢٠٠٠): <http://www.balagh.com/woman/trbiah/6f0z4e8h.htm>.

نعنع، حميدة. **الوطن في العينين**. بيروت: دار الآداب، ١٩٧٩.

# المراجع الإنجليزية


Accad, Evelyne. *The Excised.* Trans. David K. Bruner. Colorado Springs: Three Continents P, 1989.

___________. *Sexuality and War: Literary Masks of the Middle East.* NY: New York UP, 1990.

Adnan, Etel. *Sitt Marie Rose: A Novel.* Trans. Georgina Kleege. Sausalito: The Post-Apollo Press, 1982.

Al-Samman, Hanadi. *Anxiety of Erasure: Trauma, Authorship, and the Diaspora in Arab Women's Narrative.* Syracuse: Syracuse UP, forthcoming.

Bloom, Harold. *The Anxiety of Influence: A Theory of Poetry.* Oxford: Oxford UP, 1973.

Brown, Laura. "Not Outside the Range: One Feminist Perspective on Psychic Trauma." *Trauma: Explorations in Memory.* Ed. Cathy Caruth. Baltimore and London: The Johns Hopkins UP, 1995.

Burton, Richard F. *A Plain and Literal Translation of the Arabian Nights Entertainment, Now Entitled the Book of the Thousand Nights and a Night.* Benares [=Stoke Newington, UK]: n.p., 1885. 10 vols.

Caruth, Cathy, ed. *Trauma: Explorations in Memory.* Baltimore and London: The Johns Hopkins UP, 1995.

___________. *Unclaimed Experience: Trauma, Narrative, and History.* Baltimore and London: The Johns Hopkins UP, 1996.

Felman, Shoshana and Dori Laub. *Testimony: Crises of Witnessing in Literature, Psychoanalysis, and History.* NY: Routledge, 1992.

Freud, Sigmund. *Moses and Monotheism.* Trans. Katherine Jones. NY: Vintage Books, 1939.

Giladi, Avner. "Some Observations on Infanticide in Medieval Muslim Society." *International Journal of Middle East Studies* 22.2 (1990):185-200.

Gilbert, Sandra and Susan Gubar. *The Madwoman in the Attic: The Woman Writer and the Nineteenth-Century Literary Imagination.* New Haven: Yale UP, 1979.

Herman, Judith. *Trauma and Recovery.* NY: Basic Books, 1992.

Jung, Carl. *Two Essays on Analytical Psychology.* Vol. 7. Princeton: Princeton UP, 1966.

Kaplan, Caren. *Questions of Travel: Postmodern Discourses of Displacement.* Durham: Duke UP, 1996.

Kristeva, Julia. *The Kristeva Reader.* Ed. Toril Moi. NY: Columbia UP, 1986.

Malti-Douglas, Fedwa. *Men, Women, and God(s): Nawal El-Saadawi and Arab Feminist Poetics.* Berkeley: U of California P, 1995.

__________________. *Woman's Body, Woman's Word: Gender and Discourse in Arabo-Islamic Writing*. Princeton: Princeton UP, 1991.

Mernissi, Fatima. *Schererazade Goes West: Different Cultures, Different Harems*. NY: Washington Square P, 2001.

Na'na', Hamida. "Writing Away the Prison." *In the House of Silence: Autobiographical Essays by Arab Women Writers*. Ed. Fadia Faqir. Trans. Shirley Eber and Fadia Faqir. Reading: Garnet Publishing, 1998. 93-103.

Said, Edward W. *Representations of the Intellectual*. NY: Vintage Books, 1994.

El Saadawi, Nawal. *A Daughter of Isis: The Autobiography of Nawal El Saadawi*. Trans. Sherif Hetata. London and NY: Zed Books, 1999.

Stetkevych, Susanne Pinckney. *The Mute Immortals Speak: Pre-Islamic Poetry and the Poetics of Ritual*. Ithaca and London: Cornell UP, 1993.

Vees-Gulani, Susanne. *Trauma and Guilt: Literature of Wartime Bombing in Germany*. Berlin: Walter de Gruyter & Co. KG Publishers, 2003.

Woolfork, Lisa. *Embodying American Slavery in Contemporary Culture*. Illinois: U of Illinois P, 2008.

Žižek, Slavoj. *The Plague of Fantasies*. London: Verso, 1997.

# موت الذات:
# إرهاصاته في الشعر الحديث وتجلياته في الشعر المعاصر

عمرو الشريف

وهذا ليس إنسان
هذا وقت ضائع يتقاسمه المتفرجون
وحاصل جمع اللحظات التي يصرفها في كل مشهد
عمر مديد وحياة ميتة.

— جرجس شكري

تسعى هذه المقالة إلى استشراف العلاقة بين الذات الفردية، أو الفرد، والذات الجمعية، أو المجتمع، بما في ذلك السلطة، من خلال بعض النماذج الشعرية التي يمثل تسلسلها تطوراً في شكل هذه العلاقة، وكيفية تجلي هذه العلاقة الاجتماعية في الأشكال الشعرية والبلاغية المعبرة عنها. تظهر الصورة المثالية لهذه العلاقة على شكل علاقة عضوية، أي أن الذات الفردية جزء متجانس من الذات الجمعية، تتفق معها في الملامح والتوجهات العامة لها وتحيا من خلالها؛ إذ تعبر الذات الجمعية عن الذات الفردية بوصفها تجلياً أو تعبيراً عاماً عن مجموع الذوات الفردية. وتتمثل العلاقة بين الجزء والكل في أن الكل يعبر عن مجموع أجزائه. وبهذا، تحيا الذات الفردية في محيط يسمح لها بالتعبير عن نفسها، ولا يؤدي إلى اختزال فرديتها وقمعها. وتتفادى هذه الرؤيةُ الصورةَ الوجودية للعلاقة بين الفرد والمجتمع التي ترفض الرؤية الجدلية، وتؤكد أولوية وجود الإنسان بوصفه فرداً؛ وبالتالي يعدّ أي توافق بين الفرد والمجتمع فرضاً قسرياً من جهة المجتمع لشروطه على الفرد، ويكون الاغتراب هو النتيجة الحتمية لرؤية الوجوديين لتلك العلاقة؛ فالاغتراب عند الوجوديين وضع أنطولوجي لا فكاك منه، وليس وضعاً اجتماعياً يمكن فهمه وتفسيره.

أما الرؤية التي تعبر عن العلاقة الجدلية بين الفرد والمجتمع فهي الرؤية الهيجلية التي ترى المجتمع الإنساني وكل أنشطته تجلياً من تجليات الروح؛ أي أن الروح تظهر من خلال الأفراد وأنشطتهم الإبداعية. وعن طريق هذا التوافق بين الجزء والكل يصبح التناسق السمة المميزة

لهذه العلاقة، ويتجسد الكل في الجزء. وبدون تناسق الأجزاء، لا يمكن للكل أن يظهر؛ وبدون الكل لا تكتسب الأجزاء معناها. ولا تظهر هذه الصورة المتناسقة عند هيجل في العلاقة بين الذات الفردية والذات الجمعية فحسب، بل في كل أجزاء فلسفته، وبالأخص في الإستطيقا Aesthetics أو علم الجمال. ويؤكد جاك دريدا (١٩٣٠–٢٠٠٤) هذا المعنى قائلاً إن هيجل «وصف كلية الفلسفة، أي الجسد الموسوعي بأكمله، بأنه كائن حي، أو عمل فني».(١) أي أن العلاقة بين الجزء والكل، أو الروح، تبدي التناسق نفسه بين الجزء والكل الذي يعد محوراً شديد الأهمية في الفن. وفي حال حدوث هذا التناسق، يمكن وصف العمل الفني بالجمال. ولأن هيجل يرى أن التناسق بين الجزء والكل هو الصورة المثالية لكل من الفن والمجتمع، فقد «ربط بين جوهر الجمال وجوهر الفن».(٢) وقد لاحظ پول دي مان (١٩١٩–١٩٨٣) هذه العلاقة في فصل بعنوان «العلامة والرمز في إستطيقا هيجل» من كتابه **الإيديولوجيا الجمالية**، الذي تم نشره بعد موته بإشراف محرر، قائلاً إن «هيجل، إذن، هو منظِّر الرمز»،(٣) وإن «نظرية الجمال، بوصفها فكرة تاريخية وفلسفية، ترتكز عند هيجل على رؤية الفن بوصفه رمزياً».(٤) ويؤكد دي مان تلك الرابطة بين التناسق والتجسد، أو الجمال والرمز، قائلاً إن «الجمال رمزي».(٥) وذلك بالطبع لأن تجسد الكل في الجزء، أي الرمز، يعتمد التناسق بين الأجزاء – وهو الجمال – الذي يُظهر الكل.

إلا أن العلاقة بين الجزء والكل عند هيجل ليست إستطيقية بحتة، وإنما أنطولوجية، واجتماعية أيضاً. وتظهر هذه العلاقة، على المستوى الاجتماعي، على شكل العلاقة بين الذات الفردية والذات الجمعية، أو الفرد والمجتمع. غير أن تلك العلاقة الاجتماعية لا تتسم بالتناسق دوماً، ففي حال عدم ظهور هذا التناسق بصورة تلقائية، أي عندما لا يعبر المجتمع عن أفراده ولا يستطيع استيعاب مختلف من ينتمون إليه، يتم فرض مفهوم موحد على أفراد المجتمع الذين لا يتصفون بهذا التناسق. ولأن صورة المجتمع الموحدة لا تستطيع التعبير عن التنوع والاختلاف القائم بين أفراده، فإن هذا المفهوم الموحد يتم فرضه قسراً على الأفراد الفعليين الذين يحيون فيه؛ مما يؤدي إلى اغتراب هؤلاء الأفراد عن المجتمع. وليس الاغتراب وضعاً أنطولوجياً مسبقاً للذات لا يمكنها الفكاك منه، ولكنه نتاج محاولة فرض مفهوم موحد على أفراد متنوعين ومختلفين، كما أنه نتاج ظروف اجتماعية وسياسية وتاريخية محددة يمكن تحليلها والوقوف عليها. أما الذات الفردية المنعزلة عن الذات الجمعية فلا تعبر عن نفسها بالأطر الفنية نفسها التي تَنتُج عن الإحساس بالتناسق والانسجام، أي لا يمكن أن تعبر عن نفسها في شكل رمزي وفي إطار من

الجمال والتناسق. ولذلك، يظهر التشظي في الإبداع الفني لتلك الذات، وتبتعد عن إنتاج الجمال، كما أنها لا تنتج الرمز symbol المعبر عن علاقة تجسد الكل في الجزء، وإنما تنتج الأليغوريا allegory، الذي يعيد ابتعاد الدال أو المعنى المصرح به عن المدلول، أو المعنى المشار إليه، مما يعني إنتاج البعد نفسه الذي تستشعره الذات الفردية عن الذات الجمعية. أي أن الجزء المنفصل عن الكل لا ينتج الرمز أو تجسد الجزء في الكل، وإنما يُنتج انفصام الجزء عن الكل، أو الأليغوريا. وكذلك أيضاً فإن تشظي أجزاء العمل الفني يعيد إنتاج التنوع والاختلاف بين أفراد المجتمع الذي لا يستطيع المفهوم الموحد احتواءه أو دمجه. أي أن العلاقات الاجتماعية تعيد إنتاج نفسها داخل العمل الفني بأشكال مختلفة عن تلك التي أنتجتها الذات المتوحدة مع المجتمع.

وانتقالاً من المستوى الفلسفي إلى المستوى التاريخي، نجد أن ثورة يوليو في مصر قامت بإنهاء الحكم الملكي الخاضع للنزعات الاستعمارية الغربية؛ فبدأت بذلك حقبة جديدة اتسمت بالسعي نحو الحرية وبناء هوية قومية مضادة للسياسات التي كانت تسعى إلى احتواء موجات التحرر والمد القومي التي اجتاحت العالم في ذلك الوقت. وقد اتضحت ملامح الهوية الجديدة، في مختلف نواحي الثقافة والأدب، في العديد من الدول التي دخلت مرحلة ما بعد الاستعمار. وكانت إحدى السمات المميزة للأدب، في ذلك الوقت، الربط بين حرية الفرد وحرية الوطن. فالفرد يحصل على حريته الفردية التي كانت مكبلة قبل ذلك مع حصول الوطن بأكمله على تلك الحرية، إلا أن محاولة خلق هوية موحدة قوية تتمكن من مواجهة القوى الاستعمارية والمخاطر المحدقة بالديموقراطيات الوليدة الساعية نحو الحرية لم تكن يسيرة؛ نظراً لاستحالة جمع مختلف التوجهات السياسية والاجتماعية والفكرية في قالب واحد. إلا أن طبيعة النظم الثورية، وتوجسها الدائم من المخاطر التي تتهددها، كانت تحتم السيطرة التامة على أية محاولة للخروج عليها، أو حتى تكوين رأي مضاد لها. ومن هنا جاءت حتمية القضاء على أي فكر مختلف. وهكذا، تحولت الرغبة الساعية إلى الحرية، عبر جدل سلبي، إلى نقيضها، أي إلى عملية من السيطرة على كل الآراء ومحو أية توجهات مختلفة في سبيل بناء ذات موحدة قوية. وهكذا، تحوّل السعي نحو الحرية إلى قمع الاختلاف. ولم يظهر هذا الاختلاف في المراحل الأولى، ولكنه ظل قابعاً تحت مفهوم الهوية الموحدة. ولذلك كان الوعي الجديد وعياً قومياً تحررياً يؤمن بالعدالة الاجتماعية، ويسعى إلى تحقيقها، كما يسعى إلى تأكيد هويته العربية عن طريق ربط حاضره بالتراث العربي، برمته، بوصفه جزءاً من الذات الكلية. وهكذا، ظلت الذات الفردية مختزلة في الذات الجماعية.

يتعرض الوعي الجمعي، أيضاً، لصدمات عنيفة، ويكون تأثير تلك الصدمات أكثر عمقاً، وأبقى أثراً، كلما كانت غير متوقعة من الوعي الجمعي. وفي إطار خلق الهوية الساعية نحو الحرية، لم يكن الوعي الجمعي مجهزاً لاستقبال الهزائم. ولذلك كانت هزيمة يونيو من أسوأ تلك الصدمات التي تعرضت لها الذات الجمعية. وكان من آثارها إصابة تلك الذات الساعية إلى التحرر والعدالة الاجتماعية بصدمة عنيفة دمّرت المشروع القومي وطموحاته المستقبلية.

وبتدمير ذلك المشروع التحرري – ذي الجانب السلطوي – لم يعد هناك سبب يدعو إلى اختزال الاختلاف في الذات الجمعية الموحدة. ومن هنا، جاء الإحساس بتشظي الوحدة والانقسام بين الفرد والإطار الفكري العام. وحيث إن ذلك الإطار الفكري العام كان يمثل جزءاً من الوعي الفردي، فإن هذا الانقسام يظهر على شكل الثورة على المجموع أحياناً، وعلى شكل حالة من الفصام بين الفرد وذاته أحياناً أخرى. وقد اتخذت عوامل ذلك الانقسام عدة أشكال منها الثورة على حالة الضعف والوهن التي أصابت الذات الجمعية، ومنها انقسام الذات المتحدثة عند بعض الشعراء، ومنها أيضاً شكل الثورة على بعض مكونات تلك الذات الجمعية كالتراث. ومن هنا، يأتي استخدام العديد من الشعراء لعناصر التراث العربي القديم بشكل مناقض لمعناه، واختيار عناصر من هذا التراث تتضمن في معناها الثورة عليه. ولا يمكن، بالطبع، نسبة كل هذه الظواهر الثقافية إلى سبب واحد، أو تفسيرها بأنها استجابة لحالة اجتماعية محددة؛ فأيما كان تأثير العوامل الاقتصادية أو الاجتماعية، فلا يمكن رد كل الظواهر الثقافية إلى عامل سياسي أو اقتصادي واحد. ولكن يمكن النظر إليها بوصفها مظاهر عديدة تظهر في مناخ ثقافي واجتماعي عام يتخلل هذه الظواهر، وتعبر هي عن عوامل عديدة فيه.

تتبدى أولى مظاهر انقسام الوعي في انشطار الذات المتحدثة في شعر أمل دنقل(٦) ونزار قباني؛(٧) وهذا الانشطار يعني انفصال الذات الفردية عن المكون الجمعي فيها. ويعد تلك الإرهاصات المتمثلة في انفصال الذات الفردية عن الذات الكلية، تظهر آخر مراحل تطور هذا الانقسام في الوعي في ظاهرة موت الذات التي تتجلى في شعر جيل جديد من الشعراء الشبان مثل جرجس شكري(٨) وتامر فتحي.(٩) ولا يعني ذلك أن تلك الظواهر تنحصر في شعر هؤلاء الشعراء وحسب، أو أن كلاً منهم يُظهر أحدها دون الآخر؛ بل على العكس من ذلك فإنها تظهر في كتابات شعراء آخرين، وفي أشكال فنية أخرى غير الشعر. تظهر أول عناصر الانقسام في الشكل الشعري الذي ظهر به الشعر الحديث حيث كُتب معظمه في شكل القصيدة الحرة بعيداً عن السطر الشعري التقليدي الملتزم بطول محدد وعدد تفعيلات ثابت وقافية موحدة. فالذات المغتربة عن الثقافة الجمعية تبدأ في الابتعاد عن القالب التقليدي للثقافة الجمعية.

## انقسام الذات في الشعر الحديث

تحولت النزعة التحررية في الخمسينيات، بسبب رغبتها في القضاء على أية معارضة حتى تتمكن من تكوين ذات جمعية موحدة تؤهلها للوصول إلى التخلص من السيطرة الخارجية وإقامة حالة من العدالة الاجتماعية، إلى قمع لأي صوت مختلف عن محددات تلك الذات الجمعية. وبذلك استحال النقيض إلى نقيضه، وصارت الحرية قمعاً والأمل إحباطاً ويأساً. ويعبّر أمل دنقل في قصيدته «البكاء بين يدي زرقاء اليمامة» عن هذه الثنائية بين الذات الفردية التي تستنجد بزرقاء اليمامة تسألها الحقيقة التي طالما استشعرتها تلك الذات، ولكنها أبت إلا أن تسير في إطار المجموع:

أيتها النبية المقدسة..
لا تسكتي.. فقد سكتُ سنة بعد سنة
لكي أنال فضل الأمان
قيل لي «اخرس..»
فخرست.. وعميت.. وائتممت بالخصيان!
ظللت في عبيد عبس أحرس القطعان
أجتز صوفها..
أرد نوقها..
أنام في حظائر النسيان
طعامي: الكسرة.. والماء.. وبعض التمرات اليابسة
وها أنا في ساعة الطعان
ساعة أن تخاذل الكماة.. والرماة.. والفرسان
دعيت للميدان!
أنا الذي ما ذقت لحم الضأن
أنا الذي أقصيت عن مجالس الفتيان
أدعى إلى الموت.. ولم أدع إلى المجالسة!!(١٠)

ينطوي شعر دنقل هنا على ثنائية مطمورة بين الفرد المقهور المأمور بالصمت، الذي يتوجب عليه طاعة أوامر سادته والقانون القبلي الصارم الذي لا يقيم وزناً للفرد، ويعطي شيوخ القبيلة الهيمنة والسيطرة. ويتناسب السياق القبلي هنا مع فكرة السيطرة الاجتماعية؛ وبخاصة أن مفهوم الفرد نفسه مفهوم حديث لم يكن معروفاً في المجتمعات البدائية التي كان الفرد فيها جزءاً من كل ولا كيان له بمفرده. وتتضاعف تلك السيطرة عندما توصف العلاقة بأنها علاقة العبد بالسيد الذي لا يتم ذكره، إلا أن هذا العبد الذي ارتضى من العيش بأقل القليل وأنكر ذاته، هذا المهمش الذي أقصي

عن مجالس الفتيان هو نفسه الذي دُعي إلى الميدان. غير أن هذا السياق القبلي لا يسعى، بالطبع، إلى تأكيد تلك العلاقة، بل على العكس من ذلك؛ فاختيار قصة زرقاء اليمامة بصورة خاصة يسعى إلى تقويض سلطة ذلك النسق القبلي. وذلك بالإشارة إلى تلك المرأة التي استطاعت أن ترى بعينيها ما لم تره أعين كل رجال القبيلة، مما يجعلها في موقع الفرد في مواجهة المجموع. وبذلك، كان هذا الفرد المهمش – في صورة المرأة في مجتمع ذكوري – في وضع يماثل العبد الذي يأتمر بأمر السادة، والفرد الذي يسير في ركاب المجموع. هذا الفرد المهمش هو وحده على صواب بينما القبيلة كلها مخطئة. الفرد قادر على رؤية المستقبل، بينما تنكر الذات الجمعية كلها تلك الرؤية الفردية الصادقة. وهنا تتضح العلاقة بين الفرد المأمور بالصمت وبين الذات الجمعية التي تفرض هذا الصمت وتختزل الفرد، وهنا يكتسب التاريخ المؤرخة به تلك القصيدة (١٦/٦/١٩٦٧) أهمية خاصة. فقد أدت الهزيمة (في حرب الستة أيام، ٥–١٠/٦/١٩٦٧) إلى تحطيم الرؤية الجماعية وبيان صدق الرؤية الفردية؛ فالفرد يؤكد أن إرغامه على الصمت – «اخرس» – وعدم تصديق المجتمع لرؤيته الفردية، تماماً كما رفضت القبلية رؤية الزرقاء، لم تفد وإنما انتهت إلى الكارثة.

ثم تأتي الهزيمة كالضربة التي تقسم أية وحدة بين الذات الفردية والذات الجماعية، فيكتشف الفرد أن صمته لم يجد، وأن اختزال فرديته كان خطأً. وبذلك، تنقسم الذات الجمعية في النص الشعري إلى «نحن» و«هم» مضمرين في صورة ضمير فاعل وضمير مفعول ملحقين في «قلت لهم» و«قايضوا بنا»:

أيتها العرافة المقدسة..
ماذا تفيد الكلمات البائسة؟
قلت لهم ما قلت عن قوافل الغبار..
فاتهموا عينيك، يا زرقاء، بالبوار!
قلت لهم ما قلت عن مسيرة الأشجار..
فاستضحكوا من وهمك الثرثار!
وحين فوجئوا بحد السيف: قايضوا بنا..
والتمسوا النجاة والفرار!
ونحن جرحى القلب
جرحى الروح والفم
لم يبق إلا الموتُ
والحطامُ..
والدمار..(١١)

تنقسم الأنا، أو الذات، التي كانت موحدة إلى «نحن جرحي القلب» التي تظهر أول ما تظهر في شبه جملة من جار ومجرور في موقع مفعول به لا فاعل، موقع ضعف لا قوة. وتنقسم الأنا، أيضاً، إلى فاعل في صورة هؤلاء الذين رفضوا تصديق نبوءة الفرد بالخطر المحيق، ولذلك «فوجئوا» بالخطر، ثم «قايضوا» بالفرد كي يلتمسوا النجاة. وتركوه للجرذان: «فالجرذان../تلعق من دمي حساءها.. ولا أردها!».(١٢) يزداد هذا الشعور الأولى بالانقسام بين الفرد والذات الجمعية (وعبره يسقط التوافق الهيجلي بين الجزء والكل) حتى يصير شرخاً يفصل الأفراد كلهم عن الصورة المرسومة لهم، أو عن تلك الذات التي تم اختزالها في صورة «قيصر»، أو «السلطان»، أو أي دال على السلطة.

ويظهر هذا الشرخ واضحاً جلياً في قصيدة «تعليق على ما حدث» المؤرخة ١٩٧٠:

قلت لكم مراراً
إن الطوابير التي تمر
في استعراض عيد الفطر والجلاء
(فتهتف النساء في النوافذ انبهاراً)
لا تصنع انتصاراً
إن المدافع التي تصطف على الحدود، في الصحاري
لا تطلق النيران.. إلا حين تستدير للوراء
إن الرصاصة التي ندفع فيها.. ثمن الكسرة والدواء:
لا تقتل الأعداء
لكنها تقتلنا.. إذا رفعنا صوتنا جهاراً
تقتلنا أو تقتل الصغارا!(١٣)

وهنا يبدو الانقسام الذي كان مضمراً في صورة ضمير مفعول معلناً في صورة الرصاصة التي «ندفع» ثمنها إلا أنها «لا تقتل الأعداء/لكنها تقتلنا» وصورة المدافع التي «لا تطلق النيران . . . إلا حين تستدير للوراء». والتناقض الواضح الذي تحمله كل من هاتين الصورتين الشعريتين في داخلهما هو التناقض نفسه في الذات الفردية؛ فالعلاقة بين الذات الفردية والذات الجمعية لا يجب أن ينظر إليها على أنها علاقة ضدين، بل هي علاقة جدلية تدخل فيها الذات الجمعية في تركيب الذات الفردية، أي أنها جزء منها، ومن ناحية أخرى، فإن الذات المفردة هي التي تكشف عن ملامح الذات الجمعية. وهكذا، حين تثور الذات الفردية ضد الذات الجمعية فليست ثورتها مجرد رفض شيء خارج عنها، وإنما هو انقسام بداخلها

يحمل آثاراً من خارج الذات الفردية، والعلامة المميزة لهذا الانقسام الداخلي أو الفصام هي المفارقة التي تظهر بوضوح في شعر أمل دنقل، وبصفة خاصة في قصائد **العهد الآتي**.

لا يظهر هذا الانقسام في شعر أمل دنقل وحسب، وإنما يظهر أيضاً في شعر نزار قباني. ويتجلى في أوضح صورة في مرثيته «بلقيس» التي يبدأها بمفارقة واضحة يشكر بها من تسببوا في قتل زوجته:

شكراً لكم..
شكراً لكم..
فحبيبتي قتلت.. وصار بوسعكم
أن تشربوا كأساً على قبر الشهيدة
وقصيدتي اغتيلت..
وهل من أمة في الأرض..
– إلا نحن – تغتال القصيدة؟(١٤)

للوهلة الأولى، تبدو تلك المفارقة مجرد سخرية لفظية؛ فالانقسام خارجي بين الشاعر – أي الذات الفردية – والأمة – أي الذات الجمعية أو وحدة الروح المتمثلة في هذه الأمة. إلا أن تتبع القصيدة يظهر هذا الانقسام على أنه تناقض في داخل الذات نفسها، ويدفع السخرية من المستوى اللفظي إلى مستوى الحدث الذي يناقض نفسه، حيث الجزء مواجهاً، لا منخرطاً في الكل كما في النسق الهيجلي. أي أن السخرية بمختلف مستوياتها تنبع من التناقض بين الشيء وذاته، أو الفرد ونفسه، أو النواحي الفردية في الذات والنواحي التي تمتد بجذورها إلى الذات الجمعية. والمفارقة هي من أصلح الأشكال البلاغية تعبيراً عن هذا التناقض؛ إذ إن التناقض بين الدال والمدلول، أو المعنى المصرح به والمقصود هو جوهر المفارقة ذاتها. وتكشف القراءة المتأنية لقصيدة «بلقيس» عن اتساع هذا التناقض ليشمل العديد من الثنائيات التي تنتظم لتشكل فيما بينها علاقات ضدية بين عناصر كثيرة يكتسب بعضها القيمة الإيجابية، ويكتسب البعض الآخر القيمة السلبية تبعاً لعلاقته بالثنائية الأساسية بين الفرد والمجموع. وتنتشر تلك الثنائيات في شعر نزار قباني كله حتى أن التعرف على قيمتها السلبية والإيجابية يكاد يكون مفتاح قصائده كلها.

يحاول نزار قباني في «بلقيس» التوحيد بين القصيدة وموضوعها، أي بين القصيدة بوصفها نتاجاً فنياً وبين بلقيس التي ترثيها القصيدة. فكما اغتيلت بلقيس تُغتال القصيدة. والقاتل في الحالتين هو الوعي الجمعي والسلطة اللذان يمارسان القهر على الإبداع

أو الأفراد. أما الشاعر الذي لا يقدر على استيعاب موت زوجته فيحاول استحضارها والإبقاء على وجودها في القصيدة؛ فألمه وحزنه لفراق زوجته ومحبوبته يتجسد في القصيدة. وبذلك يحاول قباني الارتفاع بقصيدته من مستوى اللغة إلى مستوى الوجود الذي تسعى اللغة إلى التعبير عنه: «بلقيس.. يا وجعي../ويا وجع القصيدة حين تلمسها الأنامل».(١٥) يتجسد ألم الشاعر لفراق زوجته في القصيدة، وبذلك تصير القصيدة هي الألم نفسه، الألم الذي تسببت فيه بلقيس، وهكذا تسكن بلقيس، المتسببة في الألم، القصيدة التي هي تجسيد الألم. وإذا كانت بلقيس قد رحلت فإن وظيفة المرثية أن تبقي ذكرها، أي أن تبقي على أثر منها. ويؤكد نزار قباني تلك العلاقة بين بلقيس والشعر أكثر من مرة:

إن الذين تورطوا في القتل كان مرادهم
أن يقتلوا كلماتي!!
نامي بحفظ الله.. أيتها الجميلة
فالشعر بعدك مستحيل.(١٦)

ويؤكد، أيضاً، هذا التماهي بين القصيدة وموضوعها بين المرثية ومن ترثيها: «قتلوك في بيروت مثل أي غزالة/من بعد ما.. قتلوا الكلام..»(١٧) والإصرار على تلك المقاربة بين بلقيس والكتابة واللغة، أو الشعر، واضح وبخاصة في قوله «هل تعرفون حبيبتي بلقيس؟/فهي أهم ما كتبوه في كتب الغرام».(١٨) ويؤكد نزار قباني هذا المعنى صراحة قائلاً: «بلقيس/أيتها الشهيدة.. والقصيدة..»،(١٩) وكذلك حين يلقبها بالأيقونة؛(٢٠) فالأيقونة لا تعد مجرد تصوير كينونة مقدسة، وإنما هي تجسيد لها، أي أن الكينونة حالَّةٌ في التصوير أو التجسيد. ولكن القصيدة في الواقع هي التي تسعى إلى احتلال مكانة الأيقونة التي تتجسد فيها بلقيس، وتغدو محاولة لاستحضار وجودها الذي مازال الشاعر يستشعره:

ولا أدري أنا.. ماذا أقول؟
هل تقرعين الباب بعد دقائق؟
هل تخلعين المعطف الشتوي؟
هل تأتين باسمة..
وناضرة..
ومشرقة كأزهار الحقول؟
بلقيس..
إن زروعك الخضراء..

ما زالت على الحيطان باكية..
ووجهك لم يزل متنقلاً..
بين المرايا والستائر..
حتى سيجارتك التي أشعلتها..
لم تنطفئ..
ودخانها
ما زال يرفض أن يسافر(٢١)

فالسيجارة التي أشعلتها ولم تنطفئ بعد، والدخان الذي لم يرحل بعد، كلها أفعال أتتها بلقيس ولم تنته آثارها، وتوقع الشاعر حضورها في أية لحظة، وانتظاره أفعالها، كأن تقرع الباب وتخلع المعطف، كلها محاولات للإبقاء عليها على المستوى الشعري. وهكذا تصير القصيدة محاولة لاستحضار بلقيس والإبقاء على وجودها في حال غيابها بتوحيدهما. وهكذا أيضاً، فإن بلقيس، الزوجة الراحلة، تتوحد مع «بلقيس» القصيدة باللغة والكتابة، إلا أن حضور بلقيس السابق – حضورها الطبيعي المفتقد الآن – لا بد وأن يتغلب على ورطة «اللغة المحالة»، اللغة التي تشير إلى المعنى، ويتجسد في اللغة التي تمتلك القدرة على التجسيد والاستحضار. ولأن القدرة على استحضار الشيء والكشف عنه تعد من أهم وظائف الشعر، إن لم تكن أهمها على الإطلاق، يصير الشعر الوسيلة الملائمة لاستحضار الغائبة، بلقيس:

والشعر.. يسأل عن قصيدته
التي لم تستكمل كلماتها..
ولا أحد.. يجيب عن السؤال
الحزن يا بلقيس..
يعصر مهجتي كالبرتقالة..
الآن.. أعرف مأزق الكلمات
أعرف ورطة اللغة المحالة..
وأنا الذي اخترع الرسائل
لست أدري.. كيف أبتدئ الرسالة..
السيف يدخل لحم خاصرتي
وخاصرة العبارة..
كل الحضارة أنت يا بلقيس والأنثى حضارة..
بلقيس: أنت بشارتي الكبرى..
فمن سرق البشارة؟
أنت الكتابة قبلما كانت كتابة..(٢٢)

اللغة التي تحاول، بطبيعتها، إنتاج المعنى عن طريق الإشارة تحاول التغلب على طبيعتها، وأن تستحضر المشار إليه، أو حتى الوصول إليه، فيتم توحيد بلقيس والكتابة: فهي «الكتابة قبلما كانت كتابة». وتكون وظيفة الكتابة الثانية، أي القصيدة، استحضار الكتابة الأولى، أي بلقيس، أو التوحد معها عن طريق الصورة التي انتشرت في الآداب الأوروبية في العصور الوسطى، وكذلك في الفكر الصوفي، حيث هيمن فيهما الاعتقاد بأن الطبيعة هي كتاب الله ونتاج لغة الخلق. وتصير اللغة جسداً. فالسيف الذي «يدخل لحم خاصرتي» يدخل، أيضاً، «خاصرة العبارة». يصير مقتل بلقيس قتلاً للكلمات؛ فالشعر صار بعدها «مستحيلاً». ويكون المخرج الوحيد من استحالة الشعر، تبعاً لهذا المنطق، كتابة شعر يستحضر بلقيس في صورة مرثية لها.

وهكذا، يتم الربط بين بلقيس واللغة والكتابة والشعر والقصيدة والعديد من المحاور الأخرى التي تكتسب في شعر نزار قباني صورة إيجابية، وبالتالي يكتسب نقيضها صورة سلبية. ويتم ربط تلك النقائض بالذات الجمعية. أي إن الذات الفردية المحطمة هي التي تكتسب الصورة الإيجابية، بينما تكتسب الذات الجمعية كل الصفات السلبية بوصفها السبب في تحطيم تلك الذات الفردية. ولا يمثل هذا التعارض بين الإيجابي والسلبي تناقضاً إلا عندما تتمحور هذه المتعارضات حول عنصر واحد؛ ألا وهو العلاقة بين الذات الفردية والذات الجمعية. عندئذ، يبدأ الانقسام على الذات، والظاهرة البلاغية المصاحبة له وهي المفارقة، في الظهور. ترتبط بلقيس في شعر نزار قباني بالطبيعة، فقد:

كانت أطول النخلات في أرض العراق
كانت إذ تمشي
ترافقها طواويس
وتتبعها أيائل(٢٣)

وهي كذلك «نينوى الخضراء» و«أمواج دجلة»، وهي «مشرقة» كأزهار الحقول و«أصوات البلابل»، وهكذا فإن الطبيعة البكر الطاهرة التي لم يطرأ عليها أي تغيير تصبح قرينة بلقيس. وفي مقابل ذلك تأتي القبيلة بكناياتها السلبية:

أي أمة عربية..
تلك التي
تغتال أصوات البلابل؟
أين السموأل
والمهلهل؟

والغطاريف الأوائل؟
فقبائل قتلت قبائل..
وثعالب قتلت ثعالب..
وعناكب قتلت عناكب..
قسماً بعينيك اللتين إليها
تأوي ملايين الكواكب..
سأقول، يا قمري، عن العرب العجائب(٢٤)

وهنا يرغي نزار قباني ويزبد بحروف وبأصوات كقعقعة المعارك مهدداً بكشف الكذبة، وفضح الانقسام بين الفضائل التي تنسبها الذات العربية إلى نفسها والسلبيات التي يراها نزار قباني. وهنا، يظهر تضاد آخر بين الطبيعة والتاريخ، وهو أحد التناقضات القديمة في تاريخ الفلسفة:

ها نحن.. يا بلقيس..
ندخل مرة أخرى لعصر الجاهلية
ندخل في التوحش..
والتخلف.. والبشاعة.. والوضاعة..
ندخل مرة أخرى.. عصور البربرية..
حيث الكتابة رحلة
بين الشظية.. والشظية..
حيث اغتيال فراشة في حقلها..
صار القضية.(٢٥)

فاغتيال بلقيس المتوحدة مع الطبيعة يقف في تناقض مع البطولات الكاذبة التي سجلها التاريخ:

بلقيس:
إن هم فجروك.. فعندنا
كل الجنائز تبتدئ في كربلاء..
وتنتهي في كربلاء..
لن أقرأ التاريخ بعد اليوم
إن أصابعي اشتعلت..
وأثوابي تغطيها الدماء..
ها نحن ندخل عصرنا الحجري..
نرجع كل يوم، ألف عام للوراء.(٢٦)

وهكذا، يكتسب التاريخ - الذي يسجل قصة الذات - كناية سلبية في مواجهة الطبيعة. وتكتسب الحضارة صفة إيجابية - «كل الحضارة أنت يا بلقيس والأنثى حضارة» - في مواجهة «عصر الجاهلية» و«العصور البربرية». وتكتسب البشارة والنبوة صفات إيجابية - «بلقيس: أنت بشارتي الكبرى../فمن سرق البشارة؟» - في مواجهة الأعراب الذي وصفهم القرآن الكريم في سورة التوبة، الآية ٩٧ بأنهم «أشد كفرًا ونفاقًا» - «وسيعرف الأعراب يوماً../أنهم قتلوا الرسولة..»، وكذلك أيضاً في مواجهة الزمان العربي:

إن زماننا العربي مختص بذبح الياسمين
وبقتل كل الأنبياء..
وقتل كل المرسلين..
حتى العيون الخضر..
يأكلها العرب..(٢٧)

وترتبط بلقيس، كذلك، بمفردات الطهر والنقاء فهي «المطهرة النقية»، بينما يرتبط التاريخ العربي بمفردات العهر:

سأقول في التحقيق:
كيف غزالتي ماتت بسيف أبي لهب
كل اللصوص من الخليج إلى المحيط
يدمرون.. ويحرقون..
وينهبون.. ويرتشون..
ويعتدون على النساء..
كما يريد أبو لهب..
كل الكلاب موظفون..
ويأكلون..
ويسكرون..
على حساب أبي لهب..
لا قمحة في الأرض
تنبت دون رأي أبي لهب
لا طفل يولد عندنا
إلا وزارت أمه يوماً..
فراش أبي لهب!!(٢٨)

وهكذا ترتبط بلقيس بالطبيعة في مواجهة العرب الذين يرتبطون بالتاريخ، وبالحضارة في مواجهة البربرية، وبالنبوءة في مواجهة قتلة الأنبياء، وبالقصيدة في مواجهة من يغتالون القصيدة ويقتلون الكلمات، وبالطهر في مواجهة العهر، وهي الفرس الجميل في مواجهة «بلاد يقتلون بها الخيول»، وهي الغزالة التي «ماتت بسيف أبي لهب». وفي كل هذه الثنائيات المتضادة يظهر الانفصال التام بين الذات الفردية والذات الجماعية، إلا أن نزار قباني يدرك جيداً أن معضلته مرجعها أنه عربي، بينما يرى أن «جميع أشياء الجمال../جميعها.. ضد العرب..»، ولهذا يتساءل: «فكّرتُ: هل قتل النساء هواية عربية/أم أننا في الأصل محترفو جريمة؟».(٢٩) وهو، هنا، يسائل الذات الجمعية الظاهرة في ضمير الفاعل «أننا»؛ إلا أن تلك الذات الجمعية تضم أيضاً «أنا» مضمرة فيها. وهنا يبدأ الانقسام على الذات حين يخاطب بلقيس قائلاً:

إن قضاءنا العربي أن يغتالنا عرب..
ويأكل لحمنا عرب..
ويبقر بطننا عرب
فكيف نفر من هذا القضاء؟(٣٠)

وهكذا، تنقسم الذات على نفسها وتنقلب على ذاتها، وبالتالي يزداد اغتراب الذات الفردية عن الذات الجمعية، وتبدأ في رفضها بكل ما تمثله وما ينتسب إليها، وتحاول أن تكشف تناقضاتها:

سأقول في التحقيق:
إن اللص أصبح يرتدي ثوب المقاتل
وأقول في التحقيق:
إن القائد الموهوب أصبح كالمقاول.(٣١)

وحين يصير الوضع زائفاً متناقضاً مع ما يجب أن يكون عليه، يصبح: «هذا هو التاريخ.. يا بلقيس../كيف يفرق الإنسان../ما بين الحدائق والمزابل؟».(٣٢) وهكذا، تنقلب القيم إلى أضدادها، وتسود النزعة الساخرة المتشككة في كل القيم: «أقول: إن عفافنا عهر../وتقوانا قذارة../وأقول: إن نضالنا كذب..»،(٣٣) ينتشر ذلك الإحساس بالتناقض في شعر نزار قباني بكثرة، وخاصة في «هوامش على دفتر النكسة». وهنا، تدرك الذات الفردية تناقض الذات الجمعية مع الصورة التي تقدمها عن نفسها.

وهكذا يظهر تمرد الذات الفردية على الكل الذي تنتمي إليه، وبالتالي على نفسها، بوصفها منتمية إلى تلك الذات الجماعية في أشكال مختلفة وعلى مستويات متعددة؛ فعلى المستوى النحوي تظهر في صورة انقسام الأنا الموحدة، وعلى المستوى البلاغي تظهر في صورة المفارقة أو التناقض بين المعنى والدال، وعلى المستوى البنيوي في شكل استقطاب كل مكونات الذات إلى محورين، يرتبط أحدهما بالذات الفردية ويتميز بالإيجابية والآخر بالذات الجمعية ويتميز بالسلبية، ثم تختلط القيم السلبية والإيجابية عند اعتراف الذات الفردية بانتمائها، بشكل من الأشكال، إلى الذات الجماعية. وكذلك، على مستوى المفردات الشعرية؛ فالمرأة التي – من خلال الصورة التقليدية – تبيع نفسها وتتحول إلى عاهرة تنفصل عن ذاتها، والرجل الذي فقد ذكورته – كما يقول أمل دنقل: «ائتممت بالخصيان» – هو أيضاً رجل منفصل عن جوهره أو عن ذاته.

## موت الذات في الشعر المعاصر

تزداد ظاهرة انقسام الذات في الشعر الحديث حتى تصل إلى موتها التام في بعض كتابات الشعراء المعاصرين؛ فالعلاقة بين الذات الفردية والذات الجمعية ليست علاقة مواجهة بين نقيضين يقف كل منهما في مواجهة الآخر. الذات الجمعية مكون أساسي من مكونات الذات الفردية، وحين تنشق الذات الفردية على الذات الجمعية فإنها تنشق على نفسها. وحين تتحول الذات الجمعية، التي تعد أحد محددات أهداف الذات الفردية وكينونتها، إلى أداة لقمعها وتثور الأخيرة عليها، فإن الذات الفردية التي تطمح إلى نيل حريتها تنتهي، عبر جدل سلبي آخر، إلى ذات فاقدة للهوية والاتجاه. وتستشعر تلك الذات ضياعها. ويتجلى ذلك الضياع، صريحاً، في صورة تلك الذات في شعر العديد من الشعراء الشباب مثل جرجس شكري وتامر فتحي.

يظهر موت تلك الذات في شعر هؤلاء الشعراء على شكل التشيؤ بالمعنى الحرفي للكلمة، فالذات تتحول إلى شيء في شعرهم. تتحول الذات إلى قطعة من الملابس، مثلاً، في شعر تامر فتحي، أو إلى مطرقة أو سكين في شعر جرجس شكري. تبدو تلك التحولات في ظاهر الأمر وكأنها رمز، إلا أن تتبع هذه الأشكال من التعبير يظهر عكس ذلك تماماً. فالرمز جوهرُه الحياة، ويلعب الرمز بهذا المعنى دوراً شديد الأهمية في العلاقة بين الذات والعالم كما أكد پول دي مان، فهو لا يلغي التعارض القائم بينهما وإنما يوحدهما. فالعالم الخارج عن الذات، المختلف عنها، يصير تجسيداً للمعنى الذي تراه الذات فيه. وهذا المعنى لا يتم إضفاؤه على الرمز عشوائياً، وإنما

هو كامن فيه؛ أي أن الرمز هو رفع التعارض بين الذات والعالم، وهو بذلك نتاج جدل إيجابي. وذلك يفسر الوضع المتميز الذي يحتله الرمز في فلسفة هيجل؛ فهو، وإن كان لا يمنحه ذلك الاسم، يدرس الفن بأكمله عن طريق تتبع العلاقة بين الشكل والمضمون أو تجسد المضمون في الشكل، أي الرمز. وهنا، يتحتم إدراك الاختلاف بين مجرد الإشارة أو الدلالة على نحو ما هو حاصل في العلامة اللغوية أو العلامة الإشارية التقليدية وعلاقة التجسيد التي يعتمدها الرمز؛ فالعلاقة في حالة الدلالة تقليدية اعتباطية، أما العلاقة في حالة الرمز فهي علاقة تعتمد التشابه أو الكمون.

يعد الرمز نتاج إحساس الشاعر بمعنى متعال متجسد في شيء، وهو بذلك يضفي حياة على الأشياء. ويفترض الرمز، بذلك، أولوية المعاني المتعالية على الأشياء والتوافق بين داخل الإنسان وخارجه كما أكد پول دي مان في فصل «العلامة والرمز في جماليات هيجل». وبذلك، فإن الرمز أيضاً تعبير عن العلاقة العضوية بين الذات الفردية والذات الجمعية؛ فالذات الفردية التي تشعر بانتمائها إلى الذات الجمعية تعبر عن نفسها في شكل الرمز. ويظهر ذلك، مثلاً، في شكل تجسيد معنى ما في قصة من التراث مثلاً. أما استخدام هذه القصص بشكل مناف لمعناها الأصلي، كما يظهر في شعر أمل دنقل وقصيدة «رتل سورة النسف على رأس الوثن» للشاعر العراقي أحمد مطر، فهو تعبير الذات المنفصلة عن الذات الجمعية؛ أي أن الرمز نتاج علاقة عضوية. وهذا، بالضبط، ما يفرق بين هذه الممارسات الشعرية المعاصرة والرمزية التي عدّها بعض النقاد من المنتمين إليها؛ فبينما تعتمد الرمزية حياة الذات، تنبع تلك الأشكال الشعرية من موتها.

نشر تامر فتحي ديوانه الشعري الأول بعنوان **بالأمس فقدت زراً: قصة الملابس** عام ٢٠٠٥. ويقدم الديوان قصة حياة الإنسان منذ ميلاده حتى موته عن طريق استعارة واحدة هي الملابس. يكتب تامر فتحي في «عندما كانت الملابس صغيرة»:

كانت لشفرة المقص برودتها
وهي تمنحني جسدي
(غالباً ما نمنح الأجساد كي ندرك الوجع)
فليكن لك هذا الوجه
وهذا الاسم
وهذه العلامة أعلى الظهر
عليها مقاسك
وتعليمات الغسيل.(٣٤)

كذلك تعبر قصيدة «ديفو» عن الحزن الإنساني الدفين بسبب نقص أو عيب خلقي:

الملابس التي فقدت زراً
أو تشوهت أقمشتها
لها حزنها الخاص
تعبيرات الوجه الجامدة
عزلتها
رغبتها المعاقة بأن توضع داخل الأكياس البلاستيكية
استسلامها الكامل بأن تتحول إلى المخزن
أو إلى الأسواق الخلفية.(٣٥)

يجد كل شعور إنساني معادله الموضوعي في قصة الملابس؛ فالانتظار الممل، مثلاً، كما يقول الشاعر في ص ٢٥، هو الشماعات: «الشماعات هي الانتظار الممل/الإحساس المزيف بالارتداء». وإذا كان ما يميز قصة الملابس أنها لا تعبر، صراحةً، عن شعور أو إحساس ما، وإنما تعبر عنه من خلال صورة شعرية (وهذا ما يميز الشعر الجيد كله) فإن الصورة التي تعبر عن كل الأحاسيس والمشاعر الإنسانية هي صورة شيء جامد هو الملابس. أي أن الإنسان لا يهب الأشياء إنسانيتها على نحو ما هو حاصل في رؤية الشعراء الرومانسيين للطبيعة وتحريكهم لها وإضفاء الصبغة الإنسانية عليها، وإنما يتحول الإنسان نفسه إلى شيء:

ربما كان مسماراً أو شيئاً آخراً
ذلك الذي خلف هذا المزق ينزف بعض الخيوط
وجعل الملابس تتمدد ثانيةً أمام الخياط الطيب
لتعاود الإبر عملها
فتلملم الخيوط داخل الأقمشة
تمرق تحت النسيج
تسحب أطرافه وذاكرته
لكنها في غمرة انهماكها
تسقط بعضاً من تفاصيله
وطقوسه اليومية.(٣٦)

وهكذا، يفقد الإنسان ما يميزه من حيث هو إنسان، يفقد قدرته على التحول والتغير، وتصير حياته محتومة بتطور قصة الملابس منذ

بدايتها في المتجر حتى تتمزق: «ويبدو الموت جلياً كخرقةٍ/لمسح الأرفف/وبقايا الطعام في المطبخ.(٣٧) وإذا كانت تلك الاستعارة المميزة في شعر تامر فتحي تظهر الإنسان بمظهر الشيء فتبقى متأرجحة بين تشيؤ الإنسان وتحريك الجماد، فإن شعر جرجس شكري الذي يسبقه في الترتيب الزمني، ويأتي في موضع متقدم عنه في وضوح ظاهرة موت الذات فيه، يكمل قصة الذات حتى نهايتها، ويفوق بنبرته اللامبالية كل تعبيرات الحزن النابعة من الإحساس بالعجز أو الاغتراب التي يمتلئ بها الشعر المعاصر.

يعبر جرجس شكري عن علاقة غريبة بين الإنسان والأشياء؛ فعالمه يندر فيه ظهور الإنسان، وهو عالم جامد يقف على حافة الصمت تسكنه الأشياء، وقلما يعبر من خلاله الآخرون، وتظهر الذات الإنسانية فيه، التي قلما تظهر، في صورة ساكنة فلا تكاد تظهر حتى تختفي. يبدأ جرجس شكري ديوانه **ضرورة الكلب في المسرحية** بقصيدة «سترة»:

أنا وسترتي نخرج في نزهات شتائية
أعهد إليها بحفظ سجائري
ولا نسأل أحداً عن الطريق
أحملها في يدي حين يختنق العالم
وأحياناً تقفز إلى كتفي
كقطة
حين يغلبها الشوق
فتعض على يدي بجيوبها
وأبتسم مطمئناً
سترتي باهتة والشارع صاخب
وحين أتدلل تدفعني بقوة
فأحملها ولا نكلم أحداً
سترتي تحب الشارع مثلي
ولا أعرف كيف ولدت هذه المحبة
ولا أذكر
من أين جاءت هذه السترة
فقط حين أكره العالم
أختفي في سترتي
فتمشي هي وحيدة
لا تكلم أحداً.(٣٨)

تبدأ هذه القصة بالعلاقة بين «أنا وسترتي»؛ أي أن العلاقة ليست بين ذاتين إنسانيتين، أو حتى الذات ونفسها، وإنما بين الذات وشيء. ونلحظ أن أفعال الذات في هذه القصيدة ساكنة دائماً، مثل: «أعهد» و«أبتسم» و«أتدلل»، بل ومنفية: «لا أسأل» و«لا أذكر»، وفي بعض الأحيان لازمة لا تتطلب مفعولاً. أي أن الذات لا تقوى على الفعل. وإذا جاءت الذات بفعل ديناميكي، فإنه ناتج عن أن السترة تدفعها إلى ذلك «بقوة». أما السترة فهي التي تسيطر عليها المشاعر، فهي «تلح بالخروج» و«يغلبها الشوق»؛ أي أن السترة أكثر فاعلية من الذات الساكنة الضعيفة. والقصيدة، في النهاية، تحمل اسم «سترة»، وليس أنا. قد يكون هذا تعبيراً عن وحدة ذات لا تستطيع التواصل مع الآخرين أو عزلتها، والعزلة نتاج انفصال تلك الذات عن الذات الجمعية، إلا أن القصيدة تنتهي باختفاء أحد طرفي العلاقة، وهو الذات، أما السترة فتبقى و«تمشي هي وحيدة، لا تكلم أحداً».

تبدو نهاية الإنسان في شعر جرجس شكري عاملاً مهيمناً. يفتتح الشاعر ديوانه **رجل طيب يكلم نفسه** بقصيدة «صورة شخصية» التي تبدأ بقوله «أنا أقيم علاقات أليفة مع الأشياء»، ولكن على النقيض من «سترة»، فإن هذه الأشياء ليست خارجة عن الذات؛ لأن الصورة الشخصية هي صورة ذات صارت شيئاً. غير أن تلك الصورة لا تتضح إلا في القصيدة الأخيرة من الديوان التي تحمل عنوان الديوان نفسه. فيخاطب الرجل الطيب نفسه قائلاً:

أنا آلة تصوير
مخزن ذكريات كبير
ألتقط كل شيء
ولا أعي شيئاً
حفظت الحروب
حتى صارت ذاكرتي
مستودع بارود(٣٩)

أي أن الإنسان الذي حاول أن يرسم لنفسه صورة شخصية انتهى إلى أن تلك الصورة هي صورة شيء: آلة تصوير، تصور كل شيء ولا تقوم بأي فعل إيجابي تجاهه. ورؤية الإنسان على أنه آلة تصوير لا تشير فقط إلى سلبيته، بل أيضاً إلى أن جوهره صار التماهي مع ما حوله من الأشياء التي تكونه، وإلى جمود أفعاله التي فقدت تلقائيتها وجمدت في صورة شيء ثابت:

وأكلم نفسي أحكي للأشياء
عن بلاد قديمة
كانت تسكن هذا الهواء
ثم عبرت مثل الموسيقى
عن بشر
يحملون حيواناتهم وبيوتهم
كل صباح
يعهدون للبحر بحراستها
وغالباً ما يسقطون من معاطفهم
تاركين الهواء فارغاً
ثم أكتفي بأن أعض شفة امرأة
كل مساء
ونحن نخلع سراويلنا
ونأمر أعضاءنا بأن تعمل في صمت
حتى لا يهتز المشهد
وأكلم نفسي ثانية
أنا آلة تصوير
كل ما ألتقطه وهم فارغ
وغالباً ما تحترق أفلامي من الضحك.(٤٠)

وما يحدث كل صباح يتكرر إلى الأبد؛ حتى أصبح صورة جامدة التقطتها الذات، فعلاً فقد تلقائيته وتشيأ، وكذلك ما يحدث كل مساء. صارت كل أفعال الذات صوراً جامدة خالية من الحياة. وإذا كانت الذات تتكون من أفعالها فإن جمود تلك الأفعال وفقدانها الحياة، حتى صارت صوراً ميتة، يؤدي إلى موت الذات نفسها. ولهذا، تعد آلة التصوير صورة مناسبة جداً للذات التي فقدت حياتها وصارت تتكون من أفعال جامدة. وتدرك آلة التصوير أن كل أفعالها، أو صورها، «وهم فارغ»:

وهذا ليس إنسان
هذا وقت ضائع يتقاسمه المتفرجون
وحاصل جميع اللحظات التي يصرفها في كل مشهد
عمر مديد وحياة ميتة.(٤١)

الذات الفردية المنقسمة على نفسها صارت مواتاً. ولا يمكن التعبير عن هذا الموات بالرمز، وإنما الإنسان نفسه هو الذي

يتحول إلى شيء، وبالتالي يكتسب هذا الشيء بعضاً من الصفات التي كانت تميز الإنسان كالقدرة على الفعل.

تنقسم قصيدة «أشياء فقدت محبتها» في الديوان نفسه إلى «هو»، و«أبونا»، و«هي»، و«نحن»، و«صانعة السعادة». ويقدم كل مقطع شعري صورة شخص ما؛ إلا أن هذه الصورة تصوّر فعلاً آلياً يأتيه كل منهم، ويكرره بصورة لا نهائية حتى يفقد إنسانيته، وتتلخص صورته في ذلك الفعل الآلي؛ فهو مثلاً:

كان يسهر ويكذب علينا
حتى يفارقنا القمر
ثم نحمله إلى زوجته
وننصحها أن تقلع عن طرده
من حياتها إلى الحانة حافياً.(٤٢)

وعلى الرغم من غرابة الحدث، فالتعليق عليه جاف وخال من أية مشاعر أو تعاطف أو حتى تعبير عن الغرابة. ويوحي هذا بأن الحدث الغريب الذي يستوجب الوقوف عليه وفهمه والتعاطف معه أمسى أمراً عادياً لا يستحق الاكتراث في عالم الأناس التي صارت أشياءً. وإذا كانت هذه الأشياء أناساً، هو وهي وأبونا، فإن هؤلاء الناس يصيرون أشياءً في قصيدة «في محبة الأشياء» في ديوان **والأيدي عطلة رسمية**؛ أي أن الأشياء التي فقدت محبتها، وهي أناس، تتحول إلى أشياء فعلاً تتحلى ببعض العواطف التي تليق بالأشياء.

تحتل كلمة «محبة» مكاناً متميزاً في القصيدتين. ويرجع ذلك إلى المكانة المهمة التي تحتلها في الديانة المسيحية؛ فتعبير «الله محبة» يعني أن العلاقة بين الأقانيم الثلاثة هي علاقة محبة، وهي بذلك العلاقة التي يجب أن تتواجد بين الفرد والأفراد الآخرين الذين يكونون المجتمع، أي بين الفرد والذات الجمعية؛ إلا أن الأفراد الذين فقدوا المحبة، أي فقدوا الصلة بينهم وبين الكل الذي ينتمون إليه يتشيأون، أي تفقد أفعالهم معناها بفقدانها السياق الذي تظهر من خلاله، وتصبح مجرد تكرار روتيني، شيء جامد خال من الروح، ثم تتحول الذات المتشيئة إلى إقامة علاقات مع الأشياء التي كانت أناساً؛ فبدلاً من «هو» و«هي» تتحول عناوين القصائد إلى «المطرقة» و«الصحن».

قبل هذا التحول التام إلى شيء، تقدم قصيدتا «صاحب الرأس» و«الأيدي عطلة رسمية» صوراً ممزقة للإنسان. تبدأ القصيدة الأولى بهذه السطور:

الفم المفتوح
الآذان الصاغية
العيون التي أرهقتها الصور
تسكن رأساً يتصدع كلما تكلم صاحبه(٤٣)

في هذه السطور لا يظهر «صاحب الرأس»، وإنما تظهر العيون والآذان والفم. لا يوجد إنسان، وإنما يوجد:

أصوات تصفع بعضها
أشياء ميتة
صورة خائفة
بشر فارغون
وحياة واحدة
مسكين هذا الرأس(٤٤)

تشظى الإنسانُ وتحوَّل إلى أجزاء وأشياء وصور وأصوات دون وحدة تجمعها. كل هذه الأجزاء لا تنتمي إلى كل واحد، وإنما هي «تسكن رأساً» بوصفها مجموعة من الأشياء وضعت بجوار بعضها البعض. ويتأكد هذا المعنى مرة أخرى في «والأيدي عطلة رسمية»:

ذات مرة بكيت
فلم أجد دموعي
وخسرت عيوني إلى الأبد
ذات مرة صرخت
فهرب صوتي
وتركني عارياً
ذات مرة ضحكت
فسقط فمي وحيداً
على الأرض
وذات مرة
وذات مرة
هل كنت أنا؟(٤٥)

تلك الذات التي تفقد وحدتها تصير أجزاءً. والأجزاء بفقدها الوحدة التي تجمعها وتعطيها الحياة تفقد حياتها وتصير أشياءً. أما السمة المميزة لهذا

الشعر فهو أن التعبير عنه ليس تعبيراً تقليدياً، ولكن ما يعطي إحساساً حقيقياً بالتشظي هو إعادة خلقه على المستويين اللغوي والبلاغي:

لم أحلم
حملت رأسي وذهبت إلى النوم
هناك كان أعمى يكلم مصباحاً
عن خيط يتنزه في ثقب إبرة
وشمس تجره من قدميه
إلى حيث لا يدري.(٤٦)

الاستعارة التي تتضمنها «شمس تجره من قدميه» استعارة مختلطة mixed metaphor؛ فالشمس التي تعطي النور تجر الأعمى من قدميه. إنها استعارة لا تشكل صورة، وإنما تخلق عبثاً يستحيل تصوره. فالذات المتشظية لا تخلق صوراً يمكن تخيلها؛ لأن الصورة تعتمد نشاط الذات في خلق الوحدة بين المشبه والمشبه به، وهكذا فإن التشظي يعاد خلقه على مستوى الصورة الشعرية. وهذا يعطي الشاعر الفرصة في أن يخلق أغرب التركيبات اللغوية التي تصدم القارئ وتتركه بلا أمل في أن يستبصر صوراً مرئية يستخلص منها معنى. وإذا كانت الصور الشعرية أحد أهم مصادر الجمال في الشعر، وإذا كان الجمال يعتمد التوافق بين ملكتي الخيال والفهم، كما أوضح كانط،(٤٧) أي أن تقدم ملكة الخيال صورة متناسقة تستطيع ملكة الفهم أن تلحظ فيها هذا التناسق الذي يجعلها أشبه بالمفهوم concept دون أن تكون توحيداً تاماً لمعطيات يمكن فهمها، فإن هذا الشعر يرفض توحيد المشبه والمشبه به لخلق صورة، يرفض التناسق، وينكر على نفسه هذا الجمال. فإذا كان الجمال يعتمد التناسق بين أجزاء الصورة أو المدرك percept، وبذلك يخلق تناسقاً داخل الذات بين ملكتي الفهم والإدراك وبالتالي بين الذات والموضوع؛ أي بين الذات والعالم، وهي العلاقة التي أكدها كانط، فإن الذات المتشيئة المغتربة عن العالم لا يمكن أن تخلق هذه الصلة على المستوى الشعري عن طريق الجمال. وهذا الجمال الذي ينشأ عن طريق التناسق بين الذات والعالم هو نفسه التناسق الذي تحدثه الذات الجمعية بين الذوات الفردية، وبين الذات الفردية ومحيطها، عن طريق محو الاختلاف وفرض مفهوم موحد. ولذلك، فهذا الشعر قد يبدو غريباً وصادماً للقارئ ولكنه لا يبدو جميلاً. إلا أن درجة من درجات الاختلاف بين المشبه والمشبه به حتمية لإنتاج الصورة الشعرية، فبدون هذا الاختلاف تتماهى مكونات الاستعارة ولا توجد استعارة

أساساً. إن هذا الاختلاف كان دائماً موجوداً في التراث الشعري، إلا أن عنصر التوحيد بينهما كان يغلب على الاختلاف ليخلق صورة. وبهذا يمكن فهم هذا الشعر على أنه يُفَعِّل عنصر الاختلاف في الاستعارة حتى يدمر عناصر الوحدة ويحطم الصورة. وبذلك، فإن الذات المتشيئة المنفصلة عن التراث لا تعيد خلقه على مستوى الصورة، وإنما تبرز عوامل الاختلاف، ليس فقط بإعادة كتابة القصة بأسلوب مختلف، ولا باختيار قصص تتضمن في معناها الثورة على التراث، وإنما على المستوى الشكلي أيضاً في تحطيم الاستعارة.

وبذلك يمضي هذا الشعر في تحطيم الاستعارات أو صنع استعارات مختلطة تنكر الجمال وتقطع الطريق على الفهم وتقدم الصدمة تلو الأخرى لقارئه عن طريق تلك الصور الغريبة المتشظية، وكذلك عن طريق أسلوب المونتاج أو توالي صور متجاورة لا علاقة لها ببعضها البعض؛ فعلى سبيل المثال:

حذاء يطارد متشرداً
آخر الليل ويصرخ
أقدامي بلا تاريخ
سكين يطارد قصاباً
ويعلن التوبة
هناك كان قميصي وحيداً
يصرخ في حبل الغسيل
إلهي إلهي لماذا شنقتني؟(٤٨)

هذا التسلسل من صورة الحذاء إلى السكين إلى القميص لا تربطه رابطة، ولا يتبع منطقاً إلا منطق المونتاج أو الصور المتتابعة التي لا تمثل تطوراً بأي شكل من الأشكال. وإذا كان هناك شكل واحد يتكرر في الصور الثلاث فهو المفارقة، المتمثلة في أن يطارد الحذاء متشرداً أو أن يطعن السكين قصاباً. والعلاقة بين طرفي المفارقة بالطبع علاقة تضاد، أي أن المفارقة، تماماً كالاستعارة المختلطة، تنتج عن تفكك الوحدة التي تعتمدها الاستعارة. ففي حالة التناقض يؤدي تفكك الوحدة إلى علاقة تضاد، أما في حالة الاستعارة المختلطة فيؤدي إلى علاقة عشوائية. وتقف هذه المفارقة بالطبع على طرف النقيض من الرمز؛ فبينما العلاقة بين الدال والمدلول في الرمز علاقة حلول، أي أن المدلول حال في الدال، وهي علاقة عضوية حتى أن تلك المصطلحات اللغوية تبدو غير مناسبة للتعبير عنها، فإن العلاقة بين الدال والمدلول

في المفارقة هي علاقة عكسية، أي أن المدلول عكس الدال أو أن الدال يشير إلى نقيضه. والرمز بالطبع يظهر في المجتمعات التي تتميز بالوحدة وتكون الذات الفردية فيها جزءاً من الذات الجمعية، أما المفارقة فتظهر في الحالات التي تنقلب فيها الذات الفردية ضد الذات الجماعية التي هي جزء منها، أي تنقلب ضد نفسها. إلا أن الخلل المنطقي الذي يميز المفارقة ليس بالقوة البلاغية نفسها التي يلعبها في شعر أمل دنقل أو نزار قباني؛ لأن الخلل المنطقي يفترض وجود منطق طبيعي للأشياء يتم خرقه أو العمل ضده. إلا أن العالم العبثي الغريب في شعر جرجس شكري ليس له منطق، ولذلك لا يصدم التناقض القارئ فهو ليس خروجاً عن منطق محدد، وإنما هو استمرار لحالة التشظي وتتابع الصدمات اللذين يحكمان هذا العالم، واللذين يمكن وصفهما بأسلوب المونتاج.

قام رومان ياكوبسون بدراسة المرضى المصابين بالحُبَسَة aphasia في دراسته المهمة «وجهان للغة ونوعان من اضطرابات الكلام عند مرضي الحُبَسَة». وجد ياكوبسون أن المصابين بهذا النوع من اضطرابات الكلام لا يستطيعون النطق بما يعنون، وإنما يضطرون إلى النطق بكلمة بديلة عنه، ولكن بعضهم ينطق بكلمة تتصل بما يعنيه بعلاقة تجاور بينما ينطق الآخرون بكلمة تتصل به بعلاقة تشابه:

> يعد كل نوع من أنواع الحبسة إصابة شديدة أو بسيطة إما للقدرة على الاختيار والتبادل أو للقدرة على التوحيد والتجميع. ويتم كبت علاقة التشابه في الحالة الأولى بينما يتم كبت علاقة التجاور في الحالة الثانية. وتصير الاستعارة غريبة على الخلل الذي يصيب علاقات التشابه بينما تصبح الكناية التي تعتمد على علاقات التجاور أو المجاز التجاوري metonymy غريبة على الخلل الذي يصيب علاقات التجاور.(٤٩)

وينطلق ياكوبسون من هذه البداية إلى تحليل الإبداع الفني كله من خلاله، فيقسم المدارس الفنية والأدبية والشعرية على حسب انتمائها إلى أحد المحورين: «يوجد العديد من الدوافع التي تحدد الاختيار بين تلك البدائل في الشعر. فقد تم اكتشاف أولوية العملية الاستعارية في المدارس الرومانسية والرمزية، ولكن لم يتم اكتشاف هيمنة المجاز التجاوري على ما يسمى بالأسلوب الواقعي الذي ينتمي إلى مرحلة تقع بين انهيار الرومانسية وصعود الرمزية ويعد توجهاً مضاداً لكليهما».(٥٠) وهنا

يضرب ياكوبسون مثالاً بتولستوي الذي ينتقل من وصفه شخصية ما إلى ما يجاورها، أو من وصف جزء منها إلى وصف جزء آخر، أو ينتقل من وصف الجزء إلى الكل وما شابه. ولكن ذلك يختلف عن الأسلوب الرمزي والرومانسي الذي ينتقل من الشبيه إلى شبيهه. ويتضح هذا في الشعر الحداثي الذي يبدو فيه السياق مفككًا إلا أنه ينتقل من صورة شعرية إلى صورة أخرى تشترك معها في معنى واحد. غير أن النظر المتفحص في قصيدة «والأيدي عطلة رسمية» يجد أن تطورها لا يتبع أياً من هذين الأسلوبين اللذين حددهما ياكوبسون تبعاً لمحوري التبادل والتعاقب أو علاقات التشابه والتجاور. وبذلك، فإن هذا التطور ليس استعارياً ولاتجاورياً، وإنما يسير من صورة إلى صورة أخرى لا علاقة لها بها فيضعهما بجوار بعضهما البعض، أي يتطور بأسلوب المونتاج الذي استخدمه السرياليون من قبل. ويتناسب أسلوب المونتاج، بالطبع، مع حالة التشظي التي تخلقها الاستعارة المختلطة.

في عالم الأشياء، تصبح الأشياء هي المسيطرة. فعلى النقيض من «أشياء فقدت محبتها» التي كانت أناساً، فإن «في محبة الأشياء» في الديوان الذي يليه تقدم أشياءً فعلية تكتسب القدرة على التعبير عن نفسها، إلا أنها تحتفظ بصفتها الأساسية بوصفها أشياءً. تنقسم القصيدة إلى أربعة أجزاء أو أربعة أشياء، وهي «النشيد القومي» و«المطرقة» و«الصحن» و«زيد وعمرو». في هذا الجزء الأخير، يشعر اللغوي بفقدانه ذاته:

جيرانه يشكون الضجيج الذي يملأ البيت
حين يبدأ في تدريب أفعاله
على تأدية المعنى
ودائماً يخرج معتلاً يجر قدميه
يعتذر لهم ويؤكد أن الأسماء تموت
إذا حذفت أفعالها.(٥١)

كتب صامويل بيكيت (١٩٠٦-١٩٨٩) «الفاعل ينتج عن الفعل»؛ أي أن الفاعل على مستوى اللغة، أو على مستوى الذات الإنسانية، هو نتاج قدرته على الفعل. إلا أن هذه الرؤية المادية واللغوية تنكر في الواقع وجود تلك الذات المتعالية transcendental subject التي لا يعتمد وجودها الفعل وإنما هي وجود في ذاته. أما الوجود الذي يعتمد الفعل فينتفي بانتفاء الفعل، ويتراسل جرجس شكري مع هذه الرؤية:

حزن اللغوي واختلى إلى أفعاله
يدربها بعنف على أداء يكشف الغمة
لكنها ظلت صامتة
فعرف أن أفعاله صارت عاجزة
وفقدت الحياة المعنى.(٥٢)

وفي سكون الفعل انتفاء الذات، والأفعال الصامتة العاجزة تنفي الحياة عن الذات. وتصير الذات شيئاً كسكين كما في «النشيد القومي»:

نحن السكاكين
لنا شفرات تصرخ
ومقابضنا ميتة
نعرف أننا نذبح ونمزق
ولا تخدعنا محبة القصاب
نبتسم للذبيحة وهي تتألم
فلا تكرهونا
نحن السكاكين الكافرين
بكل محبة
خلقنا هكذا دون قلوب
وضعوا مشاعرنا في نصل حاد
وأوصانا الحداد الخالق
أن نذبح وبقوة
حتى لا نموت
فلا تكرهونا حين نذبحكم
نحن لا نعرف الألم
وأيضاً لا نبكي
فقط نذبح
فيرتفع النصل الحاد عالياً
دون خوف.(٥٣)

وهكذا، يفقد الإنسان إنسانيته ويصير شيئاً، ويصبح الشيء تعبيراً عن الإنسان، مجازاً لا رمزاً يكتسب أهميته ومعناه مما يمنحه الشاعر من معنى. وبذلك، فإن الذات التي بدأ موتها بانفصالها عن الذات الكلية، في محاولة التحرر من سيطرتها، انتهى بها الحال إلى التشيؤ، أما الذات الكلية فقد غدت وعاءً خاوياً بانفصالها عن الذوات

الفعلية التي تحيا من خلالها. وتلك الذات المتشيئة لا تعبر عن نفسها بالرمز أو الاستعارة، وإنما تعبر عن نفسها من خلال الأليغوريا والاستعارة المختلطة والمفارقة في إطار من المونتاج. وهكذا، تنتج الأشكال البلاغية والتقنيات الفنية عن علاقات اجتماعية. وهنا، تتجلى السخرية التي تحكم هذا الشعر بأكمله، وهي أن الشعر، وهو الشكل الفني الذي يخلص فيه الإنسان إلى جوهره ويعبر مباشرةً عن نفسه دون اللجوء إلى عالم الأشياء، كما أكد هيجل، يصير الشكل الفني الذي يعبر عن تشيؤ الذات وموتها. إلا أن هذه السخرية هي نفسها شهادة هذا الشعر على عصره.

**الهوامش**

(١) راجع:
Jacques Derrida, *The Truth in Painting*, trans. Geoffrey Bennington and Ian McLeod (Chicago: Chicago UP, 1987), 27.

(٢) **المرجع السابق**، ص ٢٥.

(٣) راجع:
Paul De Man, *Aesthetic Ideology*, ed. Andrzej Warminsky (Minneapolis: Minnesota UP, 1996), 95.

(٤) **المرجع السابق**، ص ٩٣.

(٥) **المرجع نفسه**.

(٦) أمل دنقل شاعر مصري ولد في قنا عام ١٩٤٠ ونشر أول مجموعة شعرية بعنوان **البكاء بين يدي زرقاء اليمامة** عام ١٩٦٩، وآخرها **أوراق الغرفة ٨** عام ١٩٨٣، وتأثر شعره بشدة بنكسة ١٩٦٧. توفي عام ١٩٨٣.

(٧) نزار قباني أحد أشهر الشعراء العرب في القرن العشرين. ولد في سوريا عام ١٩٢٣ وعمل بالسلك الدبلوماسي لفترة طويلة. اهتم في شعره بالقومية العربية والحب والدين والمرأة. توفي عام ١٩٩٨. ورغم أن نزار قباني ليس مصرياً، فإنه تأثر بالظروف نفسها التي تحكم الإطار الفكري لهذه المقالة. كذلك، فإن حضوره الشعري في العالم العربي جعله من المؤثرين والمتأثرين بالأوضاع الفكرية والسياسية والاجتماعية فيه.

(٨) جرجس شكري شاعر مصري من مواليد سوهاج عام ١٩٦٧. صدرت له دواوين **بلا مقابل أسقط أسفل حذائي** عام ١٩٩٦ و**رجل طيب يكلم نفسه** عام ١٩٩٨ و**ضرورة الكلب في المسرحية** عام ٢٠٠٠. يعمل كاتباً بمجلة **الإذاعة والتليفزيون** ومحرراً بمجلة **أدب ونقد**.

(٩) تامر فتحي من مواليد الإسكندرية عام ١٩٨٠. درس الأدب الإنجليزي.

صدر له ديوان **بالأمس فقدت زراً: قصة الملابس** والمستوحى من تجربة عمله بائع ملابس بأحد المحال بالإسكندرية.

(١٠) أمل دنقل، **الأعمال الكاملة** (القاهرة: المجلس الأعلى للثقافة، ٢٠٠٣)، ص ١٤٠.

(١١) **المرجع السابق**، ص ١٤١.

(١٢) **المرجع السابق**، ص ١٣٨.

(١٣) **المرجع نفسه**.

(١٤) نزار قباني، **الأعمال الشعرية الكاملة**، الجزء السابع (بيروت: منشورات نزار قباني، ١٩٨١)، ص ١١٠.

(١٥) **المرجع نفسه**.

(١٦) **المرجع السابق**، ص ١٢٩.

(١٧) **المرجع السابق**، ص ١١٤.

(١٨) **المرجع نفسه**.

(١٩) **المرجع السابق**، ص ١١٢.

(٢٠) **المرجع السابق**، ص ١١٣.

(٢١) **المرجع السابق**، ص ص ١١٥–١١٦.

(٢٢) **المرجع السابق**، ص ١١٢.

(٢٣) **المرجع السابق**، ص ١١٠.

(٢٤) **المرجع السابق**، ص ١١١.

(٢٥) **المرجع السابق**، ص ١١٤.

(٢٦) **المرجع السابق**، ص ١٢١.

(٢٧) **المرجع السابق**، ص ١٢٣.

(٢٨) **المرجع السابق**، ص ١٢٦.

(٢٩) **المرجع السابق**، ص ١٢٤.

(٣٠) **المرجع السابق**، ص ١٢١.

(٣١) **المرجع السابق**، ص ١١٢.

(٣٢) **المرجع نفسه**.

(٣٣) **المرجع السابق**، ص ١٢٣.

(٣٤) تامر فتحي، **بالأمس فقدت زراً: قصة الملابس** (القاهرة: شرقيات، ٢٠٠٥)، ص ٣٦.

(٣٥) **المرجع السابق**، ص ٢١.

(٣٦) **المرجع السابق**، ص ٥٣.

(٣٧) **المرجع السابق**، ص ٦٤.

(٣٨) جرجس شكري، **ضرورة الكلب في المسرحية** (القاهرة: الهيئة العامة لقصور الثقافة، ٢٠٠٠)، ص ص ١٣–١٤.

(٣٩) جرجس شكري، **رجل طيب يكلم نفسه** (القاهرة: شرقيات، ١٩٩٨)، ص ٧٧.

(٤٠) **المرجع السابق**، ص ٧٨.
(٤١) **المرجع السابق**، ص ٧٩.
(٤٢) **المرجع السابق**، ص ١٧.
(٤٣) جرجس شكري، **والأيدي عطلة رسمية** (القاهرة: شرقيات، ٢٠٠٤)، ص ١٥.
(٤٤) **المرجع السابق**، ص ١٦.
(٤٥) **المرجع السابق**، ص ٧١.
(٤٦) **المرجع السابق**، ص ٧٥.
(٤٧) راجع:
Immanuel Kant, *Critique of Judgment*, trans. James Creed Meredith (NY: The Hafber P, 1951).
(٤٨) **المرجع نفسه**.
(٤٩) راجع ترجمتي للنص في:
Roman Jakobson, *Language in Literature*, eds. Krystyna Pomorska and Stephen Rudy (Cambridge: Cambridge UP, 1987), 109.
(٥٠) **المرجع السابق**، ص ١١٣.
(٥١) جرجس شكري، **والأيدي عطلة رسمية**، ص ٣٠.
(٥٢) **المرجع نفسه**.
(٥٣) **المرجع السابق**، ص ٢٤.

# قلوب أنهكها الشتات:
# قراءة في ثنائية كمال رُحَيِّم الروائية

محمد بريري

يشير عنوان هذه القراءة إلى روايتي الأديب كمال رحيم: **قلوب منهكة** (٢٠٠٤) و**أيام الشتات** (٢٠٠٨).(١) في الرواية الأولى نتابع سيرة جلال منذ أن كان طفلاً رضيعاً إلى أن صار شاباً انتهى لتوه من دراسته الثانوية، متأهباً للالتحاق بكلية الطب بعد تفوّق مدرسي باهر. والراوي الذي يقدم أحداث الرواية هو جلال نفسه مستخدماً ضمير المتكلم. ويلاحظ القارئ في الصفحات الأولى أن النص، وإن كان واقعياً من الناحية الشكلية، فإنه يبدأ بداية غير واقعية حين يقوم الطفل الرضيع بسرد ما يدور حوله. فكأن المؤلف الضمني يسعى، من خلال هذا الانحراف الأسلوبي، إلى الوصول إلى أبعد بداية لتشكيل وعي الشخصية بما حولها.(٢) ويمضي السرد بعد هذا في تتبع المراحل التي قطعها جلال، المولود لأب مصري استشهد في حرب ١٩٥٦ – عقب ولادة جلال – وأم يهودية مصرية نشأ الابن في كنفها، وتحت رعاية والدها جدّ جلال، وفي معيّة الجدّة؛ والدتها. خالط جلال في مراحل عمره البيئة القاهرية في حي الضاهر (كما تلفظ في العامية، وأصلها «الظاهر» نسبة إلى الظاهر بيبرس) وما يحيط به من أحياء مماثلة، تسكنها بشكل عام، أطياف من الطبقة الوسطى المصرية، وتعرّف أثناء ذلك على البيئة الريفية حين زار – بصحبة أمه – جدّه لأبيه في إحدى قرى مصر القريبة من جنوب القاهرة. وتنتهي الأحداث الرئيسة في هذه الرواية برحيل جلال مع والدته كاميليا إلى فرنسا، التي كان الجدّ والجدّة قد سبقاهما إليها، وكان رحيل جلال إلى هناك إذعاناً لوالدته، بعد مقاومة منه، وبعد أن اشترط عليها أن يعود إلى مصر كي يكمل دراسته في كلية الطب. وقد كاد أن ينفذ ما خططه لنفسه، لكنه بعد أن أوشك على ركوب الطائرة عائداً إلى مصر، لم يقْوَ على مقاومة حنينه إلى أسرته التي نشأ في كنفها، وبخاصة أن أمه كانت قد توسلت إليه ألا يغادرها بعد ما بذلته من تضحيات في سبيل رعايته، عقب وفاة والده المبكرة.

وفي الرواية الثانية، **أيام الشتات**، نتابع ما يمر به جلال في باريس من نجاحات وإخفاقات، ونتعرف على شخصيات أثرت في مجرى حياته. من هذه الشخصيات عرب مسلمون، أهمهم الشيخ منجي من تونس، وأبو الشوارب من

جنوب لبنان، إلى جانب أفراد من عائلة أمه. وقد تزوج في هذه الفترة مرتين؛ الأولى من راشيل ابنة خالته التي طلّقها سريعاً، ثم من خديجة ابنة الشيخ منجي، التي ماتت عقب زواجه منها بما لا يتجاوز بضعة أسابيع. أما الأم فقد تزوجت من أحد أثرياء اليهود، وكان ينتمي إلى إحدى الأسر العريقة التي كان لها وضع متميز في مصر، من الناحيتين الاقتصادية والعائلية.(٣) وعلى كل حال فإن حنين جلال الدائم إلى مصر/حي الضاهر، وإلى محبوبته هناك، نادية، ظل يؤرّقه، فيقرّر بعد موت جدّه وجدّته أن يعود إلى مصر. وتنتهي الرواية بمشهد جلال في مطار أورلي، كما انتهت الرواية الأولى. ويلاحظ أن الراوي كثيراً ما يعود في **أيام الشتات** إلى أحداث تتعلق زمنياً بفترة سابقة يفترض أن تكون قد تمّت في **قلوب منهكة**، ،ذلك عن طريق آلية الاسترجاع.

**شتات القلوب**

تنتهي رواية **قلوب منهكة** بمشهد جلال في مطار أورلي وهو يسمع النداء على اسمه، لكنه لم يلب النداء، فقد «كانوا ينادون على شخص ميت» على حد تعبير الراوي (ص ٣٠٤). والموت الذي يتحدث عنه موت روحي نفسي يعكس حالة من العجز عن الفعل. فقد تعادل انتماؤه إلى أسرته مع انتمائه إلى حي الضاهر في القاهرة، فأصبح أسير قوتين متعاكستين ومتساويتين تقريباً، فكان أن تجمد في موضعه بعد أن شلت إرادته. عبّر الراوي عن أزمته في تلك اللحظات قائلاً: «كنت بحاجة إلى دفعة، مجرد دفعة، لمن يأخذ بيدي إلى حيث تقف الطائرة. كنت سأستجيب، سأسلم له أمري كله . . . كنت على الحافة ولم أكن بحاجة سوى إلى دفعة، لكلمة، لقشة» (**أيام الشتات**، ص ٢٠). ولقد علّل الراوي حالته في تلك اللحظات تعليلاً نفسياً: «وكأن جزءاً مني ومنذ البداية كان رافضاً الرحيل» (ص ١٥). إن هذا التشتت أو الشتات الوجداني الذي مر به في هذه اللحظات الحاسمة التي كان عليه أن يقرّر فيها تغليب أحد انتماءين على الآخر، أدّى إلى حالة من الفراغ العاطفي: «كان قلبي فارغاً، لم يعد فيه شيء أي شيء. أو أصبح ينبض كما تنبض قلوب الناس، صار يدق كالآلات، مجرد آلة تؤدي وظائفها التي يفهمها الأطباء، وليست تلك التي يعرفها الناس عن القلوب» (ص ٢٠). أما كاميليا، الأم، فلم تتمالك نفسها من شدة الفرح بعودة ابنها إليها بعد أن كان عاقداً العزم على مغادرتها، واستئناف حياته في مصر، وعدّت رجوعه معجزة من معجزات أبي حصيرة، وهو ولي من أولياء الله في عقيدة يهود مصر،(٤) وقد تمتمت لنفسها قائلة: «البركة فيك يا أبو حصيرة، البركة فيك يا أبو سرّ باتع» (**أيام الشتات**، ص ١٨). والملاحظ في هذه المناجاة لأبي حصيرة أنها لا تختلف عما تناجي به النساء المصريات المسلمات السيدة زينب أو سيدنا الحسين. وقد كان جلال، حين ينظر في

صورة أبي حصيرة المحفوظة في دولاب الجدّ في الضاهر، تنتابه مشاعر مختلطة من الرهبة، التي تصل إلى حد الخوف، والاحترام والتبجيل ( **أيام الشتات**، ص ص ٢١–٢٢). على أن التشتت بين الخوف من جهة والاحترام والتبجيل من جهة أخرى له تاريخ في سيرة جلال الدينية.

**الثقافة الدينية/الدين الثقافي**

لا يكتسب الأفراد في أي مجتمع أديانهم وأنماط تدينهم من تلقاء أنفسهم، بل من خلال ممارسات اجتماعية في المراحل العمرية المختلفة. ولقد نشأ جلال في كنف أمه وجدّه وجدّته الذين يدينون بالديانة اليهودية، وبدأ التعرف على الدين من خلال ممارسات محسوسة وألفاظ تطلق ولا يدرك معناها. ومن هنا بدأت تساؤلاته: «كان اليوم يوم سبت . . . وجدي جالس يقرأ في كتاب غلافه أسود منقوش بزخارف بارزة . . . سألت أمي عما يقرأ. قالت بصوت خافت: الكتاب المقدس . . . عندما كنت أسير مع أمي أو جدّي . . . كنت أسمع الأولاد يحلفون بالقرآن . . . وسألتها إن كان هو الذي يقرأ . . . فقالت: لا، وطلبت مني إغلاق فمي» (**قلوب منهكة**، ص ٣٠). وكان جلال قد مارس في سبت سابق بعض الطقوس الدينية مع أقرانه من أبناء اليهود، وحين روى تفاصيل هذا اليوم ذكر: «شارع سبيل الخازندار حيث معبدنا (معبد القرائين)» (**قلوب منهكة**، ص ٤٠). وقد اشترك مع الأطفال الآخرين في ترتيل مزامير داوود. وحين سأله جدّه عما إذا كان حفظ شيئاً من مزامير داوود تساءل: «مين داوود دا يا جدي؟»، فرد عليه: «داوود. وحد ميعرفش داوود؟ دا نبى من أنبيائنا». وبعد ذلك يتساءل مرة أخرى: «وسيدنا محمد هو كمان راخر نبي؟»، فيرد الجد: «بتقول إيه سيدنا مين!» وحين يتساءل جلال: «سيدنا محمد يا جدي! أصل انا بسمع الأولاد في الشارع بيتكلموا عنه. وبيحلفوا بيه كمان»، يرد: «ولا تزعل يا أستاذ جلال. ومحمد كمان نبي» (**قلوب منهكة**، ص ص ٤٠–٤٢).

من الواضح في مثل هذه المواقف أن عائلة جلال تكاد تسلّم بيهودية ابنهم، فأمه يهودية. غير أن الجد أبدى قدراً ملحوظاً من التسامح والمرونة إزاء تساؤلات جلال، على حين أن الأم أظهرت ضجرها من تساؤلات ابنها؛ ففي مرحلة لاحقة ينجذب جلال وجدانياً إلى صوت الشيخ الدمنهوري، دون أن يدرك أن ما يتلوه هو القرآن، وحين يسأل أمه عما يقوله هذا الشيخ تنهره. وإذا كانت الأم قد أفلحت في مراوغة ابنها، فإن المجتمع لا يترك مثل هذه الأمور دون مناوشة، فقد سأل جلال أحد أقرانه عما يقول الشيخ الدمنهوري فأجابه:

– دا كلام ربنا يا عبيط. دا القرآن. هو في حد مسلم ميعرفش القرآن.

– مسلم!!

– وهو انت إيه يا خايب متعرفش انك مسلم. دا انت مسلم ونص. أمك وأهلها يا حفيظ هما اللي يهود.

– يهود!

– أيوه يهود. ويا رحمن يا رحيم عليهم يوم القيامة. على النار حدف.

وحين يعود جلال إلى أمه يواجهها بأنه عرف أن ما يقرؤه الشيخ هو القرآن، وعندئذ تقول له: «ما يقرا اللي يقراه واحنا مالنا . . . وهو انت متعرفش يا حبيبي اننا يهود وكتابنا التوراة. إحنا يا جلال حاجه وهم حاجه»، غير أن جلال يقول: «أصل العيال بتقول إني مسلم وهدخل الجنة. و انتوا كلكم رايحين النار»، وعندئذ ثارت الجدّة، التي كان بينها وبين جلال عداء ومشاكسات، وانهالت عليه ضرباً، وبدأت في الصياح: «عيال مين يا وسخ يا ابن الوسخ. نار لما تلسعهم هما وأهاليهم. ومالهم اليهود يا ابن الجزمة وهو انت تطول». غير أن الجدّ يتدخل منهياً هذا الجدل، مدركاً أن المقتضيات الاجتماعية أقوى من إرادات الأفراد: «يا جلال يا بني انت مسلم. شهادة الميلاد بتاعتك مكتوب فيها كده»، ثم يضيف: «يا ابني موسى وعيسى ومحمد أخوة، واحنا هنربيك ونعلمك ونكبرك وانت حر بعدها. تدخل في دينا أهلاً وسهلاً . . . عايز تفضل مسلم انت حر» (**قلوب منهكة**، ص ص ٤٩–٥٦).

يدرك الجد إذن أن الدين ليس مسألة لاهوتية مجردة، كما يدرك أن للسياق الاجتماعي شروطه ومقتضياته التي تؤثر في اختيارات الأفراد وتوجهها، بل ربما تحدد مساراتها بشكل جبري. وقد تجلى فهم الجد للسياق الاجتماعي الثقافي وعمق تأثيره بعد سنوات من هذا الموقف الذي مر به جلال الطفل في مصر حين قرر جلال، إبان وجوده في فرنسا، الزواج من راشيل ابنة خالته إذ أبدى الجد تحفظه، بل معارضته هذه الزيجة، وكان مما قاله لحفيده: «بقول يعني لو ربنا رزقكم بعيل ولا اتنين هيعيشوا عيشة تانية غير اللي انت عشتها في مصر ويمكن يبقوا يهود . . . دا مش ممكن دا أكيد هيبقوا يهود! موافق بأه يا حلو؟»، وحين يرد جلال منفعلاً: «إيه! وهو انا رحت فين!»، يجيب الجد منفعلاً هو الآخر: «و انت تقدر تعمل إيه!»، ثم يقول «اصحى يا جلال اصحى! الحكاية حكاية الدنيا والناس اللي احنا عايشين في وسطيهم والقانون والعرف اللي بيحكمنا ويمشي كلامه علينا . . . انت هنا في فرنسا . . . لا شرع ولا دين له دخل

بأي حاجة! ولا قانون ولا عرف هيبقى في صفك» (**أيام الشتات**، ص ص ١٩٩–٢٠٠). ولقد صدقت نبوءة الجد، فلم يقض جلال مع راشيل بعد زواجه منها إلا سويعات، إذ ما إن اكتشف أنها لم تكن عذراء حتى انفصل عنها، بعد أن صدم صدمة زلزلت كيانه. ومسألة العذرية هذه يختلط فيها ما هو ديني بما هو ثقافي،(٥) وهي تمثل لدى فئات اجتماعية عريضة في مصر، وفي غير مصر، أحد المقدسات التي لا يمكن التجاوز عنها. العذرية مقدسة في الممارسات الثقافية الدينية، هذا ما أدركه الجد منذ البداية، فهو في جداله مع حفيده قال له في معرض تقديم حججه: «وكمان فيه حاجه تانيه أهم من ده كله» (**أيام الشتات**، ص ٢٠١)، لكنه لم يفصح لحفيده عن كنه هذه «الحاجة التانية». لماذا لم يفصح؟ هل لأن الرجل كان متشبعاً هو نفسه بثقافة المصريين فانساق وراء مقولة «ربنا أمر بالستر»، ناهيك عن أن هذه الثقافة ترى في الحديث عن الأمور المتعلقة بالجنس، وبخاصة مع الأبناء أو من في حكمهم، أحد المحرمات؟؛ أو لعله رأى أن هناك احتمالاً أن يكون جلال قد تجاوز ثقافياً عن مسألة غشاء البكارة.

على كل حال، أظهر الجدّ قدراً كبيراً من البصيرة في تنشئة حفيده، وأعانه على الانخراط في الثقافة الإسلامية المصرية، ففي مناسبة مولد النبي، الذي يحتفل به المصريون بطريقتهم الخاصة، يقول الراوي: «حوت اللفة . . . حصاناً وعليه فارس يشهر سيفه عالياً. كانت الأيام وقتها أيام مولد ويبدو أن جدّي أحسّ بي وأنا أتطلع إلى الأولاد والبنات، وهم يسيرون بصحبة آبائهم حاملين العرائس والأحصنة الحلاوة» (**قلوب منهكة**، ص ٦٥).

والواقع أن جلالاً لم يكن متديناً بالمعنى الحرفي المألوف: «لم أدخل مسجداً من قبل . . . ولا انحنيت قط للصلاة إلا في المناسبات، أو إذا حدث خلاف بيني وبين أمي وأردت أن أريها أني لا أزال مسلماً» (**قلوب منهكة**، ص ٢١١). كان الإسلام لديه هوية ووسيلة مقاومة وإثبات للذات، وكان قبل ذلك قد قال: «كنت قد كبرت ودخلت المدرسة الإعدادي، وأنا لا أعرف شيئاً عن الصلاة إلا من حصص الدين . . . لكن ما أن تأتي الأجازة حتى أنسى كل الذي تعلمته، كما ينسى الأولاد دروس الحساب» (**قلوب منهكة**، ص ١٣٢).

على أن هذا كله لا يعني فتور عاطفته الدينية، فالعكس هو الصحيح. هناك أكثر من موقف نمّ عن عرامة هذه العاطفة. يحكي الراوي عن رحلة صباه حين كان مشتتاً بين انتمائه اليهودي وانتمائه الإسلامي، وكان لتوه قد تلقى من جدّه قرار كونه مسلماً الذي أشير إليه فيما سبق، وكيف أنه ذهب مع جده لقضاء واجب عزاء، يحكي قائلاً: «كان الشيخ عبد الباسط عبد الصمد هو المقرئ . . . آية . . . فالثانية وحل

سكوت عميق . . . جدي نفسه كان متأثراً بالقراءة . . . أخذنا كلنا الانفعال . . . نشوة كأنها السحر . . . و انفجرت مرة واحدة في البكاء» (**قلوب منهكة**، ص ص ٥٩–٦٠). إن هذا الانخراط في البكاء يعد بمثابة التنفيس عن الانفعال بلحظة التطابق، أو الالتقاء الحميم بالهوية الدينية، بعد أن تنازعت نفس هذا الصبي هويتان مختلفتان. وكان من أثر هذا العثور على الهوية الدينية أن تماسكت شخصية جلال، ولم يعد يتأثر بالغمز واللمز الذي كان يصادفه حين يشير بعضهم إلى يهودية ذويه. لذلك حين سأل مدرس اللغة العربية عن معنى بيت شعري من الغزل الصريح، على سبيل المشاكسة، أجابه المدرس ساخراً: «روح يا خويا اسأل حد من الفاميليا. ولا اقولك روح اسأل جولدا مائير وهيه تفهمك، أظنك عارفها». لم يرتبك جلال أو يخجل من هذا الغمز السّاخر بل أجاب في ثبات: «هل تقصد أن أمي يهودية، وأنت تعايرني بها؟»، الأمر الذي صدّر الارتباك إلى المدرس فرد معتذراً: «حاشا لله لا أقصد هذا، أنا . . . أنا . . .»، ولم يكمل عبارته من فرط تلعثمه (**قلوب منهكة**، ص ١٧١).

لم يكن الدين عند جلال فكرة مجردة بقدر ما كان هوية تتجسد ثقافياً من خلال قراءة عبد الباسط عبد الصمد للقرآن، أو من خلال أشخاص بعينهم مثل الشيخ خلف الذي حين مات تجمع الناس فيما يشبه مظاهرة ضمت أطياف الشعب في حي الضاهر، واشترك الجميع، نساءً ورجالاً في تشييع جنازته، يقول الراوي: «وأدخل دفعة واحدة في بكاء وتشنج ولا أكف عن الصياح بأعلى صوتي «لا إله الا الله محمد رسول الله»، وحسن المصعوق لما أفعل يحيطني بذراعه ويرجوني أن أهدأ حتى لا أكون مضحكة للناس . . . أذكر أني ظللت نائماً حتى منتصف الليل . . . وعندما سمعت آذان الفجر نزلت إلى الجامع أصلي مع الناس» (**قلوب منهكة**، ص ٢٢٤). فهل هو يصلي وفاءً لفرائض الدين أم انخراطاً في خضم ثقافة الجماعة حينما يقول «أصلي مع الناس»؟ ويلاحظ في هذا السياق أن الشيخ خلف مثّل في الوعي العام، لدى أهل حي الضاهر وما يحيط به، نمطاً من أنماط التدين الذي لاقى قبولاً واسعاً حتى إن أم جلال، التي طالما دخلت في مشادات دينية مع ابنها، قالت عنه: «كان راجل صالح وقلبه كبير . . . دا ياما جدك شكر فيه» (**قلوب منهكة**، ص ٢٢١–٢٢٢). وحين رحل جلال إلى باريس مكرهاً أصبح الدين وسيلة لمقاومة الاغتراب: «أربعة أسابيع وأنا أصلي الجمعة في مسجد باريس الكبير. أقوم إلى الحمام وأتحمم كما يفعل المسلمون صباح هذا اليوم، وأصلي الصبح والسنة . . . عندما كنت في مصر لم تكن تشغلني هذه الطقوس» (**قلوب منهكة**، ص ٢٨٣).

بيد أن الدين لا ينفك عن الثقافة. وليس الإسلام، بوصفه ممارسات حياتية اجتماعية، واحداً، بل هو متعدد بتعدد المجتمعات

التي تعتنقه. ويتجلى ذلك حين حل عيد الأضحى وراح المصلون ومعهم جلال يرددون الأدعية المعتادة في تلك المناسبة، ويعلق جلال: «رددنا هذا الدعاء . . . غير أنه لم يخطف قلبي أو سرت في دمي دفقة من تلك الدفقات التي كانت تحدث لي هناك! في بلدي البعيد . . . لم أشعر بهذا أول أمس . . . هل العيب فيّ . . . (فرب هنا هو رب هناك) . . . أم أن المكان والزمان والوجدان وخلق الله الذين من حولي هم أيضاً من محرّكات الإيمان؟» (**أيام الشتات**، ص١٧٤). اختلف المناخ الثقافي فاختلف مذاق الشعائر الدينية التي تكتسب خصوصيات معينة باختلاف الأزمنة والأمكنة والبشر الذين يمارسونها.

**الشتات والحنين إلى حي الضاهر، أرض الميعاد**

يرتبط مصطلح «الشتات»، مثله مثل مصطلح اليهودي «التائه»، بالحنين إلى أرض الميعاد، لكنه في هذا النص يشير إلى حنين آخر؛ حنين اليهود المصريين، الذين استوطنوا فرنسا، إلى مصر؛ الوطن الأصلي الذي نزحوا منه. يضاف إلى ذلك حنين جلال وجدّه زكي اليهودي إلى العودة إلى حي الضاهر الذي تغلغلت تفاصيله المادية والمعنوية في حنايا نفسيهما. على أننا ينبغي في البداية أن نفرّق تفرقة عامة بين فئتين من اليهود المصريين؛ فئة اليهود البسطاء الذين خالطوا الحياة الشعبية في القاهرة، وفئة الأثرياء. أشار الراوي إلى هذا التقسيم، واستقرّ في وعيه منذ وقت مبكر حين عاينه لمّا صاحب جدّه في رحلته إلى المعبد اليهودي، فوصف هاتين الفئتين قائلاً:

> يهود كبار ينزلون من العربات الأمريكاني الكبيرة الفورد والكاديلاك والشيفورليه، يرتدون البلاطي الموهير والفساتين والبدلات الكحلي والرمادي وربطات العنق الفرنسية وفي أيديهم أطفال صغار شعورهم مصففة وبأطقم ثياب تؤهلهم لاحتلال أغلفة مجلات الأزياء والأناقة. يمرقون من باب المعبد شامخي الرؤوس ولا ينظرون إلى أحد. والباقون غلابة مثلنا ممن يشترون ملابسهم من محلات الموسكي وشارع كلوت بك أو ربما من الحواري التي تباع فيها الملابس المستعملة. (**قلوب منهكة**، ص ص ٤٠-٤١)

وقد أتيح لجلال أن يرى مجموعة من هؤلاء اليهود الفقراء حين زار، بصحبة جدّه، اليهودي الثرى يعقوب الذي نزح إلى فرنسا مع موجة هجرة اليهود الثانية. اعتاد هذا اليهودي الثري أن يستضيف اليهود المصريين، وحين

بدأوا في التوافد وصفهم الراوي وصفاً ينبئ عن حالة البؤس والضنك التي ظهرت على وجوههم وعلى ما يلبسونه من ثياب رثّة: «جمعتهم الغربة فلم يعرفوا بعضهم البعض إلا هنا، والفضل في ذلك يرجع إلى الأستاذ يعقوب، التقطهم واحداً بعد واحد، وجعل من شقته ملاذاً لهم، يأتون إليها ليلة السبت الأول من كل شهر يتذكرون الأيام الخوالي، ويرمي كل منهم همومه على الآخرين» (**أيام الشتات**، ص ص ١٣٦-١٣٧).

وتمارس هذه الجماعة اليهودية أثناء هذه الجلسة عادات الحديث المصرية فترتفع أصواتهم، ويقاطع بعضهم البعض أثناء الكلام، ويلوحون بأيديهم، ويروون النكات الفاحشة، وفيهم من يلعن عبد الناصر لأنه سبب الوكسة التي هم فيها، فيرد الآخر بأن إسرائيل «بنت الكلب» هي السبب. وحين جاء ذكر مبادرة السادات ظن أكثرهم، وأولهم جدّ جلال، أنهم راجعون إلى بلادهم خلال أشهر قليلة، بل وإلى أشغالهم وشققهم التي كانوا يسكنونها في القاهرة أو في المدن المصرية الأخرى. وحين يلوم يعقوب بعضهم لاستحالة أن يعود إلى مصر مرة أخرى يقول الرجل: «بس دي بلدنا يا أستاذ يعقوب! اتولدنا وكبرنا فيها، عمرك سمعت عن شجرة عجوزة قلعوها من مكانها ونفعت لما زرعوها في أرض ثانية . . . دي بلدنا يا ناس ولما الواحد يختلي بنفسه ويشغل الكاسيت ويسمع أغاني زمان يقعد يبكي زى العيال» (**أيام الشتات**، ص ١٣٩). بل إن يعقوب نفسه الذي يعيش في بحبوحة من العيش ويقطن شقة فاخرة، يحيط نفسه بجو مصري، فيستمع مع رفاقه إلى أغنيات أم كلثوم وعبد الوهاب وعبد الحليم حافظ. وفي مناسبة لاحقة دار حوار بين جلال ويعقوب، الذي تزوج من أمّ جلال، راح يُعدّد فيه يعقوب فضل اليهود في إثراء الحياة الاقتصادية والفنية والفكرية في مصر، فلما واجهه جلال بأنهم مصريون بقدر ما هم يهود أجابه يعقوب: «أمال لما هّمه مصريين قعدت الحكومة تضايقهم ليه! الحكومة مش الناس! الناس في مصر طيبين لا بيخونوا عشرة ولا يعرفوا أسية ... الحكومة منها لله هي اللي فضلت تضيق عليهم لحد ما هجّوا من البلد» (**أيام الشتات**، ص ٢٦٥).

الشتات، إذن، هو أن يجبر المرء على مغادرة الأرض التي نشأ فيها وتجّسدت تفاصيلها في وجدانه، فيكون نزوحه منها، مع شوقه الشديد إليها وتعذّر نسيانها، هو الفجيعة التي تحيل حياته إلى عذاب دائم، إذ يعاني من اغتراب عن وجوده الذي لا وجود له سواه. وتزداد معاناة مثل هذا الشخص حين يضاف إلى غربته شظف العيش، وبؤس الحياة اليومية الخالية من أية بهجة. وهذا ما كان يكابده هؤلاء اليهود الفقراء الذين اضطروا إلى مغادرة مصر.

أما شمعون، خال جلال، فهو التجسيد الحي لمأساة اليهود المغتربين في فرنسا. تخرّج الرجل من كلية التجارة بجامعة الملك

فؤاد (القاهرة حالياً) وعمل رئيساً لفرع محلات داود عدس بشارع الأزهر، لكنه حين قدم إلى فرنسا لم يوفق إلى عمل مناسب، واضطر إلى العمل كناساً، وساءت أحواله النفسية من جرّاء تدهور وضعه الاقتصادي، يقول: «أستاهل اللي أنا فيه بعد ما كنت (بيه) في مصر وتحت إيدي موظفين» (**أيام الشتات**، ص٥٩). ويصف حالة الاغتراب التي يعاني منها قائلاً: «معايا الجنسية الفرنساوية آه. لكن كدّاب اللي يقول إني مطمن وعايش بين أهلي وناسي! لا لغتي لغتهم ولا طبعهم طبعي ولا عيشتي عيشتهم . . . فين لما كنت عايش في ميدان السكاكيني وعندي عربية فيات ١١٠٠ واروح واجي كل يوم» (**أيام الشتات**، ص ٦١ ). يظهر من حديث شمعون عن نفسه أن المأزق لا ينحصر في تردّي وضعه الاقتصادي، بل يتعداه إلى الشعور الممضّ بالانفصال بين وجدانه المصري والمحيط الاجتماعي المخالف لهذا الوجدان.(٦) لذلك لام شمعون جلال قائلاً: «أنا عارف إيه بس اللي رجعك من المطار! تعالى يا فالح وانا أشاورلك على عشرة ولا عشرين واحد يهودي منّنا مستعدين يسيبوا أشغالهم ويرجعوا مصر من تاني! لا هم عايزين الكرواسون والباتيه وبنجور وهالو وبردون! بيقولوا كفاية علينا الكشري والجبنة البيضة والسميط وأهلاً يا حاج وإزيك يا بيه» (**أيام الشتات**، ص٦٠).

تتضاعف حالة الاغتراب والمعاناة من الشتات عند الجدّ زكي الذي اقتلع من حي الضاهر اقتلاعاً، ولم تغب عنه أجواء هذا الحي لحظة؛ فهو لا يكف عن التذكر الحزين لتفاصيل الحياة في هذا الحي، تفاصيلها المادية والمعنوية. حين غادر الرجل إلى باريس ترك روحه هناك في حيّ الضاهر، وظل جسده في باريس يتوق إلى تلك الروح إلى أن مات، تاركاً وصية لحفيده جلال أن يسعى إلى مواراة جسده في تراب مصر،(٧) في مدافن عائلته في البساتين. بدأت مأساة الرجل من لحظة مغادرة شقة السكاكيني. يصفه الحفيد في تلك اللحظات قائلاً: «وجهه معتم وكأنه شاخ في العمر عشر سنوات أخرى، عيناه مزمومتان ورأسه مطأطأة إلى أسفل. نفس الهيئة التي أعرفه عليها عندما يكون مكروباً» (**قلوب منهكة**، ص ١٢١). وكان الطربوش، غطاء الرأس، آخر ما حاول أن يتمسّك به، ويصطحبه معه إلى فرنسا، لكن زوجته نهرته قائلة له إنهما ذاهبان إلى باريس وليس إلى الفلاحين، بل وطلبت من ابنتها، أمّ جلال، أن تتخلّص من هذا الشيء. غير أن الجدّ رفض التفريط فيه بعد أن ظل على رأسه ثلاثين عاماً، فوعدته بأن تحتفظ له به (**قلوب منهكة**، ص ١٢٢). ويتردد ذكر الطربوش بعد ذلك عدة مرات، فمثلاً حين راحت كاميليا ابنته تلملم أشياءها استعداداً

للرحيل إلى فرنسا، تحيّرت في أمر الطربوش وقالت لجلال: «طب وطربوش جدك ده أعمل فيه إيه. دا مزيّت وميساويش نكلة. . . وانت يا عم زكي . . . بتلبس إيه على راسك دلوقتي . . . تلاقيك بتلبس برنيطة وبقيت خواجة» (**قلوب منهكة**، ص ٢٢٩).(٨)

أخطأت كاميليا التقدير فلم يغب عن بال أبيها، بمجرد وصولها مع جلال إلى فرنسا، أن يسأل عن شيئين: طربوشه القديم وصورة أبي حصيرة؛ أي مصريته ودينه، ويشكلان معاً، ودون انفصال، جوهر وجوده. وحين عاد إليه طربوشه فيما بعد

> احتضنه بين يديه، يمرّر أصابعه بحنو على حوافه ويتحسس خيوط زرّه السوداء، ويتأمله مسترجعاً أيامه التي ولت وخلفتهما بعيدين؛ الطربوش، هناك مغلق عليه في دولاب معتم . . . وهو، هنا، كالميت في مسكن هواؤه راكد رطب، وليس له من دنيا في الدنيا الكبيرة التي هو فيها، باريس التي يقولون عنها بلد النور، غير سرير وحمام ومنضدة يزدرد عليها الطعام كلما نادوا عليه. (**أيام الشتات**، ص ٢٩٥)

حين انفصل زكي عن الطربوش، وباعدت بينهما الأيام، أصبح بلا روح، بل إن المسكن آل إلى ما يشبه المقبرة. وإذا كان الطربوش قد عاد إليه، فإن كرّ الزمن جعل من المحال أن يلتئم الرأس مع رفيق العمر الضائع؛ «ففوهة الطربوش وعلى ما يبدو انكمش قطرها من (الركنة) وطول الزمن وأصبحت أقل حجماً من محيط رأسه»، وقد أدرك زكي المفارقة، فكفّ عن محاولة لبس الطربوش وقال: «ألبسه هنا! ألبسه دا إيه! هو انا عبيط! أنا با جرّبه بس، أنا هعلقه على الحيطة. فين فين يا واد يا زكي؟ أيوه هنا جنب الساعة» (**أيام الشتات**، ص ٢٩٧). أدرك زكي أن الطربوش لا يتلاءم مع الظروف الجديدة، من جهتي الزمان والمكان، ليس من سبيل إلى العودة إلى حيّ الضاهر وزمن الطرابيش. لذلك علق زكي الطربوش بجوار الساعة؛ رمز الزمان. وقد كان الطربوش آخر ما ذكر الراوي وهو في المطار في طريق عودته إلى مصر، مستعيداً ما حدث حين رتب محتويات الحقيبة: «بدأت بالبيجامة التي كان يرتديها جدي وقت أن مات، ثم بقميص رمادي بكم طويل كان أثيراً لديه، والبدلة والساعة الجوفيال، أما الطربوش فوضعته بعلبة كرتون مقواة أمسكتها باليد الثانية» (**أيام الشتات**، ص٣٨٧). ومرة أخرى يجاور الراوي بين الساعة والطربوش عن طريق ذكرهما متعاقبين.

كان حلم العودة يراود زكي إلى أن مات، ولم يكف طوال إقامته في باريس عن تذكّر وطنه مصر، ولم يكن الرجل يرى تناقضاً بين يهوديته ومصريته، بل كان شديد التعلق بهما، منتمياً إليهما معاً. وحين مازحه جلال متسائلاً عما يفعل إذا نشبت حرب بين مصر وإسرائيل، أجابه: «هو انا أقل من المسلمين بتوع الهند اللي واقفين على الحدود مع باكستان وساعة اللزوم يحاربوها» (**أيام الشتات**، ص ٢٢٢). ولا يختلف جلال عن جدّه زكي فيما كان يكابده من آلام الاغتراب، وعذاب الشوق إلى حياته السابقة في حي الضاهر. ولقد مرّ بنا كيف كان إحساسه حين مارس بعض الطقوس الدينية الإسلامية في باريس وارتباطها بالوطن وحي الضاهر.

ظل جلال يحلم بالعودة، رغم أنه حقق مع صديقه اللبناني أبو الشوارب نجاحاً اقتصادياً ملحوظاً.(٩) وقد ارتبط حنينه إلى مصر بتذكره الدائم لمحبوبته المصرية نادية، ابنة حي الضاهر، جارة السكن، التي حيل بينه وبين الارتباط بها لكونه من أم يهودية، ولم يكتف ذووها بمجرد الرفض، بل غادروا السكن ورحلوا إلى سكن آخر، ولم يفلح جلال في الاهتداء إليه بسبب تكتم أسرة نادية. وعلى الرغم من أنه تزوج مرتين؛ مرة من راشيل التي ارتبط بها تحت ضغط الشهوة الجنسية، وإغرائها له، ومرة أخرى من خديجة، ابنة الشيخ منجي، التي مال إليها ميلاً شديداً، وظن أنه يحبها، وعاش معها أياماً رائعة، فإن طيف نادية، ربيبة حي الضاهر، لم يفارق خياله، وظل يهفو إليها في كل حال. حين رأى خديجة للمرة الأولى عن قرب فتن بها: «كانت في مثل عمري تقريباً وهالني قوامها الفارع . . . وصدرها المتكور المحبوك . . . كنت أحدّق في شفتيها . . . فبدت لي شفتها العليا رقيقة على خلاف الشفة الأخرى المكتنزة والمسحوبة قليلاً إلى الأسفل»، ويمضي في التعبير عن انجذابه إلى جمال خديجة الأخّاذ، لكنه يقول: «غير أني لم أهنأ . . . عضني قلبي وأتى بنادية في بالي» (**أيام الشتات**، ص ٤٨). لم يكن طيف نادية الذي يؤرّق جلال إلا طيف الوطن. كلاهما لا يفارق روحه وإن طال الفراق. ومهما شغُل براشيل أو انجذب إلى خديجة، ومهما حقّق من نجاح عملي في باريس، فإن نادية والوطن يظلان معاً فردوسه المفقود.

حين فاتح جلال جدّه في نيته الزواج من خديجة، بارك الزيجة، ولكن حين قال له جلال: «وآه يا جدّي لو تعرف قد أيه بحبها»، قال له الجد: «اسمع يا بني أنا راجل لف بيّه الزمن ودار، وبقولك إن اللي بينك وبين خديجة ده حاجة تانية غير الحب! حاجة كبيرة. حاجة حلوة. بس مش حب» (**أيام الشتات**، ص ٢٤٦). وقد صدق حدس الجّد، رغم أن النص لا يشير إلى معرفته بقصة الحب بين حفيده ونادية.(١٠)

وسيعترف جلال، بعد ذلك، بحكمة الجّد: «كان جدّي حكيماً عندما قال: إن الذي بيني وبين خديجة شيء كبير . . . شيء جميل . . . لكنه ليس حباً . . . وإلا لماذا كان طيف نادية يلحّ عليّ» (**أيام الشتات**، ص ٢٧٧). حزن جلال حزناً عظيماً حين رحلت خديجة، لكنه يقول: «كنت لخديجة الحب الأول والأخير . . . الزوج الأول والأخير . . . أحبتني في السر والعلن، وبالقلب والجسد . . . أما أنا فلم أكن أحرص إلا على أن تعيش معي في سلام، وأن أرعاها . . . أما قلبي فلم يكن لي عليه سلطان . . . وأكل الموت خديجة، ليصير الألم ألمين . . . ألم الفراق وألم الضمير» (**أيام الشتات**، ص ٣٣٦). لم يكن هذا التعلّق بنادية إلا تعلّقاً بالوطن، أو لعل نادية تحوّلت إلى أيقونة، يتجسّد الوطن من خلالها.

**الهوية السياسية**

لاحظ بعض القراء أن رواية **قلوب منهكة** تكاد تخلو من أية إشارة إلى أحداث سياسية كبرى زلزلت كيان المصريين، مع أن جلال عاصرها أثناء وجوده بمصر.(١١) من ذلك مثلاً أنه لم يذكر شيئاً عن هزيمة **١٩٦٧** أو حرب **١٩٧٣**، اللهم إلا ما جاء بشكل عابر حين ذكر أنه رسم لوحة تعبيرية عن حرب أكتوبر دخل بها المسابقة التي أعلنت عنها مديرية التربية والتعليم (**قلوب منهكة**، ص ٢١٠)، أي إن حرب أكتوبر لم تعن له شيئاً أكثر من نشاط مدرسي. وكان قبل ذلك قد ذكر – عرضاً – شعبية عبد الناصر، وذلك بمناسبة ذهابه إلى السينما وصيحات المشاهدين الداعمة حين ظهر الزعيم في الجريدة الناطقة (**قلوب منهكة**، ص ٣٩). أما فلسطين، فوردت أيضاً بشكل عابر، ودون أن تذكر بالاسم، إذ كان يتحدث عن طربه لسماع الأغاني فقال: «وعبد الوهاب . . . يتألم ويقول: أخي جاوز الظالمون المدى، لم أفهم وقتها شيئاً مما يقول لكن قلبي كان يعرف هذه الأغنية من دون باقي الأغاني» (**قلوب منهكة**، ص٤٧).(١٢)

وينبغي قبل المضي في الكلام عن هوية الراوي جلال السياسية أن نفرّق بين المؤلف الضمني والراوي من جهة، والكاتب كمال رحيّم من جهة ثانية. إن الكاتب يقول في الإهداء: «إلى رفيق طفولتي وصباي . . . إلى الروح الطاهرة . . . روح أخي الملازم محمد رحيّم الذي غيبته عنا حرب التحرير . . . حرب أكتوبر»، وهو إهداء يُستبعد معه ألا يكون الكاتب مكترثاً بالمناسبات السياسية. أما جلال الراوي، فشأنه مختلف. الوطن لديه ليس فكرة مجردة، وليس دولة أو كياناً سياسياً، الوطن هو نادية، وصديقاه في مرحلة الصبا: حسن وفهمي اللذان كانا يؤازرانه ويدفعان عنه أذى الصبية الذين كانوا يعيرونه بأمه اليهودية، والوطن هو أيضاً أمّ حسن؛ أمه بالرضاعة. الوطن هو الناس في حي

الضاهر، هو مفردات الحياة اليومية، الحسّي منها وغير الحسّي. ولم يكن حنينه إلى مصر حنيناً إلى دولة، بل حنيناً إلى ثقافة حي الضاهر، كما تتجسّد في اللغة، لغة التخاطب اليومي، التي تُشكل الوعي على نحو خاص، فاللغة هي بيت الوجود كما يقال.

ومع ذلك، فإن جلال يذكر عن نفسه أن فلسطين، وإن انزوت في جانب قصي من عقله،(١٣) فإنها لم تغب عن شعوره ووجدانه (**أيام الشتات**، ص ١١١)، كما يذكر حماسه للقومية العربية حين كان في مصر حتى إن أصدقاءه أطلقوا عليه لقب المواطن العربي الأول (**أيام الشتات**، ص ١١٣). ولكن هذا كله كان. أما زيارة السادات للقدس، التي رحّب بها اليهود المصريون، ظناً منهم أن ذلك يفتح لهم باب العودة إلى مصر، فإنها أثارت غضب العرب والمسلمين في فرنسا، وعلى رأسهم الشيخ منجي،(١٤) صديق جلال الحميم، على حين أن جلال نفسه كان يراقب الأحداث الجارية وردود الفعل الغاضبة بغير قليل من الحياد وعدم الاكتراث حتى إنه قال للشيخ منجي الثائر: «وإيه المانع لما العرب يتصالحوا مع إسرائيل! دا الصلح خير زي ما بيقولوا» (**أيام الشتات**، ص ١١٤). وحين سئل عن موقفه من مبادرة السادات قال: «مش عارف» (**أيام الشتات**، ص ١٢٨).

هل يعني ذلك كله أن جلال أصبح مفرّغاً من أي انتماء سياسي؟ هل فقد حسّه الوطني والقومي؟ الإجابة عن ذلك هي النفي. قد تستكنّ الهوية الوطنية والقومية، لكنها لا تموت. وقد تجسّد ذلك سردياً حين كانت جدته تراقب زيارة السادات لإسرائيل في التلفزيون فعلقت قائلة: «أهو كدا السادات يبقى راجل عاقل وبتاع سياسة صحيح راح هناك يحايلهم علشان يرجعوا له سينا»، ثم تضيف: «أهو السادات يبعد بأه عن غزة وفلسطين وسوريا ومش عارفه إيه وإيه. الحاجات إللي جابت لبلده الكافية، وهناك في إسرائيل يمكن يسامحوه بعد ما يشدوا ودنه»، وعند هذا الحد يقول جلال:

> جُن جنوني، انفجرت غاضباً موبخاً قاذفاً بكلام كثير، ولاعناً إسرائيل، بل وحتى السادات الذي ذهب لهؤلاء الناس! واليهود الذين في كل مكان! . . . ما هذا الشيء الكامن بداخلي وفجرته هذه الحيزبون . . . ذلك الشيء الذي في العميق وخزته جدتي، فأطبق على صدري وأخذني في خفقة جفن إلى أبي ورفاقه الذين أبحروا ذات يوم . . . فأمسكت بهم تيارات الماء . . . ولم تدعهم إلا غرقى. (**أيام الشتات**، ص ١٢٣)

ولقد لعن جلال اليهود رغم أنه في حواراته مع الشيخ منجي كان يفرّق بين اليهود والصهاينة، وذلك في معرض دفاعه عن أمه وجدّه وجدّته وأهله من اليهود الذين لا يعتنقون الصهيونية.

ومع ذلك كله، فإن فجيعة الغربة، التي تمثل مركز الثقل الدلالي في روايتي **قلوب منهكة** و**أيام الشتات**، تكمن في جانبها الثقافي، لا السياسي. والمقصود بالثقافة هنا ممارسات الحياة اليومية، وما يتخللها من شعائر وطقوس ولغة. ولذلك فإن المؤلف الضمني كان حريصاً طوال الوقت على إنطاق الشخصيات بلهجاتهم العاميّة، سواء كانت عاميّة مصرية أم تونسية أم لبنانية.(١٥) وحين يقرّر العودة إلى مصر يحادث نفسه قائلاً:

> لم أجد حلاً إلا أن أترك حالي ومالي هنا وأعود، لا لأهلي الذين هناك ... إنما لبلدي للدنيا القديمة ... للشوارع القديمة ... وواحد شاي يا عم لبيب بس يكون كشري وعلى ميّة بيضة ... وازيك يا جلال، وفين أيامك يا ابن الحلال؟ وإيه أخبار الدنيا معاك وناوي بأه تقعد معانا هنا في الضاهر ولا هتعزل على مصر الجديدة، وازي فلان ... بخير والحمد الله، طيب وفلان ... تعيش انت بس أولاده صلاة النبي عليهم، طيب إيه رأيك بأه نروح لهم بكرة سوا بعد العصر وآهو بالمرة تعزيهم ... خلاص اتفقنا يا حاج عباس. (**أيام الشتات**، ص ٣٨٥)

في **قلوب منهكة** دارت معظم الأحداث حول أزمة الراوي من جرّاء تشتته بين هويتين؛ هوية الأم اليهودية، وهوية الأب المسلم. وقد انتهى هذا الصراع بالتحامه بهويته الإسلامية. غير أن الدين، حسب منطق الجدّ، الذي يعدّ الممثل الحقيقي لإيديولوجية النص، ليس إلا أحد مكّونات الثقافة، التي تمثل الإطار الأشمل الذي يضم داخله عناصر تتناغم أو تتصادم، ولكن في حدود هذا الإطار. فالمواطنة، لا الدين، هي أساس الانتماء. «المواطنة تعني الثقافة المشتركة كما تتجلى في التفاصيل اليومية التي يمارسها «المواطنون» في أقوالهم وأفعالهم، بغض النظر عن انتماءاتهم الدينية.

## الهوامش

(١) كمال رحيم من مواليد ١٩٤٧. حصل عام ١٩٦٨ على ليسانس الحقوق والشرطة، ثم أكمل دراساته في مجال القانون وحصل عام ١٩٨٦ على

درجة الدكتوراه من جامعة القاهرة. تدرّج في وظائف الشرطة حتى رتبة لواء. وله عدد من الكتب والدراسات القانونية. زار بحكم مناصبه في الشرطة بعض الدول العربية والأوروبية. صدر له في عام ١٩٩٧ مجموعة قصصية عنوانها **أيام في المنفى**، فازت منها قصتان في سنتين متتاليتين بالجائزة الأولى لنادي القصة عامي ١٩٩٨ و١٩٩٩. حصلت روايته الأولى **قلوب منهكة** (القاهرة: دار النيل للنشر، ٢٠٠٤) على جائزة الدولة التشجيعية عام ٢٠٠٥. كما صدرت له رواية أخرى بعنوان **أيام الشتات** (القاهرة: وكالة سفنكس للفنون والآداب، ٢٠٠٨). وكل الاستشهادات من الروايتين تحيل إلى هاتين الطبعتين مع وضع أرقام الصفحات بين قوسين.

(٢) من أول ما ترسّب في وعي جلال، وهو طفل رضيع، عنصرية الجدّة واحتقارها لكل ما هو مصري عربي إسلامي. لذلك كان أول ظهور للجدّة مرتبطاً بالفزع: «كل الذي أذكره أني قمت مفزوعاً على صوت جدّتي. كانت خنفاء وكلامها سريعاً» (**قلوب منهكة**، ص ٩ ). ومن المظاهر المبكرة لعنصرية هذه الجدّة وعنفها ما دار حول موت والد جلال، وكانت الجدّة قد تحدثت بشكل سيئ عن هذا الوالد بعد أن أبلغتهم إحدى الجارات بوفاته قائلة: «الله يرحمه بأه . . . دا شهيد ومقامه كبير عند ربنا»، فقالت الجدّة باستهانة: «شهيد!!»، فردت أمّ جلال: «أيوه شهيد . . . مش كان رايح يدافع عن بلده . . . يبقى شهيد»، فأجابت الجدّة: «أنا لا بتكلم دلوقتي عن الرحمة ولا الشهادة. كان فيه إيه يا عين أمك علشان تتجوّزيه. دا لكان مننا ولا من دينا» (**قلوب منهكة**، ص١٠).

(٣) من أجل التعرّف على مجتمع اليهود في مصر، انظر محمد أبو الغار، **يهود مصر، من الازدهار إلى الشتات** (القاهرة: دار الهلال، ١٩٩٢). وتتميز الدراسة بأنها أحاطت بالكتابات السابقة في الموضوع، ودلّت القارئ عليها. أما تجسيد الشخصية اليهودية في الأعمال السردية المصرية، فيمكن الرجوع بشأنه إلى رشاد عبدالله الشامي، **الشخصية اليهودية في أدب إحسان عبد القدوس** (القاهرة: دار الهلال، ١٩٩٢).

(٤) يقول عبد الحميد حواس وصابر العادلي عن أبي حصيرة: «أجمعت معظم الأقوال على أنه وليّ يهودي . . . وقبر الولي في حجرة تحوطها من الخارج قبور تحمل أسماء وعلامات يهودية . . . يعترف أهالي المنطقة بقدرات علاجية لأبو حصيرة . . . وسمي أبو حصيرة لأنه كان يسير على حصيرة مفروشة على سطح الماء . . . أو لأنه كان . . . يجلس على حصيرة بشارع الصاغة». و هو من أولياء منطقة دمنهور بدلتا مصر. انظر عبدالحميد حواس وصابر العادلى، «ملاحظات حول بعض الظواهر الفولكلورية بمحافظة البحيرة»، **مجلة الفنون الشعبية**، العدد ١٢ (١٩٧٠)، ص٧٠. وقد دلّنا عبد الحميد حواس مشكوراً على هذه المادة.

(٥) ومع أن الجدّة أظهرت احتقاراً لكل ما هو شرقي، فإن بعض مكونات ثقافة حي الضاهر ترسبت في نفسها، فهي على سبيل المثال تنهر حفيدتها لأنها ارتدت ثوباً غير محتشم في وجود جلال، قائلة: «إيه المسخره دى يا بت!... مانتيش شايفة ان ابن خالتك قاعد معانا» (**أيام الشتات**، ص ٧٢)، كما أن موقفها من سلوك راشيل التي فقدت عذريتها كان شبيهاً بموقف أية مصرية من حي الضاهر. يحكي الجد عنها، وكيف كانت تحدث ابنتها أم راشيل قائلة: «خلي بالك من بنتك ومتنسيش إننا في الأول والآخر ولاد بلد وجدك اسحاق كان بيلبس قفطان وجلابية، يعني الشرف عندنا غالي والعيب هو العيب» (**أيام الشتات**، ص ٢١٨). كانت الجدّة ميّالة كما هو واضح إلى المفهوم المصري عن الاحتشام.

(٦) يمثل موقف هارون، والد راشيل، حالة مختلفة، فهو نموذج للبورجوازي الصغير الذي يسعى إلى الترقّي طبقياً واقتصادياً، دون مراعاة أية قيم أخلاقية، وكانت الجدّة تشك في أنه يقوم بأعمال غير مشروعة كالتجارة في المخدرات. وما إن انفتحت مصر اقتصادياً حتى سافر إلى إسرائيل للتعاون مع إيزاك، أحد أخوال جلال، في مشروعات لاستغلال منطقة شرم الشيخ سياحياً عن طريق افتتاح نواد للقمار. تعاون معهم أيضاً يعقوب، زوج الأم، الذي وإن بدا عقلانياً متعاطفاً مع فقراء اليهود المصريين، فإنه لم يجد بأساً في التعاون مع إيزاك الذي كان يقوم ببناء المستعمرات اليهودية على أرض فلسطين (**أيام الشتات**، ص ص ٢٥٥-٢٥٩).

(٧) دار صراع عنيف بين جلال وأقاربه اليهود حول جثمان الجدّ، الذي أوصى كتابة بأن يوارى في تراب مصر، في حين أن ذويه كانوا يصرّون على نقل جثمانه إلى إسرائيل. وقد انتهى هذا الصراع بأن دفن في فرنسا، إذ حالت عقبات إدارية دون إمكان نقل الجثمان خارج فرنسا، وإن كان شمعون قد كشف لجلال – فيما بعد – عن أن إيزاك لم يكن حريصاً على دفن الجد في إسرائيل كما تظاهر؛ يقول شمعون مخاطباً جلال: «هو انت فاكر إن إيزاك أبو وش زى الكرنبايه ده يرضى يدفع فرنك واحد في حاجه زى دي! و لا حتى المسألة دي تشغله دماغ، دا كان بيهوش... عشان انت تاخد وتدي معاه وانت تتنازل عن حكاية مصر، وهو كمان يتنازل عن دفن البابا في إسرائيل! وهو في الحقيقة لا اتنازل ولا حاجة» (**أيام الشتات**، ص ٣٧١).

(٨) ولعل أول من جعل الطربوش علامة على الأصالة والانتماء الشيخ درويش في رواية نجيب محفوظ **زقاق المدق** حين حذر عباس الحلو قائلاً: «لا تمش بلا طربوش! احذر أن تعرّي رأسك في مثل هذا الجو، في مثل هذه الدنيا، فمخ الفتى يتبخّر ويطير، هذا أمر معروف في المأساة ومعناه بالإنجليزية Tragedy». راجع: **زقاق المدق** (القاهرة: مكتبة

مصر، ١٩٧٧)، ص ٤٥. خلع الطربوش يمكن أن يفهم في هذا النص بمعنى الانخلاع عن الهوية المصرية، لأن عباس الحلو سينساق وراء حميدة، فيعمل في معسكرات الإنجليز، الذين سُيقتل على أيديهم في نهاية الأمر. وقد كانت هذه النهاية المأساوية نتيجة تعرية رأسه (عقله) فأصبح عرضة لتسلّط حميدة.

(٩) حقّق جلال وأبو الشوارب نجاحاً تجارياً بفضل مساعدة راشيل، التي أرشدتهما إلى أفضل الطرق لكسب المال من عرب الخليج الذين يأتون إلى باريس، إذ كان لها خبرة طويلة، بحكم عملها في مجال السياحة، في كيفية التعامل مع هؤلاء الأثرياء. وكان الهم الأول لهؤلاء الخليجيين الحصول، بأي ثمن، على المنشطات الجنسية، والملابس النسائية المثيرة. ومع ذلك، فإن النص يشير إلى أنه حتى هؤلاء توقفوا عن التعامل مع راشيل بعد زيارة أنور السادات للقدس.

(١٠) من المحتمل، مع ذلك، أن تكون كاميليا قد أفضت إلى أبيها بقصة الحب بين جلال ونادية، التي حدثت أثناء وجودها في القاهرة، بينما كان الجدّ في فرنسا.

(١١) في تعقيبه الملحق بالنص الروائي، يقول صفوت عبد الحميد: «فالراوي لم يتعرّض لأي من الأحداث السياسية الملازمة لأحداث الرواية وخاصة أن هناك أحداثاً ضخمة وصراعات سياسية بين مصر وإسرائيل خلال هذه السنوات»، ويعدّد هذه الأحداث (**قلوب منهكة**، ص ٣١٠).

(١٢) من المعروف أن كلمات هذه الأغنية هي قصيدة للشاعر المصري على محمود طه عن فلسطين، وضع لها الموسيقار المصري محمد عبدالوهاب لحناً مؤثراً، وكانت تذاع في المناسبات القومية الخاصة بفلسطين.

(١٣) لكن النص لا يهمل وجهة النظر الفلسطينية، وذلك من خلال أبي الشوارب، جزئياً، ثم من خلال الشيخ عكرمة الذي أسهب، إلى حد ما، في عرض الحالة الفلسطينية (**أيام الشتات**، ص ص ١٧٧-١٨١). غير أن شخصية هذا الفلسطيني، الشيخ عكرمة، تبدو مقحمة على النص، وكأنه قد جيء به ليعبّر، بشكل خطابي غير مؤثر، عن صوت فلسطين. وعلى العكس من ذلك كان خطاب أبي الشوارب، وهو من جنوب لبنان، لأن القارئ عايشه من خلال السرد، في مواقف مختلفة، فهو من نسيج النص؛ أي شخصية حيّة ذات ملامح تكشّفت تدريجياً من خلال أحداث الرواية.

(١٤) نلاحظ أن الشيخ منجي اتسم بقدر من العنف والعنصرية. تجسّد ذلك من خلال تعامله الفظ مع زبائنه (وقد كان جزّاراً) ومن خلال كراهيته الشديدة لأخوال جلال اليهود. وكان الصراع العنيف محتدماً بينه وبين جدّة جلال، وكان الرجل جار سكن لعائلة جلال. وحين اصطحب جلال

جدّه إلى شقة الشيخ منجي، لاحظ الجدّ صورة معلقة على الحائط لشخص متين البنيان، تبدو على وجهه علامات التجهم (وهي صورة والد الشيخ منجي)، وكأن العنف والعدوانية صفة موروثة في عائلة الرجل. لم يكن الجدّ مرتاحاً للصورة حتى إنه قال: «يا ستار يا رب فيه ناس في الدنيا بالسحنة دي! دا زي ما يكون بيبحلق فيّه وعايز يكرشني» (**أيام الشتات**، ص ٢٧٣). وقد علّق الراوي على موقف الشيخ منجي السياسي قائلاً: «الشيخ منجي ليس كأي شيخ وكأي بشر في عدائه لليهود، ومناكفاته مع جدتي ليست مناكفات جيران وسحابات صيف، مآلها إلى الزوال! فالمسألة عنده مسألة حرام وحلال ومبدأ ودين، وإِذْنٌ لنا من الله بأن نقاتل من أخرجونا من ديارنا». يلاحظ مع ذلك أن زواج جلال من خديجة، ثم موت خديجة، وما صاحب ذلك من تزاور، سواء للاحتفال، أو للقيام بواجبات العزاء، كل ذلك أدّى إلى التخفيف المتدرج للعداء بين الجدّة والشيخ منجي، بل راحت الجدّة تتودّد للشيخ، الذي بادلها وداً بود (**أيام الشتات**، ص ٣٣٧-٣٣٨). فكأن الشيخ والجدّة قد تخلى كل منهما عن قدر من عدائه العنصري تجاه الآخر. حدث ذلك، ربما، لأن كلاً منهما اكتشف، من خلال المعايشة، أن الآخر ليس شيطاناً خالصاً.

(١٥) يتقن كمال رحيم استخدام اللهجات المصرية واللبنانية والتونسية في حوارات شخصياته الروائية. وفي لقائي الشخصي معه في ٢٠٠٩/١١/١٣ في القاهرة، سألته عن تلك الظاهرة، فرد بأنه أفاد في هذا الصدد من صديقين له من جنوب لبنان ومن تونس، وكان دائم السؤال لهما عما يوازى التعبيرات العامية المصرية في اللهجتين اللبنانية والتونسية. أما معرفته بالمجتمع اليهودي فترجع إلى صداقته في شبابه الباكر ليهودي مصري كان يتبادل معه الزيارات المنزلية. وترجع إحاطته بأحوال اليهود المصريين الذين رحلوا إلى فرنسا إلى الفترة التي عاشها في باريس حين كان يجمع المادة العلمية لرسالته الجامعية. وأشار إلى أن المشهد الذي يصور اجتماع اليهود المصريين في شقة يعقوب يكاد يكون محاكاة لما عاينه بنفسه هناك، ويذكر أن تعبير «إسرائيل بنت الكلب» كان مما تفوه به بعضهم في هذه المناسبة، كما يذكر أن هذا الاجتماع كان يختتم دائماً بالاستماع إلى أغنية عبدالحليم حافظ «سواح»، وهو ما ذكره في روايته (**أيام الشتات**، ص ١٤٢).

# «بيان التنحي» وذاكرة الهزيمة: مدخل بلاغي لتحليل الخطاب السياسي

عماد عبد اللطيف

كانت هذه السطور هي أصعب ما كتبتُ في حياتي؛
فقد كانت مصر كلها على حد الموسى.
-- محمد حسنين هيكل (متحدثاً عن «بيان التنحي»)

لغة السياسة هي لغة الدفاع عمَّا لا يمكن الدفاع عنه.
-- جورج أورويل

لدى كل أمة ذخيرة خطابية تصنع تاريخها وتشكل وعيها. وتتكون هذه الذخيرة من نصوص وكلام يشق طريقه إلى ذاكرة الأمة، ليصبح جزءاً لا يتجزأ منها. ويرتبط مثل هذا الكلام وهذه النصوص – في الغالب – بشخصيات استثنائية، وعادة ما يكون نتاج لحظات تاريخية بالغة الخصوصية؛ تكون فيها حواس الأمة كاملةً مهيأةً لتلقيه والانفعال به. ومن بين النصوص التي لا تزال حاضرة وفاعلة في الذاكرة المصرية والعربية المعاصرة «بيان التنحي» الذي ألقاه الرئيس المصري الراحل جمال عبد الناصر إثر هزيمة يونيو ١٩٦٧.(١) وهو البيان الذي سيكون موضوع هذه المقالة.

تُحاجج هذه المقالة بأن صياغة «بيان التنحي» على المستوى البلاغي كانت ذات تأثير في إنتاج الاستجابات التي أعقبت إلقاءه، والتي تمثلت أوضح ما يكون في المظاهرات الهائلة الرافضة للهزيمة والتنحي معاً. وللبرهنة على ذلك، تنخرط الدراسة في تحليل تفصيلي لبعض أهم الظواهر البلاغية في البيان، مثل التلطيف اللفظي الذي ينتمي إلى المجال المعجمي والدلالي، والضمائر الشخصية وتحولاتها التي ترتبط بالتماسك النصي والمعنوي، والاستعارة التي تقع في قلب المجاز، وطرق أداء عبد الناصر للبيان صوتياً وحركياً. ولتفسير العلاقة بين صياغة البيان بلاغياً والاستجابات التي أعقبته، سوف أحلل عمليات إنتاج البيان وتوزيعه واستهلاكه، مستعيناً بتصور متكامل عن الحدث الخطابي، أقوم بتوضيحه فيما يأتي.

## النص والمجتمع والممارسة الخطابية

تسعى هذه الدراسة إلى تقديم تحليل بلاغي لـ«بيان التنحي»، يتعامل مع البيان بوصفه حدثاً خطابياً discursive event بالمعنى الذي رسخه نورمان فيركلف أهم مؤسسي التحليل النقدي للخطاب. وللحدث الخطابي وفقاً لفيركلف ثلاثة أبعاد هي: كونه نصاً، وممارسة خطابية، وممارسة اجتماعية.(٢) ويكشف هذا التقسيم عن العلاقات المتبادلة بين النص والممارسات الخطابية والاجتماعية؛ فالنص يمثل جزءاً من الممارسات الخطابية من ناحية والممارسات الاجتماعية الأوسع من ناحية أخرى. كما يكشف عن أهمية الممارسات الخطابية، بما فيها عمليات إنتاج الخطاب وتلقيه، في صياغة النص والممارسة الاجتماعية في الوقت ذاته. ولا بد أن يتجلى الوعي بأبعاد الحدث الخطابي المختلفة أثناء عملية التحليل. وقد وضع فيركلف إزاء كل بُعد من هذه الأبعاد مستوى من مستويات التحليل. المستوى الأول هو مستوى تحليل النص، ويدرس ملامح الخطاب اللغوية وتنظيم مكوناته الملموسة، مثل المفردات والتراكيب والتماسك النصي وبنية النص. أما المستوى الثاني، فهو تحليل الممارسات الخطابية؛ أي تحليل الخطاب بوصفه شيئاً يُنتَج ويُوزَّع ويُستهلك في المجتمع. ويرى بلومارت وبولكن أن مقاربة الخطاب بوصفه ممارسة خطابية تعني أنه أثناء تحليل المفردات والتراكيب والتماسك النصي وبنية النص يجب أن يتوجه الاهتمام إلى أفعال الكلام والتماسك المعنوي والتناص، وهي عناصر تربط النص بسياقه.(٣) وأخيراً، يقوم المستوى الثالث بتحليل الممارسات الاجتماعية؛ أي المؤثرات الإيديولوجية وعمليات الهيمنة التي يُعد الخطاب مظهراً لها.

سوف أقوم بتحليل مستويات النص والممارسات الخطابية والاجتماعية في «بيان التنحي»، بدءاً بدراسة مستوى الممارسات الخطابية السابقة على إلقاء البيان: عملية إعداد البيان وما تتضمنه من اختيارات بلاغية، وعملية مراجعته وتنقيحه. ثم أدرس مستوى تحليل نص البيان، مركزاً على مجموعة من الظواهر البلاغية الحاسمة في إنجاز البيان وظيفتي الإقناع والتأثير. وفي سياق ذلك، أدرس مستوى الممارسات الاجتماعية التي وجهت عمليات إنتاج البيان وتلقيه وتأويله. ولأن أبعاد البيان المختلفة تتقاطع في كثير من المواضع، فمن الطبيعي أن تتداخل مستويات التحليل؛ فتستمر الحركة من النص إلى الممارسات الخطابية إلى الممارسات الاجتماعية والعكس.

## من المسودة إلى النص: العالَم والخطاب في لحظات التشكل

يُنسب «بيان التنحي» إلى الرئيس جمال عبد الناصر الذي ألقاه بصوته في مساء التاسع من يونيو ١٩٦٧. لكن البيان ينسب أيضاً إلى محمد

حسنين هيكل،(٤) الذي كشف عن أنه هو من قام بكتابته، وسرد تفاصيل وقائع كتابة مشروع البيان في مساء الثامن من يونيو، والنقاشات التي دارت بينه وعبد الناصر أثناء مراجعة هذا المشروع في نهار التاسع منه.(٥)

تُعد ظاهرة قيام شخص أو مجموعة من الأشخاص بكتابة مشاريع خطب رجال السياسة وبياناتهم أحد أهم ظواهر الاتصال السياسي المعاصر. فعلى الرغم من أن مهنة كتابة الخطب السياسية كانت معروفة منذ العصر اليوناني حين كان يقوم محترفو البلاغة بكتابة خطب بعض السياسيين اليونانيين مقابل أجر،(٦) فإن هذه المهنة لم تزدهر إلا منذ منتصف القرن العشرين. وقد أدى هذا الازدهار إلى نحت تسميات للقائمين بها؛ فأُطلِق على الشخص الذي يقوم بكتابة نص لكي يقوم شخص آخر بإلقائه دون إشارة إلى مؤلفه الأصلي الكاتب الخفي. أما النصوص التي يكتبها شخص – أو أشخاص – ليلقيها شخص آخر تنسب إليه فيُطلَق عليها الكتابة الخفيَّة.(٧)

تبدو مسألة الكاتب الخفي ذات حساسية خاصة في المقالة الحالية التي تتخذ من لغة البيان مادة للدراسة. وقد يمكن الادعاء بأن هذا البيان يمثِّل عبد الناصر بقدر ما يمثِّل مؤلفه الأصلي هيكل. ويبدو هذا صحيحاً تماماً لو أننا بصدد تقديم دراسة لأسلوب جمال عبد الناصر؛ لأن أية محاولة لاستخلاص سمات ما يمكن تسميته «الأسلوب الخطابي لعبد الناصر»، أو خصائصه، استناداً إلى خطبه المعدة سلفاً سوف تواجَه بمشكِل الكاتب الخفي. إلى حد أن ما قد يُقدَّم على أنه «البصمة الأسلوبية» لعبد الناصر ربما لا يعدو – في حال عدم الوعي بهذا المشكل – أن يكون البصمة الأسلوبية لكاتبه الخفي.

على الرغم من ذلك، فإن مشكل الكاتب الخفي ذو تأثير محدود على نتائج الدراسة الحالية، بالنظر إلى توجهها وغايتها. فالتوجه النقدي هنا غير معني باستخلاص السمات الأسلوبية المميِّزة للخطب، بقدر عنايته بتفسير كيف تقوم هذه الخطب بالتأثير في الجماهير المستهدَفة، وتحليل كيف تكون الصياغة اللغوية والبلاغية للبيان كاشفةً عن الأغراض التي تسعى إلى تحقيقها، والنتائج الفعلية التي ترتبت عليها. ومن هذه الزاوية، فإن تحليل البيان نقدياً لا يمكن أن يتحقق دون الأخذ في الحسبان مرحلة إنتاجه، التي تُصاغ فيها الاختيارات اللغوية والبلاغية الأساسية. أما غايتنا فهي فهم كيف تتحول البلاغة السياسية إلى أفعال سياسية، وبخاصة في لحظات الأزمات؛ وهي غاية تتجاوز العناية الشكلية بالأسلوب إلى العناية بحياة اللغة فعلياً في المجتمع. ولتحقيق هذه الغاية، لا بد أن يتجاوز البحثُ تحليلَ الظواهر اللغوية والبلاغية شكلياً إلى تحليل العلاقات الشائكة بين النص والمجتمع، ومن بينها عملية إنتاج النص وتحوله – بعد أن تمَّ إلقاؤه فعلياً – إلى خطاب.

وفي الواقع، فإن مسألة الكاتب الخفي ذات تأثير إيجابي لا سلبي في دراستنا. فمن حسن الحظ أن لدينا معلومات تفصيلية عن عملية كتابة هذا البيان منذ كان فكرةً ومشروعاً حتى أصبح نصاً ثم خطاباً.(٨) وتعطينا هذه التفاصيل فرصة نادرة لدراسة عملية تشكل الخطاب السياسي في لحظة مفصلية من تاريخ مصر المعاصر، كما أنها تتيح لنا تتبع أشكال الصراع التي توجد بين رؤيتين للعالَم تختلفان في أشياء وتتفقان في أشياء أخرى؛ هما رؤية الكاتب والحاكم. وتمكّننا من معرفة كيف أمكن «تسوية» التعارضات التي توجد بين الرؤيتين بواسطة عمليات تحاور وتفاوض مكثفة، وكيف تعكس الاختيارات اللغوية والبلاغية لكل منهما حدود رؤيته للعالم.

لقد قام هيكل بدور جذري في تشكيل توجهات السياسة المصرية وإيديولوجيتها في خمسينيات القرن الماضي وستينياته وأوائل سبعينياته. فقد قام من ناحية بكتابة معظم خطب عبد الناصر طوال فترة توليه الحكم ومعظم خطب السادات في الفترة من ١٩٧٠ حتى ١٩٧٤. كما يُنسب إليه كتابة بعض أهم الوثائق التي حملت توقيع عبد الناصر، وأسهمت بشكل محوري في تأسيس ما بات يُعرف بـ«الإيديولوجيا الناصرية»؛ أي مجموعة القيم والمبادئ والأفكار والمفاهيم التي تبنّاها نظام عبد الناصر ودافع عنها، ومن أهم هذه الوثائق كتاب **فلسفة الثورة**. إضافة إلى ذلك، كان هيكل من خلال رئاسته تحرير جريدة **الأهرام** – أكثر الجرائد العربية مبيعاً في تلك الفترة – يسهم في توجيه الرأي العام المصري والعربي على نحو ربما لم يُتح لصحفي عربي آخر في العصر الحديث. وبالمثل، كان لمقاله الأسبوعي في جريدة **الأهرام**، الذي حمل عنوان «بصراحة»، تأثير في صياغة وعي الجماهير وسياسات الحكم لم يُتح لأي مقال أسبوعي آخر.

إضافة إلى ذلك، فإن هيكل – وقت كتابة البيان – لم يكن مجرد «كاتبَ خُطب»، بل كان شريكاً أساسياً في الحكم. لقد ذكر أنه كان أحد أشخاص قلائل أتيح لهم لقاء عبد الناصر والجلوس معه في اليوم السابق على التنحي واليوم الذي تلاه. كما ذكر أن عبد الناصر أعطاه تفويضاً كاملاً حين خلد إلى النوم بعد انتهائه من إلقاء البيان، وأن رجال الدولة جميعاً، ابتداءً من رئيس مجلس الأمة وانتهاءً بوزراء الداخلية والإعلام، لم تكن لديهم وسيلة للوصول إلى عبد الناصر نفسه – بعد أن ألقى «بيان التنحي» – إلا من خلال هيكل. ومن يستمع إلى وصف هيكل الوقائع التي أعقبت إلقاء «بيان التنحي» لا يساوره شك أنه كان الحاكم الفعلي في تلك السويعات العصيبة. وهكذا، فإن هيكل عشية كتابة «بيان التنحي» لم يكن جزءاً من «لسان» السلطة ممثلةً في رئيس الدولة فحسب، بل كان جزءاً من قلبها وعقلها ويدها أيضاً.

يصف هيكل وقائع تكليفه بكتابة البيان قائلاً: «كان عبد الناصر قد طلب إلي أن أعدَّ له مشروع خطابه إلى الأمة بالتنحي . . . ولم يكن في مقدوره – إنسانياً – تلك الليلة مع أحزانه وشواغله أن يجلس ليكتب خطاباً، فاتفق معي على نقاطه، وتعهدت بأن أكتبه له.(٩) ويذكر أنه قضى ساعات مع عبد الناصر يتناقشان حول صياغة البيان، في وقت كان العالم من حولهما في حالة غليان حقيقي، وكانت مصر على حد الموسى كما وصفها هيكل. ويبرهن الانشغال لساعات كاملة في صياغة الخطاب، في هذا الوقت العصيب، على الأهمية التي كانا يوليانها هذه الصياغة.

على الرغم من «اتفاق» عبد الناصر وهيكل على «نقاط الخطاب» والتلاقي الواضح بين أفكارهما واختياراتهما، فقد قامت بعض الاختلافات بين ما سطره هيكل وما أراده عبد الناصر. بعض هذه الاختلافات كان يتعلق بمسائل محورية مثل التعبير عن مدى مسئولية عبد الناصر عن النكسة؛ فقد ذكر هيكل أن عبد الناصر «أقر ما كتبته حتى نقطة: (إنني على استعداد لتحمل نصيبي من المسئولية)، عبد الناصر قال لي: لا، اكتب ( أتحمل المسئولية كاملة)».(١٠) وقد أعاد هيكل كتابة العبارة مبقياً على تعبير «إنني على استعداد»، ومضيفاً إليه «المسئولية كاملة» بدلاً من «نصيبي من المسئولية». كما اختلفا حول مسألة من سيخلف عبد الناصر بعد تنحيه. كان رأي عبد الناصر أن يكتب هيكل اسم شمس بدران، وزير الحربية في ذلك الوقت؛ لكن هيكل رفض: «أنا حاولت أكتب اسم شمس بدران ولم يطاوعني أي قلم».(١١) وبالفعل، اقتنع عبد الناصر بحجج هيكل المفنِّدة اختيار شمس بدران، واختار بدلاً منه زكريا محيي الدين، عضو مجلس قيادة الثورة الذي شغل منصبي رئيس الوزراء ونائب رئيس الجمهورية. وبالمثل، رفض عبد الناصر اختيار هيكل تعبير «النكسة» كما سنرى لاحقاً، ثم اقتنع به في نهاية الأمر.

يبدو من الأمثلة السابقة أن شطراً كبيراً من النقاش تعلق مباشرة باختيارات بلاغية؛ مثل الاختيار بين مفردتي «النكسة» و«الهزيمة»، أو الاختيار بين تركيب «على استعداد لتحمل» و«أتحمل»، أو الاختيار بين «المسئولية» و«مسئولية»، وهي اختيارات أثرت في محصلة البيان النهائية، إضافة إلى أنها تشي بوجود اختلاف بين الكاتب والحاكم في نوع البلاغة التي يميل إلى استخدامها؛ ففي حين يبدو عبد الناصر أميل إلى إنتاج بلاغة مباشرة، تُسمِّي الأشياء بأسمائها وتقول الأشياء بأوضح الطرق وأوجزها، يبدو هيكل أميل إلى استخدام بلاغة مراوغة، تُكنِّي وتُلطِّف، وتُخفي أكثر مما تُصرح. ويظهر من صيغة البيان النهائية أن الكاتب والحاكم كليهما قد انحازا إلى بلاغة المراوغة في نهاية المطاف. وهو ما يتجلى – على سبيل المثال – في شيوع ظاهرة التلطيف اللفظي، أولى الظواهر البلاغية التي سندرسها .

## التلطيف اللفظي: اللغة وتشكيل العالم

يمكن تعريف التلطيف اللفظي euphemism في الخطاب السياسي بأنه: استخدام تعبيرات مخففة أو غامضة أو غير مباشرة للإشارة إلى ظاهرة أو سلوك أو حدث ما، بهدف توجيه إدراك مستخدمي اللغة لهذه الظاهرة أو السلوك أو الحدث وجهة معينة. ويشير هذا التعريف إلى أن التلطيف اللفظي يؤثر في إدراك البشر للواقع الذي تقدمه التعبيرات الملطِّفة، انطلاقاً من تصور يرى أن اللغة التي نستخدمها تصوغ إدراكنا للعالم بالقدر نفسه الذي تكشف عنه.(١٢) كما يفترض التعريف أن التلطيف اللفظي يحدث في حالة إمكان وجود أكثر من تعبير أو تسمية للإشارة إلى شيء واحد، أحدها يُقدم الشيء كما هو، والآخر يُقدمه ملطَّفاً، والثالث يقدمه مهوَّلاً.(١٣)

التلطيف اللفظي سمة أساسية من سمات لغة السياسة. يرجع ذلك إلى أن لغة السياسة غايتها تأسيس عالم لغوي يحقق للسياسيين الذين يُنشئونه طموحاتهم في السيطرة على السلطة والاحتفاظ بها وإضفاء الشرعية عليها. وفي سبيل تحقيق ذلك، يلجأ السياسيون ومعاونوهم إلى حشد من الظواهر اللغوية والبلاغية التي تمكنهم من تقديم تصورات عن العالم الخارجي، تحاول صياغة توجهات أفراد الشعب نحو هذا العالم، وتشكل سلوكياتهم تجاهه. ويمكن التلطيف اللفظي من إنتاج نسخ معدلة ومكيَّفة من «الواقع» أو «الحقيقة» تقوم بصياغة توجهات الجمهور وسلوكياته، بما يخدم مصالح هؤلاء السياسيين. وسوف أكون معنياً في الصفحات الآتية بالكشف عن آليات استخدام التلطيف اللفظي ووظائفه ودوره في صياغة وعي المصريين بالهزيمة.

## من الهزيمة إلى النكسة: تهوين أم استهانة؟

استخدم عبد الناصر في «بيان التنحي» تسمية «النكسة» لوصف نتيجة حرب ٥ يونيو، ١٩٦٧. خلَّفت هذه الحرب – التي حملت أيضاً اسم «حرب الأيام الستة»(١٤) – آثاراً مدمرة على جميع المستويات العسكرية والسياسية والاقتصادية.(١٥) وحين كان عبد الناصر يتهيَّأ لإلقاء «بيان التنحي»، كان قد وضح بجلاء أن الجيش المصري قد مُني بهزيمة مروِّعة. لكن البيان استخدم تعبير النكسة ولم يشر مطلقاً إلى تلك الهزيمة.

كان أول ورود لكلمة «نكسة» في «بيان التنحي» فور انتهاء عبد الناصر من العبارة الافتتاحية للبيان: «ولا نستطيع أن نخفي على أنفسنا أننا واجهنا نكسة خطيرة خلال الأيام الأخيرة، لكني واثق أننا جميعاً نستطيع – وفي مدة قصيرة – أن نجتاز موقفنا الصعب». ثم بعد ذلك وردت الكلمة أربع مرات على مدار البيان، مكوِّنة مصاحبات

لغوية مثل «درس النكسة»، و«تبعات النكسة». كما جاءت في صيغة جمع مرة واحدة مرتبطة بكلمة التضحيات.

للوهلة الأولى، يبدو استخدام تسمية نكسة جزءاً من استراتيجية خطابية للتلطيف اللفظي هدفها تقليل شعور المصريين بفداحة نتائج الحرب. هذا الشكل من التلطيف اللفظي يمكن تسميته «التهوين اللفظي»؛ ويتحقق عادة من خلال إخفاء التسمية المباشرة، دقيقة الدلالة على وضع ما، واستخدام تسمية أخرى تحمل دلالة أكثر خفة أو غموضاً. فتسمية «الهزيمة» ثقيلة الوطأة على النفس بما تحمله من دلالات مستقرة في نفوس أمة عانت الكثير من ويلات الهزائم؛ وبخاصة أن آخر هزيمتين تعرضت لهما كانتا حيتين في ذاكرة الأمة بتبعاتهما الباهظة. فقد أفقدت هزيمة عرابي الأمة استقلالها لما يزيد عن سبعين عاماً، أما جراح هزيمة ١٩٤٨، فكانت ما تزال مفتوحة ونازفة. وهكذا، كان استخدام كلمة الهزيمة اسماً لما حدث أشبه بالحفر بسكين في ذاكرة الهزائم.

بالإضافة إلى ذلك، فإن استخدام كلمة الهزيمة كان يستدعي – على سبيل التضاد – السياق النصي co-text السابق على الحرب والمتزامن معها. فقد كان الخطاب السياسي المصري بجميع تجلياته المقروءة والمرئية والمسموعة قبيل الحرب وأثناءها يعج بمفردات النصر. وكانت خطب عبد الناصر نفسه قبيل الحرب بأيام تبشر بهذا النصر، وتدعو إلى الاستعداد له. يقول في خطبته في أعضاء مجلس الأمة من القصر الجمهوري في ٢٩ مايو، ١٩٦٧:

> الفورة العربية والثورة العربية وهياج الجماهير العربية الذي نراه اليوم في كل بلد عربي، وفي كل مكان، ليس فقط لأننا عدنا إلى خليج العقبة، أو لأننا تخلصنا من قوات الطوارئ الدولية.. لا.. إنه من أجل عودة الشرف العربي.. من أجل عودة الأمل العربي.. علينا أن نستعد لننتصر، لا لنعيد مهازل سنة ١٩٤٨؛ ننتصر بعون الله وبتأييد من الله.

لقد كان استخدام كلمة الهزيمة اسماً لما حدث يغامر باستدعاء خطب التبشير بالنصر ووعود استعادة الشرف والأمل، ومقارنة ما يحكيه «بيان التنحي» بما كانت تحكيه تلك الخطب. في حين يمكن أن يكون استخدام كلمة النكسة اسماً لما حدث بوابة سحرية للهرب من تنشيط ذاكرة الجماهير الخطابية حول النصر الذي كان موعوداً. وبعد أن تخلص البيان من كلمة الهزيمة، لم يكن من المفاجئ أن يربط بين النكسة والنصر، وأن يشير بلا مواربة أو تردد إلى أن النكسة – بل النكسات – هي

خطوة أولى «على طريق النصر الحتمي الأكيد». يقول عبد الناصر في منتصف البيان: «الحرب دفاعاً عن الحق العربي ممتدة مهما كانت التضحيات والنكسات على طريق النصر الحتمى الأكيد». وهكذا تحولت الهزيمة إلى نكسة والنكسة إلى خطوة في طريق النصر.

لا تنتمي كلمة النكسة في ذاتها إلى مجال الحرب، بمثل ما تنتمي كلمات «النصر» و«الهزيمة». وهي من هذه الزاوية لا تشير إلى مفهوم محدد في مجال الحرب الدلالي. بما يعني أن دلالتها في هذا الاستخدام دلالة غامضة غير محددة، ومن ثم، تصبح منفتحة أمام التأويل، وقادرة على إخفاء الواقع الذي يكشف عنه استخدام تسمية الهزيمة. ويبدو أن اختيار تسمية غامضة للدلالة على نتيجة الحرب متسق تماماً مع الممارسات الخطابية والاجتماعية في مصر آنذاك. فقد كانت المعلومات المتاحة لدى المصريين العاديين عن الحرب قبيل إلقاء البيان مشوّشة. لم يكن أحد من أفراد الشعب المصري – عدا قلة قليلة للغاية من الشخصيات المركزية في الحكم – يعرف أبعاد ما حدث. كان الغموض يلف البلاد. وكان أفراد الشعب في حالة من الدوار بسبب التضارب بين ما تتحدث عنه أجهزة الإعلام المصرية من نصر مُبين وما تبثه الإذاعات الدولية القليلة التي كان يمكن تلقي إرسالها في مصر من وقائع هزيمة مُهينة. كان الغموض يكتنف كل شيء، وجاءت كلمة النكسة لتستثمر هذا الغموض وتضيف إليه.

إضافة إلى استثمار طاقة الغموض الكامنة في تسمية النكسة، فإن هذه المفردة ربما تحمل في ذاتها بعض مشاعر التعاطف مع من يتعرض لها. يتولد هذا التعاطف نتيجة طبيعة المجال الدلالي الذي يشيع فيه استخدام الكلمة، وهو مجال المرض؛ فنكسة المريض هي معاودته العلّة بعد النقه.(١٦) والنكسة تبدو في هذا السياق حالة مرض تتطلب الوقوف إلى جانب المريض حتى يتماثل للشفاء، أما الهزيمة فهي حالة فشل تتطلب محاسبة المسئولين عنها، وفرق كبير بين الحالتين.

ذكر هيكل أن كلمة نكسة أخذت مناقشات بينه وبين عبد الناصر. وأن عبد الناصر قال له حرفياً: «كاتب ليه نكسة؟ إذا كانت هزيمة نقول هزيمة». وعلَّل هيكل رفض عبد الناصر كلمة نكسة بأنه كان قلقاً من أن يقول الناس إن استخدام كلمة نكسة ينطوي على «تخفيف من اللي حصل». أما هيكل، فقد برر اختياره كلمة النكسة قائلاً:

> أنا باعتقد إن كلمة هزيمة في هذه اللحظة خطر، وجدت إن كلمة هزيمة هيترتب عليها حاجات كتير جداً، ثم هزيمة إزاي وفيه أطراف تانية بتقاتل؟ كان عبد الناصر قلقان إن كلمة نكسة يقول الناس إنها تخفيف من اللي حصل؛ إذا كانت

هزيمة نقول هزيمة. قلت له: أنت ماشي وسايب زكريا، فكيف يمكن أن تقول لزكريا وأنت ماشي نحن هزمنا؟ إذا قلت له نحن هزمنا فليس عليه إلا أن يقبل الهزيمة وتبعاتها، وكان هناك مقاومة وقتال فكيف تكون هزيمة؟ . . . الناس كانت رافضة لقبول الهزيمة ولكلمة الهزيمة.

يبني هيكل حجاجه عن تسمية النكسة على ثلاث حجج هي: ١- أن للاعتراف بالهزيمة تبعات لا يمكن تحملها (ربما إشارة إلى محاكمة المسئولين عنها)، ومن ثمَ فإن الأفضل هو نفي وقوعها، ٢- أن الهزيمة لم تقع لأنه توجد أطراف أخرى تحارب، ٣- أن الناس ترفض الهزيمة وكلمة الهزيمة. وقد اقتنع عبد الناصر بحجج هيكل، وأبقى على تسمية النكسة، التي جمَّلت واقعاً قبيحاً، وهوّنت لغةً ما يؤلم واقعاً، وحفظت للشعب بعض عزمه وإرادته، وضمنت لقادته كثيراً من تعاطف الشعب ومساندته.

**العدوان وآثاره: إدانة العدو واستحضار التاريخ**

لم يستخدم عبد الناصر في «بيان التنحي» تعبير «الحرب» للدلالة على الحرب التي دارت رحاها بين مصر وإسرائيل في الأيام السابقة على إلقاء البيان. وبالمثل، لم يستخدم تعبير«غزو» للإشارة إلى غزو إسرائيل الأراضي المصرية، ولا تعبير «احتلال» للإشارة إلى احتلال إسرائيل شبه جزيرة سيناء. فقد عمد البيان إلى تجاهل قائمة المصطلحات العسكرية المتعارف عليها، واستخدم قائمة أخرى من التعبيرات، كان محورها تعبير «العدوان».

لقد استخدم عبد الناصر تعبير العدوان لوصف وقائع الحرب، واستخدم تعبير آثار العدوان في وصف جميع الآثار التي خلفتها الحرب. ويبدو اختيار هذين التعبيرين منسجماً مع استراتيجية التهوين اللفظي من الهزيمة، و«التهويل اللفظي» لأفعال الخصم؛ كما يظهر بجلاء من بين سطور البيان. فالتعبير الأول يستمد قدرته التهويلية من المعنى المعجمي لكلمة عدوان التي تحمل دلالة الظلم وتجاوز الحد؛(١٧) أي أنها محمَّلة بقيم أخلاقية سلبية. إضافة إلى ذلك، فإن لكلمة عدوان تضمينات مهمة؛ فهي قد تنطوي على معنى المخاتلة والأخذ على غِرَّة، كما تنطوي على معنى الاعتداء على طرف مسالم.(١٨) وهي دلالات حرص البيان على ترسيخها في سعيه إلى إدانة ما قامت به إسرائيل من جهة، وتبرير ما آلت إليه الأحداث من جهة أخرى. وما كان يمكن للبيان أن يحقق ذلك إن استخدم مصطلح الحرب، الذي يشير إلى صراع عسكري بين طرفين يحاول كل منهما تحقيق أهداف سياسية بواسطة القوة العسكرية.

في الوقت نفسه الذي يقوم فيه تعبير العدوان بتهويل ما اقترفته إسرائيل، فإنه يقوم بتهوين الهزيمة من خلال الاتكاء على تاريخه الاستعمالي. لقد كان تعبير «العدوان الثلاثي» واسع الانتشار في أدبيات تلك الفترة للإشارة إلى حرب السويس في ١٩٥٦، وهي الحرب التي شنتها قوات إنجليزية وفرنسية وإسرائيلية على مصر إثر قرار تأميم قناة السويس. يقوم التعبير بوظيفته التهوينية من خلال التناص مع التسمية الشائعة لحرب السويس، التي تمثل نقطة مضيئة في وعي المصريين. ففي هذه الحرب، مُنيت مصر بهزيمة عسكرية، وانسحبت القوات المصرية من سيناء، لكن الحرب انتهت بنصر سياسي مصري باهر. ولم يقتصر التناص على استدعاء كلمة العدوان لوصف العمليات العسكرية، بل إن عبد الناصر أشار في البيان إلى العدوان الثلاثي في سياق حديثه عن عودة القوات المصرية إلى مضايق تيران «التي كان العدو الإسرائيلي يستعملها كأثر من آثار العدوان الثلاثي الذي وقع علينا سنة ١٩٥٦». كما أشار صراحة إلى التشابه بين حرب ١٩٦٧ وحرب ١٩٥٦ في سياق القول بأن قوى استعمارية (أمريكا وبريطانيا) حاربت إلى جوار الجيش الإسرائيلي في ١٩٦٧؛ يقول: «إن الدلائل واضحة على وجود تواطؤ استعماري معه [الجيش الإسرائيلي]؛ يحاول أن يستفيد من عبرة التواطؤ المكشوف السابق سنة ١٩٥٦، فيغطي نفسه هذه المرة بلؤم وخبث». وهكذا، فإن التناص مع العدوان الثلاثي على مصر استهدف الربط بين الحربين والانسحابين، حتى يمنح الجماهير التي لا تعرف ما حدث بالفعل مساحة أمل واسع في نصر مؤجَّل لم يدخر البيان جهداً في التبشير به. وهكذا، فبينما ترك البيان تسمية الهزيمة لأنها تغامر بالحفر في ذاكرة موجوعة، فإنه استخدم تسمية العدوان التي تتعمد الحفر في ذاكرة الانتصارات.

ينطوي «بيان التنحي» على حالات متعددة لما يُعرف بالمسكوت عنه أو مساحات الصمت.(١٩) فهناك على سبيل المثال مساحة صمت فيما يتعلق بدور القوات المسلحة المصرية في وقوع الهزيمة، ومساحة صمت مشابهة تخص الدور الذي قام به عبد الناصر تحديداً في تصعيد المواجهة مع إسرائيل. لكن أكثر مساحات الصمت لفتاً للانتباه هي المتعلقة بالنتائج الفعلية التي ترتبت على الهزيمة. فليس ثمة إشارة واحدة مباشرة إلى هذه النتائج، التي يُفترض أنها موضوعٌ أساسٌ في البيان. وكل ما استخدمه البيان للإشارة إلى هذه النتائج هو تعبير «آثار العدوان»: «أمامنا الآن عدة مهام عاجلة: المهمة الأولى: أن نزيل آثار هذا العدوان علينا، وأن نقف مع الأمة العربية موقف الصلابة والصمود. وبرغم النكسة فإن الأمة العربية بكل طاقاتها وإمكانياتها قادرة على أن تصر على إزالة آثار العدوان». يتسم تعبير «آثار العدوان» بالغموض

والتعميم. فهو لا يشير إلى أيٍّ من مظاهر الهزيمة وتجلياتها على أرض الواقع؛ فليس ثمة إشارة إلى الأرواح التي فُقدت، أو الأرض التي احتلت، أو القوات المسلحة التي دُمِّرت. واستطاع البيان القفز على نتائج الحرب بواسطة استخدام تعبير «آثار العدوان» الذي لم يظهر في النص إلا مقترناً بفعل «إزالتها». وهكذا، قفز البيان على تجليات الهزيمة ومظاهرها، مستفيداً من حيل التلطيف اللفظي ومهارات التلويح بالمستقبل.

**التنحي والاستقالة: النحت فوق ذاكرة بيضاء**

اشتهر بيان ٩ يونيو في الأدبيات السياسية بـ«بيان التنحي». وترجع هذه التسمية إلى حقيقة أن قرار عبد الناصر بالتنحي عن الحكم كان أكثر النقاط التي عالجها البيان تأثيراً في جماهير المخاطَبين. ويتجلى هذا التأثير بوضوح في خروج ملايين المصريين، إثر سماعهم البيان، للمطالبة بعدم التنحي. كما يتجلى في أن معظم الاهتمام الصحفي والإعلامي بالبيان اتجه إلى قرار التنحي. وهو ما أدى إلى تهميش نسبي للموضوع الذي كان يُفترض أن يكون محور البيان؛ أعني الهزيمة. وربما كان من العلامات الدالة على تحول عبارة التنحي إلى محور بيان ٩ يونيو أن معظم المقتطفات المسموعة أو المرئية التي توردها البرامج الوثائقية أو الأفلام التي تتناول تلك الفترة تتضمن إما عبارة التنحي فقط أو الجملة الافتتاحية للبيان بالإضافة إليها. كما تتجلى محورية فعل التنحي في بعض الاختيارات السيميوطيقية، مثل قيام فريق العمل الذي أعد خطب عبد الناصر للنشر الإلكتروني على موقعه على الإنترنت بكتابة عبارة التنحي وحدها ببنط غامق مميز يستوقف العين المتصفحة للبيان. كما اختاروا للبيان التسمية الآتية: «بيان الرئيس جمال عبد الناصر إلى الشعب والأمة بإعلان التنحي عن رئاسة الجمهورية». وهي تسمية تختزل البيان في إعلان التنحي، وتهمل الهزيمة.

اُستُخدمت كلمة «التنحي» بوصفها تلطيفاً لفظياً لمصطلح «الاستقالة»؛ وهي التسمية الدستورية لتخلي رئيس الدولة الطوعي عن الاستمرار في أداء مهام وظيفته. فالمادة ١١٠ من الدستور المؤقت الصادر في شهر مارس سنة ١٩٦٤ التي أشار عبد الناصر إلى أنه يستند إليها في قرار تنحيه عن الحكم، لا تستخدم تعبير التنحي؛ وإنما تستخدم تعبير الاستقالة. ونص هذه المادة هو: «في حالة استقالة الرئيس، أو عجزه الدائم عن العمل، أو وفاته، يتولى الرئاسة مؤقتاً النائب الأول لرئيس الجمهورية. ثم يقرر مجلس الأمة، بأغلبية ثلثي أعضائه، خلو منصب الرئيس. ويتم اختيار رئيس الجمهورية خلال مدة لا تتجاوز ستين يوماً من تاريخ خلو منصب الرياسة». والأمر نفسه ينطبق على المادة ١١١ من الدستور نفسه

التي تُنظِّم كيفية الاستقالة، ونصها: «إذا قدم الرئيس استقالته من منصبه، وجه كتاب الاستقالة إلى مجلس الأمة».(٢٠)

يبدو أن استخدام كلمة التنحي بمعنى الاستقالة لم يكن شائعاً في تلك الفترة؛ آية ذلك أن المعجم الوسيط الذي صدرت طبعته الأولى عام ١٩٦٠ وحرص مؤلفوه على أن يُضمِّنَ متنُه العديد من المعاني المستحدثة للمفردات لم يذكر هذا المعنى لكلمة التنحي. ففي مادة «نحا» يتوقف المعجم أمام المعاني الآتية لكلمة «تنحَّى»: «تنحَّى: صار في ناحية. وتنحَّى: زال وبَعُد؛ يُقال نحَّاه فتنحَّى. وتنحَّى له: قصد واعتمد».(٢١) ولم يرد ذكرٌ للتنحي بوصفه استقالة عن العمل. وربما أدّى عدم شيوع هذا الاستخدام لكلمة التنحي إلى بعض الغموض في دلالتها.(٢٢) والسؤال الذي يطرح نفسه هو: لماذا عدل المتكلم عن التسمية الدستورية إلى التسمية التلطيفية؟

هناك أهداف عملية لاختيار كلمة التنحي؛ فقد أشار شريف يونس إلى أن «الاستقالة نقل للسلطة، ويجب دستورياً أن توجه لمجلس الأمة وفقاً للمادة ١١١ من دستور ١٩٦٤ المعمول به آنذاك». ويتساءل يونس: «هل كانت صيغة التنحي الغامضة التي وردت في البيان تهدف لتجنب هذه التعقيدات الدستورية؟».(٢٣) من الواضح أن الإجابة عن هذا السؤال هي نعم. فقد سعى عبد الناصر باستخدام كلمة التنحي إلى تجنب اتباع الخطوات الدستورية التي توجبها الاستقالة؛ وهو ما أتاح له أن يختار بنفسه من يخلفه. في حين كان عليه لو استخدم مفهوم الاستقالة أن يوجه خطاباً مكتوباً إلى مجلس الأمة، ومن ثمَّ يُنظِّم المجلس عملية اختيار رئيس جديد.

لكن استخدام كلمة التنحي يؤدي وظائف أخرى تنتج عن الفرق بين التاريخ الاستعمالي لكلمة الاستقالة والتاريخ الاستعمالي لكلمة التنحي. فالأول يبدو ثرياً؛ لأنه غالباً ما يكون محملاً بذكريات شخصية بسبب ارتباطها بجانب مهم من جوانب حياة المواطن المصري اليومية، هو جانب العمل. وهكذا، فإن تلقي الجمهور كلمة الاستقالة سوف يكون محكوماً بالارتباطات النفسية والمعنوية التي تكونت لديهم نحوها من قبل. أما كلمة التنحي، فلم تكن لتُثير دلالات كامنة في نفوس المصريين، وهو ما يعني أن الذهن سوف يشرع في تشكيل ارتباطات نفسية ومعنوية جديدة لها؛ وهكذا يصبح استخدام كلمة التنحي نحتاً في ذاكرة بيضاء، هرباً من الذاكرة المشحونة.

إضافة إلى ذلك، فإن استخدام تسمية الاستقالة لوصف قرار عبد الناصر بترك الحكم كان سينطوي على تضمينات هي أن عبد الناصر مسئول عن وقوع الهزيمة، وأن تسببه في الهزيمة هو السبب في استقالته.

وفي الواقع فإن الصياغة التي استخدمها عبد الناصر في عبارة التنحي لا تتضمن أي اعتراف بأنه كان سبباً في وقوع الهزيمة، بل تصرح بوضوح أنه مسئول عن «تبعات النكسة». والفرق جلي بين تحمل المسئولية عن وقوع الهزيمة وتحمل مسئولية التخلص من آثارها. وهكذا، كان استخدام تسمية التنحي التي لا تنطوي على أية تضمينات مسبقة منسجماً مع توجه البيان نحو القفز على مسألة الاعتراف بالمسئولية عن الهزيمة.

**استعارات الهزيمة: الزحف المقدس في مفترق الطرق**

يحفل البيان بعدد من الاستعارات والتشبيهات الجزئية التي تتجمع بصفة خاصة في مفتتح البيان وخاتمته. لكن توجد استعارة مفهومية conceptual metaphor مركزية يكاد يدور حولها البيان هي استعارة «النكسة توقُّف عن المسير».(٢٤) تستوعب هذه الاستعارة الموضوعات الأساسية التي عالجها البيان. ففي إطار هذه الاستعارة تم تصوير مستقبل مصر والعالم العربي السياسي بوصفه سيراً في طريق. أما المصريون والعرب، فتم تصويرهم بوصفهم «السائرون في الطريق»، والطريق ذاته يحمل اسم الغايات التي يسعى السائرون للوصول إليها فهذا «طريق العزة» وذاك «طريق الكرامة» وثالث «طريق النصر»، إلخ. هذا السير قد يتعرض لعوامل خارجية تعوقه مثل النكسة التي تضع السائرين في «مفترق طرق»، وتحجب عنهم «الضوء» الكافي لمواصلة المسير. ومن ثم، يُصبح الهدف الأساس هو استئناف المسير بعد التخلص من «عوائق» الطريق التي تضعها قوى الاستعمار، واسترجاع البصيرة – أو البوصلة – لمعرفة أي الطرق يجب السير فيه، وتعبيد هذا الطريق أمام الشعب السائر.

منذ المفردات الأولى للبيان، يضع عبد الناصر لبنات هذه الاستعارة المركزية. يقول في مفتتح البيان: «لقد تعودنا معاً في أوقات النصر وفي أوقات المحنة، في الساعات الحلوة وفي الساعات المرة؛ أن نجلس معاً، وأن نتحدث بقلوب مفتوحة، وأن نتصارح بالحقائق، مؤمنين أنه من هذا الطريق وحده نستطيع أن نجد اتجاهنا السليم، مهما كانت الظروف عصيبة، ومهما كان الضوء خافتاً». تشير العبارة السابقة إلى الغاية التي أنشيء لأجلها البيان، والهدف الذي يسعى إلى تحقيقه. فالبيان يُقدَّم بوصفه «طريق مصارحة»، هدفه تحديد الاتجاه السليم الذي يمكن اجتيازه في مفترق الطرق الذي قادت النكسة إليه. ويتم تصوير المصارحة في هذا السياق بالبوصلة التي ستمكن عبد الناصر والشعب من العثور على الاتجاه السليم.

ترسم الفقرة الافتتاحية الأولى لوحة «المتوقفين عن المسير»، هؤلاء الباحثين عن الاتجاه السليم، على هدي ضوء خافت. ولأن المخاطَبين

بالبيان لا يعلمون أين يقفون أو لماذا، ولا يدركون كذلك ماهية الظلمة التي تشملهم أو إلى أين المسير، فقد واصلت الفقرة التالية التي تحمل معها اعترافاً مراوغاً بالهزيمة، تشكيل لوحة المتوقفين عن المسير، يقول:

> ولا نستطيع أن نخفي على أنفسنا أننا واجهنا نكسة خطيرة خلال الأيام الأخيرة، لكني واثق أننا جميعاً نستطيع – وفي مدة قصيرة – أن نجتاز موقفنا الصعب، وإن كنا نحتاج في ذلك إلى كثير من الصبر والحكمة والشجاعة الأدبية ومقدرة العمل المتفانية. لكننا – أيها الإخوة – نحتاج قبل ذلك إلى نظرة على ما وقع؛ لكي نتتبع التطورات وخط سيرها في وصولها إلى ما وصلت إليه.

يقوم تعبير «موقفنا الصعب» في المقتطف السابق بوظيفة تلطيفية؛ لكونه تهويناً لفظياً من الهزيمة. فبدلاً من أن يتحدث البيان عن «تجاوز الهزيمة» يتحدث عن «تجاوز الموقف الصعب». لكن تعبير «الموقف الصعب» إذا نُظر إليه من زاوية المعنى الحرفي يبدو منسجماً مع استعارة «النكسة توقف عن المسير»؛ فوفق هذه الاستعارة تصبح الـ«نحن» التي تشير إلى من وقعت عليهم الهزيمة عالقة في موقف صعب. ومن ثمَّ، تُصبح غاية هذه النحن هي اجتياز الموقف الصعب. وهنا، يأتي دور أول حضور لعبد الناصر بوصفه حاكماً فرداً لا يتخفى وراء ضمير النحن، وذلك من خلال ضمير ياء المتكلم «لكني واثق»، الذي جاء مقترناً بتقديم بشائر يقين وأمل للنحن المنكوسة.

لقد قرن البيان صورة الشعب العالق في موقف صعب يسعى إلى اجتيازه، والحاكم الممتلك يقين القدرة على الاجتياز، بتحديد كيفية الاجتياز وما يحتاجه من سلوكيات أو أفعال. فقد حدد عبد الناصر بيقين كامل ما يحتاجه العالقون لإنجاز الاجتياز ومواصلة المسير؛ ومن بين ما يحتاجونه تتبع خط سير الأحداث، حتى وصلتْ إلى ما وصلتْ إليه. والتعبير الأخير يستند إلى استعارة مفاهيمية هي أن الأحداث شخص يسير في طريق؛ ومن ثم، فإنه يمكن تتبع نقطة انطلاقها، وخط سيرها، ومحطة وصولها. وهي استعارة سحرية لأنها تصور الأحداث في صورة كائن يمتلك مقدرة السير وحرية اختيار الطريق. وبذلك، تأخذ الأحداث طابعاً حتمياً، لتتحول من فعل بشري مقصود إلى قدر مفروض. وهكذا، تسقط فكرة المسئولية عن الهزيمة، ودواعي مساءلة المتسببين فيها. وقد حرص البيان في جميع فقراته على إظهار طابع الهزيمة «الحتمي»؛ وبخاصة من خلال تقديم حجج عسكرية مغلوطة سواء ما يتعلق منها بمدى اشتراك

قوات أمريكية وإنجليزية في الحرب، أو ما يتعلق بالأداء العسكري المصري أثناءها الذي أشاد به عبد الناصر في أكثر من موضع.(٢٥)

استغرق تصوير عبد الناصر «خط سير الأحداث» ما يزيد على نصف مساحة البيان بأكمله؛ فمن محصلة ١٦١٧ كلمة هي مجموع مفردات البيان استغرق هذا التصوير ٨٨٨ كلمة، بنسبة ٥٥٪ تقريباً. بينما استغرق وصفه حال «المتوقفين عن المسير» ١١١ كلمة، بنسبة ٧٪ تقريباً. وهكذا، شغل تصوير ما تم اجتيازه من الطريق أضعاف المساحة التي شغلها تصوير مفترق الطرق المظلم الذي علقت فيه «النحن» أثناء سيرها خلف القائد. أما النسبة الباقية من البيان، فقد شغلها ما تبقى من الطريق؛ أعني طريق المستقبل الذي قام عبد الناصر في البيان بتعبيده ليحمل «النحن» المنكوسة إلى ساحات النصر؛ فـ«الحرب دفاعاً عن الحق العربي ممتدة مهما كانت التضحيات والنكسات على طريق النصر الحتمى الأكيد». لكن عبد الناصر بعد أن يعد بإمكان استئناف المسير، ويصوغ شكل المسير واحتياجاته وأهدافه، يعلن فجأة أنه يتنحى. لقد قرر قائد المسيرة أن يتركها في مفترق الطرق المظلم بعد أن زرع في نفوس «العالقين» أمل استئناف المسير. ليس هذا فحسب؛ بل اختار لهم قائداً جديداً للمسيرة (زكريا محيي الدين) لا تحمل ذاكرتهم له من الإيجابيات الكثير.(٢٦)

تنسجم استعارة الطريق مع أحد أكثر التعبيرات شيوعاً وإثارة للجدل في الأدبيات السياسية في فترة الخمسينيات والستينيات؛ أعني «الزحف المقدس». تمت صياغة هذا التعبير لوصف مشروع السلطة الناصرية لخلق «شعب» يتكتل خلف قائده. وقد تتبع شريف يونس جذور مفهوم الزحف المقدس الذي تمت بلورته في عام ١٩٥٣، وأثبتَ عبر تحليل معمَّق وشامل للظروف السياسية والاقتصادية والاجتماعية في تلك الفترة أن هذا الزحف المقدس كان حلم الضباط ومشروعهم السياسي. ولتحقيقه كان عليهم تفكيك أية تجمعات سياسية، وإخضاع كل التجمعات الاجتماعية لقبضتهم، من جمعيات ونقابات عمالية ومهنية وأندية وغيرها. ثم الإقناع بهذه الرؤية الاستبدادية بوصفها مثلاً أعلى عبر أدوات دعاية كانت تزداد إلحاحاً وانتشاراً.(٢٧)

وهكذا، فإن استعارة «الهزيمة توقف عن المسير» تصوِّر الهزيمة في صورة توقف الزحف المقدس؛ الذي يُحقق للشعب كينونته. ويحمل ذلك دلالة ضمنية هي أن الاعتراف بالهزيمة وقبول التنحي ليس مجرد توقف عن المسير بل هو فقدان المصريين وجودهم بوصفهم شعباً؛ لأنهم لا يشعرون بهذا الوجود إلا وهم يسيرون في «زحف مقدس» خلف قائد يمنحهم هبة هذا الوجود.(٢٨) ولأن القائد هو من ينفث في الشعب

روحه، ويمنحه عقله وقلبه، فقد كان من الطبيعي أن تتماهى الحدود الفاصلة بين «أنا» عبد الناصر، و«أنت» الشعب؛ ليتحد الكل في «نحن» مراوغة، كانت أهم أدوات البيان البلاغية في توزيع مسئولية الهزيمة، وإذكاء جذور رفضها ورفض التنحي كليهما، على نحو ما سنبرهن بالتفصيل في تحليلنا الضمائر الشخصية في البيان.

## استخدام الضمائر: استراتيجيات التضامن والمراوغة

تنقسم الضمائر الشخصية في اللغة العربية إلى ثلاثة أنواع؛ ضمائر التكلم (أنا، تاء المتكلم، ياء المتكلم، نحن، نا الفاعلين)، وضمائر الخطاب (أنتَ، أنتِ، أنتما، أنتم، أنتن، كاف الخطاب)، وضمائر الغيبة (هو، هي، هما، هم، هن، هاء الغائب). من الطبيعي أن تعود ضمائر المتكلم في البيان إلى عبد الناصر والجماعة التي يمثِّلها أو يتحدث باسمها، وأن يستخدم ضمير المفرد المتكلم (أنا) للتعبير عن نفسه، وضمير الجمع المتكلم للإشارة إلى نفسه بمعية الجماعة التي يمثلها أو يتحدث باسمها. أما المخاطَب في «بيان التنحي»، فقد تم تحديده سياقياً ونصياً بأنه الشعب المصري؛ واستخدم عبد الناصر كاف الخطاب للإشارة إليه. في حين استُخدمت ضمائر الغيبة للإشارة إلى كل ما هو خارج عملية التواصل المباشر بين المتكلم والمخاطَب؛ ومن ثم، استخدمت للإشارة إلى إسرائيل وقوى الاستعمار والدول العربية وروسيا وفرنسا وغيرها من الكيانات التي ورد ذكرها في البيان.

ربما كانت طريقة استخدام الضمائر الشخصية في «بيان التنحي» أكثر ظواهره ثراءً من وجهة النظر البلاغية. لا يرجع ذلك فحسب إلى تعدد الظواهر البلاغية المرتبطة بالضمائر في البيان مثل الالتفات والتغليب ووضع المظهر موضع المضمر؛ بل يرجع كذلك إلى الوظائف البلاغية المتعددة التي حققتها هذه الطريقة، والمهارة البلاغة المتناهية التي تكشف عنها. سوف أتناول طرق استخدام ضمائر التكلم والخطاب ووظائفها في «بيان التنحي». ويرجع استبعادي ضمائر الغيبة إلى أن هذه الدراسة معنية بالدور الذي تقوم به الضمائر في صياغة العلاقة بين المتكلم (عبد الناصر) والمخاطَب (الشعب)؛ وليست معنية بآليات وصف عبد الناصر الكينونات الغائبة. إضافة إلى اهتمامها بتحليل الصورة التي يقدمها عبد الناصر عن نفسه وعن الشعب بواسطة استخدام ضمائر التكلم ولخطاب، والآثار البلاغية لهذه الصورة. ولتحقيق ذلك سوف أقدم – بداية – حصراً عددياً بضمائر التكلم والخطاب في «بيان التنحي»: أ– ضمائر المفرد المتكلم = ٤١، ب– ضمائر الجمع المتكلم = ٨٠، ج– ضمائر الجمع المخاطب = ٥. ويكشف الحصر السابق عن بعض الظواهر اللافتة أهمها

سيطرة ضمائر الجمع المتكلم على «بيان التنحي»؛ فهي تمثل ما يزيد على ٦٤٪ من مجموع ضمائر الخطاب والتكلم. وعلى الرغم من أن البيان هو خطاب موجه من عبد الناصر إلى جماهير الشعب المصري، فإن ضمائر الخطاب لا تشغل أكثر من ٣٪ من مجموع ضمائر التكلم والخطاب. وعلى النحو ذاته، يكشف توزيع هذه الضمائر على فقرات النص أن فقرتي البيان الافتتاحيتين – وتمثل كلماتهما أقل من ٧٪ من مجموع كلمات النص – تستأثران وحدهما بما يزيد على ٢٠٪ من ضمائر الجمع المتكلم التي توجد في البيان بأكمله (٢١ من مجموع ٨٠ ضميراً)، وما يقرب من ١٥٪ من مجموع ضمائر التكلم والخطاب التي توجد في البيان (٢٢ من مجموع ١٢٦ ضميراً). وبالمقابل، تستأثر فقرة التنحي وفقرة تولية زكريا محيي الدين رئيساً للجمهورية – وتمثل كلماتهما حوالي ٧٪ من مجموع كلمات النص – بما يزيد على ٤٦٪ من مجموع ضمائر المفرد المتكلم في النص (١٩ من مجموع ٤١ ضميراً). ومن المؤكد أن الإحصاءات السابقة وطريقة توزيع الضمائر الشخصية في البيان تثير الكثير من التساؤلات، سوف نحاول طرحها والإجابة عنها فيما يأتي.

**ضمائر النحن: من الإدماج إلى التنصل من المسئولية**

ضمير الجمع المتكلم (نحن) أكثر الضمائر الشخصية مراوغة في الخطاب السياسي. فضمير المتكلم المفرد (أنا) عادة ما يعود دون التباس إلى ذات المتكلم المفردة. كذلك، عادة ما يشير ضمير المخاطَب المفرد أو الجمع إلى ذوات مخاطَبين يتم تحديدهم نصياً أو فعلياً. على خلاف ذلك، يتسم مرجع ضمير نحن في الخطاب السياسي بالكثير من الغموض؛ فهو قد يشير إلى أنا مَلَكيَّة أو مُعظَّمَة تُعبر عن نفسها بنحن الملكية، كما هو الحال في صيغة الافتتاح التقليدية في عهد الملك فاروق («نحن فاروق الأول»). لكنه قد يشير بالفعل إلى جمع من المتكلمين؛ ونحن في هذه الحال إما أن تكون نحن العامة، التي تشير إلى جميع المخاطَبين بها إضافة إلى ذات المتكلم، أو نحن الخاصة، التي تشير إلى ذات المتكلم إضافة إلى مجموعة أخرى من الأفراد ممن قد يتم تعيينهم نصياً أو فعلياً، وهم غالباً ما يكونون معاوني الرئيس ومن يشاركونه الحكم.

ينشأ غموض دلالة نحن في الخطاب السياسي نتيجة حرص السياسيين في كثير من الحالات على عدم تحديد مرجع دقيق لها. ويحقق ذلك وظيفة أساسية في الخطاب السياسي المعاصر هي وظيفة الإدماج. حيث تسعى كل سلطة سياسية مسيطرة إلى احتكار التحدث باسم الجماعة التي تحكمها؛ مما يتيح لها تقديم مصالحها وأهدافها بوصفها مصالح الجماعة بأكملها وأهدافها. كما يُحقق غيابُ المرجع وظيفةَ إبهام الفاعل؛

حين يكون للعمل المنسوب إلى النحن آثار سلبية يسعى المتكلم إلى التنصُّل من مسئوليته الفردية عنها، فيستخدم النحن العامة التي تُحمِّل المسئولية للجميع على النحو الذي يتجلى بوضوح في «بيان التنحي».

يثير الحضور الطاغي لضمائر الجمع المتكلم تساؤلات حول الوظائف التي تؤديها هذه الضمائر. من الواضح بداية أن استخدام ضمير المتكلم الجمع بهذه الكثافة في «بيان التنحي» يعكس حرص عبد الناصر الشديد على تأسيس علاقة اتحاد بينه وجماهير الشعب المصري التي تتلقى البيان. فالفقرات الافتتاحية من البيان تُهيمن عليها ضمائر الجمع المتكلم؛ سواء في موقع الفاعلية كما في «تعودنا»، «نجلس»، «نتحدث»، «نتصارح»، «نستطيع»، «نخفي»، «نجتاز»، «واجهنا»، «نحتاج»، «نتتبع»، إلخ، أو في موقع الإضافة كما في «اتجاهنا»، «أنفسنا»، «موقفنا»، إلخ. من الجلي أن علاقة الاتحاد بين عبد الناصر والشعب التي يؤسسها استخدام الضمائر تحقق وظائف بلاغية حاسمة في السياق التداولي للبيان. فنسبة الأفعال إلى النحن التي تشمل القائد والشعب تعني ضمنياً التشارك في المسئولية عن هذه الأفعال. وربما كانت الفرصة التي يتيحها ضمير الجمع للتخفف من المسئولية عن الهزيمة سبباً مباشراً لاستخدامه بدلاً من ضمير أنا في مواضع يبدو من البديهي تماماً أن يُستخدم الثاني فيها. وذلك كما في قوله «لا نستطيع أن نخفي على أنفسنا أننا واجهنا نكسة خطيرة». فالصياغة الأصلية لهذه الجملة هي «لا أستطيع أن أخفي عليكم أننا واجهنا نكسة خطيرة». وذلك لأن الشعب لم يكن يعلم ما حدث كي يخفيه، كما أنه ليس له أية مصلحة في إخفاء وقائع هزيمة لم يكن سبباً فيها. وبذلك يتيح ضمير النحن ارتداء قناع الجمع، حين يصبح وجه المتكلم المفرد مهدداً بالخذلان.

بالإضافة إلى ذلك، يخلق ضمير نحن في «بيان التنحي» حالة من التضامن بين الشعب والقائد والقوات المسلحة. فالأصل أن يشير عبد الناصر إلى القوات المسلحة مستخدماً ضمير «هم»، وأن يشير إلى الشعب الذي يخاطبه بضمير «أنتم»، وأن يشير إلى نفسه بضمير «أنا». لكنه اختار أن يستخدم ضمير نحن ليجمع الكل في واحد. ويتيح ذلك تمرير الأخطاء الفادحة التي وقعت فيها القيادة العليا للقوات المسلحة؛ وبخاصة قرار الانسحاب العشوائي من سيناء. وذلك بواسطة استخدام تعبير «قواتنا المسلحة»، الذي تكرر في البيان سبع مرات ليستحوذ وحده على ما يقرب من ٩٪ من مجموع ضمائر النحن في البيان. لكن استخدام ضمير نحن يتيح أيضاً تدعيم التضامن بين الشعب من ناحية والقوات المسلحة من ناحية أخرى؛ وهي مهمة بدت حاسمة في وقت بدأت تتكشف فيه أبعاد الهزيمة، وكان من المتوقع أن تعصف الهزيمة بثقة المصريين في جيشهم.

ربما تفسر هيمنة ضمائر الجمع للمتكلم غياب ضمائر المخاطَب بنوعيها المفرد والجمع. فالمخاطَبون أُدمجوا مع المتكلم في ضمير واحد هو نحن؛ ففقدوا بذلك وجودهم بوصفهم كياناً مستقلاً له ضمير مستقل هو أنتم؛ على الرغم من أن الأصل في البيان السياسي أنه رسالة محددة الموضوع موجَّهة من مرسل متعين إلى مستقبل متعين، لكل منهما ضميره المعياري؛ فللأول ضمير الأنا، وللثاني ضمير الأنت. لكن هيمنة النحن الإدماجية أزاحت ضمائر الخطاب من ساحة البيان فلم تتكرر بصيغها المختلفة سوى خمس مرات، تمثل ٤٪ من مجموع ضمائر التكلم والخطاب في البيان. ونظرة سريعة على المواضع التي وردت فيها ضمائر الخطاب تؤكد أن استخدامها هي أيضاً كان بهدف الإدماج وتعزيز الاتحاد بين القائد والشعب؛ فقد وردت أربعة منها في الجملتين الآتيتين:«لقد اتخذت قراراً أريدكم جميعاً أن تساعدوني عليه» و«إن قلبي كله معكم، وأريد أن تكون قلوبكم كلها معي، وليكن الله معنا جميعاً؛ أملاً في قلوبنا وضياءً وهدى». الجملة الأولى جاءت قبل إعلان قرار التنحي، ويطلب فيها عبد الناصر من الشعب مساعدته على تنفيذ قراره. وبالمثل جاء ضميرا الخطاب في الجملة الثانية التي اختتم بها عبد الناصر بيانه في سياق طلب آخر من الشعب بأن يمنحه قلبه. ربما لم يكن من قبيل المصادفة أن الضمائر الأربعة جاءت جميعاً متعلقة بفعل «أريد» المنسوب إلى أنا عبد الناصر. كما أنها جاءت كذلك في سياق طلب مباشر للتوحد والتضامن بين عبد الناصر والشعب. والجملة الأخيرة واضحة الدلالة على أن ضمائر الخطاب في «بيان التنحي» لم تعكس استقلالية ذات المتكلم عن ذات المخاطَبين بقدر ما عكست سعياً نحو الدمج بين ذواتهم؛ فقد بدأ عبد الناصر الجملة بضمير المتكلم (أنا)، ثم انتقل إلى ضمير المخاطَب (أنتم)، وأخيراً جمع بين ضميري المتكلم والمخاطَب في ضمير واحد (نحن الإدماجية). وفي سياق ذلك ذكر أن قلبه مع الشعب، وطلب من الشعب أن يكون قلبه معه، وحين اتحدت الضمائر حلَّ قلب الحاكم في قلوب الشعب، وحلَّت قلوب الشعب في قلب الحاكم، ولم يعد موجوداً سوى «قلوبنا» التي تضم في إطارها الجميع.

### عبد الناصر وأنا: استدعاء الأسطورة الفردية

فيما عدا ضمير متكلم مفرد واحد ورد في الفقرة الثانية من البيان لم يستخدم عبد الناصر صيغة «أنا» إلا بعد مرور ما يقرب من خمس البيان (٣٤٧ كلمة من مجموع ١٦١٧ كلمة). وفي حين كان معدل ورود هذه الضمائر قبل فقرة التنحي ١٪ (١٢ ضميراً داخل ١١٠٨ كلمة)، كان معدلها في فقرة التنحي وما بعدها يزيد عن ٦٪ (٢٩ ضميراً داخل ٥٠٩ كلمة). وهو ما يعني أن نسبة استخدام ضمائر المفرد المتكلم في فقرات

التنحي وما بعدها تزيد خمسة أضعاف عن نسبة استخدامها قبل فقرة التنحي. يمكن تفسير توزيع الضمائر هذا في ضوء الموضوعات التي تناولتْها أجزاء البيان، والوظائف التي استهدفتْها هذه الأجزاء. وبالنظر إلى التقسيم السابق لأجزاء البيان، سوف يتضح أن المقدمات الافتتاحية كانت تهدف إلى تأكيد التضامن بين المتكلم والمخاطَبين؛ ومن ثم، فقد شهدت كثافة عالية في استخدام ضمير نحن الذي يفيد التضامن والإدماج. أما الجزء الثاني الذي يشمل سرد الوقائع السابقة على الحرب وبعض وقائع الحرب، وما أطلق عليه عبد الناصر «دروس النكسة»، فقد استهدف إعادة بناء الماضي في أذهان الجمهور، وإعطاءهم معلومات بعينها عن الحرب، واقتراحات لمواجهة «تبعاتها». وشهد هذا الجزء تنوعاً في استخدام ضمائر المفرد المتكلم والجمع. أما الجزء الأخير، فقد تناول إعلان عبد الناصر تنحيه عن الحكم؛ أي فك العلاقة بينه والجمهور. لذا، لم يكن من الغريب أن يصاحب ذلك استخدام كثيف لضمائر المفرد المتكلم التي تميِّز الذات عن الآخرين وتضع أنا في مقابل نحن. ومع ذلك، فإن ضمير النحن لم يختف من هذا الجزء؛ بل كان يُطل برأسه بين الحين والآخر، وبخاصة في السطر الأخير من البيان، الذي يتضمن دعوة صريحة إلى إعادة الاتحاد بين المتكلم والمخاطَبين، أو بين عبد الناصر والشعب.

توجد ظاهرة أخرى لافتة في استخدام ضمائر المفرد المتكلم في البيان هي ظاهرة الالتفات من الغيبة إلى التكلم والعكس، كما يظهر في المقتطف الآتي:

> إن قوى الاستعمار تتصور أن جمال عبد الناصر هو عدوها، وأريدُ أن يكون واضحاً أمامهم أنها الأمة العربية كلها وليس جمال عبد الناصر، والقوى المعادية لحركة القومية العربية تحاول تصويرها دائماً بأنها إمبراطورية لعبد الناصر، وليس ذلك صحيحاً؛ لأن أمل الوحدة العربية بدأ قبل جمال عبد الناصر، وسوف يبقى بعد جمال عبد الناصر. ولقد كنتُ أقولُ لكم . . .

فالفقرة السابقة تتضمن خمسة التفاتات؛ ثلاثة من التكلم إلى الغيبة، يتم التحول فيها من ضمير المتكلم المفرد (أنا) إلى الاسم الظاهر الغائب (جمال عبد الناصر)؛ واثنين من الغيبة إلى التكلم؛ يتم التحول فيهما من الاسم الظاهر الغائب (جمال عبد الناصر) إلى ضمير المتكلم المفرد (أنا). إضافة إلى ذلك، تتضمن الفقرة ظاهرةً بلاغية أخرى هي استخدام الاسم المُظهَر (عبد الناصر) بدلاً من المُضمَر (هو في حالة

الغيبة، وأنا في حالة التكلم)؛ فقد تكرر اسم جمال عبد الناصر خمس مرات في عبارة واحدة، تكاد تكوّن جملة واحدة طويلة، وكان يمكن أن يُغني الضمير عن تكرار الاسم ثلاث مرات على الأقل. كما عكست العبارة حرصاً على ذكر اسم عبد الناصر كاملاً. وهكذا، احتل الاسم وحده ربع عدد كلمات العبارة (١٤ كلمة من مجموع ٥٧ كلمة).

من الواضح أن ظاهرتي الالتفات ووضع المضمر موضع المظهر هدفهما استحضار اسم جمال عبد الناصر ووضعه في صدارة النص. يرجع ذلك إلى الارتباطات الإيجابية الهائلة التي كان يستدعيها هذا الاسم في ذاكرة المصريين. وبحسب يونس، فقد «اكتسب اسم عبد الناصر، أو ناصر، أو الريس، أهمية إيديولوجية خاصة، عكست بلا شك وضعه المركزي داخل النظام».(٢٩) فنتيجة لسنوات طويلة من الدعاية الهائلة التي ربطت بين اسم جمال عبد الناصر وكل ما هو جميل وإيجابي ورائع، اكتسب الاسم قوة ذاتية جعلته أشبه بأيقونة لصفات نبيلة مثل الاستقلال والكرامة والنصر. وبذلك، اكتسب اسم عبد الناصر قوة أسطورية، كان مجرد النطق به كفيلاً باستحضارها. وغدت ذاكرة معظم المصريين في ذلك الوقت مشحونة بدلالاته القابلة للاستدعاء والتكثيف في أية لحظة.

لقد صيغت الفقرة التالية لإعلان تولية زكريا محيي الدين – وهي أطول فقرات البيان – لتستدعي هذه الدلالات تحت غطاء ما أسماه عبد الناصر «إنجازات جيل الثورة»؛ الذي:

> حقق جلاء الاستعمار البريطاني، وحقق استقلال مصر، وحدد شخصيتها العربية، وحارب سياسة مناطق النفوذ في العالم العربي، وقاد الثورة الاجتماعية، وأحدث تحولاً عميقاً في الواقع المصري أكد تحقيق سيطرة الشعب على موارد ثروته وعلى ناتج العمل الوطني، واسترد قناة السويس، ووضع أسس الانطلاق الصناعي في مصر، وبنى السد العالي ليفرش الخضرة الخصبة على الصحراء المجدبة، ومد شبكات الكهرباء المحركة فوق وادي النيل الشمالي كله، وفجر موارد البترول بعد انتظار طويل. وأهم من ذلك وضع على قيادة العمل السياسي تحالف قوى الشعب العاملة؛ الذي هو المصدر الدائم لقيادات متجددة تحمل أعلام النضال الوطني والقومي مرحلة بعد مرحلة، وتبني الاشتراكية، وتحقق وتنتصر.

وهي إنجازات اعتادت آلة النظام الدعائية، على مدار سنوات طويلة، أن تقرنها برجل واحد هو جمال عبد الناصر.

لقد لجأ عبد الناصر إلى تقنية تصدير foregrounding الاسم في لحظة حاسمة من بيانه. فقد بدأ سلسلة تكرار اسمه بعد النطق مباشرة بجملة التنحي، ثم أعقب سلسلة اسمه بسلسلة إنجازاته. وينطوي ذلك على مناورة خطابية بارعة. ففي الوقت الذي دعا فيه الشعب إلى قبول قراره بالتنحي، شرع بواسطة تكرار اسمه في استثارة الدلالات الإيجابية التي يختزنها أفراد الشعب في ذاكرتهم عنه. وعزز هذه الاستثارة بحشد سلسلة طويلة من «الإنجازات» التي حققتها مصر في فترة حكمه، والتي نُسبت إليه واقترنت باسمه. وهكذا، كان عبد الناصر يدعو الشعب إلى قبول تنحيه بإحدى يديه، بينما يلوِّح بالخسارة الهائلة التي ستلحق بالشعب لو قبل دعوته بيده الأخرى.

## العلامات غير اللغوية: من بلاغة النص إلى بلاغة الأداء

عادة ما يلجأ محللو الخطب السياسية إلى النسخ المكتوبة من هذه الخطب. وفي هذه الحالة يفقد التحليل قدراً كبيراً من إمكاناته وطاقته. فالنسخ المكتوبة من الخطب فقيرة علاماتياً مقارنة بالخطب الحيَّة. فنص الخطبة لا يتضمن إلا العلامات اللغوية المتمثِّلة فيما يقوله الخطيب، أما الخطبة الحيَّة، فهي بحر زاخر من العلامات اللغوية وغير اللغوية؛ فهي تضم كلمات الخطيب وصوته وحركاته وإشاراته وهيئته ومكانه من الجماهير ولحظات صمته وسكونه ونظرات عينيه وحضوره الجسدي. وهكذا، فإن فهم الكيفية التي تعمل بها الخطابة السياسية سوف يواجه عوائق حقيقية إذا أُغفلت العلامات غير اللغوية التي لا يقل تأثيرها عن العلامات اللغوية في الخطبة.

يبدو إغفال دور العلامات غير اللغوية في إنجاز الأثر الكلي للخطاب السياسي باهظ الكُلفة في حالة «بيان التنحي». فقد كانت براعة عبد الناصر في أداء البيان لا تقل عن براعة هيكل في كتابة نصه. وقد ذكر معظم من أجريت مقابلات معهم بخصوص البيان أن نبرة صوت عبد الناصر – وبخاصة في مفتتح البيان وخاتمته – كانت بالغة التأثير في تعاطفهم معه. وبحسب تعبير أحدهم فإن «نبرة الحزن العميق التي تبدت في صوته كانت تدفع باتجاه واحد هو اتجاه المواساة». وسوف أتوقف في تحليلي دور العلامات غير اللغوية في إنتاج التأثير الكلي لـ«بيان التنحي» أمام بعض ملامح أداء عبد الناصر الصوتي وهيئته وتوزيع نظراته بين الورقة التي كان يقرأ منها وكاميرا التلفزيون.

**نطق المفردات والتوازي النحوي: إيقاعي الحكي والشجن**

أول ما يلفت الانتباه في أداء عبد الناصر الصوتي هو الإيقاع الخافت الذي بدأ به البيان. لقد اشتُهر عبد الناصر في أدائه خطبه في السياقات العادية بصوت جهوري مرتفع، لكن صوته في عبارات البيان الافتتاحية فيه خفوت وعمق، يتناسب مع «حالة البوح» التي جعلها إطاراً للبيان. فالبوح يناسبه النبر الخافت، والإيقاع الهادئ البطيء. ولعل هذا يُفسِّر طول مساحات الصمت في العبارات الافتتاحية التي يُحدِّد فيها طبيعة بيانه بأنه مصارحة، ويعترف فيها بوقوع النكسة، وذلك مقارنة بمساحات الصمت في العبارات التالية التي يقوم فيها بتتبع «خط سير الأحداث». فالعبارات الافتتاحية تكونت من ١٠٩ كلمة تبدأ من قوله «أيها الأخوة»، حتى قوله «نتتبع التطورات وخط سيرها في وصولها إلى ما وصلت إليه». وقد استغرق نطقها مدىً زمنياً قدره ١٠٧ ثانية، بما يقارب ثانية واحدة لكل كلمة.

على خلاف ذلك، شهدت العبارات التي تناولت تطور الأحداث تغيُّراً في نبرة عبد الناصر، إذ تراجع الإيقاع الهادئ البطيء الذي ميَّز العبارات الافتتاحية، واكتسب صوته ثقةً أكبر، وأصبح أكثر جهورية وأقل خفوتاً. تبدأ هذه العبارات بقوله «إننا نعرف جميعاً كيف بدأت الأزمة»، وتنتهي عند قوله «وأمامنا الآن عدة مهام عاجلة»، وتتكون من ٨٧٩ كلمة استغرق نطقها ٤٥٥ ثانية، وذلك بما يقارب نصف ثانية لكل كلمة.

يبدو الفرق الدال إحصائياً بين المدى الزمني الذي استغرقه نطق الكلمة في العبارات الافتتاحية والمدى الزمني الذي استغرقه نطق الكلمة في العبارات التي تسرد جزءاً من تاريخ الصراع فرقاً بين طريقتين في الأداء شهدهما البيان. الطريقة الأولى كان صوت عبد الناصر فيها بطيئاً وإيقاع كلامه هادئاً خافتاً. وهو ما ينسجم مع حالة قائد يوشك أن يتحدث عن هزيمة، وما يستتبع ذلك من هيمنة نبرات الحزن والأسى والشجن، وهي جميعاً تقود إلى إطالة المدى الزمني الذي يستغرقه نطق الكلمات وزيادة الفواصل الصامتة بين أجزاء الجمل، إلى حد بدا فيه عبد الناصر – وبخاصة وهو يتحدث عن النكسة لأول مرة – كمن يُعاني لكي تخرج الكلمات من فمه.

إضافة إلى ذلك، أثَّرت ظاهرة صوتية أخرى في إطالة المدى الزمني لنطق الكلمات؛ هي ظاهرة التوازي النحوي. لقد صيغتْ العبارات الافتتاحية من البيان صياغةً بلاغيةً بارعة بهدف إنتاج إيقاع صوتي مهدهد للنفوس. وقد تحقق هذا الإيقاع من خلال مجموعة من التّوازيات النحوية. وذلك كما يتجلى في الشكل الآتي:

لقد تعودنا معاً

(١) في أوقات النصر
(٢) وفي أوقات المحنة،
(٣) في الساعات الحلوة
(٤) وفي الساعات المرة؛

(١) أن نجلس ..
(٢) وأن نتحدث ..
(٣) وأن نتصارح ..

(١) مهما كانت الظروف عصيبة،
(٢) ومهما كان الضوء خافتاً.

فالعبارة الافتتاحية الأولى تتشكل بأكملها من سلسلة من التوازيات الصوتية النحوية التي تتكرر فيها ثلاث بنيات نحوية ثابتة أربع مرات وثلاث مرات ومرتين. تتكون البنية الأولى من شبه جملة (حرف جر [في] + اسم مجرور [أوقات، الساعات] + مضاف إليه [النصر، المحنة] أو نعت للاسم المجرور [الحلوة، المرة]). أما البنية الثانية فتتكون من جملة فعلية مصدرية (أن + فعل مضارع [نجلس، نتحدث، نتصارح] + فاعل مستتر تقديره نحن). في حين تتكون البنية الثالثة من جملة فعلية شرطية (مهما + كان + اسمها [الظروف، الضوء] + خبرها [عصيبة، خافتاً]). ويزداد التناسق الإيقاعي لهذه التوازيات النحوية بفعل الجناس التام الناتج عن تكرار مفردات «الأوقات»، «الساعات»، «مهما»، «كان»، والجناس الناقص كما في مفردات «المحنة»، «الحلوة»، «المرة». وربما لم يكن من قبيل المصادفة - إضافةً إلى ذلك - أن المقاطع الأربعة التي تشكل البنية النحوية الأولى جاءت موزونة على بحر المتدارَك. فإذا حذفنا الواو التي تربط بين هذه المقاطع، نصبح أمام سلسلة متوالية من تفعيلة فَعْلُن. وبهذه الظواهر الصوتية المتعاضدة تكاد تتحول افتتاحية البيان إلى مطلع قصيدة جنائزية.

على خلاف ذلك، لم ترد مثل هذه الظواهر الصوتية في العبارات التالية التي اختصت بتتبع خط سير الأحداث، والتي استرد خلالها صوت عبد الناصر إيقاعه شبه العادي، وتلاشت إلى حد كبير نبرة الحزن التي طبعت صوته في مفتتح البيان. وتوازى تزايد سرعة نطقه الكلمات مع تصاعد في نبرة الثقة في صوته، وصلت إلى ذروتها حين كان يتحدث عما

يجب عمله لتجاوز النكسة. وبذلك أصبحنا أمام طريقة أخرى في الأداء الصوتي تقترب من أدائه الطبيعي في غير أوقات الهزيمة.

**لغة الحروف ولغة الجسد: بلاغة النصر وبلاغة الهزيمة**

تمتع عبد الناصر بقدرات متميزة على التواصل مع الجماهير. فقد استطاع بصوته العميق وحضوره الجسدي الطاغي ونظراته التي تنتقل بسلاسة من جانب إلى آخر وتوظيفه المتقن لتعبيرات الوجه والإشارات الحركية أن يمتلك قدرة كبيرة على التأثير في الآخرين. ويمكن أن نضيف إلى ذلك تمتعه بمهارات بلاغية جيدة؛ وبخاصة قدرته على مد الجسور مع الجمهور بواسطة استخدام تنويعات من ضمائر الخطاب والتكلم، ولمحات من الفكاهة والسخرية، والاستناد إلى معجم من مفردات الحياة اليومية، وبراعته في الحكي. ولعل العناصر السابقة - بالإضافة إلى توجهات سياساته المعلنة التي تماست مع أحلام كثير من المصريين والعرب وطموحاتهم، والدعاية الهائلة التي جعلت منه أسطورة تسير على قدمين - شاركت جميعاً في تشكيل ما أصبح يُعرف بـ«كاريزما» عبد الناصر التي تعني بشكل مبسط قدرته الاستثنائية على التأثير في الآخرين.

كان من الطبيعي أن تتأثر هذه القدرة الاستثنائية على التأثير في الآخرين بواقع هزيمة بعثرت أحلام النصر الموعود؛ وأحدثتْ شرخاً كبيراً في مصداقية «الزعيم». إضافة إلى ذلك، فإن إلقاء البيان أمام شاشات التلفزيون ألزم عبد الناصر - الذي اعتاد أن يخطب واقفاً - بأن يخطب جالساً خلف مكتب. وهو ما قلل من تأثير حضوره الجسدي، كما قلل من قدرته على توظيف حركات يديه وإشاراتهما؛ لأن كاميرا التلفزيون اقتصرت على تقديم ثلثي نصفه الأعلى، ولم تُظهر اليدين في كادر الصورة. كما دفعت حساسية الموقف عبد الناصر إلى الالتزام بالنص المكتوب، دون لجوء إلى ما اعتاد عليه - في خطبه السابقة على النكسة والتالية لها - من مزج بين الارتجال والقراءة من النص المكتوب. وقد حرمه التزامه الحرفي بالنص المكتوب من القدرة على الإفادة من التواصل البصري الدائم مع الجماهير التي تنظر إلى وجهه عبر شاشات التلفزيون. فقد كانت عيناه تتحركان حركةً بندولية شبه بطيئة من الورق الذي يقرأ منه إلى كاميرا التلفزيون.

على الرغم من أن العوامل السابقة ربما أدت إلى التقليل من قدرات عبد الناصر التواصلية، فإنها من المحتمل أن تكون قد أسهمت من زوايا أخرى في تدعيم تأثير البيان في الجماهير. فعلى سبيل المثال، كان اضطرار عبد الناصر إلى اعتماد النص المكتوب سبباً في

تقليل قدرات التواصل البصري، لكنه لعب دوراً كبيراً في تكريس التعاطف معه؛ لأنه أظهره في صورة قائد مطأطَأ الرأس، تهرب عيناه من الكاميرا (والناس) لتغرق في فراغ مجهول خارج إطار كادر الصورة (الورقة التي يقرأ منها). وقد كانت فقرة التنحي على وجه الخصوص أكثر الفقرات التي طأطأ فيها عبد الناصر رأسه ليقرأ من الورقة غير الظاهرة، ربما يرجع ذلك إلى الصياغة النحوية المعقدة للفقرة، وجملها الاعتراضية المربكة؛ وهو ما يحول دون الاحتفاظ بها في الذاكرة قصيرة المدى. لكن النتيجة النهائية لهذه الطأطأة هي ظهور «القائد» في صورة «المهزوم». وهي حالة ما كان للمصريين أن يسمحوا بها لرئيس استطاع أن يربط شعورهم بوجودهم – بوصفهم شعباً – بيقينهم بوجوده – بوصفه قائداً.(٣٠)

لقد أسهمت طريقة أداء البيان في تحريك ملايين الجماهير لرفض التنحي، وتشكلت بلاغة جديدة أوجدتها الهزيمة، بلاغة تجلت في اختيار المفردات والتراكيب والمجازات، وفي الأداء الصوتي والحركي، واستهدفت توجيه إدراك جموع المصريين لهزيمة يونيو، ولعلاقة عبد الناصر بها، وللمستقبل الذي ينتظرهم في حال قبولهم تنحيه، والمستقبل المغاير الذي ينتظرهم في حال رفضهم هذا التنحي. وكانت محصلة هذه البلاغة أكبر مما كان يحلم به منتجوها، فقد أسهمت «بلاغة الهزيمة» في إضفاء شرعية جماهيرية جديدة على حكم عبد الناصر أتاحت له أن يعيد بناء بعض ما دمرته الهزيمة.

## الهوامش

(١) ولد عبد الناصر في ١٨ يناير، ١٩١٨. التحق بالكلية الحربية عام ١٩٣٧، وشارك في حرب ١٩٤٨. كان العقل المدبر لحركة الضباط الأحرار التي استولت على الحكم في يوليو ١٩٥٢، وتولى منصب وزير الداخلية، ثم رئاسة الوزراء، وأخيراً رئاسة الجمهورية بعد صراع قصير على السلطة مع الرئيس الراحل محمد نجيب. وظل رئيساً للجمهورية حتى وفاته في سبتمبر ١٩٧٠. للمزيد من المعلومات عن حياة عبد الناصر والاطلاع على الإصدارين المقروء والمسموع من «بيان التنحي»، راجع: <http://www.nasser.org>. ويمكن الاطلاع على مقتطفات مرئية منه على <http://www.youtube.com>.

(٢) راجع:

Norman Fairclough, *Discourse and Social Change* (Cambridge, MA: Polity P, 1992), 71.

(٣) راجع:

Jan Blommaert and Chris Bulcaen, "Critical Discourse Analysis," *Annual Review of Anthropology* 29 (2000): 448-49.

(٤) أحد أهم الصحفيين في التاريخ العربي المعاصر. ولد في ٢٣ سبتمبر، ١٩٢٣، عمل محرراً بجريدة *The Egyptian Gazette*، ثم انتقل إلى دار أخبار اليوم عام ١٩٤٦. رأس تحرير مجلة **آخر ساعة**، كما رأس تحرير جريدة **أخبار اليوم**، قبل أن يرأس تحرير جريدة **الأهرام** في الفترة من ١٩٥٧ حتى ١٩٧٤.

(٥) حكى محمد حسنين هيكل الوقائع التفصيلية لكتابة «بيان التنحي» في ثلاث حلقات متواصلة من برنامج «مع هيكل»، الذي تبثه قناة الجزيرة القطرية، وذلك في مساءات الخميس من أيام ١٩و٢٥/٦/٢٠٠٩، و٢/٧/٢٠٠٩.

(٦) راجع تعريف الكتابة الخفية Ghost Writing في:

Theresa Enos, ed., *Encyclopedia of Rhetroic and Composition: From Ancient Times to the Information Age* (London: Routledge, 1996), 285.

(٧) راجع:

Mary E. Stuckey, *Getting into the Game: The Pre-Presidential Rhetoric of Ronald Reagan* (NY: Prager, 1989), 86.

(٨) المعلومات التي لدينا عن عملية كتابة «بيان التنحي» وصلتنا من خلال مصدر واحد هو الكاتب الذي لم يعد خفياً؛ أعني هيكل. ومن ثم، فإنه لا توجد أية وثائق تمكّننا من التحقق من صدق روايته لوقائع عملية كتابة البيان. وقد أشار هيكل نفسه أكثر من مرة إلى أن كثيراً من الأحداث التي يرويها عن واقعة كتابة البيان لم يشهدها أي شخص آخر بخلاف عبد الناصر نفسه. يمكن الرجوع إلى إشارات هيكل المتكررة لذلك في حلقات برنامج «مع هيكل».

(٩) محمد حسنين هيكل، **لمصر لا لعبد الناصر** (القاهرة: مركز الأهرام للترجمة والنشر، ١٩٨٧)، ص ٥٣. ومن اللافت استخدام هيكل تسمية «خطاب» بدلاً من «بيان».

(١٠) محمد حسنين هيكل، حلقة ٢٦/٥/٢٠٠٩ من برنامج «مع هيكل».

(١١) **المرجع السابق**.

(١٢) أتبنى في هذه المقالة صيغةً مخففةً من نظرية النسبية اللغوية Linguistic Relativism كما قدمها وورف في:

Benjamin Lee Whorf, *Language, Thought, and Reality* (NY: John Wiley, 1956).

(١٣) على سبيل المثال، تستخدم بعض المؤسسات الحكومية التي تمتلك آلية التسعير الجبري تعبيرات مثل «ترشيد» الأسعار و«تعديل» الأسعار و«تحريك» الأسعار للإشارة إلى قرارات «زيادة» الأسعار. ويشيع في الوقت ذاته أن تستخدم بعض الصحف أو الشخصيات المعارضة تعبير مثل «إشعال الأسعار» للإشارة إلى قرارات زيادة الأسعار نفسها. وتكشف

التعبيرات السابقة عن وجود ثلاث إمكانات يمكن لمستخدم اللغة الاختيار من بينها. الإمكان الأول استخدام تعبيرات مباشرة ودقيقة أقرب ما تكون إلى وصف جوهر الأشياء؛ كما هو الحال في تسمية زيادة الأسعار. وقد نحت آلان وبوريدج مصطلح الاستقامة اللفظية orthophemism للإشارة إلى هذا الاختيار. أما الإمكان الثاني، فيقوم فيه المتكلم باستخدام تعبيرات مخففة وملطفة أو غير مباشرة أو غامضة؛ كما هو الحال في تسمية ترشيد الأسعار. ويُستخدم مصطلح التلطيف اللفظي للإشارة إلى هذا الاختيار. أما الإمكان الثالث، فهو استخدام تعبيرات مبالِغة ومهوِّلة؛ كما هو الحال مع تسمية إشعال الأسعار. ويُستخدم مصطلح التهويل اللفظي Dysphemism للإشارة إلى هذا الاختيار. وعادة ما يكون التعبير المباشر تعبيراً حيادياً، بينما تُصاغ التعبيرات الملطفة أو المهولة صياغةً مجازية. لمعلومات تفصيلية عن طرق عمل التلطيف اللفظي راجع:

Keith Allan and Kate Burridge, *Forbidden Words: Taboo and the Censoring of Language* (Cambridge: Cambridge UP, 2006).

(١٤) تسمية «حرب الأيام الستة» هي التسمية الإسرائيلية المعتمَدة لما يُعرف في العالم العربي بالنكسة أو حرب يونيو. والأيام الستة هي الفترة من الخامس إلى العاشر من يونيو ١٩٦٧، وقد استطاعت إسرائيل خلالها أن تحتل الضفة الغربية وقطاع غزة والقدس الشرقية وشبه جزيرة سيناء كاملة وهضبة الجولان. وتتناص تسمية الأيام الستة مع بعض السرديات التوراتية الكبرى مثل سردية خلق العالم في مفتتح العهد القديم؛ التي تروي كيف خلق الله العالم في ستة أيام: «وَفَرَغَ اللهُ فِي الْيَوْمِ السَّابِعِ مِنْ عَمَلِهِ الَّذِي عَمِلَ. فَاسْتَرَاحَ فِي الْيَوْمِ السَّابِعِ.» انظر، **العهد القديم** (القاهرة: دار الكتاب المقدس، د. ت.)، ص ٥.

(١٥) يمكن الوقوف على الآثار العسكرية والاجتماعية والاقتصادية والسياسية لحرب ١٩٦٧ في كتاب لطفي الخولي، محرر، **حرب يونيو ١٩٦٧ بعد ٣٠ عاماً** (القاهرة: مركز الأهرام للترجمة والنشر، ١٩٩٧).

(١٦) انظر **المعجم الوسيط**، حرره إبراهيم مصطفى وآخرون، ج٢ (القاهرة: مجمع اللغة العربية، ١٩٦٠)، ص ٩٩٠.

(١٧) **المرجع السابق**، ص ٦١٠.

(١٨) من المؤكد أن اشتعال الحرب لم تكن «مفاجأة» لعبد الناصر، لأنه هو الذي نزع فتيلها بقراره سحب القوات الدولية وإغلاق مضيق العقبة أمام الملاحة الإسرائيلية. كما أنه استطاع ببصيرته التنبؤ بالتوقيت المحتمل لنشوبها، وأبلغ المسئولين العسكريين بهذا الوقت. ولم يكن الجدال السائد في تلك الفترة يدور حول ما إذا كانت مصر «ستحارب» أم لا، بل حول ما إذا كانت ستقوم بتوجيه الضربة الأولى، أم تنتظر حتى تبدأ إسرائيل الضربة الأولى، ثم تقوم

بالرد. لمعلومات إضافية حول الظروف التي أحاطت بالحرب، وتنبؤ عبد الناصر بتوقيتها. راجع عبد العظيم رمضان، **تحطيم الآلهة: قصة حرب يونيو ١٩٦٧**، ج. ١ (القاهرة: مكتبة مدبولي، ١٩٨٨)، ص ص٦٠–٩١.

(١٩) «المسكوت عنه» مصطلح قديم يشير إلى أفكار أو موضوعات يتحرز المتكلم عن الخوض فيها مباشرة لما قد ينطوي عليه الخوض فيها من مخاطر. لمزيد من المعلومات عن هذا المصطلح، راجع جابر عصفور، «بلاغة المقموعين»، **ألف**، العدد ١٢ (١٩٩٢)، ص ص ٦ –٤٩. أما مصطلح «مساحة الصمت» – أو المساحة البيضاء – فهو مصطلح يشيع في أدبيات تحليل الخطاب، ويكاد مفهومه يتطابق مع مفهوم المسكوت عنه. لتحليل مساحات الصمت في خطاب السادات السياسي، راجع عبد العليم محمد، **الخطاب الساداتي: تحليل الحقل الإيديولوجي للخطاب الساداتي** (القاهرة: كتاب الأهالي، ١٩٩٠)، ص ص ٢٣٩–٢٤٢.

(٢٠) راجع موقع **موسوعة القانون المشارك الجامعي**:

<http://www.ar.jurispedia.org/index.php/>.

(٢١) انظر **المعجم الوسيط**، ج٢، ص ٩٤٤.

(٢٢) لقد أجريت عدداً من المقابلات مع أشخاص مختلفي الثقافة ممن استمعوا إلى بيان ٩ يونيو في يوم إلقائه، وكان أحد الأسئلة الموجهة إليهم يتعلق بمدى فهمهم – في ذلك الوقت – لدلالة كلمة «أتنحى». وقد ذكر جميع المبحوثين أنهم فهموا أن الكلمة تعني «ترك الحكم» أو ما شابه إلا مبحوثة واحدة – كانت في ذلك الوقت طالبة في الفرقة الرابعة بأحد أقسام اللغات بكلية الآداب جامعة القاهرة – قالت إنها لم تعرف معنى كلمة «أتنحى»، وسألت والدها فور نطق عبارة التنحي عما يقصده عبد الناصر بالكلمة.

(٢٣) شريف يونس، **الزحف المقدس: مظاهرات التنحي وتشكل عبادة ناصر** (القاهرة: ميريت، ٢٠٠٥)، ص ١٨٣.

(٢٤) مفهوم الاستعارة كما أستخدمه أوسع من مفهومها في التراث البلاغي العربي القديم. فالمقالة تتبنى مفهوم الاستعارة كما استقر في اللغويات المعرفية على يد جورج لايكوف George Lakoff ومارك جونسون Mark Johnson وآخرين. والاستعارة عندهم هي الكلام أو التفكير في شيء ما بمفردات تنتمي إلى شيء آخر. وهي بذلك تضم الاستعارة بمعناها في البلاغة العربية القديمة التي يتم فيها نقل بعض صفات شيء ما إلى شيء آخر، إضافة إلى التشبيه الذي يتم فيه المقارنة بين بعض صفات شيء ما وصفات شيء آخر. لمزيد من الأفكار حول تأسيس نظري لكيفية الإفادة من نظرية الاستعارات المفهومية في تحليل خطاب سياسي عربي معاصر، راجع عماد عبد اللطيف، **أنا رب عائلة مصر: اللغة والسياسة والدين في خطب السادات** (القاهرة: دار الشروق، قيد النشر).

(٢٥) يحفل البيان بالكثير من المغالطات الحجاجية التي تستحق دراسة خاصة. كما يتضمَّن معلومات عسكرية مزيفة بهدف تقليل مسئولية القيادة العسكرية عن الهزيمة، وتخفيف شعور المصريين بوقعها. لحصر شامل بهذه المعلومات وتصويب لها، راجع عبد العظيم رمضان، ص ص ٢٣٦–٢٣٧.

(٢٦) يرجع ذلك إلى تولي زكريا محيي الدين منصب وزير الداخلية في وقت تزايدت فيه ظاهرة «زوار الفجر»، وتوليه رئاسة الوزارة أثناء تطبيق خطة تقشف اقتصادي في أوائل الستينيات أثَّرت بشدة على الظروف المعيشية لقطاعات ضخمة من المصريين. انظر: يونس، ص ١٨٩.

(٢٧) **المرجع السابق**، ص ٤١.

(٢٨) يمكن تأويل خروج ملايين المصريين من بيوتهم وسيرهم في الشوارع متظاهرين ضد التنحي بوصفه رفضاً رمزياً للهزيمة كما تتجلى في استعارة «الهزيمة توقف عن المسير»؛ فالمظاهرات في ذاتها شكل من أشكال السير أو «الزحف».

(٢٩) انظر: يونس، ص ١٢١.

(٣٠) يفسر يونس كيف استطاعت إدارة عبد الناصر زرع اعتقاد لدى المصريين بأن «الشعب يصبح شعباً، أو يتحقق كشعب فقط من خلال الرئيس، بل ويمكن القول إنه لا يوجد كشعب إلا به»، ص ١٥٥.

# تأملات حول الذاكرة والصدمة عند يوسف شاهين

داليا سعيد مصطفى

تتناول هذه المقالة فيلمي المخرج المصري يوسف شاهين **١١ سبتمبر**(١) **وإسكندرية .. نيويورك**(٢) من أجل طرح بعض القضايا النظرية والفنية والسياسية المتعلقة بتطويع المخرج للذاكرة وتأملاته حول مضمون الصدمة trauma على المستويين الشخصي والجماعي، حتى يثير أفكاراً وهموماً سياسية في الحاضر بخصوص العلاقة بين الولايات المتحدة الأمريكية والعالم العربي في أعقاب أحداث ١١ سبتمبر، ٢٠٠١. ولعل هذين الفيلمين من الأفلام القليلة في السينما العربية عموماً التي تناولت هذه العلاقة بالبحث والنقد. وتتّسِم سينما يوسف شاهين – بشكل عام – بمزجها بين الذاتي والجماعي، بين الواقع والفانتازيا، من أجل استكشاف قضايا سياسية تاريخية ومعاصرة ومناقشتها في آنٍ معاً.

لقد عاد شاهين في العديد من أفلامه إلى أحداث وقصص تاريخية مهمة حتى يلقي الضوء على هموم معاصرة. فنراه، مثلاً، يتخذ من معارك صلاح الدين الأيوبي ضد الغزو الصليبي إطاراً لبلورة موقفه، وإعجابه بالرئيس المصري جمال عبد الناصر ومشروعه الناصري القومي في **الناصر صلاح الدين**.(٣) ونراه في فيلمه **الوداع يا بونابرت**(٤) يعود إلى إحياء أحداث الغزو الفرنسي لمصر في نهايات القرن الثامن عشر من أجل إثارة قضية الهيمنة الاستعمارية الغربية على الشرق وارتباطها بأشكال الهيمنة الاقتصادية والثقافية الآنية. ثم نرى كيف يستدعي شاهين في فيلم **المهاجر**(٥) قصة يوسف وإخوته والرجوع إلى مرحلة مزدهرة في التاريخ الفرعوني؛ حتى يتعمق في رحلة داخل الذات التي تطلب العلم والمعرفة لكي تكتشف سعادتها الحقيقية. ونرى، أيضاً، في فيلم **المصير**(٦) كيف يتناول المخرج قضية الفيلسوف ابن رشد ومعاركه الفكرية ضد التعصب الديني، فيرجع شاهين إلى فترة مهمة من تاريخ العرب الحضاري (الأندلس في القرن الثاني عشر)؛ حتى يطرح وجهة نظره بخصوص ما يحدث على الساحة الآن من أحداث جسام أساسها التعصب الديني بشتى أنواعه.

وما سبق يُعَدُّ مجرد نماذج قليلة؛ لأنه لا يكاد يخلو فيلم ليوسف شاهين من فكرة سياسية أو تاريخية يحاول أن يربطها بقضية آنية. ولذا، أرى أن اعتماد الذاكرة وإعادة إحياء قصص ومواقف وأحداث من خلالها يُعَدُّ موضوعاً حيوياً وأساسياً في أعمال يوسف شاهين بشكل عام. وهنا، يلجأ المخرج إلى تطويع هذه الذاكرة بأشكال وتقنيات سينمائية لا تنضب. فالصورة البصرية وعناصر تكوينها من ديكور وإضاءة وملابس وماكياج وهندسة مناظر وغير ذلك، بالإضافة إلى تفاصيل الكادرات والميزانسين mise en scène تُعَدُّ من جماليات سينما هذا الفنان. كما أنه كثيراً ما يستخدم الموسيقى والشِعر والغناء والرقص لكي يفكك أشد القضايا السياسية تعقيداً ثم يعيد بناءها.

وفي هذه المقالة، أود أن أتناول مغزى استخدام شاهين الذاكرةَ وتأملاته حول موضوع الصدمة المفجعة، وسوف أشير إلى بعض التقنيات التي يلجأ إليها المخرج في هذا السياق حتى يوضح رأيه فيما يحدث الآن بين الولايات المتحدة والعالم العربي.

## صدمة ١١ سبتمبر في مقابل صدمة الاحتلال الإسرائيلي

منذ أحداث ١١ سبتمبر، اهتم العديد من الباحثين الأكاديميين والكتّاب في الولايات المتحدة بآثار تلك الصدمة على المجتمع الأمريكي في نواحٍ ومجالات متنوعة. فهناك، مثلاً، من اهتم بدراسة انعكاس ذلك الحدث على الحياة الثقافية والسياسية والفنية في الولايات المتحدة؛(٧) وهناك من اهتم بدراسة الأبعاد السيكولوجية والتوازن النفسي والعقلي عند أولئك الذين تأثروا بشكل مباشر بالحدث؛(٨) وهناك أيضاً من اهتم بتحليل حدث ١١ سبتمبر في إطار موضوع الفاجعة والذاكرة.(٩) ويجب التنويه هنا بأنه على مدار العقدين الماضيين اهتم الكثير من الأكاديميين، في مجال العلوم الإنسانية في الولايات المتحدة وبريطانيا، بتكريس منهجية دراسة مسألة الفاجعة نظرياً وتاريخياً، وليس في مجال علم النفس وعلم التحليل النفسي فحسب كما كان سائداً من قبل.(١٠) وعلى إثر ذلك، ظهرت العديد من النظريات والدراسات التي تربط موضوع الفاجعة الشخصية والجماعية بالظروف السياسية والتاريخية لدى الشعوب. فمثلاً، هناك عدة دراسات مهمة نُشرت عن الاضطراب الناشئ عن توتر ما بعد الصدمة post-traumatic stress disorder ناتجة عن الصراعات والحروب مثل المحرقة، والحربين العالميتين، وحرب ڤيتنام، وأيضاً أحداث ١١ سبتمبر، ٢٠٠١.(١١) ومن هذا المنطلق الجديد، أصبح تعريف الصدمة لا يتعلق فقط بما قد يصيب الفرد من توتر مرضي ناتج عن حادث عنيف ينطوي على تهديد حياته، ومن ثمّ يرتبط بأعراض مثل

الذعر والهلع والنسيان وفقدان القدرة على التركيز، ويمكن أن يؤدي إلى الاكتئاب والشيزوفرينيا والانتحار،(١٢) بل ترتبط الصدمة – أيضاً – بما يحيط بهذه الأعراض النفسية والعقلية من ظروف اجتماعية وسياسية وتاريخية، وبخاصة إذا كانت صدمة جماعية.(١٣) ومن هنا، تظهر أهمية الذاكرة لأن من يعاني الصدمة يودّ أن ينسى حدثاً هائلاً بعينه، ولكن تهاجم ذاكرتَه باستمرار تفاصيل مشرذمة ومتكررة حول هذا الحدث، تأتي مثلاً في هيئة كوابيس أو فلاش باك. وتكمن المعضلة، هنا، في أن من يعاني صدمة ما، لن يتمكن من التخلص من الاضطرابات الناشئة عنها إلا عندما يستطيع تذكّر تفاصيل ذلك الحدث وتسلسله الزمني، وأيضاً محاولة التعايش مع هذه الذكرى المؤلمة.(١٤) بمعنى آخر، إن الذاكرة المرتبطة بصدمة ما تكون متفسّخة ومتقطعة فيما يتعلق بالزمان والمكان والشخوص والأحداث.(١٥)

وفي العالم العربي، لم يحظَ مجال علم دراسات الصدمة Trauma Studies بالاهتمام الوافي بعد، على الرغم من أن هناك الكثير من الفواجع والصدمات الجماعية التي تستلزم الدراسة والتحليل من منطلق نظري وسياسي وتاريخي، وبخاصة الفاجعة المرتبطة بالاحتلال الإسرائيلي للأراضي الفلسطينية،(١٦) وفاجعة نكسة عام ١٩٦٧، والحرب الأهلية اللبنانية (١٩٧٥–١٩٩٠)، والحرب على العراق (٢٠٠٣)، وغير ذلك.

وتُعَدُّ السينما، عموماً، من أهم الوسائل البصرية التي استدعى فيها عدد من المخرجين في العالم مسألة الصدمة وآثارها وأسبابها ونتائجها، حيث يمكن تمثيل وطأتها وتقطّع الذاكرة من خلال تقنيات مهمة مثل: الفلاش باك، والمونتاج، واللقطات بأنواعها المختلفة. فسينما المخرج البولندي أنديه فايدا Andrzej Wajda – على سبيل المثال – قد لاقت الكثير من الاهتمام؛ بسبب تركيزه على الحروب والصراعات التي كان ضحيتها يهود بولندا في القرن العشرين وما نتج عنها من فواجع جماعية لقطاعات عريضة منهم. وهناك سينما المخرجة الإيرانية سميرة مخملباف Samira Makhmalbaf، التي اهتمت في أفلامها بربط الصدمة بالعنف الأسري والحرب؛ وبخاصة على مستوى تأثيرها في المرأة. وفي العالم العربي، اهتم العديد من المخرجين والمخرجات في فلسطين ولبنان – بشكل خاص – بتصوير فاجعة اللاجئين الفلسطينيين، وصدمة الاحتلال الإسرائيلي، والحرب الأهلية اللبنانية.

ولعل يوسف شاهين أحد السينمائيين المصريين القلائل الذين اهتموا بإبراز موضوع الصدمة المتعلقة بالهزيمة: الهزيمة الجماعية في حرب ١٩٦٧ في أفلام مثل **العصفور**(١٧) و**عودة الابن الضال**؛(١٨) وأيضاً

هزيمة الفرد وانهياره في ظل نظم برجوازية مهلهلة في أفلام مثل **باب الحديد**(١٩) و**الاختيار**.(٢٠) وعقب أحداث الحادي عشر من سبتمبر، ٢٠٠١ وتفجير برجي مركز التجارة العالمي بمدينة نيويورك، كان يوسف شاهين هو واحد من أحد عشر مخرجاً عالمياً طلب منهم المنتج الفرنسي ألان بريجا Alain Brigand أن يقدموا فيلماً قصيراً عن وجهة نظرهم في تلك الأحداث بحيث تكون مدة الفيلم ١١ دقيقة و٩ ثوان، وفي كادر واحد. وقد تم إنتاج هذا الفيلم وتقديمه في عام ٢٠٠٢ بعنوان **١١ سبتمبر**. كان شاهين هو المخرج العربي الوحيد ضمن عدد من المخرجين العالميين الذين أسهموا في هذا المشروع مثل كين لوتش Ken Loach (بريطانيا) وسميرة مخملباف (إيران) وميرا ناير Mira Nair (الهند) وعاموس جيتاي Amos Gitai (إسرائيل) وشون بن Sean Penn (الولايات المتحدة).(٢١) لقد طُلِب من هؤلاء المخرجين والمخرجات في صناعة أفلامهم أن «يتوجهوا نحو ثقافاتهم وذكرياتهم وقصصهم ولغاتهم»،(٢٢) بمعنى أن كل فيلم منها لا بد أن ينبع من ثقافة المخرج أو المخرجة والمحيط السياسي والاجتماعي والهمّ الشخصي. ولعل إحدى الملاحظات المهمة على هذه الأفلام هي أنها قد مزجت بالفعل بين السياسي والشخصي، وبين الماضي والحاضر، وبين الواقع والخيال؛ لتعبر عن رأي كل منهم في حدث تاريخي مهم مسّ حياة الآلاف من البشر، وربما سبّب للكثيرين نوعاً من الصدمة أصبحت تستدعي التفكير والتأمل.

ويحاول فيلم يوسف شاهين عن ١١ سبتمبر أن يتأمل مضمون هذه الصدمة والأسباب التي من المحتمل أن تكون قد أدت إليها. يبدأ الفيلم بمشهد تقديم شخصية المخرج يوسف شاهين (التي يلعبها الممثل نور الشريف) وهو يصور لقطة في نيويورك لبرجي مركز التجارة العالمي. ولكن بسبب عدم حصول المخرج على تصريح مسبق بالتصوير، يعترضه ضابط بوليس أمريكي ويهدده باستخدام العنف ضده إذا لم يغادر المكان فوراً. هكذا، ومنذ أول مشاهد الفيلم، يثير المخرج سؤالاً حول غطرسة القوة البوليسية الأمريكية في مواجهة الفن، وبالتالي استحالة الحوار بين رجل البوليس والمخرج السينمائي.

ثم ينتقل المخرج مباشرة في المشهد الثاني إلى بيروت؛ حيث يكون مدعواً لحضور مؤتمر صحفي حول فيلمه الجديد، في اليوم التالي لوقوع أحداث ١١ سبتمبر. يجد المخرج صعوبة في الردّ على أسئلة الصحفيين بخصوص أحداث نيويورك؛ فيطلب تأجيل المؤتمر، ثم يجلس على شاطيء البحر وحيداً يفكر في تلك الفاجعة. وفجأة، يظهر له «شبح» أحد جنود المشاة (المارينز) الأمريكيين الذين قتلوا في عام ١٩٨٣ في بيروت، في أعقاب الاجتياح الإسرائيلي للبنان عام ١٩٨٢

والتدخل العسكري الأمريكي خلال الحرب الأهلية اللبنانية. ثم من خلال هذا المشهد، يستدعي المخرج عمليتي التفجير (التي نفذها فدائيون من حزب الله) ضد ثكنات قوات المشاة الأمريكية والقوات الفرنسية في بيروت يوم ٢٣ أكتوبر، ١٩٨٣، ومقتل ٢٤١ من قوات المارينز وما يفوق الخمسين من الجنود الفرنسيين؛ أي أن أحداث عام ١٩٨٣ – التي وصفتها، أيضاً، إدارة الرئيس الأمريكي آنذاك رونالد ريجان بـ«الإرهاب» – تذكّر المخرج بأحداث ١١ سبتمبر.

يسأل جندي المارينز المخرج شاهين عن إحساسه بأحداث ١١ سبتمبر من منطلق أنه «عربي واللي عمل العَمْلة دي عرب»، ثم يبين له أنه اختار الظهور لهذا المخرج بالتحديد «عشان إنت مهتم بكل اللي بيحصل حواليك، مهتم بموتي وبوجودي. أنا موجود في مخّك إنت بس». ويكون رد المخرج: «أنا مهتم بحياة الإنسان أيّاً كان». فمن خلال هذا اللقاء، نرى مواجهة – وإن كان يغلب عليها الطابع الإنساني – بين الجندي الأمريكي الذي قُتل في أرض عربية نتيجة تدخل عسكري أمريكي، والمخرج أو الفنان العربي الذي وهب حياته وفنه من أجل قضايا تمس حياة البشر، ليس فقط في العالم العربي، ولكن بشكل وجودي وإنساني. ولعل شاهين قد اختار أن تكون هذه المواجهة مع «شبح» لكي يؤكد أن الشخصيتين هنا تُباعد بينهما مسافة محورية – وهي الموت – فمن المفترض إذن أن يتحدثا بصراحة تامة.

وهكذا، يكون الحوار هو مركز الحدث بين المخرج وجندي المارينز داني؛ حيث تدور مناقشة بينهما حول السياسة الأمريكية في العالم العربي ودعم أمريكا إسرائيل ومسؤولية الشعب الأمريكي عن الفظائع التي ترتكبها إسرائيل في حق الفلسطينيين. ثم يصطحب المخرج هذا الجندي إلى الأراضي الفلسطينية المحتلة كي يرى بعينيه لماذا يتجه الشباب الفلسطيني الذي يعيش يومياً مصائب الاحتلال الإسرائيلي إلى تفجير أجسادهم في عمليات انتحارية في المدن الإسرائيلية. ويُضمّن شاهينُ الفيلم صوراً أرشيفية لعمليات انتحارية تمّت في إسرائيل وصور بلدوزرات إسرائيلية تهدم بيوتاً فلسطينية وتقتلع أشجار الزيتون في أراضٍ فلسطينية. تقول أم المناضل الفلسطيني الشاب الذي فجّر جسده في عملية انتحارية: «الاحتلال هو العنف والإرهاب». ويشير يوسف شاهين، من خلال هذه الصور والمعاني، إلى أن الاحتلال هو في حد ذاته نكبة ونقمة على الفلسطينيين. فعندما يسأل داني عن مغزى العمليات الانتحارية ضد مدنيين، وليس ضد عسكريين فقط، يوضح له شاهين أن في أمريكا وإسرائيل حرية في اختيار من يمثل الشعب في السلطة حيث إن الناخبين يصوّتون لأشخاص بأعينهم ويعرفون سياساتهم مسبقاً؛

ولذلك فالشباب الفلسطيني الذي يقوم بعمليات انتحارية لا يستطيع أن يرفع عنهم المسؤولية لأنهم ليسوا أبرياء كلّيةً مما يحدث للفلسطينيين من جراء السياسات الأمريكية الإمبريالية والاحتلال الإسرائيلي.

من الملاحظ، هنا، أن عُمْر جندي المارينز الأمريكي يقارب عمر المقاتل الفلسطيني، ولعل هذه إشارة إلى أنهما قد قُتِلا في شبابهما في حروب ليست من صنعهما. إن اختيار المخرج إدارة الحوار مع «شبحين» يظهران له في الخيال تقنية سينمائية مهمة هنا، في محاولة من شاهين أن تتواجه عدة أطراف ممن يمسّهم – بشكل مباشر – الصراع الدائر بين أمريكا وإسرائيل والعرب؛ فيتيح مساحة لكل طرف حتى يحكي حكايته ويشرح قضيته من منظوره الخاص ودون إدانات أو أحكام مسبقة. يستدعي المخرج هنا صورتي الأمريكي والفلسطيني من خياله بعد موتهما؛ مما يسمح له بأن يكون أكثر انفتاحاً تجاههما.

من هذا المنطلق، إذن، يركز فيلم شاهين على فكرة أساسية مفادها أن الصراع الدائر بين هذه الأطراف صراع سياسي وتاريخي في المقام الأول وليس صراعاً دينياً، كما يصوره الكثير من النقاد والكتّاب في الولايات المتحدة وإسرائيل على وجه الخصوص عقب أحداث ١١ سبتمبر. كما يشير الفيلم إلى أن الفواجع التي سبّبها الاجتياح الإسرائيلي المتكرر للبنان أثناء الحرب الأهلية، والاحتلال الإسرائيلي المستمر للأراضي العربية، بالإضافة إلى الحروب التي فجرتها الولايات المتحدة في المنطقة، تفوق بكثير الفاجعة التي سببتها أحداث ١١ سبتمبر. فالنقطة الرئيسة في فيلم شاهين محاولة إلقاء الضوء على الأبعاد التاريخية لهذه الفواجع وكيفية ترابطها على نحو لا يجعلنا نفهم إحداها بمعزل عن الأخرى. وبذلك يضع الفيلم الفاجعة في سياق سردي، وهو عنصر آخر مهم في الفيلم؛ لأن مسألة التفجيرات الانتحارية – كما يشير طلال أسد – خاوية من أية رواية تاريخية بالنسبة إلى الغرب، مما يؤدي إلى وصفها التسطيحي والخطير بـ«الإرهاب».(٢٣) ويعمل أسد في كتابه على تحليل البعد التاريخي لمفهوم الإرهاب ولماذا اقترن في الآونة الأخيرة بالتفجيرات الانتحارية التي توصف بأنها إسلامية، مشيراً إلى أن العنف الناتج عن الحروب والتعذيب في السجون والمعتقلات وخطر التهديد النووي – وهو ما جعلته الديموقراطيات الغربية (وأيضاً إسرائيل) شرعياً ومقبولاً لدى شعوبها – لا بد أن نربطه أيضاً بمفهوم الإرهاب وسيطرة مشاعر الخوف على الشعوب.(٢٤)

وهكذا، ومن خلال ذلك الحوار في فيلم شاهين، يحاول كل طرف أن يبين وجهة نظره عن الخلل الذي أصاب العلاقة بين الولايات المتحدة والعالم العربي على مرّ العقود. فبعد أن كانت أمريكا تمثل حلم

الكثير من الشعوب العربية في الحرية والديموقراطية والتسامح، أصبح هناك عداء شديد بين الشعب الأمريكي والعرب. وقرب نهاية الفيلم، يدور هذا الحوار بين الجندي والمخرج:

**شاهين**: ليه مش قادرين نفهم إن الزمن مش ممكن يرجع لِوَرا؟
**الجندي**: يا ريت كان بإيدينا فعلا نرجّعه لِوَرا.
**شاهين**: أنا أقدر (ثم يضغط على زر الكمبيوتر فيعود برجا مركز التجارة إلى سابق عهدهما قبل انهيارهما).
**الجندي**: أديك قدرت ترجّع البرجين تاني بخبطة زرار، لكن هتقدر ترجّع للميت الحياة من تاني؟

وعندئذ يصمت المخرج، ويتطلع إلى وجه الجندي في حيرة، ولسان حاله يقول إنه كان يتمنى أن يُعيد هذا الجندي والشاب الفلسطيني إلى الحياة مرة أخرى، فلربما توجد وسيلة للحوار بينهما من جديد. ولكن تنهار هذه الأمنية في آخر مشاهد الفيلم، عندما يزور شاهين قبر داني في مقابر آرلنجتون بولاية واشنطن العاصمة، ويظهر له شبح الشاب الفلسطيني هذه المرة:

**الفلسطيني**: بدل ما تيجي تزورني جاي تزور قبر عسكري أمريكي جه عشان يقتلنا؟
**شاهين**: ما انتوا الاتنين ضحية لغباء البشرية.
**الفلسطيني**: بتساوي بين القاتل والضحية؟
**شاهين**: لو كان داني وأهله فهموا بدري شوية مكنش فيه حدّ فيكوا مات.
**الفلسطيني**: كان هتلر فهم. كان الأمريكان في ڤيتنام فهموا. كان الصرب والإسرائيليين فهموا. فاكر عينين أمي وأنا ماشي؟ لو انت صحيح إنسان إوعى في يوم تنساهم.

ربما استطاع الفنان أن يعيد إحياء الذاكرة، وأن يروي قصص الذين ماتوا، وربما استطاع أيضاً أن يعود بالزمن إلى الوراء من خلال الصورة المرئية، وأن يعيد تركيب الأحداث وبناءها، وأن يتخيل حوارات الضحايا وشهاداتهم، ولكنه لن يستطيع أن يمحو أحداثاً بعينها من التاريخ أو أن يتصرف في مصير ضحايا هذه الأحداث. ولعل المشهدين الأول والأخير في الفيلم يوحيان بوطأة الكارثة التي حلّت بأمريكا مع أحداث ١١ سبتمبر، حيث نرى المخرج في أول مشهد يصور مدى شموخ برجي مركز

التجارة وصلابتهما في لقطة مرتحلة travelling shot، ثم نشهد انهيار هذا الشموخ في آخر مشاهد الفيلم، حيث تنتهي الأحداث في مقابر آرلنجتون. وبذلك، نجد شاهين في هذا الفيلم يقوم برحلة بحث عن مغزى أحداث ١١ سبتمبر، وهي رحلة يربط فيها المخرج بين الماضي والحاضر، ويتنقل خلالها بين أماكن عدة من نيويورك إلى بيروت إلى واشنطن؛ فيصور كل مشهد في مكان أو مدينة مختلفة. تتنقل الأحداث وتسافر في الواقع، كما في مخيلة المخرج؛ في محاولة للتنقيب عن جوهر الصراع القائم بين أمريكا والعرب. وأعتقد أن أحد العناصر المهمة في هذا الفيلم يتمثل في أن شاهين يتيح للشخصيات الأساسية مساحة ليوضح رأيه في هذا الصراع وأسبابه وعواقبه، دون أحكام مسبقة. فالمخرج يتعاطف مع كل من داني والشاب الفلسطيني على السواء، ولكن الشاب الفلسطيني يحسم الموقف بكلمته النهائية في إشارة إلى أن شبحه ربما لن يغادر مخيلة المخرج. فهذا الشاب وأمثاله سوف يعيشون في ذاكرة المخرج السينمائية إلى الأبد.

ولعل محاولة فهم ماهية «الآخر» من الموضوعات التي اهتم يوسف شاهين بإبرازها في سينماه. والآخر في أفلامه هو مَن يختلف عن شخصيات أبطاله في الدين أو العقيدة أو العرق أو الجنس أو الطبقة الاجتماعية. ارتبطت أفلام مثل **الناصر صلاح الدين**، **إسكندرية ... ليه؟**،(٢٥) **الوداع يا بونابرت**، **المهاجر**، **اليوم السادس**،(٢٦) **إسكندرية كمان وكمان**،(٢٧) **الآخر**،(٢٨) و**إسكندرية .. نيويورك** – بشكل خاص – بمحاولة الانفتاح على الآخر وتعميق فهمنا له. ولكن هناك دائماً مرتكزاً أساسياً لهذا الحوار؛ ألا وهو المعاملة النِدّية. فالطرفان يجب أن يكونا متساويين، ولا بد من الاحترام المتبادل بينهما حتى ينشأ الحوار. ولكن إذا كان التعامل مع الآخر بمنطق القوة والعنف والغطرسة، فمما لا شك فيه (وكما يثبت لنا التاريخ بالبرهان القاطع) أن ذلك سوف يتسبب في فاجعة لأحد الطرفين أو كليهما، كما حدث في نيويورك يوم ١١ سبتمبر وكما هو حاصل يومياً في الأراضي الفلسطينية تحت الاحتلال. يقول يوسف شاهين في مقابلة معه عام ١٩٩٩ عن فيلمه **المصير**: «الخوف يمنع التفاهم. أنا لا أستطيع أن أتفاهم مع إنسان يخيفني. ولذلك فإن علاقة النِدّ بالنِدّ مهمة جداً بالنسبة لي. وهذا موضوع سأستمر في الحديث عنه حتى آخر فيلم في حياتي».(٢٩)

يعلق الناقد اللبناني وليد شميط على مفهوم الآخر في أفلام شاهين، وبخاصة فيلم **الوداع يا بونابرت**، بقوله:

> فيلم شاهين يأتي في فترة تزداد فيها عندنا نزعة التعصب والانغلاق، والحيرة في كيفية التعامل مع الغرب، وتتعاظم في الغرب نزعة الخوف من الآخر، والعنصرية البغيضة.

> وشاهين يخاطب العربي ليقول له إن النضال ضد الإمبريالية والاستعمار لا يكون بالتعصب والانغلاق والقمع على أنواعه، وإنما يكون بالديموقراطية والانفتاح على الآخر، وبإعداد النفس وامتلاك السلاح الحديث للمواجهة، وبجعل النزعة الإنسانية مصدر قوة. وهو يخاطب الغربي ليقول له إن العلاقة بيني وبينك لا يمكن أن تستقيم إلا إذا كانت مبنية على المساواة، والاحترام المتبادل، والتخلي عن نظرتك الفوقية ونزعتك الاستغلالية.(٣٠)

وقد تمت معالجة هذا الموقف من الآخر معالجة عميقة على المستويين التاريخي والثقافي في سينما شاهين. فموقفه يفكك المنظور الليبرالي للأمور الذي يجعل من الآخر أحد النقيضين، إما الصديق أو العدو، دون دراسة متعمقة للعناصر التاريخية التي تشكّل هذا الآخر. وكما سيتضح من خلال هذه المقالة، فإن الاهتمام الذي أولاه شاهين لهذا الموضوع قد اتخذ مستويات عدة انعكست في أفلامه بلغة سينمائية متعددة الأشكال.

أما فيلم المخرج الإسرائيلي عاموس جيتاي عن أحداث ١١ سبتمبر،(٣١) فهو يتعرض أيضاً للعلاقة الحميمة بين إسرائيل والولايات المتحدة، ولكن من منظور يختلف عن وجهة نظر شاهين، حيث يطرح جيتاي أسئلة وهموماً أخرى. وجيتاي هو أحد المخرجين الإسرائيليين القلائل الذين يهتمون في أفلامهم بإثارة أسئلة عن مضمون الآخر؛ فهو يناصر القضية الفلسطينية ويدين السياسات الإسرائيلية في المنطقة. يركز فيلم جيتاي عن أحداث ١١ سبتمبر على نقل صورة للحظة وقوع عملية انتحارية في تل أبيب، حيث ينجح في نقل حالة «الهيستيريا» التي تصيب رجال الأمن والإسعاف والمواطنين، وأيضاً بعض المذيعين والمذيعات بأجهزة التليفزيون. ولكن الفكرة الأساسية هنا تكمن في تحليل كاميرا جيتاي لهذه الهيستيريا بوصفها حالة مصطنعة؛ فكل شيء جاهز لحظة وقوع الانفجار: جهاز الشرطة وسيارات الإسعاف على أهبة الاستعداد، فضلاً عن وجود أجهزة الإعلام وبعض المواطنين الذين يدلون بشهادتهم عما حدث.

تحاول المذيعة في الفيلم أن يكون لها السبْق الإعلامي في نقل صورة حية على الهواء لما يحدث عقب وقوع العملية وتسأل بإلحاح كل من في الموقع إن كانت تلك عملية إرهابية أخرى، ومن هو الإرهابي الذي قام بها. يحاول أفراد جهاز الشرطة أن يدفعوها بعيداً، ولكنها تصر على التواجد في الموقع، وكل ما يهمها أن تظهر على الهواء مباشرة. ثم يأتيها صوت رئيسها في العمل يخبرها بأنها لن تظهر على الهواء لأن هناك عملاً إرهابياً حدث في نيويورك، وأن طائرات فجّرت برجي مركز

التجارة، وأن هذا الحدث هو الأهم على الإطلاق من الناحية الإعلامية. ولا تستطيع المذيعة استيعاب ما يحدث في البداية فتظل تردد عبارة أن يد الإرهاب قد نالت من نيويورك وإسرائيل في اليوم نفسه واللحظة نفسها. ولكن صوت رئيسها يأتيها مرة أخرى ليشدد على أن ما حدث في نيويورك هو الحدث الأعظم، وأن يوم ١١ سبتمبر هو يوم تاريخي لن ينمحي من الذاكرة لأن الإرهاب قد طال نيويورك.

يحاول فيلم جيتاي أن يلفت النظر إلى كيفية استغلال وسائل الإعلام المرئية في إسرائيل لموضوع «الإرهاب» والتحكم فيما يتم نقله إلى المشاهد من معلومات وصور. وفي مقابلة مع جيتاي في برلين عام ٢٠٠٧، يعلق المخرج على تسطيح البرامج الإخبارية بشكل عام (ليس فقط في إسرائيل) للقضايا المهمة بقوله: «إن برامج الأخبار المسائية أصبحت استعراضاً مرئياً للعنف بتركيزها على العناصر الدرامية، وبذلك فهي لا تُعلمنا بالكثير. فهذه البرامج أصبحت نوعاً آخر من الاستعراض بحيث إنها توهمنا بأننا بالفعل نتلقى معلومات ولكنها في الواقع تهتم في الأساس بالعنصر الاستعراضي».(٣٢) ولذلك، فمن رأي جيتاي أن السينما يمكن أن تلعب دوراً فعالاً في إظهار التناقضات المحيطة بنا، وتناقضاتنا الشخصية في العلاقة بالآخر.

يتضح من خلال فيلم جيتاي أن لفظ «إرهاب» أصبح متعارفاً عليه في وسائل الإعلام الإسرائيلية بوصفه مرادفاً لأي تفجير انتحاري، فيستخدم بوصفه أداة إدانة مسبقة للفلسطينيين بغض النظر عن مناقشة الأسباب أو المغزى. فما يمكن استنتاجه أن الفيلم يصوّر هذه اللحظة فور وقوع تفجير انتحاري بوصفها تمثيلية استعراضية أو حدثاً مفبركاً. كما يلقي الفيلم الضوء على درجة التقارب في العلاقة بين إسرائيل وأمريكا، وأن ما يحدث لأحدهما إنما هو صدى لما يحدث للآخر، وكيف أن همومهما ومصالحهما أصبحت متداخلة إلى درجة لا يمكن فصلها. يوجه فيلم جيتاي رسالة إدانة إلى وسائل الإعلام في إسرائيل وتسطيحها للأمور وهيمنتها على إعادة تشكيل الأحداث؛ لكي تنقل صورة معينة للمشاهد، ولكن الفيلم لا يتعرض لمناقشة مضمون الإرهاب الملتصق بالفلسطينيين أو موضوع الاحتلال.

لذلك، فلعله من المهم – في هذا السياق – الإشارة إلى فيلم **الجنة الآن** للمخرج الفلسطيني الأصل هاني أبو أسعد، الذي تم إنتاجه عام ٢٠٠٥.(٣٣) وتنبع أهمية هذا الفيلم من طرحه العديد من الأسئلة الملتبسة حول مغزى العمليات الانتحارية التي يقوم بها الشباب الفلسطيني ضد الإسرائيليين من وجهة نظر هؤلاء الشباب أنفسهم. يتناول فيلم **الجنة الآن** قصة الشابين خالد وسعيد اللذين ينشآن في مخيم لاجئين في نابلس، وهما

يتشاركان في أفراحهما وهمومهما حيث تربط بينهما صداقة حميمة منذ الطفولة. يتم إعلام خالد وسعيد أنه قد تم اختيارهما من قبل القيادة السياسية للقيام بعملية انتحارية في تل أبيب من ضمن قائمة المتطوعين. وينقل المخرج التفاصيل الدقيقة لتحضير خالد وسعيد لهذه المهمة من تسجيل بيانهما ووصيتهما بالفيديو، إلى الاستحمام والاستعداد للاستشهاد، إلى ربط الحزام الناسف حول جسديهما وقراءة القرآن، وغير ذلك. كما ينقل المخرج، أيضاً، ما يدور في ذهن كل منهما عن أهمية القيام بهذا النوع من النضال ضد العدو المحتل، ولكنه في الوقت ذاته ينقل وجهات نظر أخرى بين الفلسطينيين أنفسهم عن هذه القضية الشائكة. ومثلما يفعل يوسف شاهين في فيلمه، لا يصدر هاني أبو أسعد أحكاماً مسبقة على هؤلاء الشباب، ولكنه يحاول الغوص في آثار الفواجع المتواصلة التي يعيشها شباب مثل خالد وسعيد من جراء عنف الاحتلال والهواجس الشخصية التي تؤدي بهما إلى هذه النهاية. وفي نهاية الفيلم يقرر خالد بعد تفكير أنه لن يستطيع القيام بالعملية الانتحارية ويرجع أدراجه، أما سعيد فيختار أن ينفذ العملية ضد مجموعة من العسكريين في حافلة وليس ضد مدنيين.

يهتم الفيلم بإبراز فكرة أن الضغوط التي تدفع بهؤلاء الشباب الفلسطيني إلى القيام بعمليات انتحارية هي ضغوط سياسية واجتماعية وتاريخية في الأساس وليست دينية. هناك بالتأكيد عوامل دينية تعضّد من السياسية كما يشير الفيلم، ولكنه يدين بشكل مباشر وصريح أن فكرة الإرهاب التي أصبحت ملتصقة بالشباب الفلسطيني الذي يقاوم الاحتلال نابعة أساساً من منطلق ديني. فكما يقول خالد في وصيته قبل العملية: «لم يبق لنا غير أجسادنا لنحارب بها هذا الاحتلال الغاشم». ويهتم الفيلم، أيضاً، بتناول مسألة أن القرار النهائي لتنفيذ العملية الانتحارية يتخذه المناضل نفسه وبمحض إرادته وباختياره الشخصي.

تتقاطع هذه الدلالة مع فيلم يوسف شاهين في تصويره الشاب الفلسطيني الذي يقوم بعملية انتحارية، وإن كان فيلم أبو أسعد يتعمق أكثر في الفاجعة الجماعية التي يعيش تحت وطأتها هؤلاء الشباب. يأتي الفيلمان، إذن، بوصفهما رسالة سياسية ضد الاحتلال الإسرائيلي وعملائه، ويعبران عن الإصرار على أن هذا النوع من العمليات الانتحارية إنما هو لمقاومة الاحتلال لأنه يمثل فاجعة عصيبة ومستمرة يتعرض لها شعب بأكمله.

يطرح المفكر الإنجليزي تيري إيجلتون Terry Eagleton في كتابه **الإرهاب المقدس** بعض الأسئلة المهمة حول مغزى تفجير البعض لأجسادهم في عمليات انتحارية، واختلاف ذلك عن مفهوم «الاستشهاد» في سبيل الدين، وأيضاً عن خيار الإضراب عن الطعام. فمن وجهة نظر إيجلتون أن هذه

الاختيارات الثلاثة ترتبط بمفهوم حرية الفرد في اتخاذ قرار بإفناء الجسد من أجل قضية معينة، ويصيب هذا الجانب من الحرية الأنظمة السياسية بالرعب مما يجعلها تتخذ جميع الإجراءات المتعصبة والقهرية لردعه والقضاء عليه. فعلى الرغم من أن الحرية والعدالة من ركائز الحكم في الديموقراطيات الليبرالية في الغرب، فإن حرية اختيار الجسد بوصفه سلاحاً سياسياً جعل تلك الأنظمة تطلق عليها وصف إرهاب وتعلن الحرب عليها.(٣٤) وكما يوضح إيجلتون، فهناك اختلاف جوهري بين الاستشهاد لأسباب دينية والإضراب عن الطعام لأسباب سياسية من ناحية، والتفجيرات الانتحارية من ناحية أخرى، فهذا الاختيار الأخير يأتي لإفناء جسد صاحبه من أجل قتل آخرين حتى يحيا مجتمع الانتحاري وتحيا قضيته، وإن كانت عين هذا الانتحاري على «الجنة» في نهاية المطاف. أما الاستشهاد فهو يخص الفرد ذاته جسداً وروحاً إذ إنه يختاره عادة لسبب ديني وليس بغرض قتل آخرين؛ وأيضاً الإضراب عن الطعام فهو يخص الفرد وحده، وإن كان يتمنى أن يستجيب الطرف الآخر لمطالبه حتى يستطيع أن يأكل ويعيش.

ويستطرد إيجلتون بالقول إنه بالنسبة إلى الانتحاري، ربما تكون العملية الانتحارية أهم حدث في حياته، فهي التي تعطيها معنى ما وبدونها تستمر حياته تحت وطأة الفشل والقهر. فالانتحاري يتمنى لو كانت حياته لها معنى كموته، حتى لا يحتاج إلى أن يقتل نفسه وآخرين؛ فهو يقدس الحياة ويرفعها على الموت، حاله في ذلك من حال المضرب عن الطعام، فإذا حُلّت قضيته لن يختار الموت. وفي رأي إيجلتون، يرى الانتحاري اللحظة التي يفجر فيها جسده بمثابة اللحظة الخاطفة الوحيدة التي يمارس فيها حريته. فالانتحاري، مثل البطل التراجيدي في الدراما الإغريقية القديمة، يصبح المنتصر والضحية في الوقت ذاته، فهو بموته يدفع الآخرين لكي يدركوا ذلك التباين الصارخ بين فنائه وتخليد قضيته. ومن ثم، يعيش الانتحاري بشكل رمزي من خلال قضيته.(٣٥)

ولا يشير إيجلتون هنا إلى الشباب الفلسطيني الذي يقاوم الاحتلال بشكل خاص، وإنما يناقش قضية التفجيرات الانتحارية عموماً، ولكن الكثير من الأسئلة التي يطرحها تتواصل مع الأفكار التي يثيرها خالد وسعيد في فيلم **الجنة الآن**. فسعيد يقول للقائد الفلسطيني المسئول عن تنظيم العملية:

> أبوي لما صفّوه كان عمري عشر سنين. أبوي كان زلمة منيح، بس ضِعِف. الذنب في فقدان أبوي على الاحتلال. لازم يفهموا إنه حتى لما يجنّدوا عملاء ويستغلوا ضعفهم هيبقى فيه ثمن لازم يدفعوه. الحياة بدون كرامة ما تسواش . . . بيذكروك بالذل يوم ورا يوم، بالقهر، بالإهانة

... العالم قاعد متكتّف، أما إنت لحالَك، تحت كل ها القهر. بدّك تلاقي طريقة، بدّك تلاقي طريقة لتردع الباطل. هُمّه لازم يفهموا إنه إذا ما كنّاش احنا آمنين، همّه مش راح يكونوا آمنين. المسألة مش مسألة قوة، مش راح تساعد قوّتهم. أنا كمان بحاول أوصلهم هاي الرسالة، مش لاقي ... ما في طريقة تانية توصلهم الرسالة. والأنكى من هيك إنهم مقنعين كل العالم إنهم الضحية ومقنعين حالهم كمان إن همّه الضحية. كيف صارت هاي؟ همّه المحتل وهمّه الضحية؟ همّه يعني بيلعبوا دور الجلاد والضحية. وفي نفس الوقت أنا ما بيضل لي شي غير إني أكون المقتول والقاتل بردّ الفعل.

بالنسبة إلى سعيد، فإن أسوأ ما يفعله الاحتلال استغلال ضعف الناس بتجنيدهم عملاءً، وبذلك فهم «لا يضربون المقاومة فقط، ولكن أيضاً يهدّون بيوتاً، ويكسرون أخلاق شعب». يتمنى سعيد أن يجد طريقة أخرى غير تفجير جسده؛ لكي يوصل رسالته للمحتل. وإذا كان المحتل يرى نفسه الضحية فهو لم يترك لسعيد خياراً آخر. فكما يذكر إيجلتون عن مغزى العمل الانتحاري، يختار سعيد فناءه هو وأعداءه حتى يعيش شعبه وتحيا قضيته.

وهكذا، يحاول يوسف شاهين من خلال فيلم **١١ سبتمبر** أن يطرح وجهة نظره فيما يخص العلاقة بين أمريكا وإسرائيل والعرب، وقد جاء رأيه متقاطعاً مع فيلم هاني أبو أسعد **الجنة الآن**، حيث يحاول كلا المخرجين شرح كيف أن هناك عدداً من الفواجع يتصل بعضها ببعض، ويجب النظر إليها في سياقها السياسي والتاريخي. فالإمبريالية الأمريكية ومساندتها إسرائيل تولّد العنف وتؤدي إلى فاجعة جماعية عند الشعوب العربية، وسوف تنعكس هذه الفاجعة على الشعب الأمريكي كما حدث في ١١ سبتمبر. وقد جاءت رسالة شاهين في فيلمه مكثفة وسريعة وخاطفة، ولعل سيناريو الفيلم اتسم ببعض الضعف والتبسيط في أسلوب تناوله الحوار بين المخرج والجندي الأمريكي. يبدو لي وكأن شاهين أراد أن يقول الكثير في زمن الفيلم القصير (١١ دقيقة فقط)، مما جعل الفيلم لا يرتقي إلى مستوى السينماتوغرافيا التي طالما ارتأيناها في أعمال عديدة سابقة لشاهين. ولذلك، أعتقد أن المخرج قد قرر أن يعود مرة أخرى إلى بعض الموضوعات المثارة في فيلم **١١ سبتمبر** من خلال فيلمه الروائي التالي **إسكندرية .. نيويورك**.

## رحلة عبر الذاكرة: «إسكندرية .. نيويورك» وفاجعة شاهين الذاتية

على الرغم من أن فيلم **إسكندرية .. نيويورك** لا يشير إلى أحداث ١١ سبتمبر ولا يُعَدّ رد فعل لها، كما ذكر يوسف شاهين نفسه في مقابلة معه بعد عرض الفيلم،(٣٦) فإن هناك بعض القضايا السياسية التي يثيرها شاهين في هذا الفيلم والتي يمكن أن تلقي الضوء على الأسباب التي ربما أدت إلى أحداث ١١ سبتمبر. كما في فيلم **١١ سبتمبر**، يتنقل المخرج في **إسكندرية .. نيويورك** بين الماضي والحاضر عبر قصتين أساسيتين: قصة الحب التي تدور أحداثها في أمريكا الأربعينيات من القرن الماضي والتي تجمع بين يحيى الطالب المصري وجنجر الطالبة الأمريكية اللذين يلتقيان في المعهد نفسه بكاليفورنيا لدراسة المسرح؛ والقصة الثانية تجري أحداثها في نيويورك الحاضر حين يلتقي يحيى بجنجر وتخبره بأنها قد أخفت عنه أن لهما ابناً اسمه إسكندر وعمره خمسة وعشرون عاماً، وهو راقص باليه مرموق في أهم فرقة باليه بنيويورك. فعلى الرغم من أن يحيى وجنجر قد افترقا بعد انتهاء يحيى من دراسته في المعهد وعودته إلى مصر، فإنه قد التقى بجنجر في إحدى زياراته لأمريكا في السبعينيات مما نتج عنه حمل جنجر. وبعد خمسة وعشرين عاماً أخرى، يلتقي يحيى بجنجر وهو قد تخطى السبعين من العمر ليكتشف موضوع أبوته لإسكندر.

وهكذا، ومن خلال هذا اللقاء المتجدد بين يحيى وجنجر، وفي ضوء هذا الحدث الهائل في حياة يحيى وخبر أبوته لإسكندر، يبدأ كل منهما في إعادة إحياء ذكرياتهما عن لقائهما الأول في أمريكا منذ خمسين عاماً وما مرّ بهما من أحداث وما مرّ بالبلد نفسها من تغيرات وتحولات. يستخدم شاهين تكنيك الفلاش باك لعرض ذكريات يحيى وجنجر، ومن خلال تطور الأحداث يقارن بين أمريكا الأربعينيات التي كانت تحمل بالنسبة إلى يحيى – الطالب المصري الذي جاء من «آخر الدنيا» (من الإسكندرية) لطلب العلم – معاني الحب والرومانسية والانفتاح الثقافي، وأمريكا اليوم بكل ما تمثله من مفاهيم القوة العسكرية والغطرسة الإمبريالية والتحكم في مصائر الشعوب. وتبدو الرمزية هنا شديدة الوضوح؛ حيث تمثل جنجر بالنسبة إلى يحيى (في إشارة موحية للممثلة الأمريكية جنجر روجرز) الحلم الأمريكي القديم والتعاطف وإمكان الحب بين المنتمين إلى ثقافات مختلفة، ويمثل إسكندر ليحيى انتهاء هذا الحلم وانهيار أسس الفهم والحوار بين أمريكا الحاضر والعالم العربي، حيث إن إسكندر يرفض الاعتراف بيحيى أباً لأنه «عربي». وينتهي الفيلم بأغنية تتضمن كلماتها عبارة «نيويورك بتقتل أي حنين والواحد يخرج منها حزين». في رأيي أن انهيار هذا الحوار بين يحيى وإسكندر يرمز إلى جوهر الفاجعة التي حلّت بأمريكا يوم ١١ سبتمبر، كما يوحي شاهين من خلال أحداث الفيلم.

تمثل شخصية يحيى في الفيلم يوسف شاهين نفسه في شبابه، مروراً بعدّة مراحل عمرية حتى بلوغه منتصف السبعينيات من العمر. ففيلم **إسكندرية .. نيويورك** هو رابع فيلم في أعمال السيرة الذاتية ليوسف شاهين التي بدأها بفيلم **إسكندرية .. ليه؟**، وتبعها فيلم **حدوتة مصرية**،(٣٧) ثم **إسكندرية كمان وكمان**. وقد لفتت الأعمال الثلاثة الأولى في السيرة الذاتية نظر العديد من الباحثين والنقاد والمهتمين بسينما يوسف شاهين بشكل عام،(٣٨) حيث إن موضوع تقديم أفلام في العالم العربي تدور حول سيرة المخرج الذاتية، وتقديم شخصية تمثل المخرج ذاته وحياته، وتعكس فواجعه الشخصية ظاهرة فريدة من نوعها في السينما العربية.(٣٩) فربما اهتم عدد من المخرجين السينمائيين في العالم العربي بتمثيل بعض الجوانب الشخصية من حياتهم في أفلامهم مثل السوري محمد ملص والجزائري الأخضر حمينة والمصري يسري نصرالله وغيرهم،(٤٠) ولكن ما يميز أفلام يوسف شاهين الأربعة هو حديث المخرج نفسه عنها بأنها تعكس حياته إلى حدّ كبير،(٤١) على الرغم من أنه يمزج فيها بين الفانتازيا والواقع، وبين شخصيات حقيقية وأخرى من وحي الخيال. ولكن يظل القاسم المشترك في الأفلام الأربعة هو شخصية يحيى التي تمثل شاهين والتي يقدم من خلالها الكثير عن أفكاره وأحلامه وطموحاته وهواجسه الشخصية وأيضاً الملمّات والفواجع الشخصية التي وسمت جزءاً كبيراً من حياته، وهو هنا لا يفصل همّه الذاتي أبداً عن محيطه الاجتماعي والسياسي.

ففي **إسكندرية .. ليه؟**، نرى يحيى (ويلعب الدور محسن محيي الدين) الطالب الثانوي في ڤيكتوريا كولدج بالإسكندرية في أواسط الأربعينيات خلال الحرب العالمية الثانية، وهو يطمح في أن يصبح ممثلاً فيضغط على أهله متوسطي الحال حتى يوفروا له مصروفات السفر إلى أمريكا لدراسة التمثيل. وينتهي الفيلم بمشهد وصول يحيى إلى نيويورك التي طالما حلم بها من خلال الأفلام الموسيقية الأمريكية، حيث يشاهد تمثال الحرية لأول مرة. يتطلع يحيى بتمعن في وجه التمثال فيظهر له وجه امرأة قبيحة تضحك له ضحكة هيستيرية وتغمز له بعينها بينما يرى في اللحظة نفسها مجموعة من الحاخامات اليهود ينشدون نشيداً دينياً، في إشارة ساخرة إلى أن أمريكا الحلم في خيال يحيى تختلف عن الواقع الملبّد بالغيوم. وفي **حدوتة مصرية**، نرى يحيى (ويلعب الدور نور الشريف) وهو في منتصف العمر بعد أن أصبح مخرجاً كبيراً ويمر بأزمة صحية خطيرة تستدعي أن يخضع لعملية قلب مفتوح. ولقد ذكر شاهين في مقابلة معه أنه لم يكن يتوقع أن يخرج حيّاً من هذه العملية، ولذلك فلقد عدّ نجاح العملية بمثابة

فرصة جديدة له في الحياة.(٤٢) ويعكس الفيلم هذا الشعور، حيث يحلم يحيى وهو تحت تأثير المخدر في غرفة العمليات بطفولته وأحاسيسه المتناقضة تجاه أقرب النساء إليه – أمه وأخته وزوجته – في مشاهد ذكر بعض النقاد أنها تعكس تأثر شاهين بسينما المخرج الإيطالي فيدريكو فلليني Federico Fellini.(٤٣)

أما في فيلم **إسكندرية كمان وكمان**، فيلعب دور يحيى يوسف شاهين نفسه، حيث يلجأ المخرج مرة أخرى إلى الربط بين الفانتازيا والواقع من أجل التحدث عن علاقته وصداقته بالممثل الشاب عمرو (ويلعب الدور عمرو عبد الجليل) وارتباطه العاطفي والمعنوي به. اتخذ شاهين من إضراب الممثلين المصريين في عام ١٩٨٧ ضد قانون النقابات الفنية ١٠٣ واعتصامهم داخل نقابة الممثلين وإضرابهم عن الطعام إطاراً واقعياً لأحداث الفيلم. وقد كان شاهين أحد المعتصمين داخل النقابة، واستطاع من خلال هذا الفيلم أن يكشف عن الكثير من الجوانب الشخصية في علاقته بفنه وأصدقائه الفنانين، وأيضاً عن جانب حميم جداً بداخله وهو علاقته بالفنان عمرو (في إيحاء إلى الممثل محسن محيي الدين) الذي قرر أن يترك المخرج بعد عشرة أعوام من العمل المشترك.

وربما يشكّل هذا الحدث أحد الفواجع الشخصية الدفينة في حياة شاهين؛ مما دفعه إلى أن يقدم فيلماً كاملاً عن أحاسيسه ومشاعره بخصوص علاقته بصديقه الفنان الشاب. وهنا يبرز مرة أخرى مدى تسلّح شاهين بفنه وسينماه وسيناريوهات أفلامه (التي كتب العديد منها) من أجل معالجة – بل ومحاولة فهم – فواجعه الذاتية وتفكيكها. فعلى سبيل المثال، يبدأ **حدوتة مصرية** بمشهد تصوير المخرج يحيى لأحدث أفلامه؛ وذلك بالتركيز على البلاتوه والكاميرا والعاملين بالاستوديو في اللحظة نفسها التي يشعر فيها بالأزمة القلبية. ثم نرى كيف ينتهي **إسكندرية كمان وكمان** بمشهد وقوف شاهين خلف الكاميرا لتصوير اجتماع الفنانين الختامي بعد انتصار الإضراب. وتشير هذه الموتيفات، التي نراها تتكرر في عدة أفلام، إلى أن الكاميرا هي سلاح شاهين الأول والأخير. أعتقد أن أفلام السيرة الذاتية عند شاهين كانت محاولة مهمة في تاريخ السينما المصرية لمعالجة مسألة الارتباط الوثيق بين الفاجعة الجماعية والشخصية. وفي رأيي، ربما يكون فيلم **إسكندرية كمان وكمان** هو الأكثر جرأة في أعمال السيرة الذاتية، سواء على مستوى الشكل والتقنية أو المضمون. فالمخرج هنا يلجأ إلى الحلم والذاكرة والغناء والرقص بأسلوب المحاكاة الساخرة؛ لكي يكشف عن ارتباط الشخصي بالسياسي والذاتي والحميم بالجماعي.

يعلق الناقد اللبناني وليد شميط على هذه الأفلام الثلاثة بقوله:

> في **إسكندرية .. ليه؟** و**حدوتة مصرية** و**إسكندرية كمان وكمان** وضع شاهين نفسه تحت المجهر واخترق كل الجدران والحواجز والقيود وغاص في أعماق ذاته بحثاً عنها، وكأنه أراد أن يصفّي حساباته مع نفسه وهواجسه ودوافعه، ومع عائلته وفنه . . . وشاهين إذ يفتح دفاتره الشخصية العتيقة، فإنه في الوقت نفسه يغوص في واقع مصر الاجتماعي والسياسي أيضاً، فتكتسب مغامرته بُعدها الموضوعي. هذه الحلقة الجديدة في سينما يوسف شاهين، التي لا يمكن بالطبع فصلها عن سينما شاهين عموماً، تشكل بحد ذاتها تجربة فريدة في السينما العربية.(٤٤)

وإذا كان النقاّد قد اتفقوا على تعبير «السيرة الذاتية» لوصف ثلاثية يوسف شاهين، فهو يقول إنه يفضل وصف «النقد الذاتي»: «فأنا لا أعجب بنفسي وأقول يا سلام كم أنا جدع وفاهم . . . أبحث عن كل الثغرات عندي . . . أحاول أن أرى ما هي السلبيات، وسلبياتي أنا قبل سلبيات الآخرين. هل كان يمكن لي أن أتغلب عليها؟ أطرح هذا السؤال من خلال النقد الذاتي، وأحب أن أؤكد على تعبير النقد الذاتي».(٤٥) ويضيف شاهين أن فيلمه **المهاجر** كان إضافة إلى سيرته الذاتية بشكل ما:

> المهم في الفيلم هو القرار الذي يتخذه رام بترك الصحراء حيث يعيش والبحث عن العلم حيث يجده. قرر رام أن يعمل المستحيل لكي يحصل على العلم، ولكن من دون أن يستقر ويرتاح حيث يجد العلم. وهذا ما حصل معي في أمريكا. أنا تعلمت في أمريكا ولكن لم أبقَ في أمريكا . . . قراري كان أن أذهب إلى أمريكا وأتعلم شيئاً وأعود إلى بلادي وأحاول أن أكون مفيداً لشعبي أولاً. في قصة يوسف فإن يوسف يهاجر إلى مصر ويبقى في مصر، بينما أنا رجعت إلى مصر ومعي ما حصلت عليه من علم، وأحاول لغاية اليوم أن أطوّر هذا العلم. هذه هي فكرة الفيلم الأساسية.(٤٦)

وبذلك، ومع **إسكندرية .. نيويورك**، يختتم شاهين أفلام السيرة الذاتية حيث يحاول تجميع بعض الخيوط الدرامية التي عبّر عنها في الأفلام التي سبقت هذا الفيلم. وكما لعبت الذاكرة دوراً مهماً في أفلامه عن

الإسكندرية، فالمخرج يرجع بالذاكرة في **إسكندرية .. نيويورك** إلى فترة مهمة من حياته، أي إلى أمريكا الأربعينيات حين ترك أهله وأصدقاءه في الإسكندرية ليسافر إلى كاليفورنيا طالباً للعلم والمعرفة، وللحب والسعادة أيضاً. فالفيلم يلتقط الأحداث من آخر مشاهد **إسكندرية .. ليه؟**، ويقدم لنا يحيى الشاب وهو طالب في التاسعة عشرة من العمر (ويلعب الدور أحمد يحيى)؛ ثم يقدم لنا يحيى في مراحل عمرية لاحقة (ويلعب الدور محمود حميدة)، حتى بلوغه السبعينيات من العمر، وقد أصبح مخرجاً مرموقاً يطوف العالم بأفلامه التي تُعرض في المهرجانات العالمية. إذن، وكما أشرت سابقاً، تعد شخصية يحيى وحياته العنصر الأساسي الذي يربط أفلام السيرة الذاتية الأربعة؛ أما العنصر الثاني المهم الذي يجمعها فهو استخدام شاهين أساليب وتقنيات متنوعة في استكشافه هذه الرحلة الطويلة على مدار ما يقرب من ستين عاماً داخل دهاليز الذاكرة.

ولعل من أهم خصائص فيلم السيرة الذاتية عموماً أنه يركز على ذاكرة المبدع السينمائية، وعلى تقنيات الصورة البصرية لإعادة إحياء هذه الذاكرة والمعاني التي يمكن استخلاصها من تلك الرحلة. وكما يقول الراوي في رواية **الاعترافات** للكاتب اللبناني ربيع جابر: «الذاكرة حقول، حقول وقصور وكهوف ودهاليز . . . هذا ما أفعله وأنا أحكي لك: أخرج الذكريات من الغرف الخلفية، أدخل الزواريب البعيدة عن الأقدام وأحاول أن أعثر عليّ».(٤٧) وهذا على وجه التحديد هو ما يفعله يوسف شاهين في أفلام السيرة الذاتية: إنه يتعمق ويغوص في حقول الذاكرة الشخصية والجماعية ليبحث عن فواجعه وهمومه وأفراحه، ولكي يستكشف حقيقة نفسه في ضعفها وقوتها، لكي يعثر أيضاً على حقيقة علاقته بمن حوله وبالأماكن أو المدن التي ارتبط بها.

فليس صدفة، إذن، أن يكون عنوان آخر فيلم في رحلة يوسف شاهين الذاتية هو **إسكندرية .. نيويورك**، وترمز مدينة نيويورك في الفيلم إلى تجربة يحيى في أمريكا بشكل عام. يصل يحيى إلى أمريكا لدراسة التمثيل فيلتقي بجنجر الفتاة الجميلة العاشقة للسينما والمسرح. تنشأ بينهما قصة حب أثناء الدراسة، ثم يرجع يحيى إلى الإسكندرية، على الرغم من أنه كان باستطاعته العيش في أمريكا والتدريس في المعهد. ولكن يحيى يختار الرجوع إلى الإسكندرية ويبدأ مشواره السينمائي حتى يصبح مخرجاً مرموقاً. أما جنجر فلا تستطيع استكمال مشوارها في عالم الفن وتضطر تحت وطأة ظروف اقتصادية صعبة أن تتجه إلى الدعارة، ثم تتزوج فيما بعد من إيريك الأمريكي الذي يكره العرب كرهاً شديداً. يلتقي يحيى بجنجر في أمريكا في السبعينيات، أي بعد ما يقرب من خمسة وعشرين عاماً من الغياب، فيمارسان الحب مما ينتج عنه حمل جنجر دون علم يحيى. وبعد خمسة

وعشرين عاماً أخرى، يتقابل الاثنان في نيويورك الحاضر حيث تخبر جنجر يحيى بقصة ابنهما الموهوب إسكندر. يفرح يحيى فرحاً غامراً عندما يعلم بذلك وبخاصة أن زواجه لم ينتج عنه أطفال. يتحمس يحيى لمقابلة إسكندر، ولكن هذا الأخير يقابله ببرود وبعض العدوانية ولا يتقبله أباً لأنه عربي. عندما تخبر جنجر ابنها بأن يحيى هو في الحقيقة أبوه، يثور عليها:

**إسكندر**: ماما ارحميني دي آخر حاجة كنت ممكن أتصورها، ينزل لي شخص مرة واحدة من المرّيخ وتقولي لي ده أبوك وكمان يطلع عربي؟
**جنجر**: ده من أهم مخرجين العالم كله.
**إسكندر**: ولو، برضه عربي. أنا اتولدت أمريكاني وطلعت لقيت أبويا أمريكاني وأستاذي يهودي، وكل اللي بيشتغلوا في الفرقة والشو بيزينس يهود.
**جنجر**: وفين المشكلة؟ ما أديك شفت ازاي يحيى بيتعامل مع اليهود، وليه أصحاب عايشين هنا بيحبوه وبيحترموه.
**إسكندر**: ماما، مش مستعد أعترف بأب غير إيريك. يحيى ممكن يكون صديق قديم لأمي وجدير بالاحترام، مش أكتر من كده.
**جنجر**: انت لو كنت شفت دموعه وهوّه بيتكلم عنّك؟
**إسكندر**: انتي عايزاني أقبل إن يكون ليّه أب جاي من بلاد عايشة في خيم وبيركبوا فيها جمال ومتخلفين وجهلة؟
**جنجر**: انت اللي جاهل وما تعرفش أي حاجة عن الناس دي. يحيى جه يدرس هنا من خمسين سنة، عارف ليه؟ عشان أهله ما كانوش جهلة وراكبين جمال وعايشين في خيم. لأ، كان عندهم وعي إنهم يعلّموا ابنهم أحسن تعليم. بعتوه أرقى معهد في كاليفورنيا.

ولذلك، وفي محاولة منه لفهم يحيى، يشاهد إسكندر أفلام يحيى التي كانت تعرض في ذلك التوقيت بمهرجان في نيويورك. أما يحيى فيحاول أيضاً أن يفهم سرّ رفض ابنه له فيحضر حفلات الباليه التي يرقص فيها إسكندر. فالشخصيتان هنا تحاولان الالتقاء من خلال عشقهما للفن، ولكن ينتهي الفيلم بعدم حلّ معضلة إقامة حوار أو أي نوع من العلاقة بين الأب العربي والابن الأمريكي.

يذكر يوسف شاهين في مقابلة معه(٤٨) في أعقاب عرض الفيلم أن الحوار بين الولايات المتحدة والعالم العربي قد «انتهى». ويضيف أنه حاول مع آخرين على مدار ستين عاماً أن يخلق جسراً من الحوار مع أمريكا، ولكنه

اكتشف أن ذلك لم يعد ممكناً. ويعلق شاهين أن هناك الكثير من العنف في الأفلام الأمريكية الحالية على عكس أفلام هوليوود في الأربعينيات مثلاً؛ وفي رأيه أن هذه الصورة عن المجتمع الأمريكي والقوة والهيمنة الأمريكية المتمثلة في الكثير من أفلام هوليوود حالياً هي أحد العوامل التي أدت إلى تضليل الشعب الأمريكي حول غزو أمريكا لأفغانستان والعراق، وأيضاً فيما يتعلق بالقضية الفلسطينية. فالجمهور الأمريكي لم يعد يميّز بين العنف في هذه الأفلام والعنف على أرض الواقع.

وفي ردّه على سؤال عما إذا كان فيلم **إسكندرية .. نيويورك** قد جاء ردّ فعل على أحداث ١١ سبتمبر، ينفي شاهين ذلك ويوضح أن الفيلم جاء في الأساس كي يعبر عن تناقض داخله هو شخصياً يتمثل في أنه يحب أمريكا والمجتمع الأمريكي ويحب التقدم الثقافي والتكنولوجي الذي قدمه شعبها، ولكنه من ناحية أخرى يرى كيف ساعدت الإمبريالية الأمريكية على خلق الكثير من الصراعات والعنف في العالم. فهذا الشعور المتناقض تجاه أمريكا هو ما دفعه إلى عمل **إسكندرية .. نيويورك**؛ لأنه ما زال يتساءل عن أسباب حبه لأمريكا وارتباطه بها. ويذكر شاهين أيضاً أن الجزء الرئيسي في الفيلم يرجع بالذاكرة إلى فترة رومانسية من حياته عندما كان في بدايات اكتشافه الحب والمرأة. فلقد وقع في حب فتاة من أصل أيرلندي كانت تدرس معه في معهد المسرح، وكان متوقعاً أن تصبح نجمة، ولكنها للأسف أصبحت فتاة تحت الطلب فيما بعد. وعندما رجع إلى مصر تزوج وبدأ مشواره السينمائي.

في **إسكندرية .. نيويورك** يطوّع شاهين مفهوم الذاكرة من خلال الفلاش باك، وهي تقنية مهمة في التعبير عن ذكريات الشخصيات لأنها تجمع بين لحظتين زمنيتين في الماضي والحاضر، وبذلك يعبّر الفلاش باك عن تاريخ علاقات وأحداث وصور وتطورها. ففي الفيلم، يستخدم شاهين الفلاش باك حين يتحدث عن ذكريات يحيى في أمريكا الأربعينيات وذكريات جنجر عن الفترة نفسها؛ ثم ذكريات صديقة جنجر عن فترة الخمسينيات والستينيات عندما تعرضت الصديقتان لأحداث مؤلمة وواجهتا ظروفاً اقتصادية صعبة؛ وهناك أيضاً ذكريات جين زوجة يحيى وهي تحكي لإسكندر عن علاقة يحيى بأمريكا على مرّ السنوات. إذن، يعمل الفلاش باك في الفيلم على مستويات عدة وتتقاطع من خلاله ذكريات أربع شخصيات رئيسة ترسم صورة عن أمريكا في الماضي والحاضر.

ومن أهم خصائص الفلاش باك في هذا الفيلم التركيز على «ذاتية» الذاكرة، فالشخصيات تتذكر سيرتها أو تواصُل هذه السيرة مع قصص الشخصيات الأخرى وما ألمّ بها من تطورات شخصية، وإن كان داخل إطار اجتماعي وسياسي عام. ويعد الفلاش باك تكنيكاً ذا مغزى؛ لأنه يقطع تسلسل

الرواية الزمني بالرجوع إلى الماضي من أجل إلقاء الضوء على حاضر العلاقة بين أمريكا والعالم العربي أو للتحدث عن قصة معينة في الحاضر، وهو ما يرمز له شاهين بالعلاقة بين يحيى وجنجر من ناحية، ويحيى وإسكندر من ناحية أخرى. فهناك إذن مقارنة واضحة بين زمنين مختلفين في تاريخ العلاقة تعبر عنه الشخصيات من خلال رحلة عبر الذاكرة.

تذكر الباحثة الأكاديمية مورين توريم Maureen Turim في دراستها عن تقنية الفلاش باك في تاريخ السينما الأمريكية أن أفلام هوليوود في فترات تاريخية مختلفة اعتمدت أساليب تقنية عالية ومعقدة في نقلها الفلاش باك، ولكن أفلام فترة الأربعينيات من القرن الماضي اعتمدت في الكثير منها أساليب خالية من التعقيد إلى حدّ كبير.(٤٩) وتضيف توريم أن استخدام مخرجي هوليوود تقنية الفلاش باك ازدهرت في الأربعينيات خلال الحرب العالمية الثانية وبعدها لنقل ذكريات الجنود والمواطنين وخبراتهم؛ الأمر الذي يوضح تأثير الحربين العالميتين على المجتمع والفرد. كما لمعت الأفلام التي تحكي عن سيرة شخصيات غير حقيقية من خلال الفلاش باك، بوصفها نوعاً من النقد الموجه إلى المجتمع الأمريكي الرأسمالي. وتذكر توريم أفلاماً مثل **جسر واترلو** *Waterloo Bridge* (١٩٤٠) من إخراج ميرفن لورووي Mervyn Le Roy و**المواطن كين** *Citizen Kane* (١٩٤١) من إخراج أورسون ويلز Orson Welles، بوصفهما من الأفلام المؤسسة لهذا التيار. وبذلك، اختلف استخدام تقنية الفلاش باك في أفلام الأربعينيات عنها في الثلاثينيات عندما كانت أفلام «الصعود إلى الشهرة» – كما تسميها توريم – هي السائدة، مثل أفلام فريد أستير وجنجر روجرز، حينذاك كان المواطن الأمريكي ما زال مؤمناً بالحلم الأمريكي في تحقيق العدالة الاجتماعية والنجاح والشهرة.(٥٠)

وقد لجأ يوسف شاهين إلى استخدام الفلاش باك في **إسكندرية .. نيويورك** بوصفه نوعاً من استحضار ذاكرة السينما الهوليوودية في الأربعينيات. فالفيلم يستخدم تقنية سادت في السينما الأمريكية في الفترة نفسها التي يتناولها شاهين بمشاعر الحنين الجارف. وأعتقد أن هذا الحنين إلى الماضي، وهو ما نستشفّه من خلال ذكريات يحيى وجنجر، هو نقطة الضعف الرئيسة في الفيلم. فشاهين يلجأ هنا إلى جرعة زائدة من الميلودراما من أجل تصوير أمريكا الأربعينيات بوصفها الحلم الجميل ومكاناً رومانسياً سادت فيه قيم أصيلة مثل الحب والعدالة والانفتاح الثقافي. ولذلك أرى أن الميلودراما تعد الخاصة الرئيسة في هذا الفيلم مما يجعله مختلفاً اختلافاً كبيراً عن الأفلام الثلاثة الأولى في السيرة الذاتية، التي غلب عليها طابع التجريب ما بعد الحداثي، بالإضافة إلى الجرأة في استخدام تقنيات سينمائية حديثة في السرد. وربما اختار شاهين هذا الاتجاه في **إسكندرية .. نيويورك** لأنه أراد أن يوجه رسالة نقد سياسية واضحة للخلل الذي أصاب المجتمع

الأمريكي في الوقت الحاضر، مما جعل تلك القيم القديمة تتفكك وتنهار. ولكن جاءت هذه المقابلة بين الماضي والحاضر سطحية وينقصها العمق التاريخي. أعتقد أن شاهين اختار استخدام الفلاش باك بوصفه نوعاً من الأداة السياسية في مقارنته بين زمنين مختلفين في سيرة أمريكا، وأراد لرسالته السياسية أن تكون مباشرة في رمزيتها وواضحة المعالم كما فعل في فيلمه القصير عن أحداث ١١ سبتمبر.

يقول يحيى المخرج الشهير في **إسكندرية .. نيويورك** في مؤتمر صحفي تم عقده بمناسبة عرض أفلامه في نيويورك:

> أمريكا المفروض إن شعبها حرّ. تذكرة انتخابك إنت اللي بتحدد مين هوّة اللي هيحكم وسياسته تجاه العالم كله. يعني كل شخص قاعد هنا مسؤول، مش بريء أوي. ولو كنتوا عايزين كنتوا توقفوا المجازر اللي بتعملها إسرائيل في الفلسطينيين وبسلاح أمريكاني. كنتوا هتقدروا وبسهولة.

يكرر شاهين هنا الرسالة السياسية نفسها التي وجهها في فيلم **١١ سبتمبر**، ولكنه يغلف هذه الرسالة بقصة حب وقصة شاب أمريكي يجهل تاريخ العرب ويتمسك بكل الأفكار المشوّهة عنهم، بل يعد يحيى مخرجاً مجهولاً وأفلامه ليست أصلاً «على الخريطة» لأنه عربي.

## الفنون والانفتاح على الآخر

ولكن، وكما هو حاصل في معظم أفلام شاهين السابقة، لا يتخلى المخرج في **إسكندرية .. نيويورك** عن تمرير رسائله السياسية عبر جماليات الشِعر والموسيقى والرقص من خلال أسلوب التناص. وربما يكون هذا الأسلوب هو الموضوع المتميز في الفيلم حيث تتداخل وجهة نظر المخرج في العلاقة بالآخر مع نص ويليام شكسبير **مأساة هاملت**، وأيضاً مع نص جورج بيزيه Georges Bizet أوبرا **كارمن**. إن استخدام شاهين أسلوب التناص يعزز من تطويعه مفهوم الذاكرة في الفيلم ومن التوغل في فواجعه الشخصية أيضاً.

يذكر ستيوارت كلاونس Stuart Klawans أن طموح يوسف شاهين السينمائي في أفلام السيرة الذاتية الثلاثة الأولى عن الإسكندرية يتمثل في أن يجعلها متنوعة ومتشعبة الأهداف والمفاهيم مثل مسرحيات شكسبير. أراد شاهين أن تكون أفلامه مجالاً للتجريب وفوضى الفن وعفويته كما في أعمال شكسبير، «حيث يتعلم شاهين درساً في كيفية أن يكون العمل الفني شاملاً للعالم وليس في كونه مجرد قراءة لهذا

العالم».(٥١) وبذلك، جاءت أفلام الإسكندرية – في رأي كلاونس – شاملة كل ما يهم يوسف شاهين سواء على المستوى الشخصي أو الفني، وكأنه يعكس فيها مرآة ذاته وحياته.(٥٢)

أما العنصر الأساسي الآخر الذي يخلق نوعاً من الوحدة بين أفلام السيرة الذاتية الأربعة عند شاهين – إلى جانب شخصية يحيى واستخدام الذاكرة – فهو نصّ مسرحية **مأساة هاملت**. يذكر شاهين في مقابلته مع كريم بن عمرو أنه كان من أحلامه عمل فيلم مصري مقتبس عن **مأساة هاملت**، بحيث يقدم من خلاله هاملت المصري. ويضيف أنه قد أنجز بالفعل ما يقرب من ثلث السيناريو ولكنه توقف. ويرى شاهين أن **مأساة هاملت** نص شعري مسرحي متميز وعظيم، وقد أراد أن ينقل عظمة هذا النص الشعري إلى العربية من خلال فيلمه، ولكنه لم يستطع.(٥٣) ولكن ما نجح فيه شاهين في أفلام السيرة الذاتية الأربعة أن جعل من **هاملت** مجالاً لطرح مفهومه عن التواصل بين المنتمين إلى ثقافات مختلفة، بل والانفتاح على ثقافة الآخر، وخلق مساحة – من خلال هذا النص – لتصوير الفواجع الذاتية لشاهين نفسه. فما يحتويه نص **هاملت** من أحاسيس ومشاعر متناقضة وملتبسة – من حب وكره وسعادة وتعاسة وإخلاص وخيانة وانتقام – يشكّل نوعاً من الذاكرة التاريخية المتجددة على مرّ العصور لأي إنسان وجد نفسه مخدوعاً ومهاناً من أقرب الناس إليه كما حدث مع هاملت في مسرحية شكسبير. إذن، مثّلت فاجعة هاملت الشخصية مادة خصبة للتعبير عن أحاسيس ملتبسة وعميقة لدى شاهين.

ولقد استخدم شاهين مسرحية **هاملت** في أفلام السيرة الذاتية ليطرح العديد من أفكاره الفلسفية والسياسية عن ماهية الحب والانتقام والخيانة والرغبة والسيطرة والعلاقة بالآخر واكتشاف الذات. ففي **إسكندرية .. ليه؟**، نرى يحيى يبهر أستاذه الإنجليزي في المدرسة وزملاءه الطلبة باستيعابه نص **هاملت** حين يمثل مشهداً من المسرحية باللغة العربية.(٥٤) وفي **حدوتة مصرية**، يرجع يحيى بالذاكرة إلى أيام دراسته بمدرسة ڤيكتوريا كولدج وقراءته **هاملت** وكيف كان يراوده دائماً حلم تمثيل شخصية هاملت بالكامل على المسرح. وفي **إسكندرية كمان وكمان**، يبدأ الفيلم بعبارة «أكون أو لا أكون، ذلك هو السؤال» في شكل أغنية، ويصبح نصّ **هاملت** واقعاً في حياة يحيى؛ حيث يبدأ فعلياً في تصوير فيلمه عن هاملت المصري من بطولة صديقه الفنان عمرو، ولكنه يُنهي هذا المشروع عندما يرفض عمرو استكمال الفيلم ويتخلى عن يحيى.

أما في **إسكندرية .. نيويورك**، فنرى عودة إلى إثارة الحلم بتمثيل شخصية هاملت، وهو الحلم الذي طالما راود يحيى الطالب بمعهد المسرح. فلماذا هاملت بالتحديد؟ يقول يحيى لجنجر إنه شاهد الممثل

الإنجليزي الشهير جون جيلجود John Gielgud وهو يمثل دور هاملت على مسرح أوبرا القاهرة في الأربعينيات، عندما وقف جيلجود ليعلن أن هذه هي المرة الألف والأخيرة التي يمثل فيها دور هاملت. وهنا، أحس يحيى وكأن جيلجود «يسلّمه الشعلة» ليكمل مشوار هاملت من بعده. ونرى في فيلم **إسكندرية كمان وكمان** حواراً مشابهاً بين المخرج المخضرم يحيى والفنانة الناشئة نادية (التي لعبت دورها يسرا). إذن، كان نص **هاملت** يشكل ليحيى منذ صباه نوعاً من الإلهام وإمكان التواصل الثقافي وموهبة اللغة والتعبير بها عن رغبات مكبوتة. بمعنى آخر، شكّل هاملت ليحيى، على مدار تاريخه الفني، مجالاً مفتوحاً للإبداع اللغوي والتعبير عن كمّ هائل من الأحاسيس المعقدة التي نبعت أساساً من إحساس هاملت بفاجعة فقدان أبيه، وخيانة أمه وعمه له ولأبيه، الذي كان يحبه حباً عميقاً، وكذلك الرغبات الجنسية المتوارية والدفينة. وتعلق الباحثة زهر سعيد ستوفر Zahr Said Stauffer على «هوس» شاهين بشخصية هاملت في أفلام السيرة الذاتية الثلاثة الأولى بقولها إن مسرحية شكسبير قد أتاحت المجال أمام شاهين للتعبير عن حالات سيكولوجية ورغبات إيروتيكية لم يكن ليستطع التعبير عنها بشكل مباشر في هذه الأفلام.(٥٥)

وهكذا، نرى في **إسكندرية .. نيويورك** أن نص **هاملت** هو شاغل يحيى الأول خلال دراسته بالمعهد؛ فهو يرى أن إتقانه الدور مسألة جوهرية في مشوار نجاحه الدراسي وصعوده بوصفه ممثلاً فيما بعد. ويشغل هذا الموضوع حيّزاً مهماً في الفيلم؛ لأن تجربة تمثيل دور هاملت جزء رئيسي من ذاكرة يحيى الذاتية عن الفترة التي قضاها في أمريكا الأربعينيات، كما تشكّل بعداً إضافياً في ارتباطه بأمريكا وحبه لها؛ فهي المكان الذي أتاح له التعبير عن نفسه من خلال **هاملت** وأعمال شكسبير بشكل عام، فقد أتقن الدور وكان أفضل من مثّله في تاريخ المعهد، مما جعل جنجر وزملاء يحيى الآخرين يقدرونه بوصفه فناناً وممثلاً موهوباً. ومن خلال شخصية هاملت، أحس يحيى بأنه يتحقق إنسانياً وفنياً، وأن باستطاعته أن يطور هذه التجربة، فيما بعد، لكي يصبح ممثلاً متميزاً.

يتداخل هوس يحيى بنص **هاملت** في الفيلم بانبهاره بنص عالمي يشكل هو الآخر ذاكرة متجددة عن الفواجع الشخصية وأحاسيس الحب والخيانة والرغبة المتأججة بين شخصيات تنتمي إلى ثقافات مختلفة، والمقصود هنا هو أوبرا **كارمن** لبيزيه المأخوذة عن نص الكاتب الفرنسي بروسبر ميريميه Prosper Mérimée. يضمّن شاهين في **إسكندرية .. نيويورك** رقصة من **كارمن** (يؤديها أحمد

يحيى ونيللي كريم) وهي رقصة تشير بشكل رمزي إلى فاجعة يحيى الشخصية المتعلقة بعدم استمرار قصة الحب بينه وبين جنجر. ومن ناحية أخرى، يحاول يحيى أن يبرهن على أن بإمكانه تقديم هذه الأوبرا من منظور مصري. ومرة أخرى، يثبت يحيى من خلال هذا النص أنه ممثل وراقص موهوب، مثلما رأيناه يُخرج ويمثل على مسرح المدرسة في **إسكندرية .. ليه؟** نصوصاً عالمية أخرى.

إذن، يشكل فيلم **إسكندرية .. نيويورك** محطة مهمة في ذاكرة يوسف شاهين السينمائية ورحلته الذاتية لاستكشاف أبعاد علاقته الطويلة بأمريكا التي أحبها وعاش فيها تجربة متميزة في الأربعينيات من القرن الماضي، ولكنه أحس تجاهها أيضاً بمشاعر الإحباط والغضب وبخاصة في الوقت الحاضر. أعتقد أن أهمية فيلمي **١١ سبتمبر** و**إسكندرية .. نيويورك** تنبع أساساً من القضايا السياسية التي أراد شاهين أن يطرحها بخصوص العلاقة بين الولايات المتحدة والعالم العربي من خلال موتيفات وتقنيات سينمائية عديدة تعمل في مجملها على تطويع الذاكرة الذاتية والجماعية والتأمل في مسألة الفاجعة من أجل نقل وجهة نظر المخرج في هذه العلاقة. وبالتأكيد، سوف تختلف الآراء حول أهمية هذين الفيلمين من الناحية التقنية، وأنهما ربما لم يكونا على درجة عالية من الإبداع السينمائي مقارنة بأفلام أخرى في مسيرة شاهين، ولكنهما في اعتقادي سيظلان مرجعاً سينمائياً مهماً في طرح هذا النوع من القضايا السياسية التي يقل طرحها في السينما المصرية بشكل عام.

## الهوامش

(١) راجع:
Youssef Chahine, dir., *11 ’09 ’’01--September 11* [Egypt segment] (Galatée Films/Studio Canal, 2002).

(٢) يوسف شاهين، مخرج، **إسكندرية .. نيويورك** (شركة أفلام مصر العالمية للإنتاج والتوزيع وOgnon Pictures، ٢٠٠٤).

(٣) يوسف شاهين، مخرج، **الناصر صلاح الدين** (أفلام آسيا والمؤسسة العامة للسينما المصرية، ١٩٦٣).

(٤) يوسف شاهين، مخرج، **الوداع يا بونابرت** (شركة أفلام مصر العالمية للإنتاج والتوزيع، وزارة الثقافة الفرنسية، وLyric International، ١٩٨٥).

(٥) يوسف شاهين، مخرج، **المهاجر** (شركة أفلام مصر العالمية للإنتاج والتوزيع وOgnon Pictures، ١٩٩٤).

(٦) يوسف شاهين، مخرج، **المصير** (شركة أفلام مصر العالمية للإنتاج والتوزيع، ١٩٩٧).

(٧) راجع على سبيل المثال:

Jeffrey Melnick, *9/11 Culture: America under Construction* (MA: Wiley-Blackwell, 2009); Ann Keniston and Jeanne Follansbee Quinn, eds., *Literature after 9/11* (NY & London: Routledge, 2008); Daniel J. Sherman and Terry Nardin, eds., *Terror, Culture, Politics: Rethinking 9/11* (Bloomington: Indiana UP, 2005); Dana Heller, ed., *The Selling of 9/11: How a National Tragedy Became a Commodity* (NY: Palgrave Macmillan, 2005); Gene Ray, *Terror and the Sublime in Art and Critical Theory: From Auschwitz to Hiroshima to September 11* (NY: Palgrave Macmillan, 2005).

(٨) راجع على سبيل المثال:

Yuval Neria et al., eds., *9/11: Mental Health in the Wake of Terrorist Attacks* (Cambridge & NY: Cambridge UP, 2006); Yael Danieli and Robert L. Dingman, eds., *On the Ground after September 11: Mental Health Responses and Practical Knowledge Gained* (NY: Haworth Maltreatment and Trauma P, 2005); Susan W. Coates et al., *September 11: Trauma and Human Bonds* (Hillside NJ: The Analytic P, 2003).

(٩) راجع على سبيل المثال:

E. Ann Kaplan, *Trauma Culture: The Politics of Terror and Loss in Media and Literature* (New Brunswick and London: Rutgers UP, 2005); E. Ann Kaplan and Ban Wang, eds., *Trauma and Cinema: Cross-Cultural Explorations* (Seattle: U of Washington P, 2004); Judith Greenberg, ed. *Trauma at Home: After 9/11* (London: U of Nebraska P, 2003).

(١٠) قام العديد من الباحثين بتطوير نظرياتهم وأفكارهم عن موضوع الفاجعة والذاكرة من خلال الأسس النظرية والعملية التي قدمها سيجموند فرويد في كتاباته، وبخاصة في:

Sigmund Freud, *Beyond the Pleasure Principle*, trans. James Starchey (London: Hogarth P and The Institute of Psychoanalysis, 1961); *Moses and Monothesis*, trans. Katharine Jones (London: Hogarth P and The Institute of Psychoanalysis, 1939); "Trauer und Melancholie," *Sigmund Freud: Gesammelte Werke*, eds. Marie Bonaparte et al. (Frankfurt: Fischer Taschenbuch Verlag, 1999).

(١١) راجع على سبيل المثال:

Jenny Edkins, *Trauma and the Memory of Politics* (Cambridge: Cambridge UP, 2003); Anna Douglas and Thomas A. Vogler, *Witness and Memory: The Discourse of Trauma* (NY and London: Routledge, 2003); James V. Wertsch, *Voices of Collective Remembering* (Cambridge and NY:

Cambridge UP, 2002); Nancy K. Miller and Jason Tougaw, eds. *Extremities: Trauma, Testimony, and Community* (Urbana: U of Illinois P, 2002); Ruth Leys, *Trauma: Genealogy* (Chicago and London: The U of Chicago P, 2000); Cathy Caruth, *Unclaimed Experience: Trauma, Narrative, and History* (Baltimore: The Johns Hopkins UP, 1996).

(١٢) راجع:
Patricia A. Resick, *Stress and Trauma* (PA: Psychology P, 2001), 1-28.

(١٣) Caruth، ص ص ١–٩.

(١٤) Resick، ص ص ١١٧–١٣٩.

(١٥) تؤكد آن كابلان في دراستها المهمة عن موضوع الفاجعة عقب أحداث ١١ سبتمبر أنه من الصعب فصل الفاجعة الذاتية عن الجماعية. وتتناول في دراستها ما عانته هي شخصياً من صدمة مريرة على إثر أحداث ١١ سبتمبر، على الرغم من أنها لم تفقد أياً من أفراد عائلتها أو أصدقائها في ذلك اليوم. ولكن بسبب أن بيتها يقع على مقربة من برجي مركز التجارة فكانت تذهب يومياً لتلتقط الصور لذلك المكان وما حوله ولكي تحضر الفعاليات الكثيرة التي أعقبت هذا الحدث، وهو ما دفعها إلى التفكير في الأثر الذي يحلّ على المحيطين بأولئك الذين تأثروا بشكل مباشر بفاجعة ما. راجع Kaplan، ص ص ١–٢٣.

(١٦) تجدر الإشارة هنا إلى دراسة الطبيبة البريطانية من أصل فلسطيني نادية تيسير دباغ في تناولها موضوع الفاجعة المتعلقة بإقدام نسبة مرتفعة من الشباب الفلسطيني الذي يعيش تحت الاحتلال في الضفة الغربية على الانتحار. راجع:
Nadia Taysir Dabbagh, *Suicide and Palestine: Narratives of Despair* (London: Hurst & Company, 2005).

(١٧) يوسف شاهين، مخرج، **العصفور** (شركة أفلام مصر العالمية للإنتاج والتوزيع وأونسيك [الجزائر]، ١٩٧٣).

(١٨) يوسف شاهين، مخرج، **عودة الابن الضال** (شركة أفلام مصر العالمية للإنتاج والتوزيع وأونسيك [الجزائر]، ١٩٧٦).

(١٩) يوسف شاهين، مخرج، **باب الحديد** (أفلام جبريل تلحمي، ١٩٥٨).

(٢٠) يوسف شاهين، مخرج، **الاختيار** (المؤسسة العامة للسينما المصرية، ١٩٧٠).

(٢١) لقد أثار فيلم **١١ سبتمبر** انتقاداً حادّاً عند محاولة عرضه في مصر عام ٢٠٠٦ في مهرجان أفلام حوار الثقافات، وذلك بسبب مشاركة المخرج الإسرائيلي عاموس جيتاي فيه. وعلى الرغم من أن جيتاي معروف بأفلامه التي تناصر القضية الفلسطينية وتوجه انتقادات شديدة للسياسات الإسرائيلية وقوى الاحتلال، فإن رد فعل وزارة الثقافة المصرية جاء حاسماً برفض عرض الفيلم بوصفه نوعاً من أنواع

التطبيع مع إسرائيل. راجع على سبيل المثال: أحمد الجزار، «وزارة الثقافة تمنع عرض **١١ سبتمبر** بسبب مشاركة مخرج إسرائيلي في الفيلم»، **المصري اليوم**، ٢٠٠٦/٩/١٦؛ علا الشافعي، «هجوم حاد على أول مهرجان لحوار الثقافات في مصر ... اتهام منظميه بالتطبيع ... وسمير فريد يرفض الإساءة»، **الحياة**، ٢٠٠٦/١٠/٦.

(٢٢) راجع:

Alain Brigand, "The Artistic Producer's Statement," Special Features, *11 '09 ''01--September 11.*

(٢٣) راجع:

Talal Asad, *On Suicide Bombing* (NY: Columbia UP, 2007), 8.

(٢٤) **المرجع السابق**، ص ص ٣٩–٦٤.

(٢٥) يوسف شاهين، مخرج، **إسكندرية .. ليه؟** (شركة أفلام مصر العالمية للإنتاج والتوزيع، ١٩٧٨).

(٢٦) يوسف شاهين، مخرج، **اليوم السادس** (شركة أفلام مصر العالمية للإنتاج والتوزيع وLyric International، ١٩٨٦).

(٢٧) يوسف شاهين، مخرج، **إسكندرية كمان وكمان** (شركة أفلام مصر العالمية للإنتاج والتوزيع، وزارة الثقافة الفرنسية، وParis Classics، ١٩٨٩).

(٢٨) يوسف شاهين، مخرج، **الآخر** (شركة أفلام مصر العالمية للإنتاج والتوزيع وOgnon Pictures، ١٩٩٩).

(٢٩) وليد شميط، «**المصير** في زمن الأندلس»، مقابلة مع يوسف شاهين، **يوسف شاهين: حياة للسينما** (بيروت: رياض الريس للكتب والنشر، ٢٠٠١)، ص ٢٤٠.

(٣٠) **المرجع السابق**، ص ٨٦.

(٣١) راجع:

Amos Gitai, dir., *11 '09 ''01--September 11* [Israel segment].

(٣٢) راجع:

Peter Cowie, "Conversation: Amos Gitai," <http://www.amosgitai.com/html/page.asp?.docid=5&lang=1>.

(٣٣) هاني أبو أسعد، مخرج، **الجنة الآن** (Warner Independent Pictures، ٢٠٠٥).

(٣٤) راجع:

Terry Eagleton, *Holy Terror* (Oxford and NY: Oxford UP, 2005), 68-115.

(٣٥) **المرجع السابق**، ص ٩٠.

(٣٦) راجع:

Karim Benamor, "Entretien avec Youssef Chahine," September 29, 2004, <http://www.karimbenamor.com/player.asp?NID=2229/ Youssef-Chahine.asp/29/09/2004.asp>.

(٣٧) يوسف شاهين، مخرج، **حدوتة مصرية** (شركة أفلام مصر العالمية للإنتاج والتوزيع، ١٩٨٢).

(٣٨) اهتم بعض النقاد بتحليل الأعمال الثلاثة الأولى في السيرة الذاتية ليوسف شاهين بشكل مفصّل. انظر على سبيل المثال: وليد شميط، **يوسف شاهين: حياة للسينما**؛ إبراهيم العريس، **يوسف شاهين: نظرة الطفل وقبضة المتمرد** (القاهرة: دار الشروق، ٢٠٠٩). راجع كذلك:

Ibrahim Fawal, *Youssef Chahine* (London: British Film Institute, 2001); Stuart Klawans, "Nine Views in a Looking Glass: Film Trilogies by Chahine, Gitai, and Kiarostami," *Parnassus: Poetry in Review* 25.1/2 (2001): 231-52; Maureen Kiernan, "Cultural Hegemony and National Film Language: Youssef Chahine," *Alif* 15 (1995): 130-52; Christian Bosséno, ed., *Youssef Chahine: l'Alexandrin*, a special issue of *CinémAction* (Paris: Éditions du Cerf, 1985).

(٣٩) محمود قاسم، «سيرة الفنان الذاتية في السينما العربية»، **ألف**، العدد ١٥ (١٩٩٥)، ص ص ٢٣–٢٥.

(٤٠) **المرجع السابق**، ص ص ٢٥–٢٨.

(٤١) انظر حوارات يوسف شاهين الممتدة عن أفلامه (بما في ذلك أفلام السيرة الذاتية) مع وليد شميط في **يوسف شاهين: حياة للسينما**، ص ص ١١٣ – ٢٤٦.

(٤٢) **المرجع السابق**، ص ١٦١.

(٤٣) انظر نص مقابلة الكاتب عمرو عبد الحميد مع يوسف شاهين وحديثه عن فلليني (١٩٨٨) كما أعيد نشرها في: محمد الصاوي، **سينما يوسف شاهين: رحلة أيديولوجية** (الإسكندرية: دار المطبوعات الجديدة، ١٩٩٠)، ص ٤١٣.

(٤٤) شميط، ص ص ٧٤–٧٥.

(٤٥) **المرجع السابق**، ص ١٩٧.

(٤٦) **المرجع السابق**، ص ص ٢٢٣–٢٢٤.

(٤٧) ربيع جابر، **الاعترافات** (بيروت: دار الآداب للنشر والتوزيع، ٢٠٠٨)، ص ص ١١٠–١١١.

(٤٨) Benamor، د. ص.

(٤٩) راجع:

Maureen Turim, *Flashback in Film: Memory and History* (NY and London: Routledge, 1989).

(٥٠) **المرجع السابق**، ص ص ١٠٣–١١٢ و ص ص ١٢٢–١٣٣.

(٥١) Klawans، ص ٢٣٦.

(٥٢) **المرجع السابق**، ص ٢٥٢.

(٥٣) Benamor، د. ص.

(٥٤) تحلل زهر سعيد ستوفر هذا المشهد بالتحديد في فيلم **إسكندرية .. ليه؟** ومضامينه السياسية الراديكالية وأيضاً مضمونه الإيروتيكي المتواري، في فترة كان يحيى يدرس فيها في مدرسته الإنجليزية في ظل الاحتلال البريطاني لمصر. وترى الباحثة أن تمثيل يحيى لمشهد من مسرحية شكسبير باللغة العربية وإتقانه له يعد نوعاً من تحدي المحتل (المتمثل في أستاذه الإنجليزي)، ويشير أيضاً إلى رغبات إيروتيكية موحية لدى الأستاذ تجاه يحيى. راجع:

Zahr Said Stauffer, "The Politicisation of Shakespeare in Arabic in Youssef Chahine's Film Trilogy," *English Studies in Africa* 47.2 (2004): 41-55.

(٥٥) **المرجع السابق**، ص ٤٢.

# شهادة سينمائية من زمن الحرب

عرب لطفي

---

سألني صديقي المخرج السينمائي، بعد أن شاهد فيلمي الأول **بوابة الفوقا**، ما الذي ألهمك عمل هذا الفيلم؟ فأجبته مازحة: لم يكن إلهاماً، كان نوعاً من العلاج النفسي.

والحقيقة أنه بالرغم من السخرية التي شابت إجابتي فقد كانت تعبر، بمعنى ما، عن الدافع العميق والحقيقي الذي أسهم في تبلور مشروع فيلمي هذا.

لقد بدأت الفكرة تلح عليّ منذ اللحظة التي وطأت قدمي فيها مدينتي صيدا بعد أشهر من احتلال الجيش الصهيوني لها.

كنت قد غادرت مدينتي في ٢٩ مايو/آيار ١٩٨٢ إلى القاهرة، وفي نيتي الاستقرار لفترة مفتوحة. وصلت، وقابلت الأهل والأصدقاء، وأذكر أننا ذهبنا يوم ٤ يونيو/حزيران لقضاء يوم هادئ في العين السخنة، وكان يوماً جميلاً بالفعل، وتقريباً عند الساعة الخامسة أو السادسة مساءً رأيت زوجي يقترب منا، ونحن في مياه النبع، ليقول إن الأخبار في الراديو تتكلم عن بداية هجوم جوي إسرائيلي على الجنوب اللبناني.

كان ذلك بداية اجتياح شرس دمّر الكثير، وقضى على الكثير من البشر والحجر، وعلى الكثير من العلاقات الإنسانية والذكريات، وغيّر مجرى الحياة اليومية لمئات الآلاف من الناس.

عندما تحدث الكوارث يتكلم البعيدون عن الدم، ولكن ماذا عن الحياة؟! ماذا عن تدمير الحياة نفسها؟! هذا ما شغلني بعمق حين عدت إلى مدينتي في شهر سبتمبر.

لحظة دخولي الحدود اللبنانية كنت أسير وكأنني أدخل إلى عالم غير واقعي، إلى نوع من المنام الخانق المشوش الذي لا يستطيع عقلك أن يتوازن معه. إنها شوارعي نفسها، ولكن يتمشّى عليها هؤلاء الآخرون الذين كانوا دائماً كابوس حياتنا منذ الطفولة، ويختفي منها مَن تعوّدت على أن يكونوا حياة المكان. كان هذا غير طبيعي، وكنت في حالة من الذهول الداخلي. كانت كل تصرفاتي الخارجية عادية، ولكن في أعماقي كنت أتحرك داخل منام غريب.

حين وصلت إلى منزل طفولتي سعدت برؤيته أمامي كما تعودته، مما أعاد إليّ شيئاً من الإحساس بالتوازن؛ وبخاصة أنه كان قد وصلني يوم ٢٦ يونيو/حزيران، وأنا في القاهرة، خبر مغلوط مفاده أن منزلنا قد انتهى وجوده في القصف، وأذكر أن هذا الخبر بالنسبة لي كان فاجعتي الثانية بعد مقتل صديق طفولتي رشيد، وزوجته صديقتي سعاد، وطفليهما غسان وسامية بقذيفة واحدة: ماتوا كلهم، وفي لحظة واحدة لم يعودوا هناك.

يوم وصلني خبر المنزل حلمت حلماً سريالياً: رأيتني أحضن المنزل. كان حلماً غريباً وغير معقول من ناحية النسب الهندسية، ولكنه كان حقيقياً بشكل غريب. الآن، وأنا عند عتباته، أرى أنه كان خبراً مبالغاً فيه؛ لأن الإصابة هامشية والبيت لا يزال حياً، مما أعطاني شعوراً بالتماسك والاسترخاء.

**رحلتي داخل المدينة**

«لصوص المدافن لم يتركوا للمؤرخ شيئاً يدل عليّ»: هذه كلمات محمود درويش، كانت توجز ما ثار بداخلي مع كل التفاصيل التي عشتها في تلك الفترة.

في بيتنا، اكتشفت أن الحياة لم تعد كما كانت في السابق، لن يعود زوج أختي أبداً إلى هذا المنزل؛ لأنه لن يدخل لبنان ثانية (وفعلاً، لم يعد للزيارة إلا بعد سبعة عشر عاماً كانت قد تغيرت فيها أشياء كثيرة)، وابن أختي لا بد من إرساله إلى سوريا حتى يكون في أمان. أختي بقيت في المدينة لتمارس عملها وحياتها، ولكن أصبحت عائلتها مشتتة، وأصبحت اللقاءات المتقطعة طريقة أخرى في الحياة عليهم أن يعتادوا عليها.

أردت أن أبحث داخل أوراقي؛ غير أنهم فاجأوني – في منزلنا – بأنه لا بد من التخلص من الكثير من الأوراق والمستندات حتى لا تقع في يد الأعداء، وفرض عليّ هذا الاعتبارُ نوعاً من السرعة والفوضى التي أضاعت الكثير من الذكريات، إلا أنها كانت بهدف الحماية. مراسلاتي اختفت، واختفت معها ذكريات صغيرة وعوالم حميمة، أذكر منها مراسلاتي مع أخي زياد الذي كان أيضاً صديقي الحميم، وأذكر مشطاً صغيراً جداً كان قد أحضره لي محمد عودة من رحلته في فيتنام، كان مصنوعاً من حطام طائرات الفانتوم الأمريكية. لا أزال، حتى الآن، أتذكر هذا المشط، وأتذكر محمد عودة، عمي القاهري الذي كان يأخذني معه منذ طفولتي في جولاته القاهرية التي شكلت ذاكرتي مع القاهرة التي أحبها.

فقدت أشيائي الصغيرة، فقدت أماكن أحبها دمرت بالكامل، فقدت أحبائي. أصبح كل هذا، في لحظة غاشمة، جزءاً من الماضي، لم يعد له حاضر ولا مستقبل، ولم يعد لهؤلاء أثر يُستدل به عليهم سوى ذاكرتي الداخلية.

ذاكرتي الداخلية، بقايا الحكايات، بقايا الصور، بقايا الأماكن: من كل هذه الخيوط أبني فكرتي لإعادة المدينة. أن نكون هنا، وأن يعود الغائبون، ولو عبر الحكايات والصور، أن نرحل في تدفق الذاكرة الجمعية لاستعادة الحكاية.

لم تكن الفكرة بهذا الوضوح في البداية، كانت هناك حالة من التداعيات المتناثرة والانفعالات العاطفية وشعور بالتوتر.. الغضب.. المرارة.. التحدي.. الحزن.. الذهول.. الإصرار على متابعة الحياة وكأن شيئاً لم يكن. كل أنواع العواطف والانفعالات والتداعيات، كانت بطريقة أو أخرى تشكل حالة من عدم التركيز.

كنت أريد أن أفعل أي شيء لأوقف اللصوص، كنت أريد أن أصل إلى شيء، ولا أعرف ماذا أفعل. عودتي نفسها كانت نوعاً من الفعل التطميني. أردت أن أقول لنفسي أستطيع العودة إلى مدينتي متى أريد. تجولي في المدينة كان نوعاً من تهدئة النفس، وتأكيد علاقة آمنة مع المكان، ولكن كل ما يدور بداخلي كان غير محدد الملامح.

بعد أسبوع تقريباً من وصولي إلى صيدا، حصلت حادثة أضاءت في نفسي فكرة. كنت قد اتفقت مع صديقتي الحبيبة، وأستاذتي في مادة الفلسفة، فاطمة غندور كي نلتقي صباحاً كعادتنا، نتمشّى في شوارع المدينة، ونتأمل العالم عبر حوارات متناثرة أقرب إلى التداعيات. كانت فاطمة تلهمني دائماً بقدرتها على التأمل الهادئ في أكثر اللحظات صخباً، وكان لقاؤنا يُغني عالمي الداخلي دائماً، ويعطيني طاقة خاصة. كانت تأملات فاطمة مختلفة عن كل تأملات الأذكياء المحيطين بنا، لم يكن ذكاؤها عادياً؛ كان يحمل هدوءً صوفياً وقدرة على الوصول إلى جوهر الأشياء دون التشوش بالتفاصيل التي تسرق عقول الآخرين وقلوبهم، كانت دائماً تستهدف الجوهر، وكان هذا ملهماً لي.

بينما كنا نتمشّى أنا وفاطمة، سمعنا دوي انفجار هائل قريباً منا، وبدأت حالة من الهرولة والفوضى. فجَّر شاب دورية إسرائيلية. واختفى. لم يستطع أحد أن يراه. ولم تستطع القوات الإسرائيلية أن تلقي القبض عليه. بدأت القوات الصهيونية التفتيش السريع بطريقة هستيرية، والناس تتفرج عليهم، وأنا وفاطمة من الناس. فجأة سمعت فاطمة تقول بالعامية «نياله»، ومعناها التقريبي يا لسعادته، نظرت إليها متسائلة!! فقالت لي: «هذا الشاب يشعر الآن أنه

الوحيد الحر بيننا جميعاً، وهو الآن يعيش لحظة حريته الخاصة». نعم إنه الوحيد الحر بيننا، الآن. لقد أسقط الاحتلال، وحاصر حضوره المزعج. لقد أعاد هذا الشاب إلى الحياة معناها، وبطريقته أعاد إلى عالمه توازنه، واستعاد لنفسه المكان.

لم تكن هذه هي العملية الأولى ضد الاحتلال؛ كانت العمليات قد بدأت في صيدا حتى قبل سقوط بيروت، ولكن هذه العملية هي التي نبهتني لمسألة إعادة التوازن مع العالم، كيف نحاصر حصارنا، كما نصحنا محمود درويش.

هذا الشاب المقاوم وفاطمة ومحمود درويش، وكل لحظة عشتها في تلك الفترة، وحكايات الناس الكثيرة، فتحت أمامي الباب لأعيد قراءة ذاكرة مدينتي من خلال أناس كثيرين أحببتهم.

لم يحمل فيلمي كل ما بداخلي، ولكنه فتح بعض المساحات من البوح، الناقصة كثيراً، والتي لا تزال تحتاج الكثير لاستكمالها، إلا أنه كان بكل نواقصه محاولتي الأولى.

لقد كان فيلم **بوابة الفوقا** محاولتي الأولى، غير أنه لم يكن البداية.

### البدايات

أنا من مواليد مدينة صيدا في الجنوب اللبناني. وصيدا مدينة بحرية هادئة تقع جنوب بيروت، وهي بوابة الجنوب وشمال فلسطين. في هذه المدينة ولدت، ومن هذه المدينة بدأت رحلتي.

في البداية لم تكن اختياراتي اختيارات شخصية، كانت أميل إلى أن تكون قَدَراً بالمعنى البسيط للكلمة. توجد أربعة أشياء في حياتي كانت قَدَري منذ الطفولة: البحر، السياسة، العالم المفتوح على حرية الاختيار الواسعة، والسينما. لم أسعَ إلى هذه الاختيارات لأنها كانت حاضرة في حياتي منذ الولادة. كانت، كما نقول عادة، «قَدَري الخاص»، التقينا بصدفة لا تسمح لي أن أعرف من ينادي من.

نشأت في مدينة صيدا، وكان منزلنا على شاطئ البحر. نشأت وعندي قناعة عميقة أن كل إنسان في العالم له بحره الذي يتربَّى بجواره. أذكر أني بكيت حين سمعت من أحدهم، وأنا في السابعة من عمري، أن هناك أطفالاً في بلاد أخرى لم يروا البحر في حياتهم. بكيت بحرقة شفقة عليهم. لم يستطع عقلي الطفل أن يستوعب هذا النوع من الحرمان.

أذكر، أيضاً، الجزيرة البحرية الصغيرة، التي تبعد حوالي الألف متر داخل بحر مدينتنا، والتي كانت تشكل لي رفقة دائمة عن بعد، وبخاصة في ليالي الشتاء، حيث كنت أتسلى بتعداد الوقت الذي

يفصل بين النور والعتمة لفنارها الصغير. لذلك، عندما درسنا في كتب مادة التاريخ للأطفال أن الفينيقيين جاؤوا إلى لبنان في هجرات متتالية من الجزيرة العربية في عصر القحط والتصحر، واستقروا في الجزء الخصيب هنا، وأنشأوا الحضارة الفينيقية، كنت أعتقد أن جزيرتنا الصغيرة القريبة، البعيدة، الخالية سوى من الصخر والرمل، هي الجزيرة العربية. كانت الجزيرة العربية إلى هذه الدرجة قريبة مني ومن خيالي الطفولي.

كان البحر هو العالم الواسع بالنسبة لي، منه أرى الجزيرة العربية، ومن شاطئه ذات ليلة مقمرة رأيت عشتروت، إلهة الجمال، تولد من أمواجه، وتخرج باسترخاء مقتربة من الشاطئ الرملي لمدينتنا. كما شاهدت الشمس التي كانت تخرج، صباحاً، من وراء الجبل وهي تسبح في مائه عند الغروب، وكطفلة كنت أتخيل أننا ممكن لو ذهبنا في مركب وانتظرنا هناك، بعيداً، آخر البحر، سنستطيع أن نلتقي بالشمس (هذه الحكاية وضعتها في سيناريو فيلم قصير عن طفل يذهب للقاء الشمس، وللأسف لم يُنْجَز حتى الآن لاعتراضات رقابية!).

بحر مدينتي له حكاياته الكثيرة، كنت صغيرة العائلة، وكنت أسمع حكايات يرويها أخوتي عن المراكب التي ملأت البحر عام ١٩٤٨. كانت قصة مؤثرة تحكيها أختي الكبيرة: كيف أنها استيقظت في يوم ما من عام ٤٨ لتجد البحر مليئاً بالمراكب الصغيرة والمتوسطة التي تقترب من شاطئ مدينتنا، كان هذا منظراً ساحراً ومدهشاً بالنسبة لها، فركضت لتسأل أمي: «ما هذا؟» أجابتها أمي: «إنهم أهلنا من فلسطين». كانت هذه الجملة بداية رواية طويلة ممتدة لم نتوقف عن حكايتها: أملاً في نهاية سعيدة اسمها العودة، وكلما تعقدت الأحداث امتد السرد وابتدأت الحكاية تأخذ بعداً ملحمياً (مشهد المراكب كان مشهداً افتتاحياً لمشروع فيلم روائي طويل لم ينجز أيضاً).

الحكاية الفلسطينية واحدة من حكايات الجنوب اللبناني التي شكلت مصيره ومصير أهله ومصيري لكوني من أهله. لم تكن الحكاية الفلسطينية مجازر وتهجيراً قسرياً «لأهلنا» فقط، بل كانت مؤامرة على وحدة منطقة، تعوّدنا أن نتحرك فيها بحرية لنكتشف أن الأسلاك الشائكة والحدود المصطنعة أصبحت عائقاً يومياً نعيشه. كنا نسمع مقارنات أهلنا: كيف كانت الحياة قبل الصهاينة وانجلترا وفرنسا، كانت أرضاً ممتدة بلا نهاية ولا حدود، جغرافيا متكاملة.

كانت الكلمات التي أسمعها منذ الطفولة تتراكم حتى قبل أن أفهم معناها العميق: «الاستعمار»، «المؤامرة الصهيونية»، «عصابة

شتيرن»، «سايكس پيكو»، «المخيمات الفلسطينية»، «حق العودة»، «الثورة الجزائرية»، «الفدائيون»، «العدوان الثلاثي»، «الوحدة العربية»، «حرب التحرير الشعبية».

وهناك أسماء تشكل، إلى الآن، نقطة دافئة داخل وجداني؛ رغم أنها لا تمت إلى المنطقة العربية بصلة، مثلاً پاتريس لومومبا الذي لن أنساه ما حييت، ولا أعتقد أن أحداً من أهل مدينتي الصغيرة ممن عاصر تلك الفترة سينساه، لأن المدينة خرجت في مظاهرة كبرى ضد اغتيال پاتريس لومومبا «المناضل الأفريقي وبطل التحرر الوطني». أذكر حكاية ماسح الأحذية الذي رأى المظاهرة فسأل أحد المشاركين عن سبب التظاهر، فأبلغه المشارك بمقتل پاتريس لومومبا، فسأله ماسح الأحذية: «من هو پاتريس لومومبا؟»، أجابه: «إنه مناضل أفريقي ضد الاستعمار، هو مثلنا يريد أن يخرج الاستعمار من بلاده»، فما كان من ماسح الأحذية إلا أن لملم عدته وانضم بكل وجدانه للمشاركة في تأبين هذا الإنسان الذي يحمل معنا أحلامنا فقُتل غدراً.

كانت الحكايات تشكل عالماً خصباً أتحرك بداخله ويضيف إلى ذاكرتي غنى لم أجد مثله حتى في الكتب الأدبية الساحرة. كانت تدهشني بساطة الحكايات وقدرتها على التأثير. اكتشفت، عبر رحلتي مع الحكايات، كم تكون الحكاية مدهشة وساحرة حين تخرج من القلب وتلمس التفاصيل البسيطة للحياة دون سعي إلى التزييف أو التزويق. هذه المدرسة التي نهل منها الكثير من فنانينا المميزين وتأثروا بها في إبداعهم، مثلاً: فناننا الرائع ناجي العلي، ابن مخيم عين الحلوة، الذي احتضنته مدينتي الجنوبية. إن ناجي هو ابن الحكايات الصغيرة وابن الحكمة الشعبية المكثفة، خفيفة الظل وقليلة الكلفة، خرج من ثوبها المرقع لا ليرميه بل ليلبسه لحنظلة طفله الأبدي.

كان قَدَري أن أكبر في عالم تملؤه الأحداث والحكايات، وكان الطابع المنفتح لعائلتنا يساعدني على أن أكتشف العالم دون أية حواجز أو أفكار مسبقة. عائلة ممتدة فيها الأب والأم والأخوة، الأعمام والعمات، الأخوال والخالات، وأقارب العائلة وأصدقاؤها. حرية الحركة بينهم في مدينة مطمئنة ساعدتني على أن أبني وجودي كيفما يروق لي، وأختار من كل واحد منهم أشيائي التي أحبها. ومما ساعدني على الحركة، بحرية، أبٌ وأمٌ غاية في التسامح والانفتاح على العالم، لديهما عشق للحياة والتجربة، كل منهما بطريقته التي استطاعا أن ينقلاها لي ولأخوتي. كم أنا محظوظة لوجودهما في حياتي، إذ لم ألتق حتى الآن بأب وأم مثلهما، أحرار على كل المستويات، حرية المرأة

ومشاعر المساواة الاجتماعية واحترام التعددية ورفض الانغلاق واحترام الآخر وكره الظلم وعشق الصدق؛ كل هذه لم تكن قضايا للمناقشة بل كانت نمط حياة وسلوكاً يومياً.

كان بيتنا يضج بالأفكار والاهتمامات والهوايات، وكانت المعرفة بمعناها الواسع قيمة مهمة. تعلمت في بيتنا أن أحترم كل أنواع المعرفة بصرف النظر عن مصدرها. كان منزلنا يستقبل كل أنواع هواة المعرفة من الأكاديميين إلى مثقفي الشارع، ومن الرموز السياسية إلى أبناء البلد من كافة الفئات الاجتماعية.

الأدب، الشعر، السياسة، الموسيقى، السينما: كانت كلها تفاصيل حياة يومية يمارسها كل على مزاجه وسجيته، ولذلك وجدت نفسي أتحرك داخل هذا المناخ، وأستمتع بعناصره دون أن يعني هذا لي أي شيء سوى المتعة الإنسانية واكتشاف العالم. وكانت السينما، في تلك الفترة، متعة مميزة، وبخاصة أن التلفزيون (لحسن حظي) لم يصلنا إلا بعد أن بلغت سن العاشرة، مما أعطاني مساحة واسعة للاستمتاع بالسينما بكل طقوسها الجميلة. كان يوجد أربع دور عرض رئيسية في مدينتنا، ثلاث منها لأولاد عم أمي، والرابعة كان خالي يديرها لصالح صديق له في المهجر؛ مما أعطاني فرصة الذهاب متى أشاء إلى السينما خصوصاً في الأجازات. وكوني الأخت الصغرى في عائلة مهتمة بالثقافة، كان هذا يعطيني مساحة لتأمل كل النقاشات، والانحيازات الفكرية، والهوايات، والميول العاطفية التي يمارسها الكبار، والتي كانت تتفاعل داخل مصنع الأحلام الذي بدأ ينمو بداخلي. لا أستطيع أن أذكر من منهم أثّر في اختياراتي أكثر من الآخر. لكل منهم مناطقه التي أثّرت في معرفتي واهتمامي بالعالم، لكل واحد منهم أحلامه التي حضنت أحلامي وأغنتها. كان لأختي مها وأخي زياد تأثير كبير في تشكيل انحيازاتي الإنسانية واختياراتي في الحياة عاطفياً وفكرياً. أما أخي خالد فكان الشعر والتاريخ يمثلان مناطق تدفق بيننا، ولا يزال حتى الآن، أستمتع جداً بسماعه، وكان له فضل كبير في تذوقي للشعر العربي قديمه وحديثه، وفي الاهتمام العميق بتاريخ منطقتنا القديم.

لقد تنازعتني أشياء كثيرة في لحظات الاختيار، وكانت انحيازاتي مزيجاً من أشياء كثيرة أثّرت، أيضاً، في نوع عطائي طوال رحلة الحياة. لا أستطيع أن أختزل نفسي إلى كوني سينمائية فقط، ولكن من المؤكد أن السينما أعطتني مساحة كبيرة للتعبير عن ذاتي، فالسينما لم تكن منطقتي الوحيدة، ولكنها أخذت حيزاً مهماً في رحلتي مع الحياة. ولقد كان لأختي الكبيرة نبيهة دور مهم في

لفت نظري إلى إمكان أن أكون هناك داخل معمل السينما وليس فقط في صالة العرض. وهي بالمناسبة تكبرني بستة عشر عاماً؛ لذلك فحين بدأت هي مشوارها مع السينما كنت طفلة، وكان مبهراً أن أكتشف ما يمكن أن تعطيه السينما. لقد كنت، دائماً، أحب السينما بوصفها عالماً سحرياً، ولكن مع نبيهة عرفت أننا نستطيع أن نكون الساحر ذاته، وكان هذا شاعرياً جداً.

درست السينما، وعشت تجربة الانخراط في عالمها، ولكن حين بدأت الحرب الأهلية في لبنان سحبتني معها إلى المنطقة الأكثر عاطفية، وهي الوطن والحياة ومصير العالم الذي كنا نحلم بتغييره إلى الأفضل. شكلت سنوات الحرب فترة انقطاع عن ممارسة العمل السينمائي، ولكني لم أبتعد، أبداً، عن انتهاز أية لحظة كانت تعطيها الحياة لأكون في عالم السينما. أذكر في تلك الفترة حضور السينما في حياتي من خلال صديقي الحميم يسري نصر الله الذي عمل في بيروت حينها في مجال النقد السينمائي، كانت تربطنا، أنا ويسري، صداقة عميقة مليئة بالسينما وبأشياء الحياة الكثيرة التي صنعت عالمنا المشترك. التقيت هناك مع تجارب سينمائية كثيرة بتقطع تفرضه الأحداث، منها مثلاً تجربة فيلم **المنام** لمحمد ملص، عايشت جزءاً من هذه التجربة، وكان ممتعاً بالنسبة لي أن أكون في عالم السينما حتى ولو للحظات قصيرة. هناك، أيضاً، كان تصوير نبيهة لفيلم **لأن الجذور لن تموت**، وأيضاً تجارب صغيرة مع غالب شعث وزملاء آخرين كانوا يسعون إلى توثيق الحرب، ولكن كل هذه كانت لحظات مسروقة داخل إيقاع الحرب الأهلية.

كانت البداية الفعلية التي أعادتني إلى السينما هي لحظة ما بعد الاجتياح التي تحدثت عنها. وبالرغم من أن فيلمي الأول **بوابة الفوقا** صُور عام ١٩٨٩ فقد نشأت المشاعر والتداعيات التي مهدت له عام ١٩٨٢، مع بداية الغزو الإسرائيلي للبنان ووقوع مدينتي، صيدا، تحت الاحتلال.

لم تكن الفترة بين عام ١٩٨٢ وعام ١٩٨٩ مجرد تحضير؛ كانت فترة من التردد بخصوص ما أبدأ به وكيف. عملت لفترة في السينما مع المخرج محمد خان، وكنت في هذه المرحلة أعيد اكتشاف علاقتي بالسينما من الناحية العملية بعد فترة الانقطاع الطويلة. بدأت بمشروع سيناريو روائي عن لحظة الاحتلال، ثم بدأ يشدني توثيق الذاكرة بشكل أقوى، وبخاصة أني منحازة للحظة الحقيقة بشكل يجعلني، أحياناً، أجد في العمل الروائي ضعفاً ما أو شيئاً ناقصاً.

قراري النهائي ببدء العمل على الفيلم، بوصفه مشروعاً ملموساً، جاء مع الانسحاب الإسرائيلي من مدينة صيدا وحكايات الشباب المفرج عنهم من معتقل أنصار وحكايات أناس خُطف أهلهم وأصدقاؤهم. بدأت بتجميع المادة، وبدأ التحضير، ودخلت في تجربتي الأولى، وبدأت الحكايات تتدفق، تسبر غوري وأسبر غورها، وكان **بوابة الفوقا** فيلمي الأول.

فيلمي الثاني، **مرآة جميلة**، كان عن المناضلات الفلسطينيات من جيل السبعينيات. ثم جاءت أفلامي التالية بتنوعها، والحقيقة أني لو حلّلت ما يشغلني في أفلامي سأجد أن الذاكرة الممتدة، والحكاية الشعبية، والمزاج الإنساني، واكتشاف العوالم المحيطة تشكل مشتركات في أعمالي.

لا أدعي الموضوعية في أي فيلم أخرجته، ولكني كنت دائماً أمينة في بحثي عن الحكايات والتفاصيل، ولم أزيف أبداً أية فكرة أعطتها لي الشخصيات التي عرفتها وتعاملت معها، لم ألفق وثائق، ولم أدَّع العلم بشيء، بل اعتمدت أسلوب السؤال المفتوح، وحاولت دائماً أن أخلق حكاية من لحم ودم. لم أفتعل مشاعر، ولم أشحذ العطف، ولكني تفاعلت عاطفياً مع العالم الذي أصنعه. لم أدَّع الحياد يوماً، فأنا أحتقر فكرة الحياد لأنها محض ادعاء، غير أني أحاول قدر الإمكان الانحياز إلى عالم إنساني عادل، عالم ممتع وغير تسلطي.

لذلك، عشقت الثقافة الشعبية؛ لأنها تفتح مساحة واسعة للمزاج الحر ولاكتشاف أصل الأشياء؛ فهي تشكل المزاج الإنساني بوصفه أداة مقاومة للتنميط والمأسسة، واستطاع الناس عبر حركتها التلقائية وتواصلها أن يعيدوا تشكيل لغة الحكاية وصوت الموسيقى ومذاق الطعام وألوان الصورة. الثقافة الشعبية تخلق علاقة حميمة وإنسانية بين البشر، كما أنها توجه بتلقائية بسيطة، دون أن تدري، ضربة عنيفة لمشكلتين أساسيتين داخل الحضارة الإنسانية هما العنصرية والتملك الأناني.

لقد عملت على دراسة هذا الموضوع من خلال الرصد السينمائي، وبخاصة فيما يتعلق بمنطقة البحر الأحمر، وأيضاً طريق نهر النيل، في أفلامي: **سبع ليالي وصبحية**، **رانجو**، **الفرح مصري**.

حلمي الآن تحقيق رحلة طويلة على شواطئ البحر الأحمر، سعيت إليها لسنوات، ومازلت أحلم. أتمنى أن أحكي عن هذا المشروع بعد تصويره.

## فيلموجرافيا أعمال المخرجة عرب لطفي التسجيلية

٢٠٠٨: **على أجسادهم**، ١١٥ دقيقة، إنتاج مستقل. وهو عن مجزرة الطنطورة في فلسطين عام ١٩٤٨ وعن ما جرى من تطهير عرقي لاقتلاع الفلسطينيين من أرضهم.

٢٠٠٧: **احكي يا عصفورة**، ٩٢ دقيقة، إنتاج مستقل. وهو عن سبع نساء فدائيات فلسطينيات تروين حكاية الاحتلال والمقاومة الفلسطينية من خلال حياتهم.

٢٠٠٦: **غرفة مظلمة، حياة مضيئة**، ٦٢ دقيقة، إنتاج المركز القومي للسينما (مصر). وهو رحلة في عالم المصوّر محمد صبري مؤسس قسم الفوتوغرافيا في دار الهلال.

٢٠٠٥: **اللعب بالديموقراطية**، ٥٣ دقيقة، إنتاج O3 Productions. وهو عن أزمة عام ١٩٥٤ في مصر والصراع على السلطة من وجهة نظر شخصيات عايشتها من الداخل من كافة التيارات المتصارعة حينها.

٢٠٠٤: **الحاج مدبولي**، ٦٠ دقيقة، إنتاج Orbit. وهو عن صاحب أهم مكتبة في مصر الحديثة، الذي بدأ ببيع الجرائد حتى أصبح من رموز الثقافة المصرية.

٢٠٠٤: **أحمد جابر**، ٦٠ دقيقة، إنتاج Orbit. وهو عن أستاذ هندسة أسّس لمشاريع صناعية حديثة تحافظ على البيئة وتحمي إنسانية المجتمع المصري.

٢٠٠٣: **طير الحذر**، ٦٠ دقيقة، إنتاج مرآة ميديا. وهو عن الكاتب والشاعر إبراهيم نصرالله.

٢٠٠١: **حكايات من غزة**، ٦٠ دقيقة، إنتاج مرآة ميديا. وهو عن مي صايغ: كاتبة، وشاعرة، وناشطة سياسية.

٢٠٠٠: **زيارة قصيرة**، ٧٠ دقيقة، إنتاج مستقل. وهو عن زيارة مكثفة لمخيمي عين الحلوة وشاتيلا للاجئين الفلسطينيين في لبنان.

١٩٩٩: **الفرح مصري**، ٣٨ دقيقة، إنتاج قطاع قنوات النيل المتخصصة الفضائية (مصر). وهو رحلة داخل إيقاعات الأفراح في مصر بأشكالها وتنوعاتها المختلفة.

١٩٩٨: **رانجو**، ٤٠ دقيقة، إنتاج قطاع قنوات النيل المتخصصة الفضائية (مصر). وهو عن حياة ٢ مليون مصري من أصول سودانية يعيشون في مصر وموسيقاهم.

١٩٩٨: **سبع ليالي وصبحية**، ٥٠ دقيقة، إنتاج قطاع قنوات النيل المتخصصة الفضائية (مصر). وهو عن مدينة بورسعيد وآلة السمسمية المميزة لها.

١٩٩٣: **مرآة جميلة**، ٢٥ دقيقة، إنتاج القناة الرابعة البريطانية. وهو عن نساء فلسطينيات شاركن في تجربة المقاومة وحملن هم الوطن.

١٩٩١: **بوابة الفوقا**، ٩٠ دقيقة، إنتاج دائرة الثقافة بمنظمة التحرير الفلسطينية (تونس). وهو عن ذاكرة مدينة صيدا في الجنوب اللبناني (مدينة المخرجة الأم).

# عودة إلى بقايا الأطلال:
# الذاكرة والذاكرة المولّدة والتاريخ الحي في فلسطين

ليلى أبو لغد
(ترجمة حسام نايل)

---

تعني **العودةُ** في السياق الفلسطيني الرجوعَ إلى الوطن السليب. ويثير هذا التعبير المشحون، عند الفلسطينيين المشتتين، حنيناً إلى أرض الوطن التي أجبروا على الرحيل عنها في ١٩٤٨. كما يثير رغبة في التخلص من تجربة الشتات الصادمة التي فرقت العائلات وقطعت سبل العيش، واضطرت الفلسطينيين إلى الإقامة في مخيمات اللاجئين المذلّة، أو إلى مغامرات فردية حتى يقيموا حيواتهم من جديد متسلحين بما لا يكاد يتجاوز شهادات ميلادهم ومفاتيح بيوتهم التي تركوها خلفهم، موصومين بفقد بلدهم – بطريقة ما – على أيدي أناس غرباء. ويُعَدُّ الإصرار السياسي على «حق العودة» مطالبة بتصحيح خطأ أخلاقي. كما يُعَدُّ، أيضاً، مطالبة بعدم محو قصة هذا الطرد.

وبطبيعة الحال، لم يرحل كل فلسطيني عن فلسطين في ١٩٤٨؛ بل ظلّ بعضهم في الأراضي التي وقعت تحت السيطرة التوسعية المطردة للدولة الإسرائيلية التي أعلنت في ١٥ مايو، ١٩٤٨، تشبثوا بقراهم أو أقاموا بالقرب منها، أو ظلوا في مدنهم، يرقبون عالمهم وهو يتحول أمام أعينهم. عاشوا في المكان على المستوى الفيزيقي، مطرودين على المستوى الاجتماعي والسياسي، تعلموا لغة مستعمريهم وعملوا بينهم في أعمال حقيرة معظم الوقت. أما الذين رحلوا إلى مدن الضفة الغربية أو غزة، فلم يخضعوا مباشرة للحكم العسكري والإداري الإسرائيلي إلا بعد عشرين سنة، عندما احتلت إسرائيل الأجزاء المتبقية من فلسطين التاريخية بعد حرب ١٩٦٧.

ولكن معظم اللاجئين الفلسطينيين وجدوا أنفسَهم مقتلعين من وطنهم وماضيهم. فحاولوا إقامة حيوات جديدة في بلاد مختلفة، في

---

تشكر **ألف** ليلى أبو لغد وأحمد سعدي لسماحهما بترجمة ونشر هذا الفصل:
Lila Abu-Lughod, "Return to Half-Ruins: Memory, Postmemory, and Living History in Palestine." *Nakba: Palestine, 1948, and the Claims of Memory*. Eds. Ahmad Sa'di and Lila Abu-Lughod. NY: Columbia UP, 2007. 77-104. Translated with permission.

لبنان والأردن وسوريا والعراق والكويت والولايات المتحدة وانجلترا، بل وفي دول أمريكا الجنوبية. نجح بعضهم نجاحاً اقتصادياً وثقافياً، أما الكثير ممن ينتمون إلى الأجيال اللاحقة فظلوا يعيشون في مخيمات اللاجئين التي صارت – بشكل مقلق – إقامة دائمة، وقد تجمدت في مخيلتهم ذكريات الوطن.

ظلّ والدي حتى عام ١٩٩١ أحد هؤلاء المطرودين الذين لم يتمكنوا من العودة لرؤية ما حدث لبلدهم. رحلت عائلة والدي إلى الأردن، ومن هناك اقترض مالاً حتى يستقل سفينة راحلة إلى الولايات المتحدة، بحثاً عن التعليم. وهناك، أقام حياته، عمل ليدفع مصاريف الدراسة وتزوج أمي وأنجب أطفالاً، ثم ذهب إلى جامعة پرنستون – في نهاية المطاف – للحصول على درجة الدكتوراه في التاريخ العربي. وبعد مرور ثماني سنوات على خروجه تمكن من القيام برحلته الأولى إلى العالم العربي ليشغل وظيفة تابعة لليونسكو في مصر، غير أنه لم يتمكن من العودة إلى فلسطين. وعلمت من أمي أن عائلتنا قامت بزيارات متقطعة إلى الضفة الغربية والقدس. ومن هناك، كان والدي يحدق باشتياق إلى الجانب الآخر من فلسطين: ساحل يافا. ولكن بعد احتلال إسرائيل هذه المناطق في ١٩٦٧، صار ما كان يفعله مستحيلاً. ثم بعد أن حصل والدي على جواز سفر أمريكي – وكان ذلك في وقت متأخر – يعطيه حق الدخول، بوصفه سائحاً، فيما صار يُعرف الآن بإسرائيل، ظل واحداً من الفلسطينيين الذين رفضوا الذهاب إلى وطنهم السابق ورؤيته. كان والدي يكتب دون كلل عن فلسطين، ويلقي محاضرات عامة عنها، ويدرِّس تاريخها. وقد ذهب مرتين إلى بيروت للإقامة حتى يباشر من هناك مشروعات فلسطينية. وفي عام ١٩٨٢، طرده الجيش الإسرائيلي للمرة الثانية في حياته، وهي تجربة جعلته مكتئباً – وبعيداً بعداً نفسياً عنّا، عن عائلته – لبضع سنوات. فلم يكن يتخيل وضْعَ نفسه تحت رحمة وسلطة الدولة التي أغارت على بلده كلها، لم يكن يتخيل أن يقف وجهاً لوجه أمام أناس يواصلون تدمير أسلوب الحياة اليومية للفلسطينيين الذين يعيشون هناك، وأولئك الذين يعيشون في أماكن أخرى. أما الجيش الذي ألقى قنبلة عنقودية على شرفته في بيروت فقد حطم حلمه بإقامة جامعة فلسطينية مفتوحة والكثير من أحلامه الأخرى.

ثم حدث تغير؛ إذ بعد تعافيه من مرض ألمَّ به أدرك أنه قد يموت دون رؤية فلسطين مرة أخرى. ومع إدراكه لحدوث تغير طفيف في السياسات، مما يعني تخفيف القيود في الأراضي المحتلة، قرر الذهاب إليها. وأتذكر كيف كنت أستمع إلى حكاياته المثيرة حين عاد.

وكان في زيارته الأولى عام ١٩٩١ متوتراً، على الرغم من الفضول الذي كان يغشاه. قال إن صدمته الأولى عاناها عند وصوله إلى مطار اللّد حين فاجأته لافتة ترحيب تقول: «أهلاً بكم في إسرائيل». ومع ذلك كان مبتهجاً. بعد هذه الزيارة، جاء قراره عام ١٩٩٢ بـ«العودة» والرجوع. كان قد انفصل عن أمي بالطلاق في وقت سابق، وكان قد تقاعد من جامعة نورثويسترن التي كان يدرِّس فيها العلوم السياسية لمدة خمسة وعشرين عاماً. وحين جاء إلى زيارتي في إنجلترا، بعد أن وضعت توأماً، رأيت أن إحساسه بموطنه قد أفعمه بالحيوية. ثم بعد هذه الزيارة بوقت طويل، وبينما كنت أراجع أوراق مؤتمر غير مؤرخة كدَّسها فوق مكتبه، وجدت تعليقه الآتي: «معظم الناس الذين تحدثتُ معهم [ممن عادوا] يشعرون بالحزن أو الفقدان. أما أنا فأشعر بالعكس تماماً. كنت سعيداً لأني ارتبطت بأرضي من جديد، ولأني عرفت – مع التغيرات التي طرأت – أن الكثير من الثقافة الفلسطينية قد استمر حياً على الرغم من العدوان الإسرائيلي، بفضل المجهودات الكبيرة التي بذلها الفلسطينيون الذين استمسكوا بأرضهم، سواء أرض ١٩٤٨ أو الضفة الغربية وغزة».(١)

وحين وافقت أن أزوره في إسرائيل/فلسطين، بعد انتقاله إليها بخمسة أشهر، على الرغم من شعوري بالقلق، عرفت أن هذا الانتقال غيرّ من خبرته بحادثة كارثية فاصلة يسميها الفلسطينيون تسمية واضحة هي **النكبة** أو «الفجيعة». رأيت أن والدي نجح في إدخال ذكرياته عن فلسطين، مباشرةً، في الزمن الحاضر؛ لقد غرسها في التاريخ الحي. وكان إدماج الذاكرة في الحاضر التاريخي – على نحو ما فعل والدي – مما أتاح لأولاده اكتساب معرفة وتماهٍ مختلفين أيضاً. وتسعى هذه المقالة إلى استكشاف ما حدث لوالدي وما حدث لي أيضاً بسبب **عودته**. وتطلق ماريان هيرش Marianne Hirsch اسم الذاكرة المولَّدة postmemory على التجربة التي يحيا فيها المرء واقعاً يومياً تظلله ذاكرة عن ماضٍ عاشه الوالدان ينطوي على دلالة أكبر؛ وذلك في سياق تحليلها المرهف لانتقال الذاكرة المفجوعة traumatic memory عبر الأجيال عمَّن بقوا على قيد الحياة بعد كارثة المحرقة (Hirsch، ص ص ٢٢–٢٤). غير أن الموقف الذي تصفه هيرش هو موقف ذكريات الوالدين عن أحداث مرَّا بها وانقضت؛ وقد استنكر العالم هذه الإبادة الجماعية وفظائعها. وفيما يخصني يختلف الموقف، فأنا ابنة شخص عاش أحداث النكبة وتلقيتُها عنه بعد عودته إلى فلسطين؛ فالذاكرة والذاكرة المولَّدة – بالنسبة لي وبالنسبة إلى الفلسطينيين – ينطويان على قيمة تفاعلية خاصة؛ لأن الماضي لم ينقض بعدُ.

## الذكريات المحكية

كان والدي راوياً وحكاءً. ولذا، كنا – ونحن أطفال صغار – نعرف دائماً أننا فلسطينيون. وما أتذكره من حكايات عن صباه في الثلاثينيات وأوائل الأربعينيات كان يحمل عبق الحنين، وتمتزج فيه الفكاهة بالأسى. كان صعباً عليَّ أن أتخيل والدي في طفولته، حالي في ذلك من حال آخرين، فقد كان هناك عامل الاختلاف الجذري عن الحياة التي عرفتها من خلال نشأتي في الولايات المتحدة، ولعلي لم أستوعب تلك الحياة [التي عاشها والدي] إلا بشكل غير مباشر من خلال بعض سنوات الطفولة التي قضيتها في مصر والعطلات الصيفية التي كنت أقضيها مع أقاربي في الأردن، ثم بشكل أكثر مباشرة بعد أن أصبحت باحثة أنثروبولوجية وعاشرت المجتمعات العربية معاشرة حميمة. ولطالما أحببت تخيل ذلك الطفل الذي كان يعتريه الفرح بحذاء جديد في أيام العيد؛ فينام وهو يضعه تحت وسادته. وقد غمرني توحد عاطفي مع والدي حين حكى قصته مع «نمرة صفر»؛ إذ كان أبوه يعاقبه بحلاقة رأسه على الزيرو حين يخطئ، فكان والدي يتوسل إلى الحلاق أن يحلق له «نمرة واحد» حتى يجعل شعره أطول قليلاً عند منابت الشعر. ثم اعترتني دهشة من الحكايات الطريفة التي حكاها عن نفسه وهو صبي متدين في سن الحادية عشر والثانية عشر والثالثة عشر من عمره، هذا الأب العلماني الراسخ في علمانيته الذي يستنكر باستمرار «آيات الله» كما يحلو له أن يسميهم – سواء كان هذا «الآية» مسيحياً أم مسلماً أم يهودياً – هذا الأب الذي كان يلتمس لنفسه الأعذار حتى لا يصوم شهر رمضان بحجة أنه «على سفر» دائم: في المنفى،(٢) قال إنه كانت تأخذه الحماسة للتفوق على إخوته ونيل تفضيل والديه فكان يسارع إلى مساعدة الإمام الكسلان فيصعد إلى مئذنة المسجد المجاور لبيتهم في يافا ويرفع الآذان. ومع أن بواعثه على استعراض تقواه الدينية متعددة فقد كانت طريقته في التدين شديدة الذاتية: حكى لنا كيف أنه أمَّ صلاة جنازة إسلامية كاملة على روح طائره الأليف، الهدهد، بعد أن قضى نحبه حين كانوا يقضون عطلة صيفية في النبي روبين.

وقد أعطتنا حكايات والدي عن حنان أبويه ورعايتهما الأخلاقية لمحات عن طبيعة حياة العائلة في فلسطين قبل ١٩٤٨، وعن شخصية أبيه؛ ذلك الجد الذي لم نعرفه إطلاقاً. حكى والدي أنه، وهو طفل صغير، ذهب مرة إلى الحمام في منتصف الليل، وفي الظلام لم يكن يدرك أن والده موجود هناك، فظل والده صامتاً لا يتحرك، وهو الرجل الجليل، حتى لا يرتعب ابنه شبه النائم، مع ما في ذلك من حرج. غير أن والدي حكى، أيضاً، قصة اليوم الذي أرسلته فيه أمه لشراء ملح طعام، وكيف

خسر النقود وهو يلعب مقامراً في الشارع. ثم حين عاد إلى البيت متأخراً دون ملح لطعام العشاء، قالت له أمه: «انتظر حتى أخبر أبيك». فكان العقاب الصارم: الحرمان من الخروج في اليوم التالي، وكان يوم العيد الكبير، فقضى والدي يومه يطل من الشباك باكياً، وهو يرقب أصدقاءه وأقاربه يخطرون في الشارع بملابسهم الجديدة، يشترون ما لذَّ وطاب ويستمتعون بعطلة العيد. وكانت هذه الحكاية درساً أخلاقياً لنا أيضاً: لم يقامر والدي مرة أخرى على الإطلاق.

وإلى جانب هذه الحكايات، كان يقص علينا كثيراً من الحكايات السياسية التي بدأنا نتعلم منها معنى أن يكون الإنسان فلسطينياً تحت الانتداب البريطاني. فيما يرى والدي، كان الناس – في ذلك الوقت – واعين بالكاد أنهم على أهبة أحداث كارثية تجعلهم لاجئين. لم يكونوا يدركون أن الصهاينة، وليس البريطانيين، هم الخصوم الحقيقيون. ومرة أخرى، كان من العسير عليَّ تخيل والدي شاباً متمرداً يصطدم بالجيش البريطاني: والدي الأستاذ المتميز الذي يدخن الغليون، والدي المغرم بالحديث في التليفون والذي يجد متعته في اللعب مع الأطفال، والدي الذي يقرأ كل ما تقع عليه عيناه، والدي المفعم بالحيوية وهو يلقي محاضراته العامة (فيقاطعه الصهاينة ليضايقوه بوابل من الأسئلة، الأمر الذي كان يُدرُّ دموعي الحارقة التي يختلط فيها الأذى بالغضب من أجله). وتوجد نسخة من إحدى حكاياته محفوظة على شريط كاسيت، سجلها هشام أحمد فرارجه عام ٢٠٠٠، وقد سجَّل قصة حياة والدي، وإليكم حكاية اعتقاله الأول، وهي حكاية طالما سمعتها منه مراراً:

> كان البريطانيون قد فرضوا حظر التجول، كما يفعل الإسرائيليون الآن. وكنا أطفالاً في سن التاسعة أو العاشرة، وأذكر أننا كنا نلاحق جندياً ونسُبُّه، ثم فجأة اعتقلت دورية بريطانية أخي الأكبر، فساقته إلى قسم الشرطة. وهناك أشبعوه صفعاً، ثم أطلقوا سراحه. كان كل مَن يُعتقل يصبح بطلاً. وكنت أريد أن أكون بطلاً؛ فكنت أتبارى مع أخي الأكبر. ولما رأينا شرطياً يقود دراجته البخارية شتمتُه. فما كان من أولاد الزناة إلا أن جروا ورائي أنا وأصحابي! وكان أن اختفينا في أحد المخابز. شعرت أني في ورطة، فالمخبز مغلق، وكنا قد دخلناه من باب جانبي. جاء أحد الجنود البريطانيين وأمسكنا في حالة تلبس إنْ جاز التعبير، واقفين هناك لا نحرك ساكناً. قبضوا على أربعة منا. وكان الجنود يقودون أربع دراجات بخارية،

> فجعلونا نجرى أمامهم، وكان معهم سياط. كنت أرتدي جلباباً – وهو ما نلبسه عادة في الشارع – فكان عليَّ أن أرفع أطراف الجلباب وأضعها بين أسناني حتى أتمكن من الجري. شعرنا بالتعب ولكنهم ألهبونا بالسياط حتى نظل نجري. كان الناس ينادوننا من داخل منازلهم: «تعال هنا يا إبراهيم! تعال هنا يا محمد!». غير أننا كنا خائفين من أن يلاحقونا أينما توجهنا، ولهذا ذهبنا معهم.

وكما قال أبي: بعد مزيد من الصراخ، الحقيقي مرة والمفتعل مرة، تركهم البوليس لحال سبيلهم، بعد أن وبَّخهم أحد العملاء من سكان الحيّ، ثم طاردتهم دراجة بخارية أخرى على امتداد طريق العودة، فكان الجندي يلهبهم بالسوط مرة أخرى. ولا بد أن ترى – من خلال الطريقة التي حكى بها والدي القصة – الجانب المضحك الذي تثيره صورة طفل هزيل يصر على منافسة أخيه وهو يجري ممسكاً أطراف جلبابه بأسنانه حتى ينجو بحياته.

وعن المرة الثانية التي قُبض عليه فيها، قال إنه تعلم درساً لن ينساه؛ ففي هذه المرة لم يتركهم البوليس البريطاني لحال سبيلهم، بل جعلهم يعملون، إذ أمرهم أن يرفعوا بأيديهم – والدي وأصحابه – كل الحشائش الموجودة في الفناء الواسع أمام قسم البوليس، كي يصبح ساحة لملعب تنس. وقد حكى لنا هذه القصة في مرحلة متأخرة من حياته على النحو الآتي:

> كان هناك ضابط شرطة بريطاني أسميناه **أبو نياب** [شخص له أنياب كبيرة] وقد فهمت الآن، بالكاد، أنه كان سادياً. كنا نخاف منه فهو يروح ويجيء بيننا وفي يده عصا غليظة، كنا نحاول اقتلاع الحشائش فلا تطاوعنا؛ ضربنا وأمرنا بمواصلة العمل. استغرق العمل ساعتين حتى أنهيناه، فما الذي سيفعلونه بنا الآن؟ كان حظر التجول مستمراً. ولذا، طلبوا منا نقل الحشائش من جانب في الحديقة إلى جانب آخر، لمجرد أن نظل نعمل. شعرنا بالتعب الشديد وكانوا يضربوننا باستمرار. ولن أنسى ما حييت وجه أبونياب ابن الكلب الذي أشبعني ضرباً. بدأنا نصرخ فلم نكن نريد أن نُسجن. ما كنا نريده أن نصبح زعماء. وحين أفكر فيما مضى ألعن هذا النوع من الوطنية، أكان لزاماً علينا الضرب والتعذيب حتى نصبح زعماء؟(٣)

قال أبي إنه منذ ذلك الحين بدأ يستخدم الوسائل المشروعة – عقله، قلمه، موهبته في الخطابة – في نضاله ضد الاحتلال الاستعماري (الصهيوني الآن وليس البريطاني). وكفى ضرباً.

ولا أذكر، وأنا في طفولتي، استماعي إلى قصصه عن ١٩٤٨ والشهور الأخيرة قبل سقوط يافا، مسقط رأسه. فهل كنا صغاراً إلى درجة أنه لم يكلف نفسه عناء قَصِّها علينا؟ وهل كان كلامه سيعني شيئاً بالنسبة إلى أطفال لم يروا يافا مطلقاً؟ تقول أمي لي إنه حكى هذه القصص لها ولآخرين مرات كثيرة. سمعتها، وأعتقد أنها اكتسبت معنى خاصاً ومزيداً من الاتساق، بعد أن عاد والدي ليعيش في فلسطين وتمكن من رؤية يافا مرة أخرى. وكما يرى موريس هلبفاكس Maurice Halbwachs، تتطلب الذاكرة إطاراً اجتماعياً. ويرى هلبفاكس، أيضاً، أنه كلما كبر الناس سناً وتحرروا من ضرورات الحياة العائلية والمهنية صاروا – في الأغلب – أوصياء حريصين على ماضٍ تتزايد حيويته عندهم. كان والدي ناشطاً في فلسطين، ولم يكن منعزلاً على الإطلاق؛ إذ بمجرد أن انتقل إليها بدأت حكاياته تتدفق. كانت تجارب والدي في ١٩٤٨ هي التي حفزت مساعيه الطويلة في سبيل فهم ما حدث للفلسطينيين ونشره على الناس. لكن الشيء الغريب الذي حدث بعد عودة والدي إلى فلسطين أن ذكرياته أصبحت، الآن، دليلاً إلى تاريخ حي ومكان واقعي.

**من الذاكرة إلى التاريخ: التجول في يافا**

كانت يافا قلب فلسطين النابض عند والدي. وحين جئت للإقامة معه في ٢٠٠١، رأيت على حائط من حوائط شقته في رام الله، ملصقاً كبيراً ذا لون بني داكن. كان صورة فوتوغرافية تاريخية لرجل عربي ينظر بحنين إلى البحر، وفي الخلفية مدينة كبيرة، وفي أعلى الملصق مكتوب باللغة العربية «يافا ١٩٣٧». ومع هذا، فقد كان والدي يقيم في رام الله وليس في يافا؛ حيث إن المؤسسات الفلسطينية كانت تمارس عملها – على نحو متقطع – فى الضفة الغربية طوال عقد التسعينيات. فهناك كان بإمكانه العمل.

وفي أثناء زيارتي الأولى له في فلسطين عام ١٩٩٣، أحسست بالفرحة الغامرة التي كان يشعر بها لتمكنه من السيطرة على الموقف الجديد. ولعل الجانب الطيب أنه تمكن من احتواء المجتمع الذي وجده، كما أن هذا المجتمع احتواه أيضاً، سواء في الضفة الغربية أو في العديد من أجزاء فلسطين قبل ١٩٤٨. أما التوتر فكان يظهر عليه كلما اقتربنا من نقاط تفتيش الجيش الإسرائيلي: كان فمه يجف وقطرات العرق تنز من جبهته، أو يتوه لأنه لا يعرف قراءة اللوحات الإرشادية على الطريق

المكتوبة باللغة العبرية، وكان يخشى أن يسأل، وسَرَى خوفه إليَّ، فقد بدا كل شيء من حولي غريباً. أما المناظر فكانت مألوفة لتشابهها مع لبنان والأردن اللتين عرفتهما جيداً بحكم نشأتي. ملأتنا الطرق العمومية والمدن المكتظة بالعبرية بإحساس الخطر، وبصفة خاصة عندما يحتشد فيها الجنود الإسرائيليون وجنود الاحتياط ومعدات القتال بحضورها الثقيل. ومع الوقت، صار والدي معتاداً على ذلك.

كان والدي متلهفاً على أن يرينا، أنا وعائلتي الصغيرة، فلسطين كلها، من القدس إلى بيت لحم، ومن نابلس إلى الناصرة، ومن أريحا إلى عكا. كانت رحلة حافلة بالمشاهد والأصوات والتنقل بالسيارة. وأكاد ألا أتذكر مشاعري حينها ولا أستحضر صوراً من هذه الرحلة؛ فقد كنت حديثة العهد بالأمومة ومنشغلة بتوأمي ذي الخمسة أشهر ونحن في الطريق. غير أني أذكر أن الزيارات التي قمنا بها إلى أصدقائه في أنحاء فلسطين كانت حميمة، تناولنا عندهم أنواعاً من الطعام الطيب. وكما كان عهدي في طفولتي، تملكني شعور بالخجل وانتابني الصمت كلما تحول الكلام إلى حديث السياسة، أو كلما دفنت خوفي من إحراج والدي لأن عربيتي الفلسطينية لم تكن سلسة، شأن العديد منا في الشتات؛ فقد كان من الواضح أني أمريكية. ومع أن الكثير ممن قابلناهم درسوا، أو عملوا، في الولايات المتحدة أو بريطانيا، وقابلونا كلهم بترحاب شديد، فلم أشعر أني منتمية إليهم بالسهولة نفسها التي كان والدي يشعر بها.

كان والدي حريصاً على أن يرينا يافا على الأخص. وكانت جولته معنا فيها هي الجولة نفسها التي قام بها مع آخرين كثيرين، وقد ساءني قليلاً أن أكتشف ذلك فيما بعد. ولعلها تلك هي وسيلته في استرداد المدينة التي ولد فيها، واستعادة البحر الذي سَبَحَ فيه صبياً، والبيت الذي أجبر على الرحيل عنه في ١٩٤٨. في زيارته الأولى عام ١٩٩١، طلب من أصدقائه أن يأخذوه إلى يافا أولاً. شعر في البداية بالارتباك والحيرة؛ فمعظم المعالم التي كان يعرفها لم تكن موجودة. اندثر الحيُّ القريب من البحر حيث ترعرع. ومنذ عشرين عاماً، فعل أخوه ما فعله كثير من الفلسطينيين وتحدثوا عنه: طَرَقَ الباب ليستكشف أيَّ يهود – روس أم مغاربة أم يمنيين أم بولنديين – يعيشون في بيوت عائلتهم القديمة.(٤) وفجأة قال والدي إنه تعرَّف على مسجد حسن بك الذي رفع منه آذان الصلاة وهو صبي، ومن هذا المسجد استطا ع أن يتوصل إلى موقع مقهاه الذي كان. لم ينسَ والدي هذا المقهى الذي كان يعتاد التسكع بالقرب منه في الأمسيات، على أمل أن يسترق السمع إلى رواة السير الشعبية، فلم يكن يملك ثمن كوب الشاي حتى يجلس داخل المقهى ويستمع إليهم. وشيئاً فشيئاً، وهو يدور دورات واسعة حول المسجد، بدأ يهتدي إلى طريقه.

إحدى طالباته السابقات، وقد صارت أستاذة في حقل سياسة الشرق الأوسط، هي التي جعلته يراجع قراره برفض العودة. كانت تعتاد السفر إلى إسرائيل والضفة الغربية، ويذكر والدي أنها قالت له مرة: «إبراهيم، فلسطين لا تزال موجودة». وقال والدي إنه شعر بالسعادة حين وجد كلامها صحيحاً. في زيارته الأولى، سأل بعض الأطفال العرب في الشارع إنْ كانوا يعرفون شارع الملك فيصل. وفي الحال، أخذه الأطفال إليه، مع أن لافتة الشارع تشير إلى اسم مختلف تماماً. ومن هذه الواقعة، عرف أن الأمهات والآباء الفلسطينيين لا يزالون يعلمون أولادهم الأسماء القديمة للأشياء، حتى وإنْ دُفنت فلسطين ومُحيت من الوجود، حتى وإن أعادت إسرائيل كتابتها من جديد.(٥)

توجد صورة أدبية في إحدى قصص دوريس ليسينج Doris Lessing **حكايات أفريقية** *African Stories* (١٩٨١) لم تفارق مخيلتي. وكنت أكلف طلبتي بقراءة هذه القصة عام ١٩٨٥ في سياق سلسلة محاضرات في مادة «الاستعمار»: مستوطِنة بيضاء، شابة، تعيش في جنوب أفريقيا، تنظر إلى السافانا وأشجار السنط؛ فترى أشجار السنديان كثيفة الأغصان في الحكايات الخرافية الإنجليزية. لقد فعل والدي العكس. إذ بينما كنت لا أرى سوى صدوعات عميقة في منحدرات التلال الخضراء بغرض إقامة مستوطنات إسرائيلية ذات أسطح مطلية باللون الأحمر الصارخ، أو أرى أميالاً وأميالاً من الطرق العمومية التي تتشابك وتتقاطع في الامتدادات الصخرية مستحوذةً عليها عبر لافتات خضراء حديثة مكتوبة بالعبرية والإنجليزية، أو غابات مزروعة بأشجار دائمة الخضرة، غير محلية، تُخفي قرى مندثرة – بينما كنت لا أرى سوى ذلك، كان والدي يتطلع من وراء ذلك، ومن خلاله، إلى المناظر التي ألفها في شبابه.(٦)

قال والدي إنه، وهو صبي، كان يعتاد السفر إلى كل أنحاء فلسطين مع العاملين عند والده في ورشة السباكة، إذ يقومون بتوصيل مضخات المياه ومعاصر الزيتون وتركيبها وصيانتها. اكتشفت فيما بعد أنه سافر أيضاً، وهو طالب في المدرسة الثانوية المُسَيَّسة، محاولاً استقطاب زملائه الطلاب؛ مما كان يقلق أمه قلقاً شديداً كلما شرع في ركوب الأتوبيس، كما حكت لي أمي. بدا من الواضح أن والدي – وهو يقودنا بالسيارة – لا يزال يعرف طريقه في فلسطين، مع أنه كان ممنوعاً من دخولها لأكثر من أربعين سنة، وبرغم أن كل شيء قد بدا مختلفاً. أطلعنا على بساتين البرتقال التي ربما سرق منها برتقالة أو برتقالتين، وهو صغير. (وأنا أربط والدي بالبرتقال بسبب طريقته الودودة، دوماً، في تقشير البرتقال: يأكل بضعة فصوص ثم يوزع البقية على أولاده، وأعرف أنه كان من الصعب عليه رؤية برتقال يافا

في السوبر ماركت وعليه بطاقة صغيرة تقول إن منشأه إسرائيل، بينما كان هذا البرتقال جزءاً لا يتجزأ من صباه). ثم أشار إلى نباتات الصبار التي لا تزال تنتصب عنيدة ترسم حدود المناطق العربية التي كانت. ثم يشير إلى نوافذ البيوت العربية القديمة المقوسة التي لم تطلها يد التدمير، والتي تندسُّ بين المباني الجديدة التي غلبت على الضواحي والمدن. كان يبني بقايا الأطلال بخياله، بينما كنت أجهد نفسي حتى أتمثلها بين المباني الأسمنتية [الجديدة] البشعة.

بدأت جولة والدي في يافا بمصنع صغير أنشأه أبوه في ضواحي المدينة عام ١٩٢٩. ولا يزال يذكر إلى الآن حارس هذا المصنع؛ كان رجلاً أفغانياً لطيفاً ذا شارب أبيض كبير، كان يخلب ألبابهم وهم أطفال حين يقرأ كفَّ كل منهم. قال لنا والدي إن هذا الرجل كان يتمتع بالقدرة على قراءة المستقبل فأخبرهم أنهم سيضطرون كلهم إلى مغادرة يافا، أما هو نفسه – الرجل الأفغاني – فلن يغادرها. قال والدي إن الرجل الأفغاني لم يغادرها حقاً؛ فقد صدمته سيارة قبل أحداث ١٩٤٨. وشعرت أن والدي عدَّه رجلاً محظوظاً.

ركنَّا السيارة بعد أن عبرنا الشارع المزدحم إلى جانبه الآخر، عند سبيل أبي نبوت، وأشار إلى مصنع يبدو متهالكاً، كان على أيامه شركة فلسطينية محدودة للمسبوكات النحاسية والحديدية، لا يزال اسمها محفوراً على بالوعات مياه المجاري في يافا إلى يومنا هذا. وشرح لنا وهو يمتليء بمشاعر الفخر أن هذا المسبك كان يخدم المزارعين الفلسطينيين؛ يصنع لهم مضخات الديزل والمعاصر والمكابس التي يحتاجها الفلاحون لبساتين البرتقال والزيتون. لقد تعلم أبوه، في البداية، المهنة على يد بعض الألمان الذين رحلوا عن فلسطين حين استولى البريطانيون على مصنعهم أثناء الحرب العالمية الأولى، ثم استمر في العمل مع اليهود الألمان. بعد ذلك، قرر أن ينشئ شركته الخاصة مع الأقارب بوصفهم مساهمين فيها، خمسة جنيهات من هنا وخمسة من هناك وتأسست الشركة. ثم شرح لنا أنه بهذه الطريقة تمكن العرب من ألا يتكلوا على مصنع أجنبي أو يهودي. وعلى مدى عشرين سنة، هي عمر المصنع، أغلقه البريطانيون عدة مرات. ففي وقت التمرد الفلسطيني عامي ١٩٣٦–١٩٣٧، اتهم الإنجليزُ أباه بتصنيع الأسلحة سراً. فهمتُ بعد ذلك أن الوطنية سَرَتْ شعلتها في العائلة. وذات مرة، حين أغلقوا مصنعه بالشمع الأحمر، نقل أبوه سراً كل الآلات؛ هرَّبها قطعة قطعة عبر بساتين البرتقال خلف المصنع، ثم حملها على عربات الكارو إلى مكان جديد.

أوقعتهم نشاطات جدي الوطنية في المتاعب. ويذكر والدي اقتحامات رجال الشرطة والعساكر البريطانيين الليلية لمنزلهم. كان لهذا

الموقف وقع سريالي عليَّ وأنا أستحضر المشاهد العنيفة التي يصعب أن تتجاوب مع ما أعرفه عن والدي: الرجل الذي يركب الدراجة، ويقرأ الكتب، ويعتني بحديقة منزلنا في الضواحي، ويحاضر بأسلوب يفتن مستمعيه. كان البريطانيون يدخلون المنزل صاخبين، آمرين كل واحد أن يرفع يديه إلى أعلى، ثم يتوجهون رأساً إلى المطبخ ليفتشوا أجولة الدقيق والأرز بحثاً عن أسلحة. كان والدي وإخوته قد تعلموا من قبل أن يقدموا ضيوفهم الريفيين الذين يتسترون عليهم بوصفهم أولاد عم. كما اكتشفوا مبكراً أيضاً مَن يمكن أن يرتشي من المحامين وحراس السجن البريطاني لتهريب الطعام والأغطية لأبيهم. مات جدي عام ١٩٤٤، بعد أن تناوبته الاعتقالات كثيراً، ولم يكن عمر والدي قد تجاوز الخامسة عشر. ومع ذلك، استمر المصنع في الإنتاج حتى انهار كل شيء مع حرب ١٩٤٨.

وكانت المحطة الأكثر أهمية التي توقفنا عندها، في جولتنا في يافا، هي مدرسة والدي الثانوية، المدرسة التي قال عنها بسخرية مريرة إنها علمته جغرافية إنجلترا، إلى درجة أنه حين وطأت قدمه أرض لندن – بعد ذلك بسنوات عديدة – كان يعرف اسم كل شارع فيها. قال إنه في هذه المدرسة تعلم كيف يستخدم عقله، وبخاصة حين قام المدرسون بتسييسه. أما الآن فتحمل المدرسة لافتة صغيرة خارجها تشير إلى أن اسمها «مدرسة وايزمان»، ويحيطها سور من القضبان الحديدية. كانت على أيامه تُسمّى «المدرسة العامرية الحكومية الثانوية». كان والدي مغرماً بالحديث عن ذهابه – ذات مرة – مع مجموعة من الضيوف لمشاهدتها، فوجدوا شباباً أثيوبياً من المستوطنين حرَّاساً عليها، ولم يكونوا يعرفون شيئاً عن التاريخ إلى درجة أنهم لم يصدقوا أن والدي لا يتحدث العبرية حين أخبرهم أن هذه كانت مدرسته يوماً ما. وأثناء جولاته، كان يلقي نظرة فاحصة سريعة على البوابة، ويحاول مراودة حارسها حتى يدخل. نجح – ذات مرة – حين كان بصحبته بعض الأصدقاء من الولايات المتحدة، فكان عليهم أن يتركوا جوازات سفرهم الأمريكية مع الحارس. وأخذته الدهشة من أن كل شيء داخل المدرسة كان على حاله، باستثناء أن الأطفال اليهود رسموا رسومات على حوائطها الداخلية. صارت المدرسة، الآن، من مدارس التعليم المختلط بين الجنسين. أما عندما كانوا طلاباً فيها فكان عليهم أن يتسلقوا الحائط ليروا بنات مدرسة «الزهراء».

ولأن يافا كانت مدينة تجارية غير متجانسة، فلم يكن لديه زملاء ينتمون إلى عائلات عريقة. كان هو وأصحابه تواقين إلى التعلم والتحقق والإنجاز. صار بعض هؤلاء الأصحاب من أصدقاء العائلة الآن: رجائي بُصيلة، الشاعر الكفيف، وأستاذ الأدب الإنجليزي، الذي عاش في كوكومو في ولاية إنديانا؛ وشفيق الحوت الكاتب الذكي

المفعم بالحس الذي أصبح، فيما بعد، مدير مكتب منظمة التحرير الفلسطينية في بيروت. ولا يزال جميعهم يذكر المدرسين الذين علموهم تعليماً رفيعاً طبقاً لمواصفات عالية، إلى درجة أن والدي حين نجح في الذهاب إلى أمريكا وبدأ دراسته الجامعية أعفوه من اجتياز مقررات الجغرافيا والتاريخ الأوروبي. وعن هؤلاء المدرسين، قال والدي في لقاء أجري معه وقرأته، إنهم تعلموا على أيديهم، أيضاً، الفرق بين كسر قواعد المدرسة والانشغال بالعمل السياسي. كان المدرسون يقضون الوقت معهم في فناء المدرسة يجيبون عن تساؤلاتهم بشأن الإمبريالية، ويبتسمون حين يعتصمون وينظمون المظاهرات ويؤسسون اتحاد الطلبة الفلسطيني. كان هؤلاء المدرسون يدرِّسون الكيمياء والتاريخ، ويختلفون عن المعلمين الذين عرفتهم – أنا ابنته – في مدرستي الثانوية (Ahmed-Fararjeh، ص ص ٣٧–٤١).

حين عاد والدي بتفكيره إلى عامه الأخير هناك، عام ١٩٤٨، لم يكن يصدق ما حدث. كان الإنجليز يعرفون أنه ستوجد مشكلة حين ينسحبون في مايو، فأعلنوا أن امتحانات السنة النهائية سيتم تقديمها إلى شهر مارس. بذل والدي وأصحابه ما في وسعهم في المذاكرة والتحصيل، بينما الحرب دائرة في أنحاء البلاد، وعلى وجه التحديد بين يافا وتل أبيب. بعد نهاية اليوم الدراسي، كان يخرج هو وأصحابه للمساعدة، ولكنهم يقولون لأمهاتهم إنهم ذاهبون للمذاكرة معاً. قال والدي إن الطلاب كان منوطاً بهم نقاط التفتيش، فهم يعرفون الإنجليزية ويستطيعون التمييز بين الإنجليز وبين المقاتلين المهاجرين اليهود. ولكنهم لم يكونوا على دراية بأي شيء. ولم يخيل لهم أن حياتهم ستتغير تغيراً جذرياً في القريب العاجل، فقد كان همهم الأساسي اجتياز امتحانات نهاية العام، وظنوا أن مستقبلهم يتوقف على ذلك. وحين فَقَدَ شفيق – صديق والدي الحميم – أخاه، طلب والدي منه بإصرار أن يستغني عن طقوس الجنازة حتى يجتاز امتحاناته. ولما جاءوا إلى المدرسة التي تُعقد فيها امتحانات القبول بالجامعة في فلسطين، وجلسوا إلى مقاعدهم، اكتشفوا أن سطح المدرسة قد نُسف. أتمّوا امتحاناتهم على هذه الحال. وبعد الانتهاء من الامتحانات بعدة شهور، سمعوا النتائج في الراديو، وقد أذاعتها وزارة التربية والتعليم اليهودية، إذ لم يعد هناك وزارة تعليم عربية. في ذلك الوقت، كان والدي لاجئاً في نابلس بالضفة الغربية، وكان على وشك الرحيل إلى عَمَّان. أرسل تلغرافاً إلى شفيق – وكان لاجئاً في بيروت – ذكر فيه هذه المفارقة: «يا له من واقع مثير: اجتزنا الامتحانات! ونحن الآن لاجئون بلا مستقبل».

أخذتنا جولة والدي في يافا إلى شارع به مكتب بريد كولونيالي (حيث حاول والدي بلا طائل أن يسترجع صندوق بريده القديم، لا لشيء

سوى أن يشعر بالسعادة من إمكان ورود خطابات بريد مرسلة إلى يافا)، وإلى المحاكم القضائية التي كان يحلم بممارسة المحاماة فيها، متخذاً من يوسف وهبي نموذجاً، وهو النجم الذي كان يتمتع بالقدرة على استمالة الناس إلى موقفه بحسن بيانه في الأفلام المصرية. كما أخذتنا الجولة إلى محل البوظة الذي كان يذهب إليه مع أصحابه، في فترة المراهقة، لمغازلة العاملة الأوروبية فيه أكثر من تناول البوظة. لم يكن من المألوف بالنسبة لهم رؤية فتيات يعملن، مع أن الفتيات في حيِّهم، والسيدات في الحي المسيحي، يخرجن سافرات. تعبق هذه المباني بمعانٍ بالنسبة إلى والدي، يغمض إدراكُها عليَّ؛ فما كنت أرى سوى مبانٍ كولونيالية بدت أليفة إلى حد ما لوجود أمثالها في مناطق أخرى من الشرق الأوسط؛ حيث أنشأها البريطانيون والفرنسيون من أجل الحكم. وكان عندي تجاوب عاطفي مع هذه المباني في مصر حيث كنت أشعر بالراحة والاطمئنان. أما هنا فشعرت بالغربة، وذكريات والدي لم تكن الذكريات التي تؤثر فيَّ بسهولة، ربما لأنها ذكريات مشحونة بالهزيمة والعداء.

وأثناء الجولة، رأينا عمارة سكنية غير متميزة، كانت آخر مكان عاش فيه والدي. يافا وتل أبيب متجاورتان، ومع ازدياد حدة التوترات السياسية بينهما في غضون الأربعينيات انقسمتا إلى معسكرين، الأول للعرب والثاني لليهود. وفي شتاء عامي ١٩٤٧ و١٩٤٨، دار القتال بالقرب من الحدود بينهما. وكما شرح لنا والدي، صارت المنطقة المجاورة له شديدة الخطر فجأة، تطولها قذائف مدافع الهاون وطلقات الأسلحة النارية؛ فلاذت عائلته بابن عم لها يعيش في وسط المدينة. وبعد مرور أسبوعين، أدركوا أن القتال سيستمر أطول من المتوقع، وأنهم لن يتمكنوا من الرجوع إلى بيتهم في وقت قريب. وعندما نسفت عصابتا الإرجون Irgun والهاجانا Hagana بيتَ العدل غير البعيد عن منزل ابن عمهم، فقتلوا ستين شاباً ممن يرعاهم قسم الشئون الاجتماعية، وكان بصحبتهم لاعب كرة ذو شعبية ضمن المسئولين عن هؤلاء الشباب، حينئذ اعتقد والدي أنه من الأفضل انتقال العائلة إلى منطقة أخرى مجاورة. وعن هذا الحادث الأليم، يصر المؤرخون الإسرائيليون على الزعم بأن الهدف من القصف كان مقرات قيادة اللجنة الوطنية، ويؤكد والدي – الأكاديمي المؤرخ صاحب المعرفة الموسوعية ومكتبة ضخمة عن النزاع الفلسطيني الإسرائيلي – أن الهدف لم يكن في حقيقة الأمر هذا؛ لأن اللجنة الوطنية كانت قد انتقلت قبل ذلك بأسبوعين. يؤكد والدي أن الهدف كان إرهاب أهل يافا، وقد تحقق الهدف.

في الكتاب الذي حرره والدي عام ١٩٧١ تحت عنوان **تحولات فلسطين** *The Transformation of Palestine*، نشر فيه مقالة إرسكين تشايلدرز

Erskine Childers، وهو صحفي إيرلندي متميز، يصف الأمل الصهيوني – منذ أوائل القرن العشرين – في أن يختفي الفلسطينيون بأنه «أمنية مكنونة». واستناداً إلى مصادر وثائقية تتألف من إذاعات راديو صهيونية وبريطانية وعربية، يصف تشايلدرز ما حدث في يافا في الأسابيع السابقة مباشرة على الغارة. وقد صدمني الوصف حين قرأته للمرة الأولى. كان من الصعب عليَّ تخيل أن والدي وعائلته قد عاشا هذه الأحداث. ولم تحدثني جدتي عن ذلك أبداً، فحكاياتها لي عن الماضي كانت عن ليلة زفافها، وشذرات عن السحر والحياة اليومية في فلسطين، لا غير. بدأ الهجوم، فيما يروي شيلدرز، يوم ٢٥ أبريل بوحدات من الإرجون السرية تبعتها وحدات من الهاجانا الرسمية. ومع أن يافا لم تكن ضمن نصيب اليهود في قرار الأمم المتحدة بالتقسيم، فإنهم قذفوها بمدافع هاون ٣ بوصة، ولم يكن التصويب محكماً، غير أنه أحدث دماراً نفسياً. كانت يافا في مجال توجيه قنابل برميلية، وقد وصف ذلك ضابط احتياط إسرائيلي لمجلة سلاح البحرية الأمريكية المتخصصة، قائلاً إنها صُمِّمت خصيصاً لضرب المدن العربية، وكانت القنابل تتألف من «مواسير، أسطوانات خشبية أو معدنية محشوة بخليط من المتفجرات والبنزين، مزودة بإطارين من المطاط وتحتوي على فتيل تفجير»، ثم تُدَحْرَجُ في الشوارع حتى ترتطم بالحوائط ومداخل البيوت، فتنفجر قاذفةً اللهب بطريقة تتزايد تسلسلياً (Childers، ص ١٨٧). كما كان يُستخدم في إرهاب أهل يافا نفسياً عربات مزودة بمكبرات صوت تبثُّ «أصواتاً مرعبة»، كان قد تم تسجيلها من قبل، عبارة عن صرخات نساء وعويل وندب، وصفارات وأجراس ونداءات تحذيرية باللغة العربية، كي يجرى أهل يافا فينجون بحياتهم (Childers، ص ١٨٨) كما كانت النداءات تذكرهم بمذبحة دير ياسين. وأثناء ذلك، سلبت القوات اليهودية، ونهبت، كل شيء في طريقها (Childers، ص ١٩١).

كان والدي – طالب المدرسة الثانوية – قد تطوع في اللجنة الوطنية التي أنشأتها المدينة على عجل للدفاع عن يافا. وبلا تدريب، شأن العديد من أفراد القوة العسكرية الصغيرة التي يصل عددها إلى ألف وخمسمائة متطوع، كان من نصيبه سلاح قديم غير مناسب للقتال. وقال والدي إن هذا السلاح كان مفيداً مرة واحدة فقط: كان ذلك أثناء بحثه عن شقة تسكن فيها أمه وأخته، طَرَقَ الأبواب بحثاً عن شقة خالية، وفي نهاية المطاف سمع عن وجود شقة، فتوجَّه إلى السمسار، وشرح له بشكل ودود حقيقة موقفهم الذي لا رجاء فيه، ولكن الرجل رفض تأجيرها لهم بحجة أن الشقة تخص زوجين يقضيان شهر العسل، فرجاه والدي أن يؤجرها لهم مؤكداً أنهم لا يحتاجونها إلا بشكل مؤقت، وبمجرد أن يرجع الزوجان سوف يخلونها، وكان السمسار عنيداً، وبحركة مواربة أظهر والدي السلاح من تحت جاكتته،

فتمت عملية التأجير. كانت شقة حديثة، وفيها – لأول مرة بالنسبة لهم – حوض استحمام وحمام أفرنجي، ولكن أمه لم تشعر فيها بالراحة. ولم تمتد إقامتها فيها طويلاً؛ فالذعر كان شديداً، وبخاصة بعد استمرار يافا في الانهيار، وبعد أن وصلتهم أخبار عن مذبحة قرية دير ياسين.(٧) ثم تَقَرَّرَ أن تذهب النساء والأطفال إلى نابلس في انتظار أن تهدأ الأحداث. ومثلهم مثل الزوجين اللذين كانا يقضيان شهر العسل، لم يعودوا أبداً.

قضى والدي أيامه ولياليه «مدافعاً» عن يافا، وكان عمره تسعة عشر عاماً، متنقلاً بين العديد من الأماكن فيها، فصارت هذه الأماكن جزءاً من جولته في المدينة. وبدون الحس الجغرافي، لم تكن تعني الشوارع والمباني لي أيَّ شيء، ومرة أخرى عجزت عن الربط بين صورة والدي ذي الشعر الأبيض والبيريه الأسود وموسيقاه الكلاسيكية التي يبثها مذياع السيارة، وصورة هذا الشاب الذي يحدثني عنه. بذلت مجهوداً حتى أتمثل الصورة القديمة بالأبيض والأسود لشاب بشارب داكن وعيون لامعة في هذا المكان. ولكن كيف يمكنني ذلك؟ كانت صدمته في فلسطين تعيش بين جوانحي بوصفها مجرد تماهٍ جريح في الولايات المتحدة المعادية حيث ندر التعاطف مع الفلسطينيين، بل وسادت أكاذيب وعدوانية عما حدث. تذكر والدي، في نهاية شهر أبريل المشؤوم هذا، أن الطعام كان ينفد، والمخابز قد أغلقت أبوابها، بينما كان مدفع هاون موجَّهٌ من تل أبيب يهاجم المدينة بلا توقف. في ذلك الوقت، كانت الشوارع في معظم المناطق المجاورة خالية. وكان الإنجليز يحمون قوافل الناس النازحين. أما الشباب الفلسطيني فكانت مغادرتهم المدينة عن طريق البر تنطوي على مخاطرة كبيرة؛ إذ كانوا عرضة للاعتقال أو ما هو أسوأ، ولم يكن الإنجليز بقادرين على حمايتهم أو راغبين. لم يكن يوجد سوى البحر.

ثم، وهو في جولته، أشار والدي إلى مكان ألقى فيه، هو وصاحبه، سلاحيهما غير الصالحين حين همَّوا بمغادرة المدينة. كان قد فَقَدَ وسيلة الاتصال بأخيه الذي كان على جبهة أخرى، أما بقية عائلته فرحلت. في صباح الثالث من مايو، أدرك الاثنان حشداً غفيراً من الناس على صندل بحري صغير يقلع بعيداً عن الميناء باتجاه سفينة أشيع أنها سفينة النجاة الأخيرة. كان الصليب الأحمر قد أرسلها وكانت ستتجه إلى بيروت. وعندئذ، سَرَى بينهما التردد وساءلا نفسيهما ما الذي عليهما عمله. عادا إلى الشاطئ، كانا ملتحقين باللجنة الوطنية التي كانت تحثُّ الناس على عدم الرحيل مؤكدةً أن المدينة آمنة، واعدةً الناس بأن الإمدادات في الطريق (ولم تكن هناك إمدادات)، وحين عادا أدركا أن أحداً لم يبقَ. قال والدي إن إطلاق النيران كان يأتي كله من الجانب الآخر. وعند الساعة الثالثة بعد الظهر، رأوا سحابة دخان تنبعث من مدخنة السفينة. كانت السفينة تستعد للإبحار

والرحيل. تخليا عن أسلحتهما وجريا للحاق بالزورق الأخير. وعلى المركب، قابلا بحاراً بلجيكياً ظلت كلماته تتردد أصداؤها في أذن والدي على مدى خمسين عاماً: «كيف هان عليك أن تترك بلدك؟». ظل والدي يردد هذه الكلمات لنفسه مرات عديدة. مع أنه كان يعرف ألا خيار له.

تنتهي جولة يافا دائماً بالبحر. كان والدي يتجاهل اللغة العبرية التي يتكلمها الناس من حوله، ويتجاهل أزواجاً من الشباب بالبنطلونات الجينز المحزَّقة يتغازلون ويضحكون، ويتجاهل عائلات من اليهود الشرقيين محدودي الدخل خرجوا للنزهة في الهواء الطلق. رفض أن يذهب إلى مقهى الشاطئ الإسرائيلي، فأعدَّ لنفسه مكاناً على الرمال، ثم ذهب يمارس هوايته في العوم. كنت مع طفليّ على الشاطئ، كانا يرتديان قبعتين مضحكتين تحميهما من أشعة الشمس، وأدركت أنه يريد مني إظهار الإعجاب بروعة المكان. أعرف أنه يعشق البحر الذي نشأ على العوم فيه. وكان من الطريف أن يقول لزميل له عام ١٩٩٩: «نشأتي كانت بالقرب من البحر، لم أكن مقيداً بالمدينة، ولم أكن أتقيد بجماعتي التي أنتمي إليها، كنت جزءاً من عالم واسع حقاً، كنت أحلم على الدوام برؤيته» (Ahmed-Fararjeh، ص ٢٢). وقد كان: اضطر إلى الخروج ورؤية هذا العالم.

كنت طوال حياتي أرقبه وهو يحدق في البحر: من الإسكندرية، من بيروت، من أسبانيا، ومن المغرب، ومن نيوجرسي، ومن الكاريبي. كنت أراه يسبح، ماداً أصابعه الطويلة، وفيها خاتم زواجه يلمع في الشمس، أكتافه العريضة تخترق الماء عندما كان يعوم بطريقته المفضلة: سباحة الفراشة [ضربات متكررة تشبه رفرفة الفراشة]. وقد جعلنا – كلنا – نعشق البحر. أما هنا، في يافا، فقد أطلَّ على المكان الذي عَدَّه – بطريقة ما وبإصرار – بيتَه، حاله في ذلك من حال الرجل في ملصقه البني الداكن، وكنت – أنا – أستشعر أننا دخلاء. جواز سفره الأمريكي ذو اللون الأزرق هو الذي سمح له بالجلوس على الشاطئ حيث كان يسبح طفلاً مع الدلافين وسلاحف البحر، ذلك الشاطئ الذي كانت أمه تراه من نافذتها وهي تشرب قهوتها. شعره الأبيض الذي لا ينذر بخطر، والقمصان ذات الياقة المرفوعة هي التي سمحت له أن يُصنَّفَ بوصفه سائحاً أجنبياً، وليس «مواطناً» عربياً خطراً أو محتقراً. وفي المكان المخصص للسيارات على الشاطئ، سمحت له الألواح المعدنية الصفراء – التي تشير إلى أن سيارته ذات رخصة إسرائيلية والتي منحته حرية الحركة – بأن يقف بحذاء الآخرين دون أن يلفت الانتباه (السيارات المباعة للزائرين المؤقتين الذين لا يدفعون ضرائب تأخذ دوماً لوحات معدنية مرخصة مثل بقية السيارات الإسرائيلية، مما يميزها عما عداها من السيارات في الضفة الغربية أو غزة). تلك هي الألوان الساطعة في عودته إلى يافا وليس اللون البني الداكن في ملصقه.

## الذكريات بوصفها تاريخاً

وبوصف والدي أكاديمياً مهووساً بفلسطين، كان كثيراً ما يفكر في أهمية جمع ذكريات الناس عن الخروج الإجباري عام ١٩٤٨. وتبدأ مقدمته لسيرة الحياة الرائعة – التي طلبها من صديقه القديم وزميل المدرسة الثانوية رجائي بُصيلة – بتعليق عن **النكبة**، حيث كتب يقول: «مع أنها كانت حدثاً قوياً وفاجعاً، ومع أنها شكلت وجهاً مهماً من وجوه التراث الفلسطيني فهي الحدث الوحيد في التاريخ الفلسطيني الذي لم يدوَّن من وجهة نظر الضحية أساساً».(٨) وكما كتب عام ١٩٨١، علينا أن نقوم بفهم الخروج، «وإن كان في هذا الوقت المتأخر»؛ حتى نفهم التجربة الفلسطينية، حتى نكون شهوداً على تاريخ مسكوت عنه، حتى نعيد بناء هذا الحدث بكل تعقيده. وكان يهتم، دائماً، بالمشهد في اتساعه، فكتب يقول: «نعرف أن ملابسات الخروج تختلف اختلافاً كبيراً من منطقة لأخرى في فلسطين ومن طبقة اجتماعية لأخرى» (Busailah، ص ١٢٣).

تختلف سيرة الخروج الدامية، من مدينة اللّد، التي عاشها بُصيلة في يوليو عام ١٩٤٨، عن حكايات والدي الخاصة بالقتال الذي أخفق دفاعاً عن يافا، ثم الهروب عن طريق البحر. تحتوي سيرة بُصيلة على أشكال من الفهم السياسي لدى شاب راديكالي في المدرسة الثانوية، مع أوصاف لمواقف عاشها بنفسه وأخرى رويت له: قذفُ المدينة التي أغار عليها المقاتلون الصهاينة بالقنابل، شائعات عن المذابح، الخروج الإجباري الذي اضطر إليه سكان هذه المدينة جميعهم وهم حيارى لا يعرفون إلى أين يتجهون، وكان يُعتقد أن هذه المدينة لن ينال منها أحد. لم تكن مدينة اللّد ضمن حدود المنطقة المخصصة للصهاينة في قرار الأمم المتحدة بالتقسيم. غير أنها تعرضت للهجوم وطُرد سكانها في ثانيةِ حربين قصيرين مع القوات العربية دخلتهما دولة إسرائيل المعلنة حديثاً. ويصف بُصيلة عملية طردهم في الصيف ومسيرتهم الطويلة إلى المجهول بتعبيرات توراتية: إلى البريّة. وفي نهاية هذه المسيرة، على مدى يوم رهيب، انحرفوا إلى قرية عربية تسمى نعلين، على بُعد خمسة عشر ميلاً بما فيها من تعرّجات وانعطافات حتى يتجنبوا المناطق المعادية. وتنطوي ذكريات بُصيلة على لحظات من الخوف الشديد قبيل الرحيل؛ إذ حين اقتحمت القوات اليهودية البيوت، كان يختفي خلف حصيرة مطوية، يرتجف من الخوف، وكانت طلقاتهم النارية تصاحبها صرخاتُ النساء الفزعات. وتهجس ذكرياته، أيضاً، بأحداث تنمُّ عن قسوة قلبه ونكرانه الآخرين، كما حدث بعد وصوله إلى نعلين، حيث شق طريقه عائداً خلال الجموع المتخلفة عن الركب ليحضر قليلاً من الماء لصديق حميم وأمه، وكان يخفي الماء عن العطشى الذين يلتمسونه بشكل يدعو إلى الشفقة.

يتذكر بُصيلة الأحداث التي عاشها بنفسه والتي سمعها من الآخرين. ولأنه كفيف، فإن المزج بين التجربة المعيشة وما يرويه الناس له، مما يشكل ذاكرتنا، أكثر كثافة عنده. تصف سيرته لهيب الشمس والتكالب على الماء في الآبار الموحلة، كما تتضمن كلاماً عن الأجداد الذين تُركوا لأنهم لم يقدروا على مواصلة السير، وعن «أجساد خَبَتْ فيها الحياة» وأطفال تُركوا لمصيرهم في الخنادق. كتب بُصيلة يقول: «بدأت أستوعب رويداً رويداً من خلال الصراخ وما يتناهى إليَّ من جُمَل متقطعة أن بعضاً ممن لقوا حتفهم تدلت ألسنتهم، وقد علاها التراب والزغب. لم أكن أرى، مما جعلني أشعر بفزع أكبر من غيري». ثم كتب يقول: «وفيما بعد، قال أحدهم – أظن حين وصلنا إلى نعلين – أنه رأى طفلاً لا يزال حياً على صدر امرأة ميتة، كان من الواضح أنها أمه (الأم وطفلها يشبهان ما رُوي فيما بعد عن أمٍّ من دير ياسين شوهدت في القدس مع طفلها المقتول على صدرها)».

وفي محاولة العثور على النبرة المناسبة، حوَّل بُصيلة – فيما بعد – هذا الوصف الموجز إلى صورة شعرية، إذ أبدع من هذه القصة الأخيرة قصيدةً أسماها «ذكرى بعد أربعين عاماً في البرية» "Remembering After Forty Years in Wilderness"، ولم تعد كلمة البرية تدل، الآن، على الطريق الذي كان يتعثر فيه إلى نعلين فحسب، بل على عمره الطويل في المنفى، في الكويت والأردن والولايات المتحدة:

على وجه أوروبا سديم
وكانت أمريكا آنذاك في مخاضها
وقال الله ليكن نور

ولما كان نور
كان حشد من الناس يمشون على الطريق إلى نعلين
وكانت الريح تتماوت
وحلمتان ميتتان
وكان رضيع يدفن وجهه بينهما
ينتظر الرضاعة.

كانت شمس يوليو قاسية آنذاك
تشهد على ما حدث، بينما تجلت في الربيع
رحمة الرب وأمر بأن يكون نور

ولما كان نور
وفي موكب على مشهد من مدينة الله
كان طفل من دير ياسين
يضوع منه عبق زهر البرتقال
راقداً على بطنه، ميتاً بين حلمتين تتلهفان على إرضاعه.(٩)

لم يكن والدي قلقاً بشأن بنيان الذاكرة الفردية المتشظي، ومساحات الصمت وانحناء الذاكرة بفعل الزمن الحاضر أو بفعل المزج بين المعيش والمسموع، وهو القلق الذي ينتاب التحليل الأكاديمي الراهن للذاكرة الفردية أو الجمعية. لقد رأى في السير الفردية، شأن سيرة صديقه، مادةً خاماً يشتغل عليها تاريخ التجربة الفلسطينية. فكان يحثُّ الناس على الكتابة والحكي، ولو أنه كان يركز على أصدقائه المثقفين أكثر ممن كانوا قرويين وأسهموا في كتب تذكارية من قبيل الكتب التي ناقشتها دافيز Davis وسلايموڤيتش Slyomovics، أو النساء في مخيمات اللاجئين ممن حكين قصصهن لباحثين من أمثال روزماري صائغ Rosemary Sayigh، وديانا ألان Diana Allan وإيزابيل همفريز Isabelle Humphries ولالة خليلي Laleh Khalili (وكل هؤلاء ضمن *Sa'di* and Abu-Lughod, eds. *Nakba*). لم يكتف والدي بحكاية قصصه لأولاده بل نشرها في جرائد ومجلات وحكاها لمحاورين بمن فيهم أحمد فرارجه الذي جمعها في كتاب. ولعله من العوامل التي أعانته على تنشيط ذاكرته – شأنه في ذلك شأن فلسطينيين آخرين – المشروعات المعنية بإحياء ذكرى مرور خمسين عاماً على النكبة. وفي خريف حياته، عمل أيضاً على مقترح يتعلق بإنشاء «متحف الذاكرة الفلسطينية»، وهو مشروع يبدو أكثر وهمية، الآن، بعد أن أصبحت الدبابات الإسرائيلية تشق طريقها على مقربة من شقته القديمة [في رام الله]، وبعد موجات الاعتداءات الإسرائيلية منذ ٢٠٠١ التي دمرت ما تبقى من أمل ضعيف عندما كان والدي يحيا من أجل مرحلة هدوء وسيادة فلسطينية، وإن كانت مبتسرة. كان والدي يريد من هذا المتحف تقديم معروضات إثنوجرافية وأركيولوجية وفنية لإظهار استمرارية التاريخ الفلسطيني وحركته الدائبة. وكان يؤكد باستمرار أن هذا المتحف لن يكون – قطعاً – على غرار متحف المحرقة. فالنكبة يخصص لها، عن عمد، حيز صغير. وتكتمل هذه المعروضات بأرشيف الوثائق الأساسية التي يحتاج إليها البحث في التاريخ الفلسطيني.(١٠)

### تحويل البقايا المادية إلى تذكارات

دوماً يكون لموت الأب وَقْع عسير على الابنة. غير أن هذا الأب حين يوقف حياته على شيء أكبر من العائلة، فلا ريب أن موته يتخذ معنى أكبر من المعنى الفردي. مات أبي يوم ٢٣ مايو ٢٠٠١، وهو في كنف عائلته وأصدقائه. وفيما يخصني، كان الوقع الأول لموته وقعاً شخصياً قاسياً، ومثبَّتاً على الأشياء العينية [التثبيت بدلالته في التحليل النفسي]. لقد كان على ظهر كرسيه المتحرك، الأسود ذي العجلات الحمراء اللامعة، بنطلونه الخاكي، وكما كان يشير له مقلداً اللكنة العربية، ساخراً من الذات بتنكيت كاريكاتوري [عن عدم تمييز الناطقين بالعربية بين الباء المجهورة والمهموسة b/p]: «بير أوف بانتس» bair of bants [عوضاً عن پير أوف پانتس pair of pants]. كان الحزام يتدلى معوجاً. وعلى طاولة الحمام كوز الحلاقة لم يُمس وقد صار ماؤه بارداً. في كل أرجاء شقته في رام الله، ترك علامات على حياته المنقضية: أسطوانات موسيقى ڤيڤالدي التي كنا نصر – أنا وأخواتي – على تشغيلها، بينما كان شخص ذو قرابة بعيدة يلح على ضرورة تشغيل تلاوة قرآنية. كانت هناك أسطوانات أوكسجين، اثنتان من الحجم الكبير بجوار سريره، وأربعة من الحجم الصغير تصطف في الصالة، وواحدة على عربة التروللي عليها نجمة داود، مما يعني أنها مشتراة من «الجانب الآخر». كان في غرفة والدي الكثير من الأشياء الصغيرة، التي تجعل الابنة تبكي: ساعته، نظارته، حافظة نقوده، صندله، فاكهته المجففة، أكوام من أوراقه البحثية.

كل شيء توقف الآن، رعاية والدي بشكل يومي توقفت. لن تُعِدَّ له عمتي بعد الآن قهوته العربية فتأتيه بها في فنجان أخضر يميل إلى الزرقة ومزخرف يدوياً، ثم تسمع إطراءه لها. أنا وأخواتي، وقد تركنا عائلاتنا وأعمالنا كي نأتي إلى رام الله، لن نساعده بعد الآن في ارتداء ملابسه يومياً، لن نحثه بعد الآن على تناول إفطاره. ولن نفتح بعد الآن الباب لضيوفه الكثيرين، ولن نشتكي بعد الآن من كثرة الضيوف خوفاً على صحته. لن نقول له بعد الآن إن الوقت لم يحن بعد لتناول الحبوب المسكنة للألم. لن نعطي بعد الآن تعليمات الطريقة السليمة لإعداد شوربة الدجاج. لن نذهب بعد الآن لشراء الجرائد العربية والإنجليزية له، التي أصر عليها وإن لم يعد لديه قدرة على قراءتها.

وأما بعد موته مباشرة، فها نحن نغرق في تفاصيل الروح الشعبية الطقسية: أجلسنا صديقه سهيل، وأخذ ينبهنا ويشرح لنا بجدية أنه توجد عادات معينة علينا اتباعها، كما لو أننا لا نعرف شيئاً عن العالم العربي. وبينما كنا نحن – أولاده الذين تتفاوت درجة إلمامهم بالمجتمع الفلسطيني، وإن لم يكن لنا تقريباً أية تجربة في فلسطين – نجلس حزانى،

تكفّل أصدقاؤه بعمل كل شيء. كان عليهم أن يقوموا بعمل تسوية مع عالَم الجماعة الفلسطينية الغارق في السياسة أثناء الانتفاضة، وهو عالم لم نكن مهيئين للتعامل معه. كتبوا شهادة موته، وحصلوا على شهادة دفنه من الوزارات الإسرائيلية المختصة. قاموا بعمل ترتيبات الجنازة في يافا، وكذلك ترتيبات العزاء الذي يستغرق ثلاثة أيام في رام الله. وصلت كَرَاسٍ بلاستيكية إلى الشقة، ثم رُصَّت في صفوف بموازاة حوائط غرفة المعيشة وغرفة السفرة والشرفة الواسعة. نُظفت المناضد وأعدت القهوة السادة. عُلقت صوره على هيأة ملصقات. وفي المطبخ تكدست القهوة العربية وصناديق زجاجات المياه، وعلب مناديل ورقية، عرفنا أنها هدية من السلطة الوطنية الفلسطينية، وكان ذلك مما فاجأني. سيأتي عرفات من المطار مباشرة بين لفيف من المعاونين والحرس ليقدم تعازيه في هذا الأكاديمي الفلسطيني الذي بذل الكثير من أجل القضية. وُضعت الإعلانات وأجريت مقابلات صحفية، وأعدت قائمة بالمتحدثين – على سبيل التأبين – في هذه المناسبة. جاء أناس وذهبوا: علية القوم، جيران، صحفيون، سياسيون، أصدقاء من المعارف الشخصيين ومن المثقفين. وعندما وصل عمي وابن عمي من الأردن، حملوا عنا واجب تلقي العزاء؛ فهربنا إلى غرفة نوم والدنا، شاعرين بحضوره، شاعرين بالفراغ.

ثم رأينا والدي مرة أخرى يوم الجنازة. كان جسده هزيلاً، يرقد في غرفة صغيرة جامدة ذات أبواب معدنية خضراء تقع خلف مستشفى المقاصد الإسلامية في القدس، وقد جُهزِّ وفقاً لطقوس الدفن المعتادة. كان ملفوفاً في أكفان بيضاء تحدده فبدا ضئيلاً ونحيفاً. وحين ذهبت لألقي نظرة على وجهه – وكان جزء صغير منه مكشوفاً – وجدتني أبتعد فوراً. كان وجهاً بلا حياة؛ فبدت النهاية حادة في ماديتها.

وفي الوقت نفسه، تحوَّل أبي إلى رمز عند الآخرين. صحيح أن إجراءات التكفين تمت بوصفه مسلماً، ولكنه صار أيضاً بطلاً قومياً عند كل الناس. بدأنا في انتظار طويل حتى يتجمع الناس من أجل الذهاب به إلى يافا؛ فالطقس جماعي. وأثناء ذلك، كنا نترقب بتوتر أية تحركات غير عادية، ونتساءل إن «كانوا» سيمنعوننا من أخذ جثمانه. ثمة رجل يصورنا بكاميرا ڤيديو. وقد غمرتنا راحة نفسية بعد أن عرفنا أنه من تلفزيون الجزيرة، وهي قناة فضائية عربية، لم تكن معروفة خارج العالم العربي حينئذ، فقد كنا في شهر مايو قبل أشهر قليلة من أحداث ٩/١١ التي دفعت بهذه القناة إلى دائرة الوعي الغربي. وسَبَبُ هذا الترقب المتوتر الذي انتابنا أنه في المساء السابق، والبيت ممتلئ بالمعزين، تلقينا مكالمة تليفونية محبِطة. كان المتكلم يتحدث بالعربية، وبعد أن قدَّم عبارات العزاء التقليدية طلب أن يتحدث مع الشخص المسئول عن

ترتيبات الجنازة، وعرَّف نفسه بأنه من الاستخبارات الإسرائيلية، شين بيت Shin Bet. ضعفت قدماي عن حملي، ولم أفكر حينذاك إلا في حظي لكوني في منطقة خاضعة للسلطة الفلسطينية [لا إسرائيل]. كل ما تمكن هذا الضابط من عمله مكالمة تليفونية، ولم يأتِ ليطرق الباب أو يهدمه. ولم أكن أتصور الإسرائيليين إلا من خلال صور الأبيض والأسود الباهرة للكوماندوز الفرنسيين الاستعماريين الذين يهدمون الأبواب، كما في فيلم بونتيكورفو Pontecorvo اللامع **معركة الجزائر** *Battle of Algiers*. ولو كان الحدث بعد أشهر قليلة، عندما احتلت الدبابات الإسرائيلية رام الله مرة ثالثة، لكان بإمكان هذا الضابط أن يقتحم حزننا الشخصي.

وعلى الفور، أعطيتُ سماعة التليفون لأصدقاء والدي. سمعت مناقشة حامية تأتي من أقصى غرفة النوم. كانوا يتكلمون عن أنه لن يُسمح لهم بدفن والدي في يافا. كيف عرف الأمن الإسرائيلي بالموضوع؟ أذاع الراديو الفلسطيني والجرائد المحلية كل شيء: أول لاجئ فلسطيني يُدفن في مسقط رأسه. وأكد زملاء والدي أننا نمتلك الوثائق السليمة كلها: شهادة الوفاة من القدس وتصريح الدفن من الوزارة الإسرائيلية المختصة بفضل «أصدقائنا العرب الإسرائيليين» الذين ترعرعوا في النظام الإسرائيلي. ولكن ضابط الأمن كان متشبثاً بموقفه. ثم قال إنه سيعاود الاتصال مرة أخرى. اجتاحتنا حالة انفعال عميق. وبدأ الرجال يفكرون في السيناريوهات المحتملة، وكلها كانت مفزعة بالنسبة لي: قد يقومون بتوقيفنا ونحن نأخذ الجثمان من المستشفى، أو في أثناء الطريق إلى يافا، أو على مشارف الجبانة. فهل من المعقول أن نواجه الجيش الإسرائيلي وجثمان والدي يرقد تحت وهج الشمس؟ ماذا سنفعل؟ اقترح البعض أن أتصل بالقنصل العام الأمريكي في القدس. فما من سبيل آخر. فاتصلتُ به، وشرحت المشكلة التي نواجهها. كانت أمنية والدي أن يدفن في يافا، ومعنا كل الأوراق السليمة. أثنى القنصل على والدي وقدم العزاء، ثم أكد لي أنه سيتصل بالسفارة في تل أبيب. ولما لم نتلقَّ مكالمة أخرى من ضابط الشين بيت الاستخباري في هذه الليلة اعتقدنا أن هذا فأل حسن. كنت أريد لوالدي أفضل شيء يمكن عمله، أما الآخرون فكانوا على استعداد لاستغلال هذه المناسبة من أجل تأكيد حقوقهم في مواجهة التحدي الإسرائيلي.

في صباح الجمعة، خلف مستشفى المقاصد، لم يكن يوجد سوى الناس المتجمهرين، وفيما عدا ذلك لم يحدث شيء، فشعرت براحة نفسية. توافد المزيد من الناس؛ وجوه أصدقائه المألوفة، وكنا نعرفهم، وآخرون كنا نراهم في المنزل على مدى الشهور الماضية. أسعدني أن أرى بعض من أَعُدُّهم أصدقاءً، وهم أكاديميون من جيل الشباب تحدثوا معنا بالإنجليزية. وكان هناك آخرون كثيرون لم نكن نعرفهم. جاء أناس ليصافحونا. أما

الأصدقاء فاحتضن بعضهم بعضاً. ووقف رجال عند مدخل غرفة الطوارئ. ثم بدأ التهامس حين وصلت شخصيات بعينها من علية القوم أو مثيرة للجدل. جلسنا مع البعض داخل المستشفى، تحت أسقف أسمنتية عارية معروشة بأسلاك. ولم يكن في مقدوري أن أمنع نفسي من الشعور بالرثاء لهذا المستشفى العربي الفقير المتهالك، الذي يختلف تماماً عن مستشفي هَداسا Hadassah على مستوى المهارة المهنية والنشاط، حيث ذهب والدي من أجل لقاءاته الصعبة الأخيرة مع اختصاصي الرئة الحاذق واختصاصي الأورام السرطانية غير الودود.

وأخيراً، حان وقت التحرك. عربة نقل بيضاء مغلقة، بلا أية علامة عليها، توقفت فجأة أمام المشرحة، ونُقل إليها النعش. أنا وأخواتي، تشبث كل منا بالآخر ونحن نحدق من شباك العربة إلى هذا الصندوق المنعزل الخالي من أي لون. استقلّت جموع الناس سيارات وأتوبيساً جاء من رام الله، فصنعوا موكباً طويلاً. سرنا ببطء، ونحن نتلفت يميناً ويساراً، نترقب ظهور عربات الجيش الإسرائيلي الجيب أو البوليس. ولكن الطريق كان خالياً. سمعنا أن سفير الولايات المتحدة قد طمأن، مرة أخرى، شخصاً ما بأنهم سيراقبون الموقف. وشعرت بالمفارقة: والدي – بوصفه مواطناً أمريكياً – تحميه الحكومة نفسُها التي كان يلومها باستمرار؛ لأنها تدعم قاتلي أهله وتسلّحهم. ولكني كنت أشعر بالامتنان.

سارت السيارات لمسافة طويلة، على طرق عمومية، وخلال طريق خلفي في القطاع الصناعي يفضي إلى القسم العربي من يافا. وفي منطقة قريبة مزدحمة، تركنا سياراتنا ومَضينا. على الجدران ملصقات تتضمن مقالات من الجرائد عن والدي وملخصاً عن مؤهلاته وخبراته. أدركت أن الأستاذ شخصية محترمة في هذا المجتمع. وكانت لوالدي خصوصية بسبب أسلوبه الجديد: اختراق عدم فاعلية الاعتصامات، تجاهل حظر التجوال، رفض أية حدود بين الفلسطينيين – سواء في الشتات أو في المناطق المحتلة أو داخل إسرائيل – الرغبة في أن تقوم المجتمعات بدور كما كان يدعو أثناء سنواته في الولايات المتحدة.(١١) كنا في مركز جمعية يافا العربية، وهي المكان الذي حاضر فيه والدي جمهوراً كان مولعاً به إلى أبعد الحدود. هذا المكان بقايا ما كان مدينةً فلسطينيةً ذات يوم. كان يرأس الجمعية بعض الرجال الذين تحملوا – بكل تفان – عبء إسداء العون في ترتيبات الجنازة. كان دعم والدي واهتمامه بأنشطتهم يعني لهم الكثير (وضْع اليد على المباني المصادرة، إخلاء مداخل الطرق إلى البيوت المسدودة بأنقاض تل أبيب ومخلفاتها، الدفاع عن العرب المسحوقين في المناطق المتهدمة وتقديم خدمات اجتماعية للمحتاجين منهم، وبخاصة أنهم يعيشون في مستويات تختلف عن المستويات الاجتماعية المرتفعة في المناطق التي يعيش فيها اليهود).

وُضِع النعش على منضدة ضخمة في غرفة صغيرة على اليسار. وكانت توجد أكاليل من الزهور. بدا النعش فجأةً، وهو ملفوف الآن بالعلم الفلسطيني، نابضاً بالحياة. لم يعد والدي الجثةَ الهزيلة التي رأيناها من قبل. لقد اكتسب موته معنى كبيراً. وفي وقت صلاة الظهر توقفت كلمات التأبين التي كنت أسمعها بالكاد. اندفع الناس من الأبواب كي يلحقوا النعش. حمله الرجال عبر الشوارع الجانبية المؤدية إلى مسجد العجمي، تدافعوا ليأخذوا دورهم في حمل النعش. وكان ابن أختي بينهم، هو الوحيد الذي يربط شعره خلف رأسه مثل ذيل حصان، لكنه الوحيد الذي أحب والدي على الوجه الأمثل، إذ عاش معه في رام الله لمدة عامين. وفي طليعة الموكب رفع بعض الشباب العلم الفلسطيني لواءً. وكان الناس يُطلون من الشرفات العالية.

وعند المسجد، حملوه صاعدين السلالم. تساءلت متى كان آخر مرة في مسجد، لكن هذه هي المسيرة عند الموت: كان المجتمع يستوعبه والجماعة تسترده. بقيتْ كل النساء خارج المسجد، غير أني لاحظت أن عدداً من الرجال بقوا أيضاً خارج المسجد، وهم أكثر ممن دخلوا. فسألت زميلاً له من جامعة بيرزيت: «هل كل هؤلاء مسيحيون؟» فأجابني بابتسامة: «لا، يوجد الكثير من الماركسيين اللينينيين!».

وقفنا ننتظر. كانت الشمس حامية لكننا بدأنا نشعر بتحسن، فقد أمكننا رؤية البحر الآن. ثمة فتاة مراهقة ذات شعر طويل وعيون كبيرة مثل عيون الوعل، ترتدي تي شيرت وبنطلوناً من الجينز، أقامت صداقة مع أختي أثناء هذا الوقت. قالت إنها لم تكن تعرف والدنا، ثم أضافت: «ولكني لأول مرة في حياتي أشعر بالفخر لأني من يافا». وفي حقيقة الأمر، كان يوجد كثير من الناس ممن لم يعرفوا والدي، على ما خمّنت. وقد جاء هؤلاء من أرجاء فلسطين كلها، وبصفة خاصة من القسم الفلسطيني المحتل في ١٩٤٨. كان يوجد، أيضاً، قليل من اليهود الإسرائيليين المناهضين للصهاينة، وقد كان والدي بالنسبة لهم جسراً مهماً. ثم بدأت أفهم أن هناك الكثير من الناس لم يتمكنوا من المجيء؛ وهم الذين يحملون بطاقات هوية من الضفة الغربية أو غزة، إذ لم يكن مسموحاً لهم عبور نقاط التفتيش إلى «إسرائيل». وهناك، أيضاً، صديق حميم من أصدقاء والدي، وهو أستاذ كان قد انتخب في الهيئة التشريعية الفلسطينية، رفضوا التصريح له بمغادرة غزة لحضور هذه المناسبة، على الرغم من أن زوجته الأمريكية السابقة حاولت التوسط له.

عندما انتهى المصلون، بدأنا في التحرك. النعش محمول على أكتاف أمواج من الرجال، يتأرجح تأرجحاً قوياً. وفي المقدمة، من بعيد، يلوح العلم الفلسطيني، وهو يتمايل تمايلاً متحدياً. موكب ضخم من الناس السائرين معاً، يصعدون مرتفعاً وأياديهم متماسكة، يتحدثون وهم

شاعرون أنهم جزء من كل. مررنا بمطاعم السمك التي كان والدي يحب أخذ ضيوفه إليها. الأسماك مثل البرتقال عنده، كانت جزءاً من المذاقات العالقة بحس الانتماء إلى يافا. وهي مذاقات أقوى من حلوى المادلين المشهورة عند پروست Proust. المتفرجون على الموكب يرقبونه وقد أخذتهم الحيرة؛ فبعض الأطفال يلوحون معتقدين أنه موكب استعراضي. يعيش الآن كثير من الإسرائيليين فى المناطق العربية من يافا، والبعض يستمتع ببيوت مرممة ترميماً جميلاً بالبلاط والأقواس العربية، ولو أن عمتي ستنهار عندما تكتشف ذلك، فيما بعد، ونحن فى طريق العودة إلى يافا بعد أسبوع. على جانبنا السفلي الأيمن يبدو البحر متألقاً، شمس الظهيرة تسقط على راكبي الأمواج المتزلجين الذين خرجوا يستمتعون بالنسيم العليل. كان الإحساس بالبهجة شديداً: أناس كثيرون يمشون معاً خلف نعش يلفه العلم الفلسطيني، وكان مما يدعو إلى الدهشة أن أحداً لم يمنعنا من دفن والدي فى جبانة تطل على البحر في مسقط رأسه، يافا، كما تمنى.

كنت قد تأخرت عنهم، وعندما لحقت بهم في الجبانة رأيت بضعة رجال على مرتفع على يمين ثلاثة أشجار. وبينما كنت أسرع علقت قدماي، وهي في حذائي المفتوح ذي الكعب العالي، بنتوءات قبور متهدمة وغصينات. أخواتي وعمتي وقفن عند منتهى حشد الرجال. كنا نرقب والدي وقد لفه العلم، وجهه الصغير مكشوف، نراه الآن للمرة الأخيرة. سحبوه من النعش، وضعوه على أرض محفورة للتو. عادت بقاياه المادية إلى أرضه، في بقعة من أجمل بقاع الأرض (فيما عدا البيوت المنهارة ومساحات من الأرض الفضاء والتشييد المتواصل لـ«مركز پيريز للسلام»)، على هذا الجُرُف بجوار شاطئه المفضل.

وبينما كنا نشق طريقنا خلال الجبانة، سألنا صديقٌ حميم من أصدقاء والدي: «هل تريدون رؤية قبر جدكم؟» تذكر عمي مكانه، فقد كان وهو طفل يذهب إلى زيارته كل أسبوع. كان قبراً كبيراً، ولا يزال يبدو جديداً يقف بارزاً بين فتات الأحجار. ويبدو أن أحجاره من نوعية ممتازة، فهواء البحر لم يؤثر فيه مع أنه كان قاسياً على أصلب أنواع الأحجار. على جانب القبر قصيدة مكتوبة بخط منمق، وبالقرب من قاعدته رأينا اسمه: علي خميس أبو لغد. مات بعد إطلاق سراحه بوقت قصير منذ أن اعتقله البريطانيون آخر مرة بلا تُهَم. وبالقرب منه تماماً، كان قبر عمي الذي قتله الإنجليز قبل عام من رحيل العائلة، فى ١٩٤٨. وفيما بعد، عرفنا أن هذه الجبانة لم يدفن فيها أحد منذ عشرين عاماً.

حين ظهرنا من البوابة، ونحن نخطو عبر التراب والأنقاض، جاء الناس يعزّوننا واحداً فواحداً. كم كان عددهم؟ كانوا كثيرين جداً. فهل

يعرف كل هؤلاء الناس والدي؟ أم أنه كان رمزاً: ابن يافا، الفلسطيني المشهور، عاشق فلسطين، الذي حقق في النهاية حقه في العودة؟

قال محمود درويش، الشاعر الفلسطيني الكبير، وهو يتذكر والدي بعد موته بعدة أيام قليلة: «كل موتٍ هو موت أوّل، مفاجئ، صاعق، غير معروف وغير مألوف». ومع هذا، فقد طُعِّمَ موت والدي بقصص معروفة من قبل. وقد أدهشني والدي نفسه بلجوئه أثناء مرضه إلى تعبيرات غريبة لها إيحاءات دينية، وعلى سبيل المثال كان يشبِّه الألم الذي يعانيه في جانبه برفسة الملائكة، وكلما عانى من ألم السرطان وهو صابر عليه، كان يعلق شبه مازح: «نحن [الفلسطينيين] ولدنا لنعاني . . . مثل المسيح». أما الآخرون فكانوا أجرأ في استعاراتهم؛ ففلسطين ويافا هما «مواقع الذاكرة» بأصدائها المثيرة (Nora). ويشبِّه درويش فلسطين عند والدي بـ«الجحيم والفردوس معاً. ولأن سدرة المنتهى تنمو في مدينة يافا». ثم وصف حضور والدي في «قافلة الترحيل الجماعي» من يافا بأنه خطيئة أصلية، لا لاقترابه من شجرة المعرفة المحظورة بل لأنه كان بعيداً عنها بعداً كبيراً؛ مما يفسر التزامه على مدى حياته بالبحث والاجتهاد الفكري. ثم يختم درويش كلامه – كما فعل غيره – بالحديث عن عودة والدي إلى فلسطين، فيقول: «عاد ليغرس فيها شجرة المعرفة، فكان هو الشجرة». ثم يتناص مع اللغة القرآنية عن العودة عبر الموت، فيقول: «لقد ولد في يافا، وعاد إلى يافا ليبقى، هناك، إلى الأبد، قرب سدرة المنتهى».

ثم بعد سنوات قليلة، لفتت نظري تعليقات انفعالية قالها لاجئ عجوز من يافا يعيش في غزة، جمع فيها أيضاً بين الجنة ويافا. ومما يسترعي الانتباه في فيلم عمر القطان التسجيلي عام ١٩٩٥ عن سقوط يافا، وعنوانه **العودة... محارب بريطاني قديم في فلسطين**، أن رجلاً عجوزاً يقول لابنه إنه لا يستطيع تقبل ما حدث ولن يقبله. ثم يؤكد بطريقة تنطوي على ما يقترب من الكفر: «في يوم الحساب، حين يخبرني الله قائلاً: "أردتُ لك الجنة، فما قولك؟"، سأقول: "لا، أرجعني إلى بلدي، فأنا أريد الحياة في يافا". أرأيت؟ سأرفض الجنة وأقول: "من فضلك، دعني أرجع لأعيش في يافا، فهي بلدي"».

ولعل القصة الأكثر شيوعاً التي تحتضن والدي وهو ميت كانت القصة التي عبَّر عنها العلم الفلسطيني الذي غطوه به. لم يكن والدي ممن يلوِّحون بالأعلام؛ كان يكرس حياته للعدالة، كان يعشق فلسطين وأهلها، ولم يكن وطنياً فجاً، بل ظل مستقلاً على المستوى السياسي، ينتقد دائماً، ويبحث بحثاً أكاديمياً طيلة حياته. ومع هذا، لفوا نعشه في مبنى مركز جمعية يافا العربية بالعلم الفلسطيني في انتظار تشييع الجنازة. وأنا لم ألوح بعلم أبداً، ووجدت في ذلك التسييس نوعاً من المزايدة. ومع هذا، فقد

أحسست أن العلم يشحن النعشَ بكاريزما غريبة. لقد رفع الشبابُ العلمَ الفلسطيني عالياً في طليعة الموكب الجنائزي ونحن في طريقنا إلى الجبانة، وتلك إشارة تحدٍّ في بلد يعاني فيه الناس من ويلات السجن بسبب رفع هذا العلم. وبرغم ذلك، فهي حركة عادية على أرض حفلت بالكثير من جنازات «الشهداء» الشباب. ثم بعد يومين، امتدح خطيب متقد الحماسة والدي لاتخاذه قرار العودة إلى فلسطين، تاركاً وراءه رفاهية الحياة ومزاياها في أمريكا. ولأنه لم يضع شروطاً لهذه العودة، يستدل الخطيبُ من ذلك على أن «عشق الوطن لا شروط له».

أما إدوارد سعيد، الأكاديمي المتألق، وأحد أصدقاء والدي المقربين، وقد امتد عمره بعد موت والدي لمدة تقل عن ثلاث سنوات، فهو أقل رومانسية فيما يتعلق بالوطن. وفى الطقس التذكاري نفسه في رام الله عَارَضَ سعيد الصورةَ الخادعة عن الوطنية – صورة حملتها أيضاً مئات اللوحات التي ظهرت باسم منظمة التحرير الفلسطينية، والسلطة الوطنية الفلسطينية، وحركة فتح التحريرية، فيما صار تقليداً يشير إلى شهداء النضال من أجل فلسطين – عَارَضَها بالحديث عن المواطنة العالمية عند والدي. ثمّ أخذ سعيد يتكلم عن انفتاح والدي على الناس وثقافة البلد الذي قضى فيه أربعين عاماً – ألا وهو الولايات المتحدة – مع أنه كان يعارض سياساتها. كما تحدث عن فضول والدي وأسفاره العديدة: إلى الصين وپيرو والهند وبلدان أفريقيا. وفي ذلك انتقاد ضمني للمحلية أو الإقليمية التي تنشأ عن النزعة القومية. ولتخفيف جنون العظمة الذي يلازم أيضاً الوطنية، يستشهد سعيد بلازمة لوالدي تنطوي على حلاوة ومرارة في آن واحد: «نحن أناس عاديون. أناس طيبون، ولكن عاديون». وفيما بعد، سوف يكتب سعيد كيف أن والدي – على الرغم من عودته – «كان لا يزال غير متحقق وغير مستقر»، مضيفاً أن «العودة لم تغيره، مع أن شعوره بالرضى في وطنه كان أكبر من شعوره به وهو في المنفى. كانت فلسطين عنده سؤالاً لا يمكن أن يحظى بإجابة كاملة أو حتى سؤالاً يصعب التعبير عنه». غير أن سعيد لا يتمالك نفسه عن قراءة حياة والدي وموته على أساس قصة أكبر. يلحظ سعيد تنقل والدي من «ميله إلى الحياة الجماعية إلى تأمله الباطني المزاجِي، ومن نزوعه التفاؤلي والحيوية إلى الإحساس بالعجز، وهو إحساس معطل»؛ مما يجعله يستنتج الآتي: «تعبِّر حياته عن الانكسار والانتصار، عن القنوط والإنجاز، عن الإذعان والحسم في آن معاً. وبإيجاز، كانت حياته نسخة من فلسطين، عاشها بكل تعقيدها».(١٢)

أما ما لم يغفله أحد في التأبين فهو أنه حقق **عودته**: رجوعه في النهاية إلى يافا.

## الماضي في الحاضر

طبقاً لوالدي، كان الرجوع يعني تطعيم خشونة التاريخ بحكايات مرهفة، كان يعني مواجهة أصيلة مع الحاضر. ومما يثير الدهشة أنه كان يحمل على كاهله هذه المهمة بكل حماسة. وهو مَن كان يرفض العودة لوقت طويل، بدأ في تشجيع كل فلسطيني على الرجوع، حتى وإن كان سيعاني من استجوابات سلطات الاحتلال الإسرائيلية المُهينة في المطار أو الجسر: خلع الأحذية من أجل التفتيش، مصادرة الدفاتر، إفراغ محتويات حقائب السفر، تفتيش جسدي، وحتى حفاضات الأطفال الرضع وأدوات الزينة. وحين سأله أحد المحاورين على تلفزيون الجزيرة إن لم يكن شاعراً بالمرارة من أن حلمه بالرجوع قد جعله في موقف يواجه فيه الفلسطينيون مشكلات يومية ويساقون إلى مناطق تسمى ألف وباء وجيم، تفصلهم نقاطُ التفتيش العسكرية الإسرائيلية – أجاب: «لا أشعر بالمرارة مطلقاً. وعلى الأصح، أشعر أن الحضور الإسرائيلي يمثل تحدياً لنا. ومن المستحيل أن نقابل هذا التحدي بالمرارة. إنه حاجز أصارعه؛ فأنا أنادي بالمساواة، أنادي بإزالة نقاط التفتيش كلها... ومهمتنا النضال معاً حتى نغير هذا الواقع. ومجيئي هنا – وجزء كبير منه – كان من أجل تغيير هذا الواقع. فأنا لا أقاتل بعيداً عن ميدان النضال». لقد شعر والدي شعوراً قوياً، عند النهاية، أن الفلسطينيين ارتكبوا خطأ كبيراً في ١٩٤٨ حين هربوا خائفين، مع أنه يعرف – أكثر من غيره – أنهم لم يكونوا ليقدروا على فعل شيء آخر. أنفق والدي حياته وهو يستقصي كل ما يتعلق بهذا التاريخ، ومع هذا كان يقول: «كان من الواجب علينا أن نظل على الأرض، حتى وإن وصل الإسرائيليون. كان من الواجب علينا أن نبقى؛ فالنضال يتطلب مواجهة من خلال أشخاص يقاومون».(١٣)

وقد رأيت بنفسي المواجهة على أرض الواقع: رأيت جنود مكافحة الشغب المسلحين يواجهون أولاداً في سن المراهقة يقذفونهم بالحجارة. لكني رأيت، أيضاً، والدي وهو يقترب من نقاط التفتيش الإسرائيلية يشد من عوده بتوتر مستعداً للمشهد فترتسم ابتسامة متكلفة على وجه هذا الرجل المهذب الذي يُخرج جواز سفره الأمريكي بسرعة حتى يمر. وفيما بعد، جرَّبت بنفسي إسرائيل أثناء مرضه وموته، فكنا لا نقدر على الذهاب إلى أي مكان في الضفة الغربية للحصول على المسكِّنات التي أوصى بها الطبيب الإسرائيلي، وكنا نعاني من ندرة ملصقات المورفين، ناهيك عن طعامه المفضل من البروكلي وسمك السالمون، بينما كان كل هذا يتوافر على «الجانب الآخر». كنا نحتاج إلى سيارة إسعاف للحاق بمواعيد الطبيب خوفاً من نفاد أنبوبة الأوكسجين أثناء سخونة السيارة عند نقطة تفتيش متباطئة. وكان الخوف – ونحن نقترب من نقطة التفتيش – على وجه صديقته المفعم

بالحيوية، الإسرائيلية الفلسطينية من الشمال التي تعرف العبرية، وقد جاءت لتساعده على التفاوض مع المستشفى. ولم يكن مسموحاً لها – أصلاً – دخول الضفة الغربية ببطاقة هويتها الإسرائيلية، مع أنها هي وزوجها والأطفال قد عاشوا هناك. ثم المكالمة الهاتفية من الأمن الإسرائيلي، ونحن في ذروة أحزاننا، تهدد ترتيباتنا التي قمنا بها من أجل الجنازة.

إن حقيقة موت والدي الفيزيقية لا تنفصل عندي عن تفاصيل الهيمنة الإسرائيلية: بدءاً من أطراف أصابعه الزرقاء إلى الممرضين الفلسطينيين الذين دفعوه على السلالم إلى سيارة الإسعاف ولم يكونوا متأكدين من السماح لهم بالمرور السريع... بدءاً من المكالمة المتطفلة التي قام بها الضابط الإسرائيلي إلى علم ساكن لفّوه على النعش في مركز جمعية يافا... بدءاً من الشعور بالقلق من المراقبة إلى سخاء مجتمعه الذي يفوق الوصف... بدءاً من مخاوفنا على مصير مذكرة محاضرات ألقينا بها في الزبالة سهواً بينما كنا ننظف شقته إلى الرعب الذي شعرنا به في يوم موحش لم يأت فيه أحد من أصدقائه لزيارته؛ فقد جمعوا أطفالهم من المدرسة مبكراً وجلسوا يشاهدون الأخبار باهتمام ليعرفوا ما إذا كان – أو أين – سيلقي أريل شارون القنابل «انتقاماً» لحادثة ما...

لقد سمعت حكايات والدي على مدى حياتي. أما أن تمشي وأنت شاعر باليتم، تعبُر نقطة تفتيش متربة وحارة، تُسحب فيها حقائبك لمجرد أنهم لا يريدون السماح لأية سيارات فلسطينية بالعبور – فهذا شيء آخر. أن يهاجمك جنود متعجرفون بنظارات شمسية عاكسة وعضلات مفتولة ليؤخروك عن قصد – فهذا شيء آخر. أن تذهب إلى المطار مستقلاً تاكسياً عربياً في طريقك للحاق بطائرتك، فتجدهم يفتشون السيارة ببطء، ثم يغيبون في الداخل ويطول غيابهم ومعهم بطاقة هوية السائق، فيهينونك بقدرتهم على جعلك تجلس أخرس وأنت تعرف أنك بريء تماماً من أي اتهام – فهذا شيء آخر. وبينما كنت أعبر من الضفة الغربية إلى بر الأمان في القدس حتى ألحق بطائرتي، حضرتني حكايات شق الأنفاق تحت الأرض وهروب العبيد [في الولايات المتحدة] في سبيل الحرية، وتزاحمت في مخيلتي صور اللاجئين المبعدين في الحرب العالمية الثانية وهم يمشون تنوء أكتافهم بحمل ممتلكاتهم. ولكن هذه الصور لا يمكنها أن تتمثل هذا الواقع المتفرد بدمدمته العبرية التي تدَّعي، بعجرفة، حق الامتلاك. الأسلحة والجنود المنتشرون أينما تولِّي وجهَك. الفصل الكامل بين العرب واليهود. هذه التجارب والخبرات التي اكتسبتها بنفسي، أكثر من حكايات والدي، هي التي جعلتني راغبة في

الكتابة عن النكبة. ليست الكارثة الفلسطينية أثراً من الماضي: إنها حية في الحاضر، في كل منزل هدمته البلدوزرات الإسرائيلية، ومع كل حريق أشعلته طائرات الأپاتشي، ومع كل إجهاض عند نقاط التفتيش العسكرية، ومع كل قرية تمزّعت حقولها بالجدار «العازل»، ومع كل فلسطيني لا يزال يتوق إلى العودة إلى بيت لم يعد موجوداً.

**الهوامش**

(١) الرد على ليلى فانوس: لا أعرف السياق.

(٢) امتدت علمانيته إلى اختصار مادة الدين والتعليم الديني في خطته السجالية لمنهج الدراسة الجامعية الوطنية الفلسطينية، وقد رُفضت خطته. راجع الفصل السابع من عمل Hovsepian في ثبت المراجع.

(٣) كل الاستشهادات من حكايات والدي مأخوذة من تسجيلات حوارية باللغة الإنجليزية قام بها هشام أحمد فرارجه. والاستشهادات التي وردت في عمل أحمد فرارجه تشير إلى الصفحة. وبعض الحكايات والمواقف الأخرى توجد في حوار من جزءين مع زكريا محمد. وفي هذا الحوار، يذكر والدي أنه ترك يافا بالمركب في ١ مايو، وليس في ٣ مايو.

(٤) لوصف هذه الزيارات، راجع: Karmi وTamari and Hammami وAl-Qattan, "Secret Visitations". وعن عودة إدوارد سعيد إلى بيت عائلته، انظر: الفيلم التسجيلي لـBruce. وللاطلاع على عمل عن الأفلام، بما في ذلك فيلم Bruce والمطالبة ببيوت ومنازل، راجع Bishara و"Sa'di, "Catastrophe.

(٥) وبخصوص شرح بعض الأساليب التي تم بها المحو وإعادة الكتابة، راجع: Abu El-Haj وBenvenisti.

(٦) وللمزيد عن الغابات، راجع: Bardenstein وBresheeth وDavis وSlyomovics.

(٧) كانت دير ياسين قرية التزم سكانها بميثاق عدم التعدي مع الهاجانا، ومع هذا، فقد قامت قوة مشتركة من الهاجانا ومن «مقاتلون من أجل حرية إسرائيل» [LEHI وتعرف، أحياناً، بعصابة سترن] بمجزرة في دير ياسين ذهب ضحيتها – على أقل تقدير – ١١٥ رجلاً وامرأة وطفلاً، ثم رميت جثثهم في الآبار (Smith، ص ١٩٤)، والإعلام بهذه المجزرة – من خلال قوات الإرجون والهاجانا بمكبرات صوت متنقلة في مدن مثل يافا وحيفا، ومن خلال الإذاعة العربية – تسبب في ذعر رهيب. وبخصوص دراسة عن أثر مذبحة دير ياسين في الفلسطينيين انطلاقاً من مقابلات مع

اللاجئين، راجع: Nazzal. وكما بيّن Morris، لم تكن هذه المجزرة هي الوحيدة التي قامت بها القوات اليهودية. راجع، أيضاً، عمل Abdel Jawad الذي يوثق ثماني وستين مذبحة للفلسطينيين قام بها الصهاينة والقوات الإسرائيلية في عام ١٩٤٨. وقد أقام النحات الجزائري الأمريكي خليل بن ديب نصباً لضحايا دير ياسين في جنيف ونيويورك عام ٢٠٠٣، راجع أيضاً: McGowan and Ellis.

(٨) ولعله يستلهم، هنا، عنوان دراسة قام بها صديقه إدوارد سعيد، ألا وهي: «الصهيونية من منظور ضحاياها» المنشورة في كتاب سعيد عن القضية الفلسطينية، راجع: Said, *The Question of Palestine*.

(٩) يوضح بُصيلة في هامش على القصيدة أن نعلين قرية فلسطينية قام الإسرائيليون بترحيل ستين ألف فلسطيني إليها مشياً على الأقدام في يوليو ١٩٤٨.

(١٠) ويمكن الاطلاع على تفاصيل مخطط «متحف الذاكرة الفلسطينية» في مؤسسة التعاون.

(١١) أشكر روجر هيكوك Roger Heacock على توضيحه دور والدي في فلسطين، أثناء تعليقاته المؤثرة في ورشة «النكبة في الذاكرة الفلسطينية الجماعية»، في الاجتماع السادس للبحث السياسي والاجتماعي المتوسطي ضمن برنامج البحر الأبيض المتوسط، مركز روبرت شومان للدراسات العليا، مؤسسة الجامعة الأوروبية، مونتكاتيني تيرم، إيطاليا، ٢٠٠٥.

(١٢) راجع: Said, "My Guru". وللمزيد عن صداقتهما، راجع: L. Abu-Lughod.

(١٣) لقد أعطاني والدي تسجيل ڤيديو لحوار بدون عنوان، أعتقد أنه كان مع محمد خريشات في برنامج «ضيف وقضية»، قناة الجزيرة التلفزيونية، وعلى الأغلب كان عام ١٩٩١. وأشكر لوري آلن Lori Allen على تدوينه.

## المراجع العربية


درويش، محمود. «إبراهيم أبو لغد: طريق العودة هي طريق المعرفة». رثاء في تأبينه الذي أقيم في رام الله يوم ٢٦ مايو، ٢٠٠١. نشر لاحقاً في مجلة **أخبار يافا**، العدد ١١ (٣١ مايو، ٢٠٠١)، ص ٤.

زكريا، محمد. «عن يافا... والموت... والفرح... والهزيمة... والأمل. أبو لغد: خفت أن أموت دون أن أرى فلسطين فقررت العودة». **الأيام** (٢٥ و٢٦ ديسمبر ١٩٩٥)، ص ١٤ في العددين.

«متحف الذاكرة الفلسطينية: وثيقة المشروع». مؤسسة التعاون، نوفمبر ٢٠٠٠.

## المراجع الأجنبية

Abdel Jawad, Saleh. "Zionist Massacres: The Creation of the Palestinian Refugee Problem in the 1948 War." *Israel and the Palestinian Refugees*. Eds. Chaim Gans, Eyal Benvenisti, and Sari Hanafi. Berlin: Springer Verlag, 2007. 59-129.

Abu El-Haj, Nadia. *Facts on the Ground: Archaeological Practice and Territorial Self-Fashioning in Israeli Society*. Chicago: U of Chicago P, 2001.

Abu-Lughod, Lila. "About Politics, Palestine, and Friendship. A Letter to Edward from Egypt." *Edward Said: Continuing the Conversation*. Eds. Homi Bhabha and W. J. T Mitchell. Chicago: U of Chicago P, 2005. 17-25.

Ahmed-Fararjeh, Hisham. *Ibrahim Abu-Lughod: Resistance, Exile and Return. Conversations with Hisham Ahmed-Fararjeh*. Birzeit: Ibrahim Abu-Lughod Institute for International Studies, Birzeit University, 2003.

Allan, Diana K. "The Politics of Witness: Remembering and Forgetting 1948 in Shatila Camp." *Nakba: Palestine, 1948, and the Claims of Memory*. Eds. Ahmad H. Sa'di and Lila Abu-Lughod. NY: Columbia UP, 2007. 253-82.

Bardenstein, Carel B. "Trees, Forests, and the Shaping of Palestinian and Israeli Collective Memory." *Acts of Memory: Cultural Recall in the Present*. Eds. Mieke L. Bal, Jonathan Crewe, and Leo Spitzer. Hanover: UP of New England, 1997. 170-81.

Benvenisti, Meron. *Sacred Landscape: The Buried History of the Holy Land Since 1948*. Berkeley: U of California P, 2000.

Bishara, Amahl. "Examining Sentiments about and Claims to Jerusalem and its Houses." *Social Text* 75.21 (Summer 2003): 141-62.

Bresheeth, Haim. "The Continuity of Trauma and Struggle: Recent Cinematic Representations of the Nakba." *Nakba: Palestine, 1948, and the Claims of Memory*. Eds. Ahmad H. Sa'di and Lila Abu-Lughod. NY: Columbia UP, 2007. 161-87.

Bruce, Charles. *In Search of Palestine*. London: British Broadcasting Company, 1998.

Busailah, Reja-e. "The Fall of Lydda." *Arab Studies Quarterly* 3.2 (Spring 1981): 123-51.

Childers, Erskine. "The Wordless Wish: From Citizens to Refugees." *The Transformation of Palestine*. Ed. Ibrahim Abu-Lughod. Evanston, IL: Northwestern UP, 1971. 165-202.

Davis, Rochelle. "Mapping the Past, Re-creating the Homeland: Memories of Village Places in pre-1948 Palestine." *Nakba: Palestine, 1948, and the Claims of Memory*. Eds. Ahmad H. Sa'di and Lila Abu-Lughod. NY: Columbia UP, 2007. 53-75.

Halbwachs, Maurice. *On Collective Memory*. Trans. and ed. Lewis A Coser. Chicago: U of Chicago P, 1992.

Hirsch, Marianne. *Family Frames: Photography, Narrative, and Postmemory.* Cambridge: Harvard UP, 1997.

Hovsepian, Nubar. "Palestinian State Formation, Political Rent, and Education Policy: Development and the Construction of Identity." PhD Diss. City University of New York, 2004.

Humphries, Isabelle and Laleh Khalili. "Gender of Nakba Memory." *Nakba: Palestine, 1948, and the Claims of Memory*. Eds. Ahmead H. Sa'di and Lila Abu-Lughod. NY: Columbia UP, 2007. 207-228.

Karmi, Ghada. *In Search of Fatima: A Palestinian Story*. London/NY: Verso P, 2002.

Lessing, Doris. *African Stories*. NY: Simon and Schuster, 1981.

McGowan, Daniel and Marc H. Ellis, eds. *Remembering Deir Yassin: The Future of Israel and Palestine*. NY: Olive Branch P, 1998.

Morris, Benny. *The Birth of the Palestinian Refugee Problem Revisited.* Cambridge: Cambridge UP, 2004.

Nazzal, Nafez. *The Palestinian Exodus from Galilee, 1948*. Beirut: The Institute for Palestine Studies, 1978.

Nora, Pierre. "Between Memory and History: Les lieux de mémoire." Trans. Marc Roudebush. *Representations* 26 (Spring 1989): 7-24.

Proust, Marcel. *Swann's Way*. Trans. C. K. Scott Montcriff. NY: Dover Publications, 1981.

Al-Qattan, Omar. *Al-'Awda* [Going Home]. Sindibad Films and Café Productions 1995.

______________. "The Secret Visitations of Memory." *Nakba: Palestine, 1948, and the Claims of Memory*. Eds. Ahmad H. Sa'di and Lila Abu-Lughod. NY: Columbia UP, 2007. 191-206.

Sa'di, Ahmad H. "Catastrophe, Memory and Identity: Al-Nakbah as a Component of Palestinian Identity." *Israel Studies* 7.2 (2002): 175-98.

______________ and Lila Abu-Lughod, eds. *Nakba: Palestine, 1948, and the Claims of Memory*. NY: Columbia UP, 2007.

Said, Edward. *The Question of Palestine*. NY: Vintage Books, 1979.

_________. "My Guru." *London Review of Books* 23.24 (December 2001): 19-20.

Sayigh, Rosemary. "Women's Nakba Stories: Between Being and Knowing." *Nakba: Palestine, 1948, and the Claims of Memory*. Eds. Ahmad H. Sa'di and Lila Abu-Lughod. NY: Columbia UP, 2007. 135-58.

Slyomovics, Susan. "The Rape of Qula, a Destroyed Palestinian Village." *Nakba: Palestine, 1948, and the Claims of Memory*. Eds. Ahmad H. Sa'di and Lila Abu-Lughod. NY: Columbia UP, 2007. 27-51.

Smith, Charles. *Palestine and the Arab-Israeli Conflict*. Boston: Bedford/St. Martin's, 2004.

Tamari, Salim and Rema Hammami. "Virtual Return to Jaffa." *Journal of Palestine Studies* 27.4 (Summer 1998): 65-79.

# ملخصات المقالات
## (أبجدياً بالاسم الأخير)

---

## عودة إلى بقايا الأطلال:
## الذاكرة والذاكرة المولَّدة والتاريخ الحي في فلسطين

### ليلى أبو لغد
### (ترجمة حسام نايل)

هذه المقالة بلسان الابنة عن عودة والدها إبراهيم أبو لغد؛ ليحيا ثم يموت في وطنه فلسطين بعد أربعين عاماً من المنفى في الولايات المتحدة. وقد غيّرت عودته إلى أرضه من تجربته المزلزلة ومن الحدث الفاصل في حياته: النكبة. لقد طعّم ذكرياته عن فلسطين وعن يافا مباشرة في الحاضر وفي التاريخ الحي. إن تطعيم الحاضر التاريخي بذاكرته منح ابنته ليلى معرفة وهوية مختلفتين، فقد مزجت بين حكاياته وتجربتها في هذه المقالة، مركزة على ذاكرتها المولَّدة بوصفها ابنته، وخصوصية هذه الذاكرة المصاحبة لفجيعة والدها، والنكبة التي ما زالت مستمرة يومياً في فلسطين، فالذاكرة تستحضر فقدان الوطن ماضياً كما تعيش الذات هذا الفقدان حاضراً.

## أشكال الذاكرة:
## التقسيم بوصفه نموذجاً أدبياً

### آنا برنارد

تقترح هذه المقالة التأملية منهجاً لمقارنة أعمال ما يسمى «أدب التقسيم»، انطلاقاً من روايات تدور حول تقسيم الهند وفلسطين وإيرلندا. وترى المؤلفة أنه يمكن التعرف على أجناس أدبية محددة وحبكات قصصية وأساليب جمالية في مجال أدب

التقسيم. وبشكل خاص، نقع على بنية رواية الرومانس (الرواية الغرامية البطولية) ورواية النشوء (رواية تكوين الشخصية)، والسرد المتشظي. وتنزع هذه الأجناس الروائية نحو الواقع المضاد، مثيرة الحنين إلى مكان كان يمكن أن يكون، ساعية إلى إعادة التذكير ببدائل للتقسيم.

## قلوب أنهكها الشتات:
## قراءة في ثنائية كمال رُحَيّم الروائية

**محمد بريري**

ركزت هذه القراءة في روايتي كمال رُحيّم على النظر في بعض المظاهر الشكلية والمضمونية من أجل محاولة استخلاص الإيديولوجيا الكامنة التى وجّهت السرد. ويمكن تلخيص هذه الرؤية في أن الدين، رغم أهميته، ليس إلا أحد مكوّنات الثقافة بمعناها الأنثروبولوجي، أي من حيث هي لغة حية وممارسات وطقوس يومية، تكوّن باجتماعها معاً الهوية الخاصة لأفراد المجتمع. وقد كانت فجيعة الغربة، التي عانى منها بعض المصريين اليهود – من شخصيات الرواية – الذين هاجروا إلى فرنسا، راجعة إلى حنينهم إلى هويتهم الثقافية حين اضطروا إلى مغادرة الوطن الذي أكسبهم تلك الهوية. وقد انتهى تحليل الروايتين إلى أن الدعوة إلى فكرة المواطنة وجّهت كثيراً من تفاصيل السرد، مع ما تتضمنه تلك الفكرة من رفض التمييز بين المواطنين على أساس عنصري ديني.

## قراءة شهادات الفجيعة عند جونز وموريسون

**عبد النبي بن بيه**

إن الكتابة المعاصرة بمظهريها الإبداعي والمقالي مهووسة بتجلّي المقهور. ويُعَدُّ ذلك سبباً كافياً لتسمية الألفية الجديدة «زمن عودة الشبح المقهور». وعليه، فإن فِعلَي الكتابة والقراءة قد تميزا بالاستلاب والوهن وخضوع سلطة الكاتب لسلطة النص. تكشف هذه المقالة أبعاد الصدمات النفسية كما تظهر في الإنتاج الأدبي، محاولة بيان محدودية التأويل والفهم النقدي لمثل هذه النصوص، ممثلة في عملين لجيل جونز وتوني موريسون، منتهجة بذلك قراءة أخلاقية تبيّن تجربة هاتين الكاتبتين مع منظّري

الصدمات النفسيّة المبكّرة، وبخاصة تخمينات النّاقد والفيلسوف جاك دريدا. تقرأ المقالة محاورة دريدا للتجربة على أنّها جزء لا يتجزّأ من «سرديته» عن حدث الصدمة.

## وقائع متطرفة:
## مقالات وأشعار نعومي شهاب ناي

### أيبيس جوميز-ڤيجا

ترصد هذه المقالة العلاقة بين حياة الشاعرة المقيمة في الأمان النسبي في جنوب غرب الولايات المتحدة وعلاقتها الوجدانية والعائلية بفلسطين، الأرض التي تمزقها الحروب والصراعات. وبالنسبة إلى الشاعرة، فالصراع في فلسطين شخصي؛ حيث إن فلسطين وطن الأسلاف. وتتناول أشعارها موضوعات عديدة لا يراها الأمريكيون إلا على شاشة التلڤزيون، ولكنها بوصفها أمريكية-عربية تكتب أيضاً عن عالم بعيد عن فلسطين. وتعكس قصائدها حياتها في سياق أكثر أماناً مع أنها تحمل بصمة «العربي» في أمريكا في مرحلة الشك في كل عربي، بما في ذلك الشاعرة. وعبر أشعارها ومقالاتها تقوم الأديبة بالإبحار بين وقائع متطرفة وعالمين مختلفين إلى حد الاستقطاب.

## المراسلة والذاكرة:
## عود على الفجيعة في الكتابات النسائية

### وليد الحمامصي

تتناول هذه المقالة روايتي أليس ووكر **اللون البنفسجي** وحنان الشيخ **بريد بيروت** المكتوبتين عبر رسائل، موضحة أوجه الشبه بين العملين من وجهة النظر الشكلية/البنيوية، في الوقت الذي توضح فيه وظائف صيغة الرسائل وأهميتها الرمزية في كلا العملين. ويوضح الكاتب طبيعة الخطابات من حيث هي عنصر يرتبط بالبوح ويمكن كلا البطلتين من تفهم موقفيهما بشكل أعمق، حتى وإن كانت الخطابات التي تكتبها البطلتان خطابات من جانب واحد لا تتمتع بالرد مثلما في حالة الخطابات العادية.

# فجيعة الغياب، ألفة الغياب:
# تناولات الموت في نماذج من الرواية المصرية

حسين حمودة

تتناول هذه المقالة بعض جوانب من تناولات الموت في نماذج من الرواية المصرية من أعمال نجيب محفوظ وجمال الغيطاني وبهاء طاهر ونعمات البحيري وغيرهم. يتوقف البحث عند صدمة الغياب متمثلة في حدث الموت، وعند الكيفيات التي يحضر بها الموت في هذه الروايات، سواء على مستوى الوقائع الراهنة أو على مستوى الذاكرة التي تستعيد الموتى وتساوي بينهم وبين الأحياء. وترصد المقالة أثر الموت على صياغة حيوات الشخصيات التي اتصلت بمن غيبهم الموت، بما يجعل الموت يجاوز كونه حدثاً ميتافيزيقياً ليغدو حقيقة ماثلة وحية في حيوات الأحياء.

# تباريح «حزينة»

عبد الحميد حواس

تتناول هذه المقالة الثقافة الشعبية بوصفها موئل وعي الجماعة بذاتها والحافظة لمحصلة تجاربها والمبلورة لذاكرتها الجمعية، بما فيها من تجارب حزينة مفجعة و أخرى سارة. وقد أبدعت الثقافة الشعبية في سبيل استدعاء ذلك المخزون ألواناً من التعبيرات، من أبرزها فن القول. تتخذ المقالة من شخصية حزينة في رواية يحيى الطاهر عبدالله **الطوق والإسورة** مفتاحاً لأبواب فن القول الشعبية المتنوعة. وتتقصى الدراسة التنويعات اللحنية الحزينة التي تتجلى في الأنواع القولية الشعبية، ممثلة في: السرد القصصي، أغاني العمل، الأغاني النسوية المتفردة، الموال القصصي، ثم في السير الشعبية.

## الصدمة المفجعة والشهادة: «تسعة أجزاء للرغبة» بقلم هيذر رفّو

### ماجدة رومانسكا

تقدم هذه المقالة مسرحية بعنوان **تسعة أجزاء للرغبة** وهي عن الوضع العراقي الكارثي. وفي المسرحية تتحدث تسع نساء عراقيات يُقدمن شهاداتهن عن وضعهن ومآسيهن تحت القمع والحصار والغزو. وقد نجحت المسرحية جماهيرياً عند عرضها في الولايات المتحدة، وكثيراً ما كانت ممثلة واحدة تقوم بالأدوار التسعة. وتوازي صاحبة المقالة ذهنياً بين الفجيعة العراقية وفجائع تعرفت عليها من خلال خلفيتها البولندية، وتربط بين التحليل النفسي والتنظير الأدبي للصدمة الجماعية وإحساس بطلات المسرحية. كما أنها تقدم نبذة عن المؤلفة الأمريكية–العراقية التي توزعت بين انتمائها إلى بلدين متخاصمين. وتطرح المقالة أسئلة عن مدى توفيق العمل في التماهي مع الآخر، وإن كانت ترى أنه يثير التأمل في آليات التفاعل الثقافي وفي تمثل الآخر.

## قلق الاندثار:
## الكاتبة العربية بين ذكرى شهرزاد وكابوس الموءودة

### هنادي السمان

تسلط هذه المقالة الضوء على الإنتاج الأدبي لبعض الكاتبات العربيات المعاصرات في المهجر الأوروبي أو الأمريكي، وإلى التركيز على رمزين أدبيين مستمرين ومُلحين: شهرزاد التي يُصر طيفها دائماً وأبداً على الظهور في الأدب النسَّوي بين فينة وأخرى، وشبح الموءودة الذي يقضُّ مضاجع الذاكرة الفردية والجماعية للأديبات. وتطرح المقالة نظرية أدبية خاصة بكاتبات المهجر العربيات، مفادها أن الكاتبة العربية تكتب دائماً بدافع من قلق أو خوف الاندثار الذي يتولد في عقلها الباطن. وجديرٌ بالذكر أن استرجاع ذاكرة الأدب الشفهي لشهرزاد وصدمة الوأد يشكلان عاملين أساسيين لتخطي خوف الاندثار الأدبي وتجاوز الصدمة من أجل خلق نتائج إيجابية من ماض سلبي.

## موت الذات:
## إرهاصاته في الشعر الحديث وتجلياته في الشعر المعاصر

**عمرو الشريف**

تسعى هذه المقالة إلى دراسة العلاقة بين النص والمجتمع، موضحة أنه إذا ما كانت الذات الفردية تحيا من خلال علاقاتها بالذات الكلية، فإن الانقسام بينهما يؤدي إلى حالة من الفصام داخل الذات الفردية. وتتتبع هذه الدراسة ظاهرة موت الذات في الشعر الحديث والمعاصر، على العكس من الرمز الذي يظهر فى شعر المجتمعات العضوية، وترصد الدراسة كيف يعيد المجتمع إنتاج ذاته في الأشكال البلاغية التي تنتشر في الشعر المعاصر . تعيد علاقة البعد بين الدال والمدلول فى حالة الأليغوريا، والتضاد بينهما فى حالة المفارقة، إنتاج علاقة البعد بين الذات الفردية والذات الجماعية وانشقاقها عليها.

## «بيان التنحي» وذاكرة الهزيمة:
## مدخل بلاغي لتحليل الخطاب السياسي

**عماد عبد اللطيف**

تقدم هذا المقالة تحليلاً بلاغياً للبيان الذي ألقاه الرئيس المصري الراحل جمال عبد الناصر إثر هزيمة يونيو ١٩٦٧. يُحاج البحث بأن الصياغة البلاغية لبيان التنحي كانت ذات تأثير في إنتاج الاستجابات التي أعقبت إلقاءه: والتي تمثلت أوضح ما يكون في المظاهرات الهائلة الرافضة للهزيمة والتنحي معاً. تقدم المقالة تحليلاً تفصيلياً لبعض أهم الظواهر البلاغية في البيان؛ مثل التلطيف اللفظي والضمائر الشخصية وتحولاتها والاستعارات المفهومية والعلامات غير اللغوية. وغاية المقالة فهم كيف تتحول البلاغة السياسية إلى أفعال سياسية، وبخاصة في لحظات الأزمات. وتجمع المقالة بين التحليل الشكلي للظواهر اللغوية والبلاغية وتحليل العلاقات الشائكة بين النص والمجتمع.

## الجرح الذي لا يلتئم أبداً

### ڤينسنت كراپانزانو

تعالج هذه المقالة رد فعل الحركيين لمسرحية **اسم الأب** الفرنسية بقلم مسعود بن يوسف الجزائري. والحركيون جزائريون وقفوا مع الفرنسيين في حرب التحرير الجزائرية التي انتهت بخسارتهم للمعسكرين الفرنسي والجزائري. فقد قتل الآلاف منهم على يد مواطنيهم الجزائريين عند الاستقلال. أما الذين سنحت لهم فرصة الهروب إلى فرنسا، فقد فرضت عليهم الحكومة الفرنسية إقامة جبرية في مخيمات استمرت أحياناً لفترة تناهز الستة عشر عاماً. وقد رأي الحركيون في فرنسا في المسرحية إهانة لهم، وقد باءت محاولتهم بوقف عرضها بالفشل. كان اعتراضهم على تصوير ابن حركي بوصفه محاصراً بسبب قرار أبيه المأساوي، ولهذا ضل السبيل وتم التلاعب به من قبل المؤسسة العسكرية الجزائرية والإسلاميين والفرنسيين.

## استجابة أريستوفانيس للحرب الپلوپونيسية واندحار البطل الكوميدي

### ڤاسيليكي كوتيني

تقدم هذه المقالة أثر الحرب الأهلية، في اليونان القديم المعروفة بالحرب الپلوپونيسية في مسرحيات أريستوفانيس، متتبعة سيرة المؤلف وراصدة حدوث الصراع الأهلي في أعماله. وتتوصل الدراسة إلى أن أثر الحرب ونتائجها الفاجعة شكلا تدريجياً جرحاً لا للأثينيين فحسب، بل للكوميديا الأريستوفانيسية ذاتها. تركز المقالة على ثلاث مسرحيات كوميدية له: **أخارنيون**، **السلام**، **ليسيستراتي**، بالإضافة إلى مسرحية **الضفادع** التي تناقش خلاص المدينة. تشكل اللغة والموتيفات والبطل الكوميدي و(استحالة) الحل – في هذه المسرحيات – مؤشراً أدبياً للأوضاع السياسية والعسكرية.

## شهادة سينمائية من زمن الحرب

**عرب لطفي**

تتناول المخرجة تجربتها السينمائية التي تبلورت في مجتمع يعج بالصراعات السياسية وفي مرحلة شكلت فيها بلادها مركزاً أساسياً للصراع في المنطقة. هي من الجنوب اللبناني الذي هو شمال فلسطين، تنتمي إلى جغرافيا مليئة بالأحداث والأزمات. عاش أهلها كل أنواع الحروب والصراعات التي لم تتوقف أو تخف حدتها حتى الآن. هذه الجغرافيا صنعت تاريخ المخرجة وقدرها منذ الطفولة حتى الآن. عاشت لتشهد، تتأثر وتؤثر – بوصفها فرداً أو جزءاً من شعب – في قراءة هذا التاريخ واستلهامه والمشاركة في صناعته. هذه الكتابة هي محاولة لتذكر بعض من ملامح الخصوصية الفردية للمخرجة في علاقتها بالهم العام الذي صاغ وتحكم في تجربتها الإبداعية.

## تأملات حول الذاكرة والصدمة عند يوسف شاهين

**داليا سعيد مصطفى**

تتناول هذه المقالة مناقشة فيلمي المخرج المصري يوسف شاهين **١١ سبتمبر وإسكندرية .. نيويورك** من أجل طرح بعض القضايا النظرية والفنية والسياسية المتعلقة بتطويع المخرج للذاكرة وتأملاته حول مفهوم الصدمة على المستويين الشخصي والجماعي والعلاقات العربية الأمريكية في الوقت الحاضر. وهذان الفيلمان من الأفلام القليلة في السينما العربية التي تناولت هذه العلاقة بالبحث والنقد. وتشير الدراسة إلى بعض الموتيفات والتقنيات السينمائية التي يلجأ إليها المخرج في هذا السياق، وتتناول بعض التداخلات مع أفلام أخرى. وتنبع أهمية فيلمي شاهين أساساً من القضايا السياسية التي قلّ أن يتم طرحها في السينما المصرية.

## ابنة الثورة:
## سارا دولات آبادي وجماليات الذاكرة
## (مقابلة)

### إيمي أرياب مطلق

لقد أعاق مفهوم الإنتاج الثقافي في إيران الحديثة – الذي يتميز مثله مثل سياستها بالثورة والصرامة الإيديولوجية – من يعيشون خارج إيران من التعاطي مع موروثها الثري من الفنون البصرية الذي تطور في إيران الحديثة خلال القرن الماضي. في هذه المقابلة، تناقش المحاوِرة أعمال الفنانة الإيرانية الشابة الموهوبة سارا دولات آبادي (المولودة في ١٩٧٨) التي نشأت وتعلمت في إيران، وتعيش الآن في طوكيو باليابان حيث تمارس عملها. وتقدم أعمال الفنانة وحياتها نموذجاً استثنائياً، وإن كان في الوقت ذاته متكرراً، لمأزق الفنان الإيراني الحديث.

## «ذاكرة الجسد» الاجتماعية:
## الحرب والمنفى في كتابة الذات الجزائرية

### جيمس مكدوجال

تقوم المقالة بقراءة تأويلية للممارسات الثقافية الجزائرية المعاصرة بوصفها «تقنيات للعيش»، حيث تتحول ذكريات اجتماعية واسترجاعات جماعية للتجارب الفاجعة إلى أعمال أدبية وفنية بثغراتها الخاصة. وتتطرق المقالة إلى أجناس فنية ونقدية متعددة – الرواية الأدبية والموسيقى الرائجة والدراسات الأكاديمية والسير الذاتية والفكاهة ذات الطابع السياسي والصحافة – ساعية إلى ترسيمٍ الاقتصاد الرمزي الذي عبره يتم احتواء تجارب الحرب والمنفى المعطلة احتواءً نفسياً والتعبير عنها في نتاج يعكس الذات.

# الذاتية الكارثية:
# تمثيل حالة اللاموت الشبحية في لبنان

مارك وستمورلاند

تقدم هذه المقالة عدة فنانين وسينمائيين يعملون في لبنان بعد مرحلة الحرب الأهلية وكيفية استخدامهم لوسائل الإعلام والوسائط التجريبية كي يعبّروا عن كارثة اجتماعية. وتطرح المقالة مفهوم الذاتية المنسحبة المرتبطة بحالة «اللاموت»، حيث تركز هذه المشاريع التجريبية على الفجوة بين العلاقة والصورة الذهنية التي تلازمها، كي تشير إلى أشباح الحرب دون أن تتمثلها بشكل مرئي، فليست لأشباح حروب لبنان انعكاسات ولا يمكن تخيلها مباشرة. وتستكشف المقالة مدى إمكان الأطياف الرهيبة تَمثُل ما هو لامرئي وممتنع على القول ويستحيل تصويره في أوضاع يحكمها النسيان الرسمي وتجاهله للكارثة.

## تعريف بكتاب العدد
## (أبجدياً بالاسم الأخير)

**ليلى أبو لغد** أستاذة كرسي الأنثروبولوجيا والدراسات الجنوسية في جامعة كولومبيا في نيويورك. قامت بدراسات ميدانية متعددة في مصر عن النساء وسياسة الجنوسة والثقافة التعبيرية بما في ذلك وسائل الإعلام والاتصال. نشرت ثلاثة كتب، ترجم واحد منها إلى العربية بعنوان **مشاعر محجبة**، وآخر عن قصص بدوية، وثالث عن السياسة التلفزيونية في مصر. حررت العديد من الكتب، ومنها مؤخراً كتاب عن النكبة والذاكرة.

**آنا برنارد** تدرّس الدراسات ما بعد الكولونيالية بجامعة يورك في انجلترا. نشرت عدداً من المقالات في مجلات ودوريات أدبية متخصصة في الولايات المتحدة. تعكف حالياً على إنجاز كتاب عن الأشكال السردية والأليغوريا القومية في أعمال فلسطينية وإسرائيلية معاصرة.

**محمد بريري** يدرّس الأدب العربي القديم والحديث بالجامعة الأمريكية بالقاهرة وبجامعة بني سويف. صدر له كتاب عن ديوان قبيلة هذيل، ويصدر له قريباً كتاب عن الشعر الجاهلي ونزعة الشك. له عدد من المقالات والترجمات التي تتناول الأدب العربي، قديمه وحديثه، شعره ونثره.

**عبد النبي بن بيه** أستاذ مساعد في الأدب الإنجليزي والمقارن بكلية العلوم الإنسانية والاجتماعية بتونس. نشر مقالات في ميدان أدب ما بعد الاستعمار والأخلاقيات. وهو الآن بصدد بحث حول جماليات الهجرة في الأدب الأنجلوفوني والفرانكفوني المعاصر.

**أيبيس جوميز-ڤيجا** أستاذة الأدب بجامعة إلينوي الشمالية بالولايات المتحدة حيث تدرّس أدب القرن العشرين الأمريكي. تخصصت في الأدب العرقي وأدب المثليين. لها عدد من المقالات الأكاديمية ورواية ومجموعة من القصص القصيرة.

**وليد الحمامصي** مدرس مساعد بقسم الأدب الإنجليزي بجامعة القاهرة. نال درجة الماجستير في الأدب المقارن من الجامعة الأمريكية بالقاهرة. يعمل حالياً على رسالة دكتوراه عن اقتباس الأعمال الأدبية سينمائياً. له عدد من المقالات والترجمات المنشورة حول السينما والأدب ما بعد الكولونيالي ودراسات الجنوسة.

**حسين حمودة** أستاذ مساعد النقد الأدبي الحديث بكلية الآداب، جامعة القاهرة. نائب رئيس تحرير **دورية نجيب محفوظ** ومقرر لجنة الكتاب الأدبي بالمجلس الأعلى للثقافة وله دراسات نقدية عديدة وقام بتحرير وإعداد ثلاثة مجلدات عن القصة القصيرة في مصر.

**عبد الحميد حواس** مستشار أبحاث الثقافة الشعبية بمركز البحوث العربية والأفريقية، وأستاذ غير متفرغ بالمعهد العالي للفنون الشعبية بأكاديمية الفنون الجميلة. حائز على جائزة الدولة التقديرية في العلوم الاجتماعية لعام ٢٠٠٥. درّس مقررات الثقافة الشعبية في المعاهد والكليات المصرية والعربية والأمريكية. قام بدراسات منهجية وميدانية حول الأدب الشعبي. ترجم وألف العديد من الكتب والأبحاث وشارك في العديد من المؤتمرات المتخصصة.

**سارا دولات آبادي** فنانة إيرانية تعيش وتعمل في اليابان. نالت درجة الليسانس في الفنون الجميلة من جامعة أزاد بإيران. عرضت أعمالها الفنية في طهران وطوكيو ونيويورك وغيرها من مدن العالم.

**ماجدة رومانسكا** أستاذة مساعدة في كلية إيمرسون حيث تشرف على قسم دراسات المسرح. درست في جامعتي ستانفورد وكورنل. لها العديد من الكتب والمقالات. تعمل أيضاً باحثة في مركز الدراسات الروسية والأوروبية الآسيوية في جامعة هارڤارد.

**هنادي السمان** أستاذة مساعدة في اللغة العربية وآدابها في جامعة ڤرجينيا بالولايات المتحدة. تخصصت في الدراسات النسائية العربية والشرق أوسطيَّة وفي الحركات النسائية الإسلامية والعالمية وفي نظريات الأدب وتشكيل الهوية فيما بعد الاستعمار وفي الأدب المهجري. ظهرت مقالاتها بالإنجليزية في مجلات نقدية وكتب علمية. تعمل حالياً على مخطوطة كتابها الذي سيظهر قريباً بالإنجليزية بعنوان: **قلق الاندثار: الصدمة وفن الكتابة والمهجر في السرد النسوي العربي**.

**عمرو الشريف** مدرس مساعد حصل على درجة الماجستير فى الأدب الإنجليزى ويعمل على الحصول على درجة الدكتوراه في النقد الأدبي. درس بمصر والولايات المتحدة. له مقالات منشورة فى دوريات أدبية وفلسفية مختلفة تركز معظمها على العلاقة بين الاستطيقا والأدب.

**عماد عبد اللطيف** مدرس البلاغة وتحليل الخطاب بكلية الآداب، جامعة القاهرة، وعضو هيئة تحرير مجلة **اللغة**. درس بجامعة لانكستر الإنجليزية وجامعة القاهرة. يهتم بمجال الدراسات البلاغية المعاصرة، ومناهج تحليل الخطابين السياسي والديني، والتواصل بين الثقافات. نشر مؤخراً كتابين هما: **لماذا يصفق المصريون؟ أساليب التلاعب بالجماهير في السياسة والفن** و**أنا رب عائلة مصر: اللغة والدين والسياسة في خطب السادات**.

**ڤينسنت كراپانزانو** أستاذ متميز في الأدب المقارن والأنثروبولوجيا بجامعة سيتي بنيويورك. يعمل حالياً على كتاب عن الحركيين الجزائريين. له العديد من الكتب التي تجمع بين الأنثروبولوجيا والتحليل النفسي والتأويل الفلسفي، وقد قام بدراسات ميدانية في المغرب وجنوب أفريقيا والولايات المتحدة.

**ڤاسيليكي كوتيني** أستاذة مساعدة في قسم الأدب الإنجليزي والمقارن بالجامعة الأمريكية بالقاهرة. درست في اليونان والمملكة المتحدة وحصلت على الدكتوراه من جامعة لندن، متخصصة في اللغة اليونانية وآدابها. وتدور أبحاثها حول الكوميديا والميثولوجيا اليونانة وأصدائهما في الأدب المعاصر.

**عرب لطفي** مخرجة سينمائية. تدرّس صناعة الفيلم بالجامعة الأمريكية بالقاهرة. درست في معهد السينما بالقاهرة واهتمت

بـالسينما التسجيلية. لها مجموعة من الأفلام التسجيلية التي تعبّر عن حقوق المضطهدين، منها **اللعب بالديموقراطية**، و**الفرح مصري**، و**رانجو**.

**داليا سعيد مصطفى** تُدرّس الأدب والسينما في كلية دراسات الشرق الأوسط بجامعة مانشستر ببريطانيا. حصلت على الدكتوراه من جامعة مانشستر وعلى الماجستير من الجامعة الأمريكية بالقاهرة. صدر لها دراسات بالعربية والإنجليزية عن السينما المصريةوالأغنية السياسية والرواية اللبنانية، وعن تمثيل علاقات الجنوسة. ويتناول البحث الذي تقوم به حالياً صورة المدينة وتحولاتها في الرواية والسينما العربية، بالتركيز على مدينتي بيروت والقاهرة.

**إيمي أرياب مطلق** أستاذة مساعدة في قسم الأدب الإنجليزي والمقارن بالجامعة الأمريكية بالقاهرة. حصلت على الدكتوراه من جامعة پرنستون. تركز أبحاثها على الأدب والثقافة الإيرانية الحديثة المنتجة في إيران وخارجها. نشرت قصصاً قصيرة ودراسات في الأدب المعاصر.

**جيمس مكدوجال** يدرّس التاريخ بكلية ترينتي بأوكسفورد. درّس في جامعتي لندن وپرنستون. تركز أبحاثه على تاريخ شمال أفريقيا الثقافي والسياسي، وعلى الاستعمار الفرنسي والقومية والثورة في أفريقيا والشرق الأوسط.

**حسام نايل** باحث ومترجم مصري. حصل على ماجستير الآداب في النقد والبلاغة المعاصرة، جامعة القاهرة. من أعماله المنشورة: **صور دريدا** (ترجمة)، **أرشيف النص: درس في البصيرة الضالة** (تأليف)، **البنيوية والتفكيك: مداخل نقدية** (ترجمة)، **مدخل إلى التفكيك** (ترجمة)، **استراتيجيات التفكيك** (ترجمة وتأليف). ينشغل حالياً بدرس العلاقة بين النص الأدبي وأرشيف التوحيد في العالم العربي من منظور التفكيك. ومن أعماله قيد النشر: **التصوف والتفكيك: درس مقارن بين ابن عربي ودريدا** (ترجمة) و**إنقاذ الاختلاف: تفكيكات في النص الأدبي المعاصر** (تأليف).

**مارك وستمورلاند** أستاذ الأنثربولوجيا البصرية ومخرج أفلام تسجيلية. يدرّس الأنثروبولوجيا بالجامعة الأمريكية بالقاهرة.

حصل على الدكتوراه من جامعة تكساس بأوستن. عمل على مشاريع في الهند وأثيوبيا والولايات المتحدة حيث أنشأ مؤسسة هدفها توفير مشاريع عمل للأكاديميين والفنانين حول تاريخ المهمشين.